Don Kulick and Angela Terrill
A Grammar and Dictionary of Tayap

Pacific Linguistics

Managing editor
Bethwyn Evans

Editorial board members
Wayan Arka
Danielle Barth
Don Daniels
Nicholas Evans
Gwendolyn Hyslop
David Nash
Bruno Olsson
Bill Palmer
Andrew Pawley
Malcolm Ross
Dineke Schokkin
Jane Simpson

Volume 661

Don Kulick and Angela Terrill

A Grammar and Dictionary of Tayap

The Life and Death of a Papuan Language

DE GRUYTER
MOUTON

ISBN 978-1-5015-2552-0
e-ISBN (PDF) 978-1-5015-1220-9
e-ISBN (EPUB) 978-1-5015-1202-5
ISSN 1448-8310

Library of Congress Control Number: 2018967365

Bibliographic information published by the Deutsche Nationalbibliothek
The Deutsche Nationalbibliothek lists this publication in the Deutsche Nationalbibliografie;
detailed bibliographic data are available on the Internet at http://dnb.dnb.de.

© 2021 Walter de Gruyter Inc., Boston/Berlin
This volume is text- and page-identical with the hardback published in 2019.
Typesetting: Integra Software Services Pvt. Ltd.
Printing and binding: CPI books GmbH, Leck
Photo credit: Don Kulick

www.degruyter.com

ŋayi pendimor aŋgo tayap merŋa tambunkun
ripimŋa munjenumana naŋroana
eneŋa rorsemana
nunukŋa rorsemana
                                        Saraki

To the people of Gapun, past, present and future

Acknowledgements

Don's Acknowledgements:
The research on which this book is based was made possible by generous research grants by the National Endowment for the Humanities, the Wenner-Gren Foundation for Anthropological Research, the John Simon Guggenheim Memorial Foundation and the Swedish Research Council. I am grateful to my former employer, the University of Chicago, for granting me the research leave that allowed me to return to Gapun and conduct fieldwork for nine months during 2009, and for leave to visit Gapun for several months in 2010, 2012 and 2014. I am grateful to my current employer, Uppsala University, for leave to travel to the town of Madang in order to complete the final draft of this book in spring 2018.

In Papua New Guinea, I thank James Robins and Georgia Kaipu, of Papua New Guinea's National Research Institute, for their impressive skill in negotiating the bureaucracy involved in obtaining a research visa. I owe a large debt to Divine Word University in the town of Madang, which generously provided me with a place to live while I worked on the final version of this text. The late Nancy Sullivan, whose feisty and festive presence in Madang was instrumental in luring me back to Papua New Guinea after an absence of fifteen years, is deeply, sorely missed. Other people in Madang whose company and support I value are John Mackerell, John Burton, Pam Norman, Cecilia Nembou, Fidelma Takaili, Iwona Kolodziejczyk, Gert van den Berg, Patricia Paraide, David Lloyd, Edwina Jangi, Sr. Miriam Dlugosz, and Frs. Philip Gibbs, Patrick Gesch, and Garrett Roche.

I am grateful to several colleagues who generously provided me with support over the years. Many years ago, Christopher Stroud worked with me to make initial sense of Tayap, and I gratefully acknowledge his contributions to my understanding of the language. Eva Lindström shared much appreciated pre-fieldwork technical advice about audio recorders, Toughbook computers and solar panels. Two stays at ANU in Australia, one of them as a visiting fellow at ANU's Humanities Research Centre, facilitated by Nick Evans and Alan Rumsey, were extremely important in the development of this text. Andy Pawley gave me very helpful advice in relation to the dictionary, which he read through with care. Nick Evans provided important encouragement and perspicacious suggestions about the analysis at several crucial points when I felt stuck.

I am grateful to Bill Foley for reading the entire first draft of the grammar and providing invaluable feedback.

I want to take this opportunity to explicitly acknowledge the work of my co-author, Angela Terrill. Upon receiving the reader's report from an anonymous reviewer that I got back from *Pacific Linguistics* the first time I submitted the manuscript in 2011, I recognized that I needed a trained descriptive linguist to help me transform the grammar into publishable form. In 2017, I contacted Angela, who through sheer serendipity happened to be living in Uppsala, the city in Sweden where I am employed. Angela accepted my invitation to work with my manuscript, and remarkably, she managed to acquire a feel for Tayap – its idiosyncrasies and its genius – after only a few months. Angela's incisive interventions, her continual exhortations that "we need more examples", her extensive knowledge of Papuan linguistics, and her clear head and good cheer are the reason why this grammar and dictionary is now finally seeing the light of day.

My greatest debt, obviously, is to the people of Gapun, whom I have known now for over three decades. Villagers have always seen to it that I have had a house to live in (three times, in 1987, 1991 and 2009, they have built me a house), and food to eat. My debt to them is a collective one, and this documentation of their vernacular language is one way I hope they will sense some repayment of that debt. Many of the people who worked with me on the intricacies of the Tayap language are no longer alive, among them my chief language informants in the 1980s, Raya Ayarpa, Kruni Ayarpa and Mukar Raya. In 2009, I worked most intensively on the language with Monei Mbanaŋ, Samek Wanjo and Ŋgero Sair, all of whom were remarkable teachers. Others to whom I am especially grateful for my stay in Gapun in 2009 are Mbaso Monei who allowed me to live in a room in his house when I arrived in Gapun, and his older brother, the village *komiti* at the time, Opɨ Monei who organized, cajoled and supervised much of the labor that eventually built my house.

My greatest single debt during my months in Gapun since I began returning in 2006 after a fifteen-year absence is to those two men's younger sister, Ndamor Monei her husband Mbanu Ajiragi and the couple's seven sassy children Mbobot, Mopok, Poniker, Ŋawr, Ŋgayam, Kape and Kaɲirase. The house that villagers built me in 2009 was in the center of Gapun, right next to Ndamor's house. Without anyone ever asking her to do so, Ndamor quietly took it upon herself to make sure that I was always fed, and she and her daughters kept the area surrounding my house clean and free from dog feces and pig droppings. Ndamor has one of the most raucous senses of humor in the village, and now in her mid-forties, she is also one of the few women in Gapun who still has ferocious and poetic *kros*-es (harangues of anger) in Tayap. I loved both her humor and her anger – some of the most imaginative obscenities quoted in this book are Ndamor's. Living right next to Ndamor, in full hearing of everything that went on in her house at all hours of the day and night, was continually enlightening and hugely entertaining. Whenever I feel nostalgic for Gapun, it is my time spent listening to Ndamor and talking and laughing with her and her family that I miss the most.

I am grateful to the librarians in *Kungliga Biblioteket* in Stockholm, who provided me with a *forskarplats* in the reading room, where I was able to sit and write the entire first draft of this book in brisk enforced silence. I also thank the Ingmar Bergman Estate for a week long residency in August 2018. There I had the enormous privilege of putting the final touches on this manuscript sitting at the writing desk of the great auteur himself.

Finally, I thank Jonas Tillberg, for support, affection and the helicopter.

Angela's Acknowledgements:
I am grateful to Don Kulick for bringing me into this project, generously sharing his notes and recordings with me, patiently providing ever more examples, and most of all for sharing his remarkable knowledge of this intricate and fascinating language.

Don and Angela's Acknowledgements:
We both thank Ger Reesink, who revealed himself to be the reviewer of the manuscript we submitted to *Pacific Linguistics* in spring 2018. In only a few weeks, Ger had scoured the text with a gimlet eye and fine-toothed comb, noting inconsistencies, recommending literature, suggesting alternative analyses and – most considerately – remarking on the parts of the text that he particularly enjoyed. His knowledge of Papuan languages is unsurpassed and this grammar benefits from it greatly.

We are also deeply grateful to Tim Curnow who did us a wonderful service in reading the final manuscript with what must have been a microscope, and providing us with almost unbelievably detailed comments. The grammar is much the better for his thorough and meticulous input.

Authorship of this book

The first person pronoun used throughout this work refers to Don Kulick. I collected all the linguistic and ethnographic data analyzed here over the course of my thirty years' work in Gapun. As mentioned above, I wrote the entire first draft of this grammar and dictionary and submitted it for review at *Pacific Linguistics* in 2011. Shelving the project to complete other work, I took it up again in 2017, when I approached linguist Angela Terrill, who had trained in descriptive linguistics at ANU and written a grammar of the Papuan language, Lavukaleve, to collaborate with me in rewriting the text (Terrill 2003). Angela worked on the morphological and grammatical analysis in preparing the manuscript for publication.

Contents

Acknowledgements —— VII

Conventions and abbreviations —— XVIII

1   The Tayap language and its speakers —— 1
1.1   General overview of Tayap and the linguistic situation in Gapun —— 1
1.2   Past research on Tayap —— 8
1.3   Material on which this book is based —— 13
1.4   Young people's Tayap —— 17
1.5   Naming practices —— 22
1.6   Tayap linguistic profile —— 25

2   Phonology and orthography —— 27
2.1   Phonology —— 27
2.1.1   Consonants —— 27
2.1.1.1 Brief description of some of the consonant phonemes —— 27
2.1.1.2 Minimal contrasts between the consonant phonemes —— 29
2.1.2   Vowels —— 30
2.1.2.1 Vowel length expressing sympathy and pity —— 31
2.1.2.2 Vowel length expressing duration over time —— 32
2.2   Vowel sequences —— 32
2.3   Syllable structure and phonotactics —— 34
2.3.1   Syllable structure —— 34
2.4   Vowel harmony —— 35
2.5   Stress —— 37
2.6   Morpho-phonemic rules —— 41
2.7   Wordhood —— 44
2.8   Orthography —— 45

3   Word classes —— 49
3.1   Nouns —— 49
3.1.1   Definition of a noun in Tayap —— 49
3.1.1.1 Common nouns —— 49
3.1.1.2 Locational nouns —— 50
3.1.1.3 Number marking in nouns —— 51
3.1.2   The animacy/genericness distinction in nouns —— 53

3.1.2.1	Animacy/genericness marked through possessive morphemes —— 53	
3.1.3	Gender in nouns —— 55	
3.1.3.1	Gender marking —— 56	
3.1.3.2	Principles of gender assignment —— 57	
3.1.3.3	Non-particular nouns —— 60	
3.1.3.4	Gender in young people's Tayap —— 61	
3.1.4	Verbalized nouns —— 62	
3.2	Verbs —— 63	
3.3	Adjectives —— 66	
3.3.1	Number inflection in adjectives —— 69	
3.3.2	Verbalized adjectives —— 70	
3.3.3	Verbs as nominal modifiers —— 71	
3.4	Adverbs —— 72	
3.4.1	Common adverbs —— 72	
3.4.2	Adverbial functions of the suffix -*ki* —— 75	
3.4.3	Temporal adverbs —— 76	
3.4.4	Adverbials of frequency and distribution and 'not yet' —— 79	
3.4.5	Elevational and positional adverbials —— 80	
3.5	Pronouns —— 84	
3.6	Quantifiers —— 87	
3.6.1	Counting —— 87	
3.6.2	Plural markers —— 89	
3.7	Articles —— 92	
3.8	Deictics (DX) —— 93	
3.9	Interrogatives (Q) —— 96	
3.9.1	Yes/no questions —— 96	
3.9.2	Information questions —— 97	
3.10	Interjections and affect words —— 98	
3.10.1	Sounds used for calling animals and babies —— 100	
3.11	Intensifiers and discourse markers —— 100	
3.11.1	Intensifiers —— 101	
3.11.2	Discourse markers —— 103	
3.12	Mood particles —— 104	
4	**Noun phrases: Structure, modifiers, case marking and possession —— 105**	
4.1	Introduction —— 105	
4.1.1	Noun phrase structure —— 105	
4.2	Participles with the non-finite suffix -*(ŋ)gar* —— 107	

4.3	The ergative case (ERG) —— 109
4.3.1	Functions of the ergative case —— 112
4.3.1.1	Ergative clitics on intransitive verbs —— 117
4.3.2	Ergativity in the speech of young people —— 119
4.4	Peripheral cases —— 121
4.5	Possession —— 130
4.5.1	=ŋa(n) POSS with adjectives —— 132
4.5.2	Possessive modification —— 133
4.6	Peripheral case marking in young people's Tayap —— 134

5	**Basic verb morphology —— 136**
5.1	General properties of Tayap verbs —— 136
5.2	Standard negation in transitive and intransitive verbs —— 138
5.2.1	Negation of transitive verbs —— 138
5.2.2	Negation of intransitive verbs —— 141
5.3	Object (O) and subject (S/A) suffixes —— 144
5.3.1	Object suffixes —— 144
5.3.2	Subject (S/A) suffixes —— 145
5.4	Tense, aspect and mood in Tayap —— 147
5.4.1	Overview of Tayap verbal morphology —— 147
5.4.2	Irrealis —— 151
5.4.2.1	Negative (NEG) —— 151
5.4.2.2	Future (FUT) —— 151
5.4.2.3	Near future (NRFUT) —— 153
5.4.2.4	Subjunctive —— 154
5.4.3	Realis —— 154
5.4.3.1	Non-future (NF) —— 154
5.4.3.2	Perfect (PERF) —— 155
5.5	Reduplication —— 158
5.5.1	Repeated action —— 160
5.6	Reflexive and reciprocal constructions —— 162

6	**The formation of realis and irrealis verbs —— 163**
6.1	Transitive verb classes —— 163
6.1.1	Class 1: Verb stems that alternate between *p* and Ø —— 168
6.1.1.1	Exceptions to class 1 inflection —— 170
6.1.2	Class 2: Verb stems that alternate between *p* and *w* —— 172
6.1.3	Class 1 and 2 verbs in young people's Tayap —— 173
6.1.4	Class 3: Verb roots that begin with or contain *a* and alternate between *ka* and *o* in the realis —— 177

6.1.4.1	Exceptions to class 3 inflections —— 179	
6.1.5	Class 3 verbs in young people's Tayap —— 180	
6.1.6	Class 4: Verb roots that alternate between *t* and *r* —— 182	
6.1.6.1	Exception to class 4 inflection —— 185	
6.1.7	Class 5: Verb stems that are identical in realis and irrealis —— 186	
6.1.8	Class 4 and 5 verbs in young people's Tayap —— 188	
6.2	Intransitive verbs in the realis —— 190	
6.2.1	Four basic groups of intransitive verbs —— 191	
6.2.2	Subgroups of intransitive verbs —— 193	
6.2.2.1	Group IIa, verb stems that begin with *a* —— 193	
6.2.2.2	Group IIb, verb stems that alternate between *t* and *r* —— 194	
6.2.2.3	Group IVa, verb stems that begin with *a* —— 194	
6.2.2.4	Exceptions to the above classes —— 195	
6.2.3	Intransitive verbs in young people's Tayap —— 196	
7	**Mood —— 200**	
7.1	Subjunctive (SBJ) —— 200	
7.1.2	Imperative —— 202	
7.1.2.1	Intransitive imperatives —— 202	
7.1.2.2	Transitive imperatives —— 204	
7.1.2.3	The verb 'give' —— 207	
7.1.3	Jussive imperatives —— 207	
7.1.4	Indirect commands —— 208	
7.1.5	Expressing a desire for someone else to do something —— 211	
7.2	Prohibitive (PROH) —— 213	
7.3	Admonitive (ADM) —— 214	
7.4	Intentional (INTENT) —— 215	
7.5	Benefactive (BEN) —— 217	
7.6	Mood particles —— 223	
7.6.1	Expectation and impatience (EXP) —— 223	
7.6.2	Supposition (SUPP) —— 226	
7.6.3	Mirative (MIR) —— 227	
7.6.4	Surprise counter to expectation (CS) —— 228	
8	**Complex predicates —— 229**	
8.1	Complex predicates and complex clauses —— 229	
8.2	Serial verb constructions (SVC) —— 229	
8.2.1	Non-final verbs in serial verb constructions —— 231	
8.2.2	Non-final object morphemes (NFO) —— 232	

8.2.3	Verbs that always or usually occur only in SVCS —— 235	
8.2.3.1	SVCs with the grammaticalized verb k^v 'bring', 'take' —— 235	
8.2.3.2	Verbs which normally occur in SVCS —— 236	
8.2.4	Switch-function serial verb constructions —— 239	
8.2.5	Serial verb constructions in young people's Tayap —— 241	
8.3	Progressives and habituals —— 242	
8.3.1	Progressives —— 242	
8.3.1.1	Intransitive progressive —— 242	
8.3.1.2	Transitive progressive —— 245	
8.3.2	Habituals (HAB) —— 246	
9	**Simple and complex sentences —— 250**	
9.1	Simple sentences —— 250	
9.2	Complex sentences: Coordinate, subordinate and cosubordinate clauses —— 252	
9.3	Coordinated clauses —— 253	
9.3.1	Coordinated clauses with conjunctive -(y)a ('and') —— 253	
9.3.2	Coordination with -api 'afterward' (AFT) —— 256	
9.3.3	Coordination with ŋgɨ(na)napi 'therefore', 'for that reason' —— 256	
9.3.4	Coordination with ayáta 'although', 'it doesn't matter that', 'never mind that' —— 257	
9.4	Adverbial subordinate clauses —— 258	
9.4.1	Adverbial subordination with -re 'when', 'if', 'while' (SUB) —— 258	
9.4.2	Adverbial subordination with the hypothetical particles pi, pime, ndɨ (HYPO) —— 260	
9.4.3	Counterfactual (CF) —— 262	
9.4.3.1	How to form a counterfactual verb —— 265	
9.5	Relative clauses —— 268	
9.6	Finite nominalizations with consequence clitic =ŋa(n) —— 271	
9.7	Perception constructions —— 271	
9.8	Cosubordinate constructions —— 274	
9.8.1	Cosubordinate constructions with modifying suffix -ra (MOD) —— 275	
9.8.2	Cosubordinate constructions with manner suffix -kar (MANN) —— 277	
9.9	Tail-head linkage —— 280	
9.10	Complex constructions with the suffix signifying multiplicity -rar (ML) —— 282	
9.11	Complex sentences in young people's Tayap —— 283	

Tayap Texts —— 290
Tayap Text 1: Two men are chased by their lover's ghost —— 290
  English translation —— 290
  Tayap Original —— 291
Tayap Text 2: The water-spirit Ŋgayam kills the flying-fox clan —— 300
  English translation —— 300
  Tayap original —— 301
Tayap Text 3: 2-year-old boy has a close call with a deadly snake —— 308
  English translation —— 308
  Tayap original —— 309
  Commentary —— 316
Tayap Text 4: Young men kill a cassowary —— 317
  English translation —— 317
  Tayap original —— 318
  Key to transcription —— 318
  Commentary —— 324
Tayap Text 5: Girls have an adventure in the rainforest —— 327
  Key to transcription —— 329
  Tayap original —— 330

Tayap-English-Tok Pisin Dictionary —— 337
How to read the dictionary —— 337
Transitive verbs —— 338
Intransitive verbs —— 339
Complex predicates and non-final verb objects —— 341
Parentheses appearing in an entry that is not a verb —— 342
Stress —— 342
Synonyms —— 342
Obsolete words —— 343
Villagers' debates and language shift —— 343
Terms for plants and trees —— 346
Bird names —— 347
Vulgarity (tok nogut) —— 348
Words excluded from the dictionary —— 348
Tok Pisin words and expressions —— 349
Foreign words in Tayap —— 349
A note on the Tayap examples —— 351
Abbreviations and terms used in the dictionary —— 351
Animals, insects, fish and birds —— 442
Bird names —— 444

Kin terms —— 447
Parts of a house —— 448
Words pertaining to sago processing —— 449
Kinds of sago palms —— 452
Processing sago —— 454

English-Tayap finder list —— 455

Appendix 1
English translation of Georg Höltker 1938. Eine fragmentarische Wörterliste der Gapún-Sprache Newguineas. *Anthropos* **33: 279–82 —— 482**

Appendix 2
Two photographs of Gapun village taken in 1937 by Georg Höltker —— 487

References —— 489

Index —— 493

Conventions and abbreviations

Tayap examples in the grammar usually consist of four lines. The first is the Tayap speech written in bounded, unsegmented words.

The second line is the same clause or sentence in which the words have been separated into morphemes.

The third line is the interlinear gloss of the morphemes. The space separating the morphemes in the second and third lines is larger than it is in most grammars for reasons of readability. The usual manner of presentation, in which glosses for morphemes are chained together in long, complicated strings, assumes readers with a great deal of specialized knowledge, experience and patience. Separating the morphemes should make the glosses easier to process. The spacing does admittedly make it a bit harder to see individual words, but those appear in the first line of the examples.

The fourth line is the translation into English.

An example is as follows:

(1) *Merewŋgrogi munje parŋgiro*
    Merew   -ŋgro   =gi   munje   par   -ŋgɨ   -ro
    Sanae   -PL   =ERG.PL   man   bury.R   -3SG.M.R.O -3PL.R.S
    'the Sanae villagers buried the man'

Suffixes are marked by hyphens (-) and clitics are marked with an equal sign (=). In Tayap there are no prefixes, only suffixes, and enclitics rather than proclitics.

Some glossing conventions used throughout this grammar in the interlinear glosses need to be noted. Tayap verbs – and other words – have a broad range of meanings, and an *o*, for example, is consistently glossed as 'strike' in the interlinear glosses, but is translated to its context-specific meaning as 'hit', 'stab', 'kill', etc. in the translation. Similarly, the Locative case has a broad range of meanings. It is glossed as LOC when it has a locational meaning but in other contexts it may be glossed as TEMP for temporal, COM for comitative or ALL for allative.

Further conventions need explanation are as follows:

The first is the pipeline symbol | which appears in example 3 below underneath the final morpheme *-n*. This symbol means that the morpheme it glosses has more than one meaning. Disambiguation occurs through the use of pronouns or nouns, or through context.

An S is used in glossing transitive verbs to show features of the subject. With intransitive verbs, the person/number/status of subjects are marked in the language but there is no S in the gloss.

Another convention concerns Tayap's discontinuous subject markers. Some verbs have subject morphemes that occur both before and after the object morpheme. An example is as follows:

(2) ŋguyi aram tatiŋgin
 ŋgu =yi aram ta -ti -ŋgi -n
 3SG.F =ERG.F snake see.R -R.S -3SG.M.R.O -R.S
 'she saw a snake'

In this verb, the combination of *-ti* before the object morpheme and *-n* after the object morpheme encodes either a 2SG OR 3SG.F subject in realis status. The pronoun 'she' disambiguates the subject to be 3SG.F, in this case. Since it is the *combination of the two discontinuous subject morphemes* that produces meaning, the labeling convention adopted here is to gloss the first subject morpheme with 's' ('subject'), and to gloss the combined meaning of the two morphemes under the second morpheme. The object morpheme in verbs like this case occurs between the two subject markers, and is bounded by < > instead of hyphens, to show that it intervenes between the two discontinuous subject markers.

So in this grammar, the example above is written as:

(3) ŋguyi aram tatiŋgin
 ŋgu =yi aram ta -ti -ŋgi -n
 3SG.F =ERG.F snake see.R -S- <3SG.M.R.O> -2SG|3SG.F.R.S
 'she saw a snake'

The abbreviations used in the interlinear glosses otherwise generally follow the Leipzig glossing rules.

Note that the dictionary uses some different terms and abbreviations (see page 351 for those).

Conventions and abbreviations

A	subject of a transitive verb	NF	non-future
ABL	ablative	NFO	non-final object
ADJ	adjective	NRFUT	near future
ADM	admonitive	PERF	perfect
ADV	adverb	PERL	perlative
AFT	afterwards	PL	plural
ALL	allative	POSS	possessive
ATT	attribute	PREP	preposition
BEN	benefactive	PROG	progressive -*rik*
CF	counterfactual	PROH	prohibitive
COM	comitative	Q	interrogative
CS	surprise counter to expectation	R	realis
		REFL	reflexive/reciprocal
DAT	dative	S	subject
DL	dual	SBJ	subjunctive
DM	discourse marker	SG	singular
DX	deictic	SIM	simultaneous
ERG	ergative	SUB	subordinate
EXP	expectation	SUPP	supposition
F	feminine	SVC	serial verb construction
FUT	future	TAM	tense, aspect and mood
HAB	habitual	TEMP	temporal
HYPO	hypothetical	TP	Tok Pisin
INDEF	indefinite	V	verb
INST	instrumental	ᵛ	vowel that undergoes regressive assimilation to change to match the vowel of the object morpheme that follows it
INTENT	intention		
INTENS	intensifier		
IRR	irrealis		
LINK	linker -*a(k)*		
LOC	locative	X	morphological slot for object morpheme
M	masculine		
MANN	manner	XD	extended duration
MIR	mirative	1	first person
ML	multiplicity	2	second person
MOD	modifying dependent verb suffix	3	third person
		italics	Tayap
ND	nondesiderative	Roman	Tok Pisin
NEG	negative		

1 The Tayap language and its speakers

1.1 General overview of Tayap and the linguistic situation in Gapun

Tayap is the name of a Papuan language spoken by a dwindling number of people, most of whom live in a small village called Gapun (the speakers themselves call the language *Tayap mer*, which means, precisely, 'Tayap language'). Gapun is located on the Papua New Guinea mainland, between the Sepik and Ramu rivers, about thirty kilometers inland from the northern coast. The village is far from roads of any kind and is difficult to reach. It lies in a mosquito- and leech-infested swamp in the middle of the rainforest (see Map 1.1).

The Tayap language is tiny, even by the extreme standards of Papua New Guinea, where one linguist estimated that thirty five percent of the languages have fewer than five hundred speakers (Sankoff 1980: 96). As far as anyone in Gapun has been able to remember, Tayap has never had more than, at most, just over one hundred speakers. That small number seems to have remained stable for a very long time. By the 1980s, however, children were no longer learning Tayap as their first language. Instead, they were learning Tok Pisin, the most important and widely-spoken national language of Papua New Guinea.

I began my work in Gapun in 1985. At that time, the number of people who actively commanded Tayap – in the sense that they spoke it with other villagers and were able to narrate stories in it – was about ninety, out of a population of about one hundred and thirty (most but not all of whom lived in Gapun). Twenty three years later, in 2009, the population of Gapun had grown to two hundred and eight people. In addition, seventeen people who had been born and raised in Gapun had left the village (mostly because of conflicts over land rights and sorcery accusations) and moved to the village of Wongan, which is a ninety-minute trip from Gapun, by foot and then dugout canoe across a vast mangrove lagoon.

If we were to include those people in a count of Gapuners the total population would be two hundred and twenty five. And if their children, most of whom were born and raised in Wongan, were to be included, the number of people who could reasonably claim to be a Gapuner would be close to three hundred.

Any way Gapuners are counted, it is clear that their numbers have doubled over the past twenty years. However, during that same time, old people have died and children have continued to learn Tok Pisin as their first language. By 2009, fewer than twenty people still living in Gapun had grown up with Tayap as their first language.

1 The Tayap language and its speakers

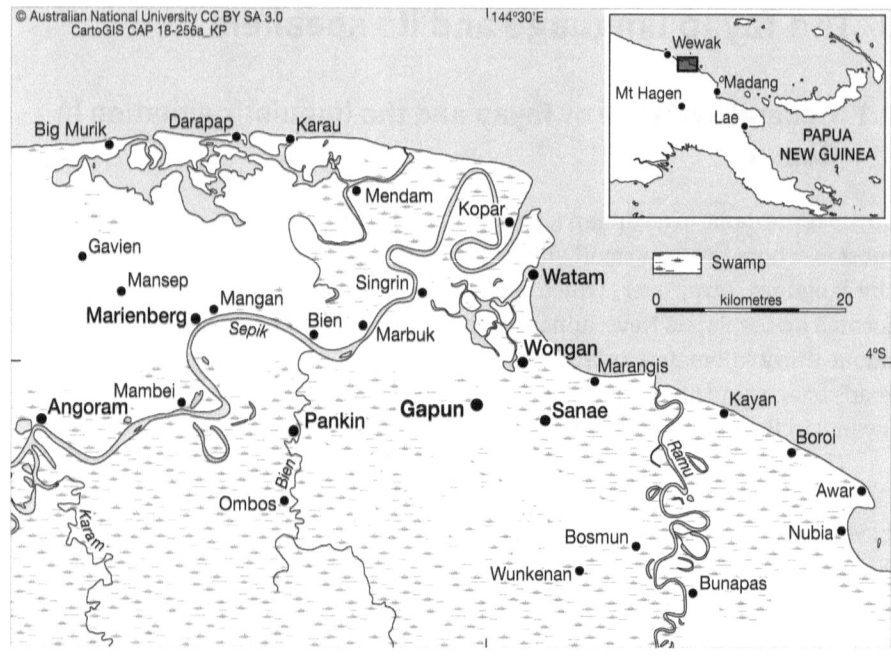

Map 1.1: Sepik-Ramu region. After Kulick (1992: 25).

Furthermore, the population of Gapun village is overwhelmingly young: ninety percent of the total population is under forty years old, and only three people in the village are over sixty years old. Today only about sixty people actively command Tayap and only about forty five use the language to any extent in their day-to-day lives.

This grammar and dictionary is an attempt to document and preserve a small part of the linguistic heritage of the Gapun people. Its publication will without doubt have little or no impact on Tayap's impending demise. Gapuners of today have little need for their vernacular. They also have little desire for it – even though no villager ever openly acknowledges this.

Many instances of language death around the world start when adults more or less consciously neglect to teach their home language to their children because they want the children to succeed in school or because the home language is socially stigmatized. This is not the situation in Gapun. No one in Gapun has ever explicitly rejected Tayap, and no one disparages it or suggests that it should be forgotten. On the contrary, Gapuners all express positive sentiments towards their vernacular language. They all say they like it. Older adults occasionally flare up and berate young people and children for not knowing it.

But despite positive sentiments toward Tayap, day-to-day village life is now overwhelmingly conducted in Tok Pisin. Village-wide meetings are in Tok Pisin, church services are in Tok Pisin, gatherings in the men's house are in Tok Pisin, chatter on the field during soccer matches is in Tok Pisin, talk among women visiting new mothers in maternity houses is in Tok Pisin. Informal conversations involving villagers over thirty-five often involve code-switching between Tayap and Tok Pisin, depending on who is present. But most conversations in Gapun, between most people, take place mostly in Tok Pisin. Even private, intimate conversations occur overwhelmingly in Tok Pisin: young men who go off together in groups to engage in secret rituals that make them feel lighter and more attractive speak Tok Pisin to one another. Husbands and wives under thirty, when they are alone together, speak Tok Pisin – a fact I know because when I asked a husband or a wife to give me their opinion on their spouse's competence in Tayap, they usually answered that they couldn't, because they almost never heard their spouse speak Tayap.

When villagers panic – for example when a drunken young man hurls himself through the village swinging a machete at anyone he sees, or when a child is bitten by a death adder in the middle of the village and no one knows where it went – on occasions like those, the overwhelming bulk of everyone's alarmed screams to one another, tellingly, is in Tok Pisin, not Tayap.

Equally tellingly, even senior villagers' admonitions to younger people to speak Tayap tend to be shouted in Tok Pisin. There is never any consistent effort to teach children Tayap; indeed, whenever young people do occasionally attempt to say something in it, any adult who hears them will often dismiss them with a chuckle or a sneer, and loudly bemoan how poorly they speak the vernacular language.

Language loss is inevitably linked to cultural change, and during the past few decades, Gapun has changed dramatically. The changes have not been economic: Gapun villagers of today are not materially much better off than their great-grandparents. Nor are villagers radically different from their post-war predecessors in terms of their understandings of their place in the world: like their grandparents, today's villagers still believe that Papua New Guineans are "the last country" and that one day, hopefully soon, Jesus will return to Earth and bestow upon them all the goods and riches that they believe He has already rewarded white people with, everywhere else in the world. (The complexity of all this is the subject of my two anthropological monographs on the village, Kulick 1992 and Kulick 2019.)

What makes villagers of today very different from the generation born in the 1940s and earlier is that the overwhelming majority of the social, cultural and ritual practices that link them to their history have vanished. The men's house cult, which for generations was the backbone of Gapun culture, is broken.

Previously important social bonds – for example, relations between joking kin, which are inherited relations to certain members of the clans into which one may marry (*njakum* in Tayap, "wanpilai" in Tok Pisin) – are no longer observed and for the most part no longer even known. Traditional healing rites, which depended on knowing, respecting, flattering and sometimes threatening the spirits of ancestors and the powers of the rainforest, are now all regarded as suspicious at best and Satanic at worst. Funerary rituals, which once engaged entire villages and were occasions for important social gatherings, great feasts and the momentous playing of the sacred flutes in the men's house – these are all moribund.

For the past fifty years, villagers have been much more interested in trying to be good Catholics (villagers began to be baptized by visiting missionaries in the early 1950s), trying to get their children educated, and trying to discover a way to make money so that they can "develop" than they have been in talking about or preserving their traditions.

Like perhaps most people around the world, Gapuners care much more about their future than they do about their past. And a price they seem destined to pay for their enthusiastic orientation towards the future is not only the loss of their traditions and history, but also the loss of their ancestral language.

The death of languages is a phenomenon that linguists, anthropologists and activists for indigenous and ethnic rights have long been aware of, and concerned about. Much early linguistic and anthropological work was devoted to "salvaging" what could be documented of traditions and languages that were fading to extinction in the early decades of the twentieth century. During the past twenty years, however, awareness of language death has turned from concern to alarm.

Linguists have realized that languages are becoming extinct at a rate seemingly unprecedented in history. It is sobering to realize, for example, that ninety percent of the indigenous languages spoken upon Cook's arrival in Australia are either dead or on the verge of dying. One overview has called the United States "a graveyard for hundreds of languages" (Nettle and Romaine 2000: 5), noting that eighty percent of the indigenous languages that still even exist there are no longer being learned by children. Thirty percent of the languages spoken in South America are thought to be "no longer viable". And so on. The most widely cited estimate of language death is the ominous prediction that ninety percent of the world's approximately six thousand languages are endangered (Krauss 1992, Evans 2010). This figure, which at first glance seems hyperbolic and unbelievable, becomes more comprehensible the moment it is realized that most people in the world speak one or more of the one hundred largest languages. Those big languages, linguists claim, are spoken by ninety six percent of the world's population.

This means that four percent of the world's population speaks the overwhelming majority of the world's languages. And those languages – thousands of them, many of them undocumented – are believed to be in danger of vanishing within the next one hundred years.

Tayap is one of those languages. And in the literature on language death that began burgeoning in the 1990s, it has sometimes been featured as a poignant example. It is discussed, for example, in Daniel Nettle and Suzanne Romaine's comprehensive overview of language extinction around the world. Those linguists cite my earlier work on Gapun (employing the spelling of "Tayap" that I used previously; Kulick 1992) to make the point that:

> Taiap is an amazingly rich language in terms of its structural diversity and particularly distinctive vocabulary, unlike any other in the Sepik. It is not clearly related to any other language in the area or indeed to any other language in Papua New Guinea as far as we can tell. (2000:13)

This celebration of Tayap's uniqueness and complexity is a buildup that leads to a somber punchline: "While further research might provide clues about the precise genetic relationship between Taiap and other languages, this is unlikely to happen. Taiap is dying", write Nettle and Romaine, employing a baleful tone that is characteristic of work on language death around the world.

No one could dispute that the disappearance of a human language is a cause for lamentation and mourning. And it would be insensitive and beside the point to critique linguists' attempts to inform a wider public about the widespread language extinction that appears to be occurring across the globe today. But even as we acknowledge and appreciate this, it is still possible to be skeptical of what has emerged as a dominant way in which linguists discuss language death – the likening of endangered languages to endangered animals and endangered plants.

Nettle and Romaine, for example, liken Tayap to a great bird. They write, "if Taiap were a rare species of bird or Ubykh [another endangered language they discuss] a dying coral reef, maybe more people would know of their plight and be concerned". And they continue, asking dramatically, "Should we be any less concerned about Taiap than we are about the passing of the California condor?" (2000: 13–14).

A question like that is difficult to answer, not least because it is far from obvious what "our" concern that Tayap is dying might actually materialize in practice, and what consequences those material expressions of "our" concern might have for anyone living in Gapun. There is also a problem with likening Tayap to a condor because exquisite as languages may be, they really are not like condors or coral reefs. Condor chicks are not sent to schools where they are taught in a cosmopolitan language they've barely ever heard, and where they learn to devalue their traditional condor ways. Coral reefs are not converted to Christianity and told that their traditional reef ways are Satanic.

To be fair, none of these things happen to languages either. But they do happen to speakers of many of the languages that linguists are so concerned about. Linguists like Nettle and Romaine who use species metaphors understand this, of course. But in the current cultural climate that exhorts people to develop concern for the environment and sustainability, many linguists seem to believe that they can elicit some kind of sympathy and support for dying languages if they talk about them in terms of biodiversity and species loss.

This way of thinking about language death is specious, however, because it directs our attention to the natural world. By encouraging us to think in terms of ecosystems rather than political systems, ecological or species metaphors elide, or at least defer, the simple realization that *language death is anything but a natural phenomenon.* On the contrary, it is a profoundly social phenomenon.

Languages die because people stop speaking them, not because they exhaust themselves in the fullness of time or are killed off by predatory languages of greater phonological scope or syntactic richness.

A better metaphor for language death, instead of seeing languages as animals or organisms, would be to think of them like political movements, philosophies or religions – that is, to consider them as social phenomena that cannot be comprehended apart from history, beliefs, economics, desire, structure and power. And that necessarily change and sometimes even disappear as the material, economic, social and cultural conditions that sustain them shift and transform.

With that in mind, and given the current state and tenor of Gapun village life, I wish to make it clear that this grammar and dictionary of Tayap is not an effort to influence the future. It is, instead, a record that documents what I am convinced soon will be the irrevocable past. Gapun villagers are ceasing to speak their language and if present trends persist, in thirty or forty years, Tayap will be gone forever. While this is inconsolably sad, it is the villagers' choice. It is a choice I have no doubt that their descendants will castigate them for, as always eventually happens with languages that die.

But I do not write this grammar and dictionary with the fantasy that its appearance will somehow change villagers' lives and make them revive their dying language. Indeed, I recognize that the opposite may – and at this point probably will – happen. The appearance of Tayap words printed in a book may foster resignation and complacency: a sense that, "Well now our language is all there in a book, so we don't really have to worry about it anymore, our children can learn it from the book when they're grown up". Tayap in a book may also solidify a view that the language is an august tongue of the ancestors far too majestic and esoteric for young people to ever even attempt to master.

So why write a book about Tayap? Partly to preserve some small part of the proverbial treasure chest of human knowledge, certainly. But mostly, I have written this grammar and dictionary primarily in the hope that a curious young Gapuner, sometime in the probably distant future, will discover it somewhere and value the fact that the obsolete language of his or her ancestors did not disappear without a trace.

The dictionary that accompanies this grammar is trilingual: Tayap, English and Tok Pisin. A few of the villagers in Gapun have had as many as ten years of schooling, most of it in English. Despite that, though (or, really, *because of that*), none of them currently possesses anything but the most rudimentary command of that language.[1] No villager today will be able to make much sense of this grammar of Tayap, but the dictionary part of this work may be entertaining and useful to them now, as opposed to some distant future. And to facilitate that usefulness, I have included definitions in the language that is replacing Tayap and in which all villagers are fluent: Tok Pisin.

I have also provided many examples of how the words in the dictionary are used in Tayap, and I have purposely included a large number of vulgarities. Gapun villagers are no different from anyone else who has ever scoured a dictionary to see if it dared to list the most obscene terms that one and one's sniggering friends could dream up. I hope that the shock of seeing some of their most vulgar words and insults immortalized in a book will provide the villagers with a great deal of guilty pleasure.

This grammar and dictionary should be of interest to linguists who study Sepik and Ramu languages and the genealogical relationships of Papuan languages more generally. It should also interest archeologists and historians who study the peopling and linguistic diversity of the Sepik region of Papua New Guinea.

---

[1] In Kulick 1992: 175–80, I discuss the kind of schooling the villagers received and argue that its sole outcome, aside from teaching some villagers a few rudimentary literacy skills, is to induce dissatisfaction with village life. Since 2009, no villager has received even this dismal minimal education. The teachers in the government-run primary school in the neighboring village of Wongan went on strike and stopped teaching in early 2009. During a brief visit to the village in March 2019, I confirmed that the school remains closed.

Tayap is relevant to both these areas of research, first because the language appears to be an isolate with no known relatives, and second, because the ancestral territory of the villagers includes the highest point in the lower Sepik basin. This territory was an island six thousand years ago, before the sea receded and the Sepik Basin formed.

These geographical and linguistic facts suggest that Tayap may be a particularly ancient, autochthonous language that was already in place before the various waves of migration from the inland to the coast began occurring thousands of years ago (Ross 2005: 46).

1.2 Past research on Tayap

The history of linguistic research on Tayap is very brief. In 1937, Gapun was visited by one of the few white men ever to make it there. This was Georg Höltker, a German S.V.D. (*Societas Verbi Divini*) missionary and anthropologist. Höltker went to Gapun in the company of another missionary based in the coastal village of Watam, and he spent three hours in the village. He took two photographs and collected a word list.

A year later, Höltker published the list of 125 words, together with the weary remark that "it will be awhile before any other researcher 'stumbles across' Gapun, if only because of the small chances of worthwhile academic yields in this tiny village community, and also because of the inconvenient and arduous route leading to this linguistic island" (1938: 280). (A translation of Höltker's short article is included here in Appendix 1, along with the two photographs he took in Appendix 2).

Höltker's brief squib remained all that was known about Tayap until the early 1970s, when the Australian linguist Don Laycock travelled around the lower Sepik to collect basic vocabulary lists that allowed him to identify and propose classifications of the many languages spoken there. Laycock never visited Gapun, but he did get as far as neighboring Wongan, and he interviewed two Gapun villagers who were staying there at the time, Kawi Waiki and Konjab Akumbi (Laycock 1973: 35).

On the basis of the word list and a few verb paradigms that he gathered from Kawi and Konjab, Laycock classified Tayap (which he called "Gapun") as a sub-phylum of the Sepik-Ramu language phylum. In the classification terminology used by Laycock and his linguistic colleagues in the 1970s, this meant that Tayap shared less than twelve percent of its basic vocabulary with other members of the phylum, and also that it exhibited marked differences from other members of the phylum – in Tayap's case, gender pronouns and other differences related to gender marking were mentioned. (The word list used by Laycock appears as an appendix to his 1973 article. A discussion of the classifying criteria used to sort out Papuan languages is in Wurm 1982: 65–72.)

Laycock included one other language in what he called the "Gapun sub-phylum level family". This was a language of over two thousand speakers, called Bungain. Bungain is geographically distant from Gapun (off to the north and west of Map 1.2, see page 13), and Gapuners have no social, cultural or economic ties or affinities with – or even knowledge of – Bungain speakers. The relationship that Laycock postulated between Tayap and Bungain was not based on any solid data or analysis – it was based on the basic vocabulary list he used, as well as some rudimentary grammatical information, such as translations of 'Give me tobacco', 'I cannot give you any, I have none', 'If I had some I would give it to you'. Laycock himself noted that all his classifications of Sepik languages were "tentative" and "impressionistic" (1973: 2). His description of the supposed similarities between Bungain and Tayap, in its entirety, consists of the following:

> The languages show complex verb morphology, after the manner of Nor-Pondo languages (subject marking by prefix in Bungain, and suffix in Gapun); but there is apparently no noun classification, and no indication of number in nouns. Gapun has a third-feminine pronoun; Bungain appears to lack this, but there is apparent gender concordance in verbs.
>
> (Laycock 1973: 35)

Aside from the remark about complex verb morphology – which is a feature shared by many Papuan languages – this description makes Bungain and Tayap sound more *dissimilar* than similar (it also turns out that Tayap, in fact, does mark number on a restricted class of nouns; see Section 3.1.3). In an attempt to assess the feasibility of Laycock's classification of Tayap and Bungain, I looked through the field data on which he based the classification, namely his field notebooks D7, D26 and D27, which are deposited in the Linguistics Department at the Australian National University, where Laycock worked.[2]

Unfortunately, the notebooks turned out to be of quite limited use, because Laycock often did not translate the vernacular words he noted down in his field notebooks. He numbered the words, but his numbering does not correspond to

---

[2] I am grateful to the collective efforts of Melissa Crowther, Mark Donohue, Nicholas Evans, Ewan Maidment, Doug Marmion, Malcom Ross and Nick Thieberger in helping me track down and obtain scanned copies of these notebooks.

the list he provides in his published article on how he classified them (Laycock 1973: 70–71).

For example, in his Bungain fieldnotes, a word Laycock does translate, as 'snake' (*atop'*), is numbered 172. But in the published list, 'snake' is word number 152. Eight untranslated words follow *atop'*, but the ninth, *kwulémbe*, Laycock translates as 'mosquito'. The problem is that in the word list published in his article, 'mosquito' comes eleven words after 'snake'. These kinds of discrepancies make it impossible to use the word list Laycock provided in his article to identify the untranslated vernacular words he noted down in his field notebooks. This is not a problem with Laycock's Tayap material, because I know the meaning of all the words he noted down. But since I know no Bungain, much of his list for that language is unrevealing.

As far as I am able to tell, there are no lexical similarities between Bungain and Tayap, beyond a couple of words that are common throughout the Sepik, such as the word for water (Bungain: *wi*; Tayap *awin*). Grammatically and morphologically, I could discern no similarities between Tayap and Bungain, and after examining the fieldnotes I was at a loss to understand the basis for his statement that "their relationship with each other is clear but not close" (Laycock and Z'graggen 1975: 757).

My own suspicion is that Laycock couldn't easily fit either Tayap or Bungain into the language families he had developed for the Sepik region, and so he simply guessed that they might be related to one another. Later researchers have suggested that Bungain may be a Torricelli phylum language (Sanders and Sanders 1980: 188). Foley (2018) classes Bungain as a member of the Marienberg Hills family, a subgroup of the Torricelli family. He bases the classification of Bungain on morphological criteria gleaned from his own fieldwork data, which he describes as "brief" (Foley 2018: 304). He provides some of this data, including a pronoun paradigm, subject agreement prefixes, morphological description and some sentence material in his major descriptive work on the Sepik-Ramu languages (2018: 197–431). None of this material is suggestive of a relationship between Bungain and Tayap.

To illustrate how different Tayap is from neighboring languages, I have added it to the "Lower Sepik family basic word list" that appears in William Foley's 1986 book, *The Papuan languages of New Guinea*. To enable the table to appear on a single page, I have omitted one of the languages in the original table (Karawari). The (K) after words in the Murik column indicates forms in the Kopar language.

Lower Sepik family: basic word list (adapted from Foley 1986: 215)

		Yimas	Angoram	Chambri	Murik	Tayap
1	'one'	mba-	mbia	mbwia-	abe	nambar
2	'two'	-rpal	-(li)par	-ri	kompari (K)	sene
3	'three'	-ramnaw	-elɨm	-ram	kerongo	manaw
4	'person'	narmaŋ		noranan	nor	----
5	'male'	panmal	pondo		puin	munje
6	'female'/ 'mother'	ŋay	nuŋor	kave	ŋai	noŋor/ama
7	'father'	apwi	apa/ano	kanu	apa	omo
8	'water'	arɨm	alɨm	arɨm	arɨm	awin
9	'fire'	awt	aluŋ	ayɨr	awr	otar
10	'sun'	tɨmal	mbwino	sɨmari	akɨn	arawer
11	'moon'	mɨla	mile	mwɨl	karewan	karep
12	'star'	awak	arenjo	suŋkwi	moai	ŋudum
13	'canoe'	kay	ke	ke	gain	yimbar
14	'louse'	nam	nam	kurɨr	iran	pakɨnd
15	'village'	num	num	num	nomot	num
16	'breast'	nɨŋay	ŋge	nɨŋke	nɨŋen	min
17	'tooth'	tɨrɨŋ	sisɨŋ	sraŋk	asarap	rewi
18	'blood'	yat	ayakone	yari	yaran	and
19	'bone'	tanɨm	salɨŋ	anamp	sarɨŋib	nɨŋ
20	'tongue'	mɨnyɨŋ	minɨŋ	tɨbulanɨŋk	menɨŋ	malɨt
21	'eye'	tuŋurɨŋ	tambli	sɨsɨŋk	nabrɨn	ŋgino
22	'nose'	tɨkay	naŋɨm	wambusu	daur	raw
23	'hair'	wapwi	mbwikmaley	yawi	dwar	pupur/ kokɨrŋgrɨd
24	'ear'	kwandumɨŋ	kwandum	kukunam	karekep	neke
25	'egg'	awŋ	awŋ	awŋk	gaug	naŋa
26	'leaf'	nɨmbrɨm	(nam)blum	nɨmpramp	nabɨrɨk	mayar
27	'tree'	yan	lor	yuwan	yarar	nɨm
28	'yesterday'/ 'tomorrow'[3]	narɨŋ	nakɨmɨn	namasɨnɨŋ	ŋarɨŋ	ewar/epi
29	'oar'	muraŋ	inap	naŋk	inaŋ	inyaŋ
30	'betel nut'	patn	parɨŋ	muntɨkɨn	porog	minjike
31	'lime'	awi	awer	ayɨr	ayr	air
32	'pig'	numbran	imbar	numpran	(nim)bren	mbor
33	'crocodile'	manba	walami	ayi	oramen	orem
34	'snake'	wakɨn	paruŋ	wan	wakɨn	aram

(continued)

---

[3] Note that 'yesterday' and 'tomorrow' are expressed by the same word in the languages cited here, something which is common also in other Papuan languages. Tayap is exceptional here.

(continued)

		Yimas	Angoram	Chambri	Murik	Tayap
35	'mosquito'	naŋgun	wawarin	naŋgun	nauk/ naŋgit (K)	at
36	'chicken'	nakwan	kilikala	nakwan	goabar	kokok
37	'sago grub'	wun	wurin	wun	kamur	kimirik
38	'sago palm'	tinum	(t)uli(no)	tinum	dun	yam
39	'sago refuse'	tiki	tikir			tawar
40	'pound sago'	pan-	pan-	pun-	pon-	mindi-
41	'wash sago'	tuku-	tuku-	tuku-	tokun-	eiw-
42	'hear'	andi-	andi-	andi-	din-	tar-
43	'hit'	tupul-	ti-	dii-	di-	o-
44	'eat'	am-	am-	am-	min-	a-
45	'go'	wa-	kal-	wa-	on-	o-
46	'feces'	milim	mindi	munjar	mindin	yewir
47	'spine of leaf'	kinin	kinin	kiniŋk	kinin	mbwag
48	'leg'	pamuŋ	namuŋ	namaŋk	namoŋ (K)	ndow
49	'big'	kipa-	kupa-	wupa-	apo-	suman
50	'cold'	tarik	popant	saruk	seripatin (K)	pokemb

There are a few clear cognates between Tayap and some of the other languages listed in this table, such as the words for 'village', 'water', 'lime' (that is, the white powder made of bivalve shells that villagers pulverize and chew together with betel nut) and 'eat'. The Tayap verb meaning 'go' is realized as *wak-* in the habitual progressive aspect and the counterfactual mood (see Sections 8.3 and 9.4.3), thus probably making it cognate with Yimas, Chambri and Murik. The Tayap word for 'woman' is cognate with Angoram's 'female', and the words for 'fire', 'pig', 'one', 'egg', perhaps 'three' and a few others are similar to some of the words in one or more of the other languages.

A few words, such as those for 'canoe' and 'oar' are borrowings – Gapuners only learned to paddle canoes after WWII, when they moved their village from its former site up on a mountain down closer to the mangrove lagoon. They did this so that it would be easier for them to transport the cash crops they heard they should grow – at the time, those were rice and peanuts – out of the village and to waiting buyers (who for the most part never materialized). All words related to canoes, paddles and fishing in the mangrove lagoon are borrowings from the Kopar language.

But despite the cognates that do exist – something that one would expect given that people in the lower Sepik have had various forms of contact with one another for a very long time – it is striking that Tayap is so different from other Lower Sepik languages. Of the fifty words listed, at least thirty five of them, or seventy percent, are unique.

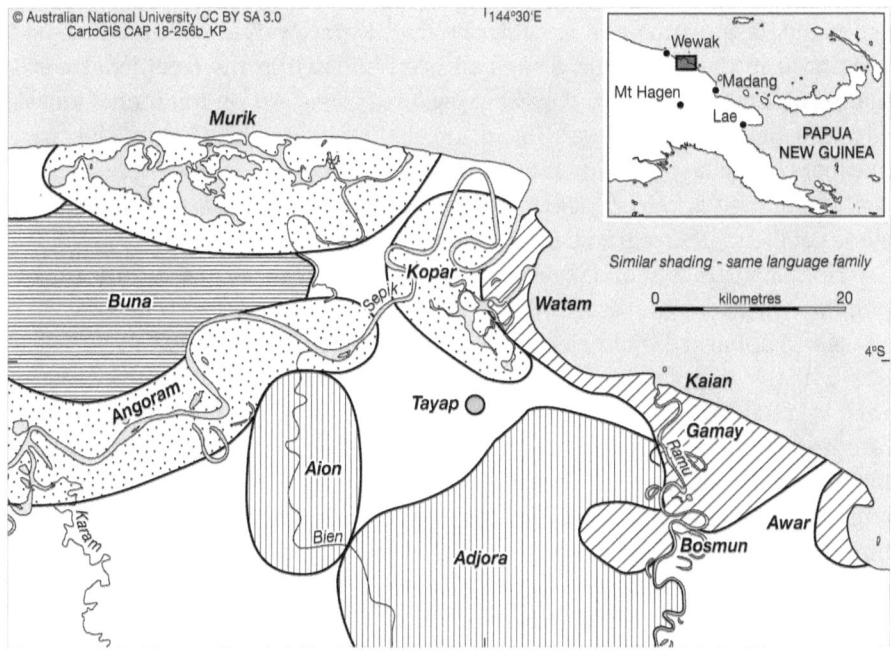

Map 1.2: Some languages of the Sepik-Ramu region. After Foley (2018: 202) and Kulick (1992: 62).

While this lack of cognates, in itself, does not necessarily prove that Tayap is an isolate, in the absence of any other evidence that it is related to other languages, it seems reasonable to classify it as a language isolate at this time (Ross 2005, Foley 2018).

1.3 Material on which this book is based

I first went to Gapun in the mid-1980s, at the suggestion of Don Laycock. I was interested in studying language shift in a place where the accounts usually offered to explain it – urbanization, social class mobility, educational aspirations – might not apply. I wanted to work on language shift in Papua New Guinea because I assumed that the tiny languages spoken there might be undergoing change. Nothing was known about the situation for Tayap, but Don had always remained curious about the language, and he reasoned cheerfully that "it's so small that something has to be happening to it". So off I went.

After a one-month reconnaissance trip to Gapun in 1985, I returned a year later and spent fifteen months in the village, gathering data on the language and on language use. During that period, I worked a great deal with senior men, especially Raya Ayarpa and his older brother, Kruni Ayarpa. Both brothers had been born in the late 1920s. They had been initiated in the traditional men's house cult of the *tambaran*, they were regarded as experts on traditional knowledge and history, and they were fluent and eloquent speakers of Tayap. They were members of the last generation to have had direct contact with the pre-colonial customs of their ancestors, either through their own experiences or through the stories of their fathers, grandfathers and other kinfolk.

I left Gapun in 1987 and wrote my PhD thesis on the social and cultural underpinnings of the language shift that was occurring there. A few years later, the thesis was published (Kulick 1992). I returned in 1991 to systematize my linguistic data with the goal of writing a grammar and dictionary. But that fieldtrip was cut short by a tragedy that occurred two months into the work: late one night, a group of armed bandits (called *ol raskol*, 'rascals', throughout Papua New Guinea) snuck into the village and attacked me in my house. They had been drawn to Gapun by a rumor that I was keeping 40,000 kina (the Papua New Guinean currency; at the time this was worth about the same in US dollars) in a metal patrol box.

In the tumult that occurred during the attack, the raskols shot a man – one of old Kruni Ayarpa's adult sons, Kawri Kruni – and he died shortly afterwards in the arms of the horrified villagers.

After murdering Kawri, the raskols fled Gapun. I left too, partly out of concern for my own safety, but also feeling that my presence in the village had come to be a dangerous liability for the villagers. My own trauma and sorrow regarding the incident led me to abandon my work on Gapun and the Tayap language (this incident and its aftermath is described in detail in Kulick 2019).

I did not return to Gapun again until fifteen years later, in 2006. During a short trip, I determined that the general law and order situation in that part of Papua New Guinea had improved, and also that the villagers were eager for me to come back. I applied for and received several research grants, and in 2009, I returned to Gapun and spent nine months in the village.

By this time, all the senior men with whom I had worked in the 1980s were long dead, and in fact, as I noted above, there remained only a few villagers who were over sixty years old. I began working on the language with one of them, Monei Mbanaŋ, a perceptive and gentle man in his mid-sixties with whom I had done a great deal of transcription work in the 1980s.

Unfortunately, two months after I arrived in Gapun, Monei grew gravely ill with what looked to me like cerebral malaria, and he died several weeks later.

Monei's death turned out to be a devastating blow to Gapun. Everyone in the village mourned the loss of their "last big man", as they all called Monei. But that mourning was riddled with conflict. Monei's adult children openly accused their maternal cousins of having paid a sorcerer to kill their father. Those accusations reignited long-smoldering hostilities. They led to village-wide brawls between different kin groups, and to uncontrolled drinking by young men, who a few years previously had been taught by men from the Sepik river village of Bien how to ferment and distill alcohol from coconut water or rotten bananas. The village was riven with threats of revenge sorcery, and by almost daily recurring uproar and violence that set everyone on edge. Social control collapsed and villagers' sense of cohesion frayed.

In the months following Monei's death, there was a powder-keg atmosphere in the village, and many villagers came to grow tired of hiding inside their houses while drunken young men strode though the village brandishing machetes, screaming obscenities in Tok Pisin and challenging others to come and fight with them. People began talking of "running away" from Gapun, and some families did actually abandon their houses and leave the village to build small homesteads for themselves in the jungle. By the end of 2009, when I left Gapun, the village was in the process of fissuring.

During this unsettling time, I collected material on Tayap by working with two other speakers. My chief language informant was Samek Wanjo, a pensive man who, in 2009, was about sixty years old. After Monei's death, Samek assumed Monei's place as the village's "biggest" man, and everyone agreed that he was one of the few remaining villagers who possessed any significant knowledge of traditions, land rights and village history.

The other person with whom I worked on Tayap was Ŋgero Sair, a thirty-five-year-old woman who is the oldest daughter of two Tayap-dominant parents. Ŋgero is one of the youngest speakers in Gapun to habitually use Tayap in her everyday conversations, and I was eager to work with her, to try to gauge any differences which might exist between her competence in Tayap, and that of older speakers. Samek and Ŋgero both turned out to be knowledgeable and nimble language informants.

With Samek I worked on vocabulary and grammar. With Ŋgero, I transcribed most of the recordings I made of naturally occurring speech.

In 1993, my linguist colleague Christopher Stroud and I published a thirty-page sketch grammar of Tayap in a volume honoring Don Laycock, who died suddenly in 1988, and whose passing was a profound loss for Papuan linguistics. Much of the analysis in that short sketch grammar is reasonable, as a first attempt to come to terms with the basic structure of the language (Kulick and Stroud 1993).

But re-reading the paper, I realized that it is an unhappily difficult text to process. Christopher and I wrote the sketch for linguists, and we were interested in facilitating the identification of underlying forms of the grammatical structures we discussed. It strikes me now that this goal – or certainly the way we tried to achieve it – obscures more about the language than it illuminates. For that reason, Angela Terrill and I have completely overhauled the analysis of Tayap presented in that paper, and we have not concerned ourselves with any attempt to identify or derive underlying forms. Anyone who might be interested in analyzing those forms – for example to determine Tayap's genetic relationships with other languages – should find sufficient material in this grammar and dictionary to do so.

The data on which this grammar and dictionary are based consists of material elicited during the following visits to Gapun: 1985 (one month), 1986–1987 (fifteen months), 1991 (two months), 2006 (six weeks), 2009 (nine months), 2010 (one month), and 2014 (two and a half months).[4] The book is also based on transcripts of naturally occurring talk that I made during all those periods of fieldwork. Those transcripts represent over one hundred hours of audio-taped talk in all kinds of situations – interactions between caregivers and children, oratories in the men's house, domestic arguments, harangues, narratives, village meetings and tuneful weeping over corpses.

All transcribed talk was written down with the help of village informants. I could never have transcribed the language by myself. At its apogee, my passive command of Tayap was respectable, and after about five months in the village in 2009, for example, I was able to follow most of what was said in the vernacular. But like village children and young adults, I never needed to actively speak Tayap – except, that is, when people from other villages came to Gapun to visit. Then, inevitably and to my great exasperation, Gapuners would ignore my

---

[4] A brief visit to Gapun in March 2019 determined that there is no longer any there there. The village has been all but abandoned. Fewer than fifty people (of which thirty were adults) were living in Gapun – this, out of total population of more than two hundred people five years earlier, in 2014. Much of the village had been reclaimed by jungle. Eight houses (the entire upper third section of the village) were incinerated in 2018, during a fight, and the victims of this violence have fled into the rainforest and built new houses there. Other villagers have taken their families and relocated to other villages, such as neighboring Wongan, or the coastal villages of Watam and Boroi.

The reason for the village's dissolution is that the disruptive binge drinking that began in earnest in 2009 has continued, and wrought devastation. Young village men have begun murdering one another in drunken frenzies. In December 2013, a village man was shot in the stomach with an arrow during a drunken brawl. He died an agonizing death a few days later. In August 2018, again during a drunken melee, a young man was shot in the head with a cruelly barbed projectile. Relatives managed to get him to a hospital in the tiny town of Angoram (a twelve hour journey away, paddling in a canoe), and the staff there managed to remove the projectile, but the man suffered severe cognitive impairments and he died a month later.

I am at a loss to imagine how the cycle of drinking and violence might be brought to an end, since murders like the ones that occurred in 2013 and 2018 only intensify the ever-more-destructive spirals of conflict that have steadily been poisoning village life for the past ten years.

In addition to resulting in unnumbered tears and profound tragedy, the dispersion of Gapun village reduces interpersonal contact between individual villagers, and it inevitably will impact on Tayap, undoubtedly hastening its demise.

protestations and insist on exhibiting me like a trained parrot. They took enormous pleasure in showing off their resident white man, and they delighted in the fact that I was able to awe their easily impressed guests with my ability to respond to commands in Tayap and mouth a few simple phrases.

Much of the material on which this description is based is stored on PARADISEC.

1.4 Young people's Tayap

In addition to language recorded through formal elicitation sessions and transcriptions of naturally occurring speech, this grammar and dictionary is also informed by fifty-six narratives from forty five young people aged fourteen to thirty that I collected and transcribed between July and November 2009.

I elicited these narratives primarily to see whether villagers younger than about thirty had any active command of Tayap at all. By mid-2009, after having lived in Gapun twenty-four hours a day for more than three months, I found that I was still unable to accurately judge this. The reason I had trouble assessing younger villagers' active competence in Tayap during this time was because whenever I asked young people if they "save toktok long tok ples" (spoke Tayap), they all told me, sure they did.

The problem was, I never heard any of them doing so. Once in a while I would hear a young person utter a few formulaic phrases in Tayap, but this was usually done to mark a situation as funny, and it was usually accompanied and followed by laughter. It also seemed to me that whenever villagers under twenty-five mouthed even a short formulaic phrase in Tayap, their tone of voice shifted to suggest that they were imitating or quoting someone else, usually to mock them (a big man's Voice of Authority, for example). Much the same happened whenever I pressed the young people who told me that they spoke Tayap, and asked them to tell me exactly what kind of things they said in the vernacular. In response, they would list a few words like *mum* and *tamwai* (sago jelly and sago pancake, respectively) and a few rudimentary formulaic phrases, such as the command to hand over some betel nut or tobacco.

At the same time, however, Tayap does continue to be heard throughout Gapun. Women and men over fifty use it habitually (even if they continually code-switch between Tayap and Tok Pisin), and a few men and women in their mid-thirties and older also use Tayap very frequently, even when speaking to their children. Even small children in the village understand the commands to go and fetch things, hit dogs, get out of the way, stop crying, etc. that adults are continually hollering at them.

Given that it was clear that Tayap was still used throughout Gapun, for a long time I thought that perhaps the young people really were quite competent in the vernacular, as they claimed to be. I fretted that I just never seemed to be in the right place at the right time to hear them when they actually spoke it.

I began to wonder whether the reason I wasn't hearing young people telling each other stories or asking each other questions in Tayap was because maybe they spoke it mostly out of the earshot of older, more fluent speakers. Maybe they felt ashamed that they weren't speaking it completely flawlessly, I conjectured. Or perhaps the vernacular, for them, had become tied to particular social events like same-sex gossip or hanging out in the rainforest – speech situations that only happened when young people were alone in groups and away from nosy and critical parents and elders.

To see whether any of this was in fact the case, I ended up spending a great deal of time with young people of both sexes between the ages of fourteen to twenty-five. I accompanied young men into the rainforest on frequent occasions, to go looking for birds to shoot with arrows or slingshots, and also when they went off together in groups to perform secret rituals that refresh their bodies.

I also spent a lot of time hanging out with young women. One place I made a point of doing this was inside maternity huts. Maternity huts are small, flimsy, hurriedly-constructed little houses on stilts, set on the periphery of the village, often near areas that villagers go off into to urinate or defecate. Women ready to give birth walk to special places in the rainforest, have their baby, then return to these maternity huts, where they are supposed to stay for up to three months (even though most young women these days find excuses to go back into their usual houses after only a few perfunctory weeks). During the entire period a woman is in a maternity hut, no man is supposed to visit her or even set eyes upon her and her newborn baby because villagers believe that the quantities of blood and uterine fluids discharged during childbirth make a woman and her newborn infant "hot" – that is to say, scalding, dangerous. Females are not as vulnerable to the effects of other women's "heat" (since they are, themselves, "hot"), and female visitors drop by a maternity hut throughout the day, usually accompanied by their younger child siblings and their own babies, if they have any. They bring food, water and gossip about the goings-on in the village from which the new mother is temporarily excluded.

It was not gender-appropriate for me to sit in the maternity huts with new mothers and other women, but the villagers regarded my enthusiasm for doing so as just a puzzling, whiteman eccentricity. Everyone in Gapun was convinced that I was going to get a fatal case of asthma from allowing myself to come in such close contact with the heat of women.

With this kind of danger in mind, whenever I wondered aloud in Gapun whether I might be coming down with a cold or a fever, a villager was always on hand to ruefully shake his or her head and remind me how foolish I was to put myself at risk of bronchial collapse by sitting next to a woman who had recently given birth. Sure, I might take special white-people's medicine to protect against the ravages of vaginal heat, they told me (this is how they assumed I could survive the blasts at all), but sooner or later, they just knew, I would start spewing blood.

Despite their expectation that I would soon be coughing out my own lungs, both women and men seemed to enjoy my visits in the maternity huts. Men enjoyed them because I took digital photos of the new babies and willingly showed them to them. Before I began doing this, no adult man had ever seen a newborn, so they were all deeply curious. Women always welcomed me because I brought gossip and stories. They also liked looking at the photos I took of them and their babies. I usually also brought along some kerosene that could be put into a tin lamp, thus sparing the new mother and her baby pitch-black nights in a lonely, wind-rattled hut.

Because I spent so many hours in the company of young women in places like maternity huts, and of young men in places like the rainforest when they performed intimate and lengthy ministrations together, I came to see, over the months, that none of these young people ever used Tayap at all. All conversations between young people under twenty-five, in all situations, were in Tok Pisin. Young people use Tayap words that are common in the villagers' speech, and that often don't have Tok Pisin equivalents (for example, words for various birds and plants in the forest). And they do sometimes use short formulaic phrases, to provoke humor or to "hide talk" from any non-villager who might be in their company or within earshot. But that is all.

Young people do not converse, narrate, gossip, argue, tell jokes, discuss erotic experiences or do anything else at all in Tayap.

Once I understood this, I became better able to make sense of the mutual recrimination that arises whenever the topic of language shift comes up in villagers' conversations. Parents blame their children for not speaking Tayap. They say in voices dripping with irony that their children have all turned white and therefore they only speak the language of white people – Tok Pisin. Young people, when mocked in this way, snap back that it's the parents' own fault their children don't speak Tayap: if they had taught them Tayap, they would be able to speak it.

Young men and women also told me that they don't speak Tayap because they are ashamed. "They laugh at us", said one twenty-one-year-old man, referring to villagers in their forties and older. "They'll say 'Oh, he's someone raised in some other village'. Or, 'Oh! A whiteman child who doesn't know the village language'. They'll make fun of us. So it's hard to answer in the vernacular and we get mixed up." ("Ol i save lap long mipela, ol bai kirap tok, 'Em wanpela mangi bilong narapela hap ia'. O 'Ye, waitman pikinini i no save long tok ples'. Na bai ol i wokim pani gen. Em nau, hat long bekim long tok ples bai mipela paul ia.")

I became curious to know if the young people's lack of Tayap, and their shame about speaking it, was due to the fact that they simply didn't command it. So to try to assess this, I began asking groups of friends, two to three at a time, to come into my house at night to narrate stories in Tayap. Because I knew by that time that young people didn't speak Tayap to one another or anyone else, I expected this task to be like pulling teeth.

Instead, to my great surprise, it was like slicing butter.

Not only were young villagers eager to narrate; all but the very youngest of them were also *able* to narrate in Tayap. Many of the narratives were short, and most of them were scaffolded by the narrator's same-sex friends, who sat on the floor with them and helped the teller remember what things were called and figure out how verbs were inflected. But what emerged in the narrative sessions was that all young people in the village have some active competence in the vernacular, and some of them have excellent active competence – even though they *never* use it.

Those young people who exhibited the highest-level proficiency in their Tayap narratives (defined as speakers who spoke relatively unhesitatingly, used a variety of pronouns, verbal statuses and verbs of motion, and who had a broad vocabulary) constitute a kind of speaker that has not been discussed in the literature on language death. They are not exactly "passive bilinguals", because they are capable of active production – in a few cases, of relatively advanced active production (Tayap Text 3, narrated by a twenty-five-year-old woman, is an example of just how advanced).

Nor are these young women and men quite the same as what the linguist Nancy Dorian, in her work on language death in Scottish Gaelic communities, once labeled "semi-speakers" (Dorian 1981). The young people of Gapun *are* like the Gaelic semi-speakers that Dorian described in that they have perfect passive competence and perfect communicative competence in the vernacular: they understand everything said to them and they respond in culturally appropriate ways. But unlike Dorian's semi-speakers (and also unlike the Australian Dyirbal semi-speakers discussed in Schmidt 1985), young people in Gapun do not use the vernacular in conversations with fluent speakers. On the contrary, with the exception of lexical items and a few formulaic phrases like those mentioned above, they never use it at all. The narratives I collected in 2009 are the only times in their lives that the young people I recorded have ever told an entire story in Tayap, and unless I return to Gapun and record some more, or unless some miracle happens and the vernacular experiences a sudden renaissance, those sessions in my house are likely the last time that anyone under twenty five will ever even attempt to narrate an entire story in Tayap.

Rather than calling them "passive bilinguals" or "semi-speakers", a more accurate name for this category of speaker might be "passive active bilingual". The convolutedness of that label seems fitting to describe a speaker who possesses sufficient grammatical and communicative competence in a second language to use that language, but who never actually does use it, because social and cultural factors make it unnecessary or undesirable to do so.

Of particular relevance for this grammar is that there is a steady and stage-bound grammatical erosion from passive active bilinguals to increasingly less competent passive bilinguals. Some of this erosion includes the following:

- The five transitive verb classes become collapsed into the morphologically simplest conjugation class, class 5.
- Verbs of motion (all of which have irregular conjugations) are avoided and reduced to 'go' and 'come'.
- TAM distinctions are reduced to the non-future tense and the present progressive aspect, which is over-extended, because it is the morphologically simplest and most regular of all TAM categories. All other aspects, tenses and moods, such as the future, are avoided.
- 2PL, 3PL and dual subjects are avoided, because the suffixes on verbs that encode them have specific forms that differ from the subject suffixes for 1SG, 1PL, 2SG and 3SG – all of which are also specific, but which are similar to one another.
- Gender concordance on verbs and with ergative case marking is often confused.
- Relative clauses and subordinate clause morphology disappear, morphemes that coordinate clauses become reduced to a single morpheme, which is over-generalized on the pattern of Tok Pisin.
- Semantic differences between different Tayap verbs are collapsed on the pattern of Tok Pisin. For example, Tayap has two verbs for 'turn': *urek-(p)-e* 'turn over' (in the sense of turning an object around or over) and *waruk-(p)-e* 'turn around', 'turn back' (in the sense of going somewhere and then turning back to return from the place from which one came). Tok Pisin uses one verb, *tainim*, 'turn', for both senses. Young speakers follow Tok Pisin semantics and use only one verb, *urek-(p)-e*, for both senses of 'turn'.

These tendencies are discussed in the appropriate sections of the grammar and in the commentaries to the Tayap texts (page 289ff).

1.5 Naming practices

Everyone in Gapun has a *numŋa nomb* 'village name', which is one of a closed class of names that are recycled every third or fourth generation. When the person who bore the name most recently has died, it becomes available for reuse. All personal names are the property of one of the five different clans to which all Gapuners belong – crocodile (*orem*), dog (*nje*), parrot (*karar*), pig (*mbor*) or flying fox (*njakep*). This means that a name expresses clan membership, which is a crucial and central facet of villagers' identity, since it regulates access to land rights (different clans have rights to different areas of land) and marriage possibilities (clans are exogamous, so one's spouse should not be a fellow clan member).

Because names signify clan membership, a person cannot give a child a name that belongs to another clan. Such an act would be a kind of theft and would result, villagers are agreed, in the ensorcellment and death of the child, of the person who named the child or of a matrilineal relative of those persons (see Kulick 1992: 98–99 for a fuller discussion).

A child's parents have little say in what their child will be called. When a baby is born and has survived a few days, one of the baby's relatives (normally a matrilineal relative such as the baby's mother's mother, the mother's uncle or one of her siblings) will let it be known that they are going to 'put a name' (*nomb ŋgur*) on the child. In due course – several weeks to a month after the child's birth – the self-appointed bestower of the name will let it be known what the child will be called. If the mother or father doesn't like the sound of the name that the relative has come up with, they can reject it and ask her or him to think of a better one. Or they can ask another relative to put another name on the child, so that the child has two competing names.

This occasionally happens even if both a child's parents are satisfied with the name that has given to their new baby: sometimes that name is a taboo name for one of the parents – it may be the name of a deceased in-law, for example, and the names of in-laws are forbidden for villagers to call, even after the in-law bearing the name has died. In a case like that, the parent who is unable to call her or his child by name will either solicit a second name, or else she or he will address the child by a nickname, which will often be a word that draws attention to a defect or disability.

Villagers do not hide or try to disguise people's physical or intellectual differences from others; on the contrary, they continually foreground such differences with names like *Ngino* (Tayap 'Eye'; the nickname of a woman with strabismus); Kela (Tok Pisin 'Baldy', the nickname of a child who fell into a fire at a young age and was left with a large scar, from which hair cannot grow, covering most of his head); or Sens (Tok Pisin 'Crazy', the nickname of a young man who is probably epileptic and who sometimes blanks out of an interaction for several minutes at a time).

Village names are anywhere from one to four syllables, with the majority consisting of two syllables. Some examples are:

SYLLABLES	FEMALE NAME	MALE NAME
1	Mbit, Mbop, Mbup	Kak, Kem, Njab
2	Kanɨm, Mopok, Yapa	Ŋgedop, Panap, Sando
3	Karepa, Mbasama, Poniker	Oŋenjar, Sakoko, Tagipa
4	Armambɨra, Somasoma, Tamgeria	Ajiragi, Antamawri, Kaŋɨrase

Since the 1950s, each villager also has a Christian name ('kristen nem' in Tok Pisin, no word in Tayap). In contrast to village names, a person's Christian name is chosen by his or her parents or by a matrilineal relative whom the parents think can come up with a better name than they can. They choose a name either that they have heard someone from another village being called, or that they have decided is a name from the Bible.

Following the pattern of their traditional naming practices, villagers avoid giving their child the same name that somebody else already has, so there is usually only one Maria, one Joseph, one Paul, etc. in Gapun at any one time.

A child's Christian name is thought up whenever the Catholic priest from the Marienberg mission station comes to the village to baptize children – an event that occurs about once every two or three years. Villagers who get too creative with Christian names are chastised and corrected by the priest. In 2009, for example, one couple had chosen the name 'Anunciata' for their three-year-old daughter, because they liked the sound of the name and they had heard from someone that it was the name of a nun somewhere. As the priest from Marienberg was about to anoint the child, the girl's godparent told him that the child's Christian name was to be 'Anunciata'. The priest stopped the ceremony.

"That's not a Christian name", he announced. The parents would have to come up with something different.

The parents were silent.

Getting no response, the priest asked who the father was. When he was identified, he asked him impatiently what other names he had considered for the girl. The father said nothing.

From somewhere in the back of the church, one of the mother's relatives suggested 'Tema'.

The priest asked the girl's father if he wanted the name 'Tema' (the girl's mother's wishes or opinions – in keeping with Catholic practice – were not solicited or considered).

The father answered by looking down at his feet and saying softly, "If you want to change it, that's alright" ("Sapos yu laik sensim bai mi bihainim yu").

"No", the priest said to him. "Do you want that name?" ("Nogat, yu laikim despela nem tu?")

The father repeated himself, "If you want to change it, that's alright".

"But do you like the name?" the priest wanted to know. ("Na yu laikim tu?")

"Yeah", said the father reluctantly and barely audibly, "Em i orait" ("It's OK").

Thus did little Anunciata become baptized as Tema, a name that the parents don't like at all, and that, consequently, has never been uttered by anyone since that moment of baptism.

In day-to-day life, most villagers are called by their village names. A handful of people, however, are usually called by their Christian name, either because they want to foreground their Catholic piety, or because their parents never really liked the village names given to their child, so they got around it by always calling the child by his or her Christian name.

For official purposes such as school enrollment or electoral rolls, villagers are identified by their Christian name and the village name of their father. So Ŋgero, one of my main language informants in 2009, is identified in official contexts as Prisila Sair.

This patrilineal naming practice is contrary to and corrosive of how villagers reckon kinship, which is matrilineally – a villager belongs to the clan of her or his mother, not her or his father. Increasingly, however, as a direct result both of Catholic teaching and government sanctioned conventions such as official naming practices, fathers are asserting rights over their children, and are beginning to "take" their children into their clans with a frequency that far exceeds past practice.

Important mythical ancestors, deities and spirits also have names, as do all the areas of Gapun's vast rainforest. The more esoteric names for the ancestors and deities vanished from Tayap in the 1990s with the last of the village's truly knowledgeable big men. Those men declined to pass on the names to their matrilineal nephews, as used to be happen, because, they told me in the 1980s, the names were powerful elements in sorcery chants and could be used to kill people. The big men who made this decision were all strongly Catholic, and they believed that their traditional knowledge was part of what was preventing Gapuners from changing into white people (Kulick 1992).

Tayap words for commonly visited areas of the rainforest remain known among villagers, because they walk through the forest every day to hunt, gather food and go to their gardens or sago swamps. The names of places rarely visited by villagers and that are several days' walk from the village are less well known, and only the oldest people in the village can recite them, after long consultations with one another.

1.6 Tayap linguistic profile

Like many Sepik languages, Tayap is a synthetic language. Verbs are the most elaborated area of the grammar. They are complex, fusional and massively suppletive, with opaque verbal morphology including unpredictable conjugation classes, both in terms of membership and formal marking. There are very many suppletive stem forms marking a basic realis-irrealis distinction as well as various other TAM categories. Person/number marking also differs depending on the verb type. This is a language of "baroque accretions" (McWhorter 2001); or what Dahl (2004) calls "mature phenomena".

There is a fundamental distinction in verbal morphology between realis and irrealis stems and suffixes, but this distinction is overridden by transitivity in the prohibitive and counterfactual forms.

Grammatical relations are marked by verbal suffixes, which distinguish S/A versus O. In some conjugations S/A is marked by discontinuous morphemes. Free pronouns and noun phrases mark the ergative case (A) compared to unmarked forms for the absolutive (S/O). As in many Papuan languages which have an ergative case, the ergative marker is optional and is frequently omitted.

There are two genders, masculine and feminine, marked not on the noun itself but on deictics, the ergative marker, suppletive verbal stems and verbal affixes. The unmarked, generic form of all nouns, including animate nouns, even humans, is feminine: however, a male referent may be masculine. Another criterion is size and shape: long, thin and large referents tend to be masculine; short, stocky and small referents tend to be feminine. Again this type of gender-assignment system is typical of the Sepik region.

Gender is only ever marked in the singular, never in the dual or plural. Nouns generally do not mark number themselves, although there is a small class of largely human nouns which mark plural, and a smaller class which mark dual. These categories, where marked, are largely marked by partial or full suppletion. Oblique cases, largely local, are marked by clitics attached to the end of the oblique NP. Two adjectives also mark number, with partially suppletive forms for singular, dual and plural. A further two adjectives have partially suppletive forms for singular and plural.

Phonologically, the language has a medium-sized consonant inventory with voiceless stops, voiced (prenasalized) stops, nasals, semivowels and a rhotic/lateral flap. There are six vowels, /a/, /i/, /ɛ/, /u/, /ɔ/ and /ə/. Stress is largely predictable, typically word final but occasionally occurring elsewhere in the word.

The expression of possession is relatively simple: a possessor is marked with a clitic, and there are no subcategories of possession.

There are two kinds of complex predicate, which can be distinguished morpho-syntactically: serial verb constructions; and complex predicates formed with the verb 'to be', which consist of progressives and habituals. There are three types of complex clause: coordinate, cosubordinate (medial-final clause chains) and subordinate clauses. Subordinate clauses consist of relative clauses, adverbial clauses, and perception constructions, as well as finite nominalizations.

2 Phonology and orthography

2.1 Phonology

Tayap forms in this and all chapters are presented in the orthography as outlined below (Section 2.8) except in the consonant and vowel phoneme tables and when cited inside square brackets.

2.1.1 Consonants

Tayap's consonantal phonemes are as follows (orthography where it differs from IPA is written inside parentheses):

	Bilabial	**Dental**	**Alveolar**	**Post-alveolar**	**Palatal**	**Velar**
stops	p	t				k
voiced stops	ᵐb (mb/b)	ⁿd (nd/d)				ᵑg (ng/g)
fricative			s			
affricate				ⁿdʒ(nj/j)		
rhotic			r (r)			
semivowels	w (labial-velar)				j (y)	
nasals	m	n				ŋ

2.1.1.1 Brief description of some of the consonant phonemes
The voiceless stops are realized as aspirated when syllable initial or medial and optionally unreleased when syllable final. For example:

> *toto* [tʰɔˈtʰɔ] 'skin'
> *ŋgwek* [ŋgwɛkʰ] ~ [ŋgwɛk̚] 'they came'
> *karep* [kʰaˈrɛpʰ] 'moon'
> *tombet* [tʰɔˈᵐbɛtʰ] ~ [tʰɔˈᵐbɛt̚] 'shelf'

Note: I wish to acknowledge the work of Caroline Crouch, who ran Tayap recordings through Praat computer software (http://www.fon.hum.uva.nl/praat/) and largely confirmed my analysis of it, but who specified the exact phonetic characteristics of the language's various phonemes.

Voiceless stops have also been heard unreleased when preceding a vowel which is repeated from one syllable to the next. In this case the first instance of the vowel is deleted and the preceding consonant unreleased, e.g.

atikɨtak [atʰɘkʰɘtʰakʰ] ~ [atˀkʰɘtʰakʰ] 'she will fall'

The voiced stops are always prenasalized word initially, and optionally medially and finally. For example:

mambrag [maᵐbɾaⁿg] ~ [mabɾag] 'spirit'

The affricate is post-alveolar and voiced and usually prenasalized. Some examples:

munje [muⁿˈdʒɛ] 'man'
minjike [miⁿdʒiˈkɛ] 'betel nut'

The rhotic is realized most often as the alveolar flap [ɾ] (thus this is considered the basic phoneme), in particular between vowels and word finally:

wurɨ [wuɾɘ] 'up'
wákare [ˈwakaɾɛ] 'no'
yimbar [jiˈᵐbaɾ] 'canoe'

However it freely alternates with the rhotic approximant [ɹ] and alveolar lateral approximant [l]. For example:

irokoŋguk [iɾɔkɔŋguk] ~ [iɹɔkɔŋguk] 'they are laughing'
rɨpam [ɾɨpam] ~ [lɨpam] 'in the olden days'

Stops and the rhotic can be pronounced with a slight central vowel release when word final. The vowel quality is /ɘ/ after an /ɘ/ vowel, and otherwise schwa. This vowel is not phonemic. For example:

otar [ɔtaɾ] ~ [ɔtaɾᵊ] 'fire'
arawer [aɾawɛɾ] ~ [aɾawɛɾᵊ] 'sun'
yimbar [jiˈᵐbaɾ] ~ [jiˈᵐbaɾᵊ] 'canoe'
karep [kʰaˈɾɛpʰ] ~ [kʰaˈɾɛpʰᵊ] 'moon'
niŋg [nɘŋg] ~ [nɘŋgᵊ] 'bone'
pakɨnd [paˈkʰɨⁿd] ~ [paˈkʰɘⁿdᵊ] 'louse'

The semivowel /w/ can be realized with slight frication, e.g.

awin [aˈwin] ~ [aˈvin] 'water'

The semivowels /y/ and /w/ are discussed below in Vowel Sequences, Section 2.2.

2.1.1.2 Minimal contrasts between the consonant phonemes
Minimal or near-minimal pairs of phonetically close phonemes are as follows:

	INITIAL	MEDIAL	FINAL
p mb/b	*paŋg* 'fiber from *tar* tree'	*apu* 'burn sth'	*pap* 'coconut'
	mbaŋ 'bang against sth'	*ambu* 'hide sth'	*tamb* 'funeral bier'
t nd/d	*tum* 'beetle'	*tatak* 'traditional decoration'	*ut* 'cane grass'
	ndum 'clear undergrowth'	*tandaŋ* 'woven screen'	*mond* 'penis'
k ŋg/g	*kandam* 'ass'	*mokɨt* 'sacred flutes'	*arik* 'really'
	ŋgadan 'sore'	*muŋgit* 'day before yesterday'	*areŋg* 'tree sp.'
k ŋ	*kamb* 'croton plant'	*takɨ* 'sleep'	*sik* 'mouth'
	ŋawmb 'large shell ring'	*taŋa* 'insect eggs'	*siŋ* 'peel sth off'
n nd/d	*nam* 'tell, say'	*ana* 'where?'	*pɨn* 'a little'
	ndam 'cluster of betel nut'	*anda* 'miss or go past sth'	*kind* 'close sth'
m mb/b	*manaw* 'three'	*mámaki* 'gnat'	*tam* 'bird'
	mbaŋaw 'areca palm sp.'	*mámbakɨ* 'net bag'	*tamb* 'funeral bier'
m n ŋ	*mai* 'enough!'	*amen* 'three days from now'	*am* 'battle' (n)
	nai 'hit someone hard'	*ani* 'who?'	*apran* 'poor thing'
	ŋa 'I/me'	*kaŋan* 'Tahitian chestnut'	*aŋ* 'pump sth'
nd/d nj/j	*ndam* 'cluster of betel nuts'	*kandaw* 'sickness'	*kind* 'close sth'
	njam 'hurriedly assembled bush house'	*kanjaŋ* 'tree sp.'	*kinj* 'tree sp.'
ŋ ŋg/g	*ŋaŋan* 'mine'	*taŋa* 'insect eggs'	*aŋ* 'pump sth'
	ŋgadan 'sore'	*taŋgar* 'nest, burrow'	*inaŋg* 'oar'
s t	*sik* 'mouth'	*mosop* 'small'	*pis* 'soundless fart'
	tɨk 'story'	*moto* 'debris in water'	*pɨt* 'wash objects'
r t	*ramb* 'carving on a slit gong drum'	*arik* 'really'	*rar* 'see'
	tamb 'funeral bier'	*atɨkɨ* 'happen'	*tat* 'needle/spine'

2.1.2 Vowels

Tayap has six vowels. The vowels are /a/, /i/, /ɛ/, /u/, /ɔ/ and /ɵ/, a non-back close-mid rounded vowel that can surface either as [ɵ] or [ø].

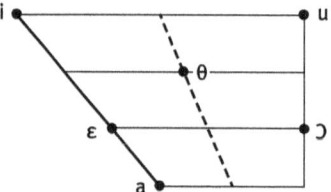

In the orthography [ɛ] is written as *e*, [ɔ] as *o* and [ɵ] as *ɨ*.

These vowels are evidenced by minimal/near-minimal sets like the following:

aŋgode 'here'   *yim* '1PL'
aŋgide 'there, a bit further away'   *yum* '3PL'
aŋgude 'there, still further away'   *yam* 'sago palm'

nek 'ladder'   *nam* 'talk'
nok 'urine'   *nɨm* 'tree'
nɨkɨr 'lap'   *num* 'village'
                           nom 'wild taro'

emb 'morning'   *ta* 'small knife'
umb 'top of sago palm'   *ti* 'type of wild sugar cane'
rɨmb 'traditional decoration' *tɨ* 'also'
                           tep 'wooden slit gong support'

The vowel *ɨ* is marginal, in that it does not appear word-initially and it does not form vowel sequences, as other vowels do. However it is a full phoneme in its own right. For example it appears in minimal sets as above, and it appears as the sole vowel in monosyllabic and mono-morphemic words:

tɨk 'story, narrative'
wɨr 'watch; guard'
tɨmɨr 'needle'
kɨmɨrɨk 'sago grub'

In addition to the six vowels that enter into phonemic contrasts, Tayap also has a mid central unrounded schwa [ə] that is inserted epenthetically between consonants at morpheme boundaries, breaking up otherwise unpermissable consonants clusters. So words like the following are pronounced with a schwa:

(2-1) a. *pwapŋgar munje* is pronounced [pwapəŋgar munjɛ]
    pwap   -ŋgar   munje
    anger -NFN.SG man
    'angry man'

   b. *okɨnetke* is pronounced [ɔkənɛtəkɛ]
    o   -kɨ   -net   =ke
    go.IRR   -IRR   -1SG.M|3SG.M.IRR   =Q
    'will he go?' or 'will I (M) go?'

Schwa also appears optionally after a word-final rhotic or stop, as mentioned above, Section 2.1.1.1.

Vowel length is non-distinctive. However, Tayap speakers use extended vowels to convey two meanings: (1) that they feel sympathy or that the hearer should feel sympathy and pity for the speaker or someone being spoken about, and (2) temporal duration.

2.1.2.1 Vowel length expressing sympathy and pity

Sympathy and pity is a sentiment that extended vowels are used to both express and elicit. This speech pattern is socialized from the beginning of a child's life. One of the earliest and most common sounds a baby will hear its mother making is the sound *yo*, uttered in a soft voice with an extended vowel and rising intonation. *Yoooooo*, held over at least three beats, means 'poor thing'. It is murmured whenever a baby starts to cry and the mother notices it and gently puts her breast in its mouth.

The expression also means 'feel sorry for X'. When an older sibling doesn't want to share food or some object with a baby, for example, a mother will elicit the older sibling's sympathy by saying *yooooo* and telling the child in a soft voice that the baby is crying for the food or object (cf. Schieffelin 1990).

This speech pattern endures in all kinds of social situations throughout life. So an adult man wanting another villager to give him a piglet might convey his desire by first mentioning that people have talked about how the addressee has several piglets, then adding that a piglet that he had been looking after had died. A likely way of saying this is:

(2-2) *ŋaŋaaaaaaaan ndɨ wasowtakara*
    ŋaŋaaaaaaaan ndɨ   wasow   -tak   -ara
    1SG.POSS   INTENS   die.R   -2SG.F|3SG.F.R -PERF
    'mine died'

Every Gapun villager would immediately understand this utterance to be a request – an indirect and veiled request, to be sure, but a request nevertheless. This understanding is raised by the extended vowel, the rising intonation and the soft voice, all of which invoke *yoooooo*.

Like Proust's famous madeleine, this prosodic package appears intended to induce affect-laden memories from earliest childhood. Its pragmatic force is to try to elicit sympathy for the speaker; sympathy that should ideally produce an action from the addressee that would result in "ending the worry" of the speaker, as villagers say in Tok Pisin ("pinisim wari"). No explicit request need ever be made. The addressee can ignore or deflect the request, but the meaning of the extended vowel and its prosodic form is clear to everyone.

2.1.2.2 Vowel length expressing duration over time

Duration over time can also be expressed through vowel length. To convey that one walked a long way, for example, one can either repeat the verb several times or extend the final vowel of the verb that the speaker wishes to highlight as extended over time. In the first case, the utterance – which is written here as it would be pronounced, with the final consonant /t/ omitted – would look as follows:

(2-3) ŋa   mbo   mbo   mbo   mbo
       1SG   go.SG.M.R   go.SG.M.R   go.SG.M.R   go.SG.M.R
       'I went, went, went, went'; i.e. I walked for a long time (see Tayap Text 1, lines 37, 40 and 45, and Tayap Text 5, lines 71–72 for further examples).

Alternatively, to express the same meaning, a speaker can extend the final vowel of the verb:

(2-4) ŋa   mbooooooo
       1SG   go.SG.M.R
       'I weeeeeeent'; i.e. I walked for a long time

2.2 Vowel sequences

Vowels may form sequences, most commonly with /i/ or /u/ as either the first or second element. Not all combinations occur, and no vowels form sequences with /ə/. Further, there are no sequences of identical vowels.

Possible vowel sequences are shown in Table 2.1.

Table 2.1 Attested vowel sequences (x means unattested, bracketed means rare).

	a	e	i	o	u	ɨ
a	x	x	ai	ao	(au)	x
e	x	x	ei	(eo)	(eu)	x
i	ia	ie	x	io	iu	x
o	x	(oe)	oi	x	x	x
u	ua	ue	x	uo	x	x
ɨ	x	x	x	x	x	x

Some examples:

> *mindia* 'stone axe'
> *aruat* 'thunder'
> *pisiek* 'she rubbed her skin'
> *tuemb* 'the day after tomorrow'
> *perei* 'say something insulting'
> *sokoi* 'tobacco'
> *nao* 'genital flesh'
> *irioki* 'dive into water'
> *minuomb* 'round pool of water'
> *teunietre* 'when I/he ran away'
> *iurok* 'mosquito sp.'

There are no sequences of more than two vowels. Any possible such sequences always involve /i/ or /u/ as the second element, and are better analyzed as sequences of VyV or VwV respectively.
For example:

> *ayab*   [aiaᵐb] 'cluster of branches of seeds or fruit'
> *mayes*   [maies] 'ceremonial spear'
> *ŋgugrugrayi* [ⁿgugrugaii] 'sleepy'
> *puwuayorom* [puuaiorom] 'beach'
> *tower*   [touer] 'quietly'
> *yɨwɨr*   [jɨuɨr] 'faeces'
> *arawer*   [arauer] 'sun'
> *awar*   [auar] 'wind from north'
> *karuwa*   [karuua] 'fish sp.'

In examples like these, the second segment is analyzed as the semivowel /y/ rather than the vowel /i/, or /w/ rather than /u/ respectively. This analysis preserves the syllable structure rules given below (Section 2.3.1). The name of the language [taiap] is thus therefore now spelt 'Tayap' rather than 'Taiap', as I spelled it previously (for an additional reason for this spelling change, see below, Section 2.8).

2.3 Syllable structure and phonotactics

2.3.1 Syllable structure

Syllable structure is $(C_1)V(C_2)$ or $C_3C_4V(C_2)$ or $(C_1)VC_5C_6$.

C_1 is any consonant
C_2 is any consonant but *y*
C_3 is any stop
C_4 is *r*
C_5 is *w*
C_6 is any stop
V is a single vowel

Although words can be generated from this schema with multiple V syllables, in practice sequences of more than two vowels do not occur (see above, Section 2.2).

So under this schema a word like *aruat* 'thunder' would be two syllables: V.CVC.

The position C_5 is analyzed as a semivowel /w/ rather than a vowel /u/ for one reason. C_6 is only ever a stop: thus an analysis of C_5 as /u/ would mean that CVC sequences with /u/ as the vowel could only ever be followed by stops. This would be a rather strange situation, so it is avoided here by instead positing a CC cluster with /w/ as the first consonant and any stop as the second.

Some examples of word shapes:

CVC	nak	'count sth'
VC	am	'battle' (n)
V.V	ei	'cry' (n)
CV	ndɨ	'emphatic particle'
C.VCV	amor	'yam sp.'
CV.VC.CV	kaikro	'landing place for canoes'
CCVC	pruk	'work'
V.CV.CVC	arawer	'sun'

CVC.CVC	rorsem	'children'
CCV.CV	Kruni	'Kruni, personal name'
VC.CV	orma	'younger sibling'
CVC	tuemb	'day after tomorrow'
CV.CV	sokoi	'tobacco'
CVC.CV	mokwa	'three pronged spear'
CVC.V.CVC	kimirik	'sago grub'
CV.CV.CV	yamiɲe	'brush turkey egg'
V.CVC	awin	'water'
V.CV	ama	'mama'

Words of the shape VNCV, where NC is a homorganic nasal-stop sequence, can in theory be distinguished from those of the shape V^{m}CV, where ^{m}C is a prenasalized stop, on the grounds that prenasalization fluctuates word-medially in Tayap, and thus could be not pronounced, whereas if the segment in question is a nasal consonant it must be pronounced.

They can also be distinguished in other ways. So for example nam'bar 'one' has stress on the syllable beginning /b/, not on the /mb/ cluster, indicating that the nasal is a full nasal consonant rather than prenasalization belonging to the voiced stop.

This analysis has implications for the orthography, and here the decision is a pragmatic one: while it is possible to distinguish NC from ^{m}C medially, in the orthography these are not distinguished. Thus, a voiced stop with no accompanying nasal indicates a voiced stop, which could alternatively be pronounced with or without nasalization. But a nasal and homorganic voiced stop cluster may refer to a NC cluster, e.g. as in nambar, or it may refer to a prenasalized stop ^{m}C.

2.4 Vowel harmony

Vowel harmony and regressive assimilation are characteristic features of Tayap verbs. The vowel of the object morpheme often influences the vowel of the verb stem or subject morpheme that precedes it.

Compare, for example, the following two forms of the verb 'set down':

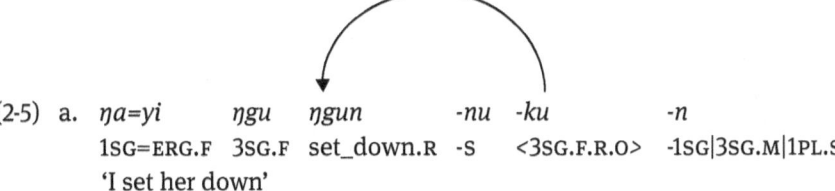

(2-5) a. ŋa=yi   ŋgu   ŋgun   -nu -ku   -n
       1SG=ERG.F 3SG.F set_down.R -S   <3SG.F.R.O> -1SG|3SG.M|1PL.S
       'I set her down'

b.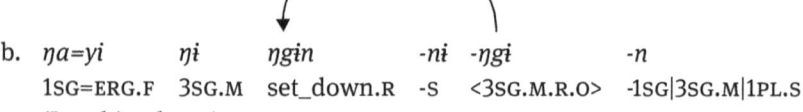
    ŋa=yi   ŋi̶   ŋgin   -ni̶   -ŋgi̶   -n
    1SG=ERG.F   3SG.M   set_down.R   -S   <3SG.M.R.O>   -1SG|3SG.M|1PL.S
    'I set him down'

The same process is evident in the subject markers of the following verb, 'collect':

(2-6) a.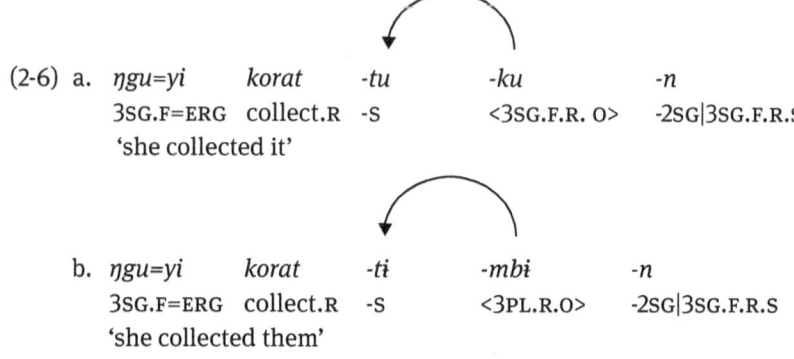
    ŋgu=yi   korat   -tu   -ku   -n
    3SG.F=ERG   collect.R   -S   <3SG.F.R. O>   -2SG|3SG.F.R.S
    'she collected it'

   b.
    ŋgu=yi   korat   -ti̶   -mbi̶   -n
    3SG.F=ERG   collect.R   -S   <3PL.R.O>   -2SG|3SG.F.R.S
    'she collected them'

Note how the vowel immediately preceding the object suffix changes according to whether the object suffix contains a mid vowel or a back vowel. That it is the vowel in the object suffix that influences the vowel in the verb stem, and not vice versa, is clear from the fact that object suffixes are invariant – they are the same for all verb stems (see Sections 3.5, 5.3.1 and 5.3.2).

In (2-6a) and (2-6b), the morpheme preceding the object is the first part of a discontinuous subject morpheme. The vowel in that morpheme, which will always be /u/ or /ə/, is often either reduced to a schwa or is omitted altogether, especially if it occurs after /n/ or medially between /k/ and /ɾ/. For example:

(2-7) a. ŋiŋi koranukun (pronounced korankun)
    ŋi̶=ŋi   kora   -nu   -ku   -n
    3SG.M=ERG   collect.R   -S   <3SG.F.R.O>   -1SG|3SG.M|1PL.S
    'he collected it'

   b. ninukun (pronounced ninkun)
    ni   -nu   -ku   -n
    do.R   -S   <3SG.F.R.O>   -1SG|3SG.M|1PL.S
    'I (M or F) did it', 'he did it', 'she did it', 'we did it'

The orthography used in this grammar and dictionary reflects the vowel deletion. *Note that in those cases when the vowel was not pronounced, it is not written in the word.*

The only other phonotactic rule involving vowels is that following the bilabial nasal /m/ or a velar stop, a vowel can acquire the semivowel /w/, a case of progressive rounding, as described for Sougb by Reesink (2002a); e.g.:

(2-8) a. *suman* 'big'   → sumwan
       b. *Mukar* (male name)   → mukwar
       c. *a-ŋgar*   → aŋgwar
           be.IRR-NFN.SG
           'being'

2.5 Stress

Stressed syllables are realized as louder and longer than unstressed syllables. Stress in Tayap is generally not phonemic, and unpredictable stress occurs rarely. In the dictionary, unpredictable stress occurs on roughly two percent of words.

Stress usually falls on the final syllable of an uninflected word (but see below for more information about stress on bound morphemes):

(2-9) *ambagái* 'men's house'   *ndugubár* 'backbone'
       karép 'moon'   *ŋayár* 'really'
       kemém 'long'   *piŋín* 'clitoris'
       koŋgód 'hour glass drum'   *pokémb* 'cold'
       orímb 'audible fart'   *puwás* 'white'
       otár 'fire'   *toŋgodíp* 'Malay apple'
       makatók 'green coconut'   *tumbúr* 'shoulder'
       minjiké 'betel nut'   *wekók* 'obscenity'

There are a number of non-predictable exceptions to the syllable-final rule. The orthography used in this grammar and dictionary marks stress explicitly on those exceptional words. Examples of two-syllable words with non-final stress:

mbímaŋ 'leech'
símbu 'maggot'

Examples of longer words with non-final stress:

(2-10) arúmbatak 'fly' pasákeke 'frog'
atáwo 'older sibling' ndagúnɨ 'furtively'
mbíoŋgi 'baby' supwáspwa 'badly'
emári 'ancestral spirit' tandímɨrit 'broom for swatting mosquitoes'
kanjígogo 'edible bamboo shoot' uráŋgeba 'large bullfrog'
nekénduko 'sharp grass' wákare 'no'

Syllables with unpredictable stress are far more common with the vowel *a* than the other vowels. In the dictionary more than three times as many instances occur with *a* as with any other vowel.

In general, stress is a property of a lexical morpheme, not an inflected word, and thus stress placement is retained under affixation. For example:

munjé 'man' munjénum 'men'
mɨrí 'forest' mɨríni 'in the forest'

There are some minimal pairs differentiated only by stress:

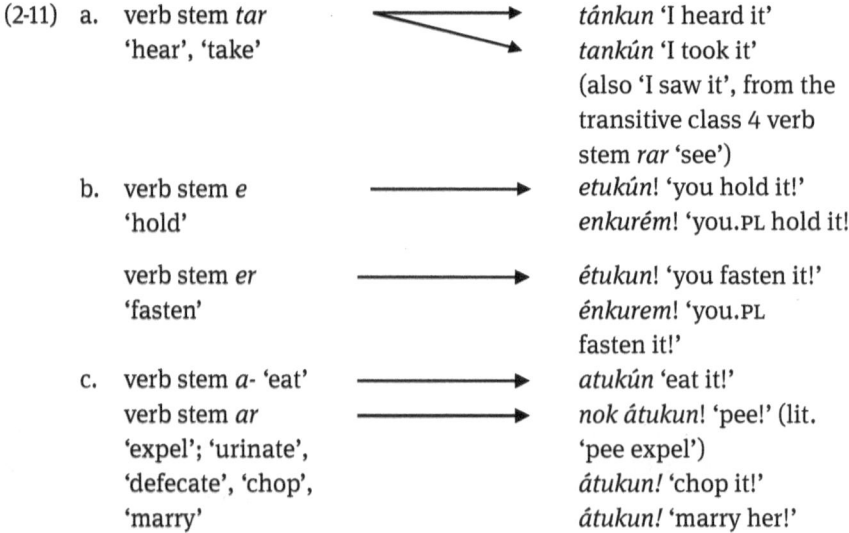

(2-11) a. verb stem *tar* ⟶ tánkun 'I heard it'
'hear', 'take' tankún 'I took it'
(also 'I saw it', from the transitive class 4 verb stem *rar* 'see')

b. verb stem *e* ⟶ etukún! 'you hold it!'
'hold' enkurém! 'you.PL hold it!'

verb stem *er* ⟶ étukun! 'you fasten it!'
'fasten' énkurem! 'you.PL fasten it!'

c. verb stem *a-* 'eat' ⟶ atukún 'eat it!'
verb stem *ar* ⟶ nok átukun! 'pee!' (lit. 'pee expel')
'expel'; 'urinate',
'defecate', 'chop', átukun! 'chop it!'
'marry' átukun! 'marry her!'

Reduplicated words retain stress on both forms (reduplication is discussed in Section 5.5):

(2-12) sumúsumú 'bat' towótowó 'four'
ndɨdɨkdɨdɨk 'lumpy' tomɨktomɨk 'spider'

Peripheral case morphemes and possessive morphemes are unstressed:

(2-13) a. *ŋguyi pitiŋárnɨ poŋgɨn*
ŋgu=yi   pitiŋár=nɨ   po   -ŋgɨ   -n
3SG.F=ERG.F machete=LOC   strike.R   -3SG.M.R.O   -SG|1PL.R.S
'she stabbed him with a machete'

b. *nɨmárŋa ŋgomar purkun*
nɨmár=ŋa   ŋgomar   pur   -ku   -n
mangrove=POSS   fish   hook.R   -3SG.F.R.O   -SG|1PL.R.S
'I (M or F) hooked a mangrove fish' (or 'he/she/we hooked a mangrove fish')

c. compare:
mbór=mat   and   mbormát
pig=POSS
'the pig's'   'a kind of banana'

ŋgí=re   and   ŋgɨré
3PL=COM
'with them'   'therefore'

Inflected verbs take stress on the final syllable of the word as a whole, with various exceptions, which are conditioned by the conjugation class of the verb, as well as by TAM and other types of affixation.

Other instances of unusual stress include the following:
(1) In verbs inflected in the perfect aspect and the intentional mood, stress falls on the syllable that precedes the perfect suffix (*-(da)ra*) and the intentional suffix (*-(n)ana*):

(2-14) a. *kakúndara*
ka   -kú   -n   -dara
eat.R   <3SG.F.R.O>   -SG|1PL.R.S   -PERF
'I (M or F) ate it' or 'he ate it' or 'she ate it' or 'we ate it'

b. *wókara*
wók   -ara
go.3SG.F.R -PERF
'she's gone'

c. *ŋa prukkɨnétana inda*
ŋa   pruk   -kɨ   -nét   -ana   inda
1SG   work.IRR   -IRR   -1SG.M|3SG.M.IRR   -INTENT   DX.M
'I (M) am going to work now'

d. *yu mum akrúnanake?*
   yu   mum   a   -krú   -nana   =ke
   2SG   sago jelly consume.IRR   -3SG.F.IRR.O   -INTENT   =Q
   'Would you eat sago jelly?' (if I offer you some)

(2) In verbs inflected in the counterfactual, stress falls on *-rik*, the counterfactual suffix:

(2-15) *akríknukun*
   ak   -rík   -nu   -ku   -n
   eat.CF   -CF   -S   <3SG.F.R.O>   -1SG|3SG.M|1PL.R.S
   'I would have eaten it'

Stress on the counterfactual suffix differentiates it from the progressive suffix *-rik-* that occurs in some progressive constructions and is always unstressed (see Sections 8.3.1 and 9.4.3).

(3) In most verbs inflected in the progressive aspect, stress falls on the final syllable of the verb stem for intransitive verbs, and on the BEN object morpheme for transitive verbs:

(2-16) a. *yu anakŋa merni warákakkut?*
   yu   anakŋa   mer=ni   warák   -ak   kut
   2SG   which   language=INST   speak.IRR   -LINK   be.SG.M.R
   'which language are you (M) speaking?'

   b. *ŋguyi ŋa oiánuk*
   ŋgu=yi   ŋa   o   -ián   uk
   3SG.F=ERG.F   1SG   strike.IRR   -1SG.BEN.O   be.3SG.F.R
   'she is hitting me'

(4) Class 4 verbs in the non-future tense take stress on the last syllable of the verb stem:

(2-17) a. *ŋiŋi namŋat aŋgi supwáspwa ŋanana nínkun*
   ŋi=ŋi   nam-ŋat   aŋgi   supwáspwa   ŋa=nana
   3SG.M=ERG.M   talk-half   DX   badly   1SG=DAT

   ní   -n   -ku   -n
   make.R   -S   <3SG.R.O>   -1SG|3SG.M|1PL.R.S
   'he said something nasty to me', lit. 'he made a nasty talk to me'

b. *ŋgigi koráttimbɨro*
    ŋgɨ=gi   korát   -tɨ -mbɨ   -ro
    3PL=ERG.PL collect.R -S <3PL.R.O> -3PL.R.S
    'they collected them'

(5) In the subjunctive mood, verb roots ending in /r/ gain the vowel /ɛ/ before the imperative ending, and that vowel is stressed, as in all imperatives, see (7) below:

(2-18) a. *rar-* (IRR) 'look' → *raré-* (SBJ, so: *raré-tet, raré-tak, raré-nkem*)
          b. *sir-* (IRR) 'descend'→ *siré-* (SBJ, so: *siré-tet, siré-tak, siré-nkem*)

(6) Intransitive verbs in irrealis dual forms take stress on the IRR morpheme:

(2-19) a. *ŋgrag ŋayarre okítike*
        ŋgrag   ŋayar=re   o   -kɨ́   -tike
        afternoon really=TEMP go.IRR -IRR -DL.IRR
        'let's the two of us go in the really late afternoon'

       b. *pereipereikítike!*
         pereiperei -kɨ́   -tike
         race.IRR   -IRR -DL.IRR
         'let's the two of us race!'

(7) With imperative verbs, stress occurs on the final syllable of the imperative stem rather than the word as a whole. For example *moser* 'buy' receives stress on the final syllable of the stem rather than the word: *mosé-tukun!* ("buy it"). See Sections 7.1.2.1 and 7.1.2.2.

(8) The subjunctive stems of class 4 verbs lose the final /r/, if they have one, of their irrealis stem and the remaining stem is always stressed. See Section 7.1.2.2.

2.6 Morpho-phonemic rules

Morpho-phonemic rules do not operate universally. For example in (2-24c) rule 3 does not apply. The conditioning factors of these rules are not known, but the rules often do apply.

    Morpho-phonemic rules involving consonants frequently involve the rhotic /r/. This is inserted at morpheme boundaries (including affixes and clitics) in the following environments:

(1) Insert /ɾ/ between a vowel and /k/ at a morpheme boundary, e.g.:

(2-19) a. *senerkɨtak*
sene -r -kɨ -tak
two -r -IRR -2SG.F|3SG.F.IRR
'it will become two'

b. *aserkrunet*
ase -r -kru -net
in_front -r -3SG.F.IRR.O -1SG.M|3SG.M.IRR.S
'he'll put it in front' or 'I (M) will put it in front'

c. *supwáspwarkɨtak*
supwáspwa -r -kɨ -tak
badly -r -IRR -2SG.F|3SG.F.IRR
'it will go badly'

(2) Insert /ɾa/ at morpheme boundary after /k/, e.g.:

(2-20) *ketukrakɨ*
ketuk -ra -kɨ
cough -ra -ADV
'having coughed...'

Note: this rule is blocked when the morpheme following the /k/ is a morpheme signaling irrealis; so *ketuk-kɨ* (cough.IRR-IRR) is permitted.

(3) Insert /ɾ/ between a consonant and a vowel at a morpheme boundary, e.g.:

(2-21) *tapratkɨŋɡiatikɨnetana*
tap -r -atkɨŋɡiatikɨnetana
carry_on_shoulders -r -he_intends_to_carry_him_down
'he intends to carry him down on his shoulders'

(4) Insert /ɾ/ between two vowels at a morpheme boundary, e.g.:

(2-22) a. *mɨndarakkut*
mɨnda -r -ak kut
tired_of -r -LINK be.SG.M.R
I (M) am fed up or 'you're (M) fed up' or 'he's fed up'

b. *worekeni̵ pimbiet*
   wo   -r =ekeni̵   pimbiet
   above -r =PERL   fly.3SG.M.R
   'it's flying above'

Other phonotactic rules involving consonants are:

(5) Insert /d/ between /n/ and /r/ at a morpheme boundary, e.g.:

(2-23) *awindre*
        awin   -d   =re
        water -d   =COM
        'with the water'

(6) The progressive form is constructed with the fully inflected verb *a* 'be' (see Section 8.3.1). The 3SG.F.R form of 'be', and the dual form, have word-initial semi-vowels: *wuk* (be.3SG.F.R) and *wuke* (be.DL.R). In the progressive, the semivowel is always deleted, resulting in examples like the following:

(2-24) a. *ŋgu akwanwuk* (pronounced [akw'anuk])
           ŋgu   a   -kwan   -wuk
           she   eat.IRR   <3SG.F.BEN.R.O>   -be.3SG.F.R
           'she is eating (it)'

        b. *mbor werri̵kwuk* (pronounced [wɛrə'kuk])
           mbor   wer   -ri̵k   wuk
           pig   dig.IRR -PROG   be.3SG.F.R
           'the pig is digging'

        c. *aiakwuk* (pronounced [aia'kuk])
           ai   -ak   wuk
           come.IRR   -LINK   be.3SG.F.R
           'it is coming'

        d. *ruru sene emrariakawkwuke* (pronounced [ɛmrariaku'kɛ])
           ruru   sene   emrari   -ak   -awk   wuke
           child.DL   two   play.IRR   -LINK   -be.HAB be.DL.R
           'the two kids are always playing'

(7) The prenasalized object suffix in indirect commands loses its prenasalization. For example:

-ŋgi- '3SG.M.R.O' is realized as -gi-
-mbɨ- '3PL.R.O' is realized as -bɨ-

(See Section 7.1.4 for more discussion and examples of indirect commands.)

(8) There is a morpho-phonemic process involving loss of word final stops, for example note the loss of final /t/ in example (2-3).

2.7 Wordhood

Words can be defined phonologically, as "a prosodic unit not smaller than a syllable" (Aikhenvald 2007: 2). Words in Tayap have the following properties:

- Whole words can be pronounced in isolation whereas units smaller than a word, i.e. bound morphemes, cannot.
- Some phonemic properties use words as defining criteria: e.g. the vowel ɨ never occurs word-initially.
- Stress usually occurs word-finally on uninflected words.
- Prenasalized stops are obligatorily prenasalized word-initially but only optionally in other environments.
- Vowel harmony operates within words.
- Reduplication only occurs within words or across a word, not across items larger than words.

Grammatical words generally coincide with phonological words in Tayap (however see Section 8.2, example (8–3) for a counter-example). Grammatical words consist of "a number of grammatical elements which (i) always occur together rather than scattered throughout the clause (...); (ii) occur in fixed order; and (iii) have a conventionalized coherence and meaning" (Aikhenvald 2007: 2).

In Tayap, verbs are grammatical words which minimally must always occur with person and/or status marking except in certain restricted morphosyntactic environments. Even the longest and most complex of the complex predicates described in Chapters 8 and 9 consist of single grammatical words, sharing as they do various properties like marking for arguments and/or realis/irrealis status. Thus the example discussed in detail in Chapter 8, *tapratkɨŋgiatikɨtakana*, 'she intends to carry him down on her shoulders', is a single phonological and grammatical word.

However grammatical words do not necessarily have to be inflected. Verbs are normally inflected, but nouns, pronouns, particles and other minor classes can occur without inflection.

2.8 Orthography

The Tayap orthography in this grammar and dictionary uses letters of the English alphabet that correspond to the language's phonemes, with two exceptions: *i* and ŋ. The phonemes /ə/ and /ŋ/ would be difficult to render using the letters used to write English or Tok Pisin. Tayap is almost never written, and any villager who does so invents his or her own nonce orthography. In my years of contact with the villagers, I have received many letters from them, always written in Tok Pisin. At the very end of these letters, though, after the writer has finished asking me for money (which is always the sole reason for sending me a letter), he or she often concludes with a line written in Tayap, to add coercive punch to the requests.

A typical example is the phrase *Aowo grag engon yu na na*, which occurred at the very end of a letter that had just instructed me to send the writer the equivalent of $8,000 (at a time when the yearly income for *the entire village* was about $500). The interjection *aowo* is an orthographic rendering of a sound used by villagers to convey worry and longing, and the rest, 'good evening to you', is a Tayap calque of Tok Pisin's "gutpela apinun long yu". The unambiguous meaning of the Tayap phrase is: 'I worry about you, so now you worry about me and send me eight thousand dollars'.

The orthography that villagers have come up with to write Tayap varies from writer to writer and from occasion to occasion. However, one convention that has developed over the years regards /ə/, which is sometimes written as *h*, and /ŋ/, which is often rendered as either *nh* or *ngh*. This convention may be the invention of Amburi Waiki, who was in his late twenties and the village prayer leader in the mid-1980s. Amburi was the only person in Gapun to write anything in Tayap at that time, and his orthography – which he himself applied erratically – was seen by others and perhaps adopted by them. (What Amburi wrote on loose pages and in school workbooks were the names of villagers who had contributed money to the village church, and the names of areas of rainforest that he wanted to note down for various reasons.)

This way of handling Tayap's phonemes results in a sentence like the following, which Amburi wrote down for me in the 1980s: *Ngha nghing ana mbet* ('I have come for them').

The problem with the orthography used to write this sentence is that it is difficult for villagers to parse and read. It makes no distinction between free and bound morphemes (*-ana*, 'for' or 'to', for example, is a bound morpheme that cannot occur on its own), and literate villagers, who have learned to read by being drilled in school with texts in English, have difficulty with the sheer number of letters used to denote simple sounds. (In the orthography used in this grammar and dictionary the sentence would be written *Ŋa ŋginana mbet*.)

A sentence produced in 2009 by a literate villager who I asked to demonstrate to me how he would write something in Tayap shows that the same problems have persisted: *Nhang nhan patir engon nhayar* ('My house is very nice'). The orthography is internally inconsistent – the word written *engon* is pronounced [ɛŋgɔn], and thus should be written *enhgon*, if the conventions of this orthography were followed consistently.

This orthography also quickly gets messy. For example, in the sentence just quoted, a common word like *ŋaŋan* ('my') is written as two words and spelled *nhang nhan*. In other instances, simple pronouns like *ŋɨ* [ŋə] ('he') and *ŋgɨ* [ŋgə] ('they') tend to stump village writers, who might write them as *nghi* and *nghgh*, respectively – although they would more likely avoid writing them or give up trying to write them.

Words with the consonant cluster /ŋg/ also pose difficulties. A name like 'Saŋgi' – which the villagers' orthography should render as something like *Sanhgi* – looks strange to the villagers when they see it written out in this way (they would in this case write 'Sangi'). Worse, a name like 'Saŋgiŋgi', which might be written something like *Sanhginhgi*, would make villagers who try to use their invented orthography throw up their hands in despair.

Because of those difficulties, which villagers perceive and talk about themselves, I do not adopt their orthographic inventions to write /ə/ and /ŋ/. Instead, I introduce two additional letters, *ɨ* and *ŋ*. These letters are ordered so that *ɨ* follows *i* in the alphabet, and *ŋ* follows *n*.

While I depart from the villagers' attempts to write /ə/ and /ŋ/, I do follow their loose convention of orthographically marking prenasalization on the voiced word-initial stops /b/ and /d/ and on the affricate /dʒ/. Villagers vary on whether or not they orthographically mark word-initial nasalization on the velar stop /g/: a word like 'cassowary', spelled *ŋgat* in this orthography, would probably be written *ngat* by most villagers.

On the other hand, though, some of them write *ŋgrag* 'evening' as *grag* (see above, the example of a villager's letter asking me for $8,000). Regardless of how they would write a word-initial /g/, however, Tayap speakers consistently prenasalize the phoneme when they pronounce it in this position. Hence, I mark this in the orthography.

This concession to village pronunciation and writing conventions means that the orthography used here is not as economical as it otherwise might have been. I could have omitted the nasalization in words beginning with /b/, /d/, /j/ and /g/ and simply noted that those phonemes are all obligatorily nasalized word-initially (this is what Christopher Stroud and I did in our 1993 sketch grammar).

In the end, though, I decided that since the only people who might conceivably ever actually use the orthography employed here are the speakers of Tayap, their perceptual biases and already-established habits were more important than an economical orthography. As I just noted, villagers who write anything in Tayap vary in whether or not they mark the prenasalization before a word-initial /g/. But they would find it counter-intuitive and odd to see or write *bor* 'pig', *je* 'dog' or *der* 'path' when they say – and would write – *mbor, nje* and *nder*.

I therefore write words the way the villagers pronounce them, with the result that there are no words in the dictionary that begin orthographically with *b, d, j* or *g*.

Word-medial and word-final prenasalized consonants are written as they are most commonly pronounced, thus the *j* in *munje* 'man' is written as prenasalized, as it is normally pronounced, versus *mbubujiram* 'bubbles from fish, crocodiles, turtles emerging from underwater', which is written unprenasalized.

This orthographic convention would also logically entail changing the spelling of the villagers' home, Gapun, to *Ŋgapun*. However, 'Gapun' is not a Tayap word. Senior men in the 1980s told me that they had heard that Germans had given the name Gapun to their village – which is called *Tayap num* 'Tayap village' in Tayap.

No one knows why 'Gapun' was chosen, but the most likely explanation is that when German cartographers and labor recruiters first appeared in the lower Sepik area in the early decades of the 1900s, they asked coastal villagers the names of inland villages which they could not reach, and they wrote down some version of the names they received in response. The Kopar-language name for Gapun, for example, is *Saŋgap*.

No great leap of imagination is required to see how a name like that, through various mis-hearings and confusions, could end up as *Gapun*. A significant percentage of the colonial records from the lower Sepik area were destroyed during WWII, so I have been unable to uncover any information that directly sheds light on the question of why Gapun is called Gapun.

But whatever the story behind the German naming of the village may be, the spelling of 'Gapun' can remain unchanged, since it is not a Tayap word.

Note that stress is marked where it is a property of a lexical morpheme (for example, *wákare* ('no'), but in the rest of the grammar it is not marked it when it is a product of complex morpho-phonemics e.g. like *kakúndara* in (2-14a) above.

Out of respect for villagers' writing habits (and also to be consistent with the analysis of the language's phonology discussed above, where no VVV clusters are permitted), I have also changed the spelling of the name of the language and people from *Taiap* – as I have spelled it in all my previous work on Gapun – to *Tayap*.

Whenever villagers write their name for themselves, they always spell it *Tayap*. And the word is a popular one to write. The front of one house near the center of the village, for example, is adorned with large letters, painted in black battery acid, that proclaims (tellingly, in Tok Pisin), NIU LUK *TAYAP* ('New Look Tayap').

Another young man, upping the linguistic ante in the direction of what many villagers have understood is the even more prestigious language, used similar material to paint the words NEW HOME *TAYAP* on a wall in his house.

A young man with whom I was walking along the beach one day, making the six-hour trip to the village of Watam to see if the local health worker there had any medicine for a bad case of scabies I had acquired in the village (she didn't), paused at one point to scratch the words NICK OUTCAST PERSON K*B*H* *ROR TAYAP MUNJE* into the sand. Translated, this means 'Nick outcast person K[ambedagam] B[lue] H[ill] child Tayap man' – the K*B*H* part of the message being a name the young villagers have given to their mountain.

Nick's scribble in the sand doesn't make much sense in either of the two languages in which it is written. But that is typical of the way that the word *Tayap* is used in young villagers' writing: it is used more as a marker or a tag than as an attempt to convey referential meaning. Nick's writing is a slightly more elaborate variant of the words *Tayap ror* (Tayap child), which is a popular tag that young men and women like to carve into trees or add after their signature at the end of a love letter. The words are modeled on the Tok Pisin word "mangi", which used to mean 'child', but which during the past thirty years has acquired the sassier meaning of 'young person' or, better, 'kid'.

3 Word classes

Tayap has two open classes of words – nouns (Section 3.1) and verbs (Section 3.2) – and a number of closed classes:

3.3 adjectives	3.8 deictics
3.4 adverbs	3.9 interrogatives
3.5 pronouns	3.10 interjections and affect words
3.6 quantifiers	3.11 intensifiers and discourse markers
3.7 articles	3.12 mood particles

The properties of Tayap's word classes are discussed in the sections below.

3.1 Nouns

3.1.1 Definition of a noun in Tayap

Nouns in Tayap have the following structural properties:
– they can function as head of a noun phrase, and are the only elements which may be sole element of an NP
– they function as arguments of a verb
– they have masculine or feminine gender

Nouns have three subclasses:
– common nouns
– locational nouns
– nouns with inherent number

These subclasses will each be described in turn.

3.1.1.1 Common nouns
Common nouns function as the heads of NPs and take masculine or feminine gender agreement. Some examples (common nouns in bold):

(3-1)   *aramre menjikan nda wisŋgɨn*
        aram=re   menjikan   nda   wis   -ŋgɨ   -n
        snake=LOC   closeby   DM   set_down.R   -3SG.M.R.O   -1SG.R.S
        'I set him down right near the snake.'

(3-2) *Pepe ŋgu tiptiek*
 Pepe   ŋgu   tiptiek
 name   3SG.F   lead.3SG.F.R
 'Pepe, she was leading'

(3-3) *otar nirkrundak*
 otar nir   -kru   -ndak
 fire   make.IRR   -3SG.R.O   -3PL.IRR.S
 'they'll make a fire'

(3-4) *Mbumjorŋi pin ŋayarni Mbananŗe Pepere*
 Mbumjor=ŋi   pin   ŋayar-ni   **Mbanaŋ**=re   **Pepe**=re
 mbumjor=ERG.M   ADV   true-ADV   name=COM   name=COM
 'A mbumjor (snake) came really close (to biting) Mbanaŋ and Pepe'

(3-5) *aram toto pisukun*
 aram **toto** pisu   -ku   -n
 snake   skin   shed.R   -3SG.M.R.O   - SG|1PL.R.S
 'the snake shed its skin'

Proper nouns do not form a subclass of nouns in Tayap. Like common nouns, they can be modified. For example:

(3-6) *Erapo ŋgwab   sawir   =ŋan   apro   sakar*
 Erapo   hole   black   =POSS   bad   INTENS
 'Fucking black-holed Erapo!'

3.1.1.2 Locational nouns

Some place names, particularly names of places in the rainforest, function as bare adjuncts, whereas all other nouns must take a peripheral case clitic, either locative, ablative or perlative. Some examples of locational nouns are as follows:

(3-7) *Kandumsik   ndow   -kru   -nana   ainda   mbek*
 Kandumsik   leg   -3SG.F.IRR.O -INTENT   DX   come.1SG.F|2SG.|1PL.R
 'I'm coming to Kandumsik [stream] (to put my legs in the water)'

> **Note:** in this example, the noun 'leg' is functioning as a transitive verb (see also example (3-26).

(3-8) aro   non   yim   mbok   Murar
       day   INDEF   1PL   go.1SG.F|2SG.F|1PL.R   Murar
       'One day we went to Murar.'

(3-9) Ngasimbara   ŋgwuk
       Ngasimbara   be.3PL.R
       'They were at Ngasimbara'

Not all place names can function as bare adjuncts, for example Turuŋgwad in the following example occurs with a locative clitic (glossed Allative):

(3-10) mun   sene   ripim   ŋgi   woke   Turuŋgwad   =re
        man.DL   two   before   3PL   go.DL.R   Turuŋgwad   =ALL
        'Once upon a time, two men, the two of them went to Turuŋgwad'

When part of a complex NP, locational nouns can take a location affix. In the following example, Murar stream occurs in a locative-marked NP. The place name Murar is the head of the NP, modified by 'stream' which then takes the locative clitic to refer to the whole NP:

(3-11) naweke ŋgoka Murar nuwombnɨ ŋgomar tarkwanŋgukre sumbwa sindernɨ emari ŋguyam katota mbot
        naw   =eke   ŋgwok   -a   Murar   nuwomb   =nɨ   ŋgomar
        grassland   =PERL   go.3PL.R   -and   Murar   stream   =LOC   fish

        tar   -kwan   -ŋguk   -re   sumbwa   sinder=nɨ
        take.IRR   -3SG.F.BEN.R.O -be.3PL.R   -SUB   ground   bare=LOC

        emári   Nguyam   katot   -a   mbot
        water_spirit   Nguyam   go_outside.SG.M.R   -and   go.SG.M.R
        'They went across the grassland to Murar stream and when they were picking up fish on the bare ground, the water spirit Nguyam went out and came'

Nouns functioning as heads of NPs are discussed in Chapter 4. Peripheral cases are discussed there in Section 4.4.

3.1.1.3 Number marking in nouns

The overwhelming majority of nouns in Tayap have only one form. Plurality is expressed through the addition of quantifiers (see Section 3.6). However, there is a closed subclass of nouns that inflect for plurality and, in a few cases, duality, by suffix and/or partial suppletion.

Nouns that are inflected for number refer to higher animates: humans, pigs and dogs.

	Singular	Dual	Plural
man	munje	mun	munjenum/munro
woman	noŋor	naŋaw	naŋro
child	ror	ruru	rorsem
mother	maya	mayaŋgre	mayaŋgro
grandmother	keke	kekeŋgre	kekeŋgud
grandfather	neni	neniŋgre	neniŋgud
older sibling	atawo	atawondodɨ	atawondodo
younger sibling	orma		ormabɨdib
great-grandparent/ancestor	amasik		amasikndodo/ amasikimb
father	omo		omosew
maternal uncle	awoi		awoiŋgud
grandchild	otan		otinimb
great-grandchild	njanimb		njanimbeda
daughter-in-law (female speaking)	oiŋga		oiŋgabɨdib/ oiŋgndodo
mother-in-law (male speaking)	otre		otrendodo
father-in-law (male speaking)	ombre		ombrendodo
husband of maternal aunt (male speaking)	eŋki		eŋkindodo
in-law	oyeŋ		oyeŋgud
mother's mother's brother	agampɨ		agampɨndodo
sister's child	romgar		rurumgrɨ
cross-sex sibling	wand		wanjmeŋ
spirit of dead person	mambrag		mambɨgir
forest being	kandap		kandipeŋ

Note: for those words with no dual form, one says 'two X' by using the plural form + *sene* 'two'. So 'two forest beings' is *kandipeŋ sene*.

Most of these kin terms, and certainly their dual and plural forms, are moribund. Several of them – *oiŋga* 'daughter-in-law, woman speaking', *njanimb* 'great-grandchild', *ombre* 'father-in-law, male speaking', *otre* 'mother-in-law, male speaking' – were produced only after several conversations among Gapun's oldest Tayap speakers. There is disagreement about whether one of them – *eŋki*, 'husband of maternal aunt, male speaking' – is even a Tayap word. Several people suggested that it might be a borrowing from the Adjora language spoken in the nearby village, Sanae. However, since old men in the 1980s told me it was, and since it has a Tayap plural, I include it here.

Villagers under forty all know common words like *munje* 'man', *noŋor* 'woman' and *ror* 'child', and they know their plural forms, but most do not know their dual forms. Most kin terms have been either forgotten or replaced with words from Tok Pisin. So *oyeŋ* 'in-law' has been replaced by Tok Pisin's "tambu", *neni* 'grandfather' has been replaced with "apa man", and *keke* 'grandmother' with "apa meri".

Words like *mambrag* 'spirit of a dead person' and *kandap* 'forest being' are kept alive by mothers who use them to frighten their small children, so everyone knows them. The plural forms, however, are not known by speakers under thirty-five.

The two non-human nouns that have plural forms are:

	SINGULAR	PLURAL
dog	nje	njenum
pig	mbor	mboreirum

3.1.2 The animacy/genericness distinction in nouns

The animate-inanimate/generic distinction is fundamental in Tayap, and is marked by two kinds of morphemes that are attached to nouns.

The first are peripheral case clitics, that denote relations like location or dative (see Section 4.4). Several of these clitics have different forms for animate and inanimate/generic referents. Note, for example, the different clitics that express movement towards something or someone – an animate referent takes =*re* and an inanimate referent takes =*nɨ* (see Section 4.4 for the complexities of the animate/inanimate division):

(3-12) a. ŋgu   Mairum   =**re**   wok
       3SG.F   Mairum   =ALL (ANIMATE)   go.3SG.F.R
       'she went to Mairum (personal name)'

   b. ŋgu   miri   =**nɨ**   wok
      3SG.F   rainforest =ALL (INANIMATE)   go.3SG.F.R
      'she went to the rainforest'

3.1.2.1 Animacy/genericness marked through possessive morphemes
Animacy/genericness is also marked on NPs by the enclitics that signal possession (see Section 4.5 for discussion of possession). The possessive clitics express animacy/

genericness and number. They have optional consonant-final forms: The conditioning factors between the vowel-final and consonant-final forms are unknown.

	SINGULAR	PLURAL
ANIMATE	=ma(t)	=mandama(t)
INANIMATE/GENERIC	=ŋa(n)	=ŋa(n)

Examples are:

(3-13) a. *mbor   =mat   ŋgagon*
    pig   =POSS   tail
    'pig's tail'

b. *Sopak   =mat   sapwar*
    Sopak   =POSS   basket
    'Sopak's basket'

c. *mɨri   =mat   mbor*
    rainforest   =POSS   pig
    'wild pig' – as opposed to a *numŋa mbor*, a domestic pig, of the village

d. *num   sami   =mat   morasi*
    village   many   =POSS   custom
    'the custom of many villages'

The possessive clitics attach to the last word of the noun phrase expressing the possessor. The order between possessor and possessed is free, so both *Sopak=ma(t) sapwar* (Sopak's basket) and *sapwar Sopak=ma(t)* (basket Sopak's), or *mɨri=ŋa mbor* (forest's pig) and *mbor mɨri=ŋa* (pig forest's) are possible. Placing the NP + POSS constituent last emphasizes it.

For animate plurals, the possessive clitic is *=mandama(t)*. For example:

(3-14) a. *Potow   =mandamat   morasi*
    Wongan   =POSS.PL   behavior
    'the behavior of the Wongan people'

b. *mbor   rorsem   =mandama   tawk*
    pig   child.PL   =POSS.PL   plate
    'the baby pigs' plate' (that they eat from)

When speaking in general terms, *=ŋa(n)* is used even with animate nouns. For example:

(3-15) a. *munjeŋa morasi*
　　　　munje　=ŋa　　morasi
　　　　man　　=POSS　behavior
　　　　'the behavior of man' (as opposed to the behavior of pigs, or dogs)

　　b. *njeŋa rewi*
　　　　nje　=ŋa　　rewi
　　　　dog　=POSS　tooth
　　　　'dog teeth', which traditionally were used as a kind of currency

　　c. *mborŋa morasi yu nirkwankut*
　　　　mbor=ŋa　　morasi　　yu　　nir　　　-kwan　　　　-kut
　　　　pig=POSS　behavior　2SG　do.IRR　-3SG.F.BEN.R.O　-be.SG.M.R
　　　　'you're acting like a pig' (lit. 'you're doing a pig's behavior')

　　d. *munjeŋan mɨrɨnɨ aku wákare, mɨri sindernɨ kut*
　　　　munje　=ŋan　　mɨrɨ　　　=nɨ　　a　　　-ku　　wákare　mɨri
　　　　man　　=POSS　rainforest　=LOC　be.IRR　-IRR　NEG　　rainforest

　　　　sinder　　=nɨ　　kut
　　　　empty　　=LOC　BE.3SG.M.R
　　　　'he isn't living in a part of the rainforest that people visit or know;
　　　　he lives in an unpopulated part of the forest'

　　e. *nime nirkwanŋgarke munjeŋa rawnɨ*
　　　　nime　　nir　　　-kwan　　　　　-ŋgarke　munje　=ŋa　　　raw　　=nɨ
　　　　thusly　do.IRR　-3SG.F.BEN.R.O　-PROH　　man　　=POSS　nose　=LOC
　　　　'you can't be doing that right in front of a person!'

3.1.3 Gender in nouns

Gender is a ubiquitous feature of Tayap. A common category in Papuan languages in general (Foley 2000: 371), in particular in non-Trans New Guinea languages (Ger Reesink pers. comm.), the pervasiveness of gender in Tayap, and the way it is marked across the grammar, differentiates it from the languages that surround it and gives it a reputation in the area as being a "hard" language.

Non-speakers of Tayap perceive the prominent role that gender marking plays in Tayap because they hear speakers telling one another to do things, and the imperative forms of intransitive verbs are inflected according to the gender (and number) of the addressee(s).

So – to use the example that Gapun villagers themselves inevitably cite whenever they explain the nature of Tayap to anyone – when you talk to a man you say *wetet* (come), and when you talk to a woman you say *wetak* (come), using gender-marked verbal affixes.

This feature of the language never ceases to astonish any Sepik villager who hears it, and people from other villages who listen to Gapuners explain that they have "two languages" invariably react as though such a language is so bizarre as to stretch the bounds of credulity (see Section 7.1.2; see also Sections 3.5 and 5.3 for gender marking on pronouns and verbal affixes).

3.1.3.1 Gender marking

Gender in Tayap is a property of nouns, but is a morphologically covert category. It is not marked not on the noun itself, but is expressed on the following targets:
(1) deixis markers (see Section 3.8); and/or
(2) ergative markers on the subjects of transitive verbs (see Section 4.3); and/or
(3) suffixes on the verb that encode subject and object (See Sections 3.5 and 5.3); and/or
(4) suppletive verb stems (see Chapter 6)

For example, compare the following intransitive constructions:

(3-16) a. *noŋor aŋgi patɨrnɨ wuk*
       noŋor   aŋgi   patɨr   =nɨ   wuk
       woman   DX.F   house   =LOC   be.3SG.F.R
       'the woman is in the house'

   b. *munje ainde patɨrnɨ kut*
      munje   ainde   patɨr   =nɨ   kut
      man   DX.M   house   =LOC   be.SG.M.R
      'the man is in the house'

Here, the gender of the subjects is expressed by both the deictic words (*aŋgi/ainde*) and the gender of the inflected verb *aku* 'be' (*wuk* 'she is' versus *kut* 'he is').

Transitive verbs mark gender in object suffixes (see Section 3.5). Some classes of transitive verbs (classes 4 and 5) signal gender and number on the subject suffix(es) as well. So compare the following non-future forms of the class 4 verb *ŋgar* 'call out to':

(3-17) a. *ŋɨŋi ŋgu ŋganukun*
       ŋɨ=ŋi   ŋgu   ŋga   -nu   -ku   -n
       3SG.M=ERG.M   3SG.F   call_out.R   -S   <3SG.F.R.O>   -1SG|3SG.M|1PL.R.S
       'he called out to her'

b. *ŋguyi ŋgu ŋgatukun*
   ŋgu   =yi   ŋgu   ŋga   -tu -ku   -n
   3SG.F =ERG.F 3SG.F call_out.R -S   <3SG.F.R.O> -2SG|3SG.F.R.S
   'she called out to her'

In both examples, the object suffix *-ku* signals a feminine object (a masculine object would be *-ŋgi*; see Section 5.3.1). But in a class 4 verb like *ŋgar*, the gender and number of the subject is also obligatorily marked: in this example, gender is encoded in the alternation between *-nu + -n* (combining to signal 1SG OR 3SG.M OR 1PL), and *-tu + -n* (combining to signal 2SG OR 3SG.F).

Notice also the different ergative markers affixed to 3SG.M (=*ŋi*) and 3SG.F (=*yi*).

Other verbs (conjugation class 3 transitive verbs and some intransitive verbs) also change their stem forms to signal the gender of the subject:

(3-18) a. *mbori pap okun*
          mbor=i   pap   o   -ku   -n
          pig=ERG.F   coconut   consume.R   <3SG.F.R.O> -3SG.F.R.S
          'the (female) pig ate coconut'

   b. *mborŋi pap kakun*
      mbor =ŋi   pap   ka   -ku
      pig   =ERG.M   coconut   consume.R   <3SG.F.R.O>

      -n
      -1SG|2SG|3SG.M|1PL.R.S
      'the (male) pig ate coconut'

Here, again, the object suffix *-ku* signals a feminine object, 'coconut', and thus remains the same in both sentences. But the verb 'consume' (*a*) is a conjugation class 3 transitive verb, and in those verbs, the verb stem changes to signal the gender (and number) of the subject, alternating between *o* and *ka* (see Section 6.1.4).

This verb-stem alternation is a source of serious difficulty for young speakers of Tayap, as is discussed in Section 6.1.5.

3.1.3.2 Principles of gender assignment

There are two genders in Tayap: feminine and masculine. Humans have natural gender, even though this can be overridden when the referent is non-particular (see below). The gender classification of all other animate nouns is decided by three criteria.

The first is particularity: the unmarked, generic form of all nouns, including animate nouns, is feminine.[1]

The second is sex: a male referent may be specified as masculine and a female referent feminine.

The third criterion is size and shape: long, thin and large referents tend to be masculine; short, stocky and small referents tend to be feminine.

Snakes (long and thin) and cassowaries (tall and imposing), therefore, are prototypically masculine; pigs (fat and stocky) are prototypically feminine. So in a sentence like 'he speared a pig', the object 'pig' will be designated by the feminine object suffix -*ku* unless the speaker specifically wants to point out that it was male, in which case the masculine object suffix -*ŋgɨ* would be used.

The difference is as follows:

(3-19) a. *ŋɨŋi mbor pokun*

ŋɨ	=ŋi	mbor	po	-ku	-n
3SG.M	=ERG.M	pig	strike.R	-3SG.F.R.O	-SG|1PL.R.S

'he speared a (female) pig'

b. *ŋɨŋi mbor poŋgin*

ŋɨ	=ŋi	mbor	po	-ŋgɨ	-n
3SG.M	=ERG.M	pig	strike.R	-3SG.M.R.O	-SG|1PL.R.S

'he speared a (male) pig'

The following chart shows the process of gender assignment in Tayap:

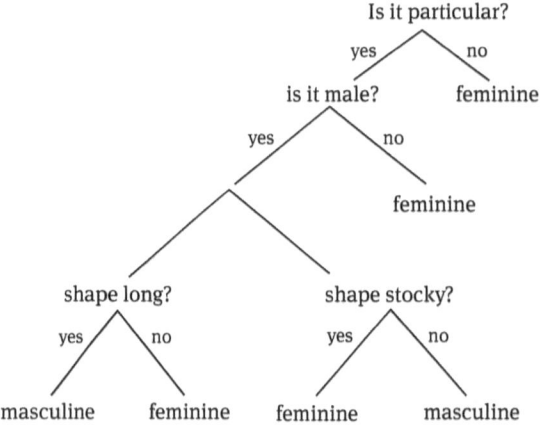

Tayap gender decision tree

---

[1] Foley (2000: 371) notes that among those Papuan languages which have gender, binary contrasts are typical, and feminine is always the unmarked gender.

As the chart suggests, even though snakes and cassowaries are commonly masculine, a short, fat snake or a squat, short-necked cassowary could be referred to using feminine forms.

The shape-based assignment of gender is not entirely predictable, however. A praying mantis is generally masculine, perhaps because its name is homophonous with 'cassowary' (i.e. *ŋgat*). And a millipede (*kakámatik*), even though it is long, is generally feminine, perhaps because it is stubby, fat, and slow moving, at least compared to a centipede (*yandum*), which is sleek and slithering (and generally masculine).

Even though nouns tend to be generally classified as feminine, there are some nouns which are always (in the case of natural phenomena and insects) or tend to be (in the case of animals and birds) masculine.

The nouns in question are:

Natural phenomena	Animals, birds and insects	
arawer 'sun'	*aram* 'snake'	*ŋgararik* 'monitor lizard'
ŋgudum 'star'	*kakarpwap* 'eagle'	*ŋgat* 'cassowary'; 'praying mantis'
nekan 'earthquake'	*kamban* 'magpie'	
aruat 'thunder'	*kekékato* 'worm'	*njakep* 'flying fox bat'
pora 'wind'	*momɨk* 'guria pigeon'	*ondom* 'hornbill'
urerŋgar 'lightning'	*nekan* 'stick insect', Note: homophonous with 'earthquake'	*orem* 'crocodile'
		pesaw 'bird of paradise'
		yandum 'centipede'

Examples are:

(3-20) *nekan   katot*
      earthquake happen.3SG.M.R
      'an earthquake (M) happened'

(3-21) *ŋayi aram taniŋgin*
      ŋa   =yi   aram   ta   -nɨ   -ŋgɨ   -n
      1SG =ERG.F snake see.R -S   <3SG.M.R.O> -1SG|3SG.M|1PL.R. S
      'I (F) saw a snake (M)'

This gender system shares some similarity with the East Sepik, Ndu family language Manambu, in which gender assignment is determined in part by the size and shape of the referent (Aikhenvald et al. 2008; see also Reesink 2003 on North Papuan languages). Aikhenvald et al. (2008: 112) note that shape-based gender assignment is a feature of languages of the Sepik area, also citing Alamblak (Bruce

1984). Other languages of the Sepik-Ramu region have gender, but very different systems: Foley (2000: 366) notes for instance that Lower Sepik languages have a phonological gender system; that is, gender assignment is based on the phonological form of the noun root.

On the other hand, the situational element to Tayap's gender system – in which gender is partly a matter of the discourse situation rather than a fixed property of a noun – is reminiscent of that of Bilua, a Papuan language spoken on Vella Lavella in the Solomon Islands. In Bilua, masculine gender is used for third-person singular masculine human referents as well as "singulative" non-human nouns. But all other nouns are marked feminine, the default form (Obata 2003: 88, 105–109).

3.1.3.3 Non-particular nouns

Nouns that otherwise could be expected to be masculine can be feminine under two circumstances.

The first is when the subject or referent of a verb is a general class of people rather than a named or known individual. For example, the following utterance is from a harangue by an older Tayap speaker who is chastising younger villagers for behaving badly. In the course of his harangue, the speaker wonders rhetorically which big man (i.e. which old, knowledgeable man) is still alive to teach young people about the good ways of the past. (The answer, he knows, is 'none'.)

His question was phrased as follows:

(3-22) *Ani   munje   suman   wuk?*
       who   man   big   be.3SG.F.R
       'Which big man is here (i.e. still living)?'

Note that the verb 'be' is inflected in 3SG.F, even though the referent is unambiguously a male. The use of the feminine form here conveys generality. It refers to the category or class of 'big men' rather than to a specific big man. If the speaker had phrased the question using the 3SG.M form of 'be', *kut*, the question would be referring to a specific named or known big man: 'Which one of the big men we all know is present here right now?'

Another example of the same phenomenon is the following (feminine forms that denote the male referent are in bold):

(3-23)   **ŋgu** *munje ŋgo* **ŋgon** *pawrɨk tatukundre, nirkwan***uk**, *noni nam***kru** *wákare*
       ŋgu   munje   ŋgo   **ŋgon**   pawrɨk   ta   **-tu**   -ku
       3SG.F   man   DM   3SG.F.POSS strength get.R -S   <3SG.F.R.O>

      -n   -dre   nir   -kwan   **-uk**
      -2SG|3SG.F.R.S   -SUB   do.IRR   <3SG.F.BEN.R.O> -be.3SG.F.R

      non=i   *nam*   **-kru**   *wákare*
      other=ERG.F   talk.IRR   -3SG.F.IRR   NEG
      'The man is of course finding his strength and doing it on his own, nobody else is telling him to'

This utterance was spoken during a tense discussion about the incessant and disruptive drinking in the village that, by late 2009, had been plaguing Gapun for some time. During a village-wide meeting, the mother of a fifteen-year-old boy shouted angrily that her husband never tried to stop their son from drinking.

In response, a man in his late thirties made the comment above, which is dismissive of the mother and supports the young man's father by implying that it wouldn't matter what the father told his son. The son, this man is saying, is old enough and would act according to his own desires anyway: no one is ordering him to drink; he does it because he wants to. But as in the previous example, (3-22), this utterance refers to a male using feminine grammatical forms.

The rhetorical effect is the same: the speaker's use of feminine grammatical forms when talking about a male conveys a meaning of generality. The speaker is not overtly disputing anything the mother says about her son or her husband, these grammatical forms say; he is making a general observation.

A non-literal but semantically more accurate translation of the man's remark would be: 'As young men get older and stronger of course they decide on their own what they want to do, they don't do things just because other people tell them to'.

3.1.3.4 Gender in young people's Tayap

Young speakers are aware that Tayap marks gender, and they know how to mark it on verb stems, object suffixes, subject suffixes and through ergative markers.

A problem they have, though, is keeping straight the forms that mark masculine gender from the ones that mark feminine gender. This problem can be exemplified by a short extract from a narrative told by an eighteen-year-old woman.

This young woman is telling a story about a crocodile that she and some other young women caught in the mangrove swamp. The women tied the 1.5 meter-long crocodile's jaws together, put it in a copra bag and brought it home. It lived for a while, then, the speaker recounts, her father killed it (forms that express gender are in bold):

(3-24) orem **aŋgi wuk** embre **sasŋi poŋgɨn**
orem　　　aŋgi　　wuk　　　　emb　　=re　　　sas　　=ŋi
crocodile　DX.F　be.3SG.F.R　morning　=TEMP　father　=ERG.M

po　　　　-ŋgɨ　　　　-n
strike.R　-3SG.M.R.O　-SG|1PL.S
'the (*female*) crocodile *was* there, in the morning (*male*) father killed *him*'

All the words and morphemes that express gender are correctly formed. The masculine ergative case morpheme on 'father' is also the correct one. But note that the grammatical gender of the crocodile here changes from feminine to masculine in the course of a single utterance. Crocodiles are generally masculine in Tayap, so the final verb here, *poŋgɨn*, is exactly what a fluent speaker would say. But the deictic word used by this young speaker, *aŋgi*, as well as the first verb, *wuk*, are semantically incorrect – they are the feminine forms, but what the speaker wants are the masculine forms: *ainde kut*.

If the speaker had been talking about a female crocodile (for example if the crocodile had been found to be carrying eggs), then the deictic *aŋgi* and the verb *wuk* would have been correct. But in that case, the final verb should have had a feminine object morpheme – it should have been *po-ku-n* (kill.R-**3SG.F.R.O**-SG|1PL.S).

This kind of gender-mixing is characteristic of young speakers. Generally speaking, the younger and less competent the speaker, the more gender will be mixed in haphazard ways like this. As in many other areas of Tayap grammar, it is clear that young speakers know *that* a particular distinction is expressed in the vernacular. They are also capable of producing some of the forms that mark the distinction. What they lack is the capacity to realize the distinction in a grammatically consistent manner.

In Young People's Dyirbal, a situation of language death in Australia, weaker speakers changed the semantic gender assignment system to a simple animacy/gender system. That is, they kept the morphology and rearranged the class assignment system (Schmidt 1985). That is the opposite situation to what is happening with Tayap: here, the assignment principles remain but what is changed is that the morphological marking has become inconsistent.

3.1.4 Verbalized nouns

Nouns (like adjectives, see Section 3.3.2) can function as verbs, with the full range of verbal morphology, with zero derivation.

(3-25) *Sandetakre priek*
      Sande   -tak   =re   priek
      Sunday (TP) -2SG.F|3SG.F.R =TEMP come_up.1SG.F|1PL.R
      'It was Sunday when we came up [to the bush camp]'

(3-26) *ŋgɨ eiarakŋgukre Kandumsik ndowkrunana ainda*
      ŋgɨ   eiar   -ak   ŋguk   -re   Kandumsik
      3PL   cry.IRR -LINK be.3PL.R -SUB Kandumsik

      ndow -kru   -nana   ainda
      leg   -3SG.F.IRR.O -INTENT DX.F
      'They [children] are crying so I'm going to Kandumsik [creek] to leg it
      [i.e. to wade into the water and net some fish].'

In the following example, it is not actually a single noun that is verbalized, but an NP – in this case a possessive NP. Verbalized nouns often carry an inchoative meaning.

(3.27) *ŋgu kapa weka numŋa noŋortakara*
      ŋgu   kapa   wek   -a   **num=ŋa**
      3SG   MIR   come.3SG.F.R -and village=POSS

      noŋor -tak   -ara
      woman   -2SG|3SG.F.R -PERF
      'She's really become a village woman' (said of a woman who moved to Gapun from another village)

3.2 Verbs

The lexical class of verbs is an open class which can be characterized as being able to host realis/irrealis status and transitivity suffixes as well as subject and object suffixes. A fully inflected verb can function as the sole word of a sentence.

There are two major subclasses of verbs: intransitive and transitive. Examples of each are:

Intransitive verb

(3-28) *ŋgu pirok*
      ŋgu   pirok
      3SG.F laugh.SG.F|1SG.PL.R
      'she laughed'

Transitive verb

(3-29) ŋayi yu tanun
 ŋa=yi   yu   ta   -n -u   -n
 1SG=ERG.F 2SG see.R -S <2SG.R.O> -SG|1PL.R.S
 'I saw you'

There are no ditransitive verbs in Tayap (see also Section 9.1). Semantically three-place predicates express the recipient of giving, for example, with the benefactive morpheme:

(3-30) is   -iata   -n
 give.SBJ -1SG.BEN.R.O -SG|1PL.R
 '(you) give it to me!'

However the recipient can be omitted, indicating that the verb in question is transitive, not ditransitive, and that the benefactive morpheme is an optional oblique argument:

(3-31) epi   i   -kru   -net
 tomorrow give.IRR -3SG.F.IRR.O -1SG.M|3SG.M.IRR.S
 'I (M) will give it (to someone) tomorrow'

Benefactive objects and regular objects cannot coocur in the same clause.

As well as being divided into transitivity classes, every Tayap verb falls into one of nine conjugation classes, based on how verbs form their non-future forms: there are five classes for transitive verbs and four for intransitives (see Chapter 6).

Verb morphology in Tayap is entirely suffixing, with morphemes for object and subject added – in that order, apart from discontinuous subject markers – to verb stems. A characteristic feature of Tayap verbs is that status is marked across the verb multiple times. The stem must occur in either an irrealis or realis form. In addition, the object and subject morphemes that get suffixed to the stem also encode realis/irrealis status.

This can be illustrated with an example from the transitive verb stem *o*, which means 'strike' (and covers actions like 'shoot', 'stab' and 'hit'). Note how irrealis vs. realis is marked across the verb (in bold):

(3-32) a. *pokun*
po -ku -n
strike.**R** -3SG.F.**R**.O -SG|1PL.**R**.S
'I (M or F)/you/he/she/we shot it'

b. *okrunet*
o -kru -net
strike.**IRR** -3SG.F.**IRR**.O -1SG.M|3SG.M.**IRR**.S
'I (M) will shoot it' or 'he will shoot it'

c. *okru wákare*
o -kru wákare
strike.**IRR** -3SG.F.**IRR**.O NEG
'(Any person or number of people) didn't shoot it' (or 'won't shoot it')[2]

The same thing happens with intransitive verbs, exemplified here with the verb *memkɨ* 'get up':

(3-33) a. *pemiet*
pem -iet
get_up.**R** -SG.M.**R**
'he got up' or 'I (M) got up' or 'you (M) got up'

b. *memkɨnet*
mem -kɨ -net
get_up.**IRR** -**IRR** -1SG.M|3SG.M.**IRR**
'I (M) will get up' or 'he will get up'

c. *memkɨ wákare*
mem -kɨ wákare
get_up.**IRR** -**IRR** NEG
'(Any pronoun, person or number of people) didn't get up' (or 'won't get up')

Status marking on verbs, while mandatory, does not always occur in predictable ways. Realis morphemes can occur as part of a verb that refers to an unreal event. An example is the counterfactual mood (CF), which is a prototypical irrealis category, because it refers to events that never occurred, such as 'If he had seen it, he would have shot it'. However in Tayap, on transitive verbs, the counterfactual is

---

[2] Note that the negative verb requires irrealis marking, see Section 5.4.2.1.

expressed by a verb stem inflected as counterfactual and suffixed by object and subject morphemes that occur in their *realis* forms, rather than in their irrealis forms, which in the case below would be *-kru-* (3SG.F.IRR.O) and *-net* (for 1SG.M.S; for the appropriate endings for other subjects, see Section 5.3):

(3-34) *wakrikkun*
 wak   -rik -ku   -n
 strike.CF -CF -3SG.F.R.O -SG|1PL.R.S
 'I (M or F)/you/he/she/we would have shot it'

For intransitive verbs, the counterfactual is expressed by a verb stem inflected as counterfactual and suffixed by group I subject morphemes, which in this grammar – for the sake of consistency with the pattern that is clear in transitive verbs – are glossed as realis. In reality, though, group I subject morphemes are the same in the realis and irrealis statuses (see Section 6.2.1).

(3-35) *memriknet*
 mem   -rik -net
 get_up.CF -CF -1SG.M|3SG.M.R
 'I (M) would have gotten up' or 'he would have gotten up'

Non-serialized independent verb stems can consist of a single vowel, like *a* 'consume', or up to four syllables, like *mundumindi* which means 'hum'.

The morphology of Tayap verbs is the subject of Chapters 5, 6 and 7.

3.3 Adjectives

Tayap has a limited, closed class of adjectives, with the following properties. They:
- modify a noun
- can take a unique plural marker (see Section 3.6.2)
- rarely occur as sole member/head of an NP (if the noun head is elided)
- never function as an argument of a verb
- do not have their own gender

They form a discrete closed class, and can be characterized on the basis of their modificational semantics, as laid out below:

EVALUATION	*apro* 'bad' *eŋgon* 'good', 'nice' *sua* 'stupid', 'rubbish'
COLOR	*karar* 'red' *kɨkɨw* 'yellow' *puwas* 'white' *ŋgɨdɨŋ* 'blue/green' *sawir* 'black'
AGE	*iro* 'new' *ewɨr* 'young' *mambɨr* 'young' (see example 3-43) *ŋgop* 'young' (used for coconuts and women's breasts) *kapar* 'senior' *kowot* 'old' *rowe* 'old' (for inanimate objects and dead ancestors)
PHYSICAL CHARACTERISTIC OR DIMENSION	*agranarmbɨr* 'hot' *ndɨdɨkdɨdɨk* 'lumpy' *pokemb* 'cold' *ŋgado/ŋgadogadi* 'bent', 'crooked' *mokop/mosop* 'small' *pisaipisai* 'soft' *suman* 'big' *seŋgrim* 'without accompaniment' *njawap* 'wet' (used for food) *pakas* 'dry' *sinder* 'empty', 'bare' *naimb* 'heavy' *mbwarpasinder* 'without a care' *tumb* 'thick', 'heavy' *tapraw* 'wide' *pasinder* 'weightless' *kikak* 'raw' *saprew* 'stuffed' *kitkit* 'muddy' *kas* 'nearly ripe', 'tough' (used *kowmb* 'deep' for cooked food) *kopik* 'streaky' *mandɨg* 'unripe' *mbabuŋ* 'burned' *prik* 'ripe' *eŋgin* 'white' (as in 'European') *pisimb* 'rotten' *taman* 'inexperienced' *uran* 'dirty', 'unkempt' *yam* 'knowledgeable' *komboj* 'dirty' (used for water) *tower* 'quiet' *mɨk* 'sharp', 'intense' *kambɨnɨm* 'pitiable' *mbutup* 'dull', 'blunt' *miŋan* 'male' *kemem* 'long' *noŋor* 'female' *kɨtiŋin* 'short' *minda* 'tired of' *awinawin* 'runny' *nipɨs* 'able' *kawrɨk/pawrɨk* 'strong', 'hard' *mɨt* 'dense'
WORDS FOR ANIMALS AND FOR ANIMAL COATS OR FEATHERS	*agránkar* 'skinny', 'emaciated' *atuŋgor* 'brown', 'tan' *pwap* 'large' (used for specific animals such as eagles and lizards) *ramborgar* 'black and white mottled' *mbatámbati* 'white and red mottled'

NUMBER	all the quantifiers listed in Section 3.6 are adjectives, although in practice the only ones ever actually used by older fluent speakers to modify nouns or noun phrases are the numbers 1–5.

Adjectives follow their head noun. Some examples:

(3-36) munje   kemem
        man   long
        'tall man'

(3-37) noŋor   kitiŋin
        woman   short
        'short woman'

(3-38) orak   apro
        thing   bad
        'bad thing'

(3-39) arawer   mik
        sun   sharp
        'hot sun' (lit. 'sharp sun')

Adjectives can function predicatively as well as attributively, although this is less common than in a language like English, because adjectives, like nouns, can become verbs (see below, Section 3.3.2). So rather than saying something like "the sun is hot" – which can be said, as *arawer mik* (lit. 'sun sharp'), as in (3-39) – speakers of Tayap more readily say *arawer miknet* (lit. 'sun sharpens', i.e. 'sun is hot').

Examples of adjectives occurring predicatively are as follows:

(3-40) a. munjema nam eŋgon aŋgi
            munje   =ma   nam   eŋgon   aŋgi
            man   =POSS talk   good   DX
            'human beings' talk is good talk' (said by a man chastising his daughter for swearing, making an implicit contrast with the grunts and howls of animals)

        b. ŋgu sumanke wekŋan?
            ŋgu   suman   =ke   wek   =ŋan
            3SG.F   big   =Q   come.3SG.F.R   =POSS
            'did she come all grown up?' (said, with a rhetorical flourish, about a woman who married into Gapun at a young age)

c. *ŋaŋan ndɨ nda mbabasak*
 ŋaŋan   ndɨ   nda   mbabasak
 1SG.POSS DM   DM   ignorant
 'mine (i.e. my children) are ignorant' (said by a father speaking about his children's knowledge of Tayap)

Adjectives can rarely function alone as the sole member of an NP; this only occurs when the head noun is understood:

(3-41) *sawir aŋgo wuk*
 black DX   be.3SG.F.R
 'this black (one) is there'

3.3.1 Number inflection in adjectives

Adjectives can take a plural suffix, as discussed in Section 3.6.2, but they can also inflect for number using partial suppletion. Like nouns, which but for a handful of exceptions do not inflect for number, the overwhelming majority of adjectives have only one form, and they do not change for number or gender. There are four exceptions to this.

Only two adjectives are inflected with partially suppletive forms in the singular, dual and plural: 'little' and 'old'. The dual and plural forms are used only for animate referents – so one says *rorsem mopri* (children little-DL, 'two little children'), but *patir mokop sene* (house little-SG two, 'two little houses').

The dual and plural forms recorded here are moribund: they were given to me in the 1980s by senior men who have since died. Today, only the oldest speakers are able to produce them:

(3-42) a. 'little'   b. 'old'
  SG *mokop*   SG *kowot*
  DL *mopri*   DL *kotiw*
  PL *mopro*   PL *koto*

In addition to 'little' and 'old', two adjectives meaning 'young' have singular and plural forms, but lack a dual form:

(3-43) a. 'young' (used for both   b. 'young' (traditionally used only for
  males and females)   females; nowadays used for both sexes)
  SG *eiwir*   SG *mambir*
  PL *eiwiro*   PL *mambro*

3.3.2 Verbalized adjectives

Like nouns, all adjectives can be zero-derived as intransitive verbs by directly suffixing them with morphemes that encode realis/irealis status, subject and other verbal categories. The verbs derived in this way are generally inchoatives; they express a change of state:

(3-44) a. *ŋgu kararkɨtak*
    ŋgu   karar   -kɨ   -tak
    3SG.F red   -IRR -2SG.F|3SG.F.IRR
    'she/it will turn red'

    b. *ŋgu mosoptakara*
       ŋgu   mosop -tak   -ara
       3SG.F small   -2SG.F|3SG.F.R -PERF
       'she/it shrank' or 'she/it got short'

    c. *ikɨn prɨktak*
       ikɨn   prɨk   -tak
       banana ripe -2SG.F|3SG.F.R
       'the banana has ripened'

    d. *arawer kɨkɨwnet, maikɨnetana*
       arawer kɨkɨw   -net   mai   -kɨ   -net
       sun   yellow -1SG.M|3SG.M.R enough -IRR -1SG.M|3SG.M.IRR

       -ana
       -INTENT
       'the sun is getting yellow and will soon be gone (i.e. it will set)'

    e. *numbwan aprotak*
       numbwan apro -tak
       thought   bad   -2SG.F|3SG.F.R
       'the thought became bad'

Similarly, in the following example, the adjective 'big' functions as a medial verb with a medial manner suffix *-kar* (Section 9.8.2):

(3-45) *ŋgomar pɨtkwanŋgukre awin sumankar puwok*
      ŋgomar pɨt   -kwan   -ŋguk   -re
      fish   wash.IRR -3SG.F.R.O -3PL.R.S -SUB

> *awin suman -kar puwok*
> water big -MANN ascend.SG.F.R
> 'While they were washing the fish, the water continued to rise' (lit. 'became big rising)

Numerals, which are also adjectives, can likewise be verbalized in this way:

(3-46) *yim imin nambartak*
yim imin nambar -tak
1PL belly one -2SG .F|3SG.F.R
'We've agreed' (lit. 'our bellies have become one')

Note, however, that adjectives inflected as progressives express a state, not a change of state:

(3-47) *yum moprokukemre, yumŋi kirawkru wákare*
yum mopro -kukem -re yum =ŋi
2PL small.PL -be.2PL.R -SUB 2PL =ERG.M

kiraw -kru wákare
know.IRR -3SG.F.IRR.O NEG
'you were all small (i.e. you were all children) then, so you don't know'

3.3.3 Verbs as nominal modifiers

Verbs can function as nominal modifiers, using the non-finite suffix *–(ŋ)gar* (see Section 4.2). For example:

(3-48) *prukŋgar noŋor*
pruk -ŋgar noŋor
work -NFN woman
'hard-working woman'

As well as simple verbs, whole clauses can function in this way:

(3-49) *sokoi aŋgar pendimor*
sokoi a -ŋgar pendimor
tobacco consume.IRR -NFN paper
'smoking paper' (i.e. paper to roll a cigarette in')

(3-50) *orak apro munje oŋgar*
orak   apro   munje   o   -ŋgar
thing   bad   man   strike.IRR -NFN
'bad thing that kills men'

(3-51) *morasi eŋgon nirŋgar munje*
morasi   eŋgon   nir   -ŋgar   munje
behavior good   do.IRR -NFN   man
'man with good behavior'

(3-52) *muta utŋgar orak*
muta   ut   -ŋgar   orak
hole   dig.IRR -NFN   thing
'thing for digging holes'

3.4 Adverbs

Tayap has many closed classes of adverbs: common, *-ki*, temporal, frequency/distributional or 'not yet', and elevational/positional adverbs. They will each be described below.

3.4.1 Common adverbs

Tayap has a small closed set of common adverbs that specify the way in which the action expressed by the verb is carried out. The full set is as follows:

aini	'like this'	*ndaguni*	'furtively', 'without permission'
aike	'thusly'		
areini	'quickly'	*ni*	'nothing'
ariuta	'slowly', 'quietly'	*ni(me)* or *ni(ki)*	'thusly'
itrubara(ni)	'a little'	*nipis*	'almost'
itruki	'slowly'	*nunum*	'running'
katkat	'quickly'	*ŋayar/ŋayor*	'really'
mapira	'harshly', 'roughly'	*pin(ini)*	'nearly', 'a little while'
mbibi(ni) or *mbibik(ni)*	'like'	*rit*	'without pausing or stopping' (used only with verbs of motion)
meŋgini	'slowly'		
moti(ni)	'again'	*sapkini*	'for no reason'
nande(n)	'thusly'	*simpakni*	'directly', 'straight'

supwáspwa	'badly'	tawaŋgenɨ	'ignorantly', 'unknowingly'
tandiw	'well'	wákarererekɨ	'yet'

Adverbs are normally placed before their head verb. Note that two adverbs can cooccur as in (3-53 f):

(3-53) a. *yumŋi supwáspwa ninkurem*
       yum =ŋi   supwáspwa ni   -n -ku   -rem
       2PL =ERG.M badly   do.R -S <3SG.F.R.O> -2PL.R.S
       'you all did it badly'

    b. *Aŋges katkat prukakkut*
       Aŋges   katkat   pruk   -ak   kut
       Aŋges   quickly work.IRR -LINK be.SG.M.R
       'Aŋges is working quickly'

    c. *ŋgon mambakɨ ndagúnɨ tatukurora*
       ŋgon   mambakɨ   ndagúnɨ
       3SG.F.POSS netbag   furtively

       ta   -tu -ku   -ro   -ra
       take.R -S   <3SG.F.R.O> -3PL.R.S -PERF
       'they stole her netbag'

    d. *ŋa ni mbet*
       ŋa   ni   mbet
       1SG nothing come.SG.M.R
       'I (M) come with nothing' (i.e. empty-handed)

    e. *yu ni kut*
       yu   ni   kut
       2SG nothing be.SG.M.R
       'you (M) are there doing nothing'

    f. *kɨkrɨwekar oŋgarke katkat katkat mbara otet*
       kɨkrɨwe-kar   o-ŋgarke   katkat   katkat   mbara   o-tet
       dawdle-MANN go.IRR-PROH quickly quickly a little go.SBJ-2SG.M.R
       'stop dawdling, go a little more quickly!' (said to a male)

    g. *Mbasamama patɨrnɨ urok, rɨt ŋayarnɨ urok*
       Mbasama =ma   patɨr =nɨ   urok,   rɨt
       Mbasama =POSS house =ALL go_inside.3SG.F|1PL.R without pausing

ŋayar -nɨ   urok
really -INTENS go_inside.3SG.F|1PL.R
'she went inside Mbasama's house, she went inside without pausing'

h. *kukununumwetet!*
ku   -ku   nunum   we   -tet!
bring -3SG.F.R.O running come.SBJ -2SG.M.R
'bring it running!' (i.e. bring it right this minute, fast)

Note also that (3-53h) has an adverb occurring between the verbs of a serial verb construction.

Like adjectives, common adverbs can function as verbs (Section 3.3.2). So just as it is possible to inflect an adjective to say something like 'it will be bad',

(3-54) *aprorkɨtak*
apro -r- -kɨ   -tak
bad   -r- -IRR   -2SG.F|3SG.F.IRR
'it will get bad' (The *r* after *apro* here and after *supwáspwa* in the next example is phonologically motivated; see Section 2.6.)

Adverbs can also be inflected to produce sentences like the following:

(3-55) a. *supwáspwarkɨtak*
supwáspwa -r- -kɨ   -tak
badly   -r- -IRR   -2SG.F|3SG.F.IRR
'it will go badly'

b. *ŋayartakara*
ŋayar -tak   -ara
really -2SG.F|3SG.F.R   -PERF
'it became the real thing'

In addition to modifying verbs, adverbs can also modify noun phrases, as in the following, in which *ŋayor* 'really' modifies the possessive NP 'illness':

(3-56) *kandawŋan munje ŋayor*
kandaw =ŋan   munje ŋayor
illness =POSS man   really
'a really sick man'

3.4.2 Adverbial functions of the suffix -kɨ

The affix -kɨ (rarely -nɨ) has multiple functions. It is one of the three irrealis affixes for intransitive verbs (see Section 5.4.2). It is also an intensifier (see Section 3.11). In addition, it expresses adverbial meanings when it is affixed to the following components:

(1) -kɨ can be affixed to nouns to express a distributive meaning; that is, that an action or event takes place on more than one individual occasion, involves an undetermined variety of the same kind of referents, or denotes the way in which something is distributed. These are usually reduplicated:

(3-57) a. *orom   -kɨ   orom   -kɨ*
           time   -ADV   time   -ADV
           'every now and again'

   b. *munje   -kɨ   munje   -kɨ*
      man   -ADV   man   -ADV
      'different men', 'a variety of men'

   c. *menjikan   -kɨ   menjikan   -kɨ*
      nearby   -ADV   nearby   -ADV
      'frequently', 'constantly' (cf. Tok Pisin's "klostu klostu")

   d. *ambagaikɨ ambagaikɨ aku wákare ainɨ*
      ambagai   -kɨ   ambagai   -kɨ   aku   wákare ai   =nɨ
      men's house -ADV men's house -ADV be.IRR NEG   here =LOC
      'there aren't a lot of different men's houses (from different clans) here'

   e. *senekɨ senekɨ isimbatan*
      sene   -kɨ   sene   -kɨ   isi   -mbata   -n
      two   -ADV two   -ADV give.SBJ -3PL.BEN.R.O -SG|1PL.R
      'give them two each'

(2) -kɨ can be suffixed to adjectives, to convey the meaning of 'still':

(3-58) a. *ror mokop kararkɨ ŋgu sisiek awinnɨ tuwŋgwar patɨrekenɨ*
           ror   mokop karar -kɨ   ŋgu   sisiek   awin   =nɨ
           child   small red   -ADV 3SG.F   descend.2SG.F|3SG.F.R water   =LOC

           tuw   -ŋgwar   patɨr   =ekenɨ
           wash   -NFN.SG house =ABL
           'the baby was still red (i.e. newborn) when she came down from (i.e. left) the maternity house'

b. *orak iroki mbatatukun*
orak   iro   -ki   mbata -tu   -ku   -n
thing new   -ADV   ruin.R - S <3SG.F.R.O> -2SG|3SG.F.R.S
'the thing was still new and you buggered it up'

(3) *-ki* can be suffixed to a verb, making that verb function as what in English would be a gerund. The form of this construction is as follows:

TRANSITIVE VERBS	IRR verb stem + REALIS or BEN object morpheme + *-ki*
INTRANSITIVE VERBS	IRR verb stem + *-ki*

Examples:

(3-59) a. *ŋaŋan nam tariaki, ŋgi Merewre ŋgwok*
ŋaŋan   nam tar   -ia   -ki   ŋgi Merew =re   ŋgwok
1SG.POSS talk hear.IRR -1SG.BEN.R.O -ADV 3PL Sanae =ALL   go.3PL.R
'Having heard my talk, they went to Sanae'

b. *nek urekekuki, Mbowdi katot Potowre*
nek   ureke   -ku   -ki   Mbowdi katot
ladder   turn.IRR   -3SG.F.R.O -ADV Mbowdi go_down.SG.M.R

Potow   =re
Wongan   =ALL
'Having turned the ladder, Mbowdi went down to Wongan'
('Ladders' are notched poles leading up into a house, and they get turned when people leave their houses so that the notches face inwards. This makes it more difficult for dogs to climb up into a house.)

c. *ketukraki, munje kowot ide orepeyin*
ketuk   -ra -ki   munje kowot ide orepe   -yi   -n
cough.IRR   -ra -ADV   man   old   DX   leave.R -1SG.R.O   -SG|1PL.R.S
'Having coughed, the old man left me'

3.4.3 Temporal adverbs

Tayap has several types of temporals, which function adverbially, and which express when an event occurred or will occur:

General temporals:	anombi	'later on in the near future'
	nunuk	'later', 'afterwards'
	nirere	'a moment ago', 'in a minute'
	ripam	'a long time previously', 'in the olden days'
	ripim	'before', 'previously'
	ripimki	'quite a while ago'
	ripimbaraki	'a fair while ago' (not as long ago as *ripimki*)
Divisions of the day:	embeb	'just before dawn' (4.30–5.30)
	emb	'morning' (5.30–7.00)
	arawer	'daytime, early afternoon' (7.00–16.00)
	ŋgrag arawer	'late afternoon' (16.00–17.00)
	ŋgrag	'early evening' (17.00–19.00)
	ikur	'night' (19.00–4.30)

The locative clitic =*re* can be used in its temporal function with these words to specify the time of an action:

(3-60) a. *ikurre yim okitike*
   ikur =re yim o -ki -tike
   night =TEMP 1PL go.IRR -IRR -DL.IRR
   'the two of us will go at night'

   b. *embre ki ŋgwokara mirini*
   emb =re ki ŋgwok -ara miri =ni
   morning =TEMP INTENS go.3PL.R -PERF rainforest =ALL
   'they went into the jungle at the break of dawn'

=*re* also carries the adverbial meaning of frequency when the temporal phrase it creates is repeated. See below, Section 3.4.4.

Calendrical time has the following nominal expressions:

aro	'day'
arawer	'day', lit. 'sun'
karep	'month', lit. 'moon'
ŋgudumŋa kit/ mbiruŋa kit	'year', lit. 'Pleiades'

=*re* is also attached to these words to specify the time of an action:

(3-61) *nunukŋa karepre oŋgrinetana oki*
       nunuk =ŋa   karep =re   o   -ŋgri
       later   =POSS moon   =TEMP strike.IRR -3SG.M.IRR.O

       -net   -ana   o   -ki
       -1SG.M|3SG.M.IRR.S -INTENT go.IRR -IRR
       'next month I'm going to go hit him'

Duration over time – 'for three days' and similar – is expressed by adding an intransitive verb ending, inflected for 3SG.F, to the number:

(3-62) *ŋgi turkar ŋgwoka arawer senetak*
       ŋgi   tur   -kar   ŋgwok   -a   arawer sene-tak
       3PL   sing_and_dance -MANN go.3PL.R -and day   two-2SG|3SG.F.R
       'they sang and danced for two days'

Days in relation to one another are expressed as:

    muŋgit   'the day before yesterday' (used generally to mean 'recently', 'in the recent past')
    ewar   'yesterday'
    ene   'today', 'now'
    epi   'tomorrow'
    tuemb   'the day after tomorrow'
    amen   '3 days hence'
    amamar   '4 days hence'
    amandukup '5 days hence'
    ndukup   '6 days hence'
    aŋgisakup '7 days hence'

The above temporals differ from the others listed so far in that unlike them, the words for days in relation to one another are *never* modified by the postposed temporal *-re*.

    Some examples of use are:

(3-63) a. *muŋgit yim prieknan ŋgi Ngasimbara patirni ŋguk*
          muŋgit   yim   priek   =ŋan, ŋgi   Ngasimbara
          recently 1PL   come_up.1SG.F|1PL.R =POSS 3PL   Ngasimbara

	patir	=*nɨ*	*ŋguk*
	house	=LOC	be.3PL.R

'recently, when we arrived Ngasimbara, they were in the house [there]'

b. *ewar ikurre ŋa mbot sasik amaikrunana*

	ewar	*ikur*	=*re*	*ŋa*	*mbot*	*sasik*
	yesterday	night	=TEMP	1SG	go.SG.M.R	bandicoot

	amai	-*kru*	-*nana*
	search_for.IRR	-3SG.F.IRR.O	-INTENT

'last night I went to hunt (lit. 'to look for') bandicoot'

Speakers younger than about forty know the words in the above list of days up to and including *tuemb* 'the day after tomorrow'. Some know, but never use, *amen* (three days from now). The words for four and five days in the future are known only by speakers over fifty. I recorded *aŋgisakup* (seven days from now) during elicitation sessions with old fluent speakers in the 1980s. Nowadays the word is obsolete, remembered by only a few of the oldest speakers in the village.

3.4.4 Adverbials of frequency and distribution and 'not yet'

Two adverbials in Tayap express frequency and distribution (-*re*), and the temporal relationship 'not yet' (*ŋgo wákare*). Note the formal parallel with the locative =*re* (see Section 3.4.3 above and Section 4.4); presumably these forms, while having different functions, have the same origin. The suffix -*re* occurs on nouns, and always involves reduplication, as the following examples show.

-*re* 'every'

(3-64) a. *Yu nimenda nirakkut arore arore. Rorsem aikindaka ambukenɨ nirakkut? Hariap kwik nirakkut.*

yu	*nimenda*	*nir*	-*ak*	*kut*	*aro*	-*re*
2SG	thus	do.IRR	-LINK	be.SG.M.R	day	-ADV

aro	-*re*	*rorsem*	*ai*	-*ki*	-*ndak*	-*a*	*ambukenɨ*
day	-ADV	child.PL	come.IRR	-IRR	-3PL.IRR	-and	what

nir	-*ak*	*kut*	*Hariap*	*kwik*	
do.IRR	-LINK	be.SG.M.R	hurry up	quick (Tok Pisin)	

```
           nir      -ak      kut
           do.IRR   -LINK    be.SG.M.R
```
'You do this all the time: the kids come and what do you always do? You're here in a hurry doing it.'

   b. *ŋa patɨrre patɨrre ekrukaŋwar noŋor wákare*
```
           ŋa    patɨr-re     patɨr-re    ekruk-aŋwar            noŋor
           1SG   house-ADV    house-ADV   walk_around.IRR-be.NFN.SG   woman

           wákare
           NEG
```
'I'm not a woman who walks around every house (gossiping).'

ŋgo wákare 'not yet'. This occurs on standard negated clauses.

(3-65) a.
```
           ŋgɨ    ai         -ki   ŋgo   wákare
           3PL    come.IRR   -IRR  yet   NEG
```
'they haven't come yet'

        b.
```
           ŋɨ      warak       -ki   ŋgo   wákare
           3SG.M   talk.IRR    -IRR  yet   NEG
```
'he hasn't spoken yet'

3.4.5 Elevational and positional adverbials

The relative geographical position of objects and people is expressed in Tayap much more frequently than it is in a language like English. When leaving someone's company, for example, one doesn't just say 'I'm going', but rather, 'I'm going up (in the direction of the rainforest)' or 'I'm going down (in the direction of the mangrove lagoon)'. Similarly, if you have just arrived back in Gapun from a trip to the village of Wongan, and someone asks you where you have been, the correct answer is not 'I was in Wongan', but 'I was down in Wongan'.

Elevational and positional relationships are lexically encoded in Tayap's rich set of verbs of motion, virtually all of which are being lost because of their irregular inflectional patterns (see Section 6.2.3). But Tayap also has a set of two free-standing elevationals and seven positionals that are used to pinpoint the location of an object or a person.

Four of these are oriented according to a spatial array consisting of two axes.

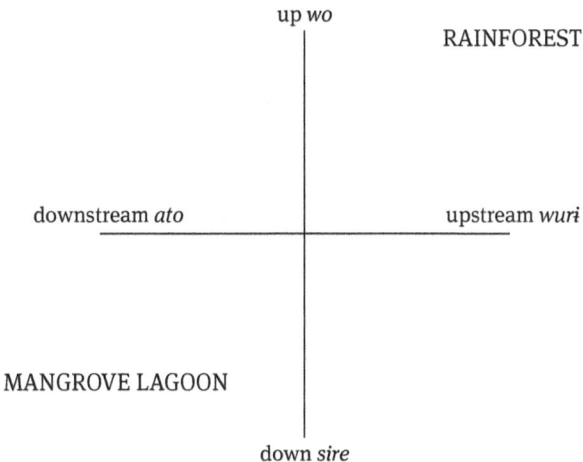

The vertical axis refers to the spatial elevationals of 'up' and 'down', for instance being up in a tree or down on the ground.

The horizontal axis refers to the geographical relationship between the rainforest and the mangrove lagoon. The mangrove lagoon that villagers have to cross to get to the neighboring village of Wongan runs to the sea and lies to the north of Gapun. The rainforest, in which the villagers live and into which they walk every day to find sago palms to process and game to hunt, lies all around the village, but most of the vast areas of their traditional land lies roughly south of Gapun. In relation to the mighty Sepik River, which can be seen from the top of the mountain where Gapun village was situated until after World War II, the mangrove lagoon is 'downstream', and the rainforest is 'upstream'. This is the sense in which villagers say they went 'down' to Wongan and then came back 'up' to Gapun. These directionals are relative to one another, so that when one has gone 'up' into the rainforest, one comes 'down' to Gapun village when one returns. Note that the terms also cover all space within the village.

The five other freestanding positionals are:

ari 'below', in the sense of 'down below' on a slope
ase 'beside', 'on the edge of', 'on the periphery of'
aro 'inside', in the sense of 'enveloped in or covered by'
ato 'outside', 'on the exterior of'
osi 'on the other side'

So, for example, in response to the question 'Where is it?', one might respond in any of the following ways:

(3-66) a. wo aŋgi wuk
up DX.F be.3SG.F.R
'it's there on top'

b. wurɨ aŋgi wuk
up DX.F be.3SG.F.R
'it's there in the upper part
of the village'

c. aro aŋgi wuk
inside DX.F be.3SG.F.R
'it's there inside'

d. ato aŋgi wuk
outside DX.F be.3SG.F.R
'it's outside there'

e. sire aŋgi wuk
down DX.F be.3SG.F.R
'it's there on the bottom/
underneath'

f. ari aŋgi wuk
below DX.F be.3SG.F.R
'it's down there'

g. ato aŋgi wuk
down DX.F be.3SG.F.R
'it's there in the lower part of
the village'

h. ase aŋgi wuk
beside DX.F be.3SG.F.R
'it's there beside
(something)'

i. osi aŋgi wuk
other side DX.F be.3SG.F.R
'it's on the other side'

These same words are adverbial modifiers, preceding verbs to modify their meaning, as in the difference between the following verbs:

(3-67) a. ŋgrɨtukun!
ŋgrɨ -tu -ku -n
put.SBJ -S <3SG.F.R.O> -2SG|3SG.F.R.S
'put it!'

b. wo ŋgrɨtukun!
wo ŋgrɨ -tu -ku -n
up put.SBJ -S <3SG.F.R.O> -2SG|3SG.F.R.S
'put it on top!'

(3-68) a. Mbam patɨrŋan pɨknɨ inde kut
Mbam patɨr =ŋan pɨk =nɨ inde kut
Mbam house =POSS veranda =LOC DX.M be.SG.M.R
'Mbam is on the veranda of the house'

b. Mbam patɨrŋan pɨknɨ inde ato kut
Mbam patɨr =ŋan pɨk =nɨ inde ato kut
Mbam house =POSS veranda =LOC DX.M outside be.SG.M.R
'Mbam is outside on the veranda of the house'

They can also be used as verbs in serial verb constructions, indicating motion, for example (see Section 8.2):

(3-69) yimbar ŋaŋan mbɨukuasetak
       yimbar   ŋaŋan   mbɨu   -ku   -ase   -tak
       canoe   mine   pull.R -3SG.F.R.O   -edge -2SG.F|3SG.F.R.S
       'She pulled my canoe outside' (i.e. she pulled it from inside the rainforest out into the open)

In addition to the freestanding elevationals and positionals, Tayap also has a number of complex positionals, all but one of which (*mborki*) are nouns attached with the locative clitic =*nɨ*.

imin=nɨ	'inside' or 'underneath' (lit. 'belly' + LOC)
kandaŋ=nɨ	'under', 'at the base of' (lit. 'base' + LOC)
mbokak=nɨ	'on top of' (lit. 'surface' + LOC)
mborki=nɨ	'outside', 'visible, out in the open'
mbwar=nɨ	'behind' or 'on' (lit. 'back' + LOC)
nunuk=nɨ	'behind' (lit. 'back side' + LOC)
orom=nɨ	'in the middle' (lit. 'middle' + LOC)
raw=nɨ	'facing' or 'in front of' (lit. 'nose' + LOC)
sek=nɨ	'underneath' (lit. 'underside' + LOC)
taw=nɨ	'beside' (lit. 'side' + LOC)

The above positionals are nouns that can occur on their own – so one can say:

(3-70) raw   =nɨ   aŋgi   wuk
       nose =LOC DX.F   be.3SG.F.R
       'it's in front'

But speakers also frequently combine locative positionals like *rawnɨ* with the freestanding elevationals and positionals, as well as more complex elements like the possessive-marked noun in (3-71a–c), to specify location. One of the tests I did for positionals was to put a plastic box in the middle of my floor and then put a torch (i.e. a flashlight) in various positions in, under, behind, etc. the box. Some of the positionals I elicited in this way are as follows (Note: *tos* 'torch' and *kontena* 'box' or 'container' are Tok Pisin words):

(3-71) a. tos   kontena =ŋa   mbwar =nɨ   wo   wuk
         torch   box   =POSS back   =LOC up   be.3SG.F.R
         'the torch is on top of the box'

   b. tos   kontena =ŋa   raw   =nɨ   ase   wuk
      torch   box   =POSS nose   =LOC beside be.3SG.F.R
      'the torch is in front of the box'

   c. tos   kontena =ŋa   kandaŋ =nɨ   aro   wuk
      torch   box   =POSS base   =LOC inside be.3SG.F.R
      'the torch is underneath the box'

In addition to the elevationals and positionals discussed above, Tayap has two further spatial adverbials that denote relative distance: *kemrak* 'far away' and *menjikan* 'nearby'. Examples are:

(3-72) a. *ŋɨ nginana kemrak puŋgot*
         ŋɨ   ŋgɨ   =nana   kemrak   puŋgot
         3SG.M   3PL   =DAT   far_away stand.SG.M.R
         'he's standing a long way from them'

   b. *paru aŋgi menjikan aŋgi wuk yuwon ndowre*
      paru   aŋgi   menjikan aŋgi   wuk   yuwon   ndow   =re
      plate   DX.F   nearby   DX.F   be.3SG.F.R 2SG.POSS   leg   =LOC
      'the plate is there near your leg'

3.5 Pronouns

Tayap has a single set of pronouns that occur in three different cases: absolutive, ergative and possessive.

The possessive pronouns are formed by adding the possessive clitic = *ŋa(n)* to the absolutive-case pronouns (with some irregularities), and the ergative pronouns are formed by adding the nominal ergative clitics (see Section 4.3) to the absolutive forms, again with some irregularities. Note that bound pronominal forms are listed below and discussed in Section 5.3.

PERSON	ABSOLUTIVE PRONOUNS	POSSESSIVE PRONOUNS	ERGATIVE PRONOUNS
1SG	ŋa	ŋaŋan	ŋayi
1PL	yim	yimon	yimŋi
2SG	yu	yuwon	yuyi

Person	Absolutive Pronouns	Possessive Pronouns	Ergative Pronouns
2PL	yum	yumon	yumŋi
3SG.F	ŋgu	ŋgon	ŋguyi
3SG.M	ŋɨ	ŋan	ŋɨŋi
3PL	ŋgɨ	ŋgan	ŋgɨgi

Note: While there are dual verb suffixes in Tayap, there is no dual free pronoun, see the discussion before examples (3-73) and (3-74) below.

There are also sets of object-marking suffixes, for the benefactive mood (Section 7.5), also used in the transitive progressive (Section 8.3.1.2), and also for non-final verbs (Section 8.2). These forms are as follows, repeated here for convenience (note that these forms are perhaps better organized by number than person, but to parallel other paradigms they are organized here by person):

Person	Benefactive Realis	Benefactive Irrealis	Non-final Object
1SG	-ia(ta)	-iti	-ai
1PL	-ma(ta)	-mati	-am
2SG	-wa(ta)	-wati	-aw
2PL	-ma(ta)	-mati	-am
3SG.F	-kwa(ta)	-kwati	-ak
3SG.M	-ŋga(ta)	-ŋgati	-at
3PL	-mba(ta)	-mbati	-amb
DL	-ma(ta)	-mati	-amb

There is a lack of parallelism between pronouns and verb morphology, in the sense that for all singular subjects, including 1SG, gender is obligatorily marked on verbs through various means that for some verb classes includes changes in the verb stem itself.

For example, note how the imperfective form of the verb 'go' (*o*) changes to express gender for singular subjects:

Person	Gender	Pronoun	Verb	
1SG	F	ŋa	mbok	'I went' (female speaking)
1SG	M	ŋa	mbot	'I went' (male speaking)
2SG	F	yu	mbok	'you went' (female referent)
2SG	M	yu	mbot	'you went' (male referent)
3SG	F	ŋgu	wok	'she went'
3SG	M	ŋɨ	mbot	'he went'

Gender is expressed in the verb here for all singular subjects. The free pronominal system, however, does not manifest a gender distinction in first or second person: feminine and masculine first-person singular are both *ŋa*; feminine and masculine second-person singular are both *yu*. The pronominal system distinguishes gender only in third-person singular (*ŋi* 'he' and *ŋgu* 'she'). For plural subjects, there is no gender distinction, neither in the pronominal system nor in the morphology of verbs.

A further divergence between the pronominal system and verb morphology is that Tayap, as noted above, has no separate dual pronoun, but it does have a dual verb inflection for both transitive verbs (*-re*) and intransitive verbs (*-tike*). This inflection signals 'we two' (1DL) or 'the two of them' (3DL).

Note, though, that 'you two' (2DL) is expressed with the second person plural (*yum*) form of the verb. Compare:

(3-73) a. DUAL
 yim o -ku -re
 1PL consume.R <3SG.F.R.O> -DL.R.S
 'the two of us ate it'

 b. PLURAL
 yim ka -ku -n
 1PL consume.R <3SG.F.R.O> -SG|1PL.R.S
 'we ate it'

 c. DUAL
 ŋgɨ wasow -tike
 3PL die.R -DL.R
 'the two of them died'

 d. PLURAL
 ŋgɨ wasow -ndak
 3PL die.R -3PL.R
 'they died'

But:

 e. yum ka -ku -rem
 2PL consume.R <3SG.F.R.O> -2PL.R.S
 'you all ate it' or 'the two of you ate it'

To specify duality for 2PL subjects, one must be explicit and say the word *sene* 'two'. So the following sentence means 'the two of you ate it':

(3-74) *yum sene kakurem*
        yum   sene   ka   -ku   -rem
        2PL   two   consume.R   <3SG.F.R.O>   -2PL.R.S
        'the two of you ate it'

A further divergence between free pronouns and verb morphology is that free pronouns operate under an ergative/absolutive alignment system whereas verbal morphology operates under a nominative/accusative system (see Section 4.3).

3.6 Quantifiers

3.6.1 Counting

The traditional counting system in Tayap was based on a person's fingers and toes. This is a well-known areal feature (Laycock 1975). The Tayap system allowed counting up to twenty, although in principle the system could count indefinitely, because after reaching twenty, one could, I was told, begin counting again on the body of another person (so 'twenty-one' could be 'two hands and two legs and one hand one finger on the other side').

This laborious system, for which there seems to have been no shorthand, disappeared rapidly after villagers began speaking Tok Pisin among themselves in the 1930s and 1940s. Today it is only vaguely remembered, and is regarded as an amusing, cumbersome and primitive curiosity by everyone in Gapun.

Villagers still use the Tayap words for 'one' through to 'five', and they sometimes combine them to denote a number between five and ten. For example, I once overheard a villager ask another in Tayap how many bags a cocoa buyer who had come to Gapun had filled (this was a typical instance of using Tayap to "hide talk" from non-villagers). The addressee, a thirty-year-old man who is a very weak speaker of Tayap and who under other circumstances never speaks it, responded by saying *manaw towotowo* (literally 'three four'), which in this context meant seven bags.

Villagers also sometimes use the Tayap word for 'ten', but never any of the others, which are always said in Tok Pisin.

The traditional system, as I recorded it from senior men in the 1980s, is as follows:

nambar	'one'
sene	'two'
manaw	'three'

towotowo	'four'
ndaram nambar	'one hand' (i.e. five)
ndaram nambar taw nonni nambar	'one hand one on the other side' (i.e. six)
ndaram nambar taw nonni sene	'one hand two on the other side' (i.e. seven)
ndaram nambar taw nonni manaw	'one hand three on the other side' (i.e. eight)
ndaram nambar taw nonni towotowo	'one hand four on the other side' (i.e. nine)
ndaram sene	'two hands' (i.e. ten)
ndaram senea[3] ndow sikrim nambar	'two hands and one toe' (i.e. eleven)
ndaram senea ndow sikrim sene	'two hands and two toes' (i.e. twelve)
ndaram senea ndow sikrim manaw	'two hands and three toes' (i.e. thirteen)
ndaram senea ndow sikrim towotowo	'two hands and four toes' (i.e. fourteen)
ndaram senea ndow nambar	'two hands and one leg' (i.e. fifteen)
ndaram senea ndow nambar taw nonni ndow sikrim nambar	'two hands and one leg one toe on the other side' (i.e. sixteen)
ndaram senea ndow nambar taw nonni ndow sikrim sene	'two hands and one leg two toes on the other side' (i.e. seventeen)
ndaram senea ndow nambar taw nonni ndow sikrim manaw	'two hands and one leg three toes on the other side' (i.e. eighteen)
ndaram senea ndow nambar taw nonni ndow sikrim towotowo	'two hands and one leg two toes on the other side' (i.e. nineteen)
ndaram senea ndow sene	'two hands and two legs' (i.e. twenty)

When numbers occur together with other adjectives, they always occur last (other modifiers can occur in any order; see Section 4.1.1). So:

(3-75) naŋaw mopri sene
naŋaw mopri sene
woman.DL little.PL two
'two little women'

There are no ordinal numerals in Tayap, and to express what English expresses as adverbial numerals ('twice', 'thrice', 'four times', etc.), Tayap uses a construction in

---

3 *senea* is *sene* ('two') with the conjunction -*a*; so 'two-and'

which the number is the main verb and the event that happens a number of times is nominalized by suffixing the irrealis verb stem with the non-finite suffix -*(ŋ)gar* (see Section 4.2). This nominalized event serves as the subject of the number-as-verb.

Examples are:

(3-76) a. *Kruniŋi rumb oŋgar manawkɨtak*
        Kruni =ŋi rumb o-ŋgar
        Kruni =ERG.M slit_gong_drum strike.IRR-NFN.SG

        manaw -kɨ -tak
        three -IRR -2SG.F|3SG.F.IRR
        'Kruni will hit the slit gong drum three times'

    b. *epi ŋa memkɨnet tuŋgwar senerkɨtak*
        epi ŋa mem-kɨ-net
        tomorrow 1SG get_up.IRR-IRR-1SG.M|3SG.M.IRR

        tuŋgwar sene -r- -kɨ -tak
        bathe.IRR.NFN.SG two -r- -IRR -IRR.2SG.F|3SG.F.IRR
        'Tomorrow I will get up and bathe twice'

    c. *ewar ŋan noŋor aikrak ndɨ, ŋiŋi ŋgu oŋgar samirɨktak*
        ewar ŋan noŋor aik -rak ndɨ
        yesterday his woman come.CF -3SG.F.CF.S.HYPO DM

        ŋɨ =ŋi ŋgu o -ŋgar sami -rɨk -tak
        3SG.M =ERG.M 3SG.F hit.IRR -NFN.SG many -CF -3SG.F.R
        'If his wife had come yesterday, he would have hit her many times'

3.6.2 Plural markers

As was discussed in Section 3.1.1.3, the only nouns in Tayap with non-singular forms are the closed class of nouns denoting some humans, and pigs and dogs. All other nouns have only one form. To indicate plurality in those nouns, the following quantifiers may be used. They immediately follow the noun to which they refer:

    samb   general marker of plurality, most often used with countable nouns
    non samb   used with unquantifiable masses like water or food
    sami   'many', 'lots of', 'plenty'
    -ŋgro   used to signify associative plurality on people or place names, pronouns and interrogative words

Examples:

(3-77) a. *Murarŋan yam samb rarkru wákare*
Murar =ŋan yam samb rar -kru wákare
Murar =POSS sago_palm PL see.IRR -3SG.F.IRR.O NEG
'we didn't see the sago palms at Murar'

b. *nam samb yunana nirkwanŋguk*
nam samb yu -nana nir -kwan -ŋguk
talk PL 2SG -DAT make.IRR -3SG.F.BEN.R.O -be.3PL.R
'they are talking about you' (lit. 'they are making lots of talk about you')

c. *ŋɨŋi awin sawir non samb kakun*
ŋɨ =ŋi awin sawir non samb
3SG.M =ERG.M water black INDEF

ka -ku -n
consume.R <3SG.F.R.O> -1SG|2SG|3SG.M|1PL.R.S
'he drank some black water'

d. *ŋa sokoi non samb kakun*
ŋa sokoi non samb
1SG tobacco INDEF

ka -ku -n
consume.R <3SG.F.R.O> -1SG|2SG|3SG.M|1PL.R.S
'I smoked some tobacco'

e. *aro sami ŋa rarŋgankut, ŋɨ tutor[4] ŋayorni awkut*
aro sami ŋa rar -ŋgan -kut
day many 1SG see.IRR -3SG.M.BEN.R.O -be.SG.M.R

ŋɨ tuto -r- -ŋayorni -awkut
3SG.M sit.R -r- -truly -be.SG.M.R.HAB
'I see him all the time, he really just sits there (and does nothing)'

Associative plurals occur: see the following example:

f. Speaker A: *Ani -ŋgro ŋgwok -ara?*
who -PL come.3PL.R -PERF
'who all came?'

---

[4] This word has an exceptional inserted *r* after the stem in some forms.

Speaker B: *Samek -ŋgro*
            Samek -PL
            'Samek and the others'

In addition to those markers of plurality discussed above, recall from Section 3.3.1 that there is a handful of adjectives that have separate dual and/or plural forms. Further, Tayap has a marker that attached to adjectives to signify 'more than one'. This plural marker (*anem*) is moribund; these days it is heard in the speech only of speakers over sixty. From one of those speakers, I elicited sentences such as the following:

(3-78) a. *numbwan eŋgon anem munjenum*
        numbwan   eŋgon   anem   munjenum
        thought   good   POSS.PL man.PL
        'men with good thoughts' (lit. 'good thoughts men')

     b. *rew suman anem munjenum*
        rew   suman   anem   munjenum
        fear   big   POSS.PL man.PL
        'cowards' (lit. 'big fears men')

In naturally occurring speech of older speakers, this marker of plurality was used most productively in the context of abuse. Indeed, I was first alerted to it when transcribing the many "kros-es" (loud public arguments, almost always started and sustained by women) that occurred in the village (Kulick 1993). There, *anem* (shortened to *nem* after the vowel in the preceding word) occurs in abusive phrases like the following:

(3-79) a. *iminkato sawirŋa nem!*
        iminkato   sawir   =ŋa   nem
        lower_intestine black =POSS ADJ.PL
        'black assholes!'

     b. *man sumanŋa nem!*
        man   suman   =ŋa   nem
        cunt big   =POSS ADJ.PL
        'big cunts!'

The retraction of what may have been a much more widely used marker of plurality to the context of vituperative abuse is an instructive instance of how particular registers of language (such as abuse) can be repositories of older, obsolescent forms that for various reasons have all but died out in the language otherwise.

3.7 Articles

Tayap has no definite article. The definiteness of a referent emerges either through the context or because it occurs together with a deictic word.

The language does, however, have a word, *non*, which means 'a' or 'some' – in the sense of 'some man' or 'some child' – and which can function as an indefinite article. The word does not mean 'one': to specify a singularity, the quantifier *nambar* 'one' is used (see Section 3.6.1). The word *non* can occur independently, as in the following request, which is heard ubiquitously in Gapun, uttered by someone asking someone else for betel nut:

(3-80) *non kukukwe*
    non   ku   -ku   -we
    INDEF   bring   -3SG.F.R.O   -come.SBJ
    'give me one/some' (lit. 'bring me one/some')

When *non* occurs after a noun, it imparts indefiniteness. If *non* does not occur, the referent will likely be interpreted as definite. An example is a sentence like the following:

(3-81) *rorŋi ŋgat tanŋgɨn*
    ror   =ŋi   ŋgat   ta   -n   -ŋgɨ   -n
    child   =ERG.M   cassowary   see.R   -S   <3SG.M.R.O> -SG|1PL.R.S

This sentence would likely be interpreted to mean 'the child saw the cassowary', but it can mean both 'the child saw *the* cassowary' and 'the child saw *a* cassowary'. The context of the utterance would usually make it clear if a definite or indefinite noun were meant.

If a speaker wanted to emphasize indefiniteness, he or she could use *non* or *non samb* (Section 3.6.2) after the nominal it modifies:

(3-82) a. *rorŋi ŋgat non tanŋgɨn*
        ror   =ŋi   ŋgat   non   ta   -n   -ŋgɨ   -n
        child   =ERG.M   cassowary   indef   see.R   -S   <3SG.M.R.O>   -SG|1PL.R.S
        'the boy saw a cassowary'

    b. *ror nonŋi ŋgat non tanŋgɨn*
        ror   non   =ŋi   ŋgat   non
        child   INDEF   =ERG.M   cassowary   INDEF

```
ta       -n  -ŋgɨ           -n
see.R    -S  <3SG.M.R.O>    -SG|1PL.R.S
```
'some (unnamed and possibly unknown) boy saw a cassowary'

3.8 Deictics (DX)

Deictics in Tayap locate a referent in space and time, and can be translated as 'this' or 'that' and 'here' or 'there'. The language has a word *ai* for 'here, and *aninɨ* for 'there'. These words are used in simple commands to put something or bring something 'here' or 'there':

(3-83) a. *ainnɨ wo ŋgritukun*
```
ai     =nɨ   wo       ŋgri     -tu  -ku           -n
here   =LOC  on_top   put.IRR  -S   <3SG.F.R.O>   -2SG|3SG.F.R.S
```
'put it here on top'

b. *anɨnɨ wo ŋgritukun*
```
anɨnɨ   wo       ŋgri     -tu  -ku           -n
there   on_top   put.IRR  -S   <3SG.F.R.O>   -2SG|3SG.F.R.S
```
'put it there on top'

Note: the locative clitic *=nɨ* on *anɨnɨ* is optional and frequently omitted (as it is in this example) probably because the word ends with *nɨ*, which is homophonous with the locative clitic.

Tayap has a six-way distinction for singular referents – three for feminine referents and three for masculine referents. As in other parts of Tayap grammar, the gender distinction collapses in the plural, and here the language maintains a two-way distinction:

	SINGULAR		
LOCATION OF REFERENT	FEMININE REFERENT	MASCULINE REFERENT	TRANSLATION
close to speaker	aŋo(de)	ainde, ai	'this one', 'here'
a bit further from speaker	aŋi(de)	anɨnde	'this one' or 'that one', 'there'
further still from speaker	aŋu(de)	anɨnɨnde	'that one', 'over there'

	PLURAL	
LOCATION OF REFERENT	BOTH FEMININE AND MASCULINE REFERENTS	TRANSLATION
close to speaker	aŋge(de)	'these', 'here'
further from speaker	aŋgɨ(de)	'those', 'there'

Note that the three-way distance distinction in the singular and two-way in the plural is highly unusual and may in fact be a simplification: the middle term in the singular could in fact be a close-to-addressee term or expressing other pragmatic factors (see e.g. Wilkins 1999).[5]

In addition to the words listed above, Tayap also has a number of slightly different deictic words. They are as follows:

Feminine	Masculine	Plural
aŋok...aŋo 'this... here'	aindet....ende[6] 'this ...here' anindet...ende/inde/ide/de 'that...there'	aŋgeb...aŋge 'these...there'
aŋudek...aŋu 'that...there'		aŋgɨb... aŋgɨb 'those... there'

The first or second words in these pairs can occur alone functioning as an argument of a verb phrase. During a disagreement between two men, for example, one protagonist responded to the other's threats to come and beat him up with the dismissive snort addressed to everybody who was listening:

(3-84) aindetŋike oyin?
  aindet =ŋi =ke o -yi -n?
  that_one =ERG.M =Q strike.IRR -1SG.IRR.O -SG|1PL.IRR.S
  'that one there is going to hit me?'

These topicalizing deictic words often co-occur, sometimes multiple times in an utterance.[7] They can be post-posed to a noun to emphasize it, for example in response to a question like 'Who did it?':

---

[5] We thank Anna Margetts for this observation.
[6] The second word here, *ende*, can also be realized as *inde*, *ide* or *de*
[7] It is possible that these instances might more felicitously be labeled "focusing", "highlighting" or "emphasizing" rather than topicalizing (Reesink 2014). More information and analysis on the functions of all these deicitics is needed.

(3-85) a. *munje aindet ende*
 man DX.M DX.M
 'this man'

 b. *noŋor aŋgok aŋgo*
 woman DX.F DX.F
 'this woman'

(3-86) a. *aindet munje ide mbábasak ende*
 DX.M man DX.M crazy DX.M
 'this man is crazy'

A third set of related deictic words are demonstrative identifiers, which indicate particularity and presence, e.g. 'it's me', or 'I'm here' (as opposed to being away somewhere). The term "demonstrative identifiers" comes from Diessel (1999). These words function in a similar way to how an adverb like *ecco* functions in the Italian *eccomi* – 'it's me' or 'here I am'. So the most common response to a question like 'Who are you?' – asked, for example when one hears someone approaching in the pitch blackness of a moonless night – is *Ŋa ainda* ('it's me').

ainda	used with	*ŋa* (1SG.M AND 1SG.F)
		yu (2SG.M AND 2SG.F)
		yim (1PL)
		yum (2PL)
ainde	used with	*ŋi* (3SG.M)
aŋgo(de)	used with	*ŋgu* (3SG.F)
aŋge(de)	used with	*ŋgi* (3SG.PL) and DL

These words are virtually obligatory with many verbs, such as *aku* 'be', in the sense that even though it would be grammatically correct to just say *ŋi kut* ('he's here'), it is pragmatically awkward. One should say *ŋi ainde kut* ('he DX.M is here').

Finally, in addition to all the deictic forms listed above, Tayap also has a quasi-deictic suffix *-me*, which means 'yes, indeed, that one (or those) as opposed to any other or others', occurring on pronouns.

-me is also used to emphasize a referent, for example:

(3-87) a. *ŋgime aŋgi ŋgwokara*
 ŋgi -me aŋgi ŋgwok -ara
 3PL -DX DX.PL go.3PL.R -PERF
 'they're indeed the ones who left' (as opposed to some other people having left)

b. *ŋgume morasi oretukun*
   ŋgu -me morasi ore   -tu -ku   -n
   3SG.F -DX deed   leave.SBJ -S <3SG.F.R.O> -2SG|3SG.F.R.S
   'Stop doing that!'

The suffix *-me* occurs just prior to the deictic *aŋgi* in one of the most frequently heard phrases in Tayap: *ŋguméŋgi*. This phrase – a contracted form of *ŋgu-me aŋgi* (3SG.F-*me* + *aŋgi*) – means 'yes, that way', 'that's right' ("em nau" in Tok Pisin).

3.9 Interrogatives (Q)

3.9.1 Yes/no questions

Yes/no questions in Tayap are formed with the clitic *=ke*. The part of speech to which *=ke* is cliticized is the focus of the question. So compare:

(3-88) a. *Amanike okinet?*
       Amani =ke o   -ki   -net?
       Amani =Q   go.IRR -IRR -1SG.M|3SG.M.IRR.S
       'Will Amani (as opposed to someone else) go?'

    b. *Amani okinetke?*
       Amani o   -ki   -net   =ke?
       Amani go.IRR -IRR -1SG.M|3SG.M.IRR.S =Q
       'Will Amani go?' (as opposed to 'will Amani stay?')

Because it expresses uncertainty, *=ke* can also be used in a context where it would be translated as 'or':

(3-89) a. *epi ŋa Mbowdike Aperke yim okitike Potowre*
       epi   ŋa   Mbowdi =ke Aper =ke yim
       tomorrow 1SG Mbowdi =Q   Aper =Q   1PL

       o   -ki   -tike   Potow=re
       go.IRR -IRR -DL.IRR Wongan=ALL
       'tomorrow I'll go with either Mbowdi or Aper to Wongan'
       (lit. 'tomorrow I Mbowdi? Aper? we two will go to Wongan')

    b. *ŋi mbaranike kut mirinike*
       ŋi   mbara   =ni   =ke
       3SG.M garden =LOC =Q

kut   miri=ni=ke
be.SG.M.R   rainforest=LOC=Q
'he's either in the garden or in the rainforest'

Note that the interrogative clitic follows the locative clitic when they co-occur, as in example (3-89b).

3.9.2 Information questions

Information questions are formed using one of the following interrogative words, many of which are readily segmentable, e.g. *anire* 'with whom' can be segmented as *ani=re* 'who=COM'; *ani=yi* is who=ERG.F; *ani=mat* is who=POSS, etc.:

ani	'who?'	ambinŋa/ ambukŋa	'which?'
aniyi	'who (did it)?'	ambukni	'how?'
animat	'whose?'	ambukrani	'how many?'/ 'how much?'
anire	'with whom?'		
ambin	'what?'	ana(kni)	'where?'
ambin ana	'why?'/ 'what for?'	anakŋa	'from where?'
ambinekeni	'from what?'	ana sokop	'when?'
ambinini/ ambin orakni	'with what?'	ambukŋa titimbŋa	'what color?'/ 'what appearance?'

Interrogatives usually occur as the second element:

(3-90) a. *yu   ambinana   mbet?*
            2SG   why   come.SG.M.R
            'why have you (M) come?'

    b. *yu   anakŋa   mbet?*
            2SG   from_where   come.SG.M.R
            'where did you (M) come from?'

    c. *ŋgu ambinini poŋgin? Taimbni*
            ŋgu   ambinini   po   -ŋgi   -n?   Taimb=ni.
            3SG.F   with_what   hit.R -3SG.M.R.O SG|1PL.R.S stick=INST
            'what did she hit him with?' 'With a stick'

    d. *kawat ambukrani yu Pasonana pikwan?*
            kawat   ambukrani   yu   Paso   =nana
            salt   how_much   2PL   Paso   =DAT

```
pi       -kwa              -n
give.R   -3SG.F.BEN.R.O    -SG|1PL.R.S
```
'how much salt did you give to Paso?'

3.10 Interjections and affect words

Tayap speakers use a number of uninflected words to express emotional states, affirmation or disagreement, as well as affective involvement with, or phatic acknowledgement of, other people. These interjections form an utterance by themselves:

ore	'Yes'. This is a Watam-language borrowing that has all but replaced Tayap's *awo*.
awo	The Tayap word for the affirmative 'Yes'. Since the 1980s, however, it has become replaced by *ore*, and the meaning of *awo* has shifted to express sarcastic agreement that would be translated in English as 'Yeah, right' or 'Like I'm so sure'. The word has also taken on connotations of confrontation and violence. It is shouted at others whom one is prepared to strike. Parents use it frequently to threaten disobedient children, and an adult engaged in a shouting match with another adult might use it to signal that her or his patience is about to give in. When it is shouted with sharp, rising volume and strong stress on the final syllable awó, the word is a warning that means: 'You haven't listened to my warnings and now I'm about to come and hit you!'
wákare	'No'. This is also the morpheme of negation, often shortened to *wak* when used to mean 'No' (as in: 'Is there any food left?' 'No'). When asked as a sharp question with rising intonation, *wákare* signifies a threat, meaning: 'So you're not doing what I told you to do? (I'm therefore going to come and hit you)'.
ario	'He/she/it is coming to get you'. This word is used to scare babies and small children. It is uttered preceded by the name of the person or thing that the caregiver wants the child to think is coming to get him or her, and is a vocative call, calling directly to the person or thing to come and get the baby (in order to hit the baby, or devour the baby).
kapambínana	'Exactly', 'Of course'

ŋguméŋgi	'That's it', 'Exactly'
yo	'Poor thing'. Always said in a soft voice with rising intonation, with exaggeratedly extended vowel pronounced over the rise (see also Section 2.1.2.1).
ŋganokeya	'Poor thing'. Refers to someone who is not present because he or she has died or left the village and gone away. Always said in a soft voice with rising intonation. It frequently either precedes or follows yo.
aowo	Word to convey longing and care for another, who is usually absent. Always said in a soft voice with rising intonation.
oiyo	'Poor me'. This is a kind of protest sound, usually growled in a voice verging on tears. It is used frequently by children when a caregiver insists they do something they don't want to do, or when another child won't give the speaker something that she or he claims is hers/his.
ey	'Oh', 'That's right'. Always said over two beats 'e-y' with rise-fall intonation, often accompanied by raised eyebrows, which also signifies agreement or affirmation.
ai	'Hey!'
wai	'Stop that!'
tse	'You've got to be kidding!'
akápore	'Oh my', 'How can this be?'
akáiya	'Listen up', 'Hold on', 'Pay attention'
yakáiya	'Oh my goodness!'. Said in response to a particularly salty joke, clever riposte or outlandish threat. Said also if one sneezes several times in a row – the sneezer says this him- or herself.
numbwanrekɨ	'Watch out!', 'Be careful!', 'Think carefully!' (lit. 'with thought')
ayáta	Two different meanings: (1) when shouted, it means: 'Enough!', 'Stop it!'; (2) when uttered in normal voice and said, for example, in response to someone saying "Poor thing, I have no food to give you", it means: 'Don't worry about it', 'Don't bother'.

ye	Two different meanings: (1) when uttered in a sudden, staccato burst, it means: 'Oh!', 'Oh no!' This sound is frequently used by caregivers to scare children. At least when children are very young, the alarmed quality of this sound can be an effective way of making them move away from an open fire or put down a sharp butcher knife. If the child is still a baby, this sound is often accompanied by the caregiver wrapping her or his arms around the baby as if to protect the baby; (2) when uttered with an extended vowel and a curled lip, it means: 'Gross'; 'Disgusting'; 'Feel shame'.
amaye	An expression moaned and cried by people experiencing extreme pain or shock, often preceded by the staccato *ye*.

3.10.1 Sounds used for calling animals and babies

Villagers also have distinctive ways of calling a number of animals and to amuse or distract pre-verbal babies:

to call a pig	close mouth, repeatedly make a sound like clearing the throat
to call a puppy	/ǁ/ – alveolar lateral click made with rounded lips
to call a grown dog	short brisk whistle held over one beat, repeated many times
to call a cat	*wsi-wsi-wsi-wsi*
to call a chicken	*tu-tu-tu-tu-tu* (high pitched)
to get a baby's attention	repeated kissing sounds
to distract a crying baby	blow air through closed lips

3.11 Intensifiers and discourse markers

A number of words and suffixes in Tayap have no referential meaning. They function to draw attention to or emphasize the word they follow. So an angry shout of *ayáta!* 'enough!' followed by the word *kai* expresses stronger disapproval than *ayáta* without the *kai*.

A second group of words function as ways for speakers to do things like plan discourse, stress particular constituents, hedge and change topics.

Tayap's intensifiers and discourse markers are as follows

3.11.1 Intensifiers

kai   intensifier used only with the command *ayáta* 'stop it'. *Kai* may be a short form of *kaitkait*, which means 'rotten shit', and is used in censorious abuse.

(3-91)   *ayáta **kai** maniŋ imin anem ayáta*
        ayáta   ***kai***   *maniŋ*   *imin*   *anem*   *ayáta!*
        stop it   INTENS   bucket   belly   POSS.PL   stop it
        You all better really stop this habit of sitting with stuffed stomachs! (*maniŋ imin* is a euphemism for *yɨwɨr imin*, which means 'shit belly', i.e. a belly filled up with feces because one has eaten so much. The speaker here is chastising his relatives, saying that they eat well but never feed him, and that such behavior must stop)

arɨk   intensifier used only with *mokop/mosop* 'little'

(3-92)   *mosop **arɨk** ŋayi ainɨ ŋguratmborinŋgɨn andnɨ kararneta mbot inde*
        mosop   ***arɨk***   *ŋa*   *=yi*   *ainɨ*
        little   INTENS   1SG   =ERG.F   like this

        ŋgur   *-at*   *mbori*   *-n*   *-ŋgɨ*   *-n*
        put.R   -3SG.M.DVO   flipflop.R   -S   <3SG.M.R.O>   -SG|1PL.R.

        and   *=nɨ*   *karar*   *-net*   *-a*   *mbot*   *inde*
        blood   =LOC   red   -1SG.M|3SG.M.R   -and   go.SG.M.R   DX.M
        'when he was really little I knocked him down like this and made him writhe and he went (away) covered red in blood'

mɨr   intensifier used to emphasize the size or quality of the noun or noun phrase that it follows:

(3-93)   a.   *yu ambinana otar suman **mɨr** aŋgo nitukun?*
            yu   *ambinana*   *otar*   *suman*   ***mɨr***   *aŋgo*
            2SG   why   fire   big   INTENS   DX.F

            ni   *-tu*   *-ku*   *-n?*
            make.R   -S   <3SG.F.R.O>   -2SG|3SG.F.R.S
            'why did you make such a big-assed fire?'

       b.   *awin   pokemb   **mɨr**   ŋayar*
            water   cold   INTENS   really
            'the water is really, really cold'

apro *sakar* negative intensifier used in the context of abuse to mean something like English 'fucking':

(3-94) a. *ŋare takwattakwatŋgarke koret ror **apro sakar** morasi aproŋa!*
ŋa =re takwat -takwat -ŋgarke koret
1SG =ALL lie -lie -PROH foreign

ror **apro sakar** morasi apro=ŋa
child bad INTENS habit bad=POSS
'Stop lying to me! You're like a fucking foreigner with bad habits' (i.e. you don't treat me like a fellow villager and tell me the truth)

b. *tokinema manŋa ŋgwab sawir manŋa **apro sakar!***
tokine=ma man=ŋa ŋgwab sawir man=ŋa **apro sakar**
catfish=POSS cunt=POSS hole black cunt=POSS bad INTENS
'Catfish cunt, fucking black cunt hole!'

This intensifier also appears to have had a plural form: in 1991, I recorded a single instance of the following, in the speech of a woman then in her mid-forties:

c. *Sakema sumanni aŋgurem **apri sakrem!***
Sake=ma suman=ni a -ŋgurem **apri sakrem**
Sake=POSS big=LOC be.IRR -NFN.2PL bad.PL INTENS.2PL
'You're all fucking being supported by Sake!' (lit. 'being on Sake's strength/bigness')

-ki intensifier affixed to adverbs, used to emphasize them (see also Section 3.4.2):

(3-95) *tandiw**ki** sirétet*
tandiw -**ki** siré -tet
well -INTENS descend.SBJ -2SG.M.R
'descend really well' (said to someone walking down the steep notched poles that lead up into houses)

-ni like *-ki*, but used more rarely, an intensifier affixed to adverbs, used to emphasize them (see also Section 3.4.2):

(3-96) *aro sami ŋa rarŋgankut ŋi tutorŋayor**ni**awkut*
aro sami ŋa rar-ŋgan-kut ŋi
day many 1SG see.IRR-3SG.M.BEN.R.O-be.SG.M.R 3SG.M

tuto -r- -ŋayor -**ni** awkut
sit.R -r- truly -INTENS be.SG.M.HAB
'I see him all the time, he really just sits there (and does nothing)'

3.11.2 Discourse markers

ŋgo   carries the sense of 'well then' or 'in that case' (cf. Tok Pisin: "pastaim"), e.g.:

(3-97) Speaker A:
*ŋa nda okinetana **ŋgo***
ŋa	nda	o	-ki	-net	-ana	**ŋgo**
1SG	DM	go.IRR	-IRR	-1SG.M|3SG.M.IRR	-INTENT	DM

'Well, I'm going to go then'

Speaker B:
*otet **ŋgo**!*
o	-tet	**ŋgo!**
go.SBJ	-2SG.M.R	DM

'Go, then/in that case'

ndɨ   discourse marker that draws attention to the noun phrase that precedes it. It conveys the gentle nuance that whatever precedes it is known or should be known by the addressee. Its meaning therefore extends from what one might translate as 'you know', 'right' or 'so', to more exasperated nuances like 'in case you weren't paying attention' or 'you perhaps don't know, but now I'm telling you'. An example expressing impatience is as follows:

(3-98)
tukur	non	**ndɨ**	we	-tak
rain	some	DM	come.SBJ	-2SG.F.R

'Come on rain, come!'

Another typical example that acknowledges previously conveyed information, and that also might be interpreted as displaying some impatience, is the following:

(3-99) Speaker A: *ŋa kebis katipkrunetana*

ŋa	kebis		
1SG	lettuce (TP)		

katip	-kru	-net	-ana
cut_up.IRR	-3SG.F.IRR.O	-1SG.M|3SG.M.IRR.S	-INTENT

'I'm going to go cut up lettuce'

Speaker B: *yu ndɨ katɨptukun*
            yu   **ndɨ** katɨp   -tu -ku   -n
            2SG DM   cut_up.SBJ -S   <3SG.F.R.O> -2SG|3SG.F.R.S
            'So cut it then'

When *ndɨ* occurs in a sentence that has at least one verb inflected in the counterfactual mood, it also functions syntactically as a marker of subordination (see Section 9.4.2).

nda   discourse marker that is likely a reduced form of the deictic morpheme *ainda* (see Section 3.8). Used like *ndɨ* to draw attention to the noun or noun phrase that precedes it, and often carries a sense similar to English 'then':

(3-100) *mboka ŋa **nda** numbwan aproyi tatɨn*
         mbok   -a   ŋa   **nda** numbwan apro =yi
         go.1SG.F|1PL.R -and 1SG DM   thought bad   =ERG.F

         ta   -t -i   -n
         get.R   -S <1SG.R.O>   -2SG.|.F3SG.F|1PL.R.S
         'we went along and then a bad thought occurred to me' (lit. 'a bad thought got me')

In a way that is similar to and probably related to the pragmatic function of Tayap's deictic words (see Section 3.8), discourse markers frequently occur multiple times in a single sentence, as in the following:

(3-101) a. *ŋa **ndɨ nda** namnak Ngemanŋi mera*
            ŋa   ndɨ nda nam   -nak   Ngeman =ŋi   mera
            1SG DM   DM   talk.R -1SG.F|1PL.R Ngeman =ERG.M SUPP
            'I thought it was Ngeman (who did it)'

        b. *yum **nda** mbor **ndɨ** ŋayi kirawkru **ŋgo** wákare*
            yum   **nda** mbor **ndɨ** ŋa   =yi   kiraw   -kru   **ŋgo** wákare
            2PL   DM   pig DM   1SG =ERG know.IRR -3SG.F.IRR.O DM   NEG
            'Well you all, I really don't know anything about that pig'

3.12 Mood particles

Tayap has four freestanding words that express expectation (*awa*), supposition (*mera*), mirative (*kapa*) and surprise counter to expectation (*nímera*). These are discussed in Section 7.6.

4 Noun phrases: Structure, modifiers, case marking and possession

4.1 Introduction

Noun phrases function as arguments of verbs: A, S, O and peripheral roles. Noun phrase function is expressed with clitics marking A. O and S arguments are unmarked, and oblique arguments are marked by clitics.

This chapter first discusses noun phrase structure, with a discussion of modifiers of the head noun. This is followed by a discussion of each case marker: ergative, locative, ablative, perlative and dative. After this comes a description of possession in Tayap. Young people's Tayap is discussed in relation to ergativity (Section 4.3.2) and peripheral case markers (Section 4.6).

4.1.1 Noun phrase structure

Noun phrase structure is as follows:

[PossP Part HEAD Mod* Quant]=case

PossP is a possessive phrase and Part is a participle; the head follows these. In the Mod(ifier) slot, either an adjective or a numeral, or both, in that order, can occur, or a relative clause, or alternatively a possessive phrase. Non-numeral quantifiers follow, and the final element of an NP is a case-marking clitic. The head noun itself can be reduplicated.

Noun phrases themselves are readily elided, but if an NP is present, its head is obligatory, or very rarely elided if retrievable from context. The head appears together with any applicable case marking. The head can be a noun, modified or not, or a pronoun. Some examples follow:
Subject NP expressed by free pronoun:

(4-1) ŋgi nam tankuro
 ŋgi nam ta -n -ku -ro
 3PL talk hear.R -S <3SG.F.R.O> -3PL.R.S
 'they heard the talk'

Numeral following the noun it modifies:

(4-2) nimir sene
 stick two
 'two sticks'

Dative-marked noun functioning as oblique:

(4-3) ŋgomar =ana ŋgwok
 fish =DAT go.3PL.R
 'they went for fish.'

Head noun modified by adjective and numeral:

(4-4) patir mokop manaw
 patir mokop manaw
 house little three
 'three little houses'

Relative clause in modifier slot:

(4-5) ŋgi ŋgomar tarkwanŋgukŋa
 ŋgi ŋgomar tar -kwan -ŋguk =ŋa
 3PL fish take.IRR -3SG.F.BEN.R.O -3PL.R =POSS
 'they who were picking up fish'

Possessive modifier preceding and numeral following the head noun:

(4-6) ŋgan nomb sene
 3PL.POSS name two
 'their two names'

The PossP element can be a possessive pronoun, e.g. *yimen nirŋgar* 'our girlfriend' or a full possessive NP:

(4-7) munjenum =mandama kokir
 man.PL =POSS.PL head
 'the heads of men'

The head can be reduplicated, in the following cases to indicate plurality. The first example has a rather complex structure, with 'spouse'-'spouse' modified by 'two', all of which is taken up in the possessive pronoun 'their':

(4-8) ŋan **ominde ominde** sene ŋgan nomb sene ŋgankun
ŋan **ominde ominde** sene ŋgan nomb sene
3SG.M spouse spouse two 3PL.POSS name two

ŋga -n -ku -n
call_out.R -S <3SG.F.R.O> -SG|1PL.R.S
'he called out his two wives' names'

(4-9) ŋgu **orak orak** rukuotitek
ŋgu **orak orak** ru -ku otitek
3SG.F thing thing throw.IRR -3SG.F.R.O.S fall.3SG.F
'she threw down her things'

Echo pronouns occur frequently with personal names, as well as with common nouns, for example:

(4-10) *Pepe ŋgu tiptiek*
Pepe 3SG.F lead.R.3SG.F|1PL.R
'Pepe, she was leading.'

(4-11) *mbumjor ŋɨ tɨ ndereke mbet*
mbumjor ŋɨ tɨ nder =eke mbet
mbumjor_snake 3SG.M too path =PERL come.SG.M.R
'the mbumjor snake he too came along the path'

> **Note:** A *mbumjor* snake is an extremely venomous black snake with shiny black skin and blue stripes, well known to villagers because of the numerous deaths for which they are responsible.

4.2 Participles with the non-finite suffix *-(ŋ)gar*

The suffix *-(ŋ)gar* forms a participle, consisting of a verb stem plus the non-finite suffix *(ŋ)gar* (realized as *-gar* after *nd, t* and sometimes *r*). Nouns formed with the *-(ŋ)gar* suffix are attributes: they denote a habitual, stative or agentive quality. Note this suffix is also used in counterfactuals (Section 9.4.3).

(4-12) a. *munje wasowŋgar aram*
   munje   wasow   -ŋgar   aram
   man   die.IRR -NFN.SG   snake
   'poisonous snake'

b. *morasi apro nirŋgar munje*
   morasi   apro   nir   -ŋgar   munje
   habit   bad   do.IRR   -NFN.SG   man
   'bad man' (lit. 'man who does bad things')

In both the examples above, the participle formed with *-(ŋ)gar* carries the meaning of habituality: the snake is (always) venomous; the man is someone who is known for habitually doing bad things. These constructions also express agentive nominalizations – i.e. expressions like 'killer of men' or 'doer of bad things'. So a sentence like the following:

(4-13) *yu yimbar andurgar*
   yu   yimbar   andur   -gar
   2SG   canoe   carve.IRR   -NFN.SG

means both 'you carve canoes' (often or habitually) and 'you are a canoe carver'; that is, the fact that you carve canoes is a characteristic by which other people know you.

The same is true of the following sentence:

(4-14) *ŋa sokoi aŋgar*
   ŋa   sokoi   a   -ŋgar
   1SG   tobacco   consume.IRR   -NFN.SG

This can be translated both as the habitual 'I smoke' (in the sense of smoking regularly or habitually) and as the stative 'I am a smoker' (as opposed to being a non-smoker).

The suffix-*(ŋ)gar* takes no TAM marking, even though it occurs in a position after the verb stem that normally would be filled with an IRR suffix (for intransitive verbs) or an object suffix inflected for TAM (for transitive verbs). The following sentence illustrates:

(4-15) *munje kowot inde ŋɨ nipis Merew =re o -ŋgar*
   man   old   DX.M   3SG.M   able   Sanae   =ALL   go.IRR   -NFN.SG
   'the old man is able to go to Sanae'

Even though the NFN suffix does not inflect for TAM, it does inflect to express person and number, according to the following pattern:

	SINGULAR	DUAL	PLURAL
1	-ŋgar	-ŋgre	-ŋgar
2	-ŋgar	-ŋgrem	-ŋgrem
3SG.M/F	-ŋgar	-ŋgre	-ŋgro

Thus, one says:

(4-16) ŋgɨ   kakau   tow   -ŋgro
        3PL   cocoa (TP)   plant.IRR   -NFN.3PL
        'they plant cocoa' (generally, habitually); 'they are cocoa planters'

(4-17) ŋɨ   kakau   tow   -ŋgar
        3SG.M   cocoa (TP)   plant.IRR   -NFN.SG|1PL
        'he plants cocoa' (generally, habitually); 'he is a cocoa planter'

Because these constructions are nominalizations and not verbs, they do not negate like verbs. They are non-verbal predications. All one does to negate them is add the negator *wákare* (see Section 5.2).

So compare:

(4-18) a.   ŋgɨ sokoi aŋgro
             ŋgɨ   sokoi   a   -ŋgro
             3PL   tobacco   consume.IRR   -NFN.3PL
             'they smoke'; 'they are smokers'

        b.   ŋgɨ sokoi aŋgro wákare
             ŋgɨ   sokoi   a   -ŋgro   wákare
             3PL   tobacco   consume.IRR   -NFN.3PL   NEG
             'they don't smoke'; 'they are not smokers'

4.3 The ergative case (ERG)

Tayap optionally marks the subject (A) of a transitive verb with an ergative case clitic, on noun phrases and free personal pronouns (note that subject and object verbal pronominal suffixes follow a nominative-accusative system, see Section 5.3).

Note the difference in the first word of the following two sentences:

(4-19) a. *Sopak wokara*
        Sopak   wok   -ara
        Sopak-Ø   go.3SG.F.R   -PERF
        'Sopak has gone'

    b. *Sopakyi taruŋ kratukun*
        Sopak =yi   taruŋ   kra   -tu -ku   -n
        Sopak =ERG.F firewood chop.R -S <3SG.F.R.O> -2SG|3SG.F.R.S
        'Sopak chopped firewood'

In (4-19a), there is no object, and the subject (S) of the sentence, Sopak, is unmarked.

In (4-19b), Sopak performs an action on an object. That object, like the subject of the previous sentence, is unmarked. But Sopak receives the ergative clitic =*yi*, which identifies her as the subject of the transitive clause.

The ergative clitics that attach to the subject NP of a transitive verb also encode gender and number. The markers that occur on NPs are:

=*ŋi*   masculine ergative
=*yi*   feminine ergative (becomes =*i* when it follows *r, t, nd, w* and often *k*)
=*gi*   plural ergative

Note that as in all other areas of Tayap grammar, gender is not indicated in the plural number, so a word like *rorsem=gi* ('children=ERG.PL') can refer to either male or female children.

These ergative clitics are also attached to the personal pronouns in a pattern that maintains the plural meaning of =*gi* but not the gendered meaning of =*ŋi* and =*yi* on 1SG and 2SG. In other words, gender is not marked in 1st and 2nd persons.

	SINGULAR	PLURAL
1	ŋa=yi	yim=ŋi
2	yu=yi	yum=ŋi
3F	ŋgu=yi	
		ŋgi=gi
3M	ŋɨ=ŋi	

Ergative clitics attach both to animate referents and to inanimate referents functioning as transitive subjects, as in the experiential constructions below:

(4-20) a. *tati poyin*
tat	**=i**	po	-yi	-n
needle	=ERG.F	strike.R	-1SG.R.O	-SG|1PL.R.S

   'the needle pierced me' (i.e. pierced my skin)

   b. *tutukyi nitin*
tutuk	**=yi**	ni	-t	-i	-n
sweat	=ERG.F	make.R	-S	<1SG.R.O>	-2SG|3SG.F.R.S

   'I am sweating' (lit. 'sweat makes me/does me')

   c. *urereŋgari nim pokun*
urereŋgar	**=i**	nim	po	-ku	-n
lightning	=ERG.F	tree	strike.R	-3SG.F.R.O	-SG|1PL.R.S

   'lightning struck a tree'

   d. *ŋa noki imin putiatan*
ŋa	**nok**	**=i**	imin
1SG	urine	=ERG.F	belly

pu	-t	-iata	-n
cut.R	-S	<1SG.BEN.R.O>	-2SG|3SG.F.R.S

   'I'm dying to pee' (lit. 'urine is cutting the belly to me'; i.e. 'my belly')

As noted above, ergative markers are clitics. They attach to the last element in a noun phrase, and not just to the head noun (cf. Spencer and Luís 2012: 2). An example of how they can attach to deictics and possessive pronouns that together with their head noun compose a noun phrase is the following:

(4-21) *awin sawirŋa ror aindetŋi tik ŋgunukun*
awin	**sawir**	**=ŋa**	**ror**	**aindet**	**=ŋi**	**tik**
water	black	=POSS	child	DX.M	=ERG.M	story

ŋgu	-nu	-ku	-n
put.R	-S	<3SG.F.R.O>	-1SG|3SG.M|1PL.M.R.S

   'that young man from Black Water told a story' (lit. 'put a story')

Ergative morphemes also cliticize to the interrogative word *ani* 'who', resulting in

ani=ŋi	'who=ERG.M'
ani=yi	'who=ERG.F'
ani-ŋgro=gi	'who-PL=ERG.PL'.

The unmarked generic form of this question word is the feminine *ani=yi* (see Section 3.9 on interrogatives, and Section 3.1.3.3 on the generic feminine).

4.3.1 Functions of the ergative case

In Tayap, ergative marking is "optional" (Foley 1986: 107; Dixon 1994: 58; McGregor 2010). This is typical in general of those Papuan languages which have an ergative case (Foley 2000: 374; McGregor 2010: 1616). In many of these languages, ergativity tends to be associated with a cluster of features, in particular agentivity, control and animacy – most particularly agentivity, such that a more agentive transitive subject is more likely to receive ergative case marking than a less agentive transitive subject.

However in Tayap, as in many other languages, ergativity seems to be sensitive to rather more factors than just agentivity.

The oldest speakers agree that most utterances that omit the ergative are perfectly fine Tayap. Speakers do not reflect on the grammatical role of the ergative markers; the way they explain them is in terms of utterance length. They say, "if you want to say it the long way, you say '*ŋayi*' [i.e. *ŋa=yi* '1SG=ERG.F']. If you want to say it shorter, you say '*ŋa*'" ("Yu laik skulim, em '*ŋayi*'. Yu laik sotim, bai yu tok '*ŋa*'").

The functions of the ergative case in Tayap are rather opaque. The following contrastive examples are intended to show that ergativity marking does not equate simply to animacy, agentivity or control.

High animacy of transitive subject argument:

(4-22) a. *ŋayi namwankuk nda*
        ŋa=yi   *nam*   *-wan*   *-kuk*   *nda*
        1SG=ERG.F talk.R -2SG.BEN.R.O -be.1SG.F.R DM
        'I'm telling you.'

    b. *ŋa wekokni adɨmrɨnakana nda*
        ŋa   *wekok*   *=nɨ*
        1SG-Ø   foul_language =LOC

        adɨ   *-mrɨ-nak-ana*   *nda*
        break.IRR -2PL.IRR.O-1SG.F|1PL.IRR.S-INTENT DM
        'I'm gonna swear at you all.'

Low animacy of transitive subject argument:

(4-23) a. *awini weka taman pombɨn*
 awin =i wek -a taman po-mbɨ-n
 water =ERG.F come.3SG.F.R -and all kill.R-3PL.R.O-SG|1PL.R.S
 'The water came and killed all of them'

 b. *numbwan eŋgontɨmbatan*
 numbwan eŋgon -tɨ -mbata -n
 thought-Ø good.R -S <3PL.BEN.R.O> -2SG|3SG.F.R.S
 'the thought made them happy'

High agentivity of transitive subject argument:

(4-24) a. *Kemŋi ewar poisirŋginre ikurre sapki kut*
 Kem =ŋi ewar poisir-ŋgɨ-n-re
 Kem =ERG.M yesterday magically_spit.R-3SG.M.R.O-SG|1PL.R.S-SUB

 ikur =re sapki kut
 night =TEMP good be.SG.M.R
 'Kem spit [a magic chant] on him yesterday and he was fine during the night'

 b. *yu tɨk aŋgi nirkrutet*
 yu tɨk aŋgi nir-kru-tet
 2SG-Ø story DX.F make.IRR-3SG.F.O.IRR-2SG.IRR
 'you will tell the story'

Low agentivity of transitive subject argument (unrealized event):

(4-25) a. *mbumjorŋi pɨn ŋayarnɨ Mbanaŋre Pepere ombrɨna*
 mbumjor =ŋi pɨn ŋayar-nɨ Mbanaŋ =re
 snake = ERG.M nearly truly-INTENS Mbanaŋ =COM

 Pepe=re o -mbrɨ -na
 Pepe=COM strike.IRR -3PL.IRR.O -INTENT
 'a snake nearly bit Mbanaŋ and Pepe.'

 b. *mbumjor pɨnɨ ŋayarnɨ Mbanaŋ oŋgrɨnana*
 mbumjor pɨnɨ ŋayar -nɨ Mbanaŋ
 snake-Ø nearly truly -INTENS Mbanaŋ

 o -ŋgrɨ -nana
 strike.IRR -3SG.M.R.O -INTENT
 'the snake really nearly bit Mbanaŋ'

High control of transitive subject argument:

(4-26) a. ŋayi namwankuk nda
ŋa =yi nam -wan -kuk nda
1SG =ERG tell.R -2SG.BEN.R.O -be.1SG.F|2SG.F|1PL.R DM
'I (F) am telling you.'

b. ŋa yureke warakakuk? ŋa Erapoke wekokni kadukun?
ŋa yu =re =ke warak -ak kuk?
1SG-Ø 2SG =LOC =Q talk.R -LINK be.SG.F.R

ŋa Erapo=ke wekok =ni
1SG-Ø Erapo=Q foul_language =LOC

kadu -ku -n?
break.R <3SG.F.R.O> -1SG|2SG|3SG.M|1 PL.R.S
'Am I talking to you? Did I swear at Erapo?'

Low control of transitive subject argument:

(4-27) a. Monakaiyi tamburni tatiŋin munaŋa saiput kukumbet
Monakai=yi tambur=ni ta -ti -ŋgi -n
Monakai=ERG.F dream=LOC see.R -S <3SG.M.R.O> -2SG|3SG.F.R.S

muna =ŋa saiput ku -ku mbet
sago_flour =POSS basket bring -3SG.F.R.O come.SG.M.R
'Monakai dreamed she saw him bringing a sago-flour-making basket'

Sentences involving affectedness – like situations of illness, hunger, thirst and desire – are normally expressed with transitive verbs, generally with the ergative marker:

(4-28) a. ŋa kandawi nitin
ŋa kandaw =i ni -t -i -n
1SG illness =ERG.F do.R -S <1SG.R.O> -2SG|3SG.F.R.S
'I'm sick' (lit. 'illness is affecting me')

b. ŋgu arei tarkru wákare sispok
ŋgu are =i tarkru wákare sisipok
3SG.F desire =ERG.F take.IRR NEG tire.3SG.F|1PL.R
'She has no desire [to do anything], she's tired' (lit. 'desire hasn't taken her')

c. *ŋgon armbɨri tatɨmɨnde yim wasowtike*

ŋgon	armbɨr	=i
3SG.F.POSS	heat	=ERG.F

ta	-tɨ	-mɨ-	-n	=dre[1]	yim	wasow	-tike
take.R	-S	<1PL.R.O>	-2SG|3SG.F.R.S	=SUB	1PL	die.R	-DL

'her heat got us and we died' (from a myth about two men who died and were resurrected, see Tayap Text 1)

d. *ŋa endekari nitin. Mum ninkurem*

ŋa	endekar	=i	ni	-t	i	-n
1SG	hunger	=ERG.F	make.R	-S	<1SG.R.O>	-2SG|3SG.F.R.S

mum	ni	-n	ku	-rem
sago_jelly	make.SBJ	-S-	<3SG.F.R.O>	-2PL.R.S

'I'm hungry (lit. 'hunger is affecting me'). You all make some sago jelly'

The ergative is frequently used when the arguments of a verb are both animate, and both present in the clause. In those instances, ergative marking is used to clearly distinguish the subject of a transitive verb from its object.

For example, the following sentence is ambiguous:

(4-29) *ŋi ŋgat poŋgin*

ŋi	ŋgat	po	-ŋgɨ	-n
3SG.M	cassowary	strike.R	-3SG.M.R.O	-SG|1PL.R.S

'he speared the cassowary' or 'the cassowary stabbed him' (with its claws)

Speakers would normally interpret the fact that the pronoun 'he' occurs in the sentence-initial position as indicating that 'he', and not 'the cassowary', is the agent in this sentence. But without ergative marking the phrase is ambiguous, and older fluent speakers say that it is poor Tayap.

The reasons for the ambiguity are:
(a) the class 1 transitive verb *o* means 'strike' or 'shoot', and here it could mean either 'penetrate or pierce with a spear' or 'penetrate or pierce with a sharp claw'; and
(b) cassowaries are typically gendered masculine, so the 3SG.M object suffix on the verb can refer to either a male person or a cassowary.

---

1 The *=re* appears as *=dre* after *n*.

For those reasons, *ŋi ŋgat poŋgin* can potentially be understood to mean either 'he speared the cassowary (with a spear)' or 'the cassowary struck him' (that is, pierced his body with the knife-like claws on its feet).

Using the ergative case marker resolves ambiguity by marking the transitive subject who performs the action. So compare:

(4-30) a. *ŋiŋi ŋgat poŋgin*
ŋi=ŋi   ŋgat   po   -ŋgɨ   -n
3SG.M=ERG.M   cassowary   shoot.R   -3SG.M.R.O   -SG|1PL.R.S
'he speared the cassowary'

b. *ŋgatŋi ŋi poŋgin*
ŋgat=ŋi   ŋi   po   -ŋgɨ   -n
cassowary=ERG.M   3SG.M   shoot.R   -3SG.M.R.O   -SG|1PL.R.S
'the cassowary speared him' (with its claws)

Note that it is *not* the case that when two NPs (A and O) are present the ergative marking must be used. The following example contains a verb that is highly transitive with two NP arguments present but there is no ergative:

(4-31) *ŋgɨ ŋgomar tarmbrar ŋgwok*
ŋgɨ   ŋgomar   tar   -mb   -rar   ŋgwok
3PL   fish   take.IRR   -3PL.R.O   -ML   go.3PL.R
'They picked up fish as they walked'

However there are also many examples in which there can be no ambiguity, and yet an ergative marker is used:

(4-32) *mbumjorŋi minjikankɨ nda kokɨr kukupemiet*
mbumjor=ŋi   minjikan   -kɨ   nda   kokɨr
Mbumjor_snake=ERG.M   nearby   -INTENS   DM   head

ku   -ku   pemiet
bring   -3SG.F.R.O   rise_up.SG.M.R
'the snake raised his head really close'

One verb that virtually always marks its subject with the ergative clitic is *kiraw-* when it conveys the meaning of 'know' (this verb also has a range of other meanings, including 'consider something', 'recognize something' and 'taste something'); note that this example has the unusual structure of a preposed head, with possessive phrase following.

(4-33) orak orak aŋgo sumbwaŋaɲi ɲi kirawtɨŋgɨn ainde
      orak   orak   aŋgo   sumbwa =ŋa   =ɲi   ɲɨ
      thing thing DX.F   ground   =POSS =ERG.M 3SG.M

      kiraw   -tɨ   -ŋgɨ   -n   ainde
      know.R -S   <3SG.M.R.O> -2SG|3SG.F.R.S DX.M
      'this thing of the ground knows about him.'

Perception verbs may or may not have subjects carrying the ergative marker. Compare the following: (4-34a), which marks the subject with the ergative clitic, and (4-34b), which doesn't:

(4-34) a. yim noni tarkru wákareŋan noni tankun
         yim   non   =i   tar   -kru   wákare =ŋan
         1PL   INDEF =ERG.F hear.IRR -3SG.F.IRR.O NEG   =POSS

         non   =i   ta   -n -ku   -n
         INDEF =ERG.F hear.R -S <3SG.F.O> -1SG|3SG.M|1PL.R.S
         'Some of us didn't hear it, some did hear it.'

      b. Akupi ŋgume ɲɨ tankun aŋgude
         Akupi   ŋgu   -me   ɲɨ
         Akupi   3SG.F -DX   3SG.M

         ta   -n -ku   -n   aŋgude
         see.R   -S <3SG.F.R.O> -1SG|3SG.M|1PL.R.S DX.F
         'He saw Akupi ['s spirit]'

4.3.1.1 Ergative clitics on intransitive verbs

The main function of ergative clitics is to mark the subject of a transitive verb. In Tayap, however, the ergative marker can also be attached to the subject of an intransitive verb.

This marked use often carries a particular nuance, which can be illustrated by an example taken from a narrative about a powerful crocodile water-spirit named Ŋgayam. In telling this story, the narrator uses the ergative with an intransitive verb:

(4-35) Ŋgayamɲi mbet
      Ŋgayam   =ɲi   mbet
      Ŋgayam   =ERG.M come.3SG.M.R
      'Ŋgayam came'

The ergative here carries the connotation of purposefulness. The implication is that Ŋgayam didn't just come – he came with a purpose, to do something, to perform some kind of action. And indeed he did: the story tells of how Ŋgayam flooded the rainforest and drowned an entire kin group as they stood gathering his children – who had the form of fish – in his jungle streams. A version of this story appears at the end of this grammar as Tayap Text 2.

Another telling instance of an ergative marker on an intransitive verb occurred once when men from the neighboring village of Sanae arrived in Gapun unannounced a few days after one of their relatives had been attacked by a Gapuner. Everyone in Gapun was fearful of the Sanae men, because it was assumed that they had come to fatally bewitch the attacker or one of his matrilineal relatives. As the Sanae men arrived in Gapun, villagers whispered to one another:

(4-36) Merewŋgrogi ŋgwek
       Merew -ŋgro =gi   ŋgwek
       Sanae   -PL   =ERG.PL come.3PL.R
       'the Sanae [men] are coming'

The use of the ergative in this case meant that the Sanae men were not just dropping by Gapun on an innocent visit to socialize. They were coming to accomplish a particular sinister purpose.

This use of the ergative to mark intentionality on intransitive verbs is also apparent in cases where the ergative is used to denote a remarked-upon *lack* of intentionality. The following example was uttered by a woman screaming abuse at her relatives because her nephew littered the ground in front of her house with seeds he blew from a homemade pea-shooter (i.e. in front of the house of the woman having the "kros", see Kulick 1992: 104–113 and Kulick 1993 for details on these kinds of antagonistic speech events):

(4-37) yumŋni mburaiakaku wákare!
       yum =ŋi   mburai   -ak   aku   wákare
       2PL =ERG.M sweep.IRR -LINK be.IRR NEG
       'you all never sweep!'

Here the ergative clitic on an intransitive verb (*mburai* 'sweep') inflected in the negative habitual aspect (see Section 8.3.2) highlights the consistent lack of intention on the part of her addressees to perform an act that she thinks they ought to consider doing occasionally.

Suter's (2010) description of optional ergativity in the Trans New Guinea language Kâte shows that the ergative marker is most likely to be used in clauses with the marked word order of OSV (as opposed to the usual SOV) or when a focus particle is used on the subject (Suter 2010: 435). In other Trans New Guinea languages, factors include animacy, agency and control (Suter 2010: 436).

As we have seen, however, there seems to be no single factor or group of factors which account for the use or absence of the ergative marker in Tayap.

4.3.2 Ergativity in the speech of young people

Young villagers under thirty who narrated stories for me in Tayap produced ergative constructions in their speech, but they had a tendency to overuse the ergative markers on intransitive verbs. The subjects of intransitive verbs like 'be', 'cry', 'stand', 'talk', 'shiver' and 'work' were all marked with ergative case marking in various young people's narratives.

Even when used in transitive verb phrases, the ergative morpheme was sometimes attached to constituents that were not the subjects of the verb. For example, one twenty-three-year-old man narrated a story about how a young girl had accused him of having raped her.

In telling the story, he said the following (note that the ellipsis denotes a series of false starts and repetitions that have been omitted, and the ergative morpheme is highlighted in bold):

(4-38) *Mosi katota namnin, 'Ŋayarke yu Yengia...morasi apro**yi** nitukun'?*
      Mosi   katot   -a   nam   -n -i   -n
      Mosi   go_down.SG.M.R -and tell.R -S <1SG.R.O> -1SG|3SG.M|1PL.R.S

      ŋayar =ke yu   Yengia morasi   apro **=yi**
      true   =Q   2SG   Yengia habit/behavior bad   =ERG.F

      ni   -tu -ku   -n
      do.R   -S   <3SG.F.R.O> -2SG|3SG.F.R.S
      'Mosi went down and told me 'Is it true that you did something bad to Yengia?''

There are semantic and grammatical errors in this sentence,[2] but of interest here is the ergative clitic, which the speaker attaches to the object noun phrase 'bad deed' instead of to the subject of the verb phrase, 'you'.

I suspect that this error occurred because the speaker seems to know that the verb *nir-* ('do' or 'make') usually co-occurs with an ergative marker. But his sense appears to be that the marker attaches to the noun or noun phrase that immediately precedes the verb; not necessarily the subject of the verb phrase.

This is a typical error made by speakers under thirty. It indicates that young speakers have parsed the ergative case marker as a formulaic part of a verb phrase involving certain verbs – in particular, the verbs 'know', 'say' and 'do'. But these speakers seem to be not entirely aware that the marker does particular syntactic and semantic work. If the ergative case clitic was really a strong marker of agency, control or animacy one might expect speakers to be aware of that, albeit subconsciously, and make mistakes accordingly; however that does not seem to be the case.

In addition to having problems with the placement and the function of the ergative clitic, young speakers also often make mistakes of gender with it. They overextend the feminine form =*yi* and use it when talking about males and plural referents. So they say things like *sas=yi* ('father=ERG.F', instead of *sas=ŋi* 'father=ERG.M') and *njenum=yi* (dog.PL=ERG.F, instead of the correct *njenum=gi* 'dog.PL=ERG.PL').

This overextension of =*yi* probably occurs because =*yi* is the ergative ending on the 1SG and 2SG pronouns (*ŋa=yi* and *yu=yi*). Speakers would have heard the *yuyi* form all their lives, every time an older speaker ordered them to carry or take or fetch or hit something. And since the narratives that people in Gapun tell one another are almost invariably accounts of personal experiences – what the narrator him or herself saw, heard, dreamt, etc. – the *ŋayi* form would also be very salient for speakers. Furthermore, the unmarked gender in Tayap is feminine see Section 3.1.3. That young speakers would overextend the feminine form, rather than the masculine =*ŋi*, is therefore not surprising.

---

2 Semantic error: the verb *nam-* 'tell' is incorrect here; the speaker wants *kotar-(p)-e-* 'ask'.

Grammatical errors: the speaker omits the ergative clitic on the subject of the verb, and also omits a locative case marker on *Yengia*, the undergoer of the verb. The grammatically correct way of phrasing the question is:

ŋayar=ke   yu=yi   morasi   apro   Yengia=ni   ni-tu-ku-n?
true=Q   2SG=ERG.F   deed   bad   Yengia=LOC do.R-S<3SG.F.R.O>2SG|3SG.F.R.S
'Is it true that you did something bad to Yengia?'

4.4 Peripheral cases

Tayap has five peripheral cases. Three of the cases mark animate and inanimate referents differently.

The *possessive* case marks possession, association and part-whole relationships, with no distinction between alienable and inalienable possession. Possession is discussed in Section 4.5.

The *locative* case has the widest semantic scope of Tayap's peripheral cases. It specifies location in time and space, covering relationships that in other languages are expressed in allative, instrumental, comitative, temporal and durative cases.

The *ablative* case expresses movement away from a person, place or object, or an action of revelation in which something that was hidden becomes visible.

The *perlative* case expresses movement along, through or by means of.

The *dative* case is used to mark recipient, purpose, comparison and a number of other relations.

All these peripheral case markers are clitics, as they occur attached to the last element of an NP with scope over the whole NP: see for example (4-40i), (4-40j), (4-42b), (4-43d), (4-43i), among others. Many of them contain optional material (shown in parentheses), the conditioning factors of which are not known. Examples (the relevant peripheral case clitics are in bold):

	Animate Referent	Inanimate Referent
possessive (POSS)	=*ma(t)* (SG) =*mandama(t)* (PL)	=*ŋa(n)*

LOCATIVE	Animate Referent	Inanimate Referent
—location of an object (LOC)	=*re* (if the object is 'with' or 'near' the referent) =*nɨ* (if the object is 'on' or if an action or event happens 'to' the referent)	=*nɨ* =*re* (when referent is a village) =Ø (mostly when referent is a named area of the rainforest)
—direction toward (glossed as ALL)	=*re*	=*nɨ* =*re* (when the referent is a village) =Ø (when referent is a named part of the rainforest or a town)

—instrumental (including marking=nɨ the language in which one is speaking) (glossed as INST)		=nɨ
—companionship, accompanied with (glossed as COM)	=re(kɨ)	=re(kɨ)
—'at the time of' (glossed as TEMP)		=re
—'for X amount of time' (glossed as TEMP)		=nɨ

	Animate Referent	Inanimate Referent
ABLATIVE (ABL) —from a person or place	=re(ŋa)	=ŋa
—falling from something	=re(ŋa)	=ekenɨ or =ŋa
—from hidden to visible	=re(ŋa)	=ŋa
	Animate Referent	**Inanimate Referent**
PERLATIVE (PERL) movement along, through or by means of	=eke(nɨ)	=eke(nɨ)
	Animate Referent	**Inanimate Referent**
DATIVE (DAT) recipient, 'for', 'about', 'for the benefit of', 'in relation to', 'for the purpose of', 'of', 'at', 'in comparison to'	=(n)ana	=(n)ana

POSSESSIVE

The possessive clitic appears on the possessor (see Section 4.5 below for a discussion of possession):

Animate possessor

(4-39) a. *ŋɨ noŋor aŋuk**ma** min eŋeweŋewnukwata*n
        ŋɨ   *noŋor*   *aŋuk* =***ma***   *min*
        3SG.M woman DX.F   =POSS breast

ŋengeweŋgew- -nu- -kwata -n
fondle.R- -S- <3SG.F.BEN.R.O> -1SG|3SG.M|1PL.R.S
'he was fondling that woman's breast'

Inanimate possessor

b. *awinŋa naŋgatik*
awin =ŋa naŋgatik
water =POSS force
'tide'

c. *arawerŋa aro*
arawer =ŋa aro
sun =POSS light
'sunlight'

d. *yimbarŋa imin*
yimbar =ŋa imin
canoe =POSS belly
'the inside of the canoe'

e. *ndaramŋa ŋgino*
ndaram =ŋa ŋgino
hand =POSS eye
'the whitish base of a fingernail'

f. *totoŋa purpur*
toto =ŋa purpur
skin =POSS hair
'body hair'

LOCATIVE
Location
(4-40) a. *paru aŋgi menjikan aŋgi wuk yuwon ndowre*
paru aŋgi menjikan aŋgi wuk yuwon ndow =**re**
plate DX.F near DX.F be.3SG.F.R 2SG.POSS leg =LOC
'the plate is there near your leg'

Event happens 'to' someone

b. *ŋayarke yu morasi apro Yengiani nitukun?*
ŋayar =ke yu morasi apro Yengia =**ni**
true =Q 2SG deed bad Yengia =LOC

```
    ni      -tu   -ku              -n?
    do.R    -S    <3.SG.F.R.O>     -2SG|3SG.F.R.S
```
'is it true that you did something bad to Yengia?'[3]

Put something 'on' someone

c. hevi *sene ŋgume ŋgi nda yuni rukupuwok*

```
    hevi (TP)           sene    ŋgume   ŋgi   nda   yu    =ni
    burdensome_deed     two     thusly  3PL   DM    2SG   =LOC

    ru              -ku              -puwok
    propel.IRR      -3SG.F.R.O       -ascend.SG.F.R
```
'they put the blame for these two things on you'

Inanimate location

d. *ŋi patirni inde wo kut*

```
    ŋi       patir    =ni    inde   wo   kut
    3SG.M    house    =LOC   DX     up   be.SG.M.R
```
'he's up in the house' (houses in Gapun are all on stilts, at least 1.5 meters off the ground)

Inanimate direction

e. Speaker A: *Yum anakni mbokem?*

```
    Yum    anak    =ni     mbokem
    2PL    where   =ALL    go.2PL.R
```
'Where are you all going?'

Speaker B: *Ŋa Samekre mbot*

```
    ŋa     Samek    =re    mbot
    1SG    Samek    =ALL   go.SG.M.R
```
'I'm going to (visit) Samek'

Speaker C: *Ŋa mirini mbot*

```
    ŋa     miri         =ni    mbot
    1SG    rainforest   =ALL   go.SG.M.R
```
'I'm going to the rainforest'

Speaker D: *Ŋa Merewre mbot*

```
    ŋa     Merew    =re    mbot
    1SG    Sanae    =ALL   go.SG.M.R
```
'I'm going to Sanae village'

---

3 This is the correct version of example (4-38), see footnote 2.

Direction toward
    f. *Kamayi kinda aŋguraktukuna ŋare wek*

Kama	=yi	kinda	aŋgur	-ak	-tu
Kama	=ERG.F	tongs	throw.R	-NFO	-S

-ku	-n	-a	ŋa	=re	wek
<3SG.F.R.O>	-2SG|3SG.F.R.S	-and	1SG	=ALL	come.3SG.F.R

    'Kama threw the tongs to me'

Language
    g. *yu anakŋa mer**ni** waraktet?*

yu	anakŋa	mer	=**ni**	warak	-tet
2SG	which	language	=INST	speak.R	-2SG.M.R

    'which language are you speaking?'

Instrumental (animacy not marked)
    h. *Sakeyi ndaram**ni** poŋgin*

Sake	=yi	ndaram	=**ni**	po-	-ŋgi-	-n
Sake	=ERG.F	hand	=INST	hit.R-	-3SG.M.R.O-	-SG|1PL.R.S

    'Sake hit him with her hand'

    i. *kokɨr traituwa ta mosop**ni** aŋgo*

kokɨr	trai	-tu	-wa	ta
head	bloodlet.SBJ	-2SG	-2SG.BEN.R.O	knife

mosop	=**ni**	aŋgo
little	=INST	DX.F

    'bloodlet your head [to relieve a headache] with this little knife here'

    j. *ŋa ŋaŋan neke**ni** tankun*

ŋa	ŋaŋan	neke	=**ni**	ta-	-n-	-ku
1SG	1SG.POSS	ear	=INST	hear.R-	-S-	<3SG.F.R.O>

-n
-1SG|3SG.M|1PL.R.S

    'I heard it with my [own] ears'

'With' animate (associative plural in this case)
    k. *yim Ngandu**re** Ainsari**re** woke mɨrini*

yim	Ngandu	=**re**	Ainsari	=**re**	woke	mɨri	=ni
1PL	Ngandu	=COM	Ainsari	=COM	go.R.DL	forest	=ALL

    'I went into the rainforest with Ngandu and Ainsari'

Note: the 1SG comitative construction requires the pronoun *yim* 'we', not *ŋa* 'I'. So one does not say 'I and X and Y did Z'; one says 'we and X and Y did Z'. This is a stylistic detail in Tayap that is not adhered to by most speakers younger than thirty.

'With' inanimate
- l. *oŋgarana kakaureki*
o	-ŋgarana	kakau	=**reki**
go.IRR	-ND	cocoa beans (TP)	=LOC

  'you shouldn't go with the cocoa beans'

Time
- m. *ŋgrag ŋayarre okitike*
ŋgrag	ŋayar	=**re**	o	-ki	-tike
early_evening	really	=TEMP	go.IRR	-IRR	DL.IRR

  'Let's the two of us go in the really early evening

Duration
- n. *Tamaw ramaŋgni akunet karep nambarni*
Tamaw	ramaŋ	=**ni**	a	-ku	-net
Tamaw	enclosure	=LOC	be.IRR	-IRR	-1SG.M|3SG.M.IRR

karep	nambar	=**ni**
moon	one	=LOC

  'Tamaw will stay inside the enclosure for one month' (mourning his wife)

Note that as described in the previous chapter (Section 3.1.1.2), locational nouns are a subclass of nouns which function as bare locatives, i.e. they either do not take case clitics at all or take them only sometimes, typically when they are in a complex NP. Some examples:

Named area of rainforest
- o. *ŋgu Kasimak ato wuk aŋgo*
ŋgu	Kasimak	ato	wuk	aŋgo
3SG.F	Kasimak-Ø	below	be.3SG.F.R	DX.F

  'she's down at Kasimak'

Direction toward named area of rainforest
- p. *yim mirini mbok, Ndurur mbok*
yim	miri	=**ni**	mbok	Ndurur	mbok
2PL	rainforest	=LOC	go.1PL|1SG.F.R	Ndurur-Ø	go.1PL|1SG.F.R

  'we went to the rainforest, we went to Ndurur'

Foreign place names can also occur as zero-marked locational nouns:

Location in town

    q. *ŋgu* Madang *aŋgi wuk*
       ŋgu   Madang   aŋgi   wuk
       3SG.F Madang-Ø DX.F be.3SG.F.R
       'she's in Madang'

ABLATIVE

From a person

(4-41) a. *weteta minjike tarkru ŋareŋa*
           we   -tet   -a   miniike   tar   -kru
           come.SBI -2SG.M.R -and betel nut take.IRR -3SG.F.IRR.O

           ŋa   =**reŋa**
           1SG   =ABL
           'come and take betel nut from me'

From a place

    b. *ŋa Merewŋa mbet inde*
       ŋa   Merew =**ŋa** mbet   inde
       1SG Sanae =ABL come.SG.M.R DX.M
       'I (M) have come from Sanae'

Falling from

    c. *noŋor otitek patirekeni*
       noŋor   otitek   patir   =**ekeni**
       woman   fall.3SG.F.R house =ABL
       'the woman fell off the house'

Inanimate from hidden to visible

    d. *ŋa tatar sapwarŋa perkun*
       ŋa   tatar   sapwar =**ŋa** per   -ku   -n
       1SG   spoon   basket   =ABL hold.R -3SG.F.R.O -SG|1PL.R.S
       'I took the spoon from my basket'

PERLATIVE

Animate

(4-42) a. *njakep nambar worekeni pimbiet*
           njakep   nambar   wo   -r-   =**ekeni** pimbiet
           flying_fox one   above -r-   =PERL   fly.SG.M.R
           'one flying fox is flying along above'

b. *mboreirum ŋaŋan patirŋan tawrekeni ekrukŋguk*

mbor	-eirum	ŋaŋan	patir	=ŋan	taw	-r-	=ekeni
pig	-PL	1SG.POSS	house	=POSS	side	-r-	=PERL

ekruk	-ŋguk
walk_about.R	be.3PL.R

'the pigs are walking about along the side of my house'

Inanimate

c. *tumbeke prike*

tumb	=eke	prike
mountain	=PERL	come_up.DL.R

'the two came up along the mountain'

d. *mirirekeni ŋgok*

miri	-r-	=ekeni	ŋgok
forest	-r-	=PERL	go.3PL.R

'they walked through the forest'

DATIVE
Recipient

(4-43) a. *minjike non isŋgatan Agrananana*

minjike	non	is	-ŋgata	-n
betel_nut	INDEF	give.SBJ	-3SG.M.BEN.R.O	-SG|1PL.R.S

Agrana	=nana
Agrana	=DAT

'Give some betel nut to Agrana'

'For'

b. *ŋa yunana aruoiakkut*

ŋa	yu	=nana	aruoi	-ak	kut
1SG	2SG	=DAT	wait.IRR	-LINK	be.SG.M.R

'I am waiting for you'

c. *ŋayi Samek ŋgodirpiŋgin makorana*

ŋa	=yi	Samek	ŋgodirpi	-ŋgi	-n
1SG	=ERG.F	Samek	request.R	-3SG.M.R.O	-SG|1PL.R

makor	=ana
sago_pounder	=DAT

'I asked Samek for the sago pounder'

'About'
    d. *Mambuyi namtukun Mairum awinnɨ tuwŋgwar patɨra**na***
Mambu	=yi	nam	-tu	-ku		-n
Mambu	=ERG.F	tell.R	-S	<3SG.F.R.O>		-2SG|3SG.F|1PL.R.S

Mairum	awin	=nɨ	tuw	-ŋgwar	patɨr	=***ana***
Mairum	water	=LOC	wash	-NFN.SG	house	=DAT

       'Mambu was angry at Mairum about the maternity house'

'Of'
    e. *pwap**ana** minda!*
pwap	=***ana***	minda
argument/anger	=DAT	tired_of

       '[I'm] sick of arguments!'

'At'
    f. *irŋgarke ŋa**nana**!*
ir	-ŋgarke	ŋa	=***nana***
laugh.IRR	-PROH	1SG	=DAT

       'don't laugh at me!'

Purpose
    g. *yim woke yam**ana***
yim	woke	yam	=***ana***
1PL	go.DL.R	sago_palm	=DAT

       'we went for the sago palm' (i.e. to check to see whether any wild pig was eating the felled sago palm, so that the pig could be ambushed and speared)

In relation to
    h. *ŋɨ ŋgɨ**nana** kemrak puŋgot*
ŋɨ	ŋgɨ	=***nana***	kemrak	puŋgot
3SG.M	3PL	=DAT	far_away	stand.SG.M.R

       'he's standing a long way from them'

In comparison to
    i. *Amburima mbor ŋɨ Krunima mbor**ana** sumannet*
Amburi	=ma	mbor	ŋɨ	Kruni	=ma
Amburi	=POSS	pig	3SG.M	Kruni	=POSS

mbor	=***ana***	suman	-net
pig	=DAT	big	-1SG.M|3SG.M.R

       'Amburi's pig, he is bigger than Kruni's'

4.5 Possession

Possession is marked by a possessive clitic on the possessor. Possessor clitics mark higher animate singular (=*ma*), higher animate plural (=*mandama*) and inanimate (=*ŋa*) possessors. Note also that Tayap has external possession constructions, discussed in Section 7.5 in the section on benefactives.

This clitic is also used to form relative clauses (Section 9.5), finite nominalizations (Section 9.6) and perception clauses (Section 9.7).

Example (4-44) shows the possessive clitic marking an NP consisting of a modified noun 'cold belly', thus demonstrating the clitic rather than affix status of these forms:

animate plural inalienable:

(4-44) *imin pokemŋan munjema tik*
       imin pokem =ŋan munje =ma tik
       belly cold   =POSS   man   =POSS story
       'the calm man's story'

For the purposes of possession, animals and humans are considered higher animates, and plants are considered inanimate. Possessive relations expressed with this construction include alienable, inalienable, body part, association and part-whole possession. There is no morpho-syntactic distinction between these categories (but see Section 7.5 for the role of benefactive object suffixes in body part possession).

Some examples:

animate singular body part (human):

(4-45) *Mbanaŋma tokimot*
       Mbanaŋ =ma   tokimot
       Mbanaŋ =POSS chest
       'Mbanaŋ's chest'

animate singular body part (animal):

(4-46) *aramma sik*
       aram   =ma   sik
       snake =POSS mouth
       'the snake's mouth'

inanimate part-whole:

(4-47) *tumbŋa kandaŋ*
      tumb   =*ŋa*   *kandaŋ*
      mountain =POSS base
      'the base of the mountain'

inanimate association:

(4-48) *miriŋa mbor*
      miri   =*ŋa*   *mbor*
      forest =POSS pig
      'a forest pig' (i.e. a wild pig)

animate plural inalienable:

(4-49) *Moipmandama kawsomb*
      Moip =*mandama* *kawsomb*
      Watam =POSS.PL   sailing_canoe
      'the Watam people's sailing canoe'

inanimate part-whole:

(4-50) *nuwombŋa taw*
      nuwomb =*ŋa*   *taw*
      stream   =POSS side
      'the side of the stream'

Recursive possession also occurs, using the possessive clitic on each possessor, with the possessee unmarked (see also example 4-44):

(4-51) *Samekma rorma mbor suman*
      Samek =*ma*   *ror*   =*ma*   *mbor*   *suman*
      Samek =POSS child =POSS pig   big
      'Samek's child's big pig'

The animate possessive clitic can be used on an inanimate noun to highlight that the noun has some kind of relation to humans:

(4-52) a. *numŋa mbor*
 num=ŋa   mbor
 village=POSS.INANIMATE   pig
 'village pig' (as opposed to a wild pig)

 b. *numma mbor*
 num   =ma   mbor
 village =POSS.ANIMATE   pig
 'pig to be eaten by the villagers' (as part of a funerary feast, for example)

(4-53) a. *miriŋa mbor*
 miri   =ŋa   mbor
 forest =POSS.INANIMATE pig
 'wild pig' (as opposed to a village pig)

 b. *mirima mbor*
 miri   =ma   mbor
 forest =POSS.ANIMATE   pig
 'pig used as payment for an area of forest'

It is possible that this variation represents the remnants of an earlier classification system, but this is all that remains of it now.

4.5.1 =ŋa(n) POSS with adjectives

The possessive clitic =ŋa(n) can also occur in construction with adjectives (see Section 3.3 for more on adjectives). However in these cases the function is clearly not possession but rather modification. For example:

(4-54) *iminkato sawirŋa*
 iminkato   sawir =ŋa
 lower_intestine   black =POSS
 'black asshole!'

(4-55) *ŋgwab mir aproŋan apro sakar*
 ŋgwab mir   apro =ŋan   apro sakar
 hole   INTENS bad   =POSS bad   INTENS
 'fucking rotten hole!'

(4-56)   ndagu mir sumanŋa
         ndagu   mir   suman   =ŋa
         steal   INTENS   big   =POSS
         'big thief'

4.5.2 Possessive modification

The possessive clitic can also occur, similarly to the above examples, but on nouns or verbs as well as adjectives, to create modifiers: for example, in (4-57)–(4-58) it occurs on a noun, rendering it a modifier, and in (4-59)–(4-61) it occurs on an adjective which here modifies a verb:

(4-57)   kandawŋa munje
         kandaw   =ŋa   munje
         sickness   =POSS   man
         'sick man'

(4-58)   sumbwaŋa noŋor
         sumbwa   =ŋa   noŋor
         ground   =POSS   woman
         'ground woman' (an insult: it means 'you're so old you have been around since when the ground emerged')

(4-59)   ei sumanŋa ror
         ei   suman   =ŋa   ror
         cry   big   =POSS   child
         'cry baby' (i.e. a child who cries a lot)

(4-60)   warak sumanŋa noŋor
         warak   suman   =ŋa   noŋor
         talk   big   =POSS   woman
         'cross woman'

(4-61)   munje apro ŋgadanŋan rukŋan
         munje   apro   ŋgadan   =ŋan   ruk   =ŋan
         man   bad   sore   =POSS   smell   =POSS
         'bad, sore-ridden, smelly man'

In (4-59) the verb *ei* 'cry' is modified by 'big', the phrase in its turn modifying the noun 'child'. Example (4-60) has the same structure: the verb is followed by the possessive-marked adjective, together modifying 'woman'. Example (4-61) is more complex. Here we have a head noun *munje* 'man', modified by adjective 'bad' and possessive-marked verbs 'sore' and 'smelly'. Note that these are the only constructions in which verbs can appear without person/status suffixes (see also Section 5.1).

4.6 Peripheral case marking in young people's Tayap

For the most part, young people retain the ability to produce correct peripheral case marking. They generally uphold the animate-inanimate distinction, and they correctly use the locative case. Locative =re sometimes causes problems when speakers have analyzed words to which it attaches as whole constituents. So *emb=re* 'in the morning' (morning=LOC) is heard so often that it has been lexicalized by many young speakers to mean 'morning', with the result that when they say 'in the morning', they add the locative clitic and produce *emb=re=re* (lit. 'in in the morning').

Animate referents generally receive correct dative and locative marking. The locative =ni on inanimate referents, however, is over-extended, probably because of interference with Tok Pisin's "long". "Long" is a preposition that covers all the meanings of Tayap's various peripheral case markers, including 'to', 'in' and 'for'. So speakers say things like:

(4-62) a. *oyaŋni* subim*nakara*
 oyaŋ =ni subim -nak -ara
 clam =LOC dive (TP) -1SG.F|1PL.R -PERF
 'we dived for clams' (lit. 'we dived to clams')

instead of

 b. *oyaŋana* amaipikun
 oyaŋ =ana amaipi -ku- -n
 clam =DAT look_for.R -3SG.F.R.O- -SG|1PL.R.S
 'we looked for clams'

(4-63) a. *Mapismat yimbarni yim mbok*
 Mapis =mat yimbar =ni yim mbok
 Mapis =POSS canoe =LOC 1PL go.3SG.F|1PL.R
 'we went inside Mapis's canoe'

instead of

 b. *Mapismat yimbarekeni yim mbok*
 Mapis =mat yimbar =ekeni yim mbok
 Mapis =POSS canoe =PERL 1PL go.3SG.F|1PL.R
 'we went by way of Mapis's canoe'

Tok Pisin also influences the syntax of the case markers. A twenty-two-year-old man produced the following sentence:

(4-64) *ŋgɨ nunuk ŋa =nɨ ŋgwek
    3PL after 1SG =LOC come.3PL.R
    'they came after me'

The individual constituents that compose this sentence are all grammatically correct. The problem is that the young man's sentence is a calque of the Tok Pisin sentence:

(4-65) ol i kam bihain long mi
    3PL PREDICATE come after PREP 1SG
    MARKER[4]
    'they came after me'

Notice that the locative clitic in the speaker's Tayap sentence in (4-64) combines with the 1SG pronoun (ŋanɨ) – just like the preposition in the Tok Pisin sentence "long mi". But while correct in Tok Pisin, the speaker's Tayap is ungrammatical. What he wants is as follows:

(4-66) ŋgɨ ŋaŋan nunuk =nɨ ŋgwek
    3PL 1SG.POSS after =LOC come.3PL.R
    'they came after me'

A final consistent error made by speakers under thirty is that they use the locative clitic to refer to named areas of the rainforest, whereas in Tayap convention these nouns are bare adjuncts. So instead of saying *yim mbok Konjamoran* ('we went to Konjamoran' – with no clitic added to Konjamoran, which is a named area of the rainforest), young speakers consistently add a locative clitic, and say either *yim mbok Konjamoran=re*, or *yim mbok Konjamoran=nɨ*, using the case marker for villages (=*re*) or for unnamed places (=*nɨ*).

Young speakers may be doing this on the pattern of Tok Pisin, where such marking, by the preposition "long", is obligatory – in Tok Pisin, 'we went to Konjamoran' would be "mipela igo long Konjamoran".

But they may also be using locative markers because it is logical to do so in Tayap: that fluent speakers do not use the locative endings on named areas of the rainforest is a marked feature of this system. An alternative explanation of why young speakers use the locative clitic here is thus that they are regularizing Tayap's case marking system.

---

4 Mihalic (1971: 23).

5 Basic verb morphology

5.1 General properties of Tayap verbs

In Tayap a single complex predicate can express the equivalent of an entire sentence in English. This is most apparent in its serial verb constructions, which can express a complex action like 'she intends to carry him down on her shoulders' in a single predicate (*tapratkiŋgiatikitakana*). Serial verb constructions like this are discussed in Chapter 8. For basic sentence structure, see Section 9.1.

Transitivity, TAM (tense, aspect and mood) and realis/irrealis status are morphologically encoded in verbs by suffixes, with the object suffix preceding the subject suffix.

In transitive verbs, this occurs in the following manner:

(5-1) a. *poŋgro*

po	*-ŋg*	*-ro*
verb stem 'strike'	-object/undergoer 'him'	-subject/actor 'they'
in realis	in realis	in realis

'they hit him'

b. *oŋgrindak*

o	*-ŋgri*	*-ndak*
verb stem 'strike'	-object/undergoer 'him'	-subject/actor 'they'
in irrealis	in irrealis	in irrealis

'they will hit him'

Intransitive verbs, too, signal both subject and status, but many of them tend to do so in a more fusional manner than is the case for transitive verbs, especially in the non-future tense (which expresses events or actions that are occurring in the present or that have occurred in the past).

An example of intransitive verbs is the verb *poror* 'sing'. Some of the forms that this verb takes in the non-future and the future tenses are as follows:

(5-2) a. *poror-net*   *poror-nak*   *poror-ŋguk*
sing.R-1SG.M|3SG.M.R   sing.R-1SG.F|1PL.R   sing.R-3PL.R
'I (M) sang' or 'he sang'   'I (F) sang' or 'we sang'   'they sang'

b. *poror-ki-net* *poror-ki-nak* *poror-ki-ndak*
sing.IRR-IRR-1SG.M|3SG.M.IRR sing.IRR-IRR-1SG.F|1PL.IRR sing.IRR-IRR-3PL.IRR

'I (M) will sing' or 'he will sing' 'I (F) will sing' or 'we will be' 'they will sing'

Verbs in Tayap are constructed around verb stems, which never occur alone (except in certain modification constructions, see Sections 4.5.1 and 4.5.2), and which also never occur without being marked for status, either realis or irrealis (although some verbs, e.g. *poror* above have the same stem for both). The root forms of these stems – that is, the forms that are available for derivational processes like nominalization, and the citation forms that are entered in the dictionary as the lexical entry for a verb – are the irrealis forms of the stem.

A note is in order on the terms "roots" and "stems" as they are used here. Roots are the lexical parts of a word, the unanalyzable part left once the affixes are all taken off. Stems are involved when inflectional affixes apply to different forms of a root (Aikhenvald 2007: 38–40). So Tayap verb roots have inflectional stems: that is, for instance, there are separate inflectional stems for realis and irrealis. In this grammar, "stem" refers to the inflectional possibilities of a verb root, and "root" designates the basic underlying lexical part of the verb.

Verbs in Tayap have the following structure:

$$V - O - (A)$$
$$V - (S)$$

Note that verbal morphology, unlike clausal relations, follows a nominative-accusative alignment system.

Verbs in Tayap mark the following elements:

Status
Has the action of the verb happened or is happening? Has it not happened?

Tense, aspect and mood (TAM)
Is the action described by the verb occurring now? Is it completed? Has it happened or will it happen? Did it not happen? Temporal and modal relations like these must be marked on the verb.

In *transitive* verbs, TAM is marked on the verb root, the object suffix and, if there is one, on the subject suffix as well.

In *intransitive* verbs, TAM is marked on the verb root and the subject suffix, when there is one. In certain situations, such as when an intransitive verb is negated, subject suffixes disappear. Modality is marked by one of the three irrealis suffixes -kɨ, -ki or -ku (see Section 5.2.2).

Subject (S/A)
With the exception of negated verbs, verbs inflected with certain mood endings (see Section 5.2 and chapter 7) and non-finite forms like participles (Section 4.2) as well as verbs in certain modification constructions (Section 4.5.1 and 4.5.2), every verb must be marked for subject (S/A).

Note that in this grammar, the subject suffixes in *transitive* sentences include S in their gloss to clearly differentiate them from the object suffixes. The subject suffixes in *intransitive* sentences do not include this S, since there is no possibility of such confusion.

The forms of the subject suffixes are discussed in Section 5.3.2.

Object (O)
Transitivity in verbs is signaled by the presence of an object suffix that either directly follows the verb stem, or, for certain verbs, that occurs between two discontinuous subject suffixes. Tayap has a number of distinct object suffixes that signal person, number and TAM. These are discussed in Section 5.3.1.

Generally speaking, verbs are formed by suffixing TAM, object (for transitive verbs) and subject morphemes onto verb stems. The system is complicated by the fact that many verbs express TAM partly or wholly through suppletion. This feature of Tayap grammar is illustrated in example (5-1). In that example, note how the verb stem alternates between *po*, when it expresses an action that has actually occurred, and *o*, when it expresses an event that has not yet happened.

As was mentioned above, main predicate verb stems never occur independently, and they never occur without being inflected for status (realis/irrealis). Despite this, though, it is easy to identify the root form of a verb. All one has to know is the verb's negated form. For this reason, let us examine verbs by looking at negation first.

5.2 Standard negation in transitive and intransitive verbs

5.2.1 Negation of transitive verbs

In order to understand what happens to a Tayap verb when it is negated, compare the following forms of the transitive verb 'consume' in the non-future and future tense:

(5-3) a. ŋɨŋi mborsip kakun
 ŋɨ   =ŋi   mborsip ka   -ku   -n
 3SG.M   =ERG.M   pork   consume.R   <3SG.F.R.O>   -1SG|2SG|3SG.M|1PL.R.S
 'he ate pork'

 b. ŋɨŋi mborsip akrunet
  ŋɨ   =ŋi   mborsip a   -kru   -net
  3SG.M   =ERG.M   pork   consume.IRR   -3SG.F.IRR.O   -1SG.M|3SG.M.IRR.S
  'he will eat pork'

 c. ŋguyi mborsip okun
  ŋgu   =yi   mborsip o   -ku   -n
  3SG.F   =ERG.F   pork   consume.R   <3SG.F.R.O>   -3SG.F.R.S
  'she ate pork'

 d. ŋguyi mborsip akrutak
  ŋgu   =yi   mborsip a   -kru   -tak
  3SG.F   =ERG.F   pork   consume.IRR   -3SG.F.IRR.O   -2SG.F|3SG.F.IRR.S
  'she will eat pork'

 e. ŋgɨgi mborsip okuro
  ŋgɨ   =gi   mborsip o   -ku   -ro
  3PL   =ERG.PL pork   consume.R   <3SG.F.R.O>   -3PL.R.S
  'they ate pork'

 f. ŋgɨgi mborsip akrundak
  ŋgɨ   =gi   mborsip a   -kru   -ndak
  3PL   =ERG.PL pork   consume.IRR   -3SG.F.IRR.O   -3PL.IRR.S
  'they will eat pork'

Leaving aside everything else that is happening with this verb, look at the verb stem. Note that the stem changes between the non-future tense, where it appears as both *ka* (for 1SG, 2SG, 3SG.M and for 1PL subjects) and *o* (for 3SG.F and 3PL subjects), and the future, where the stem is realized as *a* for every subject.

This being the case, how does one know whether the verb root of 'eat' is *ka* or *o* or *a*, or something else entirely?

This becomes clear when the verb is negated. Negation strips a verb of everything but its irrealis stem and an irrealis object suffix (for transitive verbs), or its irrealis stem and a marker of status (for intransitive verbs).

This means that the various forms of 'eat' are all negated in the same way:

(5-4) a. ŋiŋi mborsip akru wákare
ŋɨ   =ŋi   mborsip   a   -kru   wákare
3SG.M =ERG.M   pork   consume.IRR   -3SG.F.IRR.O   NEG
'he didn't eat pork'

b. ŋiŋi mborsip akru wákare
ŋɨ   =ŋi   mborsip   a   -kru   wákare
3SG.M =ERG.M   pork   consume.IRR   -3SG.F.IRR.O   NEG
'he won't eat pork'

c. ŋguyi mborsip akru wákare
ŋgu   =yi   mborsip   a   -kru   wákare
3SG.F =ERG.F   pork   consume.IRR   -3SG.F.IRR.O   NEG
'she didn't eat pork'

d. ŋguyi mborsip akru wákare
ŋgu   =yi   mborsip   a   -kru   wákare
3SG.F =ERG.F   pork   consume.IRR   -3SG.F.IRR.O   NEG
'she won't eat pork'

e. ŋgɨgi mborsip akru wákare
ŋgɨ=gi   mborsip   a   -kru   wákare
3PL=ERG.PL   pork   consume.IRR   -3SG.F.IRR.O   NEG
'they didn't eat pork'

f. ŋgɨgi mborsip akru wákare
ŋgɨ   =gi   mborsip   a   -kru   wákare
3PL   =ERGPL   pork   consume.IRR   -3SG.F.IRR.O   NEG
'they won't eat pork'

Note that 'didn't eat' (i.e. an event that did not occur in the past) and 'won't eat' (an action that will not occur in the future) are expressed with the same form, *a*, in Tayap. This is the reason this form is classified as irrealis: both the future and the negated forms of verbs are unreal events. The actions they express have either *not yet happened* (the future) or they *have not happened* or *will not happen* (the negated forms).

This invariant form of the verb stem in negation is a verb's root form.

Note that the negator *wákare* usually appears clause finally (but see e.g. examples (8-27d and 9.14b)). This feature of Tayap is common to many Papuan and Austronesian languages (Reesink 2002b).

5.2.2 Negation of intransitive verbs

Just like transitive verbs, intransitive verbs also reveal their root forms when negated. To see this, look at the full conjugation in the non-future and future tenses of the irregular verb of motion 'go':

Table 5.1: The verb *o* 'to go'

NON-FUTURE		FUTURE			
SUBJECT	VERB	SUBJECT	VERB		
ŋa 1SG 'I (male) went' or 'I'm going'	mbot go.SG.M.R	ŋa 1SG 'I (male) will go'	o go.IRR	-kɨ -IRR	-net -1SG.M|3SG.M.IRR
ŋa 1SG 'I (female) went' or 'I'm going'	mbok go.1SG.F|2SG. F|1PL.R	ŋa 1SG 'I (female) will go'	o go.IRR	-kɨ -IRR	-nak -1SG.F|1PL.IRR
yu 2SG 'you (male) went' or 'you're going'	mbot go.SG.M.R	yu 2SG 'you (male) will go'	o go.IRR	-kɨ -IRR	-tet -2SG.M.IRR
yu 2SG 'you (female) went' or 'you're going'	mbok go.1SG.F|2SG. F|1PL.R	yu 2SG 'you (female) will go'	o go.IRR	-kɨ -IRR	-tak -2SG.F|3SG.F.IRR
ŋgu 3SG.F 'she went' or 'she's going'	wok go.3SG.F.R	ŋgu 3SG.F 'she will go'	o go.IRR	-kɨ -IRR	-tak -2SG.F|3SG.F.IRR
ŋɨ 3SG.M 'he went' or 'he's going'	mbot go.SG.M.R	ŋɨ 3SG.M 'he will go'	o go.IRR	-kɨ -IRR	-net -1SG.M|3SG.M.IRR
yim 1PL 'we went' or 'we're going'	mbok go.1SG.F|2SG. F|1PL.R	yim 1PL 'we will go'	o go.IRR	-kɨ -IRR	-nak -1SG.F|1PL.IRR

(continued)

Table 5.1 (continued)

NON-FUTURE		FUTURE			
SUBJECT	VERB	SUBJECT	VERB		
yum 2PL 'you PL went' or 'you PL are going'	mbokem go.2PL.R	yum 2PL 'you PL will go'	o go.IRR	-kɨ -IRR	-nkem -2PL.IRR
ŋgɨ 3PL 'they went' or 'they're going'	ŋgwok go.3PL.R	ŋgɨ 3PL 'they will go'	o go.IRR	-kɨ -IRR	-ndak -3PL.IRR
yim sene/ ŋgɨ sene we two/ they two 'we two/they two went' or 'we two/they two are going'	woke go.DL.R	yim sene/ ŋgɨ sene we two/ they two 'we two/they two will go'	o go.IRR	-kɨ -IRR	-tike -DL.IRR

The negated form of *all* these verbs is:

(5-5) okɨ wákare
       o   -kɨ   wákare
       go.IRR   -IRR   NEG

In other words, 'I didn't go', 'they didn't go', 'we won't go', 'she will not go', etc. – all this becomes *okɨ wákare*.

As in transitive verbs, the form of the verb that appears in negation is the verb root.

An intransitive verb takes no object suffix. In negation, however, intransitive verbs exhibit a morphological structure that parallels the transitive object suffix. A negated intransitive verb signals irrealis status in both the verb stem and in the suffix that follows it. This irrealis suffix suffixed to the verb stem further marks it as irrealis.

The irrealis suffix suffixed to the verb stem is the same for all subjects, regardless of person, gender or number. Note that it occurs in contexts apart from just negation, see for example (5-9a).

The suffix occurs in one of three forms: *-ki*, *-kɨ* or *-ku*. There is some phonetic regularity in the patterning of which verb stems take which suffixes: verb stems that contain or end in front vowels tend to take *-ki* or *-kɨ*, and verb stems that contain or end in back vowels tend to take *-ku*. All the verbs that take *-ki* are verbs of motion or end in the same stem form as the verb *ai* 'come'. But like much else in Tayap, none of this is entirely predictable. All verbs suffixed by irrealis *-ki*, for example, may be verbs of motion or verbs that end with *-ai*. But not all verbs of motion take *-ki*. And there are many exceptions to the front vowel/back vowel pattern.

Examples of intransitive verb stems that take *-kɨ*:

ar	'go inside'	ŋawŋ	'bark'
atɨ	'appear'	ŋawriŋ	'growl like a dog'
eiar	'cry'	ŋguru	'snore'
emrari	'play'	o	'go'
ir	'laugh'	paindak	'prevent pregnancy'
isuwok	'sneeze'	piŋ	'jump'
kawr	'howl'	poror	'sing'
korar	'assemble to meet'	pruk	'work'
mem	'stand'	rar	'look around'
mɨndɨ	'growl like a pig'	ta	'sleep'
mur	'work sago'	warak	'talk'
nam	'tell'	wur	'go up to a place'

Examples of intransitive verb stems that take *-ki*:

ai	'come'
as	'come down from a place'; 'come outside'
pereipereiki	'race'
raraiki	'become visible'
sir	'go down from a house or tree'
wi	'rise'

Examples of intransitive verb stems that take *-ku*:

a	'be'	turu	'dance'
ambru	'bellow like a cassowary'	tutu	'sit'
ambu	'hide'	tuw	'bathe'
andru	'meow, moan, chirp'	wuw	'ascend' e.g. a tree or up into a house
mungu	'stand'		

Of all the irrealis modal markers for intransitive verb stems, the most productive is -*kɨ* (which in addition to being a modal marker also has a range of other functions in Tayap; see Section 3.4.2).

In the dictionary, intransitive verbs are listed with -*ki*/ -*kɨ* / -*ku* attached.

5.3 Object (o) and subject (s/a) suffixes

5.3.1 Object suffixes

Before going on to discuss the range of TAM distinctions made in Tayap, it will be useful to distinguish the various forms of the object and subject suffixes that, together with the verb stems, encode TAM on a verb.

Taking the object suffixes first, note how their forms in irrealis are simply the realis forms with an *r* inserted before the vowel in all cases except 1SG, which retains the same form in both statuses. Interestingly, only the 3PL is distinguished from the other non-singular suffixes in both paradigms:

	REALIS OBJECT SUFFIXES			IRREALIS OBJECT SUFFIXES		
	SINGULAR	DUAL	PLURAL	SINGULAR	DUAL	PLURAL
1	-*i*	-*mɨ*	-*mɨ*	-*i*	-*mrɨ*	-*mrɨ*
2	-*u*	-*mɨ*	-*mɨ*	-*ru*	-*mrɨ*	-*mrɨ*
3F	-*ku*			-*kru*		
		-*mɨ*	-*mbɨ*		-*mrɨ*	-*mbrɨ*
3M	-*ŋgɨ*			-*ŋgrɨ*		

Example:

(5-6) a. *ewar ŋgigi ŋɨ poŋgro*
       ewar   ŋgɨ   =gi   ŋɨ   po   -ŋgɨ   -ro
       yesterday 3PL   =ERG.PL 3SG.M strike.R -3SG.M.R.O -3PL.R.S
       'yesterday they hit him'

     b. *epi ŋgigi ŋɨ oŋgrɨndak*
        epi   ŋgɨ   =gi   ŋɨ   o   -ŋgrɨ   -ndak
        tomorrow 3PL   =ERG.PL 3SG.M strike.IRR -3SG.M.IRR.O -3PL.IRR.S
        'tomorrow they will hit him'

5.3.2 Subject (S/A) suffixes

Tayap's subject (S/A) suffixes can be compared in Tables 5.2 and 5.3 below. Irrealis subject suffixes only mark gender for singular subjects, and realis subject suffixes do not mark gender at all. Both paradigms collapse second person non-singular, they distinguish third person plural, and they collapse first and third person dual. Note that these complex syncretisms are different in different paradigms (see Section 3.5 for other pronoun paradigms, including the free pronouns and benefactive suffixes).

Table 5.2: Subject suffixes on transitive verbs

	IRREALIS SUBJECT SUFFIXES FOR TRANSITIVE VERBS			REALIS SUBJECT SUFFIXES FOR TRANSITIVE VERBS		
	SG	DL	PL	SG	DL	PL
1F	-nak					
		-tike	-nak	-n	-re	-n
1M	-net					
2F	-tak					
		-nkem	-nkem	-n	-rem	-rem
2M	-tet					
3F	-tak					
		-tike	-ndak/tuko	-n	-re	-ro
3M	-net					

Examples:

(5-7) a. *ŋi epi ŋgakreŋan pupur arkrunet*
    ŋi   epi   ŋgakre =ŋan   pupur
    3SG.M tomorrow jaw   =POSS   hair

    ar   -kru   -net
    shave.IRR -3SG.F.IRR.O -1SG.M|3SG.M.IRR.S
    'tomorrow he will shave off his beard'

b. *ŋi ewar ŋgakreŋan pupur karkun*
    ŋi   ewar   ŋgakre =ŋan   pupur
    he   yesterday jaw   =POSS   hair

```
kar        -ku              -n
shave.R    <3SG.F.R.O>      -1SG|2SG|3SG.M|1PL.R.S
'yesterday he shaved off his beard'
```

For *intransitive* verbs, the irrealis subject markers are the same as those for transitive verbs. The *realis* subject markers vary depending on the group to which the verb root belongs, and many are irregular. These subject markers are discussed in Section 6.2.

Table 5.3: Subject suffixes on intransitive verbs

	IRREALIS SUBJECT SUFFIXES FOR INTRANSITIVE VERBS			REALIS SUBJECT SUFFIXES FOR INTRANSITIVE VERBS		
	SG	DL	PL	SG	DL	PL
1F	-nak					
		-tike	-nak		see 6.2.1	
1M	-net					
2F	-tak					
		-nkem	-nkem		see 6.2.1	
2M	-tet					
3F	-tak					
		-tike	-ndak/tuko		see 6.2.1	
3M	-net					

Examples:

(5-8) a. *kaimwa imbɨkɨtak*
```
      kaimwa      imbɨ        -kɨ       -tak
      cockatoo    fly.IRR     -IRR      -2SG.F|3SG.F.IRR
      'the cockatoo will fly'
```

b. *kaimwa pimbiek*
```
      kaimwa      pimb        -iek
      cockatoo    fly.R       -1SG.F|3SG.F|1PL.R
      'the cockatoo flew'
```

In addition to the object and subject suffixes listed in the tables above, Tayap also has a set of benefactive object suffixes and a set of counterfactual subject suffixes.

These are listed in Section 3.5 and discussed in Section 7.5. Counterfactuals are discussed in Section 9.4.3. Non-final object markers are discussed in Section 8.2.2.

5.4 Tense, aspect and mood in Tayap

5.4.1 Overview of Tayap verbal morphology

It should be clear by now that the fundamental distinction in Tayap's verbal morphology system is between real and unreal events. Verb stems marked as realis or irrealis combine with other suffixes that also are marked for TAM to make tense distinctions, to express the progressive and habitual aspect, and to encode modal notions like desire and prohibition.

The basic combinations, which can be modified by verbal suffixes and compounding to produce more tenses and aspects, are as follows:

Table 5.4: Overview of verbal morphology

TRANSITIVE VERBS						
Verb stem	Object suffix	Modal marker	Subject suffix	Verbal suffix or Negation	→	TAM
IRR	IRR		Ø	NEG	→	NEG
IRR	IRR		IRR	Ø	→	FUT
IRR	IRR		IRR	-(n)ana	→	NRFUT
IRR/CF	R	(-rɨk-)	R (discontinuous subject suffixes optional)	Ø	→	CF
IRR/SBJ	R		R	Ø	→	SBJ
R	R		R	Ø	→	NF
R	R		R	-(da)ra	→	PERF

INTRANSITIVE VERBS					
Verb	Modal marker	Subject suffix	Verbal suffix or Negation	→	TAM
IRR	IRR	Ø	NEG	→	NEG
IRR	IRR	IRR	Ø	→	FUT
IRR	IRR	IRR	-(n)ana	→	NRFUT

(continued)

Table 5.4 (continued)

INTRANSITIVE VERBS					
Verb	Modal marker	Subject suffix	Verbal suffix or Negation	→	TAM
CF	(-rɨk-)	IRR OR CF	∅	→	CF
SBJ	∅	R	∅	→	SBJ
R	∅	R	∅	→	NF
R	∅	R	-(da)ra	→	PERF

Notice in the above table that irrealis and realis suffixes do not always combine in expected ways. While some verb forms (like verbs in the non-future or the future) are composed of verb stems, object suffixes and subject suffixes that all are marked for either realis or irrealis, other verb forms (the prohibitive (Section 7.2) and counterfactual (Section 9.4.3)) mix these suffixes, and have, for example, intransitive verb stems marked for irrealis, but object and subject suffixes inflected in their realis forms.

If an action or event has occurred, is occurring or occurs regularly, Tayap encodes the following distinctions:

Perfect (PERF)   actions or events that are completed; e.g. 'He died'; 'They have finished the work' (see Section 5.4.3.2).

Non-future (NF)   actions or events that are occurring at the moment of speaking or that have occurred but are either ongoing or unmarked in terms of their termination or completedness; e.g. 'She is in the house'; 'They ate the pig meat we gave them'. This is also the form used to make gnomic statements like 'Birds fly' (see Section 5.4.3.1).

Progressive (PROG)   actions or events that are not fully realized because they are occurring at either the moment of speaking or they were occurring at the same time some other action happened; e.g. 'I am sitting here eating sago jelly'; 'He was eating sago jelly when they arrived'. The progressive can also express events that recur regularly (discussed in Section 8.3.1).

Habitual (HAB)   actions or events that occur all the time; e.g. 'She is always smoking' (discussed in Section 8.3.2).

If an action or event (a) has not occurred or won't occur; (b) has not yet occurred but may occur or is expected to occur, or (c) might have occurred but didn't, Tayap marks the following distinctions:

Negative (NEG) actions or events that have not occurred or will not occur; e.g. 'I didn't spear the pig', 'He won't go to Wongan' (see Section 5.2).

Future (FUT) actions or events that are anticipated to occur in the future; e.g. 'He will go hunting tomorrow' (see Section 5.4.2.2).

Near future (NRFUT) actions or events that are anticipated to occur in the immediate future; e.g. 'They're going to leave now' (see Section 5.4.2.3).

Counterfactual (CF) actions or events that might have occurred but didn't, e.g. 'If they had seen me, they would have beaten me up'; or that are impossible, e.g. 'if you were young I would marry you' (expressed by a subordinate construction: see Section 9.4.3)

Subjunctive (SBJ) speaker's desire that something happen (or not happen), or that another person do something (or not do something); e.g. 'You go!' or 'May X not happen' (see Section 7.1).

The following is a schematic representation of Tayap's TAM system.

150 — 5 Basic verb morphology

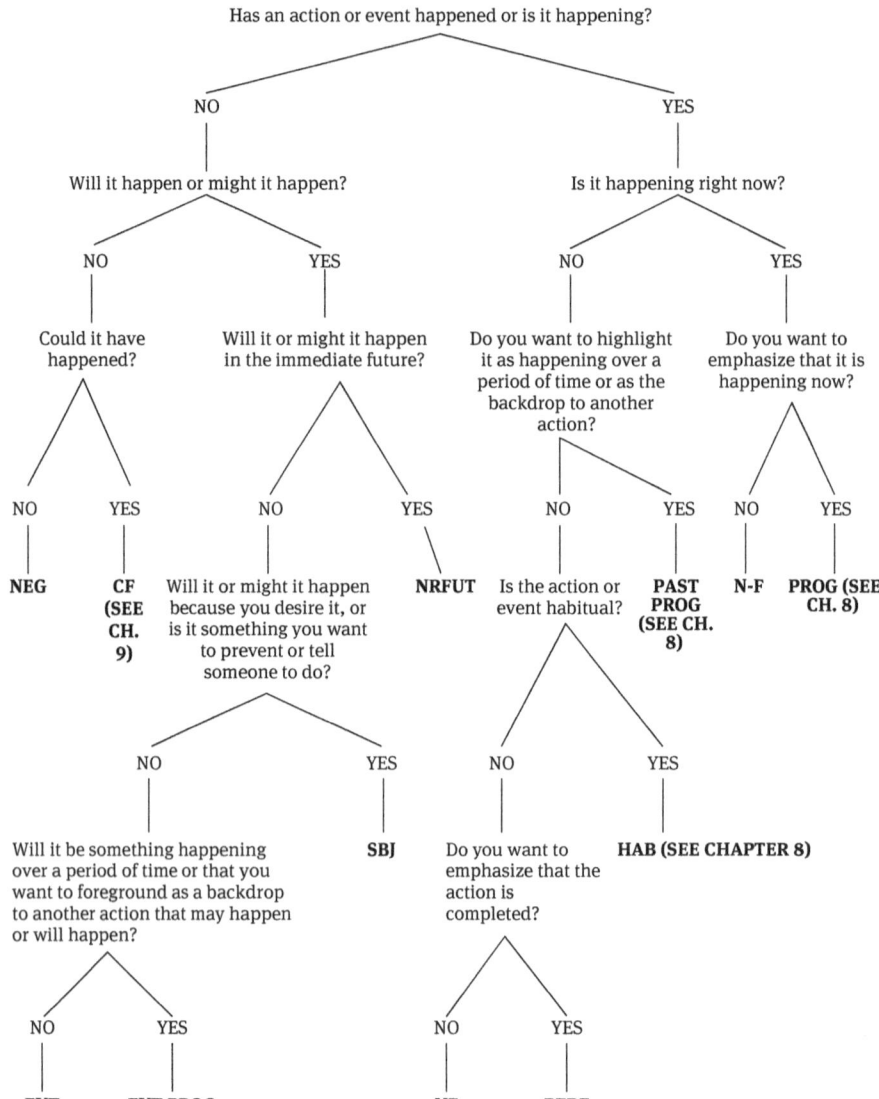

5.4.2 Irrealis

5.4.2.1 Negative (NEG)
The formation and scope of the negative has been discussed in Section 5.2.

5.4.2.2 Future (FUT)
Like the negative, the future is formed on the basis of the (irrealis) verb stem. Compare:

	NEGATIVE		FUTURE	
INTRANSITIVE	o-ki	wákare	o-ki	-net
	go.IRR-IRR	NEG	go.IRR-IRR	-1SG.M|3SG.M.IRR.S
	'X (any subject) didn't/ won't go'		'He will go' or 'I (M) will go'	
TRANSITIVE	a-kru	wákare	a-kru	-net
	consume.IRR-3SG.F.IRR.O	NEG	consume.IRR-3SG.F.IRR.O	-1SG.M|3SG.M.IRR.S
	'X(any subject) didn't/ won't consume it'		'He will consume it' or 'I (M) will consume it'	

With *intransitive* verbs, the future is formed by suffixing an irrealis subject suffix to the irrealis modal suffix that follows the verb stem.

With *transitive* verbs, the irrealis subject suffix (Section 5.2.2) is added after the irrealis object suffix.

So future is formed in Tayap according to the following patterns:

INTRANSITIVE VERBS	IRR verb stem + IRR suffixes -*ki*, -*kɨ* or -*ku* + IRR subject
TRANSITIVE VERBS	IRR verb stem + IRR object + IRR subject

Examples:
INTRANSITIVE
(5-9) a. *yim epi mindikitike*
   yim `*epi* *mindi* -*ki* -*tike*
   1PL tomorrow work_sago.IRR -IRR -DL.IRR
   'tomorrow the two of us will work sago'

b. *tukur aikittakre, ŋa patɨrnɨ arkinet*

tukur	ai	-ki	-tak	-re	ŋa	patɨr	=nɨ
rain	come.IRR	-IRR	-2SG.F|3SG.F.IRR	-SUB	1SG	house	=LOC

ar	-ki	-net
go_inside.IRR	-IRR	-1SG.M|3SG.M.IRR

'if it rains, I (M) am going inside the house'

c. *epi ŋa embre kɨ memkɨnak*

epi	ŋa	emb	=re	=kɨ
tomorrow	1SG	morning	=TEMP	=INTENS

mem	-kɨ	-nak
get_up.IRR	-IRR	-1SG.F|1PL.IRR

'tomorrow I (F) will get up right at dawn'

TRANSITIVE

(5-10) a. *Maiwaŋi mbaranɨ yu aruonet*

Maiwa=ŋi	mbara=nɨ	yu
Maiwa=ERG.M	garden=LOC	2SG

aruo	-ru	-net
wait.IRR	-2SG.IRR.O	-1SG.M|3SG.M.IRR.S

'Maiwa will wait for you in the garden'

b. *yim Mbur rarkrutikeya muna ŋgon urakkukuaikitike*

yim	Mbur	rar	-kru	-tike	-ya
1PL	Mbur	see.IRR	-3SG.F.IRR.O	-DL.IRR.S	-and

muna	ŋgon
sago_flour	3SG.F.POSS

urak-	-ku	-ku	ai	-ki	-tike
carry_on_shoulder.IRR	-bring	-3SG.F.R.O	come.IRR	-IRR	-DL.IRR.S

'the two of us are going to help Mbur carry her sago (and come to the village)'

c. *epi ŋayi yum ombrɨnet*

epi	ŋa=yi	yum
tomorrow	1SG=ERG.F	2PL

o-	-mbrɨ-	-net
strike.IRR	-2PL.IRR.O-	-1SG.M|3SG.M.IRR.S

'tomorrow I (M) am going to hit you all'

The future encodes an unreal event, but also locates an event in time. It contrasts with the near future in terms of the action's expected occurrence in relation to the moment of speaking: the near future is expected to occur soon in relation to the moment of speaking; the future is expected to occur at some other point in the future – a time that may or may not be specified by a temporal adverb like 'this evening', 'tomorrow' or 'later'.

5.4.2.3 Near future (NRFUT)

The near future is formed by suffixing morpheme *-ana* (*-nana* after a vowel) to a verb inflected for future tense:

INTRANSITIVE VERBS	IRR verb stem + IRR -*ki*, -*kɨ* or -*ku* + IRR subject + -*(n)ana*
TRANSITIVE VERBS	IRR verb stem + IRR object + IRR subject + -*(n)ana*

Examples:

INTRANSITIVE

(5-11) a. *ŋa prukkɨnetana inda*

  ŋa   pruk   -kɨ   -net   -ana   inda
  1SG   work.IRR -IRR -1SG.M|3SG.M.IRR.S -INTENT   DX.M

  'I (M) am going to work now' (which is why I am getting up to go)

TRANSITIVE

  b. *yu mum akrutetanake?*

  yu   mum   a   -kru   -tet   -ana   =ke
  2SG   sago_jelly eat.IRR -3SG.F.IRR.O -2SG.M.IRR.S -INTENT =Q

  'Are you (M) going to eat sago jelly?' (if I fix a plate of it for you?)

The suffix -*(n)ana* expresses intention (see Section 7.4). But Tayap distinguishes between a near future tense and an intentional mood. Pure intentionality, with no morphological marking for time, is signaled on both transitive and intransitive verbs by omitting the subject suffixes in the inflected future verb and affixing -*(n)ana* directly to the irrealis object marker (for transitive verbs) and directly to the irrealis modal marker (for intransitive verbs). So compare:

INTENTION

(5-12) a. *yu mum akrunanake?*

yu	mum	a	-kru	-nana	=ke
2SG	sago_jelly	eat.IRR	-3SG.F.IRR.O	-INTENT	=Q

'Would you eat sago jelly?' (if I offer you some)

Note: The gender of 'you' here is unspecified, since there is no subject suffix on the verb.

NEAR FUTURE

b. *yu mum akrutetanake?*

yu	mum	a	-kru	-tet	-ana	=ke
2SG	sago_jelly	eat.IRR	-3SG.F.IRR.O	-2SG.M.IRR.S-	-INTENT	=Q

'Are you (M) going to eat the sago jelly?' (that is sitting in front of you getting cold)

The only difference between these two questions is that in the first example (5-12a) there is no subject suffix on the verb.

In practice, it can be difficult or meaningless to try to distinguish between the near future and intention. Just as an English expression like 'I'm going to leave now' conflates the desire or intention to leave with an action that is about to occur, so does a Tayap sentence inflected in the near future tense imply a desire or intention.

However, the difference between English and Tayap here is that unlike English, Tayap can also clearly morphologically distinguish between an action that is intended or desired and one that is about to occur.

5.4.2.4 Subjunctive

The subjunctive mood is discussed in detail in Section 7.1.

5.4.3 Realis

5.4.3.1 Non-future (NF)

The non-future signifies that the action denoted by the verb is either ongoing or has already happened. Because the non-future can refer to both the present and the past, and also to express general truths, it is the most frequently occurring verb form in Tayap. Unhappily for younger speakers, it is also the most irregular and unpredictable verb form. Transitive verbs in the non-future can be separated into five distinct conjugation classes. Intransitive verbs are less regular, but fall into four conjugation classes that contain several subgroups and exceptions.

It is not possible to predict – for example, on the basis of the phonological shape of a verb root – the class of a transitive verb or the inflectional pattern of an intransitive verb. The only way to know the non-future inflection of a verb is by hearing it inflected by a fluent speaker.

The formation of verbs in the realis status is a feature of Tayap grammar that requires lengthy explanation. It is the subject of Chapter 6.

5.4.3.2 Perfect (PERF)

The perfect is used to mark an action as having been completed. It is formed by adding the following suffixes to a verb inflected in the non-future tense:

-*da(ra)*   after *n*. Conditioning factors between -*da* and -*dara* are unknown
-*(a)ra*   after all other phonemes (-*ra* if the verb ends in a vowel; -*ara* otherwise)

The perfect foregrounds the difference between an action or event in process and one that is completed; the difference between being on one's way and having arrived:

(5-13) a. ŋɨ   mbet
           3SG.M   come.SG.M.R
           'he is coming' or 'he came'

       b. ŋɨ   mbet   -ara
           3SG.M   come.SG.M.R   -PERF
           'he has come', 'he has arrived'

Perfect tense is used to foreground the completedness of an action or event, e.g.

(5-14) *karep wokara aro senenɨ ŋa yu aropowun* Wewak
        karep   wok   -ara   aro   sene   =nɨ   ŋa   yu
        moon   go.3SG.F.R   -PERF   day   two   =LOC   1SG   2SG

        aropo   -wu   -n   Wewak
        wait.R   -2SG.R.O   -SG|1PL.R.S   Wewak
        'last month (lit. 'moon has gone') I waited for you for two days in [the town of] Wewak'

The perfect also marks relations of completedness between different events. For example, a young mother telling the story of how she thought a death adder had bitten her son said the following (see Tayap Text 3, from which this sentence is extracted):

(5-15) ŋa nda namnak aramŋi nda poŋgindara wasowkinetana
       ŋa   nda   nam   -nak   aram   =ŋi   nda
       1SG   DM   talk.R -1SG.F|1PL.R snake =ERG.M DM

       po   -ŋgɨ   -n   -dara
       strike.R -3SG.M.R.O -SG|1PL.R.S -PERF

       wasow   -kɨ   -net   -ana
       die.IRR -IRR   -1SG.M|3SG.M.IRR -INTENT
      'I thought the snake had bitten him and that he was going to die' (lit. 'I thought the snake had bitten him and he will die in the near future').

Another example of how the perfect is used to distinguish different kinds of completedness is an extract from a conversation in which a man in his fifties was commenting to others about how young people no longer speak Tayap. This man says that if young Gapuners go to another village and the people there want to attack them and beat them up, they won't be able to communicate with one another to organize their defense. "What language will you speak to one another?", he asks rhetorically:

(5-16) eŋgin mernɨ namkɨtak, ŋgigi tatukrora
       eŋgin   mer   =nɨ   nam   -kɨ   -tak   ŋgi=gi
       white_people language =LOC talk.IRR -IRR -2SG.F|3SG.F.IRR 3PL=ERG.PL

       ta   -tu   -ku   -ro   -ra
       perceive.R -S   <3SG.F.R.O> -3PL.R.S -PERF
      'If one speaks Tok Pisin, they've already understood your plans' (lit. 'You will speak in Tok Pisin, they've already understood it'). (Note the use of the feminine subject ending -tak to denote a non-specific, general referent; see Section 3.1.3.3.)

Notice here that the use of the perfect here carries the meaning of 'already' – the foreign villagers will have understood the unfortunate Tok Pisin-speaking Tayap villagers' plans before they are even finished being articulated.

    There are significant differences in how the perfect is used in the speech of fluent speakers and how it is used by speakers younger than thirty. For fluent speakers of Tayap, the perfect combines elements of tense (time in the past) and aspect (relevance to now) and is used to mark an action as having been completed.

For young speakers, the scope of the perfect suffix has been expanded. In addition to functioning grammatically to express temporal relations, it also functions syntactically to coordinate clauses.

Tayap has several clause coordinating suffixes, including the suffix *-api*, which means 'afterward' (see Section 9.3.2). This suffix is not used by speakers younger than thirty. Instead, one of the ways those speakers coordinate clauses is with the use of the perfect suffix.

Here are the two ways a fluent speaker might say 'After she talked to Akep, Mbopai left':

(5-17) a. *Akepre waraktakapi, Mbopai wok*
Akep =re warak -tak -api Mbopai wok
Akep =LOC talk.R -2SG.F|3SG.F.R -AFT Mbopai go.3SG.F.R
'after she talked to Akep, Mbopai left'

b. *Akepre warakrapi, Mbopai wok*
Akep =re warak -r- -api Mbopai wok
Akep =LOC talk.IRR -r- -AFT Mbopai go.3SG.F.R
'after she talked to Akep, Mbopai left'

The perfect is not used in either of these two sentences. The sentences do not foreground the completedness of the action of talking; they foreground the temporal relationship between the actions expressed in the clauses. They mark the subordinate clause ('after she talked') as the background or condition for the main clause ('she left').

Here is how a nineteen-year-old speaker of Tayap formulated (5-17):

(5-18) *Akepre waraktakara, ŋgu wok*
Akep =re warak -tak -ara ŋgu wok
Akep =LOC talk.R -2SG.F|3SG.F.R -PERF 3SG.F go.3SG.F.R
'she finished talking to Akep, she left'

In this speaker's Tayap, what should be the coordinating suffix *-api* is instead realized as the perfect suffix *-ara*. That such a substitution can occur is partly because the younger speaker calques on Tok Pisin while speaking Tayap.

In Tok Pisin, the word "pinis", which derives from English 'finish', is both an aspect marker and a clause-coordinating adverbial. As a marker of aspect, it follows a verb to indicate completed action. So compare:

(5-19) mi go   vs.   mi go pinis
       'I am going' or 'I went'   'I have gone'

       ol i toktok   vs.   ol i toktok pinis
       'they talk' or 'they talked'   'they've finished talking'

As a clause-coordinating conjunction, "pinis" forms an utterance in itself and is said with rising intonation:

(5-20) Mipela toktok igo igo.   Pinis,   mipela i go nambaut
       we   talk   DURATION   'finished' we   go   around
       'we spoke for a while and when we were finished talking, we went our separate ways'

Young speakers of Tayap model their use of the perfect on these dual functions of Tok Pisin's "pinis" and they use the perfect suffix to signify both a completed action and clause coordination. They even pronounce verbs onto which they have suffixed the perfect suffix as they would the Tok Pisin equivalent with "pinis", i.e. they use the same rising intonation that they use when speaking Tok Pisin.

5.5 Reduplication

The reduplication of verbs is another way of expressing temporality and epistemic stance (usually disapproval). The repetition or iteration of an action, for example, is expressed by repeating the verb stem:

(5-21) a. *ketukketukkwankut*
           ketuk   ketuk   -kwan   -kut
           cough.IRR   cough.IRR   -3SG.F.BEN.O -be.SG.M.R
           'he is coughing and coughing'

       b. *mbarow sene mborimborikar woke awin motoreke*
           mbarow   sene   mbori   mbori   -r-   kar   woke
           mbarow_fish   two   flipflop.IRR flipflop.IRR -r-   -MANN   go.DL.R

           awin   moto   =reke
           water   dirty   =PERL
           'two mbarow fish flipflopped flipflopped along puddles of water'

In the following example part of the benefactive suffix is reduplicated:

   c. ŋa omoŋi namsamb piapiapiatan nam ŋgume namwankuk
       ŋa   omo   =ŋi   nam -samb pi   -ia
       1SG father =ERG.M talk -PL   give.R -1SG.BEN.R.O

       pi   -ia   pi   -iata   -n   nam   ŋgume
       give.R -1SG.BEN.R.O give.R -1SG.BEN.R.O -SG|1PL.R talk   thus

       nam   -wan   -kuk
       talk.IRR -2SG.BEN.R.O -be.1SG|2SG.F.R
       'The talk that father gave, gave, gave me [i.e. the talk that he imparted to me repeatedly], I (F) am telling you that talk'

   d. ŋare takwattakwatŋgarke koret ror apro sakar morasi aproŋa
       ŋa   =re   takwat takwat -ŋgarke koret   ror   apro sakar
       1SG =LOC lie.IRR lie.IRR -PROH   foreign child bad INTENS

       morasi   apro=ŋa
       habit   bad=POSS
       'You can't keep telling lies to me! You're like a fucking foreigner with bad habits'

The following example has reduplication of an inflected verb:

   e. trausis ŋaŋan isiriisiriwok
       trausis   ŋaŋan   isiri   isiri   wok
       trousers (TP) 1SG.POSS fall_off.IRR fall_off.IRR go.3SG.F.R
       'My trousers keep falling down

Reduplication of a verb can also carry the meaning that the action expressed by the verb happens over a length of time.

(5-22) a. yu weteta wetukwar wetukwar kukuwe tumbekeni
           yu   we   -tet   -a   wetu   -kwar   wetu   -kwar
           2SG come.SBJ -2SG.M.R -and wank.IRR -MANN wank.IRR -MANN

           ku   -ku   we   tumb   =ekeni
           bring -3SG.F.R.O come.SBJ mountain =PERL
           'you (M) come and wank wank your way up the mountain'
           (hollered by a woman in anger about a man she said always cheated her. The meaning is something like 'come and jerk yourself off all the way up the mountain')

5.5.1 Repeated action

There are a number of ways of showing an action is repeated. The following example shows repetition, rather than reduplication strictly speaking, of a verb:

> b. *ŋgɨ amkwar ŋgwoka ŋgwoka ŋayi ŋgɨ orepemɨn*
>
> | ŋgɨ | am | -kwar | ŋgwok | -a | ŋgwok | -a |
> |---|---|---|---|---|---|---|
> | 3PL | fight | -MANN | go.3PL.R | -and | go.3PL.R | -and |
>
> | ŋa | =yi | ŋgɨ | orepe | -mɨ | -n |
> |---|---|---|---|---|---|
> | 1SG | =ERG.F | 3PL | leave.R | -3PL.R.O | -SG\|1PL.R.S |
>
> 'they were fighting for a long time and I (gender unspecified) left them'

In addition to simply repeating a verb to convey that an action or event occurred several times or extended over a period of time, Tayap has a verbal suffix (*-ítŋo*) that marks an action or event as occurring repeatedly and exaggeratedly over a continuous, extended period of time. The meaning of this form corresponds to the durative "igo" construction in Tok Pisin – e.g. "em i krai igo igo igo"; 'he cried and cried and cried'. The suffix only occurs on intransitive verbs and this restricted usage may have limited the form's transmission.

Speakers under forty understand the meaning of verbs that have the *-ítŋo* suffix, but they never produce the forms themselves. In 2009, even speakers over fifty had trouble thinking of examples. Perhaps the forms occurred mainly in ritual narrative and singing or tuneful weeping over corpses – verbal skills that for the most part have become moribund in Gapun.

In the 1980s, I recorded the suffix *-ítŋo* for verbs that were repeated over an extended period of time, for example in the following verbs:

emrar-ítŋo	*poror-ítŋo*
play.IRR-XD	sing.IRR-XD
ketuk-ítŋo	*simber-ítŋo*
cough.IRR-XD	chew_betel_nut.IRR-XD
warak-ítŋo	
talk.IRR-XD	

I was also told that an alternative form that meant the same thing was the irrealis verb stem + *-ít-* + *ŋayar*, which is an adverb meaning 'really'. Senior men told me that both forms below express the same meaning – perhaps because the first form may be a contraction of the second:

emrar-ítŋo	or emrar-it	ŋayar
play.IRR-XD	play.IRR-XD?	really

The *-ítŋo* suffix that I recorded in the 1980s no longer occurs in the speech of anyone in Gapun.

Today, to the very limited extent that the idea of repeated actions over an extended period is encoded by a verbal suffix at all, this is done by adding the suffix *-ŋo*, or its variants *-eŋo*, *-erŋo* and *-irŋo* directly to the irrealis stem of an intransitive verb. The suffix is the same for all subjects; a verb with this suffix takes no subject endings, and the verb is always repeated.

(5-23) a. *pororŋo pororŋo ŋgakre mbɨdtak*

poror -ŋo poror -ŋo ŋgakre mbɨd -tak
sing.IRR -XD sing.IRR -XD jaw hurt.R -2SG.F|3SG.F.R

'X (i.e. any subject) sang and sang so much that X's jaw hurt'

b. *rarerŋo rarerŋo emb otitek*

rar -erŋo rar -erŋo emb otitek
look.IRR -XD look.IRR -XD morning fall.3SG.F.R

'X (i.e. any subject) looked and looked (for example, in a dream) until morning came'

c. *ketukŋo ketukŋo potak mbɨdtiatan*

ketuk -ŋo ketuk -ŋo potak
cough.IRR -XD cough.IRR -XD throat

mbɨd- -ti -iata -n
pain.IRR -S <1SG.BEN.R.O> -2SG|3SG.F.R.S

'I (gender unspecified) coughed and coughed so much that my throat hurt'

d. *indirŋo indirŋo man mbɨdtukwatan*

indi -rŋo indi -rŋo man
fuck.IRR -XD fuck.IRR -XD vagina

mbɨd -tu -kwata -n
pain.IRR -S <3G.F.BEN.R.O> -2SG|3SG.F.R.S

'She (or 'they' or 'we') fucked and fucked so much that her vagina hurt'

5.6 Reflexive and reciprocal constructions

Reflexive and reciprocal constructions are formed by adding the suffix -*ano* (-*ŋano* after a vowel) to the subject pronoun.

In reflexive constructions, the valency of a verb is decreased, so a verb that normally takes two arguments – a subject and object – instead only takes one. There is no explicit grammatical marking of this decreasing valency other than in the fact that a verb in a reflexive construction is always intransitive.

(5-24) a. *awin nanukni ŋaŋano taniet*
    awin nanuk =ni   ŋa   -ŋano   ta   -niet
    mirror   =LOC 1SG -REFL   see.R -1SG.M|3SG.M.R
    'I saw myself in the mirror'

Non singular subjects in this construction convey reciprocity:

  b. *yimano yim tatike*
    yim -ano   yim   ta   -tike
    1PL -REFL 1PL   see.R -DL.R
    'the two of us saw ourselves' or 'saw each other'

  c. *ŋgiŋano amurukuke*
    ŋgi -ŋano   amuru   -kuke
    3PL -REFL   fight.R -DL.R
    'the two of them are fighting each other'

This construction can also be used for emphasis, to convey that the subject does the action alone:

(5-25) a. *yuŋano nitukun!*
    yu   -ŋano   ni   -tu -ku   -n!
    you   -REFL   do.SBJ -S   <3SG.F.R.O> -2SG|3SG.F.R.S
    'Do it yourself!'

  b. *ŋgiŋanoki kirawtukuro*
    ŋgi -ŋano   -ki   kiraw   -tu -ku   -ro
    3PL -REFL   -EMPH   know.R -S   <3SG.F.R.O> -3PL.R.S
    'they realize it themselves'

6 The formation of realis and irrealis verbs

Perhaps the single most complex feature of Tayap's grammar is the formation of verbs in the realis status. The realis stem forms are only used in forming the non-future tense and the perfect aspect. However, because the realis status is what speakers use to refer to actions and events that have occurred in the past or are occurring in the present – as well as to make gnomic statements like 'birds fly' – it is the single most frequently occurring inflectional form in the speech of fluent Tayap speakers.

In the speech of younger, less fluent speakers, the non-future tense is still used, but the weakest speakers do their best to get around it as much as they can. To manage this, they overextend the progressive aspect, which is easier to inflect, partly because the verb stem inflects in its irrealis form and thus remains consistent, and partly because the suffixes that encode person and number that follow the verb stem have minimal variation (see Section 5.3).

The realis status is another kettle of fish. Its inflectional forms are irregular both in terms of the kinds of changes that occur in verb stems, and also in terms of their relative predictability. Transitive and intransitive verbs have very different inflectional patterns.

The following section (Section 6.1) discusses transitive verbs; intransitive verbs are discussed separately in Section 6.2.

6.1 Transitive verb classes

All transitive verbs belong to one of five conjugation classes. Class 1 and 5 have the biggest membership: in the dictionary there are 76 class 1 verbs and 73 class 5 verbs, with the other classes smaller: class 2 with 23, class 3 with 21 and class 4 with 38 verbs.

The classes are distinguishable by two interrelated patterned changes that occur on the verb stem:

1. the pattern of alternation between the stem's form in the non-future tense and its form in the irrealis status (for example when it is negated or when it denotes the future);
    and
2. the nature of the stem changes that occur in the non-future

In addition to these two kinds of patterned changes to the verb stem, three of the five conjugation classes – classes 3, 4 and 5 – also mark the subject twice with a discontinuous subject marker.

It was demonstrated in Section 5.2 how the root of a verb can be deduced from knowing the form it takes when it is negated. With that in mind, notice once again how the root of a verb like *o* 'strike' changes between the irrealis and the realis stem forms, seen here in the contrast between future and non-future tenses:

(6-1) a. FUTURE ŋguyi okrutak

		VERB STEM	OBJECT	SUBJECT
ŋgu	=yi	o	-kru	-tak
3SG.F	=ERG.F	strike.IRR	-3SG.F.IRR.O	-2SG.F|3SG.F.IRR.S

'she will hit it/her'

b. NON-FUTURE ŋguyi pokun

		VERB STEM	OBJECT	SUBJECT
ŋgu	=yi	po	-ku	-n
3SG.F	=ERG.F	strike.R	-3SG.F.IRR.O-	-SG|1PL.R.S

'she hit it/her'

Now look at another transitive verb class, this one exemplified by the verb root *wuw* 'carry on shoulder':

(6-2) a. FUTURE ŋguyi wuwkrutak

		VERB STEM	OBJECT	SUBJECT
ŋgu	=yi	wuw	-kru	-tak
3SG.F	=ERG.F	carry_on_shoulder.IRR	-3SG.F.IRR.O	-2SG.F|3SG.F.IRR.S

'she will carry it/her on (her) shoulder'

b. NON-FUTURE ŋguyi puwkun

		VERB STEM	OBJECT	SUBJECT
ŋgu	=yi	puw	-ku	-n
3SG.F	=ERG.F	carry_on_shoulder.R	-3SG.F.R.O	-SG|1PL.R.S

'she carried it/her on (her) shoulder

Once again, note the way the verb stem alternates.

This kind of alternation is patterned and consistent, and it provides the basis for distinguishing class 1 verbs (that alternate between the Ø form of the verb stem in irrealis and *-p-* in realis), and class 2 verbs, which consist of verb stems that alternate between *-w-* in irrealis and *-p-* in realis (the hyphens indicate that both phonemes can occur word-initially or word-medially, depending on the verb in question).

Contrast both of those verb classes with conjugation class 3, which is characterized by a stem alternation between irrealis *a* and realis *ka* and *o* (depending on the subject of the verb).

(6-3) a. FUTURE   *ŋguyi akrutak*

		VERB STEM	OBJECT	SUBJECT
ŋgu	=yi	a	-kru	-tak
3SG.F	=ERG.F	consume.IRR	-3SG.F.IRR.O	-2SG.F|3SG.F.IRR.S

'she will eat it'

b. NON-FUTURE   *ŋguyi okun*

		VERB STEM	OBJECT	SUBJECT
ŋgu	=yi	o	-ku	-n
3SG.F	=ERG.F	consume.R	<3SG.F.R.O>	-SG|1PL.R.S

'she ate it'

c. FUTURE   *ŋiŋi akrunet*

		VERB STEM	OBJECT	SUBJECT
ŋi̇	=ŋi	a	-kru	-net
3SG.M	=ERG.M	consume.IRR	-3SG.F.IRR.O	-1SG.M|3SG.M.IRR.S

'he will eat it'

d. NON-FUTURE *ŋiŋi kakun*

		VERB STEM	OBJECT	SUBJECT
ŋi̇	=ŋi	ka	-ku	-n
3SG.M	=ERG.M	consume.R	<3SG.F.R.O>	-SG|1PL.R.S

'he ate it'

Verb stems in the fourth class of transitive verbs, class 4 verbs, alternate between *r* in irrealis and *t* in realis. They also have an extra subject morpheme in the non-future that alternates between $-n^V-$ and $-t^V-$ and that marks person, gender and number. An example is *rar* 'see':

(6-4) a. FUTURE *ŋguyi nje rarkrutak*

				VERB STEM	OBJECT	SUBJECT
ŋgu	*=yi*	*nje*	*rar*		*-kru*	*-tak*
3SG.F	=ERG.F	dog	see.IRR		-3SG.F.IRR.O	-2SG.F|3SG.F.IRR.S

'she will see the dog'

b. NON-FUTURE *ŋguyi nje tatukun*

				VERB STEM	SUBJECT	OBJECT
ŋgu	*=yi*	*nje*	*ta*		*-tu*	*-ku*
3SG.F	=ERG.F	dog	see.R		-S-	<3SG.F.R.O>
SUBJECT						

-n
-2SG\|3SG.F.R.S
'she saw the dog'

c. FUTURE *ŋiŋi nje rarkrutak*

				VERB STEM	OBJECT	SUBJECT
ŋɨ	*=ŋi*	*nje*	*rar*		*-kru*	*-net*
3SG.M	=ERG.M	dog	see.IRR		-3SG.F.IRR.O	-1SG.M|3SG.M.IRR.S

'he will see the dog'

d. NON-FUTURE *ŋiŋi nje tanukun*

				VERB STEM	SUBJECT	OBJECT
ŋɨ	*=ŋi*	*nje*	*ta*		*-nu*	*-ku*
3SG.M	=ERG.M	dog	see.R		-S	<3SG.F.R.O>
SUBJECT						

-n
-1SG\|1PL\|3SG.M.R.S
'he saw the dog'

The final class of transitive verbs, class 5, is the simplest verb class. In class 5 verbs, the stem remains the same and does not change between the irrealis and realis statuses. This regularity and simplicity is certainly one reason why all foreign verbs that get incorporated into Tayap become inflected as class 5 verbs.[1] It is also why speakers younger than thirty tend to conjugate all transitive verbs as though they belonged to this verb class.

---

[1] The single exception to this generalization is the verb *mwanambrir* 'be jealous of'. This is a Kopar-language verb that has become incorporated into Tayap as a class 4 verb, undoubtedly because of its phonetic form (its root ends in an *r*).

Like class 4 verbs, class 5 verbs are inflected in the non-future tense with discontinuous subject morphemes. Together these mark the subject of a verb. An example of a class 5 transitive verb is *ep* 'return' or 'give back':

(6-5) a. FUTURE *ŋguyi pande epkrutak*

			VERB STEM	OBJECT	SUBJECT
ŋgu	*=yi*	*pande*	*ep*	*-kru*	*-tak*
3SG.F	=ERG.F	axe	give_back.IRR	-3SG.F.IRR.O	-2SG.F|3SG.F.IRR.S

'she will return the axe'

b. NON-FUTURE *ŋguyi pande eptukun*

			VERB STEM	SUBJECT	OBJECT
ŋgu	*=yi*	*pande*	*ep*	*-tu*	*-ku-*
3SG.F	=ERG.F	AXE	give_back.IRR	-S	<3SG.F.R.O>
SUBJECT					

-n
-2SG|3SG.F.R.S
'she returned the axe'

c. NON-FUTURE *ɲiɲi pande epnukun*

			VERB STEM	SUBJECT	OBJECT
ɲi	*=ɲi*	*pande*	*ep*	*-nu*	*-ku-*
3SG.M	=ERG.M	AXE	give_back.IRR	-S	<3SG.F.R.O>
SUBJECT					

-n
-1SG|3SG.M|
1PL.R.S
'he returned the axe'

All transitive verbs can be assigned to one of the five verb conjugation classes based on:
(a) the pattern of alternation that occurs between the realis and irrealis verb stems;
(b) the phonetic shape of the verb stem in its realis forms.

What makes this system difficult for young speakers of the language is that there is little predictability about which verbs fall into which conjugation classes. For example, most verb stems that begin with *a* are class 3 verbs. However, some, like *and-(p)-o* 'awaken', and *amai-(p)-i* 'search for' are not (they are both class 1 verbs).

Another example: it is impossible to know, if one only hears the non-future form of a verb like *parkun* 'I filled it up', whether the verb is a class 1 verb (in which case the stem would be *ar*), a class 2 verb (in which case the stem would be *war*) or a class 5 verb, in which case the stem would be *par*. (It turns out that 'fill up' is a class 2 verb.)

A similar problem presents itself with a verb like 'let go', 'release'. Even if one knows that a future form of this verb is *orekrutak*, 'she will release it' (or 'you (F) will release it'), one can only guess as to whether its non-future form will be *porekun* (class 1) or *oretukun* (class 5), both of which are entirely possible – but both of which are wrong. It turns out that the verb is a class 1 verb, but the expected *p* appears *after* the *e*, rather than before the *o*, thus rendering *orepekun* ('she released it').

What follows below is detailed discussion of the five classes for transitive verbs.

6.1.1 Class 1: Verb stems that alternate between *p* and ∅

Verbs in this class consist of roots that contain the vowels *o*, *e*, *i* and *u* – in other words, every vowel except *a* and *i*. Verb roots frequently contain several of those vowels, and it is not predictable which of the vowels will appear with the *p*.

In the realis stem, one of the above vowels in the root appears with a *p*. In the irrealis, the *p* and the vowel that follows it does not appear. An example of a class 1 verb is 'strike', which has already been mentioned above (6-1a and b).

In the presentation that follows, the non-future forms are given first as examples of the realis stem, and they are followed by future forms of the same verb as examples of the irrealis stem, in order to clearly illustrate the contrasts that define the different verb classes.

(6-6) a. *o* 'strike' (REALIS)

ŋa =yi po -ku -n
1SG =ERG.F strike.R -3SG.F.R.O -SG|1PL.R.S
'I (M or F) hit it/her'

yuyi	po-ku-n	'you (M or F) hit it/her'
ŋguyi	po-ku-n	'she hit it/her'
ŋiɲi	po-ku-n	'he hit it/her'
yimɲi	po-ku-n	'we hit it/her'
yumɲi	po-ku-rem	'you PL hit it/her'
ŋgigi	po-ku-ro	'they hit it/her'
yim seneyi	po-ku-re	'we two hit it/her'

b. *o* 'strike' (IRREALIS)

ŋa =yi o -kru -net
1SG =ERG.F strike.IRR -3SG.F.IRR.O -1SG.M|3SG.M.IRR.S
'I (M) will hit it/her'

ŋayi	o-kru-nak	'I (F) will hit it/her'
yuyi	o-kru-tet	'you (M) will hit it/her'
yuyi	o-kru-tak	'you (F) will hit it/her'
ŋguyi	o-kru-tak	'she will hit it/her'
ŋiŋi	o-kru-net	'he will hit it/her'
yimyi	o-kru-nak	'we will hit it/her'
yumyi	o-kru-nkem	'you PL will hit it/her'
ŋgigi	o-kru-ndak	'they will hit it/her'
yim seneyi	o-kru-tike	'we two will hit it/her'

The negated form of this verb is *o* + IRR object + *wákare*.

(6-7) a. *o   -kru   wákare*
　　　　hit.IRR -3SG.F.IRR.O   NEG
　　　　'X [i.e. any subject] didn't hit it/her' (or 'won't hit it/her')

　　b. *o   -mbrɨ   wákare*
　　　　hit.IRR -3PL.IRR.O   NEG
　　　　'X [i.e. any subject] didn't hit them' (or 'won't hit them')

　　c. *o   -ru   wákare*
　　　　hit.IRR -2SG.IRR.O   NEG
　　　　'X [i.e. any subject] didn't hit you' (or 'won't hit you')

Examples of other class 1 verbs are:

<u>verbs with a root containing an *e*</u>
andei-(p)-e 'step on'
e 'hold'
er 'close', 'braid'
ke-(p)-e 'pull out', 'extract'
kotar-(p)-e 'ask', 'request'
mbur-(p)-e 'bend'
ore-(p)-e 'let go', 'release'
urek-(p)-e 'turn over'
wawar-(p)-e 'hang up'; 'suspend'
wemb-(p)-e 'chase'

<u>verbs with a root containing an *i*</u>
amai-(p)-i 'search for'
i 'think'

<u>verbs with a root containing an *o*</u>
and-(p)-o 'awaken', 'rouse from sleep'
aru-(p)-o 'await'
kɨnd-(p)-o 'close', 'block'
njaw-(p)-o 'peel'
o 'strike', 'shoot'
trar-(p)-o 'boil meat'
tu-(p)-o 'plant'

<u>verbs with a root containing a *u*</u>
undu 'dig away dirt in search of' (e.g. a brush turkey egg)

(continued)

ir 'laugh at'
mamanj-(p)-i 'show'
mburai-(p)-i 'sweep'
ruwond-(p)-i 'smoke' (i.e. cure)
wit-(p)-i 'string'
wos-(p)-i 'throw away'

A glance through the above examples should make it apparent that it is not possible to predict which vowel in a verb stem will be preceded by a *p* in the realis form.

In the dictionary, verbs are listed under their root forms; that is, in the barest irrealis forms they take when they are negated. A verb like 'strike', therefore, is listed under *o*, along with an entry defining it as a class 1 transitive verb. That 'class 1' means that the verb listed, in its realis form, has a *p* either preceding it, or following it (this position is specified in the entry). If the *p* appears in the middle of the stem, this is indicated by parentheses. For example, the root form of 'ask' is written *kotar-(p)-e*.

Note that this convention is used for citing verbs as *lexemes* in citation form; it is not used in the example sentences.

6.1.1.1 Exceptions to class 1 inflection

There are only five class 1 verbs which have exceptional inflection, and three of these are highly similar. Those three exceptions are:

ŋgadɨr 'pass by'
ŋgadɨr 'defeat'
ŋgodɨr 'request'

These three verbs all have a realis stem with ends in *pi*; however in the irrealis stem, not only is the *p* absent, there is also no *i*. So for example:

(6-8)   NON-FUTURE   FUTURE

        ŋgadɨrpi   -mɨ   -ro   ŋgadɨr   -mrɨ   -ndak
        pass_by.R -1PL.R.O -3PL.R.S   pass_by.IRR -1PL.IRR.O -3PL.IRR.S
        'they passed by us'   'they will pass us by'

Note that if this verb had followed the conventions of class 1, the root would be *ŋgadɨr-(p)-i*, and the future inflection would be *ŋgadɨrimrɨndak*. Instead, there is a Ø where the vowel would be in a class 1 inflection.

The fourth exception is the verb *mbudji* 'send' or 'sell'. This verb root has the stem form *mbuspi* in realis, rendering the following:

(6-9)	NON-FUTURE	FUTURE
	'X sent it'	'X will send it'
ŋayi (1SG.M)	mbuspi-ku-n	mbudji-kru-net
ŋayi (1SG.F)	mbuspi-ku-n	mbudji-kru-nak
yuyi (2SG.M)	mbuspi-ku-n	mbudji-kru-tet
yuyi (2SG.F)	mbuspi-ku-n	mbudji-kru-tak
ŋguyi (3SG.F)	mbuspi-ku-n	mbudji-kru-net
ŋɨŋi (3SG.M)	mbuspi-ku-n	mbudji-kru-tak
yimŋi (1PL)	mbuspi-ku-n	mbudji-kru-nak
yumŋi (2PL)	mbuspi-ku-rem	mbudji-kru-nkem
ŋgɨgi (3PL)	mbuspi-ku-ro	mbudji-kru-ndak
DL	mbuspi-ku-re	mbudji-kru-tike

Negated verb:

(6-10) mbudji   -kru   wákare
        send.IRR -3SG.F.IRR.O NEG
        'X [any subject] didn't send it' (or 'won't send it')

The final exception is the verb *wos-(p)-i* 'get rid of', 'throw away'. This verb is exceptional because in its *irrealis* form, it does not retain the final vowel of the stem (so instead of the predicted *wosi* in IRR, we just have *wos*) this is similar in fact to the first three exceptions:

(6-11)	NON-FUTURE	FUTURE
	'X got rid of it'	'X will get rid of it'
ŋayi (1SG.M)	wospi-ku-n	wos-kru-net
ŋayi (1SG.F)	wospi-ku-n	wos-kru-nak
yuyi (2SG.M)	wospi-ku-n	wos-kru-tet
yuyi (2SG.F)	wospi-ku-n	wos-kru-tak
ŋguyi (3SG.F)	wospi-ku-n	wos-kru-net
ŋɨŋi (3SG.M)	wospi-ku-n	wos-kru-tak
yimŋi (1PL)	wospi-ku-n	wos-kru-nak
yumŋi (2PL)	wospi-ku-rem	wos-kru-nkem
ŋgɨgi (3PL)	wospi-ku-ro	wos-kru-ndak
DL	wospi-ku-re	wos-kru-tike

Negated verb:

(6-12) wos   -kru   wákare
        get_rid_of.IRR -3SG.F.IRR.O   NEG
        'X [any subject] didn't/won't get rid of it'

6.1.2 Class 2: Verb stems that alternate between *p* and *w*

Class 2 verbs consist of verbs that begin with or contain the semivowel *w*. In the realis, this semivowel is replaced by a *p*.

A typical class 2 verb is *woi* 'sweep'.

(6-13) a. *woi* 'sweep' (NON-FUTURE)

ŋa   =yi   poi   -ku   -n
1SG   =ERG.F   sweep.R   -3SG.F.R.O -SG|1PL.R.S
'I (M or F) swept it'

yuyi	poi-ku-n	'you (M or F) swept it'
ŋguyi	poi-ku-n	'she swept it'
ŋɨɲi	poi-ku-n	'he swept it'
yimɲi	poi-ku-n	'we swept it'
yumɲi	poi-ku-rem	'you swept it'
ŋgigi	poi-ku-ro	'they swept it'
yim seneyi	poi-ku-re	'the two of us swept it'

b. *woi* 'sweep' (FUTURE)

ŋa   =yi   woi   -kru   -net
1SG   =ERG.F   sweep.IRR   -3SG.F.IRR.O -1SG.M|3SG.M.IRR.S
'I (M) will sweep it'

ŋayi	woi-kru-nak	'I (F) will sweep it'
yuyi	woi-kru-tet	'you (M) will sweep it'
yuyi	woi-kru-tak	'you (F) will sweep it'
ŋguyi	woi-kru-tak	'she will sweep it'
ŋɨɲi	woi-kru-net	'he will sweep it'
yimɲi	woi-kru-nak	'we will sweep it'
yumɲi	woi-kru-nkem	'you PL will sweep it'
ŋgigi	woi-kru-ndak	'they will sweep it'
yim seneyi	woi-kru-tike	'the two of us will sweep it'

The negated form of this verb is *woi* + IRR object + *wákare*.

(6-14) a. woi   -kru   wákare
           sweep.IRR   -3SG.F.IRR.O   NEG
           'X [i.e. any subject] didn't sweep it' (or 'won't sweep it')

    b. woi   -mbri   wákare
       sweep.IRR   -3PL.IRR.O   NEG
       'X [i.e. any subject] didn't sweep them' (or 'won't sweep them')

Examples of other class 2 verbs are:

utɨr-(p/w)-or	'cut into small pieces', 'slice up'
war	'bury'; 'put inside e.g. a basket'; 'scrape or grate, e.g. coconut'
wi-(p/w)-o	'put on top of something'
woi	'roll up'
wur	'dislodge'; 'strain sago'; 'braid a grass skirt'; 'catch something by hooking it'
wuw	'dig a hole'

Just because a verb begins with a semivowel in its root form does not mean that it is a class 2 verb. The following verbs, for example, all begin with *w*, but are not class 2 verbs:

wawar-(p)-e	'hang up', e.g. on a hook (class 1)
wemb-(p)-er	'chase' (class 1)
wure	'worry about'; 'be concerned about' (class 5)

For that reason, the entries in the dictionary make it clear (a) which verbs are class 2 verbs and (b) where in the verb the *p/w* alternation occurs. The verbs are entered in their root form, so a verb like 'sweep' *(p/w)-oi* is entered as *woi* (again, because the negated form of the verb is *woi* + IRREALIS OBJECT). The designation as a 'class 2' verb means that it displays *p/w* alternation.

If the alternation is *word initial*, this isn't marked. If it is *word internal*, this is shown, as it is in the above examples in parenthesis (see *utɨr-(p/w)-or* and *wi-(p/w)-o* above as examples).

6.1.3 Class 1 and 2 verbs in young people's Tayap

All verbs that have different stems in their irrealis and realis forms pose problems for young speakers of Tayap. What generally happens whenever young speakers are unsure of a form is that they take the irrealis stem (which is the same as the verb root) and inflect that stem with realis morphology – that is, with object and subject morphemes marked for realis status.

So a class 2 verb like *war* 'fill' will be inflected as

(6-15) a. **war   -ku   -n*
fill.IRR -3SG.F.R.O -SG|1PL.R.S
'I filled it'

instead of the correct form, which is:

b. *par   -ku   -n*
fill.R -3SG.F.R.O -SG|1PL.R.S
'I filled it'

An incorrect form like **warkun* indicates that the speaker is using the verb root, *war*, as the basis for inflection. All young people do this, and this kind of error demonstrates a central feature of how young speakers produce Tayap verb morphology: they clearly perceive the morphological structure of verbs but they are unable to produce them correctly.

The speaker who produced **warkun* possibly had a sense that the verb she wanted is associated with both the semivowel *w* and the plosive *p*. Having heard *parkun* ('I filled it'), *warkrutak* ('she will fill it', or 'you (F) will fill it') and *warkru wákare* ('X won't fill it) all her life, the speaker who produced this utterance probably intuitively knew the different forms that this verb can take. She has not analyzed the different sounds as signifying different tenses and statuses, and so what she ends up producing is a verb that mixes together realis and irrealis forms and results in an ungrammatical neologism.

Young speakers who attempt to inflect class 1 or 2 verbs that they do not automatically know do one of three things:

The first thing they can do is illustrated by the above example: they include both the irrealis and realis forms in the same verb. Other examples are **wurpukun* (instead of *puwkun*; from *wuw* 'carry on shoulder') and **woipokun* (instead of *poikun*; from *woi* 'roll').

The second strategy is to conjugate the class 1 or 2 verb as though it were a class 5 verb. This means treating the verb root as though it is invariant, and also using a discontinuous subject marker in the non-future. So a class 1 verb like *kotar-(p)-e* 'ask' becomes **kotar* and is inflected as:

(6-16) a. **kotar -tu -ku   -n*
ask.IRR -S <3SG.F.R.O> -2SG|3SG.R.S
'she asked her'

instead of the correct form:

> b. kotarpe   -ku   -n
>   ask.R   -3SG.F.R.O   -SG|1PL.R.S
>   'she asked her'

The ungrammatical verb *kotar-tu-ku-n* is a perfectly correctly formed class 5 verb (see below, Section 6.1.7). The problem is that the verb in question, *kotar-(p)-e-*, is a class 1 verb, not a class 5 verb.

At the same time, however, it is important to note that anyone hearing the ungrammatical verb *kotar-tu-ku-n* will have no trouble understanding its meaning. The verb root *kotar* means 'query'. It derives the noun 'question' (as *kotarŋgar*) and the intransitive verb 'ask', *kotarki*. Because this basic meaning of the verb root is known to everyone, it does not make a great deal of difference for comprehension if the verb is conjugated as a class 1 verb or as a class 5 verb.

This kind of separable relationship between the meaning of a verb root and the details of its inflection will likely lead to the attrition of class 1 and 2 verbs. When it doesn't matter is if a verb is inflected as *mbuspiŋgin* (class 1, *mbus-(p)-i* 'send') or *mbustiŋgin* ('send' inflected as a class 5 verb), the less regular inflection will inexorably decline in use in the speech of young speakers who have not learned it.

At the same time as young speakers simplify Tayap verbal morphology in this way – that is, treating verbs of other classes as though they were all class 5 verbs – there is also a competing tendency to insert a *p* in verbs that do not take one. So some young speakers produce forms like the following:

(6-17) a. *moserpi   -ku   -n
          buy.R   -3SG.F.R.O   -SG|1PL.R.S
          'I bought it'

instead of

> b. mose   -nu   -ku   -n
>   buy.R   -S   <3SG.F.R.O>   -1SG.M|3SG.M|1PL.R.S
>   'I bought it'
>   verb root *moser* (class 4)

(6-18) a. *andpi   -ku   -n
          follow.R <3SG.F.R.O>   - SG|1PL.R.S
          'I followed her'

instead of

b. *kandu*   -*ku*   -*n*
   follow.R   <3SG.F.R.O>   -1SG|2SG|3SG.M|1PL.R.S
   'I followed her'
   verb root *andu-* (class 3)

Both (6-17a and 6-18a) are inflected as class 1 verbs in the non-future tense, despite the fact that *moser* 'buy' is a class 4 verb and *andu* 'follow' is a class 3 verb. These cases exhibit the *opposite* of the tendency just discussed: instead of collapsing class 1 and 2 verbs into class 5 verbs, verbs from other classes become incorporated into class 1 and 2 verbs.

There may have always been some free variation in Tayap on this count. In the speech of the oldest Tayap speakers, for example, I recorded two words for the verb 'sweep'; one *mburai* (class 5) and the other *mburai-(p)-i* (class 1). The difference in non-future inflection between these two verbs is the element that directly follows the stem: in the first verb that is *n* or *t* plus a vowel, in the second verb it is a *p*.

So using the first verb, one would say that a woman *mburai**tu**kun* her house; using the second, one would say she *mburai**pi**kun*.

When I asked if these two forms meant anything different the oldest speakers in the village told me no, they were exact synonyms. And that they were both correct.

The co-existence of two different forms of the same verb suggests that there may have always been some accepted variation in the classification of verbs as class 5 or class 1 verbs. If this is the case, then it seems that some young speakers have honed in on that variation and exploited it. They inflect verbs as class 1 verbs (i.e. inserting a *p* in the non-future) much less frequently than they simply collapse all verbs into class 5 verbs. But the fact that they can create class 1 verbs out of verb roots from other classes shows, once again, that young speakers possess a broad repertoire of grammatical competence in Tayap. What they lack is productive ability.

The third strategy that young speakers use when they are unsure of how to conjugate a class 1 or 2 verb in the non-future is to inflect it in the progressive aspect. This often makes little semantic sense. But as is discussed in Section 8.3.1, the progressive aspect is an "easy" inflectional form – all one needs to know is three things: (1) the irrealis stem form of the verb; (2) the benefactive object (which in most cases will be -*kwan* '3SG.F.BEN.R.O'); and (3) the correct form of the verb 'be'. This relative morphological transparency appeals to younger speakers and allows them to use verbs they otherwise would have a hard time inflecting.

Thus, rather than tackling the class 2 verb *war* 'grate', to generate the correct non-future form *parkun* 'I grated it', or the class 1 verb *o* 'shoot', to generate the correct non-future form *pokun* 'I shot it', young speakers telling stories about their actions and adventures say things like the following:

(6-19) a. war   -kwan   -kuk
           grate.IRR   -3SG.F.BEN.R.O   -be.1SG.F.R.S
           'I (F) was grating it'

     b. o   -kwan   -kut
         strike.IRR   -3SG.F.BEN.R.O   - be.SG.M.R.S
         'I (M) was shooting it'

These are perfectly formed progressives. However, the context in which they occurred demanded the non-future tense. But by inflecting the verbs in the progressive aspect, the speakers who needed them were at least able to use them. This phenomenon illustrates a general rule of grammatical decay in Tayap, namely: the weaker the speaker, the more instances of the progressive aspect that speaker will use (see also Section 8.3.1).

6.1.4 Class 3: Verb roots that begin with or contain *a* and alternate between *ka* and *o* in the realis

The majority of the verbs in this class begin with *a*, but some do not, although they all contain an *a* in the verb root. In the realis status, these verbs have suppletive or partially suppletive stems:

ŋa 'I'
yu 'you'
ŋi 'he'   } *a* in the root becomes *ka*
yim 'we'
yum 'you PL'

ŋgu 'she'
ŋgi 'they'   } *a* in the root becomes *o*
DL

In the irrealis status, the *a* is unaltered.
An example of a class 3 verb is *a* 'consume'.

(6-20) a. *a* 'consume' (NON-FUTURE)
           ŋa   =yi   ka   -ku   -n
           1SG   =ERG.F   consume.R   <3SG.F.R.O>   -SG|1PL.R.S
           'I (M or F) ate it'

yuyi	ka-ku-n	'you ate it' (M or F subject)
ŋguyi	o-ku-n	'she ate it'
ɲiɲi	ka-ku-n	'he ate it'
yimɲi	ka-ku-n	'we ate it'
yumɲi	ka-ku-rem	'you PL ate it'
ŋgigi	o-ku-ro	'they ate it'
yim seneyi	o-ku-re	'we two ate it'

b. *a-* 'consume' (FUTURE)

ŋa	=yi	a	-kru	-net
1SG	=ERG.F	consume.IRR	-3SG.F.IRR.O	-1SG.M|3SG.M.IRR.S

'I (M) will eat it'

ŋayi	a-kru-nak	'I (F) will eat it'
yuyi	a-kru-tet	'you (M) will eat it'
yuyi	a-kru-tak	'you (F) will eat it'
ŋguyi	a-kru-tak	'she will eat it'
ɲiɲi	a-kru-net	'he will eat it'
yimɲi	a-kru-nak	'we will eat it'
yumɲi	a-kru-nkem	'you PL will eat it'
ŋgigi	a-kru-ndak	'they will eat it'
yim seneyi	a-kru-tike	'we two will eat it'

The negated form of this verb is *a* + IRR object + *wákare*.

(6-21) a. | a | -kru | wákare |
| consume.IRR | -3SG.F.IRR.O | NEG |

'X didn't eat it' (or 'won't eat it')

b. | a | -mbɨ | wákare |
| consume.IRR | -3PL.IRR.O | NEG |

'X didn't eat them' (or 'won't eat them')

c. | a | -ŋgrɨ | wákare |
| consume.IRR | -3SG.M.IRR.O | NEG |

'X didn't eat him' (or 'won't eat him')

Examples of other class 3 verbs are:

adu	'break'
apu	'burn'; 'scorch'
ambu	'hide'

andu	'roof a house'; 'gather vegetables'
aŋgu	'pull'
ar	'marry'; 'cut'; 'urinate'; 'defecate'
wirar	'put inside'

6.1.4.1 Exceptions to class 3 inflections

One exceptional class 3 verb is *amɨra* 'bite'. This verb contains two instances of *a*. In a way that is diagnostic of this verb class, one of them (the second *a*) alternates between *ka* and *o*.

What is exceptional is that for 3SG.F, 3PL and DL, the first *a* also changes, as follows:

(6-22)	ŋayi	*amɨr-ka-ku-n*	'I (M or F) bit it'
	yuyi	*amɨr-ka-ku-n*	'you (M or F) bit it'
	ŋiɲi	*amɨr-ka-ku-n*	'he bit it'
	ŋguyi	**o**mɨr-**o**-ku-n	'she bit it'
	yimɲi	*amɨr-ka-ku-n*	'we bit it'
	yumɲi	*amɨr-ka-ku-rem*	'you PL bit it'
	ŋgigi	**o**mɨr-**o**-ku-ro	'they bit it'
	yim seneyi	**o**mɨr-**o**-ku-re	'we two bit it'

There are two possible reasons for this exception. One is that *amɨra* might be a compound verb consisting of two morphemes: the verb *a* 'consume' prefixed with *amɨr*. *Amɨr* does not occur by itself, but Tayap does have an adverbial particle, *mɨr*, which is an intensifier (see Section 3.11.1). So the verb 'bite' might mean something like 'consume with intensity', 'chomp down on', and that word may have acquired a prothetic *a* at some point.[2] This would explain why the word-initial *a* is not consistently treated as part of a verb – one would expect **kamɨr-ka-**

---

[2] This analysis has wider implications for the way that verbs generally have been analyzed throughout this grammar. Both William Foley and Ger Reesink have suggested that Tayap verbs may be similar in structure to the verbs in a language like Kalam, which are constructed around semantic cores that often consist of one or two phonemes (for example, *d-* 'hold', *g-* 'make/happen', *ñ-* 'transfer', *pk-* 'hit') and that classify the event as being of a certain type. These verb roots are modified by verb adjuncts that specify features like manner or effect (see Pawley 2006 for a concise summary). A Tayap verb like *amɨra* 'bite' certainly suggests a similar structure, as do class 1 transitive verbs like *e* 'hold' and *ore-(p)-e* 'let go/release', which suggest a root like *e* 'possess' that is modified by verbal adjuncts (see the examples of verbs after example 6-7). We have not pursued this line of enquiry principally because of the difficulty in applying a semantic core to the apparent generic verbs in Tayap: it isn't clear how one might decide on a semantic

ku-n. It would also explain the reason for the *o* forms: they would be motivated by phonetics (they undergo regressive assimilation with the *o* forms of the inflected verb *a*) rather than morphology.

The second reason could be morphological. The intransitive verb *adɨokɨ* 'trip' behaves like 'bite', in that the initial *a* changes to *o* for 3SG.F, 3PL and dual, but it does not change to *ka*. Like 'bite', 'trip' seems to consist of two conjoined verbs – the initial *adɨ* and the final *okɨ*, which is the verb 'go'. So we get *ŋa adɨmbot* '1SG.M tripped', but *ŋgu odɨwok* 'she tripped'. This suggests that the *ka/o* alteration manifests differently on some complex verb combinations.

Whatever the explanation for a verb like 'bite' may be, it is one that gives speakers trouble. Many quite competent speakers, even if they inflect the second *a* correctly (that is, even if they alternate between *ka* and *o* when inflecting that part of the verb), will often not inflect the initial vowel on *amɨr*. So they will say *ŋguyi amɨr-o-ku-n* 'she bit it' instead of the correct *ŋguyi omɨr-o-ku-n*. Older speakers condemn this as poor Tayap, even if some of them sometimes use this form themselves in unmonitored speech.

In the dictionary, class 3 verbs, like all other verbs, are entered under the form they take when negated.

Thus, a verb like 'consume' is entered as *a*. And 'bite' is *amɨra*.

6.1.5 Class 3 verbs in young people's Tayap

In general, realis forms of class 3 verbs present significant problems to speakers under thirty, who have not acquired the sense of how to pattern the *ka/o* variation. These young speakers tend to correctly identify the stem of these verbs as containing an *a*. But when conjugating those verbs in the non-future tense, they often bypass the *ka/o* alternation and produce a form using the irrealis stem, such as the following:

(6-23) a.   **a-ku-re*

　　　　　　 a　　　　　　　　　　　　　　 -*ku*　　　　　 -*re*
　　　　　　 IRR verb stem 'consume'　 <3SG.F.R.O>　 - DL.R.S
　　　　　　 'the two of us ate it' (the correct form is *o-ku-re*; from the verb stem *a* 'eat')

---

core wide enough to include verbs like 'await' and 'strike', or 'bury' and 'strain sago' but narrow enough to exclude those verbs that do not fall into these classes.

b. *and-pe-ku-n
   and   -pe   -ku   -n
   IRR verb stem 'follow'   -class 1 -p- insertion -3SG.F.R.O   -SG|1PL.R.S
   'I followed it' (the correct form is *kandu-ku-n*; from the verb root *andu* 'follow')

Interestingly, when speakers produce forms like these, they often clearly perceive that something is wrong. In one narrative, for example, a twenty-four-year-old man attempted to inflect the class 3 verb *apu* 'cook' in the first-person non-future. The correct form of this verb is:

(6-24) kapu   -ku   -n
        cook.R   <3SG.F.R.O>   -1SG|2SG|3SG.M|1PL.R.S
        'I cooked it'

Instead of *kapukun*, the young man says the following (the slash in the Tayap sentence indicates a false start):

(6-25) ŋa tamwai *ap/kapoktukundara
        ŋa   tamwai   *ap/kapok -tu -ku   -n   -dara
        1SG   sago_pancake   *'cook'.R -S   <3SG.F.R.O> -2SG|3SG.F.R.S -PERF
        'I cooked three sago pancakes'...

This short utterance contains two morphological errors (it is also an example of the over-extension of the perfect aspect, discussed in Section 5.4.3.2).

First, the young man inflects this verb as a class 5 verb, inserting the subject morpheme *-tu*, which does not occur in non-future transitive verbs belonging to classes 1–3. Furthermore, he gets that morpheme wrong: he wants *-nu*, not *-tu* (see below, Sections 6.1.6–6.1.7).

But it is the verb root that is of interest here, and this is where the speaker runs into problems that he clearly perceives but cannot surmount. He starts by producing "*ap*", which indicates that he knows the root form of verb that he wants (*apu*). He also clearly senses that the verb he intends is a class 3 verb, and will take a *ka* in the non-future. But the stem he then produces is a nonsensical form, "*kapok*".

As soon as he says "*kapoktukundara*", the young man stops himself and looks at a friend, who is the same age as him and who is sitting together with the two of us in my house. The young man signals to his friend with his eyes and a flick of his chin that he wants assistance in inflecting this verb.

The following conversation then ensues, with the ellipses indicating that the speakers trail off in a tone of uncertainty (A is the young man, B is his friend):

(6-26) B (trying to help A but also unable to conjugate the verb): *kapu*...
A: *kapu*...(laughs, giving up)
B: *kapu*...
A: *apotukun* (laughs, guessing)

This process of arriving at the conjugation of class 3 verbs is common among speakers under thirty, and it is illustrative of how they produce morphology in Tayap. It is clear that the root form of the verb is salient to this speaker, as is the fact that the verb changes its stem in the non-future. The process of transforming *apu* to *kapukun*, however, is beyond the reach of these two speakers. What they jointly produce is a series of verbal forms that interestingly contain fragments of all possible permutations of a class 3 verb: the root form *a*; the *ka* inflection; and even the *o* inflection (realized here as the *o* in the made-up verb **apotukun*).

These speakers' passive competence in Tayap clearly gives them possession of all the morphological elements that constitute these verbs. But they lack the means to produce them themselves.

6.1.6 Class 4: Verb roots that alternate between *t* and *r*

Verb roots in this class all begin and/or end with *r*.

In the realis, the *r* of the root changes to a *t*, if it is verb-stem initial. If the *r* occurs at the end of the stem, it is deleted.

Class 4 verbs also do something that the transitive verbs in classes 1–3 do not do: they mark the subject of the verb twice: once with the final subject morphemes that we have already seen in verbs from classes 1–3, and again with a second set of morphemes that occur directly after the verb stem:

ŋa 'I' (M and F)
ŋi 'he'   } -n^v-
yim 'we'
yum 'you PL'

yu 'you' (M and F)
ŋgu 'she'   } -t^v-
ŋgɨ 'they'
DL

Note: The vowel denoted by the raised ^{v} after *n* and *t* is frequently realized as a schwa [ə] or is omitted entirely, see Section 2.4.

The realis stems of class 4 verbs are formed in the following way (note that when glossing the two discontinuous subject morphemes, the first subject morpheme is glossed simply with 's' and the second morpheme with the combined meaning of the two discontinuous morphemes):

VERB STEM.R + SUBJECT.R + OBJECT.R + SUBJECT.R

The object appears in between the two subject markers. This is glossed in angle brackets to show that it intervenes between the discontinuous subject markers. An example of a class 4 verb with a root-initial r is *rambu* 'mark' (in the sense, for example, of 'carve a pattern into an hourglass drum'):

(6-27) a. *rambu-* 'mark' (NON-FUTURE)

ŋa =yi tambu -nu -ku -n
1SG =ERG.F mark.R -S <3SG.F.R.O> -1SG|3SG.M|1PL.R.S
'I (M or F) marked it'

yuyi	tambu-tu-ku-n	'you (M or F) marked it'
ŋguyi	tambu-tu-ku-n	'she marked it'
ɲiɲi	tambu-nu-ku-n	'he marked it'
yimɲi	tambu-nu-ku-n	'we marked it'
yumɲi	tambu-nu-ku-rem	'you PL marked it'
ŋgigi	tambu-tu-ku-ro	'they marked it'
yim seneyi	tambu-tu-ku-re	'we two marked it'

b. *rambu-* 'mark' (FUTURE)

ŋa =yi rambu -kru -net
1SG =ERG.F mark.R -3SG.F.IRR.O -1SG.M|3SG.M.IRR.S
'I (M) will mark it'

ŋayi	rambu-kru-nak	'I (F) will mark it'
yuyi	rambu-kru-tet	'you (M) will mark it'
yuyi	rambu-kru-tak	'you (F) will mark it'
ŋguyi	rambu-kru-tak	'she will mark it'
ɲiɲi	rambu-kru-net	'he will mark it'
yimɲi	rambu-kru-nak	'we will mark it'
yumɲi	rambu-kru-nkem	'you PL will mark it'
ŋgigi	rambu-kru-ndak	'they will mark it'
yim seneyi	rambu-kru-tike	'we two will mark it'

The negated form of this verb is *rambu* + IRR object + *wákare*.

(6-28) a. *rambu   -kru   wákare*
  mark.IRR -3SG.F.IRR.O NEG
  'X didn't mark it' (or 'won't mark it')

    b. *rambu   -mbɨ   wákare*
  mark.IRR -3PL.IRR.O NEG
  'X didn't mark them' (or 'won't mark them')

An example of a class 4 verb with a root-final *r* is *nir* 'do' or 'make':

(6-29) a. *nir* 'do' (NON-FUTURE)
  ŋa =yi ni -nu -ku -n
  1SG =ERG.F do.R -S <3SG.F.R.O> -1SG|3SG.M|1PL.R.S
  'I (M or F) did it'

yuyi	*ni-tu-ku-n*	'you (M or F) did it'
ŋguyi	*ni-tu-ku-n*	'she did it'
ŋɨŋi	*ni-nu-ku-n*	'he did it'
yimŋi	*ni-nu-ku-n*	'we did it'
yumŋi	*ni-nu-ku-rem*	'you PL did it'
ŋgɨgi	*ni-tu-ku-ro*	'they did it'
yim seneyi	*ni-tu-ku-re*	'we two did it'

    b. *nir* 'do' (FUTURE)
  ŋa =yi nir -kru -net
  1SG =ERG.F do.IRR -3SG.F.IRR.O -1SG.M|3SG.M.IRR.S
  'I (M) will do it'

ŋayi	*nir-kru-nak*	'I (F) will do it'
yuyi	*nir-kru-tet*	'you (M) will do it'
yuyi	*nir-kru-tak*	'you (F) will do it'
ŋguyi	*nir-kru-tak*	'she will do it'
ŋɨŋi	*nir-kru-net*	'he will do it'
yimyŋi	*nir-kru-nak*	'we will do it'
yumŋi	*nir-kru-nkem*	'you PL will do it'
ŋgɨgi	*nir-kru-ndak*	'they will do it'
yim seneyi	*nir-kru-tike*	'we two will do it'

The negated form of this verb is *nir* + IRR object + *wákare*.

(6-30) nir   -kru   wákare
        do.IRR -3SG.F.IRR.O   NEG
        'X didn't do it' (or 'won't do it')

Other examples of class 4 verbs are:

korar	'collect'
krar	'chop'
kundar	'cover'
mbar	'plant' (e.g. house posts into the ground)
moser	'buy'
niŋgar	'distribute'
ŋgar	'call out to'
ŋgur	'put'
rar	'see'
roŋgu	'extract from inside the ground or from a hole in a tree'
ru	'wash something'
ruŋgu	'pluck'
rupu	'put on a traditional loincloth or skirt'
rur	'sharpen'
sisir	'sew'
tar	'hear' or 'fetch'
teter	'desire'
wiwir	'blow on'

6.1.6.1 Exception to class 4 inflection

There is a single exception to the class 4 inflection: the verb *ru* 'propel', 'expel', 'throw'. This verb does not take the first part of the discontinuous subject marker:

(6-31) a. *yir tukun*
           yir   tu   -ku   -n
           spear   propel.R   <3SG.F.R.O>   -SG|1PL.R.S
           'he threw the spear'

       b. *munjenum aŋge tewtukoya nok tukuro*
           munjenum   aŋge   tew   -tuko   -ya
           man.PL   DX.PL   fear.R -3PL.R -and

           nok   tu   -ku   -ro
           urine   propel.R   <3SG.F.R.O>   -3PL.R.S
           'the men were so afraid they peed themselves'

In the dictionary, class 4 verbs, like all other verbs, are entered under the form they take when negated. This means that verbs with word-initial *r-* are entered under that letter. So a verb like 'see' is *rar*.

6.1.7 Class 5: Verb stems that are identical in realis and irrealis

This is the largest class of verbs in Tayap. It is the least complex class, because verb stems in this class do not change in the realis status. Foreign verbs – which these days means Tok Pisin verbs – are incorporated into this class.

For example, the Tok Pisin verb "winim" ('blow') would appear in a Tayap sentence as follows:

(6-32) *ŋguyi otar* winim*tukun*

ŋgu	=yi	otar	winim	-tu	-ku	-n
3SG.F	=ERG.F	fire	blow	-S	<3SG.F.R.O>	-2SG|3SG.F.R.S

'she blew on the fire'

Nothing in the verb stem changes in the non-future. But like class 4 verbs, the subject of the verb is marked twice, once at the end of the inflected verb, and once in the middle, between the verb stem and the object morpheme, with the following morphemes:

ŋa 'I' (M and F)
ŋi 'he'
yim 'we'
yum 'you PL'
} -*n*ᵛ-

yu 'you' (M and F)
ŋgu 'she'
ŋgi 'they'
DL
} -*t*ᵛ-

Note: The vowel denoted by the raised ᵛ after *n* and *t* is frequently realized as a schwa [ə] or is omitted entirely, see Section 2.4.

An example of a class 5 verb is *nam-* 'tell':

(6-33) a. *nam* 'talk' (NON-FUTURE)

ŋa	=yi	nam	-nu	-ku	-n
1SG	=ERG.F	talk.R	-S	<3SG.F.R.O>	-1SG|3SG.M|1PL.R.S

'I (M or F) told her'

yuyi	nam-tu-ku-n	'you (M or F) told her'
ŋguyi	nam-tu-ku-n	'she told her'
ŋɨŋi	nam-nu-ku-n	'he told her'
yimŋi	nam-nu-ku-n	'we told her'
yumŋi	nam-nu-ku-rem	'you PL told her'
ŋgigi	nam-tu-ku-ro	'they told her'
yim seneyi	nam-tu-ku-re	'we two told her'

    b. *nam* 'tell' (FUTURE)

       ŋa=yi   nam   -kru   -net
       1SG=ERG.F talk.R -3SG.F.IRR.O -1SG.M|3SG.M.IRR.S
       'I (M) will tell her'

ŋayi	nam-kru-nak	'I (F) will tell her'
yuyi	nam-kru-tet	'you (M) will tell her'
yuyi	nam-kru-tak	'you (F) will tell her'
ŋguyi	nam-kru-tak	'she will tell her'
ŋɨŋi	nam-kru-net	'he will tell her'
yimŋi	nam-kru-nak	'we will tell her'
yumŋi	nam-kru-nkem	'you PL will tell her'
ŋgigi	nam-kru-ndak	'they will tell her'
yim seneyi	nam-kru-tike	'we two will tell her'

The negated form of this verb is *nam* + IRR object + *wákare*.

(6-34) a. nam   -kru   wákare
             talk.IRR -3SG.F.IRR.O NEG
             'X didn't tell her'

        b. nam   -mbrɨ   wákare
           talk.IRR -3PL.IRR.O NEG
           'X didn't tell them'

Other examples of class 5 verbs are:

mbɨbiu 'stretch', 'elongate'	*ndok* 'decorate'
mburai 'sweep'	*riri* 'roll vigorously between hands'
adádadɨ 'break off'	*simb* 'organize'
ep 'return an object'	*takwat* 'lie'
katɨp 'cut into small pieces'	*tɨk* 'suppress'
krakrɨ 'break, tear or fold into small bits'	*tumbu* 'capture'

nak 'count'
ndede 'roll off'

trai 'blood let'

6.1.8 Class 4 and 5 verbs in young people's Tayap

The tendency for young speakers to collapse all of Tayap's verb classes into class 5 verbs has already been mentioned several times. The reason for this tendency is simple: the stems of class 5 verbs always remain the same. There is no stem alternation between the realis and the irrealis – no *p* insertion, no *ka/o* alternation, no changes at all.

Class 4 verbs, of course, do undergo stem change between realis and irrealis; indeed, this alternation is what distinguishes them from class 5 verbs. Young people have a difficult time with those changes, and they predictably deal with them by simply ignoring them.

In other words, the *t/r* alternation is overlooked and verbs in the non-future tense are inflected using their irrealis stem forms. This renders verbs like the following:

(6-35) a. *ru   -nu   -ku   -n
         sharpen.IRR -S   <3SG.F.R.O>   -1SG|3SG.M|1PL.R.S
         'I sharpened it'

instead of

b. tu   -nu   -ku   -n
   sharpen.IRR -S-   <3SG.F.R.O>   -1SG|3SG.M|1PL.R.S
   'I sharpened it'

verb root *ru* (class 4)

c. *mbar   -tu   -ku   -n
   stand.IRR -S   <3SG.F.R.O>   -2SG|3SG.F.R.S
   'she stood it up'

instead of

d. mba   -tu   -ku   -n
   stand.IRR -S   <3SG.F.R.O>   -2SG|3SG.F.R.S
   'she stood it up'

verb root *mbar* (class 4)

When young speakers inflect class 4 and class 5 verbs, they sometimes omit the first part of the discontinuous subject morpheme (that is, the -n^V- or -t^V- segment of the verb) and they produce verbs like the following:

(6-36) a. *nam   -gɨ   -n
         talk.R -3SG.M.R.O -SG|1PL.R.S
         'I told him'

instead of

     b.   nam   -nɨ -ŋgɨ   -n
           talk.R -S   <3SG.M.R.O> -1SG|3SG.M|1PL.R.S
           'I told him'
           verb root *nam* (class 5)

More commonly, though, speakers retain the form of the discontinuous subject marking. But the weakest speakers collapse the distinction between -n^V (1SG, 1PL, 2PL, 3SG.M) and -t^V (2SG, 3SG.F, 3PL, DL) in one of two ways:

(1) they replace both -n^V and -t^V with -p^V.

So *namtukun*, which means 'You/she told her', and *namnukun* 'I/he/we told her' both become *nam**p**ukun*;

or else

(2) they collapse the distinction between -n^V and -t^V such that -n^V disappears completely and all forms take -t^V.

So *namnukun* becomes *namtukun*. This is what the young speaker quoted in example (6-25) does – he uses a -t^V form when what is wanted is a -n^V form.

The reason for this it that the imperative verb forms that are most often addressed to children and young people – and to which they need to pay attention if they are not to be chastised, threatened or hit by the older person telling them to do something – are forms that contain -t^V. So children and young people will hear older speakers telling them *yu nam**t**ukun* ('you tell her!') or *yu ŋgri**t**ukun* ('you put it!').

When young speakers struggle to inflect a verb, this imperative form often ends up being the one they produce. It is as though they wrack their brains for the proper form, and come up with the form by which they are addressed. The problem, of course, is that that form denotes particular subjects, and 'I' is not one of them.

6.2 Intransitive verbs in the realis

Intransitive verbs in the realis status display many of the same kinds of stem changes as characterize transitive verbs. For example, some verb stems alternate between *p* and Ø, like class 1 transitive verbs, between *p* and *w*, like class 2 transitive verbs, between *a* and *ka* or *o*, like class 3 transitive verbs, or between *t* and *r*, like class 4 transitive verbs.

Other alternations exist only for intransitive verbs – for example an alternation between *m* in the irrealis and *p* in the realis, as in *memkɨnet* → *pemiet* ('I will get up' → 'I got up').

As is the case with transitive verbs, none of these variations are predictable, and there are many verbs, especially verbs of motion, that are irregular. In these verbs, stem changes between irrealis and realis do not adhere to any of the conventions discussed above.

Intransitive verbs in Tayap do not group into distinct conjugation classes as neatly as transitive verbs do. Recall that transitive verbs, whatever changes their verb stems may undergo, all take the same object morphemes. Their subject morphemes also remain largely the same; the only difference being that class 4 and 5 verbs take discontinuous subject morphemes. But even those discontinuous subject morphemes have regular and predictable forms.

Intransitive verbs are different. There is little or no patterned correspondence between how a verb stem alters between irrealis and realis – say, for example the *m/p* alternation just mentioned – and the subject endings taken by that verb. Compare, for example, the following two verbs, 'get up' and 'stand':

FUTURE
(6-37) a. *memkɨnet*
  mem   -kɨ   -net
  get_up.IRR   -IRR   -1SG.M|3SG.M.IRR
  'I (M) will get up' or 'he will get up'

NON-FUTURE
b. *pemiet*
  pem   -iet
  get_up.R   -SG.M.R
  'I (M) got up', 'he got up' 'you (M) got up'

FUTURE

(6-38) a. *muŋukunet*
       muŋu   -*ku*   -*net*
       stand_up.IRR -IRR -1SG.M|3SG.M.IRR
       'I (M) will stand up' or 'he will stand up'

NON-FUTURE

b. *puŋot*
    puŋ   -*ot*
    stand_up.R -SG.M.R
    'I (M) stood up', 'he stood up', 'you (M) stood up'

Notice that even though both of these verb stems alternate between *m* in irrealis and *p* in the realis, their final subject endings in the non-future are different from one another: -*iet* in one case and -*ot* in the other. This lack of patterned relation between stem alternation and subject endings is the reason intransitive verbs are not classified here into "conjugation classes".

Instead, they are labeled with the looser term "conjugation groups" and identified here and in the dictionary by the variation in endings that they exhibit in the 1SG masculine and feminine.

6.2.1 Four basic groups of intransitive verbs

Intransitive verbs have four basic sets of suffixes used on the realis stem to encode the person, gender and number of the subject. They are as follows:

	INTRANSITIVE VERB REALIS SUBJECT ENDING WITH EXAMPLE			
	Group I -*net*/-*nak* *ketukki* 'cough'	Group II -*iet*/-*iek* *eiwki* 'wash sago'	Group III -*pet*/-*pek* *waruk-(p)-eki* 'turn back'	Group IV -*ot*/-*ok* *irki* 'laugh'
ŋa 1SG	*ketuk-net* (M) *ketuk-nak* (F)	*peiw-iet* (M) *peiw-iek* (F)	*waruk-pet* (M) *waruk-pek* (F)	*pir-ot* (M) *pir-ok* (F)
yu 2SG	*ketuk-tet* (M) *ketuk-tak* (F)	*peiw-iet* (M) *peiw-iek* (F)	*waruk-pet* (M) *waruk-pek* (F)	*pir-ot* (M) *pir-ok* (F)

(continued)

	INTRANSITIVE VERB REALIS SUBJECT ENDING WITH EXAMPLE			
	Group I -net/-nak ketukɨ 'cough'	Group II -iet/-iek eiwkɨ 'wash sago'	Group III -pet/-pek waruk-(p)-ekɨ 'turn back'	Group IV -ot/-ok irkɨ 'laugh'
ŋɨ 3SG.M	ketuk-net	peiw-iet	waruk-pet	pir-ot
ŋgu 3SG.F	ketuk-tak	peiw-iek	waruk-pek	pir-ok
yim 1PL	ketuk-nak	peiw-iek	waruk-pek	pir-ok
yum 2PL	ketuk-nkem	peiw-kem	waruk-pekem	pir-kem
ŋgɨ 3PL	ketuk-tuko	peiw-ko	waruk-peko	pir-ko
DL	ketuk-tike	peiw-ke	waruk-peke	pir-ke

Note: In this grammar and in the dictionary, the root form of the intransitive verb is *usually* (see 8.2.1) written with its irrealis marker (-kɨ, -ki or -ku), for two reasons: (a) in order to make it easier to tell the difference between intransitive verbs and transitive verbs, which do not have irrealis markers; and (b) to indicate which of the three irrealis morphemes is used on specific intransitive verbs. In addition, note that the various stem alternations such as (p/Ø), (p/w), (p/m), etc. are indicated in the dictionary, under the proper entry. So the entry for *eiwkɨ*, for example, looks like this: **eiwkɨ** *v.i.* (**peiwiet/peiwiek, ŋgɨ peiwko**), wash sago pith; *wasim saksak*.

It is evident that all the endings in the four groups listed above are variants of the following endings:

1SG.F, 2SG.F, 1PL → k
1SG.M, 2SG.M → t
2PL → kem
3PL → ko
DL → ke

Most intransitive verbs in Tayap fall into one of the above conjugation groups of verbs. Below are some examples of verb roots that are inflected according to the patterns listed above:

Group I, -net/-nak
Most verbs that have been zero-derived from nouns are inflected according to this pattern.

eiarkɨ 'cry'
isuwokkɨ 'sneeze'

Group II, -iet/-iek
Many, but not all, verbs with roots that begin with *p* in the realis are inflected according to this pattern.

indɨkɨ 'fuck'
imbɨkɨ 'fly'

mbabuŋkɨ 'scorch'
ŋgrukkɨ 'snore'
pisimbkɨ 'rot'
prukkɨ 'work'
punatkɨ 'mourn'
pwapkɨ 'get angry'
waikɨ 'walk around'
warakkɨ 'converse'

ipɨkɨ 'burn'
osikɨ 'cross over'
memkɨ 'get up'
papku 'pierce'
tuwku 'wash'
warkɨ 'net'
wawku 'stick to', 'adhere'

Group III, -pet/-pek
emrarkɨ 'play'
ke-(p/w)-ekɨ 'remove', 'extract'
kotarkɨ 'ask'
mbur-(p)-ekɨ 'bend'
urek-(p)-ekɨ 'turn'
wawar-(p)-eikɨ 'hang up'

Group IV, -ot/-ok
aru-(p)-okɨ 'wait'
erkɨ 'intertwine'
muŋguku 'stand'
nunum-(p)-okɨ 'run'
rɨr-(p)-orkɨ 'kick legs about', e.g. in a tantrum
wuwku 'ascend'

6.2.2 Subgroups of intransitive verbs

In addition to the basic inflectional patterns outlined above, there are also subgroups and exceptions. The subgroups are as follows:

6.2.2.1 Group IIa, verb stems that begin with *a*

If the verb takes the group II -iet/-iek endings and the root begins with *a*, the following alternations occur in the realis, exemplified by *arkɨ-* 'go down'.

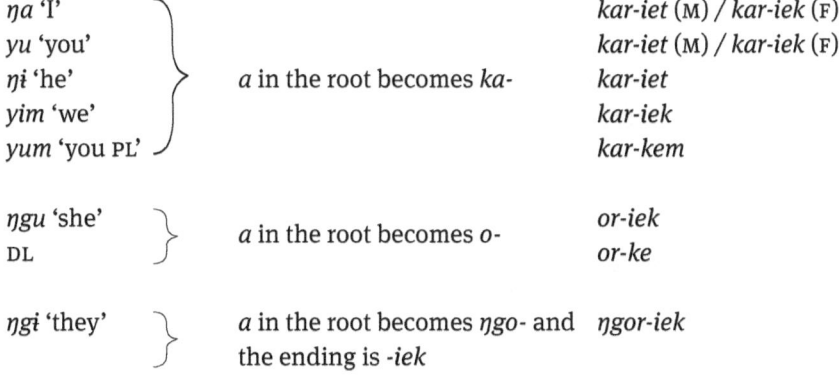

ŋa 'I'   kar-iet (M) / kar-iek (F)
yu 'you'   kar-iet (M) / kar-iek (F)
ŋɨ 'he'   *a* in the root becomes *ka-*   kar-iet
yim 'we'   kar-iek
yum 'you PL'   kar-kem

ŋgu 'she'   *a* in the root becomes *o-*   or-iek
DL   or-ke

ŋgɨ 'they'   *a* in the root becomes *ŋgo-* and ŋgor-iek
                 the ending is *-iek*

Several of the verbs in this subgroup have two equally possible forms in the 3PL form: either the above form with *ŋgo-* + *-iek*, or *o-* + *-ko*.

Consider for example *amuku* 'fight':

(6-39) *ŋa* 'I'   *kam-iet* (M) / *kam-iek* (F)
   yu 'you'   *kam-iet* (M) / *kam-iek* (F)
   ŋɨ 'he'   *kam-iet*
   ŋgu 'she'   *om-iek*
   yim 'we'   *kam-iek*
   yum 'you PL' *kam-kem*
   ŋgɨ 'they'   *ŋgom-iek* or *om-ko*
   DL   *om-ke*

6.2.2.2 Group IIb, verb stems that alternate between *t* and *r*

Like class 4 transitive verbs, some intransitive verb stems that begin with *r* change to *t* in the realis. The subject part includes an element that varies between *t* and *n*. For example:

(6-40) *rewkɨ* 'be afraid'
   ŋa 'I'   *tew-niet* (M) / *tew-niek* (F)
   yu 'you'   *tew-niet* (M) / *tew-niek* (F)
   ŋɨ 'he'   *tew-niet*
   ŋgu 'she'   *tew-tiek*
   yim 'we'   *tew-niek*
   yum 'you PL' *tew-nkem*
   ŋgɨ 'they'   *tew-tuko*
   DL   *tew-tike*

6.2.2.3 Group IVa, verb stems that begin with *a*

Here the alternation is the same as in group IIa, above, with the difference that those forms of the verb that there are realized as *o* (i.e. the inflections for 3SG.F and DL) are here realized as *u*, with some other variations. For example:

	arkɨ 'go inside'	*atɨkɨ* 'appear', 'go down'
ŋa 'I'	*kar-ot* (M) / *kar-ok* (F)	*kat-ot* (M) / *kat-ok* (F)
yu 'you'	*kar-ot* (M) / *kar-ok* (F)	*kat-ot* (M) / *kat-ok* (F)
ŋgu 'she'	*ur-ok*	*ut-ok*
ŋɨ 'he'	*kar-ot*	*kat-ot*
yim 'we'	*kar-ok*	*kat-ok*

yum 'you PL'	kar-kem	katɨ-kem
ŋgɨ 'they'	ŋgur-ok	ŋgut-ok
DL	ur-ke	uti-ke

6.2.2.4 Exceptions to the above classes

Exceptions that do not fit any of the above patterns are as follows:

	aiki 'come'	okɨ 'go'	aku 'be'	aski 'come outside'/'come down'
ŋa 'I'	mb-et (M) mb-ek (F)	mb-ot (M) mb-ok (F)	ku-t (M) ku-k (F)	kas-et (M) kas-ek (F)
yu 'you'	mb-et (M) mb-ek (F)	mb-ot (M) mb-ok (F)	ku-t (M) ku-k (F)	kas-et (M) kas-ek (F)
ŋgu 'she'	w-ek	w-ok	wu-k³	us-ek
ɲɨ 'he'	mb-et	mb-ot	ku-t	kas-et
yim 'we'	mb-ek	mb-ok	ku-k	kas-ek
yum 'you PL'	mb-ekem	mb-okem	ku-kem	kas-kem
ŋgɨ 'they'	ŋg-wek	ŋg-wok	ŋg-wuk	ŋgus-ek
DL	we-ke	wo-ke	wu-ke	us-ke

	sirki 'descend'	taki 'sleep'	tutuku 'sit'	wurkɨ 'go up'
ŋa 'I'	si-niet (M) si-niek (F)	ta-t (M) ta-k (F)	tut-ot (M) tut-ok (F)	pr-iet (M) pr-iek (F)
yu 'you'	si-siet (M) si-siek (F)	ta-t (M) ta-k (F)	tut-ot (M) tut-ok (F)	pr-iet (M) pr-iek (F)
ŋgu 'she'	si-siek	ta-k	tut-ok	pr-iek
ɲɨ 'he'	si-niet	ta-t	tut-ot	pr-iet
yim 'we'	si-niek	ta-k	tut-ok	pr-iek
yum 'you PL'	si-nkem	ta-kem	tutu-kem	pr-ɨkem
ŋgɨ 'they'	si-siko	ta-ko	tutu-ko	pɨr-ko
DL	si-sike	ta-ke	tutu-ke	pɨr-ke

---

3 This form is always realized as -uk in e.g. progressive constructions. See e.g. (8-27c, 8-29b and 8-30b).

6.2.3 Intransitive verbs in young people's Tayap

Intransitive verbs present young speakers with even greater problems than transitive verbs. The unpredictable nature of the subject endings, as well as many of the stem changes between the irrealis and the realis forms, leave increased scope for uncertainty and mistakes.

Many of the mistakes that young speakers make when inflecting intransitive verbs are similar to the errors they make when they try to inflect transitive verbs. Verb stem alternations are often disregarded, and young speakers inflect verbs by mixing irrealis stems with realis subject endings. Examples are:

(6-41) a. *muŋg   -ot
          stand.IRR -SG.M.R
          'he stood'

instead of

       b. puŋg   -ot
          stand.R -SG.M.R
          'he stood'
          verb root *muŋguku* 'stand'

(6-42) a. *rip   -tike
          go_first.IRR -DL.R
          'they two went first'

instead of

       b. tip   -tike
          go_first.R -DL.R
          'they two went first'
          verb root *ripki* 'stand'

(6-43) a. *amb   -tak
          hide.IRR -2SG|3SG.F.R
          'she hid'

instead of

b. *ombiek*
   hide.R.3SG.F.|1PL.R
   'she hid'
   verb root *ambuku* 'hide'

Looking at the verb stems in the (b) examples here and comparing them to the forms that young speakers produce in the corresponding (a) examples, it is clear that the young speakers have a strong sense of the root forms of the verbs they want to inflect. Once again, though, they lack the ability to produce the correct inflections. In many cases, the forms they produce are intelligible – anyone hearing *muŋgot* or *riptike* in the context of a story would have little difficulty understanding it. Other verbs that undergo both stem changes and less common inflectional forms, like *ambuku* 'hide', present greater challenges to comprehension.

Example (6-43) above with *ambuku* 'hide' illustrates another feature of how young speakers inflect intransitive verbs. Just as these speakers show a strong tendency to collapse all classes of transitive verbs and inflect them as though they were class 5 verbs, so do they tend, when they inflect intransitive verbs, to treat them all as though they belonged to group I (see Section 6.2.1).

So an irregular verb like *taki* 'sleep' will be realized as *tatet* 'you (M) slept' instead of the correct *tat*, and a verb with a regular but non-transparent inflectional pattern like the one above, *ombiek* 'she hid', will be regularized to *ambtak*.

Group I intransitive verbs take subject endings that are the most common ones for intransitive verbs. Three characteristics of the subject endings in this group make them particularly salient for young speakers. The first is that they are, precisely, the most common subject endings that affix to intransitive verbs.

The second reason for their salience is the fact that they are identical in form to the subject endings that affix to verbs in the future tense. So compare the following:

Pronoun	Subject endings for group I intransitive verbs in realis	Subject endings for all verbs (both intransitive and transitive) inflected in irrealis (see Table 5.2 and 5.3)
ŋa 'I'	-*net* (M)	-*net* (M)
	-*nak* (F)	-*nak* (F)
yu 'you'	-*tet* (M)	-*tet* (M)
	-*tak* (F)	-*tak* (F)

(continued)

Pronoun	Subject endings for group I intransitive verbs in realis	Subject endings for all verbs (both intransitive and transitive) inflected in irrealis (see Table 5.2 and 5.3)
ŋgu 'she'	-tak	-tak
ŋi 'he'	-net	-net
yim 'we'	-nak	-nak
yum 'you PL'	-nkem	-nkem
ŋgi 'they'	-tuko	-tuko/-ndak
DL	-tike	-tike/-nkem

That these endings occur so frequently in Tayap makes them readily available for young speakers to access when they are trying to conjugate a verb with the correct subject ending.

The third reason why the subject endings listed above are particularly salient for young speakers is because several of the forms are also identical to the imperative endings of intransitive verbs – even those verbs that have other subject endings in the realis.

So in the imperative mood, even a verb as irregular as *okɨ* 'go' takes a regular ending and becomes *o-tet* ('go.SBJ-2SG.M.R') or *o-tak* ('go.SBJ-2SG.F.R') or *o-nkem* ('go.SBJ-2PL.R').

Following this pattern, the imperative command telling a female to hide is *amb-tak* (from the verb root *ambuku*). This is exactly the form that the speaker who wanted to say 'she hid' produced in a narrative. The form is incorrect, but the reason she chose it, and not some other form, is clear.

Intransitive verbs of motion present special problems for young speakers of Tayap. A language like English uses a wide range of prepositions to encode various kinds of motion. So English speakers say 'go up', 'go down', 'go across', 'go around', 'go first', 'go inside' and so on. Tayap has separate verbs for all of those motions (and many more): *wurkɨ* 'go up in a direction', *wuwku* 'ascend', *askɨ* 'go down in a direction', *sirkɨ* 'descend', *utak-(p)-oskɨ* 'go across', *ripikɨ* 'go first', *arkɨ* 'go inside'. All those verbs either change their stem form – often dramatically – in the realis status and/or they have irregular and unpredictable inflections. An example is the common verb 'go', which has a stem form of *okɨ* in the irrealis, but which in the realis becomes *mbot* 'he goes' (or 'I (M) go' or 'you (M) go'), *wok* 'she goes', *ŋgwok* 'they go', etc.

The unpredictability and irregularity of verbs of motion has resulted in their becoming relatively scarce in the speech of speakers under thirty. The weakest speakers get by with just two verbs of motion: *okɨ* 'go' and *aikɨ* 'come'. The nature of speakers' narratives sometimes forces them to attempt other verbs, like *sirkɨ* 'descend' (if the narrator has someone up a tree) or *arkɨ* 'go inside' (if the narrator is talking about going inside a particular area of rainforest where a pig has been speared or a venomous snake spotted). But young speakers' attempts to inflect those verbs are often either not correct or are arrived at only after discussion with friends.

Even the common verbs 'go' and 'come' present many young speakers with problems as soon as they have to inflect the verb for a person other than the singular 'I', 'you', 'he', 'she' or 'we' (whose subject ending is always the same as the 1SG.F ending). The inflections for 2PL, 3PL and dual – all of which are quite different from the other subject endings – tend to be avoided, and when they do occur they tend to be either wrong or the result of much back-and-forth negotiation among the narrator and his or her friends.

The dual form, in particular, seems moribund. It should have occurred in many of the narratives I collected, because many young people talked about how they did something in the rainforest or the mangrove swamp together with one close friend. The overwhelming tendency in those narratives, though, was to use the 1PL 'we' form of the verb instead of the dual – so speakers said *yim mbok* 'we went' or *yim kuk* 'we were', when what they wanted was *yim woke* 'we two went' and *yim wuke* 'we two were'.

A final strong tendency in regards to intransitive verbs is phonological. Young speakers frequently reduce the number of vowels that occur in a verb. Particularly vulnerable is word medial *i*, which often gets eliminated, and the vowel cluster *ie*, which often gets reduced to *e*. So for example a verb with a vowel cluster like *tewtiek* 'she ran away' becomes *tewtek* or *tetwek*. *Priek* 'she went down' becomes *prek*, and so on.

This is a phonological process that probably has been going on in Tayap for some time. In the 1980s, I recorded senior men who consistently said things like *katititet* 'he fell'. In other words, their versions of these verbs had *more* word-medial vowels than are present in the speech of even the oldest speakers today. What seems to have happened in Tayap is that medial syllables have undergone a steady process of reduction.

(6-44) 'he fell'   *katititet* → *katitet* → *katet*
senior men's Tayap in the 1980s   fluent speakers' Tayap in 2009   young people's Tayap in 2009

7 Mood

Mood is the name given to the ways a language grammatically encodes a speaker's attitude toward an utterance. How does a speaker issue a command or express a wish? Voice a doubt or assert a fact? English accomplishes many of these kinds of speech acts with modal verbs like 'can', 'will' and 'must'. Tayap expresses them with particular kinds of verbal morphology. The declarative or indicative mood (i.e. making a statement) has been presented this grammar. It is not morphologically marked in Tayap. The interrogative mood is expressed with the interrogative clitic =*ke*, discussed in Section 3.9.

Other moods that are indicated through particular morphology on a verb are as follows:
- Subjunctive (including imperative, jussive, indirect commands and wishes) (Section 7.1)
- Prohibitive (Section 7.2)
- Admonitive (Section 7.3)
- Intentional (Section 7.4)
- Benefactive (Section 7.5)

Other free-form mood particles are also discussed (Section 7.6).

Note that the realis/irrealis distinction which is fundamental to so much of Tayap's verbal morphology is considered in this work to be a status distinction rather than a mood distinction, and as such is discussed in Chapters 5 and 6 rather than here. Note also that the realis/irrealis distinction is not available to non-indicative moods apart from the benefactive.

7.1 Subjunctive (SBJ)

Tayap has a distinct set of verb forms that encode a speaker's desire that another person do something. The underlying syntactic structure in which a subjunctive appears is a subordinate clause (i.e. 'I want that X do Y'), but a separate set of subjunctive forms can also occur in a main clause. Since those forms only occur in indirect commands, they are discussed below in Section 7.1.5.

The inflectional pattern for intransitive and transitive verbs in the subjunctive mood is as follows:

TRANSITIVE VERBS	subjunctive verb stem inflected as class 5 verb + realis subject and object endings
INTRANSITIVE VERBS	subjunctive verb stem + realis subject ending

Below are the subjunctive inflections for the intransitive verb *aiki* 'come' and the class 3 transitive verb *a* 'eat'. To clearly see the difference between the subjunctive and the indicative, the indicative inflections of those verbs appear in the two right-hand columns:

(7-1)

	SUBJUNCTIVE		INDICATIVE	
	INTRANSITIVE	TRANSITIVE	INTRANSITIVE	TRANSITIVE
Pronoun	*aiki* 'come'	*a* 'eat'	*aiki* 'come'	*a* 'eat'
	'…that X come'	'…that X eat it'	'X came'	'X ate'
ŋa (M) 'I'	we-net	a-nu-ku-n	mbet	ka-ku-n
ŋa (F) 'I'	we-nak	a-nu-ku-n	mbek	ka-ku-n
yu 'you'	we-tet	a-tu-ku-n	mbet	ka-ku-n
	we-tak	a-tu-ku-n	mbek	ka-ku-n
ŋgu 'she'	we-tak	a-tu-ku-n	wek	o-ku-n
ɲɨ 'he'	we-net	a-nu-ku-n	mbet	ka-ku-n
yim 'we'	we-nak	a-nu-ku-n	mbek	ka-ku-n
yum 'you PL'	we-nkem	a-nu-ku-rem	mbekem	ka-ku-rem
ŋgɨ 'they'	we-ndak	a-tu-ku-ro	ŋgwek	o-ku-ro
DL	we-tike	a-tu-ku-re	weke	o-ku-re

Note (for *we-tet* / *we-tak*): These are the 2SG imperative forms of these verbs.

Note (for *we-nkem*): These are the 2PL imperative forms of these verbs.

A verb like *aiki* 'come' notwithstanding, the subjunctive stem form of most verbs has the same realization as the verb's irrealis stem form. The exceptions to this pattern are discussed in Sections 7.1.2.1 and 7.1.2.2 below.

The subjunctive in Tayap is used to express the following speech acts:
(a) direct imperatives ('Take this food to Kapiru!');
(b) jussive imperatives ('Let her go');
(c) indirect commands ('Tell them to hit him'; 'Make them go away');
(d) wishes ('I want you all to go to Sanae')

Each of these four uses of the subjunctive involves different grammatical and syntactic components. A direct imperative can, by itself, constitute a sentence. Jussive imperatives involve the fixed expression *ŋganokaw*, which does not change for person or number. Indirect commands can be expressed in two ways, one using the subjunctive in both the main clause and the subordinate clause; and one just juxtaposing two independent clauses in the declarative mood. The expression of a wish, similarly, has several forms, only one of which involves the subjunctive.

7.1.2 Imperative

The imperative mood expresses a command that is directly addressed to one person ('you come!') or to several people ('you all come!'). In Tayap there are two kinds of imperatives: positive imperatives – commands to do something – and negative imperatives, commands to *not* do something.

Negative imperatives have a particular morphology and are discussed under prohibitives and admonitives (see Sections 7.2 and 7.3).

Positive imperatives – a command that an addressee perform some action – are realized differently for intransitive and transitive verbs.

7.1.2.1 Intransitive imperatives

The imperative forms of intransitive verbs are the single most salient grammatical feature of Tayap, both for the speakers of Tayap and for everyone else in the lower Sepik area who has ever heard of the language. Whenever Tayap speakers talk about their vernacular, they merrily tell anyone who is willing to listen that Tayap "is broken into a woman's language and a man's language" ("i bruk long tok ples bilong ol meri na tok ples bilong ol man"). If you want to talk to a woman, they explain patiently, you have to use the "women's language" ("tok ples bilong ol meri"). If you want to talk to a man, you have to use the "tok ples bilong ol man".

Anyone who has followed this grammar this far knows that Tayap does indeed have a number of gender-specific forms, such as the difference in first-person forms for intransitive verbs inflected in the non-future tense (a male says *ŋa mbot* 'I went'; a female says *ŋa mbok*; see Section 6.2). But this particular gendered distinction is not primarily what the villagers have in mind when they talk about how their language is broken in two.

Instead, the villagers who describe Tayap in that way are referring to a single feature of grammar, namely the different forms that the imperative of an intransitive verb takes when it is addressed to a woman or to a man. The dramatic way villagers describe this feature of their grammar, however – that you have to speak to men and women using their specific "languages" – makes it seem as though the entire Tayap language is "broken" in two.

The villagers' exegesis carries the unspoken implication that even parts of speech like nouns have female and male forms, and that both those forms must be mastered in order to be able to talk at all. Non-Gapuners who listen to Gapun villagers describe Tayap in this way always react with understandable dismay, and they inevitably shake their heads in wonder that a human language could possibly be so complex. Some of them then go off and augment the complexity further, informing others that, in fact, Tayap is "broken" into four languages: one for women, one for men, one for girls and one for boys.

Gapuners' story about Tayap's difference from other vernacular languages must have arisen because no other language in the area marks gender on the imperative forms of intransitive verbs. This is a salient feature of language because whenever villagers from different places meet, one way many of them enjoy spending time is to quiz one another on what one calls common objects – 'betel nut', 'lime' (for chewing betel nut), 'tobacco', 'pig', 'dog' and 'sago jelly' are the inevitable ones – in their respective vernaculars.

Once these words have been exchanged, many people then go on to ask about simple verbs: "How do you tell someone to come?", they ask each other; "How do you say 'go'?". Anyone asking a Tayap speaker that question will receive the spiel about the vernacular being "broken in two" in response, and so the story about the bizarreness of the little language that really is two – or is it four? – separate languages gets perpetuated and spread throughout the lower Sepik area.

Despite the hype, however, the imperative form of an intransitive verb is a simple construction. All it involves is (a) a verb stem inflected to express a speaker's wish that another person do something – in other words, a verb stem inflected in the subjunctive mood – and (b) a subject ending that marks gender and number. So the imperative for any intransitive verb is formed in the following way (recall that 2nd person dual uses the plural form; see the discussion that precedes example (3-73)):

subjunctive verb stem } + -tet (2SG.M.R)
+ -tak (2SG.F.R)
+ -nkem (2PL.R|DL)

The subjunctive stem of a verb is almost always the same as the form that verb takes in the irrealis status. Examples are:

(7-2) a. MALE   o-tet   muŋgo-tet   pruk-tet
         ADDRESSEE   go.SBJ-2SG.M.R   stand.SBJ-2SG.M.R   work.SBJ-2SG.M.R
                     'You go!'   'You stand!'   'You work!'

      b. FEMALE   o-tak   muŋgo-tak   pruk-tak
         ADDRESSEE   go.SBJ-2SG.F.R   stand.SBJ-2SG.F.R   work.SBJ-2SG.F.R
                     'You go!'   'You stand!'   'You work!'

	c. PLURAL ADDRESSEES	o-nkem go.SBJ-2PL.R 'You all go!'	muŋgo-nkem stand.SBJ-2PL.R 'You all stand!'	pruk-nkem work.SBJ-2PL.R 'You all work!'

In all the examples above, the stem form of the verb in the subjunctive is identical to the stem form of those verbs in the irrealis status. There are exceptions to this pattern (for intransitive verbs; transitive verbs have exceptions discussed in 7.1.2.2), however, such as the following, where the verbs have a subjunctive-specific form:

(7-3) a. *ai* (IRR) 'come' → *we-* (SBJ, so: *we-tet, we-tak, we-nkem*; see example 7-1 above)
b. *tutu* (IRR) 'sit' → *tuto-* (SBJ, so: *tuto-tet, tuto-tak, tuto-nkem*)

Verb roots ending in *r* gain the vowel *e* before the imperative ending, which is also stressed:

(7-4) a. *rar* (IRR) ' look' → *raré-* (SBJ, so: *raré-tet, raré-tak, raré-nkem*)
b. *sir* (IRR) 'descend'→ *siré-* (SBJ, so: *siré-tet, siré-tak, siré-nkem*)

If these exceptions only occurred in the imperative mood, it would be possible to simply classify them as exceptions and maintain that the stem form of an imperative verb is its irrealis form. However, the stem forms of verbs in the imperative mood are also the forms that occur for verbs inflected to express an indirect command (see below 7.1.4). This fact indicates that the underlying form for imperative forms is a subjunctive wish – in other words, 'You go!' takes the grammatical form of '(I want that) you go!'.

For that reason, the stem forms of verbs inflected in the imperative are classified as subjunctive rather than irrealis, even though their realization in speech is most often identical with the irrealis forms.

7.1.2.2 Transitive imperatives

The command form of a transitive verb does not mark the gender of the subject – so villagers' claims that Tayap is "broken in two" doesn't even extend to the imperative forms of transitive verbs. But transitive imperatives do mark the number of the subject and the usual person, number and gender of the object of the verb. They are formed according to the following pattern:

When the addressee is singular:

SUBJUNCTIVE VERB STEM + -tᵛ + REALIS OBJECT + -n

Examples:

(7-5) a. *atukun!*
a -tu -ku -n!
consume.SBJ -S <3SG.F.R.O> -2SG|3SG.F.R.S
'eat it!'

b. *ŋgritukun!*
ŋgri -tu -ku -n!
put.SBJ -S <3SG.F.R.O> -2SG|3SG.F.R.S
'put it!'

c. *ŋgritiŋgin!*
ŋgri -ti -ŋgɨ -n!
put.SBJ -S <3SG.M.R.O> -2SG|3SG.F.R.S
'put him!'

d. *otin!*
o -t -i -n!
strike.SBJ -S <1SG.R.O> -2SG|3SG.F.R.S
'hit me!'

When the addressee is plural:

SUBJUNCTIVE VERB STEM + -nᵛ + REALIS OBJECT + -rem

Examples:

(7-6) a. *ankurem!*
a -n -ku -rem!
consume.SBJ -S <3SG.F.R.O> -2PL.R.S
'you PL eat it!'

b. *munje ide onŋgirem!*
munje ide o -n -ŋgɨ -rem!
man DX.M strike.SBJ -S <3SG.M.R.O> -2PL.R.S
'you PL hit that man!'

c. *oniyem!*
    o   -n   -i   -yem!
    strike.SBJ -S   <1SG.R.O>   -2PL.R.S
    'you PL hit me!'
    Note: After the 1SG object morpheme, *-rem* → *-yem*

An exception to the pattern above is that the subjunctive stems of class 4 verbs lose the final *r*, if they have one, of their irrealis stem. The remaining stem is always stressed. This renders forms such as the following:

			SINGULAR	PLURAL
(7-7)	a.	*korar* 'collect' →	*korá-tukun!*	*korá-nkurem!*
			'you collect it!'	'you PL collect it!'
	b.	*nir* 'do' →	*ní-tukun!*	*ní-nkurem!*
			'you do it!'	'you PL do it!'
	c.	*ŋgar* 'call out' →	*ŋgá-tukun!*	*ŋgá-nkurem!*
			'you call out to her!'	'you PL call out to her!'
	d.	*krar* 'chop' →	*krá-tukun!*	*krá-nkurem!*
			'you chop it!'	'you PL chop it!'
	e.	*moser* 'buy' →	*mosé-tukun!*	*mosé-nkurem!*
			'you buy it!'	'you PL buy it!'

There are three further exceptions among class 4 verbs.
(1) The first is the verb *rar* ('look'). Like its intransitive equivalent (see above example 7-4) this verb retains the final *r* of its irrealis stem and gains the vowel *e* on the end of the subjunctive stem, before the imperative ending, rendering *rarétukun* 'look at it!' and *rarénkurem* 'you PL look at it!'.
(2) The second is the verb *tar*, which means both 'listen, hear' and 'take, fetch'. This verb has the same form for both meanings in all other forms. But in the subjunctive mood, the verb has two different forms. One behaves like class 4 verbs ending in *r* (that is, the *r* disappears), and the other behaves like *rar* (i.e. the *r* stays and gains the vowel *e* before the imperative endings):

(7-8)   *tar* 'listen/hear'   *tar* 'take, fetch'
        tá-tukun!   *taré-tukun!*
        'you listen (to it)!'   'you take it!'

        tá-nkurem!   *taré-nkurem!*
        'you PL listen (to it)!   'you PL take it'

(3) The third exception is the verb *ŋgur* ('put'). This verb stem undergoes both metathesis and its vowel becomes fronted, rendering *ŋgri*. Thus, the imperative forms are *ŋgrítukun* 'you put it!' and *ŋgrínkurem* 'you PL put it!'.

7.1.2.3 The verb 'give'

The imperative form of the transitive verb *i* 'give' takes the form of *is* in the singular and *in* in the plural. 'Give' optionally but usually takes the BEN object forms (see Section 3.2). Examples of some of the imperative forms of 'give' are:

(7-9) SINGULAR ADDRESSEE
     is-iata-n
     give.SBJ-1SG.BEN.O.R-SG|1PL.R
     'you give it to me!'

     PLURAL ADDRESSEE
     in-iat-rem
     give.SBJ-1SG.BEN.O.R-2PL.R
     'you PL give it to me!'

     is-kwata-n
     give.SBJ-3SG.F.BEN.O.R-SG|1PL.R
     'you give it to her!'

     in-kwat-rem
     give.SBJ-3SG.F.BEN.O.R -2PL.R
     'you PL give it to her!'

     is-mbata-n
     give.SBJ-3PL.BEN.O.R-SG|1PL.R
     'you give it to them!'

     in-mbat-rem
     give.SBJ-3PL.BEN.O.R-2PL.R
     'you PL give it to them!'

7.1.3 Jussive imperatives

The jussive imperative 'Let X do Y' is formed with a fixed expression *ŋganokaw*, used for both singular and plural addressees. This expression consists of two parts: the word *ŋganok*, which seems to have no independent meaning but which also occurs in another fixed expression *ŋganokeya* ('poor thing'; see Section 3.10), and the subjunctive stem form of the verb 'be' (*aw*).

Ŋganokaw can be followed by a verb in the subordinate clause inflected in either the subjunctive mood (7-10 a-c) or the future tense (examples 7-10 d-e):

(7-10) a. *ŋganokaw Ndair ambaigaini awnet*
      ŋganokaw Ndair ambagai =ni aw -net
      let   Ndair men's_house =LOC be.SBJ -1SG.M|3SG.M.R
      'let Ndair stay in the men's house'

b. *ŋganokaw ŋiŋi amainukun*
   ŋganokaw   ŋi   =ŋi
   let   3SG   =ERG.M

   amai   *-nu*   *-ku-*   *-n*
   look_for.SBJ   -S   <3SG.F.R.O>   -1SG|3SG.M|1PL.R.S
   'let him look for it'

c. *ŋganokaw Mbanaŋana minjike isŋgatan*
   ŋganokaw   Mbanaŋ   =ana   minjike   is   -ŋgata
   let   Mbanaŋ   =DAT   betel_nut   give.SBJ   -3SG.M.BEN.O.R

   -n
   -SG|1PL.R.S
   'let (him or her) give betel nut to Mbanaŋ'

d. *ŋganokaw and atikitak ŋan*
   ŋganokaw   and   ati   -ki   -tak   ŋan
   let   blood   fall_down.IRR   -IRR   -2SG.F|3SG.F.R   3SG.M.POSS
   'let him bleed' (lit. 'let his blood flow')

e. *ŋganokaw ndugubar mbidkwatitak*
   ŋganokaw   ndugubar   mbid   -kwati   -tak
   let   backbone   pain.IRR   -3SG.F.BEN.O.IRR   -2SG.F|3SG.F.R
   'let her backbone hurt' (i.e. 'I don't care')

7.1.4 Indirect commands

An indirect command is a command to tell somebody else to do something, for example, 'Tell Kasek to go to Wongan' or 'Send them home'. The corresponding direct form of these commands – i.e. 'Go to Wongan!' or 'Go home!' – is discussed above in Section 7.1.2.

In Tayap, indirect commands can be formed in two ways. The first is a paratactic structure: two fully inflected independent clauses, a command clause followed by a future clause, are juxtaposed with no conjunctive morpheme connecting them. For example:

		TELL CLAUSE		COMMAND CLAUSE		
(7-11)		'Tell Kasek		to go'		
a.	*Kasek*	*nam-ti-ŋgi-n*	*ŋi*	*ŋgo*	*o-ki-net*	
	Kasek	talk.SBJ-S<3SG.M.R.O>	3SG.M	DM	go.IRR-IRR-1SG.	
		2SG|3SG.F.R.S			M|3SG.M.R	
	lit. 'tell Kasek...		...he will go'			

b. 'You all tell Mbowdi   to hit them'
   Mbowdi   nam-ni-ŋgi-rem   *ŋɨ   o-mbri-net*
   Mbowdi   talk.SBJ-S<3SG.M.R.O>   3SG.M   strike.IRR-3PL.IRR.O-1SG.M|
            2PL.R.S   3SG.M.R.S
   lit. 'you all tell Mbowdi...   ...he will hit them'

The second way of formulating an indirect command involves inflecting both the verb in the "tell" clause and the verb in the "command" clause in the subjunctive mood. Contrast example (7-11a) above with the following:

(7-12) *Kasek   nam   -gi   o   -net*
        Kasek   talk.SBJ   -3SG.M.R.O   go.SBJ   -1SG.M|3SG.M.R
        'Tell Kasek to go'

Notice that the verb 'talk/tell' in the main clause of (7-12), has no subject morpheme. Comparing 'tell' in (7-11a) with 'tell' in (7-12), we see the following differences:

(7-13) FULL FORM   REDUCED FORM
        nam-ti-ŋgi-n   *nam-gi*
        talk.SBJ-S<3SG.M.R.O>2SG|3SG.F.R.S   talk.SBJ-3SG.M.R.O
        'tell him'   'tell him'

Not only does the reduced form in (7-13) take no subject morpheme; the object morpheme suffixed to the verb stem is realized without prenasalization. This means that what is normally realized as -*ŋgi* '3SG.M.R.O' → -*gi* and what is normally realized as -*mbi* '3PL.R.O' → -*bi*. All other object morphemes retain their regular realis forms.

Now look at the verb in the subordinate clause in (7-12). This form – *o-net* – is what is discussed above in Section 7.1 as the subjunctive form of a verb.

Indirect commands are normally introduced with a verb such as *nam* 'talk/tell'. So, again, to express an indirect command, one usually says either (7-14) or (7-15):

        IMPERATIVE   FUTURE
(7-14) *Kasek   nam-ti-ŋgi-n*   *ŋɨ   ŋgo   o-ki-net*
        Kasek   talk.SBJ-S<3SG.M.R.O>   3SG.M   DM   go.IRR-IRR-1SG.M|3SG.M.R
               2SG|3SG.F.R.S
        'tell Kasek to go' (lit. 'tell Kasek he will go')

	REDUCED FORM	SUBJUNCTIVE
(7-15)	*Kasek nam-gɨ*	*o-net*
	Kasek talk.SBJ-3SG.M.R.O	go.SBJ-1SG.M|3SG.M.R
	'tell Kasek to go' (lit. 'tell Kasek that he go')	

However, indirect commands can also be formulated without an explicit introductory speech verb. In such cases, the indirect command is expressed in a way that makes no explicit mention of who is responsible for carrying out the action.

An example of this was uttered during a discussion of the school in the neighboring village of Wongan that village children had gone to until March 2009, when the teachers suddenly refused to work anymore. The speaker here means that he wants other villagers to get rid of the striking teachers, whom he refers to as 'old' and one of whom he calls by name (the name has been changed):

(7-16) *Aŋɨ rowesamb aŋɨ taman wosmbɨ ondak. Nelson tɨ onet*

Aŋɨ	rowe	-samb	aŋɨ	taman	wos	-mbɨ
DX.PL	old	-PL	DX.PL	all	get_rid_of.SBJ	-3PL.R.O

o	-ndak	Nelson	tɨ	o	-net
go.SBJ	-3PL.R	Nelson	too	go.SBJ	-1SG.M|3SG.M.R

'[Tell] every one of those old teachers to piss off. [Tell] Nelson too to go'.

These could also be analyzed as jussives as described above without *ŋganokaw*, thus "Let the teachers piss off. Let Nelson go too".

Negative indirect commands, like 'I didn't tell Mbawi to go', are formed by negating the main verb (note that it is intransitive) and suffixing the verb in the subordinate clause with the intentional suffix (see Section 7.4 for discussion of how the intentional suffix is used):

(7-17) a. *Sakeyi namkɨ wákare Kunji eŋgrɨnana*

Sake	=yi	nam	-kɨ	wákare	Kunji
Sake	=ERG.F	talk.IRR	-IRR	NEG	Kunji

e	-ŋgrɨ	-nana
hold.IRR	-3SG.M.IRR.O	-INTENT

'Sake didn't say to hold Kunji'

b. *Mbityi namkɨ wákare Kruniŋi Sombaŋ okrunana*

Mbit	=yi	nam	-kɨ	wákare	Kruni	=ŋi
Mbit	=ERG.F	talk.IRR	-IRR	NEG	Kruni	=ERG.M

Sombaŋ	*o*	*-kru*	*-nana*
Sombaŋ	strike.IRR	-3SG.F.IRR.O	-INTENT

'Mbit didn't tell Kruni to hit Sombaŋ'

Commands telling someone else to tell another person *not* to do something, are expressed with the prohibitive, discussed below in Section 7.2.

(7-18) *Mawi namtɨŋgɨn (or nam-gɨ) oŋgarke*

Mawi	nam	-tɨ	-ŋgɨ	-n
Mawi	talk.SBJ	-S	<3SG.M.R.O>	-2SG|3SG.F.R.S

(or	*nam-gɨ*)		*o-ŋgarke*
	talk.SBJ.3SG.M.R.O		go.IRR-PROH

'Tell Mawi not to go'

7.1.5 Expressing a desire for someone else to do something

The final use of the subjunctive in Tayap is in constructions in which a speaker expresses a desire that some action be performed by someone else or something else. Here the subjunctive occurs in the "desire" clause, after an expression of cognition in the main clause. It is the appearance of the verb in its subjunctive form that generates the meaning of the verb in the main clause as one of desire, rather than cognition.

(7-19) a. *ŋa numbwan pikun ŋɨ onet Merewre*

ŋa	numbwan	pi	-ku	-n
1SG	thought	strike.R	-3SG.F.R.O	-SG|1PL.R.S

ŋɨ	o	-net	Merew	=re
3SG.M	go.SBJ	-1SG.M|3SG.M.R	Sanae	=ALL

'I want him to go to Sanae' (lit. 'I struck the thought that he go to Sanae')

b. *ŋɨ numbwan pawrɨktak Arut wetak Tayapre*

ŋɨ	numbwan	pawrɨk	-tak		Arut
3SG.M	thought	strong.R	-2SG.F|3SG.F.R		Arut

we	-tak	*Tayap=re*
come.SBJ	-2SG.F|3SG.F.R	Gapun=ALL

'he really wants Arut to come to Gapun' (lit. 'the thought strongs him that Arut come to Gapun')

This construction using an expression of cognition in the main clause and a subjunctive in the subordinate clause is unusual – examples (7-19a) and (7-19b) are from elicitation sessions with senior men in the 1980s. I have not encountered this construction in any of the conversations or speeches that I have transcribed. Instead, desire predicates are constructed in one of two ways, none of them involving the subjunctive.

The first way of forming a desire predicate is with the verb phrase '*arei* + ergative + *tar*', which literally means 'desire takes'. This is a moribund construction: like examples (7-19a-b) above, my only recorded instances of it are in elicitation sessions in the 1980s with senior informants.

The construction is realized without overt marking on the main clause, and the verb in the subordinate clause is inflected for future tense:

(7-20) *ŋi areiyi tatiŋgin ŋa okinet Potowre*
  ŋi   arei   =yi   ta   -ti   -ŋgi   -n
  3SG.M desire =ERG.F take.R   -S   <3SG.M.R.O> -2SG|3SG.F.R.S

  ŋa   o   -ki   -net   Potow   =re
  1SG go.IRR -IRR -1SG.M|3SG.M.R   Wongan =ALL
  'he wants me to go to Wongan' (lit. 'desire takes him, I will go to Wongan')

The most common way to express the desire that someone or something else do something that you want is to use the verb *nam*, which has the primary meaning of 'talk' or 'tell', but which is also used to mean 'think' (this kind of semantic conflation between verbs like "talk", "tell", "think" and "desire" is common in Papuan languages; Reesink 1993).

Desire predicates with *nam* are constructed the same way as the example above, that is to say with the verb in the subordinate clause inflected in the future tense. Speakers also often use the adverb *nande* 'thusly' to draw attention to the verb of desire, producing sentences like the following:

(7-21) *ŋa nande namnet yu okitet Ombágire*
  ŋa   nande   nam   -net   yu   o   -ki   -tet
  1SG thusly   talk.R -1SG.M|3SG.M.R   2PL go.IRR -IRR -2SG.M

  Ombági=re
  Pankin=ALL
  'I want you to go to Pankin' (lit. 'I say/think thusly: you will go to Pankin')

7.2 Prohibitive (PROH)

In contrast to the imperative mood, which expresses the speaker's command for the addressee to perform a particular action, the prohibitive is a command to *not* perform an action. It can be translated as 'Don't do X', 'Don't dare do X' or 'X is prohibited'. The prohibitive cannot be negated. It is formed as follows:

PERSON
ŋa 'I'
yu 'you'
ŋgu 'she'   IRR verb root + (BEN R object) + *-ŋgarke*
ŋi 'he'
yim 'we'

yum 'you PL' →   IRR verb root + (BEN R object) + *-ŋgremke*
ŋgɨ 'they'   →   IRR verb root + (BEN R object) + *-ŋgroke*
DL   →   IRR verb root + (BEN R object) + *-ŋgreke*

If a speaker includes the benefactive object in this construction, the action is marked as ongoing, in the progressive aspect, so it means 'Don't be doing X!'

(7-22) a. *emarar   -ŋgarke!*
       play.IRR   -PROH.SG|1PL
       'you can't play!' or 'it's forbidden to play!'; said for example to a child during a church service

  b. *minjike   tar   -ŋgroke!*
       betel_nut take.IRR -PROH.3PL
       'they can't take the betel nut!'

  c. *numbwan   mbabasak   -ŋgarke!*
       thought   crazy.IRR   -PROH.SG|1PL
       'don't forget!'

  d. *nime nirkwanŋgarke munjeŋa rawni!*
       nime   nir   -kwa   -ŋgarke   munje   =ŋa
       thusly do.IRR   -3SG.F.BEN.R.O   -PROH.SG1PL   man   =POSS

     raw   =nɨ
     nose =LOC
     'you can't be doing that right in front of a person!'

e. ai   =nɨ   a   -ŋgwarke!
   here =LOC be.IRR   -PROH.SG|1PL
   'you can't be here!'

7.3 Admonitive (ADM)

A structure that is morphologically almost identical to the prohibitive occurs in the modal construction that expresses the non-desirability of an action.

This modality in Tayap has its exact equivalent in the Tok Pisin expression "nogut X", where X denotes an action that the speaker doesn't want to happen, regrets happening, is uncertain has happened or will happen, or when the speaker anticipates or senses that something undesirable will ensue from the action's occurrence. This is a difficult expression to translate, because it can be a warning, as in 'X better not happen/have happened'; a negative hope, as in 'I hope X doesn't happen' (or, 'I hoped X wouldn't happen'); a concern, as in 'May X not happen'; or a meditation, like 'What if X should happen?'. The admonitive cannot be negated.

In Tayap, this construction differs from the prohibitive only in that the final -*ke* of the prohibitive markers is -*ana* in the admonitive, and that there is no benefactive in it:

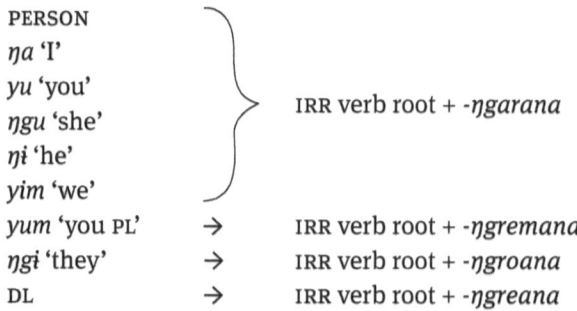

```
PERSON
ŋa 'I'
yu 'you'
ŋgu 'she'            }  IRR verb root + -ŋgarana
ɲi 'he'
yim 'we'
yum 'you PL'    →    IRR verb root + -ŋgremana
ŋgɨ 'they'      →    IRR verb root + -ŋgroana
DL              →    IRR verb root + -ŋgreana
```

Examples:

(7-23) a. ror   aŋgu   eiar   -ŋgarana
          child   DX.F   cry.IRR   -ADM.SG|1PL
          'that girl better not cry' (or else!) or 'let's hope that girl doesn't cry'

       b. yum   awin   tar   -ŋgremana
          2PL   water   take.IRR   -ADM.2PL
          'you all better not take away the water' or 'let's hope you all don't take away the water'

c. *numbwan   reki   yu   ŋgon   niŋg   adɨ   -ŋgarana*
   thought   with   2SG   3SG.F.POSS   bone   break.IRR   -ADM.SG|1PL

   aŋgi
   DX.F
   'look out, be careful you don't break her bone'

The difference between the prohibitive and the admonitive can be illustrated by the following examples:

(7-24) a. *wasow* 'die'
          wasow-ŋgarke   *wasow-ŋgarana*
          die.IRR-PROH   die.IRR-ADM.SG|1PL
          'Don't die!', said in anguish to   'May you not die'; said to someone
          someone who is dying   who is sick

     b. *warak* 'converse'
        warak-ŋgarke   *warak-ŋgarana*
        converse.IRR-PROH   converse.IRR-ADM.SG|1PL
        'Don't talk!', said to someone   'Let's hope you don't talk' or 'You
        who is talking   better not talk'; said to someone who
                                           knows a secret about another person
                                           and is going to visit that person; the
                                           speaker is expressing the hope that
                                           the person addressed won't open his
                                           or her mouth and spill the beans

7.4 Intentional (INTENT)

The intentional mood expresses two kinds of events. The first is actions that are or were intended or desired but that have not been completed or that didn't occur or won't occur. The second kind of event expressed by the intentional mood is an inevitable action: an action that often, in retrospect, ended in a foreseeable way.

An example of this latter sense is the response of a woman seeing a photograph I had taken of a gravely ill Monei Mbanaŋ; he had been sick for weeks and I photographed him as he was about to be carried to a canoe and taken to a hospital, where he died a few days later. Upon seeing this photograph months after Monei had died, looking at a desiccated and paralyzed Monei, this woman murmured *waso-kɨ-nana* (die.IRR-IRR-INTENT) 'he's about to/intending to die', in a soft, rising voice expressing sorrow.

The intentional mood was mentioned earlier in the section on the near future tense (5.4.2.3) because it is constructed in a similar way, with the bound morpheme

-*ana* (-*nana* after a vowel; this form is often reduced and realized as -*na*) affixed directly to the irrealis object marker (for transitive verbs) or directly to the irrealis marker -*ki*-, -*kɨ*- or -*ku*- (for intransitive verbs). So the structure is as follows:

TRANSITIVE VERBS	IRR verb stem + IRR object + -(n)ana
INTRANSITIVE VERBS	IRR verb stem + IRR morpheme + -(n)ana

Examples of the intentional mood are:

(7-25) a. *ewar ŋa sokoi akrunana, sokoi wákare*
   ewar   ŋa   sokoi   a   -kru   -nana
   yesterday 1SG tobacco consume.IRR -3SG.F.R.O -INTENT

   sokoi   wákare
   tobacco NEG
   'yesterday I (M or F) wanted to smoke, but there was no tobacco'

 b. *rɨpɨm ŋa naŋro manaw armbrɨnana, ŋa numbwan pikun pruk mɨk, ŋa mndanet*
   rɨpɨm   ŋa   naŋro   manaw   ar   -mbri   -nana
   earlier 1SG   woman.PL   three   marry.IRR- -3PL.IRR.O INTENT

   ŋa   numbwan pi   -ku   -n   pruk   mɨk
   1SG   thought realize.R -3SG.F.R.O   -SG|1PL.R.S   work   intense

   ŋa   mɨnda   -net
   1SG   tired_of.R   -1SG.M|3SG.M.R.S
   'before, I (M) wanted to marry three woman, but I realized that that would be hard work, so I changed my mind' (lit. 'I became fed up/tired'; *ŋa mɨndanet* translates as "mi les" in Tok Pisin)

 c. *Aŋgara mum akrunana, ŋginana mɨndiki wokara*
   Aŋgara   mum   a   -kru   -nana   ŋginana
   Aŋgara sago_jelly consume.IRR -3SG.F.IRR.O -INTENT   therefore

   mɨndɨ   -ki   wok   -ara
   work_sago.IRR   -IRR   go.3SG.F.R -PERF
   'Aŋgara wanted to eat sago jelly, that's why she went to go work sago'

The fact that a meaning of intention or desirability is foregrounded in this construction means that it can also be translated as 'in order to' or 'with the intention of', as in the following, consisting of two juxtaposed main clauses:

(7-26) a. *ŋɨ mbet ŋa rarɨnana*
        ŋɨ   mbet   ŋa   rar   -i   -nana
        3SG.M come.3SG.M.R 1SG see.IRR -1SG.IRR.O -INTENT
        'he has come to see me'

    b. *ŋgɨ kotarŋgrɨnana ŋgwok*
        ŋgɨ   kotar   -ŋgrɨ   -nana   ŋgwok
        3PL   ask.IRR -3SG.M.IRR.O -INTENT go.3PL.R
        'they went to ask him'

Like the prohibitive and the admonitive, verbs inflected with the intentional suffix cannot be negated. Instead negative intention is expressed by negating another verb of the sentence (7-27), or by a word like *mɨnda* 'tired of', 'sick of' that expresses negative affect (7-28):

(7-27) a. *ŋa aiki wákare ŋɨ rarŋgrɨnana*
        ŋa   ai   -ki   wákare   ŋɨ   rar   -ŋgrɨ   -nana
        1SG   come.IRR -IRR NEG   3SG.M see.IRR -3SG.M.IRR.O -INTENT
        'I haven't come to see him'

(7-28) a. *ŋgɨ mɨnda mum akrunana*
        ŋgɨ   mɨnda   mum   a   -kru   -nana
        3PL   tired_of sago jelly eat.IRR -3SG.F.IRR.O -INTENT
        'they don't want to eat sago jelly' (lit. 'they're tired of eating sago jelly')

The intentional suffix is also used in negative indirect commands (see Section 7.1.4).

7.5 Benefactive (BEN)

Tayap has a set of benefactive object morphemes that denote
(a) that the action or event denoted by the verb has direct relevance to or consequences for the participant encoded in the benefactive object morpheme.
and/or
(b) external possession – that is, the morphemes encode the relationship of possessor-possessed as a core relation of the verb, and they treat the possessor of what is semantically the object of the verb as, itself, the object of the verb, in this case the benefactive object (Payne and Barshi 1999).

Note that the benefactive object suffixes are also used in progressives, see Section 8.3.1.2.

Possession in general is discussed in Section 4.5. Ditransitive verbs are discussed in Section 3.2, where it is shown that they are not a structural class of verbs but rather are transitive verbs with an optional oblique argument.

The difference between benefactive object morphemes and non-benefactive object morphemes can illustrated with the following examples, both of which can be translated to mean 'he speared my pig':

(7-29) a. *ŋɨŋi ŋaŋan mbor pokun*

ŋɨ	=ŋi	ŋaŋan	mbor	po	-ku	-n
3SG.M	=ERG.M	1SG.POSS	pig	strike.R	-3SG.F.R.O	-SG|1PL.R.S

'he speared my pig'

b. *ŋɨŋi ŋaŋan mbor poia(ta)n*

ŋɨ	=ŋi	ŋaŋan	mbor	po	-ia(ta)	-n
3SG.M	=ERG.M	1SG.POSS	pig	strike.R	-1SG.BEN.R.O	-SG|1PL.R.S

'he speared my pig'

Note: The morpheme (*ta*) marks the benefactive object morpheme as realis. It is shown in parentheses to indicate that it is optional and frequently omitted in speech. In fact, it is not unusual that everything after the first part of the benefactive object morpheme is omitted. So the verb in (7-29b), for example, will often occur as [pɔia].

Even though these two sentences can be translated the same way in English, they are not synonymous in Tayap. The first example is the unmarked construction: it is a simple declarative sentence consisting of a transitive class 1 verb stem (*po*) suffixed by a 3SG.F object morpheme denoting the pig (-*ku*) and a subject ending (-*n*) denoting 'he', all inflected for realis.

The second example is marked. It contains the same verb stem inflected for realis, but instead of the object morpheme that refers to the pig that was shot, what follows is a morpheme that means 'mine', 'the one belonging to me' or 'the one whose being shot had consequences for me'. Morphemes that encode this relation often also encode the notion of benefit, and in keeping with other linguistic work on Papuan languages (e.g. Foley 1991: 307–11), here they are labeled "benefactive", even if the label is not entirely satisfying, because the actions encoded by the verb do not necessarily entail benefit. In (7-29a)–(7-29b) above, for example, the spearing of my pig may be *malefactive*, and it may have happened contrary to the speaker's knowledge, will or desire.

The BEN morphemes highlight a relationship of possession and/or the consequences that an action or event have on the person or thing denoted by the morphemes. In (7-29a) and (7-29b) above, a relation of possession is expressed in both examples, by means of the possessive pronoun *ŋaŋan* 'my'. But while possession is *evident* in the first example, it is *emphasized* in the second, partly through the possessive pronoun (which can be omitted in this construction) and partly through the benefactive morphology affixed to the verb stem.

Benefactive morphemes often occur on a transitive verb like 'give'. Here the possessive meaning of 'what belongs to me' or 'what should belong to me' is evident.

(7-30) *isia(ta)n*
      is   *-ia(ta)*   *-n*
      give.SBJ -1SG.BEN.R.O SG|1PL.R.S
      'give it to me'

Benefactive object morphemes also appear when one talks about possessed items such as body parts:

(7-31) a. *kokɨr mbɨdtia(ta)n*
        kokɨr *mbɨd* *-t* *-ia(ta)*   *-n*
        head   pain.R -S <1SG.BEN.R.O> -2SG|3SG.F.R.S
        'my head hurts' (lit. 'head pains me')

     b. *kokɨr mbɨdtukwa(ta)n*
        kokɨr *mbɨd* *-tu* *-kwa(ta)*   *-n*
        head   pain.R -S <3SG.F.BEN.R.O> -2SG|3SG.F.R.S
        'her head hurts' (lit. 'head pains her')

     c. *ŋan niŋ odiŋga(ta)n*
        ŋan *niŋ* *odɨ*   *-ŋga(ta)*   *-n*
        his   bone break.R <3SG.M.BEN.R.O> -2SG|3SG.F.R.S
        'she broke his bone'

     d. *ŋaŋan niŋ kadia(ta)n*
        ŋaŋan *niŋ* *kadɨ*   *-ia(ta)*   *-n*
        my   bone break.R <1SG.BEN.R.O> -2SG|3SG.M.R.S
        'he broke my bone'

     e. *munje ninde ngugubar mbɨdtiŋga(ta)n*
        munje *ainde* *ndugubar* *mbɨd* *-ti*
        man   DX.M   spine   pain.R -S

        -ŋga(ta)   *-n*
        <3SGR.M.BEN.R.O> -2SG|3SG.F.R.S
        'the man's spine hurts'

Note: *adu* 'break' is a class 3 transitive verb; hence the verb stem variation in these examples (7-31c and d; see Section 6.1.4)

Although as already noted, the benefactive morphemes do not necessarily carry a positive meaning of benefit (something that is apparent from examples (7-31c – 7-31d) about bone-breaking), they often do express the meaning of doing something for the benefit of someone, even though it is often difficult in practice to separate the sense of beneficiary from that of possession.

A command like the following means both 'Get rid of the rubbish that is in her house' and 'Get rid of the house's rubbish for her benefit':

(7-32) *patirŋa pipia aŋgo wostukwa(ta)n*
 patir =ŋa pipia aŋgo
 house =POSS rubbish (TP) DX.F

 wos -tu -kwa(ta) -n
 get_rid_of.SBJ -S <3SG.F.BEN.R.O> -2SG|3SG.F.R.S
 'get rid of this rubbish in her house'; 'get rid of this house's rubbish for her'

The following command is similar: it means both 'Light my cigarette' and 'Light my cigarette for me'.

(7-33) *ŋaŋan sokoi wototia(ta)n*
 ŋaŋan sokoi woto -t -ia(ta) -n
 1SG.POSS cigarette light.IRR -S <1SG.BEN.R.O> -2SG|3SG.F.R.S
 'light my cigarette'; 'light my cigarette for me'

Because they foreground a relationship of possession or one in which an agent has been affected by an action or event, benefactive object morphemes can be affixed to any verb stem – even an intransitive, stative verb like 'be'.

One old woman once told a story of how she upbraided her teenage son for taking money out of her net bag without her permission. "Yesterday you cried for me to give you money", she recounted herself saying, "and I gave you two kina to buy biscuits, which you bought and ate"[1].

After having established her prior generosity, the woman continued, saying in a self-pitying voice:

---

[1] The kina, from the Tok Pisin word for 'clam', is Papua New Guinea's main unit of currency.

(7-34) ŋaŋan tri kina ŋayar aŋgi wuiatan
ŋaŋan   tri   kina   ŋayar   aŋgi   wu   **-iata**   -n
1SG.POSS three   kina   really   DX.F   be.R.3SG.F -1SG.BEN.R.O   -SG|1PL.R
'my 3 kina is there'; i.e. it's all I have left

Here the benefactive morphemes foreground the speaker as both possessing and being directly affected by the presence of the three kina. Not only are her three kina there; they are three kina that are there specifically for her benefit and use.

Earlier, this same speaker, also talking about herself, said:

(7-35) saki tutor ŋayar kuka nda ikur sisiatan
saki   tutor   ŋayar   kuk   -a   nda   ikur
nothing   sitting   truly   be.1SG.F|2SG.F|1PL.R   -and   then   evening

sis   **-iata**   -n
fall.R   -1SG.BEN.R.O   -SG|1PL.R
'I (F) sat there doing nothing at all and the evening fell on me'

Verbs constructed with the benefactive morphemes are formed according to the following pattern:
(7-36)

	VERB STEM INFLECTED FOR STATUS	FIRST PART OF DIS-CONTINUOUS SUBJECT MORPHEME WHERE APPROPRIATE*	BENEFACTIVE OBJECT MORPHEME	SUBJECT MORPHEME INFLECTED FOR STATUS
REALIS				
a.	po strike.R		-iata -1SG.BEN.R.O	-n -SG|1PL.R.S
b.	wos throw_away.R	-tu -s	-kwata <3SG.BEN.R.O>	-n -2SG.3SG.F.R.S
c.	sis descend.R		-iata -1SG.BEN.R.O	-n -SG|1PL.R
IRREALIS				
d.	moser buy-IRR		-wati -2SG.BEN.R.O	-ndak -3PL.IRR.S
e.	i give.IRR		-mbati -3PL.BEN.R.O	-ke -DL.IRR.S
f.	adɨk break.CF	-tɨ -s	-ŋga <3SG.M.BEN.R.O>	-n -2SG.3SG.F.R.S

*For example, in class 4 and class 5 transitive verbs inflected in the non-future tense, and in verbs inflected in the counterfactual (see Sections 6.1.6–6.1.7 and 9.4.3)

Because benefactive morphemes are object/undergoer-like morphemes, they occur in the expected object slot in a verb's architecture, thus precluding the appearance of the object marker. Note that a coreferential NP can appear with the object marker: see for example (7-37a) below. And like the other object morphemes that have been discussed and exemplified throughout this grammar, the benefactive object morphemes are marked as either realis or irrealis.

The forms of the benefactive object marker can be compared to those of the (non-benefactive) object morphemes:

	NON-BENEFACTIVE OBJECT MORPHEMES		BENEFACTIVE OBJECT MORPHEMES	
	REALIS	IRREALIS	REALIS	IRREALIS
1SG	-i	-i	-ia(ta)	-iati
2SG	-u	-ru	-wa(ta)	-wati
3SG.F	-ku	-kru	-kwa(ta)	-kwati
3SG.M	-ŋgɨ	-ŋgrɨ	-ŋga(ta)	-ŋgati
1PL	-mɨ	-mrɨ	-ma(ta)	-mati
2PL	-mɨ	-mrɨ	-ma(ta)	-mati
3PL	-mbɨ	-mbrɨ	-mba(ta)	-mbati
DL	-mɨ	-mrɨ	-ma(ta)	-mati

As mentioned above, the realis markers in parenthesis (*ta*) are optional and frequently omitted.

Examples of how these morphemes appear in various TAM categories are as follows:

(7-37) a. *Njabŋi Kruni eŋgune eŋgune ŋginŋgatan*
 Njab=ŋi Kruni eŋgune eŋgune
 Njab=ERG Kruni flattery flattery

 ŋgɨ -n **-ŋgata** -n
 put.R -S <3SG.M.BEN.R.O> -1SG|3SG.M|1PL.R.S
 'Njab buttered up Kruni'

 b. *pitiŋar isian epi motini iwatinet*
 pitiŋar is -ia -n epi motini
 machete give.SBJ -1SG.BEN.R.O -SG|1PL.R.S tomorrow again

 i **-wati** -net
 give.IRR -2SG.BEN.IRR.O -1SG.M|3SG.M.IRR.S
 'give me the machete, tomorrow I (M) will give it back to you'

c. *ŋɨ nɨpis wákare okɨya yuwon oŋgab moserwatinana*
   ŋɨ   nɨpis   wákare   o   -kɨ   -ya   yuwon   oŋgab
   3SG.M able   NEG   go.IRR   -IRR   -and   2SG.POSS pot

   moser   -**wati**   -nana
   buy.IRR   -2SG.BEN.IRR.O   -INTENT
   'he's not able to go and buy a pot for you'

d. *ŋa rewkɨ wákare pi, Mbupyi nɨŋ adɨktian*
   ŋa   rew   -kɨ   wákare   pi   Mbup   =yi   nɨŋ
   1SG   flee.IRR -IRR   NEG   HYPO   Mbup   =ERG.F   bone

   adɨk   -t   -**ia**   -n
   break.CF   -S   <1SG.BEN.R.O>   -2SG|3SG.F.R.S
   'If I (M or F) hadn't run away, Mbup would have broken my bone'

e. *Aŋgara awkrak pi, ŋa korot iknu**kwata**n*
   Aŋgara awkrak   pi   ŋa   korot
   Aŋgara   be.3SG.F.CF HYPO   1SG   net

   ik   -nu   -**kwata**   -n
   give.CF   - S   <3SG.F.BEN.R.O>   -1SG|3SG.M|1PL.R.S
   'If Aŋgara had been here, I would have given her the net'

7.6 Mood particles

Tayap also has four freestanding particles – *awa*, *mera*, *kapa* and *nímera* – that express expectation, supposition and surprise. Two of these particles – *awa* and *mera* – occur with both verbs and other parts of speech. *Kapa* modifies only nouns and adjectives and *nímera* occurs with only verbs.

7.6.1 Expectation and impatience (EXP)

The particle *awa*, which occurs initially or in the case of (7-39), after the subject, carries a connotation of expectation tinged with slight or potential impatience or disapproval. In the 1980s, senior men translated some occurrences of *awa* for me with the Tok Pisin word "watpo" ('what for'). "Watpo" is a demand that one can easily imagine being shouted at black plantation workers by white colonial overseers. In the speech of the senior Gapun men, it was an interrogative that retained an aggressive or exasperated tone that didn't so much mean 'why?' as it meant, 'Why in the world…? or 'Why the hell…?'.

By 2009, *awa* was rarely heard in Tayap speech, and the instances of the word I heard in the speech of senior villagers did not express overt disapproval. However, they did seem to indicate that what was being referred to was anticipated or overdue. So note the difference in meaning between two sentences, one of which uses the simple interrogative, and the other which uses the modal particle *awa*:

(7-38) a. Speaker A: *wek-ara*
come.3SG.F.R-PERF
'she has arrived'

Speaker B: *Ndamor=ke?*
Ndamor=Q
'who, Ndamor?'

b. Speaker A: *wek-ara*
come.3SG.F.R-PERF
'she has arrived'

Speaker B: *Ndamor **awa**?*
Ndamor EXP
'it must be Ndamor?'

Another example occurred when an old woman was waiting for a piece of meat to be heated on a fire. At one point during a conversation about other things, she asked a girl who was looking after the meat:

(7-39) *ŋgu **awa** mborsip tandiu pipiek?*
3SG.F EXP pork well cook.3SG.F.R
'is the pork cooked enough?'

Once again, this question is not simply a request for information; it expresses an expectation. In the next example, given to me by a senior man in the 1980s, men in Gapun were ready to fight men from the neighboring village of Sanae. All prepared to fight, the Gapun men could ask one another in anticipatory excitement:

(7-40) ***awa** ŋgi ai -ki -ndak?*
EXP 3PL come.IRR -IRR -3PL.IRR
'Will they come?'; i.e. 'Do you think they'll really come?'

When it occurs together with a negated verb, the sense of expectation is heightened. Contrast the following two sentences:

(7-41) a. ***awa*** *mbet*
       EXP   come.R.1SG.M|3SG.M.R
       'he should come' (i.e. 'I expect he will come')

   a. ***awa*** *ai-ki wákare*
       EXP   come.IRR-IRR   NEG
       'he must have arrived'

Because it carries a sense of expectation, this construction is similar in meaning to the admonitive mood discussed in Section 7.3. For example, the following two sentences both mean something similar:

(7-42) a. ***awa*** *Kemma orasambgi nirru wákare*
       awa   *Kem*   *=ma*   *ora*   *samb*   *=gi*
       EXP   Kem   =POSS   thing   PL   =ERG.PL

       nir   *-ru*   *wákare*
       make.IRR   -2SG.IRR.O   NEG
       'it must be Kem's things [i.e. his connections with the spirit world] that are making you sick' (in Tok Pisin: "Nogut ol samting bilong Kem i mekim yu")

   b. *Kemma orasambgi nirŋgarana*
      Kem   *=ma*   *ora*   *samb*   *=gi*   *nir*   *-ŋgarana*
      Kem   =POSS   thing   PL   =ERG.PL   make.IRR   -ADM.SG|1PL
      'it wouldn't be good if it's Kem's things [i.e. his connections with the spirit world] that are making you sick' (same Tok Pisin translation as above).[2]

---

[2] This example is marked by non-agreement between the plural noun (*orasamb*, 'things') and the plural ergative morpheme *(=gi)* affixed to the noun, and the singular inflection (*-ŋgarana*) on the verb 'make' (*nir*). One would expect the plural ending –*ŋgroana* (so '*nirŋgroana*' see Section 7.3).

It is probable that this example takes the form it does because the plural noun *orak samb* ('things') is usually treated as a singular entity. So speakers say:

   ŋgan orasamb wuk aŋgi
   ŋgan   *orak*   *samb*   *wuk*   *aŋgi*
   3PL.POSS   thing   PL   be.3SG.F.R   DX
   'their things are there' (lit. 'their things is there')

Although they clearly are not identical in meaning, sentences like these two both express an anxiety in relation to, or an expectation about, an event.

7.6.2 Supposition (SUPP)

Another particle, *mera*, marks the epistemic status of an action or event as something that has been assumed but that the speaker believes does not correspond to what actually happened. In other words, it is what Tayap speakers use to convey a meaning like 'I thought Paita had gone to Wongan'. A statement like that in English conveys a belief that regardless of whether or not Paita did go to Wongan, the speaker expected him to but believes that he did not.

The modal particle *mera* that carries this meaning follows whatever part of speech is the focus of the assumption. So it can occur after a noun, as in the following:

(7-43) ŋa ndɨ nda namnak Ngemanŋi **mera**
 ŋa   ndɨ   nda   nam   -nak   Ngeman   =ŋi   **mera**
 1SG DM   DM   talk.R -1SG.F|1PL.R Ngeman =ERG.M SUPP
 'I (F) thought it was Ngeman' (who did it, but it wasn't)

Most commonly, *mera* follows a verb, thereby reframing what would have been a statement as a supposition. For example:

(7-44) ŋa namnet ŋɨ Potore okinet **mera**
 ŋa   nam   -net   ŋɨ   Poto   =re
 1SG talk.R -1SG.M|3SG.M.R 3SG.M Wongan =ALL

 o   -ki   -net   **mera**
 go.IRR -IRR -1SG.M|3SG.M.IRR   SUPP
 'I (M) thought he would go to Wongan' (but he didn't)

Without the modal particle, this sentence would mean 'I thought: he will go to Wongan'. *Mera* turns the statement into an assumption that, moreover, the speaker believes did not come to pass. Note that these constructions always involve the use of a phrase like 'I thought' or 'I lied' as exemplified here.

The particle is also to express the action of having been fooled or lied to. So 'they lied to us that you were dead' is:

(7-45) ŋgigi yim takwattɨmɨro yu wasowtet **mera**
ŋgi=gi   yim   takwat-tɨ-mɨ-ro   yu   wasow-tet   **mera**
3PL=ERG.PL   1PL   lie.R-S<1PL.R.O>3PL.R.S   2SG   die.R-2SG.M.R   SUPP
'they lied to us that you (M) were dead' (lit. 'they lied to us, you were dead we thought')

7.6.3 Mirative (MIR)

Kapa encodes surprise. It follows nominals and the closest colloquial English translation would be the expression 'that damned X' in both its positive and negative valences; so both 'That damned kid really did well' and 'That damned cat peed on my sofa'. *Kapa* follows pronouns, nouns and noun phrases, as in the following examples:

(7-46) a. ŋgu **kapa** weka numŋan noŋortakara
ŋgu   **kapa**   wek   -a   num   =ŋa
3SG.F   MIR   come.3SG.F.R   -and   village   =POSS

noŋor   -tak   -ara
woman   -2SG|3SG.F.R   -PERF

'she came to our village and really turned into a village woman' (said about a woman from Pankin village who married into Gapun forty years ago and is the only foreigner in memory ever to learn absolutely flawless Tayap)

b. ŋa mbota kuta emb **kapa** otɨtek katkatkɨ
ŋa   mbot   -a   kut   -a   emb
1SG   go.SG.M.R   -LINK   be.SG.M.R   -and   morning

kapa   otɨtek   katkat   -kɨ
MIR   fall.3SG.F.R   quickly   -INTENS

'I (M) went and was there (waiting for a wild pig to wander into a trap) and the damned morning came really quick' (before a pig could come)

c. ŋa **kapa** markar mbot, yu markɨ wákare
ŋa   **kapa**   mar   -kar   mbot   yu   mar   -kɨ   wákare
1SG   MIR   row.IRR   -MANN   go.SG.M.R   2SG   row.IRR   -IRR   NEG
'I (M or F) am the only damned one who rowed, you didn't row'

7.6.4 Surprise counter to expectation (CS)

Nímera expresses surprise that a situation has turned out contrary to one's expectations. It is a combination of the adverb, *ni*, which expresses a negative state – the state of doing nothing or having nothing (see Section 3.4.1) – with the suppositional particle *mera* (see above Section 7.6.2).

An example that senior speakers used to explain the particle is as follows: You tell another person to complete some work and then you leave them, thinking that the person will not do the work. When you return, you find that the person actually *has* done the work, at which point you might say:

(7-47) ŋa   ndɨ   yu   **nímera**   kut   inda
        1SG DM   2SG CS   be.R.SG.M.R DX.M
        'I thought you (M) just were here' (doing nothing, but you weren't, you actually worked) (lit: 'I was like, you just were here')

Another example is that people have come to your house and you expect them to help you do some work, but they don't. You might say:

(7-48) yum   **nímera**   a   -ku   -nana   mbekem?
        2PL   CS   be.IRR -IRR   INTENT   come.2PL.R
        'So you've all come just to be here?' (and do nothing even though I expected you to work?)

A final example is that you are carving something and you want to make it look like an object you have seen before – perhaps a small statue with a traditional pattern. In the course of carving the piece, though, it ends up looking very different from what you expected. *Nímera* here expresses the surprise you feel at this:

(7-49) ŋa ndɨ **nímera** nirkrunana wákare ŋa ninukun
        ŋa   ndɨ   **nímera**   nir   -kru   -nana
        1SG   DM   CS   make.IRR   -3SG.F.IRR.O -INTENT

        wákare ŋa   ni   -nu   -ku   -n
        NEG   1SG   make.R   -S   <3SG.F.R.O>   -1SG|3SG.M|1PL.R.S
        'I thought it would turn out differently than the way it turned out' (lit. 'I intended to make it [one way], no, I made it [another way]')

8 Complex predicates

8.1 Complex predicates and complex clauses

In Tayap, the major division in complex structures is between combining verbs versus combining clauses. Verb combining in Tayap is accomplished through complex predicates, which can be serial verb constructions or complex predicates involving the verb 'to be'. Clause combining is of three types: Coordinate, subordinate and cosubordinate constructions.

This chapter deals with complex predicates, and the following chapter (Chapter 9) deals with clause combining.

8.2 Serial verb constructions (SVC)

From the previous chapters, it should be amply evident that Tayap has an exuberance of verb forms. Until now, the presentation of Tayap verb forms has for the most part concentrated on what we might somewhat understatedly call 'simple verbs': single, independent verbs that can take the full range of TAM marking, as well as the full range of subject and object affixes, and function as sole predicates.

In addition to these 'simple' verbs, though, Tayap has the possibility of joining together verb stems in serial verb constructions (SVCs) or complex predicates with the verb 'to be' in habituals and progressives (discussed below, Section 8.3).

Tayap SVCs are sequences of verb stems that encode a complex series of actions. An example is *tapratkɨŋgiatɨkɨtakana*, a single complex predicate that means 'she will carry him down on her shoulders':

(8-1) *tapr   -at   -kɨ -ŋgi*
   carry_on_shoulders.IRR -3SG.M.NFO -bring -3SG.M.R.O

   -atɨ   -kɨ -tak   -ana
   -go_down.IRR -IRR -3SG.F.IRR -INTENT
   'she will carry him down on her shoulders'

tapr ↓	-at ↓	kɨ ↓	-ŋgɨ ↓	-ati-kɨ-tak-ana ↓
verb stem *tap* 'carry on shoulders', with *r* inserted at morpheme boundary (see 2.6)	object suffix that occurs only with non-final verbs, *-at*, inflected for 3SG.M (see Section 8.2.2)	verb root k^v 'bring', which can only occur together with a verb of motion (see below)	object suffix used with final verbs, inflected for 3SG.M.R (Section 5.3.1)	independent verb of motion *ati* 'go down' inflected in the irrealis status for 3SG.F subject intentional

Serial verb constructions like **tapratkɨŋgiatikɨtakana**, consist of three distinct verb stems: two non-final verbs (*tap* 'carry on shoulders' and k^v 'bring[1]'), and the final verb of motion *atikɨ* 'go down'. The two non-final verbs take no marking for TAM, but, being transitive, they do both take object morphemes. Note that those two object morphemes *-at* and *-ŋgɨ* both encode 3SG.M. Furthermore, the second one *-ŋgɨ* is inflected for TAM (in this case, realis status, since it is a non-final object suffix, as will be discussed in Section 8.2.2 below).

Two characteristics mark this word as a single predicate:
(1) the subject of the verb is shared, and encoded only once, on the final verb, and the object of the first verb and subject of the second are shared; and
(2) the complex predicate can only be negated as a whole. Even though it consists of three distinct verb stems, *tap*, k^v and *atikɨ*, only the final verb (the same one that takes the subject marking) is negated.

So the negated form of this verb is:

(8-2) tapr   -at   kɨ   -ŋgɨ
       carry_on_shoulders.IRR -3SG.M.NFO bring -3SG.M.R.O

   ati   -kɨ   wákare
   go_down.IRR   -IRR   NEG
   '(she) won't (or didn't) carry him down on her shoulders'

Further, *tapratkɨŋgiatikɨtakana* is a single phonological word (see Section 2.7). Note, however, that the boundary between the non-final object (NFO, which in this case is *-at*; see below 8.2.2) and the main final verb that takes subject marking

---

[1] The vowel harmonizes to the vowel of the object.

is permeable, and can be interrupted by question morphemes and even separate words, as in the following:

(8-3) kopi *tarak masinni ŋakrawokwankuk*
      kopi   tar   -ak   masin=nɨ
      coffee (TP) take.IRR -3SG.F.NFO machine (TP)=LOC

      ŋakrawo -kwan   kuk
      shell.IRR -3SG.F.BEN.R.O be.SG.F|1PL.R
      'we used to take the coffee to a machine and shell it'

In this situation the form is no longer a single phonological word but still a single predicate.

Serial verb constructions are composed of one or more non-final verb(s) and a final verb. The non-final verbs are always formally irrealis, but the final verb can take the full range of Tayap's TAM inflections. TAM and subject marking occurs once across the construction, on the final verb, and the non-final verb(s) are marked only for their object, if transitive.

According to Haspelmath (2016: 296), a serial verb construction is "a monoclausal construction consisting of multiple independent verbs with no element linking them and with no predicate-argument relation between the verbs". It is important to make clear that non-final and final verbs are both independent, and there is not a relationship of syntactic dependency between the verbs of a serial verb construction. Instead, there is a sharing of features (TAM, subject marking and negation). The differences between non-final and final verbs are positional, a factor of where they fall in the clause, rather than related to dependency.

8.2.1 Non-final verbs in serial verb constructions

Intransitive verbs used as non-final verbs take their irrealis stem (while not taking an irrealis suffix -*kɨ*, -*ki* or -*ku*), and do not take any further marking. In the next example, the non-final verb *rar* 'see' appears in its irrealis stem form, with no further marking, and is immediately followed by the final verb of the serial verb construction. Note that in this example, together these two verbs form a complex predicate, which is then marked with a conjunction 'and', forming a coordinated clause (see Section 9.3):

(8-4) *rarmboka tankun*
      rar   mbok   -a
      see.IRR go.1SG.F|1PL.R -and

```
ta       -n  -ku        -n
see.R    -S  <3SG.F.R.O> -SG|3SG.M|1PL.R.S
```
'... I was looking and I saw it ...' (lit. 'seeing go and seeing it...')

On transitive verbs used as non-final verbs, again the irrealis stem is used, and the object is marked using a realis form, regardless of the status marking on the final verb to follow. For example (non-final verb in bold):

(8-5) manŋa ŋgwab nambar **krar**kuotike
```
man   =ŋa    ŋgwab  nambar  krar        -ku         otike
cunt  =POSS  hole   one     break.IRR   -3SG.F.R.O  fall.DL.R
```
'the two of them broke open the same cunt hole and fell out' (i.e. they are brothers)

Note that these non-final verbs are not truncated forms of full verbs. Compare the form of the class 4 transitive verb 'break', in bold print in the following example (this is a coordinated construction, see Section 9.3) with its non-final form above in example (8-5):

(8-6) manŋa ŋgwab nambar kratukureya otike
```
man   =ŋa    ŋgwab  nambar
cunt  =POSS  hole   one
```

```
kra       -tu  -ku          -re       -ya   otike
break.R   -S   <3SG.F.R.O>  -DL.R.S   -and  fall.DL.R
```
'the two of them broke open the same cunt hole and fell out'

Examples (8-5) and (8-6) have more or less the same meaning. But notice that the only element that is the same in both verbs is the realis object suffix *-ku*. The stem of the fully inflected verb (8-6) *kra* 'break' has a TAM-appropriate stem (in this case, since it is expressing an event that occurred in the past, the stem appears in its realis form).

The non-final forms in serial verb constructions (8-5) will always appear in irrealis form, and TAM will be carried by the verb that follows it. The final verb has the full range of possibilities of any normal verb outside of serial verb constructions.

8.2.2 Non-final object morphemes (NFO)

The object suffixes that can affix to non-final verbs have two forms: they are either the regular forms that occur on independent transitive verbs (see Section 5.3.1), or they are drawn from a particular set of object forms that only occur on non-final verbs. This set of non-final object suffixes is as follows; note that there is no distinction between dual and plural forms in this paradigm:

	SINGULAR	DUAL/PLURAL
1	-ai	-am
2	-aw	-am
3SG.F	-ak	-amb
3SG.M	-at	

Example:

(8-7) *tandiwki rarambotimbin*
 tandiw -ki rar **-amb** o -ti -mbi -n
 well -EMPH look.IRR -3PL.NFO shoot.SBJ -S <3PL.R.O> -2SG3SG.F.R.S
 'aim well and shoot them!'

These non-final object morphemes are the functional equivalent of the object suffixes used with the final verbs of serial verb constructions or indeed any verb outside of serial verb constructions. They are also more or less interchangeable with them. Looking again at example (8-7), above, it is possible to substitute *-amb* (3PL.NFO) with *-mbi* (3PL.R.O), the regular object suffix used in independent verbs:

(8-8) *tandiwki rarmbiotimbin*
 tandiw -ki rar **-mbi** o -ti- -mbi -n!
 well -EMPH look.IRR -3PL.R.O shoot.SBJ -S- <3PL.R.O> -2SG|3SG.F.R. S
 'aim well and shoot them!'

It is not possible, however, to substitute *-mbi* with *-amb* in other clauses. There are two main differences between the non-final and other forms of the object morphemes:
(1) Whenever one occurs, a non-final verb object suffix always occurs in the first object position of a complex predicate. Another non-final object can occur in the second or subsequent object slot, but a non-final object suffix is blocked from appearing after an independent object morpheme has occurred.
(2) Non-final object morphemes do not inflect for realis and irrealis. Unlike the forms used with independent verbs – where *-ku*, for example, expresses 3SG.F.**R**.O and *-kru* expresses 3SG.F.**IRR**.O – the non-final object forms *always*

occur in the forms listed above. Like the verbs to which they affix, which are unaffixed for realis/irrealis status, the non-final object suffixes are unmarked with regard to status.

It is not always clear how to determine which object morpheme – the non-final verb object morpheme or the other form – will be used in any given instance.

So in *tapratkɨŋgɨatɨkɨtakana* (repeated from (8-1)) notice that the non-final object *-at* 3SG.M.NFO occurs after the first verb, and the form that occurs with other verbs, *-ŋgɨ* 3SG.M.R.O occurs after the second non-final verb:

(8-9)   *tapratkɨŋgɨatɨkɨtakana*
      tapr   *-at*   *kɨ*   *-ŋgɨ*
      carry_on_shoulders.IRR   -3SG.M.NFO   bring   -3SG.M.R.O

      atɨ   *-kɨ*   *tak*   *-ana*
      go_down.IRR   -IRR   3SG.F.R   -INTENT
      'she will carry him down on her shoulders'

The subject of a complex predicate like *tapratkɨŋgɨatɨkɨtakana* is encoded on the inflected final verb, and it is this final verb that would be negated to negate the predicate. To see this clearly, below are examples of this same complex predicate inflected for different subjects. Note the differences in the subject suffix (in bold) just prior to the final intentional suffix – everything else in the verb remains the same. Example (8-10d), repeated from (8-2), gives the negated verb, where, as always, there is no subject marked.

(8-10)   a.   *tapratkɨŋgɨatɨkɨ* **-net**   *-ana*
                           -1SG.M|3SG.M.IRR   -INTENT
                'I (M) will carry him down on my shoulders or 'he will carry him down on his shoulders'

         b.   *tapratkɨŋgɨatɨkɨ* **-nak**   *-ana*
                          -1SG.F|1PL.IRR   -INTENT
               'I (F) will carry him down on her shoulders' or 'we will carry him down on our shoulders'

         c.   *tapratkɨŋgɨatɨkɨ* **-ndak**   *-ana*
                          -3PL.IRR   -INTENT
               'they will carry him down on their shoulders'

         d.   *tapratkɨŋgɨatɨkɨ*   *wákare*
                                NEG
               '(any subject) won't (or didn't) carry him down on her shoulders'

8.2.3 Verbs that always or usually occur only in SVCs

8.2.3.1 SVCs with the grammaticalized verb k^v 'bring', 'take'

The verb stem k^v only ever occurs as a non-final verb within a SVC. It expresses that an object will be brought to the deictic center or taken away from the deictic center in a way that is specified by the verb of motion that follows it.

Tayap has a number of verbs that express different ways of carrying objects. They include:

andruwe 'carry on head'
erorar 'carry on back'
ser-(p)-e 'carry in hand'
tap 'carry on shoulders'
wuw 'carry on one shoulder'

Verbs like these express specific ways of carrying an object. The verb stem k^v, on the other hand, does not specify how an object is carried. It simply means 'bring' or 'take' in both the narrow sense of physically carrying something, and in the more extended sense of, for instance, 'bringing the visitors down (or taking them down) to the end of the village to send them off'. Tayap speakers use the Tok Pisin word "kisim" as a more or less exact equivalent.

Unlike all other verbs in the language, k^v never functions as a final verb of a serial verb construction, nor indeed any other verb type:
- it never occurs without another verb following it in a serial verb construction;
- it is not marked for tense;
- it does not take subject morphemes (although it does take object marking);
- and it cannot be independently negated.

Whenever it is used, k^v must occur as part of a serial verb construction, in construction with other non-final verbs and/or fully inflected final verbs.

K^v 'bring' is one of the most commonly occurring verbs in Tayap, since villagers are constantly telling children and others to bring them things (k^v + object morpheme + *aiki* 'come') or take things away (k^v + object morpheme + *oki* 'go').

Examples of its use are as follows (k^v in bold):

(8-11) k^v 'bring', 'take'
    a. *ŋaŋan sapwar kukuwe!*
       ŋaŋan   sapwar   **ku**   -ku   we
       1SG.POSS basket bring -3SG.F.R.O come.SBJ
       'bring my basket!'

b. *Njime kiŋgiwe!*
 Njime **ki** -ŋgi we
 Njime bring -3SG.M.R.O come.SBJ
 'Bring Njime!' (i.e. carry him over here)

c. *ŋaŋan sapwar kukuŋgwokara*
 ŋaŋan sapwar **ku** -ku ŋgwok -ara
 1SG.POSS basket take -3SG.F.R.O go.3PL.R -PERF
 'they took my basket' (lit. 'they left taking my basket')

As the only obligatorily non-final verb in the language, it is likely that *kʸ* has been grammaticalized from an earlier independent verb stem. Note that according to Haspelmath (1995), constructions like those described here for Tayap with *kʸ* should not be considered SVCs since *kʸ* is not an independent verb. However, while *kʸ* is indeed not an independent verb, it is useful to consider it with other verbs functioning in SVCs. It takes object marking like a normal verb; it also has verbal semantics. Further, *kʸ* can form part of longer sequences of verbs in a complex predicate, like in example (8-1) in which *kʸ* is the second of three predicates functioning together as a complex whole: here it is functionally identical to the other non-final verb of the SVC, clearly acting equivalently to other verbs in the language.

Alternatively, the morpheme *kʸ* could be thought of as a converb, or an auxiliary. However with a converb one would expect a situation of adverbial subordination (Haspelmath 2005: 3), and with an auxiliary one would expect tense, aspectual, modal, voice or polarity semantics (Schachter and Shopen 2007: 41), all of which are lacking here.

Kʸ could also be thought of as an incorporated adverb. The best analysis, however, would seem to be to regard *kʸ* as a grammaticalized non-final verb.

8.2.3.2 Verbs which normally occur in SVCs

With the exception of the grammaticalized verb *kʸ* ('bring', 'take'), just discussed, all Tayap verbs can be used independently, outside of serial verb constructions. A number of verbs associated with motion, however, almost always appear as non-final verbs in serial verb constructions.

The most commonly occurring verbs of this type are the following (all verbs in the SVC are in bold):

(8-12) *ru* 'propel', 'expel'
 a. *Raya moŋar rukuotitek numatni*
 Raya moŋar **ru** -ku **otitek** numat =ni
 Raya stone propel.IRR -3SG.F.R.O fall.3SG.F.R ground =ALL
 'Raya threw the stone on the ground.'

b. *riŋgiwotet!*
ri	*-ŋgi*	***wotet***
propel.IRR	-3SG.M.R.O	go_up.2SG.M.R

   'throw him up!'

c. *nambɨrnɨ riŋgiwokɨŋgimbet*
nambɨr	*=nɨ*	***ri***	*-ŋgi*	*wo*	***ki***	*-ŋgi*
breast	=LOC	propel.IRR	-3SG.M.R.O	up	bring	-3SG.M.R.O

   mbet
   go.SG.M.R

   'he lifted him onto his chest and brought him' (or 'I (M) or you (M) lifted him onto my/your chest and brought him')

d. *rukuaritak!*
ru	*-ku*	***aritak***
propel.IRR	-3SG.F.R.O	go_down.SBJ.3SG.M.R

   'throw it away!'

(8-13) *Moip naŋro kosepyi manŋa iru utɨpormbatanŋan rorsem ŋgime* ***wer****amb* ***otɨtek****ŋan yɨwɨrgwabekenɨ*

Moip	*naŋro*	*kosep*	*=yi*	*man*	*=ŋa*	*iru*
Watam	women	crab	=ERG	cunt	=POSS	clitoris

utɨpor	*-mbata*	*-n*	*=ŋan*	*rorsem*	*ŋgi*	*-me*
slice_up.R	-3PL.BEN.R.O	-SG|1PL.R.S	=POSS	children	3PL	-DX

wer	*-amb*	***otɨtek***	*=ŋan*	*yɨwɨrgwab*	*=ekenɨ*
pull_out.IRR	-3PL.NFO	fall.3SG.F.R	=POSS	asshole	=PERL

'They pulled those two kids out the assholes of Watam women whose clits have been sliced up by a crab' (lit, 'the crab sliced the women, (someone) pulled out the children, they fell')[2]

---

[2] It isn't entirely clear why the verb *otɨtek* 'fall' here is inflected in 3SG.F (one might expect *ŋgotɨtek* 'fell.3PL.R'). One reason may be that the speaker, who was shouting angrily in affect, produced an ungrammatical utterance. Another reason may be that the verb 'fall', when it is used as part of a SVC, as it is here, has become a formulaic expression, and is realized as *otɨtek* for all subjects, regardless of gender or number. In example (8-13), the plural meaning of the verb is conveyed by the NFO (*-amb*). Compare examples (8-12a) and (8-22).

(8-14) ŋayi awin worerkuwok
ŋa   =yi   awin   **worer**   -ku   **wok**
1SG   =ERG.F water   capsize.IRR   -3SG.F.R.O go.3SG.F.R
'I poured the water' (lit. 'I capsized the water, it went')

(8-15) oremŋi mbor motikkuwok
orem   =ŋi   mbor   **motik**   -ku   **wok**
crocodile =ERG.M   pig   swallow.IRR -3SG.F.R.O go.3SG.F.R
'the crocodile swallowed the pig'

war 'put into'

(8-16) embatotoni warakkukumbet
embatoto   =ni
cloth   =LOC

war   -ak   **ku**   -ku   **mbet**
put_into.IRR -3SG.F.NFO   bring -3SG.F.R.O come.3SG.M.R
'he put her in a piece of cloth and brought her'

While the final verb is commonly a verb of motion, it does not have to be. Examples are as follows (all verbs in bold):

(8-17) a. sapwar yuwon krarkuwawarpekun
           sapwar   yuwon   **krar**   -ku
           basket   2SG.POSS   break.IRR   -3SG.F.R.O

           wawarpe   -ku   -n
           hang_up.R -3SG.F.R.O   -SG|1PL.R.S
           'she tore up your basket and hung it up'

       b. epi ŋgɨ tapɨtak towoikunirkrundak
           epi   ŋgɨ   tapɨtak   **towoi** -ku
           tomorrow   3PL   baked_sago   try.IRR -3SG.F.R.O

           nir   -kru   -ndak
           make.IRR   -3SG.F.IRR.O   -3PL.IRR.S
           'tomorrow they will try to make baked sago'

       c. ewar yu bisket moserkukakun
           ewar   yu   bisket
           yesterday   2SG   biscuit (TP)

> ***moser*** -ku ka -ku -n
> buy.IRR -3SG.F.R.O consume.R <3SG.F.R.O> -SG|1PL.R.S
> 'yesterday you bought biscuits and ate them'

(8-18) *sapwar yuwon krarkuwawarekru wakare*
sapwar yuwon ***krar*** -ku
basket your break.IRR -3SG.F.R.O

waware -kru wákare
hang_up.IRR -3SG.F.IRR.O NEG
'she didn't rip up your basket and hang it up'

It is possible to think of these non-final/final sequences, here described as serial verb constructions, as cosubordinate (medial-final) clause chaining constructions, but an analysis of SVCs reflects better the fact that they occur within single clauses rather than across clauses. The SVC as a whole generally forms a single grammatical word, and NP arguments and negation are shared across the construction. Also, medial verbs have overt linking morphology, which verbs in serial verb constructions do not (see Section 9.8 for a discussion of medial-final clause chaining, i.e. cosubordinate constructions).

8.2.4 Switch-function serial verb constructions

Switch-function serial verb constructions (the term is from Aikhenvald 2006), in which the object of the non-final verb is shared with the subject of the final verb are common in Tayap.
    Examples are:

(8-19) *ŋayi awin worerkuwok*
ŋa =yi awin ***worer*** -ku ***wok***
1SG =ERG.F water capsize.IRR -3SG.F.R.O GO.3SG.F.R
'I (F or M) poured water' (lit. I capsized water, it went)

(8-20) *ewar ŋgi yimbar worerkuwok*
ewar ŋgi yimbar ***worer*** -ku ***wok***
yesterday 3PL canoe capsize.IRR -3SG.F.R.O go.3SG.F.R
'Yesterday they capsized the canoe' (lit. I capsized the canoe, it went)

(8-21) *ewar ŋiŋi marasin mitikuwok*

ewar	ŋi	=ŋi	marasin	**miti**	-ku
yesterday	3SG.M	=ERG.M	medicine (TP)	swallow.IRR	-3SG.F.R.O

wok
go.3SG.F.R

'Yesterday he swallowed the medicine' (lit. He swallowed the medicine, it went)

So these are constructions in which the subject marking on the final verb agrees with the object of the preceding transitive verb (in other words: in example (8-21) it agrees with the -*ku* '3SG.F.R.O' of the first part of the SVC; both refer to the 'medicine', the object of 'swallow' and the subject of 'go'. Other examples of these types of constructions are (8-12a), (8-14) and (8-15) above.[3]

These constructions occasion confusion in speakers (even older, fluent speakers) when they are brought to their attention. When I asked speakers whether an example like (8-21) ought not to be *miti-ku-mbot* (that is, with a final verb that agrees with the masculine subject of the previous verb, so go.3SG.M.R), they would pause, consider and agree. But then they would produce sentences like (8-21), where the final verb agrees with the object of the previous verb and not its subject. Occasionally during elicitation sessions, they would become flustered and contradict themselves when producing gender agreement. An example is:

(8-22) *ŋayi munje inde awinni riŋotitek*

ŋa	=yi	munje	inde	awin	=ni
1SG	=ERG.F	man	DX	water	=LOC

ri	-ŋgi	otitek
propel.IRR	-3.SG.M.R.O	fall.3SG.F.R

'I (M or F) threw the man in the water'

In this example the man, masculine, is marked as such in the object affix on the verb 'propel'. But the same argument is marked as feminine in the subject of the second verb 'fall'.

---

[3] These constructions are not uncommon in the languages of the world (Haspelmath 2016), as well as in Papuan languages (Roberts 1997). Note that they are regular serial verb constructions rather than switch reference constructions.

8.2.5 Serial verb constructions in young people's Tayap

The general rule for serialized verbs in young people's Tayap, unsurprisingly, is: the more complex the verb, the less likely it is that it will appear in the speech of young people.

The first casualties, on that rule, are complex predicates like *tapratkɨŋgiatɨkɨtakana*, which require mastery of numerous derivational and morphological processes that are beyond the reach of young speakers.

A handful of the most fluent passive active speakers under thirty produced impressively complex forms like the following:

(8-23) a.

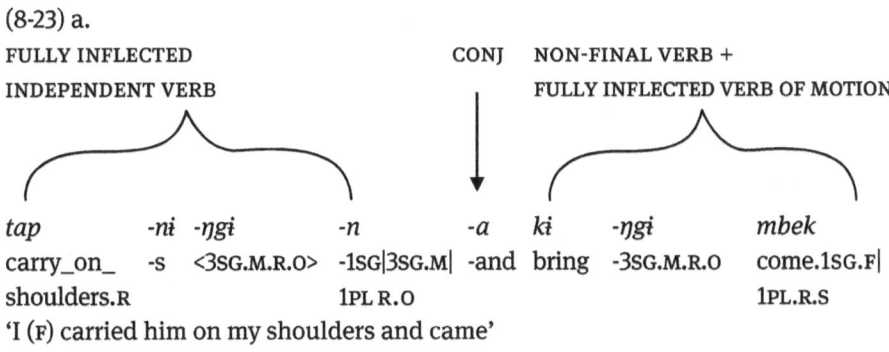

FULLY INFLECTED INDEPENDENT VERB				CONJ	NON-FINAL VERB + FULLY INFLECTED VERB OF MOTION		
tap	-nɨ -ŋgi		-n	-a	kɨ -ŋgi		mbek
carry_on_shoulders.R	-S	<3SG.M.R.O>	-1SG|3SG.M|1PL R.O	-and	bring	-3SG.M.R.O	come.1SG.F|1PL.R.S

'I (F) carried him on my shoulders and came'

b.

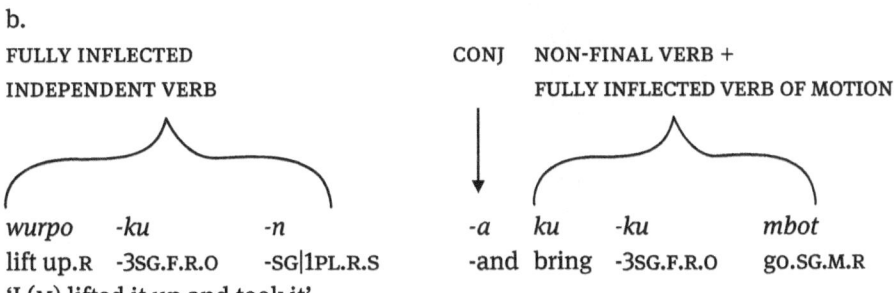

FULLY INFLECTED INDEPENDENT VERB			CONJ	NON-FINAL VERB + FULLY INFLECTED VERB OF MOTION		
wurpo	-ku	-n	-a	ku	-ku	mbot
lift up.R	-3SG.F.R.O	-SG|1PL.R.S	-and	bring	-3SG.F.R.O	go.SG.M.R

'I (M) lifted it up and took it'

Both (8-23a) and (8-23b) consist of an independent verb + the coordinating suffix *-a* followed by a non-final + final verb in a serial verb construction. Even these most complex forms, however, are always built around the grammaticalized verb *kʸ* and the simple verbs of motion 'go' and 'come' – in other words, they are built around the verbs 'bring' and 'take away'.

Even the weakest speakers can produce SVCs like *ku-ku-we* ('bring it and come') or *ku-ku-priek* ('she brought it up [to the village, from the mangrove swamp]') because they have heard them numerous times every day since they were born, as imperatives directed at them and others, and as important parts of narratives.

8.3 Progressives and habituals

Progressive and habitual constructions are formed by means of complex predicates with the verb 'to be'. They are formed in a similar fashion to each other. Intransitive progressives and habituals use the linking morpheme -*a(k)* 'LINK' to join the predicates, while transitive progressives and habituals combine the two predicates directly.

These complex predicates are not analyzed as serial verb constructions because of the use of the linker morpheme in intransitive constructions (cf. Haspelmath 2016: 296). Further, they are not coordinated clauses since they are more closely grammaticalized than that analysis would suggest.

They are therefore considered to be complex predicates in their own right.

8.3.1 Progressives

The progressive marks events that are occurring either at the moment of speaking (as in 'I am eating a sago pancake') or as a backdrop to another action in narration (for example 'he was eating a sago pancake when they arrived' or 'she will be cooking when they come'). It can also express a recurring event or action, as in 'I used to see Sopak in Wongan, but now I don't anymore'.

The progressive is a complex predicate. It consists of two separate verb stems: an irrealis verb stem + linker (in the case of intransitives) + the verb 'be', which is inflected for person, number, TAM and status.

8.3.1.1 Intransitive progressive
The progressive aspect for the majority of intransitive verbs is formed as follows:

irrealis verb stem
+
-*a(k)*[4] 'LINK'
+
verb 'be'[5], inflected for TAM, status and subject

---

[4] Realized as -*ak* before a vowel, -*a* elsewhere.
[5] Note that in the progressive and habitual the verb 'be' has forms *wuk* realized as *uk* and *wuke* realized as *uke*.

Examples:

(8-24) a. *yim prukakuk*
    yim   pruk   -a   kuk
    1PL   work.IRR   -LINK   be.1PL.R
    'we are working'

   b. *yu anakŋa merni warakakkut?*
    yu   anakŋa   mer   =ni   warak   -a   kut
    2SG   which   language   =INST   speak.IRR   -LINK   be.SG.M.R
    'what language are you (M) speaking?'

   c. *kambromtukur suman aiakuk*
    kambromtukur   suman   ai   -ak   uk
    huge rain   big   come.IRR   -LINK   be.3SG.F.R
    'a massive rainstorm is coming'

Intransitive verb roots that end in *-i* or *-w*, such as *mindi* 'work sago', *imbi* 'fly', *ipi* 'burn', *eiw* 'wash sago', *tuw* (bathe), as well as a few verbs with roots that both end in *r* and that exhibit class 2 (*p/w*) alternation in their realis-irrealis stems, form the progressive as follows:

irrealis verb stem
+
-rik/-ruk 'PROG'
+
verb 'be', inflected for TAM and subject

Examples:

(8-25) a. *mindirikkút*
    mindi   -rik   kút
    pound sago pith.IRR   -PROG   be.SG.M.R
    'he is pounding sago pith'

   b. *tam aŋgu imbirikúk aŋgu*
    tam   aŋgu   imbi   -rik   úk   aŋgu
    bird   DX.F   fly.IRR   -PROG   be.3SG.F.R   DX.F
    'that bird is flying'

c. *rewrikkút inde*
   rew   -rik   kút   inde
   fear.IRR -PROG   be.SG.M.R   DX.F
   'he's afraid'

d. *warrikúk*
   war   -rik   úk
   net.IRR -PROG   be.3SG.F.R
   'she's netting (fish)'

e. *mbor werrikúk*
   mbor wer   -rik   úk
   pig   dig.IRR   -PROG   be.3SG.F.R
   'the pig is digging'

f. *ŋgu tuwrukúk*
   ŋgu   tuw   -ruk   úk
   3SG.F bathe.IRR -PROG   be.3SG.F.R
   'she is bathing'

g. *yim amrukkúk*
   yim   am   -ruk   kúk
   1PL   fight.IRR -PROG   be.1SG.F|2SG.F|1PL.R
   'we are fighting'

The progressive morpheme *-rik* has the same form as the counterfactual morpheme (see Section 9.4.3). The counterfactual morpheme, however, is always stressed, whereas the progressive *-rik* is always unstressed.

Progressive verbs formed with *-rik* also have a different stress pattern from progressive verbs formed with *-ak*. Verbs with *-ak* take stress on the final syllable of the verb stem. Progressive verbs formed with *-rik* or *-ruk* take stress on the final syllable of the inflected verb.

Temporality on progressive verbs is expressed by the fully inflected final verb 'be'. Thus, a future progressive is formed as follows:

(8-26) *ŋgi pororakakundak*
   ŋgi   poror   -ak   akundak
   3PL   sing.IRR   -LINK   be.3PL.IRR
   'they will be singing'

8.3.1.2 Transitive progressive

The progressive aspect for transitive verbs is formed in the same manner as for intransitive verbs, except that in the place of the progressive morpheme, a benefactive object morpheme appears. The pattern is as follows:

> irrealis verb stem
> +
> benefactive object
> +
> verb 'be', inflected for TAM, status and subject

Benefactive object morphemes are a distinct set of object morphemes that normally foreground possession or the fact that the action expressed by the verb impacts on a particular entity. They are discussed in Section 7.5.

In the progressive, these morphemes always occur with a final *n*. They encode the features of the transitive object, and have none of the associations with possession or that the verb impacts particularly upon the entity. Their forms are:

	SINGULAR	DUAL	PLURAL
1	-ian	-man	-man
2	-wan	-man	-man
3F	-kwan		
		-man	-mban
3M	-ŋgan		

Examples:

(8-27) a. *ŋa mum akwankut*
 ŋa mum a -kwan kut
 1SG sago jelly consume.IRR -3SG.F.BEN.O be.SG.M.R
 'I (M) am eating sago jelly'

b. *oremŋi munjenum ambankut*
 orem =ŋi munjenum a -mban kut
 crocodile =ERG.M man.PL consume.IRR -3PL.BEN.O be.SG.M.R
 'the crocodile is eating the men'

c. *ŋguyi ŋa oianuk*
 ŋgu =yi ŋa o -ian uk
 3SG.F =ERG.F 1SG strike.IRR -1SG.BEN.O be.3SG.F.R
 'she is hitting me'

d. *ripim ŋa Sopak rarkwankut Potore, ene wákare rarkru*

ripim	ŋa	Sopak	rar	-kwan	kut	Potow	=re
before	1SG	Sopak	see.IRR	-3SG.F.BEN.O	be.SG.M.R	Wongan	=LOC

ene	wákare	rar	-kru
nowadays	NEG	see.IRR	-3SG.F.IRR.O

'I (M) used to see (lit. 'am seeing') Sopak in Wongan, but now I don't anymore'

Transitive and intransitive progressive verbs are favored by the weakest speakers of Tayap, and they are over-extended to express temporal relationships that more correctly would be expressed by the non-future tense. As was discussed in Chapter 6, the non-future forms of Tayap verbs are irregular and complicated to construct. In comparison, the progressive is easy: all one needs to know in order to form it is the following:
(1) the irrealis verb stem (which doesn't change for speaker or referent);
(2) the object (which will frequently be -*kwan*, the 3SG.F.BEN.O form); and
(3) the correct form of the verb 'be', which would be heard hundreds of times every day in the village.

This means that if you know the IRR verb stem and the object (which, again, will usually be the 3SG.F.BEN.O form, -*kwan*), you have two-thirds of the verb formed. All you need to complete it is the correct form of the verb 'be'.

The weaker a speaker is, the more she or he will avoid talking about any subject other than 'I', 'you', 'he', 'she' or 'we' – which means that there are only three endings to choose from: -*kuk* (which expresses 1SG.F, 2SG.F and 1PL), -*kut* (1SG.M, 2SG.M and 3SG.M) and -*(w)uk* (3SG.F).

8.3.2 Habituals (HAB)

The habitual aspect marks an action as one that occurs all the time. To signal habituality, speakers can use the progressive aspect, which has just been discussed above. However, if they want to *emphasize* the habitually recurring nature of an action or event, they use the habitual aspect.

An example of the habitual in use is the following comment, made about a three-year-old child who loved to eat and who always managed to be on hand when meals in several households were being served:

(8-28) *ŋi mum akwanawkkut*

ŋi	mum	a	-kwan	awk	kut
3SG.M	sago_jelly	consume.IRR	-3SG.F.BEN.O	be.HAB	be.SG.M.R

'he is always eating sago jelly'

This habitual form can also carry the implication that the person who 'is always eating sago jelly' doesn't readily eat other forms of sago, such as sago pancakes.

The habitual is formed in exactly the same way as the progressive, except that 'be' at the end of the verb is inflected with a specific form that expresses habituality, *awk-*, followed by an inflected form of 'be'. Thus, intransitive verbs that express the habitual progressive are formed as follows:

$$\text{irrealis verb stem}$$
$$+$$
$$\text{linker } -a(k)^6$$
$$+$$
$$\text{HAB 'be', inflected for TAM, status and subject}$$
$$+$$
$$\text{verb 'be', inflected for TAM, status and subject}$$

Examples:

(8-29) a. *arore arore ruru sene emrariakawkuke*
　　　　 aro-re　　aro-re　　ruru　　　sene
　　　　 day-ADV　day-ADV　child.DL　two

　　　　 emrari　　-ak　　awk　　uke
　　　　 play.IRR　-LINK　be.HAB　be.DL.R
　　　　 'every day all those two kids do is play'

　　 b. *arore arore noŋor aŋgu sapkini pororakawkuk*
　　　　 aro-re　　aro-re　　noŋor　　aŋgu　　sapkini
　　　　 day-ADV　day-ADV　woman　　DX.F　　for_no_reason

　　　　 poror　　-ak　　awk　　uk
　　　　 sing.IRR　-LINK　be.HAB　be.3SG.F.R
　　　　 'every day that woman is always singing for no reason'

---

6 Realized as *-ak* before a vowel, *-a* elsewhere.

With transitive verbs, the habitual is formed as follows:

irrealis verb stem
+
benefactive object morpheme
in its progressive form (i.e. ending in *n*)
+
HAB 'be', inflected for TAM, status and subject
+
verb 'be', inflected for TAM, status and subject

Examples:

(8-30) a. *ŋɨŋi ndagro sisirkwanawkkut inde*
 ŋɨ =ŋi ndagro sisir -kwan awk
 3SG.M =ERG.M palm leaf sew.IRR -3SG.F.BEN.O be.HAB

 kut inde
 be.SG.M.R DX.M
 'he is always sewing palm leaves' (to make roofing shingles)

 b. *Oŋaraŋyi orákaŋgar apukwanawkuk*
 Oŋaraŋ =yi orákaŋgar apu -kwan awk
 Oŋaraŋ =ERG.F food cook.IRR -3SG.F.BEN.O be.HAB

 uk
 be.3SG.F.R
 'Oŋaraŋ is always cooking food'

Besides 'be', only two other verbs in Tayap – 'come' and 'go' – have suppletive habitual stem forms:

ai	→	*aiak*
come.IRR		come.HAB
o	→	*wak*
go.IRR		go.HAB

These habitual stems combine directly with the habitual form of 'be', as follows:

(8-31) a. *aro sami yim wakawkkuk⁷ Potore*
 aro sami yim wak awk kuk Potow =re
 day many 1PL go.HAB be.HAB go.1SG.F|3SG.F|1PL.R Wongan =LOC
 'we go to Wongan every day'

 b. *ŋgɨ arore arore ŋare sokoy aiakawkŋgwuk⁸ moserkrunana*
 ŋgɨ aro -re aro -re ŋa =re sokoi
 3PL day -ADV day -ADV 1SG =LOC tobacco

 aiak awk ŋgwuk
 come.HAB be.HAB be.3PL.R

 moser -kru -nana
 buy.IRR -3SG.F.IRR.O -INTENT
 'they come to me every day to buy tobacco'

Habituality can also be expressed not using a complex predicate like those discussed above, but by using an inflected form of the verb 'to be' as a simple predicate. Habitual verbs can express habituality in a variety of temporalities. It is possible to say that an action will always be happening in the future, for example. This is done by taking the habitual stem *awk-* and inflecting it for future tense. So compare:

(8-32) a. *a-ku-tak* b. *awk-ku-tak*
 be.IRR-IRR-3SG.F.IRR be.HAB-IRR-3SG.F.IRR
 'it will be' 'it will habitually be'

---

7 often shortened to *wakuk*
8 Often shortened to *aiakŋguk*

9 Simple and complex sentences

This final chapter of the grammar describes simple and complex sentences, tail-head linkage, and the way in which young speakers typically form complex clauses.

Complex sentences are of three main types: coordinated clauses, cosubordinate clauses and subordinate clauses.

Coordinated clauses are independent clauses joined by various conjunctions.

Cosubordinate clauses themselves are of two types: modifying and manner structures.

Subordinate clauses are also of three types: adverbial clauses (including counterfactual clauses), relative clauses and perception constructions.

Tayap also has finite nominalizations, and these are discussed after the discussion of relative clauses.

9.1 Simple sentences

A simple sentence in Tayap may consist of no more than an inflected verb. Thus, a complex predicate like the serial verb construction discussed throughout the previous chapter, *tapratkiŋgiatikitakana* 'she intends to carry him down on her shoulders' is a fully formed sentence in Tayap. A simpler example is:

(9-1) *puko*
come_up.3PL.R
'they came up'

Word order is relatively flexible, since the grammatical relations of core constituents and other elements are expressed through morphology and potentially marked on NPs by case clitics like the ergative. However, Tayap is a verb-final language and the unmarked order of elements in a declarative intransitive sentence is Subject-Verb (SV), and in a declarative transitive sentence Subject-Object-Verb (AOV):

	SUBJECT	VERB
(9-2) a.	*prerikin*	*pipiek-ara*
	sweet_potato	burn.3SG.F|1PL.R-PERF
	'the sweet potato burned'	

	SUBJECT	OBJECT	VERB
b.	*Merew-ŋgro=gi*	*munje*	*par-ŋgi-ro*
	Sanae-PL=ERG.PL	man	bury.R-3SG.M.R.O-3PL.R.S

'the Sanae villagers buried the man'

In transitive clauses that contain a subject, an object, and an oblique argument, the order of object and oblique is fairly free, with the caveat that the object never follows the verb, while the oblique argument can. Also, the subject normally occurs in the sentence-initial position. Some examples of various word orders follow:

		SUBJECT	DIRECT OBJECT	VERB		OBLIQUE
(9-3)	a.	*Sopak=yi*	*orákaŋgar*	*ni-tu-ku-n*		*yim=ana*
		Sopak=ERG.F	food	make.R-S<3SG.F.R.O>2SG|3SG.F.R.S		1PL=DAT

'Sopak made us food'

		SUBJECT	DIRECT OBJECT	OBLIQUE	VERB
	b.	*Sopak=yi*	*orákaŋgar*	*yim=ana*	*ni-tu-ku-n*
		Sopak=ERG.F	food	1PL=DAT	make.R-S<3SG.F.R.O>2SG|3SG.F.R.S

'Sopak made us food'

		SUBJECT	OBLIQUE	DIRECT OBJECT	VERB
	c.	*Sopak=yi*	*yim=ana*	*orákaŋgar*	*ni-tu-ku-n*
		Sopak=ERG.F	1PL=DAT	food	make.R-S<3SG.F.R.O>2SG|3SG.F.R.S

'Sopak made us food'

(9-4)	OBJECT	VERB	SUBJECT			
	pomiŋ	*ta-tu-ku-re*	*omindeominde*	*sene*	*ŋan*	
	conch	hear.R-S<3SG.F.R.O>DL.R.S	spouse.PL	two	3SG.M.POSS	

'his two wives heard the conch shell'

Verbless clauses also exist. The subject precedes the complement. For example:

(9-5) *ŋa ainda*
  1SG DX
  'It's me'

(9-6) omɨndeomɨnde yum=ke?
    spouse.PL   2PL=Q
    'Are you my lovers?'

Negated verbless clauses use the general negator *wákare*, which occurs finally:

(9-7) ŋa tam ror wákare
    ŋa   tam   ror   wákare
    1SG   bird   child NEG
    'I'm not a baby bird'

9.2 Complex sentences: Coordinate, subordinate and cosubordinate clauses

Complex sentences consist of coordinate, cosubordinate or subordinate structures. The following suffixes and free morphemes function to express these clause types.

Clause-coordinating suffixes (conjunctions): Sections 9.3.1, 9.3.2		*-(y)a* 'and' *-api* 'then', 'afterwards'
Clause-coordinating words: Sections 9.3.3, 9.3.4	*ŋgi(na)napi* *ayáta*	'therefore', 'for that reason' 'never mind that', 'even though', 'it doesn't matter that'
Clause-subordinating suffix and words: Section 9.4	*-re* *pi* *pime* *ndɨ*	'if', 'when', 'while', 'because' hypothetical
Clause-cosubordinating suffixes (medial-final chains) Section 9.8		*-ra* 'modifier' *-kar* 'manner'
Other complex clause combining (see Section 9.10)		*-rar* 'multiplicative'

9.3 Coordinated clauses

9.3.1 Coordinated clauses with conjunctive –(y)a ('and')

The simplest way to link verbs in Tayap is to add a conjunctive morpheme -a (realized as -ya after a vowel) glossed as 'and' to fully inflected verbs that occur in a series. Verbs linked in this manner express sequentiality: X happened, then Y happened, then Z happened, and so on.

For example:

(9-8) a. *Konjab adɨmbota sindineta turonɨ siniet*
       Konjab adɨmbot -a sindi -net -a
       Konjab trip.SG.M.R -and slip.R -1SG.M|3SG.M.R -and

       turo =nɨ siniet
       slope =LOC go_down.SG.M.R
       'Konjab tripped, lost his footing and slid down the slope'

   b. *yu urekteta raretet!*
       yu urek -tet -a rare -tet
       2SG turn.SBJ -2SG.M.R -and look.SBJ -2SG.M.R
       'turn around and look!'

All the clauses linked together in this way are independent clauses. For example:

(9-9) *mbuspimbroya nda ŋgɨ prike*
      mbuspi -mb -ro -ya nda ŋgɨ prike
      send.R -3PL.R.O -3PL.R-S -and DM 3PL come_up.DL.R
      'They sent them off and the two came [back] up [to Gapun].'

(9-10) a. *yum aikiya ŋanana orákaŋgar apukru wákare*
       yum ai-ki -ya ŋa =nana orákaŋgar
       2PL come.IRR-IRR -and 1SG =DAT food

       apu -kru wákare
       cook.IRR -3SG.F.IRR.O NEG
       'you all didn't come and cook any food for me'

   b. *ŋiŋi okɨya minjike moserkruya aikɨya ŋare mbudjikru wákare*
       ŋɨ =ŋi o -ki -ya minjike moser -kru
       3SG.M =ERG.M go.IRR -IRR -and betel_nut buy.IRR -3SG.F.IRR.O

-ya	ai	-ki	-ya	ŋa	=re	mbudji	-kru	wákare
-and	come.IRR	-IRR	-and	1SG	=ALL	sell.IRR	-3SG.F.IRR.O	NEG

'he didn't go and buy betel nut and come and sell it to me'

Note that in both examples in (9-10), even though the negating word *wákare* appears only once, the scope of negation covers all verbs, and all verbs appear in the irrealis form that they take when negated:

ai-ki
come.IRR-IRR
apu-kru
cook.IRR-3SG.F.IRR.O

o-kɨ
go.IRR-IRR
moser-kru
buy.IRR-3SG.F.IRR.O

ai-ki
come.IRR-IRR
mbudji-kru
sell.IRR-3SG.F.IRR.O

wákare
NEG

However, the scope of negation can also cover just the final independent clause: see below, example (9-11c).

Note that these structures are considered to be series of independent coordinated clauses. It is possible to consider them as single complex predications, particularly as the scope of negation can cover the whole coordinated series. But an analysis of coordinated clauses is preferred here, since each of the verbs is a fully inflected independent verb, which can take its own overt NP arguments as individual clauses do, and which can stand on its own. In addition, there is an overt linker joining the clauses, making an analysis of a single predicate less viable (Haspelmath 2016: 296).

It is also possible to consider these sequences as medial-final chaining (cosubordinate) constructions (Longacre 2007: 398). However, the non-final verbs receive the full range of inflections, as do the final verbs. In medial-final chains the non-final verbs are cosubordinate (see below, Section 9.8). For those reasons it seems best to treat these sequences as independent coordinated clauses.

Coordinate clauses do not have to share subjects, and as examples (9-11c and d) show, they can be independently negated:

(9-11) a. ŋgigi ŋa utawtioya ŋa katitet awinnɨ
        ŋgɨ   =gi   ŋa   utaw   -t -i   -o   -ya
        3PL   =ERG.PL 1SG   push.R -S <1SG.R.O> -3PL.R.S -and

        ŋa   katitet   awin   =nɨ
        1SG   fall.1SG|3SG.M|1PL.R water =ALL
        'they pushed me and I fell in the water'

    b. noŋoryi tatɨŋgɨna mbor wemperkureya munjeŋi pokun
        noŋor   =yi   ta   -tɨ -ŋgɨ   -n   -a   mbor
        woman   =ERG-F see.R -S <3SG.M.R.O> -2SG.F|3SG.F.R.S -and pig

        wemper -ku-   -re   -ya   munje =ŋi
        chase.R -3SG.F.R.O DL.R.S- -and   man   =ERG.M

        po   -ku-   -n
        strike.R -3SG.F.R.O -SG|1PL.R.S
        'the woman saw him and the two of them chased the pig and the man speared it'

    c. Kamayi awin andrupekuna non worerraatɨkɨ wákare
        Kama   =yi   awin   andrupe   -ku   -n   -a
        Kama   =ERG.F water carry_on_head.R -3SG.F.R.O -SG|1PL.R.S -and

        worer   -ra   atɨ   -kɨ   wákare
        capsize.IRR -MOD fall.IRR -IRR   NEG
        'Kama carried some water and none of it spilled'

    d. ŋgigi ŋa utawi wakarere ŋa katitet awinnɨ
        ŋgɨ   =gi   ŋa   utaw   -i   wákare -re
        3PL   =ERG.PL 1SG   push.IRR -1SG.IRR.O NEG   -SUB

        ŋa   katitet   awin   =nɨ
        1SG   fall.1SG|3SG.M|1PL.R water =ALL
        'they didn't push me and I fell in the water'

All these examples contain separate clauses, each one headed by fully inflected independent verbs. The first two examples express a sequential relationship between the actions: they pushed me *and then* I fell (9-11a); the woman saw the man, *and then* the two of them chased the pig, *and then* the man speared the pig (9-11b). This relationship of sequentiality is the most common implication of clauses joined with *-a*.

But as (9-11c) shows, *-a* can also coordinate clauses that express a simultaneous rather than sequential relationship between the actions: Kama carried the water *and while she was carrying it*, none of it spilled.

9.3.2 Coordination with *-api* 'afterward' (AFT)

The suffix *-api* links clauses that encode actions that occur consecutively, one after the other. It is affixed to a verb that is fully inflected for person, number and TAM and takes its own arguments. The suffix marks that verb as an action that was or will be completed before the action in the clause that follows it occurred or will occur.

Like *-a*, *-api* can link clauses that involve either the same subject or different subjects. Again, it joins full independent clauses.

Examples are:

(9-12) a. ŋa tuwkunet**api** aikinet yure
ŋa   tuw   -ku   -net   **-api**
1SG   wash.IRR -IRR   -1SG.M|3SG.M.IRR   -AFT

ai   -ki   -net   yu   =re
come.IRR   -IRR   -1SG.M|3SG.M.IRR   2SG   =ALL
'I'll wash first, then I'll come to you'

b. ŋgomiek   **-api**   karep   pwiek
fight.3PL.R   -AFT   moon   rise.3SG.F.R
'after they fought, the moon rose'

9.3.3 Coordination with *ŋgi(na)napi* 'therefore', 'for that reason'

Some speakers pronounce this form *ŋgu(na)napi*, which indicates that it might be analyzed as *ŋgu* (3SG.F)+ the coordinating suffix *-api*. So: 'after it'.

Nginanapi (or *ŋginapi*) is a freestanding word. It introduces a clause that expresses cause or reason, thereby combining two main clauses:

(9-13) a. ngigi Kama ngarkwanŋguk ngarkwanŋguk, **ŋginapi** ŋgu wek
ŋgi   =gi   Kama   ŋgar   -kwan   -ŋguk
3PL   =ERG.PL   Kama   call_out.IRR   -3SG.F.BEN.O   -be.3PL.R.S

ŋgar   -kwan   -ŋguk   **ŋginapi** ŋgu   wek
call_out.IRR -3SG.F.BEN.O -be.3PL.R.S therefore 3SG.F come.3SG.F.R
'They kept calling out to Kama and that's why she came'

b. *ewar ŋgadan utok,* **ŋginapi** *nɨ waikɨ wákare*
ewar   ŋgadan   utok   **ŋginapi**   nɨ   wai
yesterday   sore   appear.3SG.F.R therefore   3SG.M   walk.IRR

-kɨ   wákare
-IRR   NEG
'Yesterday a sore appeared [on his leg] and therefore he didn't walk'

9.3.4 Coordination with *ayáta* 'although', 'it doesn't matter that', 'never mind that'

Ayáta is a word most familiar to the villagers as an interjection of impatience or dismissal, in its meaning of 'Stop it! or 'Never mind' (see Section 3.10). It is this latter sense of dismissal that is expressed when the word is used in a sentence as a clause-coordinating conjunction.

(9-14) a. **ayáta** *nɨ munje suman, nime ŋa namŋgarke*
ayáta   nɨ   munje   suman   nime   ŋa   nam   -garke
although   3SG.M   man   big   thusly 1SG   talk.IRR -PROH
'It doesn't matter that he's a big man, he can't talk to me like that'

Note the position of the negative in the following sentence, and note also that its scope covers both 'go' and 'see' verbs, which are both in their negative stripped down form.

b. **ayáta** *nɨ aikinana waraknet, ŋa wákare inda okɨ rarŋrɨ*
ayáta   nɨ   ai   -kɨ   -nana   warak -net
although   3SG.M   come.IRR   -IRR   -INTENT   talk.R -1SG.M|3SG.M.R

ŋa   wákare   inda   o   -kɨ   rar   -ŋrɨ
1SG   NEG   DX.M   go.IRR   -IRR   see.IRR   -3SG.M.IRR.O
'Never mind that he talked about coming, I'm not going to go see him'

c. **ayáta** *ŋgɨ aikɨ wákare, yim orákaŋgar nɨrkrunak*
ŋgɨ   **ayáta**   ai   -kɨ   wákare   yim   orákaŋgar
3PL   although   come.IRR   -IRR   NEG   1PL   food

```
nir          -kru           -nak
make.IRR     -3SG.F.IRR.O   -1SG.F|1PL.IRR.S
```
'Even though they didn't come, we'll make food'

Sentences with *ayáta* can also occur in construction with the verb in the clause that follows *ayáta* in the prohibitive mood. For example:

(9-15) a. ***ayáta** tukur aiŋgarke, yim okitikenana*

```
ayáta      tukur   ai         -ŋgarke  yim   o        -ki    -tike
although   rain    come.IRR   -PROH    1PL   go.IRR   -IRR   -DL.IRR

-nana
-INTENT
```
'Even if it rains, we'll go'

b. ***ayáta** ikur katkat sirŋgarke, ŋgɨ aikindakana aŋgi*

```
ayáta      ikur      katkat    sir           -ŋgarke   ŋgɨ
although   evening   quickly   go_down.IRR   -PROH     3PL

ai-ki-ndak-ana              aŋgi
come.IRR-IRR-3PL.IRR-INTENT DX
```
'Even if night comes quickly, they're going to come'

9.4 Adverbial subordinate clauses

9.4.1 Adverbial subordination with *-re* 'when', 'if', 'while' (SUB)

The suffix *-re* (realized as *-de* after *n*) attaches as a suffix to fully inflected verbs and marks a verb as expressing the background condition in relation to which the action indicated in the main clause occurs. This backgrounding nature of subordination is emphasized by the order of the subordinate and main clauses in Tayap: the subordinate clause always precedes the main clause.

In English, these are clauses that would be expressed with the subordinating conjunctions 'if' and 'when'. Unlike English, though, Tayap makes no distinction between 'if' and 'when', at least when referring to unreal events; both are expressed by *-re*.

These clauses are semantically subordinate in that they specify a precondition for the action of the main clause to occur. They are not considered medial-final (cosubordinate) constructions, as the non-final verbs are structurally quite different, for instance they are not obligatorily irrealis (Section 9.8).

Examples are as follows:

(9-16) a. *ŋa aŋgok akrunetre, kambwan ambukrunet*
ŋa   aŋgok   a   -kru   -net   **-re**
1SG DX.F   consume.IRR -3SG.F.IRR.O -1SG.M|3SG.M.IRR.S -SUB

  kambwan ambu   -kru   -net
  vomit   throw_up.IRR -3SG.F.IRR.O -1SG.M|3SG.M.IRR.S
  'If I (M) eat that I will vomit'

b. *poŋgrore, wasownet*
po   -ŋg   -ro   **-re**   wasow   -net
strike.R -3SG.M.R.O -3PL.R.S -SUB   die.R   -1SG.M|3SG.M.R
'when they shot him, he died'

c. *ɲiɲi namŋat aŋgi supwáspwa ŋanana ninkunde, ŋa ŋgunana maikarpet*
ɲi   =ɲi   nam   -ŋat   aŋgi   supwáspwa   ŋa   =nana
3SG.M =ERG.M   talk -half DX.F   badly   1SG   =DAT

ni   -n -ku   -n   **-de** ŋa   ŋgu =nana
do.R -S <3SG.F.R.O> -1SG.M|3SG.M|1PL.R.S -SUB   1SG 3SG.F =DAT

maikar-pet
shame.R-SG.M.R
'when he said that bad thing to me, I (M) became ashamed'

When verbs in both subordinate and main clauses are constructed in the progressive (see Section 8.3.1) the meaning of *-re* is 'while' and the actions indicated by the verbs occur simultaneously, not sequentially.

(9-17) a. *ŋa prukakkutre, ɲi pororakut*
ŋa   pruk   -ak   kut   **-re** ɲi
1SG work.IRR -LINK be.3SG.M.R -SUB   3SG.M

poror   -ak   kut
sing.IRR -LINK be.3SG.M.R
'when I (M) am working, he sings'

b. *ŋa mindirikutre, tukur aiki wákare*
ŋa   mindiri   kut   **-re** tukur ai   -ki
1SG   pound_sago.IRR be.3SG.M.R -SUB   rain   come.IRR -IRR

```
         wákare
         NEG
         'While I (M) was pounding sago, it didn't rain'

     c.  ŋgatŋi awin akwankutre, ŋa poŋgɨn
         ŋgat      =ŋi     awin   a              -kwan
         cassowary =ERG.M  water  consume.IRR    -3SG.F.BEN.O.R

         kut        -re    ŋa    po         -ŋgɨ         -n
         be.SG.M.R  -SUB   1SG   strike.R   -3SG.M.R.O   -SG|1PL.R.S
         'the cassowary was drinking water when I (M or F) speared him'
```

Negative conditionals occur paratactically without *-re*, perhaps because the negation word *wákare* already ends in *re*:

```
(9-18)  yu ŋaŋan nam tariati wákare, ŋayi yu adrunet
        yu    ŋaŋan     nam    tar          -iati            wákare
        2SG   1SG.POSS  talk   listen.IRR   -1SG.BEN.O.IRR   NEG

        ŋa    =yi      yu    adu       -ru         -net
        1SG   =ERG.F   2SG   hit.IRR   -2SG.IRR.O  -1SG.M|3SG.M.IRR
        'If you (M or F) don't listen to my talk, I (M) am going to hit you'
```

9.4.2 Adverbial subordination with the hypothetical particles *pi, pime, ndɨ* (HYPO)

Counterfactual events are expressed by a main clause ('I would have killed the snake') and a subordinate clause ('if I had seen it in time'). As discussed in the following section, Section 9.4.3, counterfactual constructions, in addition to being formed with a particular inflectional morphology, also obligatorily take a particle that can be glossed as 'hypothetical'.

This particle, which can be either *pi, pime* or *ndɨ* marks the clause in which it appears as the subordinate clause. These particles all have their own stress.

Like the previous clauses, these clauses are semantically subordinate.

For example:

```
(9-19)  a.  pipiŋgabu aŋgwar pime, oŋgab wawarwekrɨknukun
            pipiŋgabu  a        -ŋgwar    pime,   oŋgab
            hook       be.IRR   -NFN.SG   HYPO    pot
```

```
        wawarwek      -rik   -nu   -ku              -n
        hang_up.CF    -CF    -S    <3SG.F.R.O>      -1SG.M|3SG.M|1PL.R.S
        'If there had been a hook, I would have hung up the pot'
```

b. *ŋɨ mbɨd tarkru wákare **ndɨ**, mɨndɨrɨknet*

```
        ŋɨ       mbɨd    tar      -kru           wákare    ndɨ
        3SG.M    pain    get.IRR  -3SG.F.IRR.O   NEG       HYPO

        mɨndɨ             -rik   -net
        work_sago.CF      -CF    -1SG.M|3SG.M.R
        'If he hadn't gotten a pain, he would have worked sago'
```

Unlike the clause-linking constituents *-a*, *-api* and *-re*, the hypothetical particles *pi*, *pime* and *ndɨ* are not bound morphemes. They are free morphemes that tend to be clause final, as the following examples show:

(9-20) a. *Mbanuŋ ewar awknet pi, wakŋgɨn*

```
        Mbanuŋ    ewar         awk     -net            pi
        1SG       yesterday    be.CF   -1SG.M|3SG.M.R  HYPO

        wak-        -ŋgɨ          -n
        -strike.CF- -3SG.M.R.O-   -1SG.M|3SG.M|1PL.R.S
        'If Mbanuŋ had been here yesterday, I would have hit him'
```

b. *yu noŋor mambɨr pi, arrɨknun*

```
        yu       noŋor    mambɨr    pi
        2SG      woman    young     HYPO

        ar       -rik  -n  -u           -n
        marry    -CF   -S  <2SG.R.O>    -1SG.M| 3SG.M|1PLR.S
        'If you were young, I would marry you'
```

When appearing with a verb inflected in the intentional mood (see Sections 5.4.2.3 and Section 7.4), *pi* (or *ndɨ*, which is also sometimes used in this context) means 'If X want(s) to do Y...'. For example:

(9-21) a. *Kiki Potowre atɨkɨnana pi, namku wetak*

```
        Kiki    Potow     =re      atɨ              -kɨ    -nana      pi
        Kiki    Wongan    =ALL     go_down.IRR      -IRR   -INTENT    HYPO

        nam        -ku              we           -tak
        talk.SBJ   -3SG.F.R.O       come.SBJ     -3SG.F.R.S
        'If Kiki wants to go down to Wongan, tell her to come'
```

(9-22) a. *Yu mum akrunana pi, oteta Sopakyi mum iwatitak*
   yu   *mum*   *a*   *-kru*   *-nana*   *pi*
   2SG   sago_jelly   consume.IRR   -3SG.F.IRR.O   -INTENT   HYPO

   o   *-tet*   *-a*   *Sopak*   *=yi*   *mum*
   go.SBJ   -2SG.M   -and   Sopak   =ERG.F   sago_jelly

   i   *-wati*   *-tak*
   give.IRR   -2SG.BEN.O.IRR   -2SG.F|3SG.F.IRR.S
   'If you want to eat sago jelly, go and Sopak will give you some sago jelly'

Ndɨ behaves slightly differently to *pi* and *pime*. *Ndɨ* is also a discourse marker that highlights the noun phrase that it follows in ongoing talk (see Section 3.11.2). However, when it occurs in a clause with a verb inflected in counterfactual mood, *ndɨ* conveys a hypothetical meaning.

  Ndɨ is also the particle that usually follows the negation *wákare* in a negative counterfactual sentence, for example:

(9-23) *ewar tukur aiki wákare ndɨ yim patɨr andɨkrɨkkun*
   ewar   *tukur*   *ai*   *-ki*   *wákare*   *ndɨ*
   yesterday   rain   come.IRR   -IRR   NEG   HYPO

   yim   *patɨr*   *andɨk*   *-rɨk*   *-ku*   *-n*
   1PL   house   roof.CF   -CF   -3SG.F.R.O   -SG|1PL.R.S
   'If it hadn't rained yesterday, we would have roofed the house'

9.4.3 Counterfactual (CF)

The counterfactual expresses an action or event that could have happened but did not or cannot happen, as in 'If he had gone hunting yesterday, he would have speared a cassowary', or 'If you had been young, I would marry you'. Some of the ways of constructing the counterfactual have become moribund in Tayap. There are a number of morphologically rather complex subtypes. The counterfactual has the largest degree of variation documented for any verb form in Tayap. Already in the 1980s, I was told by senior men that a clause like 'would have gone' could be expressed as *wakret*, *waknet*, *wakrɨknet* or *wakrɨkret*, and that all of those verbs meant exactly the same thing.

  By 2009, the oldest fluent speakers were constructing counterfactual sentences differently from what I had recorded in the 1980s. Those oldest speakers were still able to produce counterfactual morphology, but they only inflected one of the verbs in a counterfactual construction consisting of two clauses. Most speakers under fifty, however, could not do even this. Those speakers constructed counterfactual sentences without using any counterfactual morphology.

And even relatively fluent Tayap speakers younger than forty have stopped using Tayap in the main clause of a counterfactual construction.

Senior men in the 1980s expressed the counterfactual as follows:

IF-CLAUSE	THEN-CLAUSE
verb inflected with counterfactual morphology + hypothetical particle *pi, pime* or *ndɨ*	verb inflected with counterfactual morphology

Example:

(9-24) *njenum Mbowdirekɨ muŋgit wakndak pi, ŋgɨ ŋgat non wakŋgro*
  njenum   Mbowdi =rekɨ   muŋgit   wak¹   -ndak   pi,
  dog.PL   Mbowdi =COM   recently   go.CF   -3PL.IRR   HYPO

  ŋgɨ   ŋgat   non   wak   -ŋg   -ro
  3PL   cassowary   INDEF   strike.CF   -3SG.M.R.O   -3PL.R.S
  'If the dogs had gone with Mbowdi the other day, they would have speared a cassowary'

By 2009, the oldest fluent speakers were expressing counterfactuality by nominalizing the verb in the if-clause with the non-finite suffix *-(ŋ)gar* (see Section 4.2):

IF-CLAUSE	THEN-CLAUSE
irr verb stem affixed with *-ŋgar* + hypothetical particle *pi, pime* or *ndɨ*	verb inflected with counterfactual morphology

Example:

(9-25) *Mairumyi ŋanana sokoi mokɨr iŋgar pime, tuwakrɨknukun*
  Mairum =yi   ŋa =nana   sokoi   mokɨr   i   -ŋgar   pime
  Mairum =ERG.F   1SG =DAT   tobacco   seedling   give.IRR   -NFN.SG   HYPO

---

1 Note that the counterfactual form of *okɨ* ('go') is exceptional. See Section 9.4.3.1.

> *tuwak -rɨk -nu -ku   -n*
> plant.CF -CF -S <3SG.F.R.O> -1SG|3SG.M|1PL.R.S
> 'If Mairum had given me a tobacco seedling, I would have planted it' (lit. 'Mairum hypothetically a giver of a tobacco seedling, I would have planted it')

Counterfactual morphology is still used in the example above, but unlike the senior men in the 1980s, the oldest speakers of Tayap in 2009 only used it for the verb of the then-clause. In this case, the counterfactual meaning of the if-clause is borne by the hypothetical particle *pi*, *pime* or *ndɨ*, not by verb morphology. Constructing a counterfactual sentence like this was a possibility earlier, and I have a few recorded examples of this form from the 1980s. But they are rare. The overwhelming majority of the examples I recorded in the 1980s inflected the verbs in both the if-clause and the then-clause with the counterfactual morphology.

Counterfactual morphology is completely absent in the language of fluent speakers between the ages of forty and fifty-five in 2009. They consistently express counterfactuality without using any counterfactual morphology at all:

IF-CLAUSE	THEN-CLAUSE
IRR verb stem affixed with -*ŋgar* for all subjects + hypothetical particle *pi*, *pime* or *ndɨ*	verb inflected in future tense

Example:

(9-26) *ŋgigi Mbanaŋ rarŋgar pi, wemberŋgrɨndak*
  ŋgi =gi   Mbanaŋ rar   -ŋgar   pi,
  3PL =ERG.PL Mbanaŋ perceive.IRR -NFN.SG HYPO

  wember -ŋgrɨ   -ndak
  chase.IRR -3SG.M.IRR.O -3PL.IRR.S
  'If they had seen Mbanaŋ, they would have chased him' (lit. 'Those hypothetically who are see-ers of Mbanaŋ, *they will chase him*')

This trend continues in the speech of speakers in their early forties and younger. On the few occasions when these speakers formulate a counterfactual statement, the entire then-clause is in Tok Pisin, not Tayap:

IF-CLAUSE	THEN-CLAUSE
IRR verb stem affixed with -*ŋgar* for all subjects + hypothetical particle *pi*, *pime* or *ndɨ*	entire clause in Tok Pisin, with verb inflected in the present or future tense

Example:

(9-27) ŋaŋano aŋgwar ndɨ, yu kisim bikpela bagarap long moning
ŋa -ŋano a -ŋgwar ndɨ,
1SG -REFL be.IRR -NFN.SG HYPO

yu kisim bikpela bagarap long moning
2SG get big damage PREP morning (all Tok Pisin)
'If I had been there myself, you would have gotten hurt in the morning'
(lit. 'Me myself hypothetically present, you get big damage in the morning'; i.e. I would have beaten you up)

It is possible that the counterfactual has been on its way out of Tayap for quite some time. That, at any rate, may be one explanation for the fact that already in the 1980s it exhibited the widest variation of any verbal morphology.

Another explanation could be that the various forms, even if they had the same literal meaning, had different stylistic nuances. If so, those nuances had already been lost even in the speech of senior men in the 1980s.

9.4.3.1 How to form a counterfactual verb

Counterfactual morphology is quite specific. Intransitive verbs use their irrealis stems, and transitive verbs their realis stems.

The actual stem form of many intransitive verbs is the same as their irrealis form. But other verb stems have suppletive forms. They change in regular ways, but most of the forms occur nowhere else in Tayap (an exception is the counterfactual form for *o* 'go', which is the same as that verb's habitual stem, see Section 8.3.2). The changes to the verb stems are as follows:

class 1 & class 2 verb stems that contain *e* → *wek*
class 1 & class 2 verb stems that contain *o* → *wak*
class 1 & class 2 verb stems that contain *i* → *ik*
class 3 verb stems, *a* → *ak*

EXCEPTIONS: (1) the verb 'be', *a*-, becomes *awk* in CF
(2) the verb 'marry', *ar*-, remains the same and does not change to *ak* in CF

The following is a full list of how counterfactual intransitive verbs are formed.

SUBJECT PRONOUN	VERB STEM	COUNTERFACTUAL AFFIX	SUBJECT ENDING
ŋa 'I'			-ret (CF) or -net (IRR) (M speaker) -rak (CF) or -nak (IRR) (F speaker)
yu 'you'	VERB STEM INFLECTED FOR COUNTERFACTUAL (IN MOST CASES THIS IS THE SAME AS THE STEM IN IRREALIS)	+ (-rɨk) +	-ret (CF) or -net (IRR) (M referent) -rak (CF) or -nak (IRR) (F referent)
ŋɨ 'he'			-ret (CF) or -net (IRR)
ŋgu 'she'			-rak (CF) or -tak (IRR)
yim 'we'			-nak
yum 'you PL'			-nkem
ŋgɨ 'they'			-ndak
DL			-(ti)ke

Note that the counterfactual -rɨk is always stressed, in which point it differs from the formally identical progressive marker also -rɨk (see Section 8.3.1.1).

The counterfactual affix -rɨk is optional in those cases where the form of the verb stem in the counterfactual differs from its form in the irrealis. So, for example, a verb like 'be' is realized as *a* in its irrealis form, but in the counterfactual, it becomes *awk*. This partially suppletive stem change makes the counterfactual morpheme -rɨk redundant. Therefore, it can be omitted. But it doesn't have to be omitted.

The phrase 'she would have been' can thus be expressed in any of the following four ways:

awk-rɨk-rak
awk-rɨk-tak
awk-rak
awk-tak

Transitive verbs display a similar range of variation. They can be formed in ways that either include or exclude the following morphemes in parentheses. Note the realis forms of the subject and object affixes:

verb stem.CF + (-rik) + (-nʸ/-tʸ) + object.R + subject.R
                counterfactual   subject suffix
                suffix   for transitive
                                 classes 4 and 5
                                 (see Section
                                 6.1.6)

So a verb like 'I would have eaten it' has the following forms, all of which senior speakers insist mean the same:

verb stem.CF	+ (-rik)	+ (-nʸ/-tʸ)	+ object.R	+ subject.R		
ak-	-rik	-nu-	<ku>	-n	→	akriknukun[2]
ak-	-rik		-ku	-n	→	akrikkun
ak-		-nu-	<ku>	-n	→	aknukun
ak-			-ku	-n	→	akkun

As with intransitive verbs, all these options for variation only apply to verbs that alter their stems in the counterfactual. They don't apply to a verb like *moser* 'buy', for example, because that verb has the same stem form in both the irrealis and the counterfactual (since *moser* isn't a class 1, 2 or 3 verb; see the discussion above about which verbs change their stem form in the counterfactual).[3] In this case, where the stem does not change to express the counterfactual, the counterfactual morpheme *-rik* is needed – even if the *-nʸ/-tʸ* subject morphemes are optional.

So the full range of inflectional options listed above applies to verbs like *o* 'hit' or *wawar-(p/w)-e* 'hang up', because to express counterfactuality, those verb stems change and become *wak* and *wawarwek* respectively. In those instances, once again, the counterfactual affix *-rik* is redundant, since the stem change already signals counterfactuality.

Negative counterfactual actions are expressed by simply negating the relevant subordinate verb as in a main clause, and following this with one of the hypothetical particles (most commonly *ndi*), then expressing the main clause in the counterfactual as usual:

---

[2] In the morphological combination *-riknukun*, the morpheme-medial *n* and *u* undergo metathesis, resulting in [rəkunkun]
[3] To lessen the risk for confusion, the verb stem of such verbs is glossed as CF in counterfactual constructions, even though the stem is identical with its IRR form. An example is (9-23).

(9-28) a. *ŋayi rarŋgri wákare pi, aramŋi amïraknin*

ŋa=yi	rar-ŋgri		wákare	pi,	aram=ŋi
1SG=ERG.F	perceive.IRR-3SG.M.IRR.O		NEG	HYPO	snake=ERG.M

amïrak-	-n	-i		-n
bite.CF-	-S-	<1SG.R.O>		-1SG|3SG.M|1PL.R.S

'If I hadn't seen it, the snake would have bitten me'

b. *Kono wasowki wákare ndi, ŋayi ŋgu arriknukun*

Kono	wasow	-ki	wákare	ndi	ŋa	=yi	ŋgu
Kono	die.IRR	-IRR	NEG	HYPO	1SG	=ERG.F	3SG.F

ar	-rik	-nu	-ku-		-n
marry.CF	-CF	-S	<3SG.F.R.O>		-1SG|3SG.M|1PL.R.S

'If Kono hadn't died, I would have married her'

9.5 Relative clauses

A relative clause is a clause which modifies a noun phrase, which "delimits the reference of an NP by specifying the role of the referent of that NP in the situation described by the [relative clause]" (Andrews 2007: 206). Relative clauses in Tayap are nominalized, marked with the inanimate possessive clitic =ŋa(n) which appears on the verb of the relative clause. This possessive clitic =ŋa(n) is added to a fully inflected verb, which then functions as a subordinate relative clause. The common argument or head ("domain nominal" in Andrews' 2007 terms) of a relative and a main clause can be in S, A, O or oblique function in the relative clause and in the main clause.

Tayap relative clauses are external. The relative clause generally directly follows the common argument in the main clause. This is the position held by a nominal modifier (e.g. adjective) as well (see Chapter 4).

The common argument may also be expressed with a deictic (Section 3.8) functioning resumptively with respect to the head noun, and typically following the common argument directly: for example, consider (9-29a-b). In both examples there are two resumptive pronouns, in (9-29a) following the relative clause and as the final part of the main clause and in (9-29b) following the common argument and as the final part of the main clause. Note that these resumptive pronouns agree in gender and number with the common argument. They are not an obligatory part of relative clauses: see for example (9-29c) and (9-29f), which do not have them.

Note that the verb of the relative clause is fully inflected, and the relative clause contains all the usual components of a clause. The relative clause may even contain a complex predicate: see for example (9-29f) which has a relative clause with a serial verb construction involving k^v 'bring' in construction with a verb (see Section 8.2.3.1).

Relative clauses would appear to always be restrictive. No non-restrictive relative clauses have been found in the data. In the following example the possessive marker is in bold and the head noun in the main clause underlined.

(9-29) a. nɨm puŋgokawuk**ŋan** aŋgi kopi aŋgi
<u>nɨm</u>   puŋgok   -a   wuk   =**ŋan**   aŋgi   kopi   aŋgi
tree   stand.3SG.F.R -LINK   be.3SG.F.R =POSS   DX.F   coffee (TP)   DX.F
'the tree which is standing there is coffee'

b. mum aŋgi ewar yimŋi kakun**ŋan** eŋgon aŋgi
<u>mum</u>   aŋgi   ewar   yim   =ŋi
sago_jelly   DX.F   yesterday   1PL   =ERG.M

ka   -ku   -n   =**ŋan**   eŋgon   aŋgi
eat.R <3SG.F.R.O>   -1SG|3SG.M|1PL.R.S   =POSS   good   DX.F
'the sago jelly that we ate yesterday was good'

c. yu ato kut**ŋa** nirkru wakare?
<u>yu</u>   ato   kut   =**ŋa**   nir   -kru   wákare
2SG   down   be.SG.M.R   =POSS   do.IRR   -3SG.F.IRR.O   NEG
'you who were down there didn't do it?'

d. ŋayi kirawŋgar munje ainde tam ŋan ndagúnɨ tatɨŋgatro**ŋan**
ŋa   =yi   kiraw   -ŋgar   <u>munje</u>   ainde   tam   ŋan
1SG   =ERG.F   know.IRR   -NFN.SG   man   DX.M   bird   3SG.M.POSS

ndagúnɨ   ta   -tɨ   -ŋgat   -ro   =**ŋan**
furtively   take.R   -S   <3SG.M.BEN.O.R>   -3PL.R.S   =POSS
'I know the man whose bird they stole'

e. munje ainde Sopakyi mámbakɨr piŋgatan**ŋan** ainde mbet inde
<u>munje</u> ainde   Sopak =yi   mámbakɨr   pi   -ŋgata   -n
man   DX.M   Sopak =ERG.F   netbag   give.R -3SG.M.BEN.O.R   -SG|1PL.R.S

=**ŋan**   ainde   mbet   inde
=POSS   DX.M   come. SG.M.R   DX.M
'the man to whom Sopak gave the netbag is coming'

f. ŋgɨgi Ayarpa poŋgro sawáraŋga ŋgan kukuŋgwek**ŋanɨ**
ŋgɨ   =gi   Ayarpa   po   -ŋg   -ro   <u>sawáraŋga</u>
3PL   =ERG.PL   Ayarpa   strike.R   -3SG.M.R.O   -3PL.S   mace

	ŋgan	ku	-ku	ŋgwek		=ŋa	=ni̇
	3PL.POSS	bring	-3SG.F.R.O	come.3PL.R.S		=POSS	=INST

'they hit Ayarpa with their mace that they brought'

Note in the above example that the relative clause clearly appears inside the NP, with the instrumental clitic coming after the relative clause.

g. ŋayi kirawŋgar noŋor aŋgu munjeŋi pokunŋa

ŋa	=yi	kiraw	-ŋgar	noŋor	aŋgu	munje	=ŋi
1SG	=ERG.F	know.IRR	-NFN	woman	DX.F	man	=ERG.M

po	-ku	-n	=ŋa
strike.R	-3SG.F.R.O	-SG|1PL.R.S	=POSS

'I know the woman whose husband hit her'

h. ŋgume nunuk pokroŋan ŋayi kirawkru wákare anakŋan tatukro

ŋgume	nunuk	po	-k	-ro	=ŋan	ŋa	=yi
DX	later	strike.R	-3SG.F.R.O	-3PL.S	=POSS	1SG	=ERG.F

kiraw	-kru	wákare	anak	=ŋan	ta	-tu
know.IRR	-3SG.F.R.O	NEG	where	=ABL	take.R	-S

-ku	-ro
<3SG.F.R.O>	-3PL.S

'I don't know where they got the one they killed later from'
Ie, 'the one they struck later, I don't know where they got it from'

Relative clauses are not very common and the corpus contains few examples to show whether the common argument is syntactically a part of the relative clause or part of the main clause. However the main clause of (9-29d) can be negated using *wákare* before *munje* (and changing the verb *kiraw* to *kirawŋgri*). This suggests that *munje* belongs syntactically in the relative clause rather than the main clause. However more examples are needed to be certain.

Tayap used to have another relativizing suffix: the morpheme *-gin* (or perhaps it was a clitic *=gin*, there is not enough evidence to show). This morpheme seems to be synonymous with, and occurs in exactly the same morphological slot as, *=ŋa(n)*. For example:

(9-30) patir aŋgu ŋaŋan omoŋi perkun**gin** otitekara

patir	aŋgu	ŋaŋan	omo	=ŋi	per	-ku
house	DX.F	1SG.POSS	father	=ERG.M	build.R	-3SG.F.R.O

	-n	-gin	otitek-ara
	-SG|1PL.R.S	-REL	fall.3SG.F.R-PERF

'the house there that my father built has collapsed'

The morpheme appears both in naturally occurring talk and in elicitation sessions that I recorded in the 1980s. By 2009, however, it was no longer used by anybody.

9.6 Finite nominalizations with consequence clitic =ŋa(n)

Finite nominalizations are constructed, like relative clauses, with the possessive clitic, and carry the meaning of consequence; that a particular state has been brought into existence because of an action. For example:

(9-31) kokɨr mbɨdtia ŋaŋan noŋor kokɨr kratianŋa

kokɨr	mbɨd	-t	-ia⁴		ŋaŋan	noŋor	kokɨr
head	pain.R	-S	<1SG.BEN.R.O>		1SG.POSS	woman	head

kra	-t	-ia		-n	=ŋa
break.R	-S	<1SG.BEN.R.O>		-2SG|3SG.F.R.S	=POSS

'my head hurts because my wife hit me on the head'

9.7 Perception constructions

Sentences that describe an act of perceiving, like seeing or smelling, can be expressed in two ways in Tayap: either paratactically as two separate clauses, or with a nominalized construction.

In the perception construction, the perceiver is subject of the main clause, and the person or thing perceived is object. In the subordinate (nominalized) clause, always placed after the main clause, the action expressing the circumstances of the perception is indicated. Coreferential with the main clause object is the thing perceived, which may be subject or object in the subordinate clause.

The two possibilities are exemplified below:

---

4 This is a reduced form of *mbɨd-t-iata-n* (pain.R-S<1SG.BEN.O.R>2SG|3SG.F.R.S). See the note that directly follows example (7-29) in Chapter 7.

Paratactically combined clauses:[5]

(9-32) a. *ewar Njimeŋi noŋor sene tanmbɨn ŋgɨ mɨrɨnɨ woke*
         ewar   Njime   =ŋi   noŋor   sene   ta   -n   -mbɨ
         yesterday Njime   =ERG.M   woman   two   see.R   -S   <3PL.R.O>

         -n   ŋgɨ   mɨrɨ   =nɨ   woke
         -1SG.M| 3SG.M|1PL.R.S   3PL   rainforest   =ALL   go.DL.R
         'yesterday Njime saw two women go into the rainforest'
         (lit. 'yesterday Njime saw two women[5], they went into the rainforest')

Perception construction:

(9-32) b. *ewar Njimeŋi noŋor sene tanmbɨn ŋgɨ mɨrɨnɨ wokeŋa*
         ewar   Njime   =ŋi   noŋor   sene   ta   -n   -mbɨ
         yesterday Njime   =ERG.M   woman   two   see.R   -S   <3PL.R.O>

         -n   mɨrɨ   =nɨ   woke   =ŋa
         -1SG.M| 3SG.M|1PL.R.S   rainforest   =ALL   go.DL.R   =POSS
         'yesterday Njime saw two women going into the rainforest'
         (lit. 'yesterday Njime saw the two women, their going into the rainforest')

As (9-32b) shows, the main verb of perception is inflected for the perceiver of the action, and the verb expressing the perceived action is inflected for the actor who performs that action. That action is nominalized with the possessive clitic =ŋa(n).

(9-33) *ambagaiyi tatukun maya wopikunŋan*
        ambagai   =yi   ta   -tu   -ku   -n   maya
        men's house =ERG.F see.R -S   <3SG.F.R.O>   -2SG|3SG.F.R.S mother

        wospi   -ku   -n   =ŋan
        eject.R -3SG.F.R.O -SG|1PL.R.S =POSS
        'The men's house saw [i.e. it witnessed] the old woman being ejected.'
        (lit: the men's house saw her, our ejecting the mother'

---

5 Note that number agreement is not consistent in examples (9-32a) and (9-32b): the speaker uses the form 'woman (SG) two' rather than the dual form *naŋaw* or the plural *naŋro*, and the object agreement is plural rather than dual. These two examples were from an elicitation session and the inconsistency was noticed too late to be queried directly.

One argument, the subject or the object of the main clause, is coreferent with either the subject or object of the nominalized clause. The verb of the nominalized clause is fully inflected. These clauses, while marked with the possessive clitic (as relative clauses are), are structurally different from relative clauses.

Relative clauses modify NPs, and they occur in the modifier slot within an NP. These nominalized clauses, on the contrary, while they share an argument with their main clause, do not modify an NP but rather modify an entire main clause, within the specific semantic domain of perception. The shared argument of the clauses is expressed only once, in the main clause, while the nominalized clause consists only of the nominalized predicate and any arguments.

These are not complement clauses either, as the nominalized clause does not function as an argument of the main clause, but rather as a modifier. This can clearly be seen for example in (9-32b), in which it can't be the case that the nominalized clause is functioning as an argument of the main clause. The main clause verb has 3PL object marking, so the object must be the women, not the clause describing them going into the forest.

Other potential candidates for complement clauses, including constructions of saying and telling, are expressed with verbal morphology involving indirect commands (see Section 7.1.4).

Further examples:

(9-34) a. *Sopakyi Nik tatŋgin mbor pokunŋa*
Sopak =yi Nik ta -t -ŋgi -n
Sopak =ERG.F Nik perceive.R -S <3SG.M.R.O> -2SG|3SG.F.R.S

mbor po -ku -n =ŋa
pig strike.R -3SG.F.R.O -SG1PL.R.S =POSS
'Sopak saw Nik spearing the pig'

b. *ŋayi ŋgu tankun patɨrnɨ urokŋa*
ŋa =yi ŋgu ta -n -ku -n
1SG =ERG.F 3SG.F see.R -S <3SG.F.R.O> -1SG|3SG.M|1PL.R.S

patɨr =nɨ urok =ŋa
house =ALL go_inside.3SG.F|1PL.R =POSS
'I saw her going inside the house'

In (9-34a) the main clause is *Sopakyi Nik tatŋgin* 'Sopak saw Nik', and the subordinate perception clause *mbor pokunŋa* '[Nik] spearing the pig'. Thus the clause structure as a whole is 'Sopak saw Nik [spearing the pig]'. The clause is not modifying Nik, as it would be in a relative clause, but rather the perception clause predicates what is perceived.

In negative perception clauses like 'I didn't see X doing Y', the perception verb is negated and the verb that expresses the perceived action is inflected in its realis form and relativized with =ŋa(n):

(9-35) a. *Tamboŋyi Mbume rarkru wákare yiwɨr wospikunŋa*
      Tamboŋ =yi   Mbume rar   -kru   wákare yiwɨr
      Tamboŋ =ERG.F   Mbume see.IRR -3SG.F.IRR.O NEG   shit

      wospi   -ku   -n   =ŋa
      get_rid_of.R -3SG.F.R.O -SG|1PL.R.S =POSS
      'Tamboŋ didn't see Mbume getting rid of the shit'

  b. *Mburi Mairum rarkru wákare ŋgon patɨr poikunŋa*
     Mbur =i   Mairum rar   -kru   wákare ŋgon
     Mbur =ERG.F Mairum see.IRR -3SG.F.IRR.O NEG   3.SG.F.POSS

     patɨr   poi   -ku   -n   =ŋa
     house   sweep.R   -3SG.F.R.O -SG1PL.R.S =POSS
     'Mbur didn't see Mairum sweeping her (Mairum's) house'

  c. *ŋayi kirawru wákare yu mbetŋa*
     ŋa   =yi   kiraw   -ru   wákare yu   mbet   =ŋa
     1SG =ERG   know.IRR   -2SG.IRR.O   NEG   2SG come.SG.M.R =POSS
     'I didn't know you (M) had come'

9.8 Cosubordinate constructions

A further type of clause combining construction in Tayap consists of medial verbs appearing with modifying suffixes and then linked to independent final verbs, which are always verbs of motion. These are cosubordinate constructions, also called clause chaining constructions: the terms are used interchangeably here.

In these clauses, a medial verb appears in its irrealis or realis stem form, without a subject marker, with an object marker if transitive, and one of three linking suffixes: *-ra* (modifier), *-kar* (manner), or *-rar* (multiple), followed by an independent verb. These structures form medial-final chains (Longacre 2007). Van Valin and La Polla (1997) call this type of clause linkage cosubordination, i.e. dependency without embedding.

Nothing can occur between the medial verb and the final verb. Also such clauses cannot contain cataphoric pronominal reference (i.e. cannot refer forward to something in a later clause). So medial chains are not subordinate, but neither are they coordinate as their medial verbs are dependent on the final verb of the chain for status marking.

In all three types of clause chains, negation occurs once and has scope over the whole construction.

Tayap cosubordinate constructions differ from serial verb constructions in that medial verbs have an obligatory linking suffix, whereas non-final verbs in serial verb constructions do not, and serial verb constructions generally form a single phonological word whereas cosubordinate constructions do not (see Section 8.2 for discussion of serial verb constructions).

One unusual facet of Tayap's medial-final constructions is that they do not typically form the long chains that Papuan languages in general are so famous for. The majority of medial-final chains in Tayap consist of a single medial verb followed by a final verb. This might be in part because the final verb has to be a verb of motion.

An alternative analysis of these constructions, in particular -r and -kar, is that they are adverbial suffixes, rendering an adverb from a verb. However a cosubordinate analysis is preferred here as negation operates across clause boundaries to cover the whole construction rather than negating the putative adverb directly (see below, Section 9.8.2).

9.8.1 Cosubordinate constructions with modifying suffix -ra (MOD)

Consider the -ra[6] construction first, in comparison with two independent clauses linked by a conjunction:

Coordinated construction:

(9-36) a. ŋi piŋneta katot
      ŋi   piŋ   -net   -a   katot
      3SG.M jump.R -SG.M.R.S -and go_down.SG.M.R
      'he hopped and went down'

Cosubordinate construction:

b. ŋi piŋra katot
   ŋi   piŋ   -ra   katot
   3SG.M jump.R -MOD go_down.SG.M.R
   'he jumped down'

Coordinated construction:

---

[6] Two verb roots realize -ra as -wa. Those roots are ke-(p/w)-eki 'fall out' (realized in the MOD form as ke-wa) and adioki 'trip' (realized as adi-wa).

(9-37) a. *ŋgu mamrartaka wok*
ŋgu   mamrar -tak   -a   wok
3SG.F shake.R -2SG.F|3SG.F.R.S -and go.3SG.F.R
'she shook and went/as she went'

Cosubordinate construction:

b. *ŋgu mamrara wok*
ŋgu   mamrar -ra   wok
3SG.F shake.R   -MOD go.3SG.F.R
'she shivered'

The difference in meaning between these two forms is subtle. Speakers say that the fully inflected forms – those in (9-36a) and (9-37a) above – are synonymous with the *-ra* forms – those in (9-36b) and (9-37b). Some verbs – 'jump' for example – regularly occur in both forms. At the same time, however, it is clear that the morpheme *-ra* does not just link two verbs in a temporal sequence like the conjunction *–(y)a* does (Section 9.3.1). Instead, *-ra* modifies both the verb to which it affixes and the verb of motion that follows it, creating a new lexical predicate out of two independent verbs.

In an important sense, all complex predicates create new lexical verbs by linking together a series of different verbs. But the difference in this case is this: other kinds of sequences in Tayap create complex predicates by conjoining verbs that retain their separate lexical meaning even as they link together in sequences with other verbs. Their meaning is additive – each verb contributes its particular meaning to the final compound construction. So a sequence like *tapratkiŋgiatikitakana* (Section 8.1ff) that was discussed in the previous chapter is composed of separate constituents that each add their own meaning to the action being expressed, resulting in a verb that means 'she will carry him down on her shoulders'.

Complex clauses created with the *-ra* suffix, on the other hand, are not additive, they are transformative. A complex clause created with *-ra* is not so much the sum of its parts as it is a new semantic entity. Although many verbs formed with *-ra* do retain a transparent relation to the independent verbs that derive them, others have meanings that are completely different from the two verbs that compose them. So 'faint', for example, is *wasowra aiki-* (*wasow* 'die' + *-ra* + *aiki* 'come').[7]

Another way in which the *-ra* suffix transforms verbs is that it reduces their valency. Compare the verb *worer* 'capsize' in constructions formed with *-ra*, and

---

[7] This suffix occurs on at least one noun: the way to express that a body part has 'fallen asleep', as one says in English, is to use the derived verb *siwididimra oki*, which comes from the word for small black ants; so *siwididim* 'ants' + *-ra* + *oki* 'go'.

in serial verb constructions formed with a non-final verb + a final verb like those discussed in Section 8.2:

(9-38) a. *ewar yimbar worerara wok*
ewar　　　yimbar　worer　　　　-ara　　wok
yesterday　canoe　　capsize.IRR　-MOD　go.3SG.F.R
'yesterday the canoe tipped over'

b. *ewar ŋgɨ yimbar worerkuwok*
ewar　　　ŋgɨ　yimbar　worer　　　　-ku　　　　wok
yesterday　3PL　canoe　　capsize.IRR　-3SG.F.R.O-　go.3SG.F.R
'yesterday they tipped over the canoe'

(9-39) a. *awin worerara wok*
awin　　worer　　　　-ara　　wok
water　capsize.IRR　-MOD　go.3SG.F.R
'the water spilled'

b. *ŋayi awin worerkuwok*
ŋa　　=yi　　　awin　　worer　　　　-ku　　　　　wok
1SG　=ERG　water　capsize.IRR　-3SG.F.R.O　go.3SG.F.R
'I poured the water'

Notice how the first sentences in these pairs (9-38a) and (9-39a) only has one argument – the subject, 'canoe' in (9-38a) and 'water' in (9-39a). The second sentences have two arguments – subject ('they' and 'I') and object ('canoe' and 'water').

Negation on verbs marked with *-ra* is only marked on the independent verb that carries TAM, but its scope is both/all verb stems. So the negation of a verb like 'jump' is:

(9-40) *ɲɨ　　　piŋ　　　-ra　　atɨ　　　　　-kɨ　　wákare*
3SG.M　jump.R　-MOD　go_down.IRR　-IRR　NEG
'he didn't jump down' or 'he won't jump down'

9.8.2 Cosubordinate constructions with manner suffix *-kar* (MANN)

Like clause chains constructed with *-ra*, those formed with *-kar* also add a morpheme directly onto the irrealis stem of a verb that precedes a verb of motion, thus creating a medial verb. Unlike the *-ra* forms, however, constructions formed with *-kar* or its allophonic variant *-kwar* (the environment triggering the alternation is unknown) maintain the separate meanings of the modified verb and the verb of motion that follows it. The suffix *-kar* creates a manner medial verb, one that answers the question 'How or in what manner did X go/come, etc.?'

Verbs constructed with *-kar* are constructed in the following way:

IRR verb stem + *-kar/-kwar* + fully inflected verb of motion

Verbs formed with *-kar* encode the simultaneity of both actions for the duration of both actions. In English, this temporal relationship would be rendered with the adverbial 'as', as in 'They were laughing as they washed the dishes', or participle clauses, as in 'Laughing, they washed the dishes'. In other words, the first action, laughing, occurred simultaneously with, and continued for the same length of time as, the second action, washing the dishes.

This foregrounding of duration and simultaneity results in awkward literal translations, as in the following example:

(9-41) nda   mbɨd   non   rekɨ   ai   -kar   wek
        DM   pain   INDEF   with   come.IRR   -MANN   come.3SG.F.R
        'she came feeling pain as she came'

A more idiomatic translation would be with an English adverbial phrase; something that highlighted the experience of pain as during travel, like 'In pain, she made her way here'.

Cosubordinate constructions created with the *-kar* suffix also highlight an action or process that has begun and is continuing, especially when the construction is used with an inanimate subject. In English, this kind of phrase would use a verb of inception, like 'begin' or 'start', or a verb of intensification or process, like 'growing' or 'becoming'; for example: 'his anger was growing'.

The verb of motion that follows the medial verb created with the *-kar* suffix is most commonly either 'go' (*okɨ*) or 'come' (*aikɨ*), although any verb of motion may occur in this slot. Examples are:

(9-42) a.   ŋgu   warak   -kar   wek
             3SG.F   talk.IRR   -MANN   come.3SG.F.R
             'she came talking'

        b.   ɲɨ   ŋgar   -kwar   mbot
             3SG.M   call_out.IRR   -MANN   go.SG.M.R
             'he called out as he went along'

The sense of development and process means that these verb forms can co-occur with other chained forms, such as the -*ra* forms, for example:

(9-43) *minjike =ŋa mbatep pwak -ra o -kar wek*
betel_nut =POSS unit drop.IRR -MOD go.IRR -MANN come.3SG.F.R
'the flowers on the betel nut (palm) are in the process of opening'

This suggests that the -*ra* clause and the -*kar* clause are syntactically equivalent, both equally dependent on the final verb *wek* 'come'.

The directionality of the verb of motion ('go' or 'come') can express a difference in meaning, as in the following:

(9-44) a. *toto andɨ -kar wek*
skin swell.IRR -MANN come.3SG.F.R
'(my) skin is swelling up' (in various places because bees have stung me)

b. *toto andɨ -kar wok*
skin swell.IRR -MANN go.3SG.F.R
'(my) skin is swelling up' (from a central point and spreading outwards)

This kind of semantic difference encoded by different verbs of motion may have been more productive in the past, and subtle nuances may have been eroded and lost over the course of the last few decades. Today, senior speakers insist that with only a few exceptions, such as (9-44a) and (9-44b) above, verbs formed with 'go' and 'come' have the same meaning and can be used interchangeably.

Chains with -*kar* are negated by placing the negative marker after the independent verb. So the negated form of example (9-42a) is:

(9-45) *ŋgu warak -kar ai -ki wákare*
3SG.F talk.IRR -MANN come.IRR -IRR NEG
'she was not talking as she came'

The scope of negation in manner constructions has to include the medial verb. Thus, the negated sentence means that the woman probably still came (the sentence probably would not have been uttered if she hadn't come); she just didn't come talking.

This seems to indicate that -*kar* (and in fact -*ra*) are complex verbal constructions rather than adverbials, since negation of adverbials would be expressed with the negator directly after the adverbial, not as here at the end of the clause.

9.9 Tail-head linkage

Tayap makes extensive use of tail-head linkage, a phenomenon in which the last verb of one sentence is repeated as the first verb of the next sentence. It is a coherence device for structuring discourse and is very common among Papuan languages (de Vries 2005). In de Vries's terms, Tayap's tail-head linkage is the chained type, utilizing the basic complex clause structures of the language, namely coordination and subordination.

Some examples, which are taken from the Tayap Texts at the end of this grammar, are presented below (see those texts for many more examples of this phenomenon).

The following excerpt is a continuous stretch of speech taken from a narrated story that is presented in its entirety in Text 1. The repeated inflected verbs are in bold.

(9-46) a. *mbuspimbroya nda ŋgi prike.*
            mbuspi   -mb   -ro   -ya   nda   ŋgi   **prike**
            send.R- -3PL.R.O   -3PL.R.S -and   DM   3PL   come_up.DL.R
            'They sent them off and the two came [back] up [to Gapun].'

        b. *Prikeya wekeya nawni Kirmar.*
            Prike   -ya   weke   -ya   naw   =ni   Kirmar
            come_up.DL.R   -and   come.DL.R   -and   grassland   =LOC   Kirmar
            'They came (back) up and came to the Kirmar grassland.'

Further examples:

(9-47) a. *Noŋor ti wasowtaka ŋgon mambrag noŋor aŋgo wok. Woka ainimengi nambirni puko.*
            Noŋor   ti   wasow   -tak   -a
            woman   too   die.R   -2SG.F|3SG.F.R   -and

            ŋgon   mambrag   noŋor
            3SG.F.POSS   spirit   woman

            aŋgo   **wok.**   **Wok**   -a   aini   -me   -ŋgi
            DX.F   go.3SG.F.R   go.3SG.F.R   -and   here   -DX   -DX.F

            nambir   =ni   **puko**
            chest   =LOC   come_up.3PL.R
            'The woman too had died, and her spirit was going. It was going and thus they came up towards it.'

b. *Kirmar nambɨrni pukoya⁸ ŋgu kotarpembɨn:*

Kirmar	*nambɨr*	*=ni*	***puko***	*-ya*	*ŋgu*
Kirmar	chest	=LOC	come_up.3PL.R	-and	3SG.F

kotarpe	*-mbɨ*	*-n*
ask.R	-3PL.R.O	-SG|1PL.R.S

'They came up towards (lit. 'to the chest') Kirmar and she asked them:'

The next sequence is a continuous stretch of speech taken from Tayap Text 3, which describes a walk through the rainforest in which a young boy is nearly bitten by a snake. Note the tail-head linkage at (9-48 b-c), and (9-48 c-d). In both cases the verb of the previous clause is repeated, with different inflections.

(9-48) a. *Nda Abramŋi nɨmŋat tankun*

Nda	*Abram*	*=ŋi*	*nɨm*	*=ŋa*	*at*
DM	Abram	=ERG.M	tree	=POSS	piece

ta	*-nu*	*-ku*	*-n*
take.R	-S	<3SG.F.R.O>	-1SG|2SG|3SG.M|1PL.R.S

'Then Abram [Masito's husband] took a stick'

b. *aram nime poŋgin.*

aram	*nime*	***po***	*-ŋgɨ*	*-n*
snake	thus	strike.R	-3SG.M.R.O	-SG|1PL.R.S

'hit the snake with that.'

c. *Poŋgina, wasonet.*

Po	*-ŋgɨ*	*-n*	*-a*	***waso-net***.
strike.R	-3SG.M.R.O-	SG|1PL.R.S	-and	die.R-1SG.M|3SG.M.R

'He hit it, and it died.'

d. *Wasowneta ainɨmende*

Waso	***-net***	*-a*	*ainɨ*	*-me*	*-nde*
die.R	-1SG.M|3SG.M.R	-and	here	-DX	-DX.M

'It died and there...'

In most cases of tail-head linkage, only the verb is repeated. The second instance of the verb usually occurs with a conjunction marker to connect it to the clause that follows. However, other material can be repeated too: an example is the oblique NP repeated with the verb in lines (9-47 a-b).

9.10 Complex constructions with the suffix signifying multiplicity -*rar* (ML)

The final suffix occurring on complex sentences is -*rar*. This suffix signifies that the action denoted by the verb occurred in relation to multiple objects – so 'look at many things' instead of just 'look', or 'shoot at many things' instead of just 'shoot'. The suffix -*rar* is always used on transitive verbs. The object morpheme is always in the realis form. TAM is marked on the final, independent verb of motion that follows the medial verb. Even though the action of the verb happens multiple times, the object is still singular. So the structure of this form is as follows:

> transitive verb stem IRR + object R + -*rar* + verb of motion inflected for subject, TAM and status

Examples are as follows:

(9-49) a. *tar   -ku   -rar mbet*
          take.IRR -3SG.F.R.O -ML   come.SG.M.R
          'he collected several as he came' (or 'I (M)' or 'you (M)')

   b. *o   -ku   -rar mbot*
      shoot.IRR -3SG.F.R.O -ML   go.SG.M.R
      'he shot various things as he went' (or 'I (M)' or 'you (M)')

If the object slot is filled by a BEN object rather than a direct object, then -*rar* is realized as -*tar* (see examples 9-49c and d below):

> transitive verb stem IRR + BEN object R + -*tar* + verb of motion inflected for subject, TAM and status

   c. *kokɨr krar   -mba   -tar weke*
      head   break.IRR   -3PL.BEN.R.O -ML   come.DL.R
      'the two of them cracked open all their heads'

   d. *ŋɨ   =ŋi   noŋor   ŋan   mbɨd*
      3SG.M   =ERG.M   woman   3SG.M.POSS   pain

      i   -kwa   -tar mbet
      give.IRR -3SG.F.BEN.R.O -ML   come.3SG.M.R
      'he beat up his wife' (lit. 'he gave his woman pain multiple times')

Verbs constructed with -*rar* are negated by negating the final, fully inflected verb in the series. And like -*kar* verbs, the scope of negation covers the whole construction. So the negated form of (9-49a), above, is:

(9-50) tar   -ku   -rar ai-ki   wákare
        take.IRR   -3SG.F.R.O   -ML   come.IRR-IRR   NEG
        'he didn't come collecting several'

9.11 Complex sentences in young people's Tayap

Young people use a great deal of tail-head linkage in their narratives. The narrator of Text 4, for example – a twenty-year-old man with good passive Tayap but limited active command of the language – uses tail-head linkage in fifty percent of his clause conjunctions. Compare this with between roughly ten to twelve percent in Texts 1–3, which were narrated by more fluent speakers.

Subordinate and cosubordinate clauses are beyond the capability of most Tayap speakers younger than thirty. A few of the most skilled passive active speakers (such as the twenty-five-year-old narrator of Tayap Text 3) can use the subordinating morpheme -*re* to produce 'when' clauses (see lines 26 and 51 in Tayap Text 3). But hypothetical morphemes – like the counterfactual mood that often accompanies it – are mostly dead, and in fifty five of the fifty six narratives by young people that I collected in Gapun, there is not a single instance of relativization.[8]

Young people's narratives are strings of events presented paratactically – X did Y, Z happened, Q did P. Sometimes, the events are narrated with no clause-linking morphology, as in the following extract, from a narrative told by a twenty-three-year-old man (hesitations, false starts and interruptions and encouragements by another speaker have been edited out of this extract):

---

8 The single exception is a complex narrative in flawless Tayap told by a twenty-nine-year-old young woman named Mbonika Amburi (the same Mbonika who features as a six-year-old girl in the opening vignette of Kulick 1992). Mbonika is the paradigm example of the passive active speaker. She never speaks more than a few formulaic phrases of Tayap to anyone, and knowing her well and seeing her every day, I had come to assume that her command of the vernacular was minimal. After being astonished by the fluency of her Tayap narrative, I asked her why she never spoke the language. She is ashamed, she told me. She feared that if she spoke Tayap and said something wrong, the old people in the village would laugh at her. "They'll criticize", she told me. "They'll say, 'You all speak Tok Pisin too much and so you don't know the vernacular'. For that reason, I'm ashamed to speak the vernacular" ("Ol bai wokim koments, 'Tok Pisin i planti na yupela i no save long tok ples'. Na olsem na mi save sem long tok ples.")

(9-51) ...*Yim kuk. Yim kuk, ŋa embre, ŋa mbot. Paita ŋɨ mbet. ŋa taina, yim mbok. Yim mbok, Mbasamayi mum nirkwankuk. ŋa mbot tutotakut...*

Yim	kuk.		Yim	kuk		ŋa	emb	=re	ŋa
1PL	be.1SG.F1PL.R		1PL	be.1SG.F|1PL.R		1SG	morning	=TEMP	1SG

mbot,	Paita	ŋɨ	mbet	ŋa	*ta-ina[9]
go.SG.M.R	Paita	3SG.M	come.SG.M.R	1SG	see.R-??

yim	mbok.	Yim	mbok,	Mbasama	=yi	mum
1PL	go.1SG.F|1PL.R	1PL	go.1SG.F|1PL.R	Mbasama	=ERG.F	sago_jelly

nir	-kwan	-kuk	
do.IRR	-3SG.F.BEN.O.R-	be.1SG.F.R ('I (F) was making');[10]	

ŋa	mbot	tutot	-ak	-kut
1SG	go.SG.M.R	sit.SG.M.IRR	-LINK	-be.SG.M.R

'We were (there). We were (there), in the morning, I went, Paita he came, he saw me [or I saw him], we went. We went, Mbasama was making sago jelly. I went was sitting down...'

Leaving aside the morphological and TAM errors made by this speaker (all of which are typical of the kinds of errors made by young speakers), note that he does not use a single coordinating, cosubordinating or subordinating morpheme throughout this entire stretch of speech. The verb phrases that make up the narrative are simply placed one after the other with no linkage between them. (The final *a* of the nonce word *taina* could be a coordinating morpheme, but this is hard to know since the word doesn't mean anything.)

Much more commonly than simply listing verb phrases one after the other, young speakers link clauses with the coordinating conjunction *-(y)a*. Here is an extract from a narrative about a pig hunt by a twenty-six-year-old man who is one of the more advanced younger speakers in the village:

(9-52) ... *Ŋa motɨnɨ warukpeta mbet. Mbeta mborma ndow tankuna anpekuna mbot. Ŋa mbot yɨwɨr rar/yɨwɨr tankun, mbot, yɨwɨrkɨ and. Na ŋa ŋganet...*

Ŋa	motɨnɨ	waruk	-pet	-a	mbet
1SG	again	turn_back.R	-SG.M.R	-and	come.SG.M.R

---

[9] The correct form is either *tanin* 'he saw me' or *tanŋgin* 'I saw him'.
[10] The speaker wants a non-future verb here – *nɨtukun* 'she made'. But even the progressive verb he uses is incorrectly inflected. The form he wants is *nirkwanuk* 'she was making'.

```
Mbet             -a    mbor  =ma    ndow
come.SG.M.R      -and  pig   =POSS  leg

ta      -n   -ku              -n               -a
see.R   -S   <3SG.F.R.O>      -1SG|3SG.M.R.S   -and

*anpe         -ku             -n          -a
follow.R      <3SG.F.R.O>     -SG|1PL.R.S -and

mbot        Ŋa   mbot       yiwɨr  rar/yiwɨr
go.SG.M.R   1SG  go.SG.M.R  shit   see.IRR/shit

ta      -n   -ku            -n              mbot       yiwɨr-ki     and
see.R   -S   <3SG.F.R.O>    -1SG|3SG.M.R.S  go.SG.M.R  shit-INTENS  blood

Na        ŋa   ŋga         -net
and (TP)  1SG  call_out.R  -1SG.M|3SG.M.R
```
'...I turned back and came. I was coming and I saw the pig's tracks and I followed them. I came shit I see/I saw shit, I went and there was lots of shit, blood. And [Tok Pisin] I called out...'

This speaker has the typical problem with the class 3 transitive verb *andu* 'follow' (see Section 6.1.5). The form he wants is *kandukun*, not the nonce form he creates by using the verb root as the basis for the non-future inflection. But regardless of his difficulty inflecting some verbs, he nevertheless is able to link verb phrases into a coherent narrative. He does this with a single morphological tool, however: the coordinating conjunction *-(y)a*.

This morpheme has been over-extended in the speech of most young speakers to do the work of all coordinating, cosubordinating and subordinating morphemes. The reason for this over-extension is probably twofold.

First, *-a* occurs frequently in Tayap, as a way to link coordinated clauses (see Section 9.3.1).

Second, the suffix *-a*, especially when it appears in speech after verbs ending in *n* – verbs like *tankun* and **andpekun* in the narrative above – sounds a lot like (and behaves syntactically a lot like) Tok Pisin's conjunction "na", which means 'and'. That Tok Pisin is never far from the minds of young Tayap speakers is evident at the end of the above narrative, when the speaker briefly code-switches into Tok Pisin, precisely to link two clauses.

Cosubordinate verbs formed with the multiple suffix, *-rar*, do not appear in the narratives I collected from speakers younger than thirty, and verbs formed with the modifying *-ra* suffix only occur when they have become lexicalized, in verbs like *worer-ara wok* 'pour' or *wasow-ra wek* 'faint'.

The only kind of cosubordinate construction that young speakers do sometimes use is verbs formed with the medial manner suffix *-kar*. A small number of verbs recur in the different narratives. These verbs always encode motion, never process or development, and they are verbs that have probably been lexicalized, like *rar-kar mbot* ('I looked and came'), *mar-kar ŋgwok* ('they rowed away'), and *amai-kwar wek* ('I was searching as I came').

However, the *-kar* form remains productive for at least some speakers, who produced verbs like the following:

(9-53) a. miri   adu   -kwar   *weske
          forest   break.IRR   -MANN   come_outside.DL
          'the two of us came crashing out of the forest'; **weske* has no meaning; the speaker wants *uske*, from the verb root *aski-*.

   b. naw   apu   -kwar   ŋgwek
      grassland   burn.IRR   -MANN   come.3PL.R
      'they burned and came'; a morphologically correctly formed but semantically incorrect verb – the speaker was talking about men lighting fire to a grassland to drive game out towards men waiting with spears, and she wants *otar war-kwar ŋgwek*: 'fire light.IRR-MANN come'; lit. 'they lit fire while coming'.

   c. ŋgat   sene   am   -kwar   ŋgwek
      cassowary   two   fight.IRR   -MANN   come.3PL.R
      'the two cassowaries were fighting with one another as they came'; the speaker wants the dual form of 'come', *weke*.

Even though each one of the examples in (9-53 a-c) contains a grammatical error of one sort or another, they indicate that at least some young speakers can derive medial verbs and form complex predicates with the *-kar* suffix.

A few speakers over-extend the subordinating suffix *-re* to coordinate clauses. The following is an example of this, from a narrative told by an eighteen-year-old woman (hesitations, false starts and interruptions by other speakers have been edited out, and the name in the example has been changed):

(9-54) ...yim taman sumbwani katek. Sumbwani katekre, ani, Sopak pemiekre nande namtak...
       yim   taman   sumbwa   =ni   katek   sumbwa   =ni
       1PL   all   ground   =ALL   fall.1SG.F|1PL.R   ground   =ALL

katek	-re	ani	Sopak	pemiek	-re	nande
fall.1SG.F|1PL.R	SUB	who	Sopak	get up.SG.F1PL.R	-SUB	thusly

nam -tak
talk.R -2SG.F|3SG.F

'we all fell to the ground. When we fell to the ground, who (was it), Sopak, when she got up she said...'

This speaker's use of the clause subordinating morpheme -*re* (Section 9.4.1) is morphologically correct – that is, it is placed correctly after the main verb in a clause that thus becomes marked as subordinate. But it is semantically awkward. A more fluent speaker would tell the story using the coordinating morpheme -*a* (Section 9.3.1) in all instances where this speaker uses the subordinating morpheme. This particular speaker uses -*re* more than all other young speakers combined. It seems that she has identified the morpheme as a synonym for the coordinating suffix -*a*.

Three other kinds of clause linkage appear in young people's narratives. The first is the use of the perfect suffix to coordinate clauses, discussed in Section 5.4.3.2.

The second is linkage accomplished with the word 'okay', which has become part of Tok Pisin (as "oke") via English.

Here is an example from the narrative of a twenty-one-year-old man telling a story about buying alcohol:

(9-55) *piatana ŋa mbot ŋgɨreki* **oke** *Jastinŋi botol nambar mosenkun* **oke** *Simbɨraŋi non mosenkun* **oke** *ŋa ŋaŋan nambar kukumbota ŋgɨreki akruna*

pi	-iata	-n	-a	ŋa	mbot	ŋgɨ	=reki	**oke**
give.R	-1SG.BEN.R.O	-SG|1PL.R.S	-and	1SG	go.SG.M.R	they	=COM	okay

Jastin	=ŋi	botol	nambar	mose	-n	-ku
Jastin	=ERG.M	bottle (TP)	one	buy.R	-S	<3SG.F.R.O>

-n	**oke**	Simbɨra	=ŋi	non	mose	-n	-ku
-1SG|3SG.M|1PL.R.S	okay	Simbɨra	=ERG.M	one	buy.R	-S	<3SG.F.R.O>

-n	**oke**	ŋa	ŋaŋan	nambar	ku	-ku
-1SG|3SG.M|1PL.R.S	okay	1SG	1SG.POSS	one	bring	-3SG.F.R.O

mbot	-a	ŋgɨ	=reki	a	-kru	-na
go.SG.M.R.S-	-and	3PL	=COM	consume.IRR	-3SG.F.IRR.O	-INTENT

'...he gave me and I went with them, OK Jastin bought one bottle, OK Simbɨra bought one, OK I took mine and went with them to drink...'

Note that 'okay' here performs the role of both -*a* (which this speaker uses proficiently, as can be seen in lines 1 and 4 of this extract) and the clause coordinating suffix -*api*, which links clauses that encode actions that occur one after the other (Section 9.3.2).

The third way young villagers sometimes link clauses is with the Tayap word *mai*, which means 'enough', and the discourse marker *nda*. For many young speakers, these two words have replaced the -*api* suffix as a way of indicating that one action was completed before the next action began.

This usage can be exemplified with an extract from a narrative told by a nineteen-year-old woman:

(9-56) ...*ŋayi wakuna wakuna **mai**, **nda** sowor ninkun. Sowor nitukuna **mai**, amayi mum nitukuna **nda** yim kakun uretrekɨ.*

ŋa	=*yi*	*pap*	**wa*	-*ku*	-*n*	-*a*
1SG	=ERG.F	coconut	grate.R	-3SG.F.R.O	-SG|1PL.R.S	-and

**wa*	-*ku*	-*n*	-*a*	**mai**	**nda**	**sowor*
grate.R	-3SG.F.R.O	-SG|1PL.R.S	-and	enough	DM	little boiling

ni	-*n*	-*ku*	-*n*		**Sowor*
do.R	-S	<3SG.F.R.O>	-1SG|3SG.M|1PL.R.S		little boiling

ni	-*tu*	-*ku*	-*n*	-*a*	**mai**
do.R	-S	<3SG.F.R.O>	-2SG|3SG.F.R.S	-and	enough

ama	=*yi*	*mum*
mama	=ERG.F	sago_jelly

ni	-*tu*	-*ku*	-*n*	-*a*	**nda**	*yim*
do.R	-S	<3SG.F.R.O>	-2SG|3SG.F.R.S	-and	DM	1PL

ka	-*ku*	-*n*	*uret*	=*rekɨ*
eat.R	<3SG.F.R.O>	-1SG|1PL.R.S	bamboo shoots	=COM

'...I grated the coconut and, I grated it and enough, I made a boiling. She made a boiling, enough, then mama made sago jelly then we ate it with bamboo shoots'

There are several grammatical errors in this short extract: the class 2 transitive verb *war* 'grate' is inflected in a way typical of young speakers (see Section 6.1.3). The expression *sowor ninkun* doesn't exist – the speaker wants a verb, *soworpokun* ('I boiled a little', from the verb root *sowor-(p)-o* 'boil a small amount'). And the speaker produces two different inflections for her **sowor* construction:

'I did it' (*ninkun*) and 'she did it' (*nitukun*), so it is never clear exactly who boiled the small amount of bamboo shoots she talks about.

As far as syntax is concerned, note how the speaker uses *mai* ('enough') to express the completion of one action before the following action begins, and how the discourse marker *nda* marks the beginning of the following action. This is precisely the kind of clause coordination done by the Tayap suffix *-api*, and in the speech of a fluent speaker, the young woman's sentence would look like this:

(9-57) *ŋayi pap parkunapi, uret soworpokun*

ŋa	=yi	pap	par	-ku	-n	-api,
1SG	=ERG.F	coconut	grate.R	-3SG.F.R.O	-SG|1PL.R.S	-AFT

uret	soworpo	-ku	-n
bamboo_shoot	boil_small_amount.R	-3SG.F.R.O	-SG|1PL.R.S

'I grated the coconut, after I had grated it, I boiled a little bamboo shoots'

That the utterance that this young woman actually produces in (9-56) is so far removed from correct Tayap – in terms of vocabulary, verb inflection and morphology – is sobering.

It is a chill reminder that a tenacious and unique little language spoken by very few people for a very long time is now on its way to oblivion.

Tayap Texts

Tayap Text 1: Two men are chased by their lover's ghost
Narrated by Raya Ayarpa in 1987

English translation

I am going to tell the story of the old ancestors of Mbwadum. Once upon a time (lit. before, in the old days) two men went to the Turuŋgwad clan. Kanjaŋ village. For mangrove slugs. They were going to go and they went to their lover and asked her: "Are you OK? We're going to go for mangrove slugs at the Turuŋgwad clan".

She told them, "The two of you go. I'm not a baby bird who is going to swallow a seed and die".

Hearing her talk, they went. With their best dog, they went to the Turuŋgwad clan. In Kanjaŋ village. Thus they went and the people of the Turuŋgwad clan gave them gifts. They gave them the gift of two sticks of dried slug meat and they sent them on their way and the two of them came back up [home].

The two came up and went and came up to the Kirmar grassland.

The woman too had died and her ghost went there. She went they came up. They came up toward the grassland. They came up toward the Krimar grassland and she asked them, "So the two of you come now, do you?"

The two answered, "Yes". They asked her, "Where are you going?"

"I have children who are crying, so I'm going to Kandumsik stream to try and net some fish".

"OK. You go on then, in that case".

She passed by them and put down her things, turned and cleared her throat and said, "Who are you? Are you my lovers? It's me".

They threw down their two sticks of slugs and then she chased them. She chased them and brought them [towards the village]. She chased them and brought them.

The dog stood and was fighting with the spirit woman while the two ancestors picked up speed and came. The dog was fighting, fighting, fighting with the spirit woman. Leaving her, he then came to the two ancestors. He came, came, came, came, came, he came down to them.

The spirit woman came close to them and he [the dog] stood and fought. He was fighting with the spirit as the two ancestors came [towards the village].They continued in that way [i.e. the dog and woman fighting, the men fleeing] for a long time in the forest far away from the village, and finally they came and appeared at the bottom of Mbwadum mountain. They came up along the mountain.

Children were below playing on the slope, they were shooting arrows at little coconuts. They were shooting arrows at little coconuts when the two men came up to them. They told them: "Call out to us!". The children called out to them: "O! O! O! O! O! O!"

They [the men] fell and rolled down and died, their two bodies lay there below. Their dog died together with them.

The spirit woman, she had brought them thusly and she stood there and then she turned and left them.

Leaving them, she went away. The two men were laying there and they [other men], thinking this must have something to do with ghosts, got a branch and spit magic chants on it and as they were trying to bring them back, the two men got up.

The others asked them: "What did this to you?"

"The ghost, our girlfriend, chased us and came and her heat [i.e. her power] affected us and so we died".

"OK", said the others, "Come on then [back to the village]".

Tayap Original

1. *Ŋa Mbwadum arumandama tik*
   Ŋa   Mbwadum   aru=mandama   tik
   1SG   Mbwadum   ancestor=POSS.PL   story

2. *ŋgurkrunetana aŋgi.*
   ŋgur-kru-net-ana   aŋgi
   put.IRR-3SG.F.IRR.O-1SG.M|3SG.M.IRR.S- INTENT   DX
   I am going to tell the story of the old ancestors of Mbwadum.

3. *Mun sene ripim ŋgi woke Turuŋgwadre.*
   Mun   sene   ripim   ŋgi   woke   Turuŋgwad=re
   man.DL   two   before   3PL   go.DL.R Turuŋgwad=ALL
   Once upon a time, two men went to the Turuŋgwad (clan) (in) Kanjaŋ village.

4. *Kanjaŋ num.*
   Kanjaŋ   num
   Kanjaŋ   village
   In Kanjaŋ village.

5. *Kandipana. Ngɨ okɨnana wokeya ŋgan*
   Kandip=ana   Ngɨ   o-kɨ-nana   woke-ya   ŋgan
   mangrove_slugs=DAT 3PL   go.IRR-IRR-INTENT   go.DL-and   3PL.POSS
   For mangrove slugs. They were about to go and they went to their

6. *nireŋgar kotarpekure: "Yu sapkike? Yim nda okɨtikenana*
   nireŋgar   kotarpe-ku-re   Yu   sapkɨ=ke   Yim   nda
   lover   ask.R-3SG.F.R.O-DL.R 2SG   good=Q   1PL   DM
   lover and asked her: "Are you OK? We're going to go

7. *okɨtikenana kandipana Turuŋgwadre*
   o-kɨ-tike-nana   kandip=ana   Turuŋgwad=re.
   go.IRR-IRR-DL.IRR-INTENT   mangrove_slugs=DAT   Turuŋgwad =ALL
   to get mangrove slugs in Turuŋgwad".

8. *Ngu namtɨmbɨn,*
   Ngu   namtɨmbɨn
   3SG.F   tell.R-S<3PL.R.O>2SG.F|3SG.F.R.S
   She told them,

9. *"Yum onkem. Na tam ror wákare nɨm iru*
   Yum   o-nkem   Na   tam   ror   wákare   nɨm   iru
   2PL   go.SUB-2PL.R   1SG   bird   child   NEG   tree   seed
   "You go. I'm not a baby bird that I will

10. *motɨkuokɨre wasowkɨ"*
    motɨk-ku-o-kɨ-re   wasow-kɨ
    swallow.IRR-3SG.F.R.O-go.IRR-IRR-SUB   die.IRR -IRR
    swallow tree seeds and die".

11. *Ngɨ nam tarkwakɨ, woke.*
    Ngɨ   nam   tar-kwa-kɨ   woke
    3PL   talk   hear.IRR-3SG.F.BEN.R.O-ADV   go.DL.R
    Hearing her talk, the two left.

12. *Ngan nje nambarrekɨ woke. Turuŋgwadre. Kanjaŋ num.*
    Ngan   nje   nambar-rekɨ   woke   Turuŋgwad=re.   Kanjaŋ num.
    3PL.POSS   dog   one-COM   go.DL.R   Turuŋgwad=ALL   Kanjaŋ village
    The two went with their best dog. To the Turuŋgwad (clan). (In) Kanjaŋ village.

13. *Ngi ainimengi wokeya,*
    Ngi   aini-me-ngi   woke-ya
    3PL   here-DX-DX.F   go.DL.R-and
    Thus they went and

14. *Turuŋgwadgi oraitimbro.*
    Turuŋgwad=gi   orai-t-imb-ro
    Turuŋgwad=ERG.PL   bestow.R-S<3PL.R.O>3PL.S
    the Turuŋgwad people gave them gifts.

15. *Oraitimbroya kandipŋa nimir senereki*
    Orai-t-imb-ro-ya   kandip=ŋa   nimir sene=reki
    bestow.R-S<3PL.R.O>3PL.S-and   mangrove_slug=POSS   stick two=COM
    They gave them a present of two sticks strung full of mangrove slugs

16. *mbuspimbroya nda ŋgi prike.*
    mbuspi-mb-ro-ya   nda   ŋgi   prike
    send.R-3PL.R.O-3PL.R-S-and   DM   3PL   come_up.DL.R
    They sent them off and the two came [back] up [to Gapun].

17. *Prikeya wekeya nawni Kirmar.*
    Prike-ya   weke-ya   naw=ni   Kirmar
    come_up.DL.R-and   come.DL.R-and   grassland=LOC   Kirmar
    They came (back) up and came to the Kirmar grassland.

18. *Noŋor ti wasowtaka ŋgon mambrag noŋor aŋgo*
    Noŋor   ti   wasow-tak-a   ŋgon   mambrag   noŋor
    woman   too   die.R-2SG.F|3SG.F.R-and   3SG.F.POSS   spirit   woman

    aŋgo
    DX.F
    The woman too had died, and her spirit

19. *wok. Woka ainimengi nambirni puko.*
    wok.   Wok-a   aini-me-ŋgi   nambir=ni   puko
    go.3SG.F.R   go.3SG.F.R-and   here-DX-DX.F   chest=LOC   come_up.3PL.R
    was going. It was going and thus they came up towards it.

20. *Kirmar nambɨrnɨ pukoya ŋgu kotarpembɨn:*
    | Kirmar | nambɨr=nɨ | puko-ya | ŋgu | kotarpe-mbɨ-n |

    Kirmar nambɨr=nɨ puko-ya ŋgu kotarpe-mbɨ-n
    Kirmar chest=LOC come_up.3PL.R-and 3SG.F ask.R-3PL.R.O-SG|1PL.R.S
    They came up towards (lit. 'with their chest facing') Kirmar and she asked them:

21. *"Yum mbekemke?" Ngi namtike: "Awo".*
    Yum mbekem=ke Ngi nam-tike: "Awo".
    2PL come.2PL.R=Q 3PL talk.R-DL.R yes
    "Have you come?" The two said, "Yes".

22. *Ngɨgi ŋgu kotarpekure: "Yu anaknɨ?"*
    Ngɨ=gi ŋgu kotarpe-ku-re: "Yu anaknɨ?".
    3PL=ERG.PL 3SG.F ask.R-3SG.F.O-3PL.R.S 2SG to_where
    The two asked her: "Where are you going?"

23. *"Ngɨ eiaraknɡukre Kandumsik ndowkrunana ainda*
    Ngɨ eiar-ak-ŋguk-re Kandumsik ndow-kru-nana
    3PL cry.IRR-LINK-be.3PL.R-SUB Kandumsik leg-3SG.F.IRR.O-INTENT

    ainda
    DX.F

24. *mbek". "Ey. Nda otak ndɨ ŋgo".*
    mbek. Ey Nda o-tak ndɨ ŋgo
    come.1SG.F.R alright DM go.SBJ-3SG.F.R DM DM
    "They [children] are crying so I'm going to Kandumsik [creek] to leg it [i.e. to net some fish]". "Alright then, you go".

25. *Ngadirmbɨutoka orasamb*
    Ngadir-mbɨ-utok-a orasamb
    pass.R-3PL.R.O-go_down.3SG.F.R-and thing.PL
    She passed them and went down,

26. *orewirukuwoka urekpeka*
    orewiru-ku-wok-a urekpek-a
    throw_down.IRR- 3SG.F.R.O-go.3SG.F.R-and turn.3SG.F|1PL.R-and
    threw down her things, turned,

27. *kakrartɨmbɨna namtak: "Yum anɨŋgro?"*
    kakrar-tɨ-mbɨ-n-a   nam-tak: "Yum
    clear_throat.R-S<3PL.R.O>SG|1PL.R.S-and   talk.R-2SG.F|3SG.F.R   2PL

    ani-ŋgro?"
    who-PL
    cleared her throat and said: "Who are you?"

28. *"Omɨndeomɨnde yumke? Ŋa ainda".*
    Omɨndeomɨnde   yum=ke?   Ŋa   ainda
    spouse.PL   2PL=Q   1SG   DX
    "Are you my lovers? It's me"

29. *Ŋgɨ tɨ ainɨmeŋgɨ kandipŋa sene*
    Ŋgɨ   tɨ   ainɨ-me-ŋgɨ   kandip=ŋa   sene
    3PL   too   here- DX-DX.F   mangrove_slugs=POSS   two

30. *aŋguraktukureya nda ŋguyi ŋgɨ*
    aŋgurak-tu-ku-re-ya   nda   ŋgu=yi   ŋgɨ
    throw.R-S<3SG.F.R.O>DL.R-and   DM   3SG.F=ERG.F   3PL

31. *wempermbɨn.*
    wemper-mbɨ-n
    chase.R-3PL.R.O-SG|1PL.R.S
    They threw down their two [sticks] of mangrove slugs and she chased them.

32. *Ŋguyi ŋgɨ wempermbɨn kɨmbɨwek.*
    Ŋgu=yi   ŋgɨ   wemper-mbɨ-n   ki-mbɨ-wek
    3SG.F=ERG.F   3PL   chase.R-3PL.R.O-SG|1PL.R.S bring-3PL.R.O-come.3SG.F.R
    She chased them and brought them [towards the village]

33. *Ŋguyi ŋgɨ wempermbɨn kɨmbɨwek*
    Ŋgu=yi   ŋgɨ   wemper-mbɨ-n   ki-mbɨ-wek
    3SG.F=ERG.F   3PL   chase.R-3PL.R.O-SG|1PL.R.S bring-3PL.R.O-come.3SG.F.R

34. *kɨmbɨwek. Nje pungota*
    ki-mbɨ-wek   Nje   pungot-a
    bring-3PL.R.O-come.3SG.F.R   dog   stand.1SG.M|3SG.M.R-and

35. *mambrag noŋorre amurukutre, omosew sene*
    mambrag   noŋor=re   amuru-kut-re   omosew   sene
    spirit   dog=COM   fight.R-be.SG.M.R-SUB   father.PL two
    She chased them and brought them, brought them. The dog stood and while he was fighting with the ghost, the two ancestors

36. *ŋgɨ ŋguruŋ tatukureya weke.*
    ŋgɨ   ŋguruŋ   ta-tu-ku-re-ya   weke
    3PL   speed   take.R-S<3G.F.R.O>DL.R.S-and   come.DL.R
    they picked up speed and came.

37. *Nje ɲɨ amuruku amuruku amuruku*
    Nje   ɲɨ   amuru-ku   amuru-ku   amuru-ku
    dog   3SG.M   fight.R-be.SG.M.R   fight.R-be.SG.M.R   fight.R-be.SG.M.R

38. *mambrag noŋor.*
    mambrag   noŋor
    spirit   woman
    The dog, he was fighting for a long time with the ghost.

39. *Orekukɨ nunuk omosew senere mbet.*
    Ore-ku-kɨ   nunuk   omosew   sene=re   mbet
    leave.IRR-3SG.F.R.O-ADV   behind   father.PL two=COM   come.SG.M.R
    Leaving her, he [the dog] came behind the two ancestors.

40. *Mbe mbe mbe mbe mbe,*
    Mbe   mbe   mbe   mbe   mbe
    come.SG.M.R   come.SG.M.R   come.SG.M.R   come.SG.M.R   come.SG.M.R
    He came over a long distance

41. *ŋgɨre kaset.*
    ŋgɨ=re   kaset
    3PL=COM   come_out.SG.M.R
    He came out [of the rainforest] with them.

42. *Mambrag noŋor ŋgu ŋgɨre menjikantak,*
    Mambrag   noŋor   ŋgu   ŋgɨ=re   menjikan-tak
    spirit   woman   3SG.F   3PL=ALL   close-2SG.F|3SG.F.R
    The ghost got close to them,

43. *puŋgota kamiet.*
    puŋgot-a   kamiet
    stand.SG.M.R-and   fight.SG.M.R
    he [the dog] stood and fought.

44. *Amurukutre mambragre* [pause] *na omosew sene*
    Amuru-kut-re   mambrag=re   na   omosew   sene
    fight.R-be.SG.M.R-SUB   spirit=COM   and (TP)   father.PL   two
    While he was fighting with the dog [pause] and the two ancestors

45. *aikar weke. Nime nirkar nirkar nirkar*
    ai-kar   weke.   Nime   nir-kar   nir-kar
    come.IRR-MANN   come.DL.R   thus   do.IRR-MANN   do.IRR-MANN

    nir-kar
    do.IRR-MANN
    continued to come. Thus did they do it,

46. *nirkar, miri kemem aŋgokeke, ŋgweka*
    nir-kar   miri   kemem   aŋgok=eke   ŋgwek-a
    do.IRR-MANN   forest   long   DX=PERL   come.3PL.R-and
    a big rainforest they came through and

47. *nda ŋgusek tumbŋa kandaŋni Mbwadum.*
    nda   ŋgusek   tumb=ŋa   kandaŋ=ni   Mbwadum
    DM   appear.3PL.R   mountain=POSS   base=LOC   Mbwadum
    they appeared at the base of Mbwadum mountain.

48. *Tumbeke prike. Rorsem ŋgi ari emrariakŋguk*
    Tumb=eke   prike   Rorsem   ŋgi   ari
    mountain= PERL   come_up.DL.R   child.PL   3PL   below

    emrari-ak-ŋguk
    play.IRR-and -be.3PL.R

49. *tokroni, papkrim ondirkwanŋguk.*
    tokro=ni   papkrim   ondir-kwan-ŋguk
    slope=LOC   little_coconut   shoot.IRR-3SG.BEN.R.O-be.3PL.R
    They came up along the mountain. Children were playing below on the slope, they were [playing a game] shooting [arrows at] a little coconut.

50. *Papkrim ondɨrkwanŋguk, ŋgi ŋgire uske.*
    papkrim   ondɨr-kwan-ŋguk.   ŋgi   ŋgi=re   uske
    little_coconut shoot.IRR-3SG.BEN.R.O-be.3PL.R   3PL   3PL=ALL   appear.DL.R
    They were shooting a little coconut, and the two appeared to them.

51. *Namtɨmbre: "Rorsem! Yimana sandaw onkurem!".*
    Nam-tɨ-mb-re: Rorsem   yim=ana   sandaw   o-nkurem!
    talk.R.S<3PL.R.O>DL.R.S   child.PL 1PL=DAT   shout   strike.SBJ-2PL.R
    They told them: "Children, shout for us!"

52. *Rorsem sandaw pokuro: "O! O! O! O! O! O!"*
    Rorsem   sandaw   po-ku-ro   "O! O! O! O! O! O!"
    child.PL   shout   strike.R-3SG.F.R.O-3PL.R.S
    The children shouted, "O! O! O! O! O! O!"

53. *Ngi ti adɨwamborirkara orkeya*
    Ngi   ti   adɨ-wa-mborir-kar-a   orke-ya
    3PL   too   trip.IRR-MOD-roll.IRR-MOD-and go_down.DL-and

54. *wasowtikeya pisimb sene aini ari wuke.*
    wasow-tike-ya   pisimb   sene   ai=ni   ari   wuke
    die.R-DL.R-and   corpse   two   here=LOC   below   be.DL.R
    The two fell down and rolled down [the slope] and they died and their corpses lay there below.

55. *Ngan nje ti ndakop wasownet. Mambrag*
    Ngan   nje   ti   ndakop   wasow-net   Mambrag
    3PL.POSS   dog   too   together   die.R-1SG.M|3SG.M.R   spirit
    Their dog too died together with them.

56. *noŋor ŋgu kɨmbɨweka ainɨmeŋgi*
    noŋor   ŋgu   kɨ-mbɨ-weka   ainɨ-me-ŋgi
    woman   3SG.F   bring-3PL.R.O-come.3SG.F.R   here- DX-DX.F

57. *puŋgoka nda warukpek, orepembɨn.*
    puŋgok-a   nda   warukpek   orepe-mbɨ-n.
    stand.SG.F.R-and   DM   turn.SG.F.R leave.R-3PL.R.O-SG|1PL.R.S
    The ghost woman she brought them and she thus stood and turned and left them.

58. *Orembɨkɨ, nda ŋgu wok.*
    Ore-mbɨ-kɨ,   nda   ŋgu   wok
    leave.R-3PL.R.O-ADV   DM   3SG.F   go.3SG.F.R
    Leaving them, she went.

59. *Ngɨ nda wurkeya ŋgɨ nda mambrag tawnɨ*
    Ngɨ   nda   wurke-ya   ŋgɨ   nda   mambrag   taw=nɨ
    3PL   DM   be.DL.R-and   3PL   DM   spirit   side=LOC

60. *ŋgutukuroya nɨmnduko*
    ŋgu-tu-ku-ro-ya   nɨmnduko
    put.R-S<3SG.F.R.O>3PL.R.S-and   tree_branch

61. *poisɨrtukroya tawaitɨmbrore,*
    poisɨr-tu-ku-ro-ya   tawai-tɨ-mb-ro-re
    spit_chant.R-S<3SG.F.R.O>3PL.R.S-and   try.R-S<3PL.R.O>3PL.R.S-SUB
    The two were there and they [the men who saw them lying there dead] decided that this was a spirit matter, they spit magic chants on a tree branch and tried [to waken] them and

62. *ŋgɨ pemke. Kotarpembro: "Yum ambini*
    ŋgɨ   pemke.   Kotarpe-mb-ro: Yum   ambin-i
    3PL   get_up.DL.R   ask.R.3PL.R.O-3PL.R.S   2PL   what-ERG.F
    they got up. They asked the two:

63. *"Yum ambini nitɨmɨn?"*
    Yum   ambin=i   ni-tɨ-mɨ-n
    3PL   what=ERG.F   make.R-S<2PL.R.O>2SG|3SG.F.R.S
    "What happened to you?"

64. *"Yim mambrag noŋori yimen nireŋgari*
    Yim   mambrag   noŋor=i   yimen   nireŋgar=i
    1PL   spirit   woman=ERG.F   1PL.POSS   lover=ERG.F
    We, our spirit lover

65. *wempermɨna wekeya ŋgon*
    wemper-mɨ-n-a   weke-ya   ŋgon
    chase.R-1PL.R.O-SG|1PL.R.S-and   come.DL.R-and   3SG.F.POSS
    chased us and we came, her

66. *armbɨri tatminde yim wasowtike".*
    armbɨr=i   ta-ti-mi-n-de   yim   wasow-tike
    heat=ERG.F   take.R-S<1PL.R.O>SG|1PL.R.S-SUB   1PL   die.R-DL.R
    heat got us and we died"

67. *"Sapki nda. Wenkem nda".*
    Sapki   nda   we-nkem   nda
    good   DM   come.SBJ-2PL.R   DM
    "OK. Come on then"

Tayap Text 2: The water-spirit Ŋgayam kills the flying-fox clan
Narrated by Samek Wanjo in 2010

English translation

Long ago the ancestors of Kokokane together with the ancestors of Mbwadum were in Kokokane village and they went for fish. They went across the grassland to Murar stream and they picked up fish – on the bare ground they were picking up fish. The water-spirit Ŋgayam had left [and took the water in the stream with him]. He went outside to destroy the Watam people's sailing canoe. He destroyed it in the ocean. They were going to Manam. When they were going across he broke their sailing canoe in the middle and took a piece of it and brought it – he brought it inside to his home in the middle of the water, he put it.

The people from Kokokane and Mbwadum were picking up fish when he came back. His two wives who were hanging up from a branch of a wild ball tree [they had the shape of turtles and the villagers had captured them and hung them up].

They [the villagers] picked up fish as they walked on the bare ground. Two mbarow fish flipflopped and went along in puddles of water they jumped along and fell into the big water and they went with news. They went, and telling their father [i.e. Ŋgayam], the two of them came back, they all came back together.

He [Ŋgayam] came with the water and came inside [the rainforest]. He came and ascended. He ascended the stream – the water grew more massive. They were picking up fish, the men and women ancestors. They saw good water [coming] and this made them happy, [they said:] "Oh, we'll bathe in this good water, we'll wash the fish."

They were washing dirt from the fish. While they were washing the fish, the water was rising.

The water was rising, the water-spirit was coming closer. The sound of a conch shell rose up. He blew a conch shell, and [the beating of] an hourglass drum he came up. He came close and the two women left their wild ball branch and came down and with their two small machetes – machetes made of the bark of a sago palm tree. With them, they cracked open the heads of the ancestors. They killed them. They went and killed all of them. They killed them all, all of them died. Not a single one was left.

The ones [i.e. the ancestors] who [had collected fish and] were walking back along the grasslands, their basket of fish [came alive] and killed them all. They all died in the grassland as they came. A few who came back up to the village remained alive. The water came and killed all of them [i.e. the ones who hadn't yet come back to the village].

The water-spirit came and together with his children they killed them all [i.e. they killed all the ancestors]. There were no more left of the ancestors of Kokokane and Mbwadum. His [i.e. Ngayam's] two wives, as they called their two names they cut up [the ancestors] with their machete, the machete of sago palm bark: "Tutup, Tutup, Kaioka, Kaioka", [they called out, saying their own names], "Tutup, Tutup, Kaioka, Kaioka".

Tayap original

1. *Ripɨm aru munjenum Kokokanerekɨ Mbwadum ŋgwuka,*
   Ripɨm   aru   munjenum   Kokokane=rekɨ   Mbwadum   ŋgwuk-a
   long_ago   ancestor man.PL   Kokokane=COM   Mbwadum   be.3PL.R-and
   Once upon a time, ancestors from Kokokane, together with ancestors from Mbawdum were and

2. *Kokokaneŋa numnɨ ŋgwuka ŋomarana ŋgwok.*
   Kokokane=ŋa   num=nɨ   ŋgwuk-a   ŋomar=ana   ŋgwok
   Kokokane=POSS   village=LOC   be.3PL.R-and   fish=DAT   go.3PL.R
   they were in Kokokane village and they went to fish

3. *Naweke ŋgoka, Murar nuwombnɨ ŋgomar*
   Naw=eke   ŋgok-a   Murar   nuwomb=nɨ   ŋgomar
   grassland=PERL   go.3PL.R-and   Murar   creek=LOC   fish
   They went across the grassland and in Murar creek,

4. *tarkwaŋukre sumbwa sinderni ŋgomar*
   tar-kwa-ŋguk-re   sumbwa   sinder=ni   ŋgomar
   take.IRR-3SG.F.BEN.O-be.3PL.R.S-SUB   ground   bare=LOC   fish
   and when they were picking up fish on the bare ground,

5. *tarkwaŋguk, emári Ngayam katota*
   tar-kwa-ŋguk   emári   Ngayam   katot-a
   take.IRR-3SG.F.BEN.O-be.3PL.R.S   water_spirit   Ngayam   go_out.SG.M.R-and
   they were picking up fish, the water spirit Ngayam went out and

6. *mbot. Mbota Moipmandama kawsomb*
   mbot   Mbot-a   Moip-mandama   kawsomb
   go.SG.M.R   go.SG.M.R-and   Watam-POSS.PL   sailing_canoe

7. *krarkrunana katot.*
   krar-kru-nana   katot
   break.IRR.3SG.F.IRR.O-INTENT   go_out.SG.M.R
   went. He went to destroy the Watam villagers' sailing canoe.

8. *Marani krankun.*
   Mara=ni   kra-n-ku-n
   ocean=LOC   break.R-S<3SG.F.R.O>SG|1PL.R.S
   He destroyed it at sea.

9. *Ngi Mainambre okinana ŋgwok.*
   Ngi   Mainamb=re   o-ki-nana   ŋgwok
   3PL   Manam=ALL   go.IRR-IRR-INTENT   go.3PL.R
   They were intending to go to Manam [island].

10. *Oski ŋgwokre oromni kranmbatan*
    Oski   ŋgwok-re   orom=ni   kra-n-mbata-n
    across   go.3PL.R-SUB   middle=LOC   break.R-S<3SG.F.BEN.R.O>1SG|3SG.
                                           M|1PL.R.S
    When they went across in the middle [of the ocean], he destroyed theirs [i.e. their canoe].

11. *kawsombŋa taw ŋgume kukumbeta*
    kawsomb=ŋa   taw   ŋgume   ku-ku-mbet-a
    sailing_canoe=POSS   side   thus   bring-3SG.F.R.O-come.SG.M.R-and
    He brought a side of their sailing canoe.

12. *kukukarota ŋan numnɨ.*
    ku-ku-karot-a   ŋan   num=nɨ
    bring-3SG.F.R.O-go_inside.SG.M.R-and   3SG.M.POSS village=LOC
    He brought a side of their sailing canoe, he brought it inside to his village.

13. *Awin oromnɨ, ŋgunkuna wuk.*
    Awin   orom=nɨ   ŋgu-n-ku-n-a   wuk
    water   middle=LOC   put.R-S<3SG.F.R.O>1SG|3SG.M|1PL.R.S-LINK   be.3SG.F.R
    In the middle of the water, he put it and it was there.

14. *Kokokanerekɨ Mbwadum ŋgomar tarkwaŋguka motɨ mbetre.*
    Kokokane=rekɨ   Mbwadum   ŋgomar   tar-kwa-ŋguk-a
    Kokokane=COM   Mbwadum   fish   take.IRR-3SG.F.BEN.O-be.3PL.R.S-and

15. *motɨ mbetre. Ŋan noŋor sene*
    motɨ   mbet-re   Ŋan   noŋor   sene
    again   come.3SG.M.R-SUB   3SG.M.POSS   woman   two
    The villagers from Kokokane and Mbwadum were taking fish when he came back. His two wives

16. *wawarpembreya wuke tamroŋa ndukonɨ wukeŋa.*
    wawarpe-mb-re-ya   wuke   tamro=ŋa   nduko=nɨ   wuke=ŋa.
    hang.R-3PL.R.O-   be.DL.R   wild_ball=POSS   branch=LOC   be.DL.R=POSS
    DL.R.S-and
    were hanging from the branch of a wild ball tree [the wives had the form of turtles and the villagers had captured them and hung them up]

17. *Ŋgɨ ŋgomar tarmbrar ŋgwoka, sumbwa sindernɨ.*
    Ŋgɨ   ŋgomar   tar-mb-rar   ŋgwok-a   sumbwa   sinder=nɨ.
    3PL   fish   take.IRR-3PL.R.O-ML   go.3PL.R-and   ground   bare=LOC
    They [the villagers] collected the fish from the bare ground.

18. *Mbarow sene mborimborikar woke awin motoreke woke*
    Mbarow   sene   mborimbori-kar   woke   awin   moto=reke   woke
    mbarow_fish   two   flipflop.IRR-MANN   go.DL.R   water   dirty=PERL   go.DL.R
    Two mbarow fish flipflopped through the dirty water

19. *piŋkar wokeya awin sumannɨ woke otɨkeya*
    piŋ-kar   woke-ya   awin   suman=nɨ   woke   otɨke-ya
    jump.IRR-MANN   go.DL.R-and   water   big=ALL   go.DL.R   fall.DL.R-and

20. *namreki woke. Woke omo namgiki, namgiki*
    nam=reki woke.   Woke   omo   nam-gi-ki
    talk=COM go.DL.R go.DL.R father talk.R-3SG.M.R.O-ADV
    they jumped and went to the big water with the news. Telling their father,

21. *namgiki motini weke ndakop ŋgwek.*
    nam-gi-ki   motini weke   ndakop   ŋgwek
    talk.R-3SG.M.R.O-ADV   again   come.DL.R together come.3PL.R
    telling him, they came back together [with *Ŋgayam*].

22. *Awinreki mbeta karot. Karota*
    Awin=reki   mbet-a   karot   Karot-a
    water=COM   come.SG.M.R-and   go_inside.SG.M.R   go_inside.SG.M.R-and
    He went with water, he came inside [the creek]. He came inside and

23. *puwot. Puwota nuwombni awin sumantaka*
    puwot   Puwot-a   nuwomb=ni   awin   suman-tak-a
    ascend.SG.M.R   ascend.SG.M.R-and   creek=LOC   water   big-2SG.F|3SG.F.R-and
    he rose. He rose and the water in the creek began to rise and

24. *ŋgi ŋgomar tarkwanŋgukŋa aru munjenumreki naŋro.*
    ŋgi   ŋgomar   tar-kwan-ŋguk-ŋa   aru   munjenum=reki
    3PL   fish   take.IRR-3SG.F.BEN.R.O-be.3PL.R-REL   ancestor   man.PL=COM
    the ancestor men and women who were collecting fish.

25. *naŋro. Awin eŋgon tatukroya numbwan*
    naŋro   Awin   eŋgon   ta-tu-ku-ro-ya   numbwan
    woman.PL   water   good   see.R-S<3SG.F.R.O>3PL.R.S-and   thought

26. *eŋgontimbatan: "O yim awin*
    eŋgon-ti-mbata-n   O   yim   awin
    good-S<3PL.BEN.R.O>2SG|3SG.F.R.S   Oh   1PL   water
    They saw the good water and had good thoughts, "Oh, we'll

27. *tuwkunak eŋgonni,*
    tuw-ku-nak   eŋgon=ni
    wash.IRR-IRR-1SG.F|1PL.IRR   good=LOC
    bathe in the good water,

28. ŋgomar pitmbrinak sumbwanana.
    ŋgomar   pit-mbri-nak   sumbwa=nana
    fish   wash.IRR-3PL.IRR.O-1SG.F|1PL.IRR   ground=DAT
    we'll wash the dirt from the fish".

29. Ngomar pitkwanŋgukre awin sumankar puwok
    Ngomar   pit-kwan-ŋguk-re   awin   suman-kar   puwok
    fish   wash.IRR-3SG.F.R.O-3PL.R.S-SUB   water   big-MANN   ascend.SG.F.R
    While they were washing the fish, the water continued to come in

30. Awin sumankar woka munje emári mbeta
    Awin   suman-kar   wok-a   munje   emári
    water   big-MANN   go.3SG.F.R-and   man   water_spirit

    munje   mbet-a
    man   come.SG.M.R-and

31. menjikannet. Pomiŋ pemiek.
    menjikan-net   Pomiŋ   pemiek
    close-1SG.M|3SG.M.R   conch   get_up.1SG.F|3SG.F.R
    The water got bigger and the water spirit got closer. The [sound of a] conch shell rose up.

32. Pomiŋ ninkun.
    Pomiŋ   ni-n-ku-n
    conch   do.R-S<3SG.F.R.O>SG|3SG.M|1PL.R.S
    He blew a conch shell.

33. Pomiŋ tatukure omindeominde sene ŋan.
    Pomiŋ   ta-tu-ku-re   omindeominde   sene   ŋan
    conch   hear.R-S<3SG.F.R.O>DL.R.S-SUB   wives   two   3SG.M.POSS
    His two wives heard the conch shell.

34. Pomiŋreki koŋodreki ŋureki piet.
    Pomiŋ=reki   koŋod=reki   ŋgu=reki   piet
    conch=COM   hourglass_drum=COM   3SG.F=COM   come_up.SG.M.R
    With the [sound of] a conch shell and [the beating of] an hourglass drum, he came up.

35. *Mbeta menjikan. Noŋor sene tamroŋa nduko*
    Mbet-a   menjikan noŋor sene tamro=ŋa   nduko
    come.SG.M.R-and   close   wife   two   wild_ball=POSS   branch
    He came closer. His two wives

36. *orekusisikeya ŋgan pitiŋarŋa at*
    ore-ku-sisike-ya   ŋgan   pitiŋar=ŋa   at
    leave.IRR-3SG.F.R.O-descend.DL.R-and   3pl. POSS machete=POSS   half
    descended from the wild ball tree and

37. *senereki karamŋa pitiŋar ŋguni aru*
    sene-reki   karam=ŋa   pitiŋar   ŋgu=ni   aru
    two-COM   sago_palm_bark=POSS   machete   3SG.F=INSTR   ancestor
    with their machetes their sago-palm-bark machetes

38. *munjenummandama kokir krakrirmbatar weke*
    munjmenum=mandama   kokir   krakrir-mba-tar   weke
    man.PL=POSS.PL   head   break.IRR-3PL.O.R-ML   come.DL.R
    the two split open the heads of the ancestors. The two killed them.

39. *Pombre. Pombreya weke.*
    Po-mb-re   Po-mb-re-ya   weke
    strike.R-3PL.R-DL.R   strike.R-3PL.R-DL.R-and   come.DL.R
    The two killed them. The two killed them and came.

40. *Taman pombro. Taman waswituko. Moti non*
    Taman   po-mb-ro   Taman   waswi-tuko   Moti   non
    all   strike.R-3PL.R-3PL.R   all   die_like_flies.R-3PL.R again   one/some
    They killed them all. They all died like flies. There wasn't a single one left.

41. *aku wákare. Non nawŋa oromni waikar ŋgwekŋan,*
    a-ku   wákare   Non   naw=ŋa   orom=ni   wai-kar
    be.IRR-IRR   NEG   one/some   grassland=POSS   middle=LOC   walk.IRR-
                                                                          MANN
    There wasn't a single one left. The ones who were walking in the middle of the grassland

42. *ŋgwekŋan, ŋgomarŋa kondewi ombrar*
    ŋgwek=ŋan   ŋgomar=ŋa   kondew=i   o-mb-rar
    come.3PL.R=POSS   fish=POSS   container=ERG.F   strike.IRR-3PL.R.O-ML
    the containers of fish [came alive and] killed

43. *wek. Nawɨ waswirkar ŋgwek.*
    wek   Naw=nɨ   waswir-kar   ŋgwek
    come.3SG.F.R grassland=LOC   die_like_flies.IRR-MANN   come.3PL.R
    them all. They died like flies in the grassland.

44. *Non numnɨ ŋgwekŋa, ŋgɨ purko*
    Non   num=nɨ   ŋgwek=ŋa   ŋgɨ   purko
    one/some   village=ALL   come.3PL.R=POSS   3PL.R   come_up.3PL.R
    The ones who went to the village, they came up

45. *numnɨ ŋgwuk. Awɨnɨ weka taman*
    num=nɨ   ŋgwuk   Awɨn=ɨ   wek-a   taman
    village=LOC   be.3PL.R   water=ERG.F   come.3SG.F.R-and   all
    the village, they remained alive. The water came and

46. *pombɨn. Emárɨ munje mbeta ŋan*
    po-mbɨ-n   Emárɨ   munje   mbet-a
    strike.R-3PL.R.O-SG|1PL.R.S   water_spirit   man   come.SG.M-and
    killed them all. The water spirit came and

47. *ŋan rorsemrekɨ taman pombɨna*
    ŋan   rorsem=rekɨ   taman   po-mbɨ-n-a
    3SG.M.POSS   children=COM   all   strike.R-3PL.R.O-SG|1PL.R.S-and
    together with his children killed them all and

48. *wákaretuko Kokokanerekɨ*
    wákare-tuko   Kokokane=rekɨ
    NEG-3PL.R   Kokokane=COM
    there were no more [people] of Kokokane

49. *Mbwadum. Ɲan omɨndeomɨnde sene ŋan nomb sene*
    Mbwadum   Ɲan   omɨndeomɨnde   sene   ŋan   nomb   sene
    Mbwadum   3SG.M.POSS   wives   two   3PL.POSS   name   two
    and Mbwadum. His [i.e. Ngayam's] two wives,

50. *ŋgarkukɨ pɨtɨŋarnɨ karamŋa*
    ŋgar-ku-kɨ   pɨtɨŋar=nɨ   karam=ŋa
    call_out.IRR-3SG.F.R.O-ADV   machete=INSTR   sago_palm_bark=POSS
    as the two called their two names,

51. *pitiŋarni utimbrar weke:*
    pitiŋar=ni   uti-mb-rar   weke
    machete=INSTR slice.IRR-3PL.R.O-ML   come.DL.R
    sliced up everyone with their machetes made of sago palm bark:

52. *"Tutup, Tutup, Kaioka, Kaioka. Tutup, Tutup, Kaioka, Kaioka"*
    "Tutup, Tutup, Kaioka, Kaioka. Tutup, Tutup, Kaioka, Kaioka"

Tayap Text 3: 2-year-old boy has a close call with a deadly snake

Narrated by Masito Monei in 2009

The following narrative is an example of the Tayap spoken by a high-proficiency passive active bilingual. The narrator, Masito Monei, was 25 years old when she told this story, and she is the youngest relatively fluent speaker in Gapun.[1]

Words in Tok Pisin are in italics in the English translation below. Commentary follows the Tayap text.

English translation

One day we went to Murar. We went and Kama and her kids and her husband [did too] *and* us. We were there and we came back [i.e. we came up to Gapun]. It was *Sunday* and we came up. We came and on the path. On the path Kama and her family went first, they went first. They came and they were [already] at Ŋgasimbara. *And* we with the two kids the two of us [narrator and her husband] came later.

We came and a mbumjor [a deadly venomous snake] was closeby – a snake, a mbumjor – it was like that in front of us. *And* I was carrying Mbanaŋ [narrator's 2 year old son] and coming, and I put him down right near the snake. I set him down and I told him, "You walk and go. "Walk on your own".

Me and Pepe [narrator's 6 year old daughter]. Pepe was walking in the lead. He [Mbanaŋ] was behind her. The two of them walked and walked, and were close to the mbumjor. The mbumjor too was coming on the path. *And* he had been inside the forest and was coming outside [onto the path]. The two of them were walking along the path. They came and the mbumjor raised its head really close and he was going to strike them. He stood up like this....

---

[1] This is the same Masito, in 2010 a mother of four, whose language socialization as a baby I discussed in Kulick 1992.

When Pepe saw the snake, she ran away. *And* Mbanaŋ was standing there. He was standing there looking for the snake. And the thing it was doing – it was really close to Mbanaŋ's chest, it was going to strike him right there. It was that close. I was looking around and I saw it. I thought that the mbumjor had struck him. I threw down my things. I ran and snatched him away from the snake's mouth.

The mbumjor really nearly struck Mbanaŋ. It had its head up and it was about to strike Mbanaŋ. I went and saw Mbanaŋ. I was going to leave him there and run away, but I didn't. I went and with my hand I snatched him away. I told him, "The snake is about to bite you!" I thought that it had bitten him and that he was going to die. It was a terrible thought. I *checked* his leg, and there was no bite. Abram [narrator's husband] took a stick and killed the snake. He struck it and it died. It died and he left it there and we came.

We came and at Ŋgasimbara we saw Kama and her family. I told them, "A mbumjor nearly bit Mbanaŋ and Pepe. They were a hair's breath away from dying". Then we came back again to the village. *That's all.*

Tayap original

1. *Aro non yim mbok Murar.*
   Aro   non   yim   mbok   Murar
   day   one   1PL   go.1SG.F|1PL.R   Murar
   One day we went to Murar.

2. *Yim mboka Kamare ŋgon rorsemreki*
   Yim   mbok-a   Kama=re   ŋgon   rorsem=reki
   1PL   go.1SG.F|1PL.R-and   Kama=COM   3SG.F.POSS   child.PL=COM
   We went and Kama and her children

3. *Kamare ominre na yim.*
   Kama=re   omin=re   na   yim
   Kama=COM   spouse=COM   and (Tok Pisin)   1PL
   with Kama, her husband and (Tok Pisin) us.

4. *Yim kuka priek.*
   Yim   kuk-a   priek
   1PL   be.1SG.F|1PL.R-and   come_up.1SG.F|1PL.R
   We were there [in Murar] and we came up [back to the village]

5. *Sandetakre priek. Mbeka*
    Sande-tak=re   priek   Mbek-a
    Sunday-2SG.F|3SG.F.R=TEMP come_up.1SG.F|1PL.R go.1SG.F|1PL.R-and
    It was Sunday when we came up. We went and

6. *nderŋa oromnɨ. Nderŋa oromŋa Kamaŋgro*
    nder=ŋa   orom=nɨ   Nder=ŋa   orom=ŋa   Kama-ŋgro
    path=POSS   middle=LOC   path=POSS   middle=POSS   Kama-PL
    in the middle of the path. The middle of the path, Kama and her family

7. *tuptukro / ŋgɨ tuptukoya ŋgwek*
    *tuptukro   ŋgɨ   tuptuko-ya   ŋgwek
    lead.3PL.R   3PL   lead.3PL.R-and   come.3PL.R
    *lead / they came first. (Note: the / indicates a false start)

8. *Ngweka Ngasimbara ŋgwuk.*
    Ngwek-a   Ngasimbara   ŋgwuk.
    come.3PL.R-and   Ngasimbara   be.3PL.R
    They came and were [already] at Ngasimbara

9. Na *yim ruru senerekɨ nunuk wekeya.*
    Na   yim   ruru   sene=rekɨ   nunuk   weke-ya
    And (Tok Pisin)   1PL   child.DL   two=COM   behind   come.DL.R-and
    And (Tok Pisin) the two of us came behind them with our two kids and

10. *Yim mbeka nda mbumjorre*
    Yim   mbek-a   nda   mbumjor=re
    1PL   come.1SG.F|1PL.R-and   DM   mbumjor_snake=LOC
    We were coming and a mbumjor snake

11. *menjikan menjikan aram, mbumjor ide, ŋɨ nanden*
    menjikan   menjikan   aram   mbumjor   ide   ŋɨ   nanden
    closeby   closeby   snake   mbumojor   DX   3SG.M   thus
    closeby, closeby the snake, a mbumjor, he was there

12. *rawnɨ.* Na *Mbanaŋ tapnɨŋgɨna*
    raw=nɨ   Na (Tok Pisin)   Mbanaŋ   tap-nɨ-ŋgɨ-n-a
    nose=LOC   and   Mbanaŋ   carry.R-S<3SG.M.R.O>-SG|1PL.R.S-and
    in front. And I carried Mbanaŋ

13. kiŋgimbeka, aramre menjikan nda
    ki-ŋgi-mbek-a   aram=re   menjikan   nda
    bring-3SG.M.R.O- come.1SG.F|1PL.R-and   snake=LOC   closeby   DX
    brought him, and while the snake was close,

14. wisŋgin.
    wis-ŋgi-n
    set_down.R-3SG.M.R.O-SG|1PL.R.S
    I set him down.

15. Sireŋginŋgina
    Sire-ŋgi-n-ŋgi-n-a
    down-put.R-S<3SG.M.R.O>SG|1PL.R.S-SG|1PL.R.S-and
    I put him down and

16. namniŋgin "Waiteta
    nam-ni-ŋgi-n   wai-tet-a
    talk.R-S<3SG.M.R.O>SG|1PL.R.S   walk.SBJ-2SG.M|3SG.M.R-and
    I told him, "Walk and

17. otet. Neker otet". Ña Pepe-re...
    o-tet   Neker   o-tet   Ña   Pepe=re
    go.SBJ-2SG.M|3SG.M.R alone   go.SBJ-2SG.M|3SG.M.R   1SG   Pepe=COM
    go. Walk by yourself". Me and Pepe [speaker's 6-year old daughter]...

18. Pepe ŋgu tiptiek. Ñi nunuk.
    Pepe   ŋgu   tiptiek   Ñi   nunuk
    Pepe   3SG.F   lead.2SG.F|3SG.F.R   3SG.M   behind
    Pepe she was in front. He was [walking] behind [her].

19. Weke, weke menjikan mbumjorre. Mbumjor ŋi ti
    Weke   weke   menjikan   mbumjor=re   Mbumjor   ŋi   ti
    come.DL.R   come.DL.R   closeby   mbumjor=LOC   mbumjor   3SG.M   too
    The two of them came, the snake closeby. The mbumjor too, he

20. ndereke nanden mbet. Na ŋi mirini
    nder=eke   nanden   mbet   Na   ŋi
    path=PERL   thus   come.SG.M.R   And (Tok Pisin)   3SG.M
    came along the path. And he

21. *mirini kuta kaset. Ŋgi ndereke*
    miri=ni   kut-a   kaset   Ŋgi   nder=eke
    forest=LOC be.SG.M.R-and come_outside.SG.M.R 3PL path=PERL
    came outside [on the path] from the forest. The two of them [i.e. the two children]

22. *waitike weke. Wekeya mbumjorŋi menjikanki*
    wai-tike   weke   Weke-ya   mbumjor=ni   menjikan-ki
    walk.R-DL.R come.DL.R come.DL.R-and mbumjor=ERG.M closeby-INTENS
    walked along the path. They came and the mbumjor was really close

23. *nda kokir kukupemieta*
    nda   kokir   ku-ku-pemiet-a
    DM   head   bring-3SG.F.R.O-get_up.SG.M.R-and
    his head raised and

24. *ombrina ninbin.*
    o-mbri-na   ni-n-bi-n
    strike.IRR-3PL.IRR.O-INTENT do.R-S<3PL.R.O>SG|1PL.R.S
    and was about to strike.

25. *Nande inde puŋgota…Pepe ŋgu*
    Nande   inde   puŋgot-a   Pepe   ŋgu
    thus   DX   stand.R.SG.M.R-and   Pepe   3SG.F
    He was standing like this and…Pepe she

26. *aram tatiŋginre tewtiek*
    aram   ta-ti-ŋgi-n-re   tewtiek
    snake see.R-S<3SG.M.R.O>2SG|3SG.F.R.S-SUB   flee.SG.F|1PL.R
    saw the snake and she ran away

27. *Na Mbanaŋ puŋgotakut.*
    Na (Tok Pisin)   Mbanaŋ   puŋgot-a-kut.
    and   Mbanaŋ   stand.SG.M.R-LINK-be.SG.M.R
    And Mbanaŋ was standing there.

28. *Puŋgota rarŋgankut aram inde…*
    Puŋgot-a   rar-ŋgan-kut   aram   inde
    stand.SG.M.R-and look.IRR-3SG.M.BEN.R.O-be.SG.M.R snake   DX
    He stood there and was looking for the snake

29. *aŋguk orak aŋgu ambin nirkwan/*
    aŋguk   orak   aŋgu   ambin   nir-kwan/
    DX   thing   DX   what   do.IRR-3SG.BEN.IRR.O
    the thing, what it was doing/

30. *ŋi nda menjikan Mbanaŋma tokimot*
    ŋi   nda   menjikan   Mbanaŋ=ma   tokimot
    3SG.M   DM   closeby   Mbanaŋ=POSS   chest
    on Mbanaŋ's chest

31. *oŋatinana aini stret*
    o-ŋgati-nana   ai=ni   stret (Tok Pisin)
    strike.IRR-3SG.M.BEN.IRR.O-INTENT   here=LOC
    it really almost bit him right here.

32. *Nande nende menjikan, Ŋa nda*
    Nande   nende   menjikan   Ŋa   nda
    thus   thus   closeby   1SG   DM
    It was so close I

33. *rarmboka tankun.*
    rar-mbok-a   ta-n-ku-n
    see.IRR-go.1SG.F|1PL.R-and   see.R-S<3SG.F.R.O>SG|3SG.M|1PL.R.S
    was looking and I saw it.

34. *Ŋa namnak mbumjorŋi*
    Ŋa   nam-nak   mbumjor=ŋi
    1SG   talk.R-1SG.F|1PL.R   mbumjor=ERG.M
    I thought the mbumjor

35. *poŋginara. Orak orak*
    po-ŋgi-n-ara   Orak   orak
    strike.R-3SG.F.R.O-SG|1PL.R.S-PERF   thing   thing
    had bitten him. I

36. *rukuotitek, nunumpuwok*
    ru-ku-otitek   nunum-puwok
    propel.R-3SG.F.R.O-fall.3SG.F.R.S   running-ascend.SG.F|1PL.R
    threw down my things, ran up

37. *sakini aramma sikni mbiuningin*
    sakini   aram=ma   sik=ni   mbiu-ni-ŋgi-n
    nothing   snake=POSS   mouth=LOC   stretch.R-S<3SG.M.R.O>-SG|1PL.R.S
    pulled him from the snake's mouth.

38. *Mbumjor pini ŋayarni Mbanaŋ oŋgrinana.*
    Mbumjor   pini   ŋayar-ni   Mbanaŋ   o-ŋgri-nana
    mbumjor   ADV   true-ADV   Mbanaŋ   strike.IRR-3SG.IRR.O-INTENT
    The mbumjor was this close to biting Mbanaŋ.

39. *Ni nda kokir pemieka nda Mbanaŋ*
    Ni   nda   kokir   pemiek-a   nda   Mbanaŋ
    3SG.M   DM   head   get_up.SG.M.R-and   DM   Mbanaŋ
    His head was raised and

40. *oŋgrinana menjikan. Ŋa mboka*
    o-ŋgri-nana   menjikan   Ŋa   mbok-a
    strike.IRR-3SG.IRR.O-INTENT   closeby   1SG   go.1SG.F|1PL.R-and
    he wanted to strike Mbanaŋ. I went

41. *Mbanaŋ taningin.*
    Mbanaŋ   ta-ni-ŋgi-n
    Mbanaŋ   see.R-S<3SG.M.R.O>SG|3SG.M|1PL.R.S
    and I saw Mbanaŋ.

42. *Namningin: "Aram aŋgidekmeŋgi*
    Nam-ni-ŋgi-n   aram   aŋgidek-me-ŋgi
    talk.R-S<3SG.M.R.O>SG|3SG.M|1PL.R.S   snake   DX.F-DX-DX.F
    I said, "The snake there

43. *orunetana". Ŋa nda namnak*
    o-ru-net-ana   Ŋa   nda   nam-nak
    strike.IRR-2SG.IRR.O-1SG.M|3SG.M.R.S-INTENT   1SG   DM   talk.R-1SG.F|1PL.R
    is going to strike you". I thought

44. *ni nda poŋginara*
    ni   nda   po-ŋgi-n-ara
    3SG.M   DM   strike.r-3SG.M.R.O-SG|1PL.R.S-PERF
    it had bitten him and

45. wasowkinetana. Numbwan aprotak.
    wasow-ki-net-ana.					Numbwan		apro-tak
    die.IRR-IRR-1SG.M|3SG.M.IRR-INTENT	thought		bad-2SG.F|3SG.F.R
    he was going to die. A bad thought arose.

46. Ŋa ndow sekimkwankuk, wákare
    Ŋa		ndow	sekim-kwan-kuk						wákare
    1SG		leg		check (TP)-3SG.F.BEN.R.O-be.1SG.F|1PL.R		NEG
    I was checking his leg, no [the snake hadn't bitten Mbanaŋ]

47. Nda Abramŋi nimŋat tankun
    Nda		Abram=ŋi		nim=ŋa-at			ta-n-ku-n
    DM		Abram=ERG.M		tree=POSS-piece		take.R-S<3SG.F.R.O>SG|3SG.M|1PL.R.S
    Then Abram [Masito's husband] took a stick

48. aram nime poŋgin.
    aram	nime	po-ŋgi-n
    snake	thus	strike.R-3SG.M.R.O-SG|1PL.R.S
    hit the snake with that.

49. Poŋgina, wasonet.
    Po-ŋgi-n-a								waso-net.
    strike.R-3SG.M.R.O-SG|1PL.R.S-and		die.R-1SG.M|3SG.M.R
    He hit it, and it died.

50. Wasowneta ainimende
    Waso-net-a					aini-me-nde
    die.R-1SG.M|3SG.M.R-and		here-DX-DX.M
    It died and there

51. ŋgratkutre, yim mbek
    ŋgra-t-kut-re								yim		mbek.
    put.IRR-3SG.M.NFO-BE.SG.M.R-SUB				1PL		come.1SG.F|1PL.R
    he put it, we came.

52. Mbeka Ŋgasimbara Kamare
    Mbek-a							Ŋgasimbara		Kama=re
    come.1SG.F|1PL.R-and			Ŋgasimbara		Kama=COM
    We came to Ŋgasimbara,

53. *tanɨmbɨn. Namnɨmbɨn,*
    ta-nɨ-mbɨ-n.   Nam-nɨ-mbɨ-n
    see.R-S<3PL.R.O>SG|1PL.R.S   talk.R-S<3PL.R.O>SG|1PL.R.S
    we saw Kama and everyone. I told them,

54. "*Mbumjorŋi pɨn ŋayarnɨ Mbanaŋre Pepere*
    Mbumjor=ŋi   pɨn   ŋayar-nɨ   Mbanaŋ=re   Pepe=re
    mbumjor=ERG.M   ADV   true-ADV   Mbanaŋ=COM   Pepe=COM
    "A mbumjor came really close to biting Mbanaŋ and Pepe

55. *ombrɨna. Pɨn ŋayarnɨ wasowtike*".
    o-mbrɨ-na   Pɨn   ŋayar-nɨ   wasow-tike
    strike.IRR-3PL.IRR.O-INTENT   ADV   true-ADV   die.R-DL.R
    The two of them came really close to dying".

56. *Motɨnɨ nda ainɨme mbek numnɨ.*
    Motɨnɨ   nda   ainɨ-me   mbek   num=nɨ
    again   DM   here-DX   come.1SG.F|1PL.R   village=ALL
    Then we came back to the village.

57. Em tasol (Tok Pisin)
    Em   tasol
    3SG   just
    That's all.

Commentary

The narrator of this story is an example of a young passive active speaker, a villager who never speaks more than a few formulaic phases of Tayap. She speaks Tok Pisin to everyone: her children, her husband, her old mother, her siblings, and even her mother-in-law, with whom she interacts every day, and who is a Tayap-dominant woman in her late fifties. Despite the fact that this young woman never speaks Tayap, she not only possesses solid grammatical competence in the language; she is also able to activate that competence to produce narratives of relatively great complexity. She is the youngest villager able to do this; her husband, who is 6 years older, was able to produce a coherent narrative only with her active intervention.

Gapuners would judge this narrative to be a good story in terms of structure, content and performance. It adheres to the village narrative convention of having the protagonist or protagonists go off into the rainforest, have something happen there, and then return, at the end of the story, back to the village. It contains detail and a variety of perspectives. It is dramatic.

Grammatically, the narrative is complex. It contains a number of different verbs of motion besides 'go' and 'come' (lines 4–5, 16, 21, 22, 36), serial verbs (lines 13, 15, 23, 36) and clauses coordinated with the clause subordinating morpheme -*re* (lines 26, 51). All verbs but one are correctly inflected for subject – this speaker makes none of the errors that most other young speakers make, discussed throughout the grammar. The one inflectional error she does make is *tuptukro* 'they went first' in line 7; but she corrects herself and produces the correct form a few words later. Her pronunciation of the word, /tuptuko/, deviates a bit from the more usual *tiptuko*, but it is within the range of acceptable variation.

The only grammatical mistakes made by the speaker both occur with regard to the gender of the snake. For most of the narrative, the snake is correctly gendered masculine. But three times, in lines 29, 33, and 42, it becomes feminine (even if line 29 is ambiguous, because it isn't entirely clear what the speaker is referring to).

Tayap Text 4: Young men kill a cassowary
Narrated by a 20-year-old young man in 2009

The following text is an example of the kind of young people's Tayap that has been discussed throughout the grammar. The narrator, a twenty-year-old young man, is one of the youngest of ten children. His mother is one of the most Tayap-dominant speakers in the village, and his father, who died several years ago, also spoke Tayap just as much as, if not more than, he spoke Tok Pisin.

This young man has flawless passive competence in Tayap, but his ability to actively speak the language is limited. He is still able to narrate the broad outlines of a story, but the story he tells is difficult to follow. Referents are jumbled, verbs are inflected incorrectly and the narrative is punctuated with nervous laughter and hesitations, as the young man plans out what he will say. At several points, the speaker is simply unable to inflect a verb, and he is prompted by his 30-year-old brother-in-law, who was sitting with us, listening to the young man's story.

The following English translation of the young man's story reflects its disfluent nature. (All the names of people in this story have been changed).

Commentary follows the Tayap text.

English translation

We went into the forest. We went and it was getting dark. We went and Waiki [laughs] (fight?) [laughs]. Waiki and Mbini (fight?) eh...ssss [sound of frustration].

Speaker B, speaker's thirty-year-old brother-in-law: The two of them fought.

The two of them fought [laughs]. Waiki, Mbini hand here on the chest pounded him. He pounded him and tree/tree/tree branch [laughs] with a tree branch. *Wait* [said in Tok Pisin]...he fell. He fell and he got up and Konjab/Konjab Konjab... Konjab...Konjab...he got up and Konjab [whispers to himself, for 15 seconds, rehearsing the words] pounded Konjab. Pounded him. Konjab cried. He cried and he...he...hand...[meaningless]/eh/ssss...[16 second hesitation, laughs]. He shook hands [laughs]. He shook hands and they enough...[laughs] enough...

Speaker B: The two had enough [i.e. they finished fighting]

The two had enough. And we were there. We were there and in the morning we went with the dogs. We went with the dogs and the dog...the dog chase/chased a cassowary/cassowary. He chased/he was and we brought her, we brought her and we brought her [12 second hesitation] and (get up??)/the dogs [laughs]. The dogs, the dogs, *wait* [in Tok Pisin]...The dogs [whispers to himself, rehearsing] they got up/they got up. They got up, we went and we went and speared the cassowary. We speared him and we/we/we we two tied his legs with a rope and then we they [meaningless] came. They came, they came, we came. We came and at the stream we/we will put [quietly to himself, rehearsing] at the stream/the stream's will put...will put...the stream we brought him and the stream's side will put...will put [laughs, 6 second pause].

Speaker B: Just [inaudible]

[laughs] We...[laughs] on the stream's side burn...we brought him and on the stream's side

Speaker B: We burned him [i.e. singed the feathers off the dead cassowary]

We burned him. We burned him and chop/will chop...[laughs] We chopped him...we chopped him [laughs]. We chopped him and we came. We came to Ŋgarmembag. That's enough.

Tayap original

KEY TO TRANSCRIPTION

Italics	Tayap	*	ungrammatical or incorrect Tayap
roman	Tok Pisin	??	nonce morpheme or word
/	false start or self-correction	[ ]	author's comments
...	pause or hestitation		

1. *Yim mbok mirini. Yim mboka ikur nda sisiek nda.*

Yim	*mbok*	*miri=ni.*	*Yim*	*mbok-a*	*ikur*	*nda*	*sisiek*
1PL	go.1PL.R	forest=ALL	1PL	go.1SG.F |1PL.R-and	night	DM	fall.3SG.F.R

   We went into the forest. We went and night fell.

2. *nda. Yim mboka Waikire* [laughs] *amini*...[laughs].
   nda   Yim   mbok-a   Waiki=re   *amini
   DM   1PL   go.1SG.F|1PL.R-and   Waiki=COM   fight?
   We went and Waiki [laughs] fi...[laughs].

3. *Waikire Mbinire amini...eh...ssss....*
   Waiki=re   Mbini=re   *amini
   Waiki=COM   Mbini=COM   fight?
   Waiki and Mbini fi...eh...ssss [sounds of frustration]

4. Speaker B, a thirty-year-old brother-in-law listening to this story:
   Amurukuke
   Amuru-kuke
   fight.R-DL.R
   The two had a fight.

5. *Amurukuke* [laughs]. *Waiki Mbini ndaram aini nambirni*
   Amuru-kuke   Waiki   Mbini   ndaram   ai=ni   nambir=ni
   fight.R-DL.R   Waiki   Mbini   hand   here=LOC   chest=LOC
   The two had a fight [laughs]. Waiki hand

6. *tawaitiŋgin.*   *Tawaitiŋgina*
   *tawai-ti-ŋgi-n   *Tawai-ti-ŋgi-n-a
   hit.R-S<3SG.M.R.O>2SG|3SG.F.R.S   hit.R-S<3SG.M.R.O>2SG|3SG.F.R.S-and
   She hit him and she hit Mbini in the chest here [Waiki is a young man,
   as is Mbini]

7. *nim/nim/nimŋa* [laughs] *ndukoni nimŋa ndukoni* wet...
   nim/nim/nim=ŋa   nduko=ni   nim=ŋa   nduko=ni   wet
   tree/tree/tree=POSS branch=INSTR   tree=POSS   branch=INSTR   wait (Tok Pisin)
   with a tree branch [laughs] with a tree branch wait...

8. na (Tok Pisin) *Konjab/Konjab katet. Kateta ŋi pemieta*
   na (Tok Pisin) Konjab/Konjab katet.   Katet-a   ŋi   pemiet-a
   and (Tok Pisin) Konjab/Konjab fall.   fall.SG.M.R-and   3SG.M   get_up.SG.M.R-and
   SG.M.R
   ... and Konjab/Konjab He fell down. He fell down and he got up and

9. *Konjab/Konjab...Konjab...Konjabyi...ŋɨ pemieta Konjab* [speaker whispers to himself for 15 seconds]
    Konjab/Konjab   Konjab   Konjab=yi*   ŋɨ   pemiet-a   Konjab
    Konjab/Konjab   Konjab   Konjab=ERG.F   3SG.M   get_up.SG.   Konjab
    M.R.-and

    Konjab/Konjab...Konjab...Konjab he got up and Konjab [speaker whispers to himself for 15 seconds]

10. *Konjab kadɨgin. Kadɨgin.*
    Konjab   kadɨ-gɨ-n
    Konjab   hit.R<3SG.M.R.O>1SG|2SG|3SG.M|1PL.R.S

    Kadɨ-gɨ-n
    hit.R<3SG.M.R.O>1SG|2SG|3SG.M|1PL.R.S

11. *Kadɨgin. Konjabyi eiarnet.*
    Kadɨ-gɨ-n   Konjab=yi*   eiar-net
    hit.R<3SG.M.R.O>1SG|2SG|3SG.M|1PL.R.S   Konjab=ERG.F   cry.R-1SG.M|3SG.M.R
    Konjab hit him. He hit him. He hit him [the three 'hit' verbs are repeated in a soft tone that suggests the speaker is trying them out to hear whether they sound correct]. Konjab cried.

12. *Eiarneta, ŋɨ...ŋɨ ndaram...sit/eh/ssss...* [16 second hesitation]
    Eiar-net-a   ŋɨ   ŋɨ   ndaram   sit/eh/sss
    cry.R-1SG.M|3SG.M.R-and   3SG.M   3SG.M   hand   ?/eh/ssss
    He cried and he...he...hand..sit/eh/ssss... [16 second hesitation]

13. [laughs] *ndaram pekuna* [laughs] *ndaram pekuna...*
    ndaram   *pe-ku-n-a   ndaram   *pe-ku-n-a
    hand   hold.R-3SG.F.R.O-SG|1PL.R.S   hand   hold.R-3SG.F.R.O-SG|1PL.R.S-and
    [laughs] he held hand and he held hand and [laughs]
    [Speaker means to say that Konjab and his antagonist shook hands]

14. *ŋgɨ mai...*[laughs] *mai...*
    ŋgɨ   mai   mai
    3PL   enough   enough
    they enough...[laughs] enough

15. Speaker B: *Maitike*
    Mai-tike
    enough-DL.R
    The two of them had enough [i.e. they finished fighting]

16. *Maitike. Nda yim kuk. Yim kuka*
    Mai-tike.   Nda   yim   kuk   yim   kuk-a
    enough-DL.R   DM   1PL   be.1SG.F|1PL.R 1PL   be.1SG.F|1PL.R-and
    The two of them had enough. Then we were there. We were there and

17. *embre yim mbok, njereki mbok.*
    emb=re   yim   mbok   nje=reki   mbok
    morning=TEMP   1PL   go.1SG.F|1PL.R   dog=COM   go.1SG.F|1PL.R
    in the morning we went, we went with dogs [to hunt]

18. *Njereki mboka, nje...nje ŋgat/ŋgat*
    Nje=reki   mbok-a   nje   nje   ŋgat/ŋgat
    dog=COM   go.1SG.F|1PL.R-and   dog   dog   cassowary/cassowary
    We went with dogs, dogs...dogs cassowary/cassowary

19. *wem/werpekun. Werpeki/kuta*
    wem/*werpe-ku-n.   *Werpe-ki/kut-a
    chas/chase.R-3SG.F.R.O-SG|1PL.R.S   chase.R-IRR??/be.SG.M.R-and
    he chased it. He was chasing it

20. *kuku/kukumbok, kukumboka*
    *ku-ku/ku-ku-mbok   *ku-ku-mbok-a
    bring-3SG.F.R.O/bring-3SG.F.R.O-go.1SG.F|1PL.R   bring-3SG.F.R.O-go.1SG.F|1PL.R-and
    we brought her, we brought her and

21. *kukumboka* [12 second hesitation] *peŋ/*njenumyi* [laughs]
    *ku-ku-mbok-a   peŋ   *njenum-yi
    bring-3SG.F.R.O-go.1SG.F|1PL.R-and   get_up??   dog.PL-ERG.F
    we brought her and [12 second hesitation] *peŋ*/the dogs [laughs]

22. *nejnumyi njenumyi...wet...njenumyi*
    *nejnum=yi   *njenum=yi   wet   *njenum=yi
    dog.PL=ERG.F   dog.PL=ERG.F   wait (Tok Pisin)   dog.PL=ERG.F
    dogs dogs...wait...dogs [all these mix the plural noun with the feminine singular ergative suffix]

23. [whispers to himself, rehearsing] *pemko/pemko. Pemko. Yim mboka*
    pemko/pemko   Pemko   Yim   mbok-a
    get_up.3PL.R/get_up.3PL.R   get_up.3PL.R   1PL   go.1SG.F|1PL.R-and
    [whispers to himself, rehearsing] they got up/they got up. They got up. We went and

24. *yim mboka ŋgat poŋgin.*
    yim   mbok-a   ŋgat   po-ŋgi-n.
    1PL   go.1SG.F|1PL.R-and   cassowary   strike.R-3SG.M.R.O-SG|1PL.R.S
    we went and speared a cassowary.

25. *Poŋgina yim/yim/yim ndow ŋan ŋgripni*
    Po-ŋgi-n-a   yim/yim/yim   ndow   ŋan   ŋgrip=ni
    strike.R-3SG.M.R.O-   1PL/1PL/1PL   leg   3SG.M.POSS   rope=INSTR
    SG|1PL.R.S-and

26. *perkure nda yim urk/urk/ŋgwek.*
    *per-ku-re   nda   yim   urk/urk// *ŋgwek
    tie.R-3SG.F.R.O-DL.R   DM   1PL   ??/??/come.3PL.R
    We speared him and we/we/we two tied his legs and then we ??/??/they came.

27. *Ngwek, ŋgwek yim mbek.*
    *Ngwek   *ŋgwek   yim   mbek
    come.3PL.R   come.3PL.R   1PL   come.1SG.F|1PL.R

28. *Mbeka nuwombni yim/yim* [quietly to himself] *ŋgir-ki ssss* [sound of frustration]
    Mbek-a   nuwomb=ni   yim/yim   *ŋgir-ki
    come.1SG.F|1PL.R-and   stream=LOC   1PL/1PL   put?-IRR
    We went and at the stream we/we [quietly to himself, rehearsing] pu sssssss [sound of frustration]

29. *nuwombni/nuwombŋa tawni ŋgri...ŋgri...nuwomb*
    nuwomb=ni/nuwomb=ŋa   taw=ni   ŋgri   ŋgri   nuwomb
    stream=LOC/stream=POSS   side=LOC   put.IRR   put.IRR   stream
    at the stream/on the side of the stream will put...will put...stream

30. *kiŋgimbeka tawni ŋgri...ŋgri...*[6 second pause]
    ki-ŋgi-mbek-a   taw=ni   ŋgri   ŋgri
    bring-3SG.M.R.O-come.1SG.F|1PL.R-and   side=LOC   put.IRR   put.IRR
    we brought him and on the side will put...will put...[6 second pause]

31. Speaker B: *sakini* [inaudible]
    sakini
    just
    Just [inaudible]

32. [laughs] *yim*...[laughs]...*nuwombŋa tawni apru*...
    yim   nuwomb=ŋa   taw=ni   *apru
    1PL   stream=POSS   side=LOC   burn
    [laughs] we...[laughs]...at the side of the stream will bu...

33. *kiŋgimbeka nuwombŋa tawni*
    ki-ŋgi-mbek-a   nuwomb=ŋa   taw=ni
    bring-3SG.M.R.O-come.1SG.F|1PL.R-and   stream=POSS   side=LOC
    we brought him and came and at the side of the stream

34. Speaker B: *Kapŋgin*
    Kap-ŋgi-n
    burn.R<3SG.M.R.O>1SG|2SG|3SG.M|1PL.R.S
    We burned him [i.e. singed off the cassowary's feathers]

35. *Kapŋgin. Kapŋgina*
    Kap-ŋgi-n   Kap-ŋgi-n-a
    burn.R<3SG.M.R.O>1SG|2SG|3SG.   burn.R<3SG.M.R.O>1SG|2SG|3SG.
    M|1PL.R.S   M|1PL.R.S-and
    We burned him. We burned him and

36. *yim krar/krara/...*
    yim   krar/krar-a/ [laughs]
    1PL   chop.IRR/chop.IRR-and
    we will chop/will chop and [laughs]

37. *krarpiŋ...krarpiŋ...*[laughs] *krarpiŋna,*
    *krar-p-iŋ   *krar-p-iŋ   *krar-p-iŋ-n-a
    chop.IRR-R-3SG.M.R.O   chop.IRR-R-3SG.M.R.O   chop.IRR-R-3SG.M.R.O-
                                                    SG|1PL.R.S-and
    will/do chop him...will/do chop him...[laughs]..(we) will/do chop him and

38. *yim mbek. Yim mbek Ngarmembag. Nda mai.*
    yim   mbek   Yim   mbek   Ngarmembag   Nda   mai
    1PL   come.1SG.F|1PL.R   1PL   come.1SG.F|1PL.R   Ngarmembag   DM   enough
    we came. We came to Ngarmembag. That's enough.

Immediately after they finished telling their story in Tayap, I always asked young speakers to re-tell the story in Tok Pisin. I did this for two reasons. First, I did it in order to compare the fluency and complexity of the narratives – in order to check, for example, whether a speaker told a brief, simple narrative in Tayap because she or he was someone whose narrative style was brief and simple in any language, or whether a brief and simple story in Tayap was an artefact of limited active competence in the language.

The second reason I elicited the same story in Tok Pisin was to be able to make educated guesses about what a speaker had attempted to say in Tayap in those instances where the forms she or he used were far from the grammatically correct ones.

Here is the story this speaker told immediately after he concluded his Tayap narrative:

Yumi go long bus. Yumi go long bus nau apinun wantaim tudak i godaun. Tudak i godaun nau, Pita, Waiki. Em Konjab taitim han bilong em ia na em i tok, "Yu kam. Traim paitim bros bilong mi". Em kirap i kam tasol, putim han long bros bilong man na em pundaun i godaun long [no ken harim] bilong settri. Em pundaun i godaun nau, em kirap nau na em tok, "Spirit nogut hatim bel bilong mi". Em kirap paitim Mbini. Em paitim Mbini, tupela kirap, sekhan pinis, moning ia mipela i go long bus. I go long bus tasol ol dok raunim muruk. Ol dok raunim muruk, kisim em i go, ol sanapim em. Yumi go, Sando i go sutim em. Sutim em, mipela karim em i kam long Umba, baret ia. Em mipela pasim em, hangamapim em, pinis, yumi kukim em pinis, brukim em pinis, yumi kam gen long ples.

We went into the forest. We went into the forest in the afternoon as it was getting dark. It was getting dark. Pita – Waiki [Pita's Tayap name]. Konjab raised his fists and said, "Come on. Try to hit me on the chest". He got up and put his hands on his chest and he fell down on the [unintelligible] of a shade tree. He fell down and then he got up and said, "A bad spirit is making me angry". He got up and hit Mbini. He hit Mbini, the two of them shook hands, and in the morning we went into the forest. We went into the forest and the dogs found and chased a cassowary. They chased the cassowary, brought it [i.e. chased it towards the young men] and they cornered it. We went, Sando went and speared it. He speared it and we carried it to the Umba stream. We tied it up, hung it up, burned off its feathers and butchered it, then we came back again to the village.

Commentary

The narrator of the cassowary story, like most of his peers, avoids any tense or status besides the imperfective. To a certain extent, this limitation is an artefact of the kinds of stories speakers tell – a story in Gapun ("stori" in Tok Pisin, *tik* in Tayap) is definitionally a telling of some event that happened in the past. 'Stories' are not about future plans or actions. They are highly conventionalized narratives that are always about what the teller or someone else did – almost always in the rainforest – and they conclude with the protagonist(s) returning to the village after the adventure is over. The story told by this young speaker adheres to those conventions.

However, good story-tellers can also include different actor perspectives and they can refer to events that have happened or may happen outside the temporal frame established by the narrative. That Masito Monei does this in Tayap Text 3 is one of the qualities that would make her story a satisfying one in the opinion of villagers.

Young speakers like the young man who narrated the cassowary hunt are unable to do this. They never use verbs inflected for the future or the counterfactual; instead, everything is in the imperfective and occasionally the perfective. The problem for these speakers, as is discussed in Chapter 6, is that the imperfective in Tayap is a difficult aspect, full of irregular and unpredictable inflections.

These problems are evident in this narrative. The narrator does an impressive job inflecting some of the verbs he chooses. He correctly inflects intransitive verbs like *memki* 'get up' (lines 8–9, 23) and transitive verbs like the class 3 verb *adi-* 'pound' (lines 10–11) that would stump many other young speakers.

But with other verbs, the narrator's story demonstrates the same kinds of errors that are common in the speech of young speakers of Tayap. He has a tendency, for example, to inflect verbs of other verb classes as though they were all class 5 verbs. In line 5, for example, *tawai-(p)-i* 'hit'/ 'pound' is a class 1 verb. This means that the correct inflection in the imperfective is:

tawaipiŋgɨn
tawaipi-   -ŋgɨ-   -n
hit.R-   -3SG.M.R.O-   -SG|1PL.R.S
'Any singular subject hit him', or 'we hit him'

Instead, the speaker produces the verb as a class 5 verb:

tawaitɨŋgɨn
tawai-   -tɨ   -ŋgɨ   -n
hit.R-   -S   <3SG.M.R.O >   -2SG|3SG.F.S
'You hit him', or 'she hit him'

In addition to inflecting the verb in the wrong verb class, the speaker also mixes up the subject morphemes. If the verb were a class 5 verb, the first segment of its discontinuous subject marker would be -n^v- (which denotes 3SG.M) not -t^v- (which denotes 3SG.F; see Section 6.1.7).

Other verbs simply stump him. 'Chase' – the class 1 verb *wemb-(p)-er* (line 19) – is inflected unsuccessfully. The class 3 verb *apu* 'cook', singe' (lines 32–35) gives this speaker the same problems it gave the young speaker quoted in Section 6.1.5).

The class 4 verb *krar* 'chop' (lines 36–37) is inflected, after several attempts, as though it were a class 1 verb (see Section 6.1.3). This verb is, furthermore, semantically incorrect. The speaker wants the class 2 verb *wuw* 'butcher'. He chooses *krar-* on the pattern of Tok Pisin, where one could use the verb "brukim", 'chop', to describe the butchering of a carcass. "Brukim" is also what one does with firewood – and this is the link to *krar*, which is the verb in Tayap used to denote the chopping of firewood. Through this series of associations: Tok Pisin's 'chop' ("brukim") → Tayap's 'chop' (*krar*), the narrator ends up choosing a verb that is semantically appropriate in Tok Pisin but not in Tayap. We will see another example of this same error in Tayap Text 5, lines 27–30.

This is an example of one of the processes of lexical reduction that Tayap is undergoing in the speech of young villagers.

Another feature of this speaker's narrative that is common in the narratives of young people is the avoidance of plural verb inflections. As noted in Section 5.3.2, speakers do inflect verbs with the 1PL (an inflection that is identical to the 1SG.F form). But they avoid inflecting verbs in the 2PL, 3PL and dual forms, because these forms have specific inflections that differ quite markedly from the inflections for the other persons and numbers.

The verb in line 13 for example, *er* 'hold', should be in the dual form, since it refers to two people shaking hands (it is correct to use this verb to denote this action; so in Tayap one doesn't 'shake hands', one 'holds hands' to signal reconciliation). Thus, narrator should say:

pe-ku-re		*pe-ku-n*
hold.R-3SG.F.R.O-DL.R	*instead of*	hold. R-3SG.F.R.O-DL.SG|1PL.R.S
'the two held hands'		'he held hand'

That the speaker does not produce this form is typical. Another dual form is given to him by his brother-in-law (line 4). While he clearly recognizes this form and repeats it immediately, he produces no other dual forms himself.

The one instance in which the speaker does attempt a plural verb inflection, he inflects it correctly (line 23, *pemko* 'they got up'). However, this verb is incorrect. It is a substitute for what the speaker wants – as evidenced partly by the verb he does use (which has phonetic, semantic and inflectional similarlities to second part of the serial verb he should have used), and partly by the verb he uses in the Tok Pisin version of his story, which is "sanapim", 'corner'.

The verb the speaker was searching for is a serial verb, *weX-(p/m)-unguku* 'corner'. This is a complicated verb to inflect because it requires both a dependent object morpheme and an understanding of the *p/m* alternation undergone by the verb stem. What the speaker wanted in this instance was the following:

wetpuŋguko
wet-	*-t-*	*-puŋguko*
corner.IRR-	-3SG.M.NFO-	-stand.3PL.R

'they cornered him' (i.e. the dogs cornered the cassowary)

A serial verb like this is not in the repetoire of most young speakers of Tayap. Some young men did produce it automatically in stories about hunting, but those who did produce it had clearly absorbed it as a fixed construction. Anyone who hesitated and tried to actively construct this verb always failed.

The last thing to note about the way this speaker uses verbs is the phonological reduction of the verb 'fall' (line 8). This reduced form, *katet*, is the form used by younger speakers. It differs from what older speakers say, which is *katɨtet* 'he fell'. For more on this, see Section 6.2.3.

Apart from difficulties with verbs, this speaker also evidences common problems that young people have with Tayap's ergative construction. Like many other young speakers, the narrator of the cassowary story uses the ergative hapazardly; and the gender and number distinctions encoded by Tayap's three different ergative morphemes are lost. The narrator uses a single form of the ergative morpheme, the feminine singular form, *-yi*. This speaker affixes this morpheme both to masculine referents (for instance, in lines 9 and 11, *Konjab-yi*) and plural referents (*njenum-yi* in lines 21–22 should be *njenum-gi*).

The final observation to make about this speaker's Tayap is that he is stronger than many of his peers when it comes to gender concordance. As I noted above, he does have a problem with the gender of ergative morphemes. But he correctly inflects intransitive verbs for gender (e.g. lines 1, 8–9, 11–12), and most of the object morphemes he uses in transitive verbs are the correct ones. The single error he makes is in the gender of the cassowary, which starts out as feminine (lines 19–21; *-ku* is the feminine object morpheme; the speaker wants *-ŋgi*, the masculine morpheme), but then switches to the correct masculine form (lines 24, 25, 30, 33, 35, 37; recall that cassowaries are generally masculine in Tayap, see Section 3.1.3).

Tayap Text 5: Girls have an adventure in the rainforest
Narrated in 2009 by

Speaker A, 14 years old
Speaker B, 15 years old
Speaker C, 17 years old

The narrative in Text 5 represents the end of the line for the Tayap language. It was told by a fourteen- year old girl (speaker A), assisted by her friend (speaker B) and her older sister (speaker C).

I knew all three of these girls well. I knew, therefore, that their passive competence in Tayap was highly developed: the mother of the two sisters, and both parents of speaker B, use a great deal of Tayap in day-to-day life, and all three girls have no trouble understanding orders and following narratives in the language. Despite this, the girls had little active competence in Tayap. The only things they ever regularly uttered in Tayap were curse words like *kwem petiek* (wanker) or *ŋgwab* (hole), which they delighted in hurling at each other and other children numerous times during the course of a day.

To spare the girls what I feared might be the embarrassment of trying to speak in Tayap and failing, I had not considered asking them to try to narrate a story. They, however, had other ideas.

They knew that young women and men in their twenties regularly came up into my house at night to tell stories in Tayap, and caught up in the excitement of that, the three girls announced to me one afternoon that they, too, intended to come and tell a story. And so they did. Each speaker told a short story, in the collaborative and argumentative manner that characterizes the story below.

The stories produced by these young speakers are a glimpse into the future of Tayap. The Tayap spoken by these girls is what the language will look like at the very end of its life, when verb classes have imploded, when inflections for person and number are jumbled, and when Tayap's vocabulary has been more or less completely replaced with Tok Pisin.

The speakers collectively make many of the errors discussed in the grammar, including:
- overextension of the present progressive (lines 22, 26, 32–35, 45–46)
- inability to inflect class 2 and 3 verbs (lines 11–12, 31–36, 42, 61–65)
- semantic reduction of Tayap verbs on the model of Tok Pisin (lines 26–29)
- Tok Pisin verbs inflected with Tayap morphology (lines 11, 13, 23, 57)
- inability to correctly inflect verbs for subject (lines 13–15, 17, 21–22, 29, 35, 42, 61)
- loss of verbs of motion (lines 43–44)
- insecurity about the ergative (line 9)

In addition to those grammatical errors, this story is told disfluently and incoherently. In order to make any sense of it at all, I present, first, the same story told by Speaker A in Tok Pisin.

As I mentioned in my commentary on Tayap Text 4, I always asked young speakers to re-tell in Tok Pisin what they had just narrated in Tayap, so that I could be reasonably certain of what it is they had wanted to say in Tayap, even if the forms they used were incorrect or incomprehensible.

Here is fourteen-year-old speaker A's narrative in Tok Pisin, followed by an English translation. All the names in the narrative have been changed:

Mi, Nensi, Mbabe, Marai. Mipela go, Nensi holim susu bilong Mbabe. Nensi kirap, sakim Mbabe i godaun. Mbabe kirap krai. Nensi wantaim Marai kirap laitim smok. Tupela smok i go, Mbabe kam. Mbabe kam mipela i go brukim kanjígogo *istap,* kanjígogo *i katim han bilong mi. Brukim pinis, mipela i kam. Kam kukim pinis, katim, Marai wantaim Mbabe putim long Andon na mi go antap long kokonas. Mi go antap long kokonas na mi tokim Nensi, lukluk na kam lukim wara long Kombirum. Mi tokim Nensi, Nensi kam autsait lukim pinis mipela i godaun nau na mipela i go. Andon tokim mipela yupela i go brukim kru pankin. Nensi i go brukim kru pankin. Mi, Mbabe, Marai, mipela i go brukim aibika. Brukim i kam, Marai i giamanim mitupela Mbabe. Mitupela kirap ron i kam. Ron i kam nau mipela i kam long ples.*

Me, Nensi, Mbabe, Marai. We went, Nensi held Mbabe's tit. Nensi got up and pushed Mbabe and she fell. Mbabe got up and cried. Nensi and Marai lit cigarettes. The two of them were smoking and Mbabe came. Mbabe came and we went to collect *bamboo shoots*. We were collecting them and a *bamboo shoot* cut my hand. We collected them and we came back. We came and cooked them, and when we did that, Marai and Mbabe put some aside for Raimon and I went up a tree to get some coconuts. I went up and I told Nensi, "Look and come and see the water at Kombirum". She came out and looked at it and then we left. Raimon told us to go and pluck some pumpkin greens. Nensi went and plucked pumpkin greens. Me, Mbabe, Marai, we went to pluck *aibika*. We plucked it and Marai tricked me and Mbabe. We ran and came back. Ran and came back and we came back to the village.

This narrative is the kind of story that villagers of all ages tell each other all the time, concerning actions and adventures in the rainforest. Like other narrators, the girl telling this story assumes that the listener knows the protagonists and can fill in, or subsequently ask about, the details not made explicit in the telling – for example, why the man, Raimon, was in the same part of the rainforest as the girls, and what kind of trick Marai played on the speaker and her friend Mbabe.

The speaker told her story in Tok Pisin fluently and without hesitation. Even including laughter and a few interruptions by the other girls present, which I have edited out, the Tok Pisin narrative took the speaker 1 minute and 10 seconds to tell.

In contrast, the following story she told in Tayap took her 5 minutes and 30 seconds – 5 times as long – to tell.

KEY TO TRANSCRIPTION

bold	Tayap	...	pause or hestitation
italics	Tok Pisin	*	ungrammatical or incorrect Tayap
/	false start or self-correction	??	nonce morpheme
=	simultaneous talk; i.e. talk that follows the equal sign is spoken at the same time as the next speaker's talk that is proceeded by =	( )	implied but unexpressed meaning
		[ ]	author's comments
		between thick lines	grammatically correct Tayap

	TAYAP-TOK PISIN ORIGINAL	ENGLISH TRANSLATION
1	A: **Ŋa, Nensi, Mbabe, Marai. Yim Maprinum** [lap] *wet...*	A: **Me, Nensi, Mbabe, Marai.** [Marai is the speaker's older sister, speaker C, and Mbabe is her friend, speaker B] **We Maprinum** [laughs] *wait...*
2	B: *Yu no ken lap na toktok*	B: *You can't laugh and talk at the same time.*
3	A: **Yim tumb** ... *olsem wanem mi paul ia.* 1PL mountain	A: **We mountain**...*what, I'm getting it wrong.*
4	B: **tumb=nɨ** o/ mountain=ALL ?? [perhaps some form of **okɨ** 'go']	B: **to the mountain** o/
5	C: **Yim tumb=nɨ** 1PL mountain=ALL	C: **We to the mountain**
6	B: **pri/priek** go_up.1SG.F|1PL.R	B: **we went/went up**
7	A: **Yim tumb=nɨ priek**...*wet...* 1PL mountain=ALL go_up.1SG.F|1PL.R	A: **We went up to the mountain**...*wait...*
8	B: **Kanjɨgo amai**..*eh...Raimon* bamboo shoots find	B: **Bamboo shoots find**...*eh...Raimon*
9	A: **Nensi=yi/ Nensi/ Mbabe=yi** Nensi=ERG.F/Nensi Mbabe=ERG.F **min/Nensi** breast/Nensi	A: **Nensi (did) / Nensi/ Mbabe (did) breast/ Nensi**
10	B: *Yu katim, yu katim. Raimon, Raimon. Raimon =pastaim*	B: *You're shortening it, you're shortening it. Raimon. Raimon, Raimon =first*
11	A: =*holim*-**tu-ku-n**. hold-S<3SG.F.R.O>2SG| 3SG.F.R.S *Eh! Yu inap yu.* **Nensi=yi** Nensi=ERG.F **Mbabe** Mbabe *sakim*-**tu-ku-n**, push-S<3SG.F.R.O>2SG|3SG.F.R.S **Mbabe eiar-tak** [*lap*]. **Mbabe** Mbabe cry.SG.F.R Mbabe **eiar-tak. Yim Marai=re** cry.SG.F.R 1PL Marai=COM **Nensi=re sokoi** Nensi=COM tobacco ***o-tu-ku-n** hit.SBJ-S<3SG.F.R.O>2SG| 3SG.F.R.S	A: = **held** it. **Hey! you stop it** [to B]. **Nensi pushed Mbabe, Mbabe cried** [laughs]. **Mbabe cried. Me and Marai and Nensi *hit** [speaker means 'rolled'] **tobacco** The Tayap verb for 'hold' here would be: **per-ku-n** hold.R-3SG.F.R.O-SG|1PL.R.S 'she held it' The Tayap verb for 'push' here would be: **utak-tu-ku-n-a** push.R-S<3SG.F.R.O>2SG|3SG.F.R.S-and **otitek** fall.3SG.F.R. The verb **otukun** is the imperative form of 'hit.'

12	C: ***woipo-ku-n** roll.R-3SG.F.R.O-SG|1PL.R.S	C [correcting A]: ***we rolled it*** **Note:** the correct inflection for the class 2 verb **woi** 'roll' is: **poi-ku-n** roll-3SG.F.R.O-sg|1PL.R.S 'we rolled it'
13	A: **Yim kanjigo** 1PL bamboo shoots *painim*-**tu-ku-n** look for-S<3SG.F.R.O>2SG| 3SG.F.R.S	A: **We** looked for **bamboo shoots**
14	B: *****Amai-ru-ku-n** look _for-2SG.IRR.O-3SG.F.R.O-SG|1PL.R.S	B: ***we look for*** **Note:** speaker wants **amai-kru-nana** look_for.irr -3SG.F.IRR.O-INTENT **priek** go_up.1SG.F|1PL.R
15	A: **Amai-tak** [lap] look _for.R-SG.F.R	A: **She looked for** [laughs] **Note:** speaker wants **amai-nak** look_for.R-1SG.F|1PL.R 'we looked for'
16	B: *Eh* [*i no ken harim*]	B: *Eh* [inaudible].
17	A: **yim amai-tak.** *Em tasol* [*lap*] 1PL look _for.SG.F.R	A: **We she looked for.** *That's all* [laughs] The correct Tayap form is either: **yim amai-nak** 1PL look_for.R-1SG.F|1PL.R 'we looked for' or **yim amaipi-ku-n** 1PL look_for.R-3SG.F.R.O-SG|1PL.R.S 'we looked for it'
18	B: *Em tasol ah? Yopla.*	B. *That's all ah? You've got to be kidding.*
19	A: *Wet, mi paul ia.*	A: *Wait, I'm getting it wrong.*
20	B: *Yu no ken lap na toktok.*	B: *You can't laugh and talk.*

21 A: **Yim** *****amai-tak**...
    1PL   look_for.SG.F.R
    eh, olsem wanem?

A: **We she looked for**...*eh, what?*

22 C: **Amai-kwan-uk-a,**
    look_for.IRR-3SG.F.BE.R.O-3SG.F.S-and

    amai-kwan-ŋguk-a,
    look_for.IRR-3SG.F.BE.R.O-3SG.F.S-and

    =kanjígogo   wákare
    bamboo shoots   NEG

C: **She looked for and they looked for and there were no bamboo shoots**

Note: speaker wants
amaipi-ku-n-a,
look_for.R-3SG.F.R.O-SG|1PL.R.S-and
amaipi-ku-n,
look_for.R-3SG.F.R.O-SG|1PL.R.S
wákare
NEG

'we looked and looked for it but there was none'.

23 A: **=Kanjígogo=yi/**
    bamboo shoot=ERG.F
    Kanjígogo   ŋaŋan
    bamboo shoot   1SG.POSS
    ndaram *katim...eh...[lap]*
    hand

A: **Bamboo shoot did/Bamboo shoot** *cut my hand*...*eh*...[laughs]

24 B: **Ni-tu-ku-n,**
    do.SBJ-S<3SG.F.R.O>2SG| 3SG.F.R.S
    ni-tu-ku-n
    do.SBJ-S<3SG.F.R.O>2SG| 3SG.F.R.S

B: **Do it, do it** [i.e. tell the story]

25 A: **Kanjígogo=yi**
    Bamboo shoot=ERG.F

A: **Bamboo shoot (did)**

26 C: **ŋaŋan   ndaram**
    1SG.POSS hand
    *****krar-kwan-uk**
    chop.IRR-3SG.F.BEN.R.O-3SG.F.R.S

C: **She *was cutting my hand**

Note: the correct 3SG form of this verb would be
krar-kwan-uk
chop.IRR-3SG.F.BEN.R.O-be.3SG.F.S
'it was chopping it'

However, both the verb 'chop' and the progressive status are incorrect here. Speaker wants:

pu-tu-ku-n
cut.R-S<3SG.F.R.O>2SG|3SG.F.R.S
'it cut it [my hand]'

27 A: **ŋaŋan ndaram** *kat*

A: **my hand** *cut*

28	C:***krar-tu-ku-n** chop.IRR-S<3SG.F.R.O>2SG|3SG.F.R.S	C: ***it will has cut it**
29	A:*Wet, yu no ken/* **krar-tu-ku-n.** chop.IRR-S-<3SG.F.R.O>-2SG| 3SG.F.R.S **Yim *wek,** 1PL come.3SG.F.R	A: *Wait, you can't/* ***it will has cut it.** **We *came**
30	C: **Mbek** come.1SG.F.|1PL.R	C: **We came**
31	A: *O em inap.* **Yim mbek...***wet*...**kanjígogo apwar...apwar...***eh, olsem wanem?*	A: *Oh that's enough.* **We came...***wait...* **bamboo shoots *cook...*cook...**eh, what (should I say)?
32	B: ***ap-ran-kuk** cook.IRR-??-BE.3SG.F.R	B: ***we cooking**
33	A: *Uh huh* [*em laik tok yes*]. ***Ap-war...****wet pastaim mi paul.* cook-?? **Kanjígogo *ap-wan...***eh*... bamboo shoots cook-??	A: *Yeah* [affirmative sound], ***cooking...****wait a minute, I'm mixed up.* **Bamboo shoots *cooking...**eh*...
		Note: speaker wants *either* **apu-kwan-kuk** cook.IRR-3SG.F.BEN.R.O-be.SG.F|1PL.R 'we are/were cooking it' or **kapu-ku-n** cook.R-3SG.F.R.O-1SG|2SG|3SG.M|1PL.S 'We cooked it'
34	B:***Ap-wa...a...** cook-??	B: ***Cook...co...**
35	C: ***Ap-waŋ-kuk-a** cook-??-be.SG.F|1PL.R-and	C: **We were *cooking** [you (?)/for you (?)]
36	A: *Eh,* **kanjígogo** bamboo shoots ***apwar...**[lap] cook-??	A: *Eh,* **bamboo shoots *cook...**[laughs]
37	C: **Raimon**=re **Teresia**=re Raimon=COM Teresia=COM	C: **with Raimon and Teresia**
38	A: *Wet. Tsk.*	A: *Wait. Tsk.*
39	Don: *Larim em stori*	Don: *Let her tell the story*
40	C: *Bai mi helpim em nau, klostu klostu.*	C: *I'm gonna keep helping her, everything she says.*
41	Don: *Larim em stori.*	D: *Let her tell the story.*

42	A: Ŋa...*ssss...* **yim kanjígogo** 1SG 1PL bamboo shoot **ap-wan...ke...***eh, husat ia...* **yim** cook-??...?? 1PL **Nensi-re Mbabe otar nambar,** Nensi-COM Mbabe fire one **ŋa otar nambar, Marai** 1SG fire one Marai **nambar. Ŋa *mai-tak,** one 1SG enough-SG.F.R *kokonas/* **pap=nɨ** *ata/eh!* coconut=LOC ??	A: I...*sss* [sound of impatience and frustration] **we *cook bamboo shoots..??... eh, who ... Nensi and Mbabe had [or lit] a fire, I had [or lit] a fire, Marai had [or lit] one. I *had enough [or 'was finished']**, *coconut/cononut...??/eh!*
43	C: **wo-kuk.** above-be.SG.F.R	C: **it was above.**
		Note: speaker wants **puwok** go_up.SG.F|1PL.R 'I went up' [the tree]
44	A: *Eh,* **wokuk. Wokuk.** *Wara...eh...olsem wanem?*	A: *Eh,* **it was above. It was above.** *Water... eh...what?*
45	C: **awin rar-kwan...** water see.IRR-3SG.F.BEN.R.O	C: ***was looking at water**
		Note: speaker wants **awin ta-n-ku-n** water see.R-S<3SG.F.R.O> 1SG|3SG.M|1PL.R.S 'I saw water'
46	A: **awin *rar-kwan...kuk** water see.IRR-3SG.F.BEN.R.O... be.SG.F.R	A: ***we...were looking at water**
47	B: **awin potak=i** water throat=ERG.F	B: **thirsty**
48	A: **Ŋa Nensi=yi**/ *Nensi...eh...* 1SG Nensi=ERG.F *olsem wanem? Yu wet, mi paul. Wet mi paul ia.* **Marai=re Mbabe=re** Marai=COM Mbabe=COM **kanjígo** bamboo shoots	A: **I Nensi did**/*Nensi...eh...what? You wait, I'm mixed-up. Wait, I'm mixed-up.* **With Marai and Mbabe bamboo shoots**
49	C: *Raimon*	C: *Raimon*

50	A: *Raimon* [lap]. *Wet mi paul ia. Wet, yu stop. Wet pastaim.*	A: *Raimon* [laughs]. *Wait, I'm mixed-up. Wait* [to C, who is laughing]. *Stop it. Wait a little.*
51	B: *Eh! Yu no ken lap na toktok!*	B: *Eh! You can't laugh and talk!*
52	A: **Kanjígo** Raimon *olsem wanem? Sssss.*	A: **Bamboo shoots** Raimon, *what? Sssss.*
53	B: [*ino ken harim*]	B: [inaudible]
54	A: **Mbabe=re Marai Raimon-mat** Mbabe=COM Marai Raimon-POSS [*lap*]. *Wet pastaim.*	A: **With Mbabe Marai Raimon's** [laughs]. *Wait a minute.*
55	C: *Don, meri bilong sem ia* [*lap*].	C: [sarcastically about her sister] *Don, she's such a bashful girl* [laughs].
56	B: [*lap*]	B: [laughs]

57	A: *Yu no ken lap. Wet.* **Kanjígogo**
	                bamboo shoots
	    Raimon **givim-tu-ku-n**...[*lap*]
	              give.S<3SG.F.R.O>2SG|
	              3SG.F.R.S
		A: *Don't laugh. Wait.* **Bamboo shoots.**
		Raimon *gave **it** [laughs, 7 second pause]
		
		Note: speaker wants
		pi-ŋata-n
		give.R-3G.S.M.BEN.R.O-SG|1PL.R.S
		'we gave him'

58	Don: *Yu wokim, yu brukim bus. Wokim tasol.*	D: *Tell it, you tell it however you can. Just tell it.*
59	A: [*lap*] **kanjígo** Raimon [*lap*]. *Inap, mi les lok toktok.*	A: [laughs] **Bamboo shoots** Raimon [laughs]. *Enough, I'm tired of talking.*
60	B: *Pasim maus na em bai toktok isi tasol. Yu stori!*	B: *Shut up* [said to C] *and she'll speak slowly. You tell the story!*
61	A: **Raimon=ŋi Nensi** Raimon=ERG.M Nensi **nam-tu-ku-n** talk.S<3SG.F.R.O>2SG| 3SG.F.R.S *kru pankin* **ada**...*ah*... plu...	A: **Raimon told Nensi to plu...** *pumpkin vine* **Note:** the subject of the verb 'say' is Raimon, a male, so the speaker wants **nam-nu-ku-n** talk.R-S<3SG.F.R.O>1SG|3SG.M|1PL.R.S 'he told her'
62	C: ***and-tu-ku-n.** pluck-S<3SG.F.R.O>2SG| 3SG.F.R.S	C: ***pluck it**
63	A: *Eh,***and-tu-ku-n** pluck-S<3SG.F.R.O>2SG| 3SG.F.R.S **yim** *aibika* 1PL	A: *Eh, ***you pluck it off, we** *aibika* [a spinach-like vegetable] **Note:** speaker wants **andu-tu-ku-n** pluck.SBJ-S<3SG.F.R.O>2SG| 3SG.F.R.S 'Pluck it!'

		Note: The Tayap word for *aibika* (a spinach-like vegetable) is ŋgat.
64	B: *and-tu-ku-n pluck-S<3SG.F.R.O>2SG| 3SG.F.R.S	B: **You pluck it**
		Note: andu- 'pluck'/'collect vegetables' is a class 3 verb, so speaker wants **kandu-ku-n** pluck.R-3SG.F.R.OSG|1PL.R.S 'we plucked (leaves of *aibika*)'
65	A: *Uh huh,* *and-tu-ku-n. pluck-S<3SG.F.R.O>2SG| 3SG.F.R.S **Marai=yi takwat** Marai=ERG.F lie/trick	A: Yeah, ***you pluck it.*** **Marai trick**
66	C: **-tɨ-mɨ-n** S<1PL.R.O>2SG| 3SG.F.R.S	C: **-ed us**
67	A: **-tɨ-mɨ-n.** S<1PL.R.O>2SG| 3SG.F.R.S *Na* **yim** 1PL	A: **-ed us.** *And* **we**
68	C: **motɨnɨ** again	C: **again**
69	Don: *Larim em stori.*	Don: [to C] *Let her tell the story.*
70	A: **Yim motɨnɨ** 1PL again	A: **We again**
71	B: **mbek** come.1SG.F|1PL.R	B: **we came**
72	A: **mbek. Mbek** come.1SG.F|1PL.R come.1SG.F|1PL.R *na* [lap]. **Yim** 1PL **kasek** come_down.SG.F|1PL.R **num=nɨ.** *Em tasol.* [lap] village=ALL	A: **we came back. We came** *and* [laughs] **We came down to the village.** *That's all.* [laughs]

Tayap-English-Tok Pisin Dictionary

How to read the dictionary

The Tayap alphabet has 21 letters: a, b, d, e, g, i, ɨ, j, k, l, m, n, ŋ, o, p, r, s, t, u, w, y. No words begin with ɨ, and words underlyingly beginning with b, d, g and j are prenasalized and pronounced as [mb], [d], [ŋg] and [nj]. As explained in Section 2.8 of the *Grammar*, this prenasalization is marked orthographically, with the result that there are no words that begin with the letters b, g, or j, beginning instead with mb, ŋg and nj. Only one word – a loan word from the neighboring Adjora language – begins with d.

A dictionary entry contains the following information:

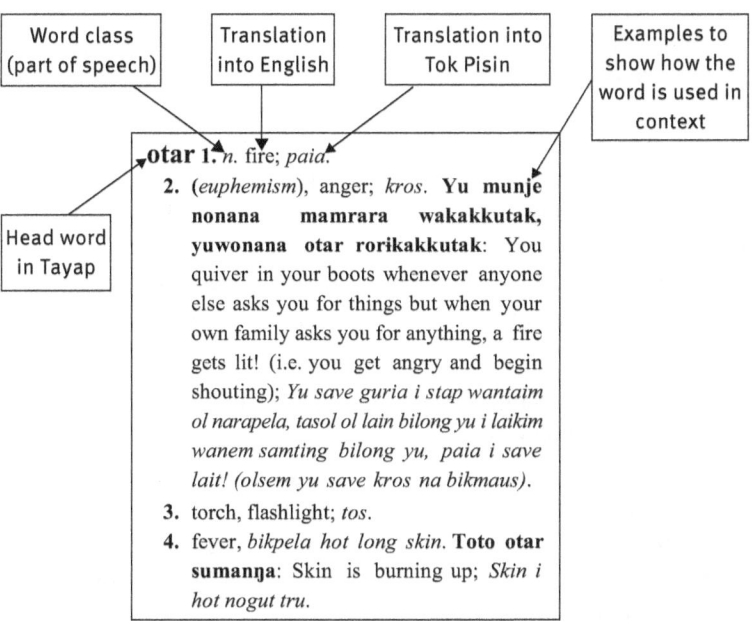

Only unbound, freestanding words are listed in the dictionary. Tayap's bound morphemes are discussed in the relevant sections of the *Grammar*.

Tayap verbs are identified as transitive or intransitive. Verbs also commonly occur in serial verb constructions. Those that almost exclusively occur in such constructions are marked as such (see below; see also Chapter 8).

Verbs appear in the dictionary alphabetized according to the form the verb stem takes when it is negated (See Section 5.2).

https://doi.org/10.1515/9781501512209-011

Transitive verbs

The entries for transitive verbs identify them by their verb class, as those are distinguished in Chapter 6 of the *Grammar*. In terms of how they appear in the dictionary, this means the following:

(a) Class 1 transitive verbs that alternate between ø in irrealis and **p** in realis are listed in their ø form *if that form is word initial*.

So a verb like 'hit', which in realis/irrealis alternates between **p** and ø word-initially (**po-ku-ro** 'strike.R-3SG.F.R.O-3PL.R.S' [they hit it], but **o-kru-ndak** 'strike.IRR-3SG.F.IRR-3PL.IRR' [they will hit it]) appears in the dictionary as **o**, because that is the negated form of this verb (so **o-kru wákare** 'strike.IRR-3SG.F.IRR.O NEG' [X (any subject) didn't/won't hit her or it'], **o-ŋgri wákare**, 'strike.IRR-3SG.M.IRR.O NEG' [X (any subject) didn't/won't hit him], and so on). The realis/irrealis alternation undergone by the stem is noted in the entry that follows the verb.

If the alternation between **p** and ø occurs at the end of the verb stem, the entry notes the **p** in parentheses. So **ruwond-(p)-i** 'smoke something' (in the sense of putting it over a hearth and letting smoke dry it) should be read to mean that **p** only occurs in the realis form of the verb. Thus: 'they smoked it' is **ruwondpi-ku-ro** (smoke.R-3SG.F.R.O-3PL.R.S), but 'they will smoke it' is **ruwondi-kru-ndak** (smoke.IRR-3SG.F.IRR.O-3PL.IRR.S) – note, no **p**.

The negated form of this verb is **ruwondi-kru wákare** [X (any subject) didn't/won't smoke it], **ruwondi-mbri wákare** [X (any subject) didn't/won't smoke them], and so on.

(b) Class 2 transitive verbs that alternate between **w** in irrealis and **p** in realis are listed in their **w** form *if that form is word initial*.

So a verb like 'sweep' (**poi-ku-ro** 'sweep.R-3SG.F.R.O-3PL.R.S' [they swept it], but **woi-kru-ndak** 'sweep.IRR-3SG.F.IRR.O-3PL.IRR.O' [they will sweep it]) appears as **woi**, because that is the negated form of this verb (so **woi-kru wákare**). The realis/irrealis alternation undergone by the stem is noted in the entry that follows the verb.

If the alternation between **w** and **p** occurs at the end of the verb stem, the entry notes this alteration in parentheses. So **utir-(p/w)-or** 'cut into small pieces', should be read to mean that **p** occurs in the realis form of the verb, and **w** occurs in that same slot in irrealis. So 'they cut it into small pieces' is **utirpor-ku-ro** (cut_into_small_pieces.R-3SG.F.R.O-3PL.R.S), 'they will cut it into small pieces' is **utirwor-kru-ndak** (cut_into_small._pieces.IRR-3SG.F.IRR.O-3PL.IRR.S).

The negated form of this verb is the irrealis verb stem + irrealis object: **utirwor-kru wákare, utirwor-ŋgri wákare**, and so on.

(c) Class 3 transitive verbs that begin with or contain **a** and alternate between **ka** and **o** in realis are listed in their **a** form and their class is noted. So 'eat' appears as **a**, because the negated form is **a-kru wákare** [X (any subject) didn't/won't eat it], **a-ŋgɨ wákare** [X (any subject) didn't/won't eat him], and so on).

(d) Class 4 transitive verbs that alternate between **r** in irrealis and **t** in realis are listed in their **r** form *if that form is word initial.*

So a verb like 'make' (**ni-tu-ku-ro** 'make.R-S<3SG.F.R.O>3PL.R.S' [they made it], but **nir-kru-ndak** 'make.IRR-3SG.F.IRR.O-3PL.IRR.S' [they will make it]) appears as **nir-**, because that is the negated form of this verb (so **nir-kru wákare** [X (any subject) didn't/won't make it], and so on).

If the alternation between **r** and **t** occurs at the end of the verb stem, the word is listed with an **r** ending, but the realis/irrealis alternation undergone by the stem is noted in the entry. So the entry for **ŋgar** 'call out to' notes that the verb is class 4 verb, which means that the **r** undergoes the alternation discussed in Section 6.1.6 of the *Grammar*.

(e) Class 5 transitive verbs do not undergo any changes in the verb stem between realis and irrealis. Hence, the verb stem appearing as the dictionary entry is the same regardless of whether the verb is realis or irrealis.

Intransitive verbs

Intransitive verbs are alphabetized according to their irrealis stem form + the irrealis ending (**-ki, -kɨ** or **-ku**) that affixes to the stem when it is negated.

If the verb stem itself changes between realis and irrealis, the stem change is noted in parentheses after the main entry.

For example, the entry for 'laugh' looks like this:

irkɨ *v.i.* (**pirot/ pirok**), laugh; *lap*.

This entry should be read to mean the following:

(1) The irrealis form of this intransitive verb is **irkɨ**, consisting of the verb stem **ir** + the irrealis suffix **-kɨ**. This is the form the verb takes when it is negated – so one says **irkɨ wákare** 'X (any subject) didn't/won't laugh'.

The irrealis suffix **-kɨ** is a morpheme separate from the verb stem, but it is provided in the dictionary entry because, as discussed in Section 5.2.2 of the *Grammar*, there is no way of knowing what the suffix is unless one hears it (or sees it here).

The form of the verb stem that appears in negation is also the form that constitutes the basis of all non-realis status and mood inflections; for example, **ir-kɨ-ndak** 'laugh.IRR-IRR-3PL.IRR' [they will laugh], and **ir-ŋgarana** 'laugh.IRR-ND' [X (any subject) better not laugh].

(2) The forms in the parentheses following the entry are the verb's realis forms. If the forms are regular, only a few will be listed, in order to allow a reader to identify them by looking at Sections 6.2.1 and 6.2.2 of the *Grammar*. In the case of 'laugh', a glance at Section 6.2.1 reveals that the endings **-ot** and **-ok** indicate that 'laugh' is a Group IV intransitive verb, and that **pirot** means 'I (M) laughed', 'you (M) laughed', or 'he laughed'; **pirok** means 'I (F) laughed', 'you (F) laughed', 'she laughed' or 'we laughed'. The forms that verbs that belong to this Group take for all other persons are found in that Section.

If the intransitive verb is irregular in realis, the irregular forms will be listed in the parentheses following the entry.

Another example of an entry for an intransitive verb, this time for one whose stem form does *not* change between realis and irrealis, is 'say', 'talk'. The entry for this verb looks like this:

namkɨ *v.i.* (**-net/-nak**), say, talk; *tok*.

This entry should be read to mean the following:
(1) The irrealis form of this intransitive verb is **namkɨ**, consisting of the verb stem **nam** + the irrealis suffix **-kɨ**. This is the form the verb takes when it is negated – so one says **namkɨ wákare** 'X (any subject) didn't/won't talk'.

Once again, the irrealis suffix **-kɨ** is a morpheme separate from the verb stem, but it is provided in the dictionary entry because there is no way of knowing what the suffix is unless one sees it here.

The form of the verb stem that appears under negation is also the form that constitutes the basis of all non-realis status and mood inflections; for example, **nam-kɨ-ndak** 'talk.IRR-IRR-3PL.IRR' [they will talk], and **nam-ŋg rana** 'talk.IRR-ND' [X (any subject) better not talk].

(2) In those cases where all that follows an entry for an intransitive verb is parentheses with endings like (**-net/-nak**), this means that the verb stem remains the same between realis and irrealis. The realis person-endings of these verbs can be reckoned through the following steps:
   (a) remove the irrealis suffix **-ki**, **-kɨ** or **-ku** (in the case of 'say' or 'talk', it is **-kɨ**). This leaves only the verb stem (**nam**);
   (b) suffix the appropriate subject endings to that stem.

The endings (**-net/-nak**) provided in the entry for 'say, 'talk' indicate what those approriate subject endings are. The parentheses indicates that **nam** takes the endings (**-net/-nak**) in realis. These endings are detailed in Sections 6.2.1 and 6.2.2 of the *Grammar*. In this case, (**-net/-nak**) indicate that **nam** is a Group I intransitive verb. Checking Section 6.2.1, one sees that the full realis conjugation of **nam** is as follows :

1SGM	ŋa	nam	-net (M)	'I (M) said'
1SGF	ŋa	nam	-nak (F)	'I (F) said'
2SGM	yu	nam	-tet (M)	'you (M) said'
2SGF	yu	nam	-tak (F)	'you (F) said'
3SGF	ŋgu	nam	-tak	'she said'
3SGM	ni	nam	-net	'he said'
1PL	yim	nam-	-nak	'we said'
2PL	yum	nam	-nkem	'you *pl.* said'
3PL	ŋgɨ	nam	-tuko	'they said'
DL	yim sene/ ŋgɨ sene	nam	-tike	'we two said'/ 'they two said'

Note: for a discussion of how the dual forms are used in Tayap, see Section 3.5 and the discussion of examples (3-73) and (3-74).

Another example would be an intransitive verb in the dictionary followed by the endings (**-iet/-iek** – for example **papku** 'pierce'. These endings show that the verb inflects like a Group II intransitive verb (see Section 6.2.1).

Complex predicates and non-final verb objects

The dictionary also lists forms frequently occurring in complex predicates. These consist of cosubordinate verbs suffixed occuring with either **-ra** ('modifier') or **-kar** ('manner'), and often followed by a verb of motion (see Section 9.8). The verb of motion that follows these verbs in the dictionary entry is either **okɨ** 'go' or **aiki** 'come', depending on which one would most be most common in village speech. However, these verbs of motion can be substituted by any other.

Several entries are for commonly-occurring serial verbs constructed with non-final object suffixes. Those suffixes change for the object of the verb; it is therefore not possible to write them in non-specified form. In those cases, the capital 'X' indicates that the morphological slot represented by X must be filled with an object suffix – unless otherwise specified, this will be a non-final object suffix.

An example is the entry for the following verb, which means 'humiliate', 'embarrass', 'defeat':

timbraXokɨ *v.i. irr.* (serial verb construction conjugated like **okɨ**, Note: the X is a non-final object suffix).

This entry should be read as follows:
(a) this intransitive verb is irregular, and is conjugated like **okɨ** (see the dictionary entry for **okɨ** for the pattern);
(b) the **X** slot will be filled with the appropriate non-final object suffix when the verb is inflected (these are discussed in Section 8.2.2 of the *Grammar*).

So 'we defeated him' would be **timbra*t*wok** (non-final object suffix underlined) but 'we defeated her' would be **timbra*k*wok**. 'We defeated them' would be **timbra*mb*wok**, and so on.

Parentheses appearing in an entry that is not a verb

If a Tayap word that is *not* a verb contains any letters inside parentheses, this means that the word occurs both with or without those elements, and that the meaning of the word remains the same regardless of whether the full form or the shorter form is used. So **ana(knɨ)** 'where?' occurs in both the full form **anaknɨ** and also as **ana**. **Aŋgu(de)** 'there' occurs as both **aŋgude** and **aŋgu**.

Stress

Stress is marked only on words that deviate from the general rule that stress falls on the final syllable of a word (see Section 2.5 of the *Grammar*).

Synonyms

Where no example or explanation is given between two cross-referenced words that mean the same thing, I have been unable to elicit any difference in meaning. Examples are **ŋakraw** and **ndadab**, both of which mean 'peel', i.e. the skin of a fruit or vegetable that has been removed. My questions about difference in meaning were consistently answered with a version of the following: "If you want to say **ŋakraw**, you'll say **ŋakraw**. If you want to say **ndadab** you'll say **ndadab**. They mean the same" ("Yu laik tok **ŋakraw** bai yu tok **ŋakraw**. Na yu laik tok **ndadab** bai yu tok **ndadab**. Em wankain mining tasol"). Or I would sometimes be told "wanpela mining na tok i bruk": there's one meaning but the talk (i.e. the language) is broken, or fractured.

In some cases – for example, two different verbs that mean 'sweep': **mburai** (class 5) and **mburai-(p)-i** (class 1) – the words are true synonyms (although in this case, it is clear that the verb is **mburai**; in the class 1 form it is constructed with **i-** 'give').

In other cases, the difference in the meaning of two words may have been lost. I suspect, for example, that the two words for 'bridge', **koŋgrik** and **nimirkokir**, at one time referred to different kinds of bridges – made of different material, spanning different bodies of water or constructed in different ways. However, I was unable to elicit any difference in meaning from the most senior speakers in the village. Whatever difference may have existed is now forgotten.

Obsolete words

The same is true of some of the other vocabulary items included here. I have labeled 'obsolete' a few words that I recorded in the 1980s but that in 2009 were either unknown or no longer used. Other words have been retained without comment, but their meaning today is hazy. For example, there are four named winds in Tayap: **awar**, **ŋgamai**, **mbunim** and **mbankap**. On this all older villagers are agreed. They are also agreed that the winds are differentiated primarily by the directions of their origin. What they absolutely could not agree upon, however, was what those directions of origin are. One senior speaker was adamant that the **ŋgamai** wind, for example, came from the mountain to the south of Gapun. Another senior speaker was equally adamant that the wind came from the sea, which lies to the north of Gapun. Likewise, the **awar** wind was held by some speakers to come from the mountain (i.e. the south) and others to come from the mangrove lake (i.e. the north). Speakers argued vigorously with one another whenever this topic came up, but they never resolved it.

By sheer luck, the four winds are listed and defined in Georg Höltker's 1938 wordlist. For having been gathered in three hours by someone who had never before heard Tayap (and who would never hear it again), Höltker's list of 125 words is impressively accurate. So in the end, I decided to base the definition I give here on the definitions listed by Höltker, partly because he would have spoken to language informants who still lived in a completely Tayap-speaking village, and also because one of the oldest speakers still alive in Gapun defined the winds as Höltker does in his wordlist.

Villagers' debates and language shift

Something similar to the 'wind problem' occurred with a word that I would have thought was common and uncontroversial – the word for 'rainbow'. One morning after a night of heavy rain, a large rainbow appeared in the sky. On my way to wash my clothes in one of the village waterholes, I saw the rainbow and realized that I didn't know what it was called in Tayap. So I asked the first person I saw – a fluent speaker of Tayap in his late thirties – what one calls a rainbow in Tayap.

"Renbo", he responded, without missing a beat.

Um, no, I told him, that must be the Tok Pisin word – the Tayap word had to be something else. The man told me that in that case, he didn't know, and that I should go ask his father, sixty-five-year-old Monei Mbanaŋ, who was my main language informant at the time. I went off to find Monei and thus did my innocent query launch a month of acrimonious debate from one end of the village to the other.

I found Monei sitting on his veranda and I asked him the word for rainbow. He pondered for awhile. He told me he couldn't remember the word offhand; he needed to think about it. He thought for several days. Finally, he told me that 'rainbow' had no single word in Tayap; instead, 'rainbow' was expressed by the verb phrase **akin tamtiek**, 'cloud is marked with color'. This sounded reasonable to me, and I duly recorded it. But when I repeated it to other speakers to check their reactions, I was universally met with disdain. "Em giaman" – 'He's lying', everyone sneered, using their favorite expression to dismiss another speaker's expertise in Tayap. Even though no one could think of the correct term themselves, they all told me they knew that the phrase Monei had volunteered was wrong.

Days went by and no one could come up with 'rainbow'. Older villagers explained to me that their parents and older relatives had warned them about rainbows, saying they should never walk underneath one, because if they did, their minds would become clouded and confused. But even though they remembered these cautions, no senior speaker could recall the word for 'rainbow' that their parents and relatives had used while articulating them. The word for 'rainbow', villagers told me, "i hait" – it was hiding. (In the villagers' defense, I should note that rainbows are not exactly common occurrences in Gapun – I only saw that one the entire eight months I was there in 2009).

Eventually Monei's old wife, Sopak Waiki, told me that she had a dream in which the true word for 'rainbow' had been whispered to her by a dead ancestor. The word, she revealed, was **minuomb** – a word that otherwise means 'large round lake'. Sopak said that the way to say 'rainbow' in Tayap was to say **akinni minuomb utok**, 'a round lake appeared in the clouds'.

I told other senior speakers of Sopak's revelation. They were unmoved. "Em giaman", they all pronounced, impassively.

A few days later, one of the oldest men in the village told me that he had remembered the word – it was **wagurmos**.

The other speakers' judgement fell predictably: "Em giaman", they all said. They explained that **wagurmos** meant the white film one sees in the sky at night

– that is, the Milky Way. It doesn't mean 'rainbow' at all. Many older speakers also took the opportunity to disparage the linguistic knowledge of the old man who had offered **wagurmos**. That speaker may be old, they said belittlingly, but he's "lapun nating" – he's grown old without having learned anything. All he has, people said, is "bebi sens" – the sense of a baby.

Weeks passed and frustration grew. But finally, having heard about the senior speakers' search for 'rainbow', a young man in his 30s one day came and told me that he had once heard his grandfather, Kruni Ayarpa, say the word for 'rainbow'. Kruni had been one of my language informants in the 1980s; he died in the early 1990s. For the last few decades of his life, Kruni had been universally respected and vaguely feared as an elder who knew everything about Gapun's history and who spoke flawless and eloquent Tayap. The young man reported that as a child, he had once been together with Kruni when women from the neighboring village of Wongan mentioned rainbows, which are called *mamor* in their Kopar language. They asked Kruni what the word in Tayap was. Kruni told them that it was **mamar**.

Rather than being a breakthrough, this word, too, was rejected. "It means 'banana'", all the old people responded dryly when, without telling them why, I asked them to define **mamar**. And indeed, it does mean a kind of banana. But in the end, unable to come up with a word or expression that satisfied them all, and undoubtedly growing annoyed at my persistence in questioning them, the older villagers begrudgingly agreed that **mamar** must be the word for 'rainbow' too, since Kruni apparently had claimed it was.

My own conclusion is that **mamar** probably was the Tayap word for 'rainbow'. Tayap and Kopar share quite a few nouns, because speakers of the two languages have been in contact with one another for a very long time. The kind of slight phonetic variation between *mamor* and **mamar** are common in the words shared by the two languages. For example:

	Tayap	Kopar
crocodile	**orem**	*oreo*
cockatoo	**kaimwa**	*keimwa*
turtle	**pawp**	*pup*
lorikeet	**njijerik**	*njijeriŋ*
hook	**pipiŋgabu**	*bibigabu*

For those all those reasons, I have entered 'rainbow' as one of the definitions of **mamar**. I recount the little epic of finally getting that word, though, in order to illustrate the fact that not all of the entries contained in this dictionary will satisfy all the current speakers of Tayap.

In fact, this inability to satisfy all the current speakers of a Tayap is a feature of the language that may be contributing to its demise. I was continually struck by how vigorously (and, to my mind, how gratuitously) senior speakers of Tayap discounted and ridiculed one another's linguistic competence. Early on, I stopped trying to discuss Tayap in groups of old people because any discussion of any aspect of the language would inevitably result in bickering. Speakers might eventually grouchily agree on whatever it was I was asking them about, but later on, they would always arrange a private moment with me to heartily dismiss the knowledge and opinions of their fellow speakers.

While it escapes no one's attention that Tayap is a tiny language spoken nowhere else but in Gapun (and by Gapun villagers living in the neighboring village of Wongan), knowledge about language is regarded as a private, rather than a communal, possession. This way of thinking about language is an extension of the villagers' more general ethos of ownership. Gapun villagers would shake their heads in absolute bewilderment at the persistent Western stereotypes about how a rainforest-dwelling people like themselves supposedly eschew ownership and share their natural resources in a kind of prelapsarian socialist ecological bliss.

On the contrary. In Gapun, *nothing* is communal, nothing is equally owned and shared by everyone. Everything – every area of land, every sago palm, every coconut palm, every mango tree, every pot, plate, axe, machete, discarded spear shaft, broken kerosene lamp, and every anything else one can think of – is owned by someone (including people's names and the right to bestow them, as well as knowledge of myths, songs, and curing chants). Villagers guard their rights of ownership energetically and they defend them loudly (see Kulick 1992 for an extended discussion of this that is as relevant today as it was twenty years ago).

This understanding of possession and ownership has consequences for language: it means that the sociolinguistic truism of a common "shared" language has little purchase in Gapun. In their own view, villagers don't "share" a language. Instead, each speaker *owns* his or her own version of the language. And the older those speakers become, the more they regard their version as the proper one and everyone else's as "giaman" (false, a lie; **takwat** in Tayap). This absence of a language ideology that regards a common language as something "shared" means that speakers are predisposed to not regard the loss of Tayap as particularly traumatic. Fluent elder speakers still have 'their' Tayap; if younger speakers don't possess a version of it as, well, "wari bilong ol". That's their problem.

Terms for plants and trees

This dictionary would have been much longer if I had been able to include the vernacular's extensive lexicon for plants and trees. Unfortunately, I am not a botanist and even with the help of specialist books like *Handbooks of the Flora of Papua New Guinea* (Womersley 1978; Henty 1985) I was never able, for the most part, to distinguish between – let alone identify or describe – the numerous plants, vines, bushes, roots, trees and grasses that exist in the villagers' rainforest. Walking through the forest, villagers would often point in the distance and mention the name of whatever tree or vine they happened to notice. I usually had no idea what they were pointing at – to the untrained eye, vegetation in a rainforest looks an awful lot alike.

After telling me the name of whatever it was they had pointed at, villagers would often then add that the thing they had drawn my attention to was similar to another kind of plant they had gestured towards on some previous occasion, but "not too much" (i no tumas). This is the equivalent of taking a Gapun villager who perhaps has never seen an automobile to a busy Los Angeles freeway interchange, waving in its general direction and saying, "We call that one a Honda. It's like a Toyota, but not too much".

Needless to say, the information imparted on those rainforest promenades was almost invariably lost on me. Even when I was sure that I was looking at the same tree or vine or bush that the speaker was pointing at, I was usually unable to distinguish it in any meaningful way from most other trees, vines, and bushes growing around it. And it seemed unhelpful to include entries in this dictionary like "tallish tree with long leaves and smooth bark".

Where the plant or tree is culturally, socially, medicinally or gustatorily salient, or is used for a specific purpose – or when even a layperson like myself was able to identify it (a fern, for instance) – I have included it, defining it usually it by its salient characteristic, use or purpose rather than by its appearance. An exception to this are the words used by the villagers for the nine kinds of sago palms they pound and wash to extract their staple food from.

Many of the less commonly-used words for plants and trees, like the vernacular words for birds (listed separately), are disappearing. At the same time, however, quite a few of those words will be retained for the forseeable future, because the language that is replacing Tayap, Tok Pisin, has no equivalent terms.

Bird names

A separate list of words for birds appears at the end of this dictionary. For the sake of completeness, however, the words for birds are also listed in the appropriate places in the dictionary. See the note in the section on words for birds at the end for an explanation of those entries.

Vulgarity (tok nogut)

I have purposely included numerous examples of what the villagers usually refer to by the Tok Pisin words "tok nogut", which means 'bad talk', or 'vulgarity' (the Tayap equivalent is **wekok**).

One reason I do this is for the pure entertainment value of such talk – as I mention at the beginning of the grammar, Gapun villagers are no different from anyone else who has ever scoured a dictionary to check to see which scandalous words have been enshrined in print.

But in addition to this more purient consideration, there is also the issue of linguistic preservation. 'Bad talk' is disappearing in the Tayap language, not because people don't swear anymore (they swear all the time: one of a child's first phrases these days is "kaikai kan", 'eat cunt', to express opposition or dissatisfaction), but because the majority of the swearing, even by people who otherwise speak excellent Tayap, now is in Tok Pisin.

The gist of this swearing is the same – in Tayap, most swearing involves some variation of 'cunt', 'asshole' or 'prick', and so it does also in Tok Pisin. The difference is that swearing in Tayap can be poetic, consisting of complex verbal constructions, like 'His mother gave birth to him through her asshole together with a pile of shit, while lightning flashed!' (**Ŋan mayayi yiwirŋan ŋgwabekeni pomborreki tatiŋiŋan mamraireki!**'), or 'Your big cunthole is fucking sagging!' (**Ŋgwab mir rumbrutak otitekŋa apro sakar!** – the image the verb phrase **rumbrutak otitekŋa** conjures for the villagers is loose mud on a riverbank sagging down towards the water).

Swearing in Tok Pisin consists of relatively unimaginative noun phrases ("kan pekpek" 'cunt shit' and "wul pekpek" 'shit hole' are favorites). These words have the same affective force as the Tayap curses, but from a linguistic perspective, they are boring.

My inclusion of so much swearing is to remind the villagers that Tayap has an impressive, lyrical arsenal of vulgarity at its disposal. The loss of imaginative swearing is as lamentable as the loss of any other domain of language use and linguistic creativity.

Words excluded from the dictionary

The only words that have been intentionally excluded from this dictionary are words relating to practices that men do not want women to know about. If I had included the words referring to those practices, I would have had to define them, and doing so would have involved revealing information that men want to keep hidden. As far as I have been able to determine, there is little that men do that women do not in fact know everything there is to know about. But neverminding that, I respect the wishes of the men in Gapun to maintain a sphere of mystery, and so words pertaining to their secret practices shall remain secret here.

On the other hand, I have included the few 'secret' words that villagers use to 'hide talk' from those very few foreign villagers who have ever learned any Tayap. Those secret words may be remnants of a more extensive secret code register that has fallen into disuse. The words refer to commonplace objects like betel nut and tobacco that village men and women request from each other, using codewords that they think no foreigner who might be present will understand. I decided to include the few words that villagers still use in this register because they otherwise are very likely to disappear soon without leaving any trace at all.

Tok Pisin words and expressions

Tok Pisin expressions and orthography in this dictionary sometimes differ from the two standard sources, Francis Mihalic's 1971 *The Jacaranda Dictionary and Grammar of Melanesian Pidgin*, and the more recent, less comprehensive, *Oxford Tok Pisin-English Dictionary* (Volker, Jackson, Baing and Deutrom 2008). Those differences reflect village idioms and pronunciation and I include them here simply to document some of the variation that exists in Papua New Guinea in relation to Tok Pisin. So, for instance, I write "gorngorn" instead of Mihalic's gorgor (a type of ginger).

Sometimes the words in the Tok Pisin dictionaries are not used in Gapun. An example is the word given in both dictionaries for "centipede" – "plantihan" (lit. 'plenty-hand'). I have never heard any villager use this word, which is not surprising, since the Tayap name for those much-feared venomous insects, **yandum**, is known by even the smallest child. If a Tok Pisin word included in the *Jacaranda* or *Oxford* dictionaries is not used in Gapun, I have not included it here. Instead, I have either used a word that at least some villagers recognize, or I have supplied a description in Tok Pisin that should be intelligible to the villagers.

Foreign words in Tayap

Several commonly used nouns, adjectives and verbs stems have been incorporated into Tayap from two nearby vernaculars, which are called Kopar and Adjora in the linguistic literature. The Kopar language is spoken in three villages: in neighboring Wongan and in the Sepik river villages of Kopar and Singrin.

Today, the language is in bad shape and is disappearing even more quickly than Tayap. Young men and women in their twenties seem not even to understand much Kopar, let alone speak it. But it is still spoken by adults, though, especially women over forty.

Adjora, in contrast, is a much more robust language. This is partly undoubtedly due to the fact that the population of Adjora-speaking villages is large. Already in the 1970s, Adjora had about 2,347 speakers, according to Laycock and Z'graggen (1975:739). This population has no doubt grown exponentially since then.[1] In addition to sheer numbers, the persistence of the Adjora language is also surely linked to the fact that the people of Adjora-speaking villages, such as the nearby Sanae, consciously and proudly maintain key components of their traditional culture, such as parts of the men's house cult and many of the practices relating to mortuary rituals. (Partly for this reason, the villagers of Gapun regard Adjora-speaking villages as the source of all sorcery and the cause of every death in Gapun). While my informal observations indicate that Adjora may be losing ground among young people in Sanae village, and perhaps also in the villages of Tarengi and Wunkenan, the language is still spoken by probably several thousand people in villages to the east of Gapun extending to the Ramu river.

It was not always clear which words in Tayap are of foreign origin because (a) the words are fully integrated into the Tayap grammar, so foreign verb roots, for instance, are with few exceptions declined as class 5 Tayap verbs, and (b) speakers under sixty tended not to be aware that a particular word was not of Tayap origin. I know that a certain word is of foreign origin only because either its phonetic shape struck me as unusual and I specifically queried people about it (one of the words for mushroom, **oŋgisu**, is an example), or because an older villager brought it to my attention (an example is the verb for being jealous, **mwanambri**).

---

[1] I checked Laycock's list of villages speaking Adjora (1973: 38) against the official PNG Census from 2000, which is the most recent census for the country. Six of the twenty one villages listed by Laycock do not appear in that census, presumably because they have changed their names since the early 1970s, they have become absorbed into other villages, or they no longer exist. The remaining fifteen villages list a total population of 3,271. This is much lower than I would have expected. Gapun's population has more than doubled since the 1970s, and the population of Sanae, the only Adjora-speaking village I have personal familiarity with, has certainly grown substantially since I first went to the area in the mid-1980s. The problem is that the data on which Laycock based his speaker estimates is not reliable – he himself comments on the difficulty of estimating speaker numbers in areas that had either never been censused, or had been censused many years previous to his work. "The figures", he wrote, "cannot represent with complete accuracy the number of native speakers of any of the languages, except those that are very small" (1973:56).

Whenever I tried to confirm the foreignness of a word with other older speakers, I frequently encountered the problem that those speakers disagreed among themselves. Whenever the disagreements remained unresolved, I have based my entry in this dictionary on the judgement of Samek Wanjo.

A note on the Tayap examples

Because this text is likely to be the only documentation that will ever appear of the Tayap language, I have taken care to supplement many definitions with illustrative sentences in Tayap. Those sentences are drawn from my elicitation sessions and from the recordings of naturally occurring talk that I have made over the course of the past thirty years. They will be of interest primarily to Gapun villagers, but any linguist interested in Tayap should be able to segment them and understand their morphology and grammar by referring to the grammar section of this book.

Abbreviations and terms used in the dictionary

adj.	adjective	*lit.*	literally
Adjora	word of Adjora-language origin	*masc.*	masculine
adv.	adverb	*mood part.*	mood particle
dir.	directional	*n.*	noun
dl.	dual	*part.*	particle
d.v.	dependent verb	*per. case*	peripheral case
dx.	diectic word	*pl.*	plural
emph.	emphatic	*pos.*	positional
fem.	feminine	*pro.*	pronoun
ERG	ergative clitic	*temp.*	temporal
excl.	exclamation	*v.i.*	intransitive verb
intens.	intensifier	*voc.*	vocative
interj.	interjection	*v.t.*	transitive verb
interrog.	interrogative	*Watam*	word of Watam-language origin
irr.	irregular		
inv.	invariant form; i.e. a form that remains the same regardless of person, number or TMA.	X	morphological slot to be filled with an object morpheme
Kopar	word of Kopar-language origin	†	moribund form

A

a *v.t.* (class 3), consume by eating, drinking or smoking; *kaikai, dring, smok*. **Yu orakaŋgar kakunda?**: Have you eaten (*lit.* 'have you eaten food?'); *Yu kaikai pinis?*; **Ŋgɨ sokoi aŋgwar wákare**: They don't smoke (*lit.* 'they don't smoke tobacco'); *Ol i no save smok*.

abambɨ[†] *n.* ex-wife (used by the ex-in-laws of the woman) (*obsolete*); *man i lusim meri bai mama na papa bilong man kolim ex-meri long despela nem*.

abar *n.* overgrown rainforest, *tik bus*. See also **mbarmɨt**.

abarkɨ *v.i.* (**-tet/-tak**), become overgrown with bush; *kamap bus*. **Nder abartak**: The path is overgrown; *Rot i kamap bus*.

adádadɨ *v.t.* (class 3), **1.** fold something, e.g. a sheet or piece of cloth; *poltim olsem wanpela bedsit o wanpela laplap*.
2. break something into small bits, e.g. a biscuit; *brukim liklik liklik, olsem wanpela biskit*. **Nɨŋ adaditɨŋatan!**: Break his bones! *Brukim brukim ol bun bilong em!*.
3. hit something or someone several times, pummel; *paitim*. **Adadaditɨgɨn!**: Pummel him!; *Paitim em gut!*

adadit *n.*, joint; *join*. **Akaɲɲa adadit**: crook of arm; *join bilong han*; **Ndaramɲa adadit**: wrist, *join bilong han*; **Ndowɲa adadit**: ankle; *join bilong lek*.

adaikɨ *v.i. irr.* (ŋa **adɨbet/adɨbek**; yu **adɨbet/adɨbek**; ɲɨ **adɨbet**, ŋgu **adɨwek**, yɨm **adɨbek**, yum **adɨbekem**, ŋgɨ **adɨgwek**, yɨm sene **adɨbeke**), remain, *stap*. **Ŋa oŋgar nɨpɨs wákare ŋa adɨbet inda, yum neker onkem**: I'm not able to go, I'm remaining, you all go by yourselves; *Mi no nap igo, mi bai stap, yupela wan i go*.

adɨokɨ *v.i.* (conjugated like **okɨ**: ŋa **adɨmbot/adɨmbok**; yu **adɨmbot/adɨmbok**; ɲɨ **adɨmbot**; ŋgu **odɨwok**; yɨm **adɨmbok**; yum **adɨmbokem**; ŋgɨ **odɨŋwok**; yɨm sene **odɨwoké**), **1.** fall down, collapse; *pundaun*. **Ŋɨ adɨmbota tat**: He collapsed and slept; *Em (man) pundaun na slip*; **Ŋgu odɨwok**: She fell; *Em (meri) pundaun*.
2. trip, be tripped up; *pundaun*. **Nɨmɲa itawni ndow kadukuna, adɨmbot**: I tripped on the roots of the tree and I fell; *Rop bilong diwai bampim leg bilong mi na mi pundaun*.

adu *v.t.* (class 3), **1.** hit something; *paitim*.
2. intoxicate someone; *spakim*. **Minjikeyi ɲɨ odɨgɨn**: The betel nut intoxicated him; *Buai spakim em*.
3. snap finger; *pairapim pinga*. **Ŋɨ ndaram adukwankut**: He is snapping his fingers; *Em pairapim pinga bilong em*.
4. kneel; *brukim skru*. **Ewar ŋgu mɨŋgɨp odukun**: Yesterday she kneeled (*lit.* 'she kneeled on her knees'); *Asde em i brukim skru*.
5. swear at; *tok nogutim*. **Ŋgu wekoknɨ odukun**: She swore at her; *Em tok nogutim em*.
6. laugh at; *lap long*. **Ŋa ironɨ kadɨgɨn**: I laughed at him; *Mi lap long em*.
7. hang up; *hangamapim*. **Embatoto adantukun!** Hang up the piece of cloth! *Hangamapim laplap!*

adur *v.t.* (class 5), smash through something; *brukim*. **Ŋa tɨ memkɨnaka sapkɨnɨ mɨrɨ adurkrunak**: I'll also make an attempt, even though I have no knowledge of what to do (*lit.* I will get up and smash through the undergrowth); *Mi tu bai kirap brukim bus tasol*.

adurɨokɨ *v.i.* (conjugated like **okɨ**), be smashed, shattered; *brukbruk*. **Oŋgab aŋgɨ adurɨwok**: That pot is smashed; *Kanaka sosbin i brukbruk*.

aduwarɨ *v.t.* (class 5), smash up against something; *brukim*. **Taruŋnat aŋgɨ aduwarɨtukun!** Smash the piece of firewood against something to make it smaller! *Brukim hap paiwut!*

agampɨ *n.*; *voc.* (*pl.* **agampɨndodo**), mother's mother's brother; *brata bilong mama bilong mama*.

agídada *n.* [Adjora], an exceptionally good and true friend; *poroman i save pas tru long yu.*

agin *n.* gecko; *geko, liklik palai bilong haus.*

agráŋkar *adj.* [Adjora], skinny, emaciated, usually used to describe pigs; *bun nating, ol man i save toktok long ol pik.* The Tayap equivalent is **niŋ sinder** (*lit.* 'bone nothing'; just bones).

agu *n.* large termites that make mounds rising from the ground (**kwaw**); *waitpela anis a save wokim ol bikpela haus bilong ol long ol long kunai o insait long bus.*

ai 1. *n.* here, *long ia.* **Aini wuk**: It is here; *Em i stap long ia.* **Aini ase ŋgritukun**: Put it here on the outside; *Putim long arrere.* **Yu aiŋa wákare**: You aren't from here; *yu no bilong despela hap.*

2. *interj.* Hey!, *Yu harim!*

aiamb *n.* cluster of branches with fruit, betel nut or anything that has large seeds that grow in clusters; *han diwai i gat buai o wanem kain prut*: **Minjikeŋa aiyamb suman**: large cluster of betel nut; *bikpela han buai.*

aianj-(p)-e *v.t.* (class 1), singe leaves to make them pliable; *boinim.* See also **aranj-(p)-e-**.

aiawaŋ *n.* placenta; *bilum i stap insait long bel bilong ol meri o ol animol.*

aiawaŋar *n.* Anopheles mosquito; *bilakpela natnat i gat makmak long ol pinga.*

aike *adv.* this way, like this; *olsem.* **Aike wetak**: Come this way; *I kam olsem.* **Aike etukun**: Hold it like this; *Holim olsem.*

aikesim *n.* a kind of tree with soft bark that attracts sago grubs and mushrooms; *diwai i nogat strong ol binatang bilong saksak na ol talinga i save kamap long en.*

aikeitam *n.* Black Bittern (*Birds of New Guinea* plate 3, #1–2, 5, 7, 10).

aiki *v.i. irr.* (**ŋa mbet/mbek; yu mbet/mbek; ŋi mbet; ŋgu wek; yum mbekem; yim mbek; ŋgi ŋgwek; yime sene weke**): come, *kam.*

ainde *dx. masc.* here, close to speaker; *em ia, samting i stap klostu long husat i toktok i stap.*

aini *adv.* like this; *olsem.* **Aini we(tak/tet)**: Come this way; *I kam olsem.*

aiŋgar *n.* arrival; *ikam bilong wanpela man o meri, o bilong wanpela samting (pik o dok o wanem wanem samting).*

air *n.* **1.** powder that looks like pulverized white chalk that is made from baked clamshells. One dips a ginger pepper in it and chews it, together with a betelnut; *kambang.*

2. unattractive white film on skin or other living object; *waitpela das long skin o long wanpela samting.* **Toto airŋan**: unhealthy skin covered in white, chalky color; *skin i gat das.*

airkut *n.* the gourd into which **air** (lime powder) used to be put, not grown in Gapun anymore, and last used by senior men in the 1980s. These gourds have been replaced by plastic jars; *skin kambang bilong ol tumbuna bilong putim kambang, ol Gapun i no save growim nau, na nogat man i save usim.*

airuramb *n.* the day after a funerary feast, when all the work and rituals are completed and all the visitors from other villages have departed; *de bilong malolo, bihain long wanpela pati, olgeta wok i pinis na ol manmeri bilong ol narapela hap ol i go pinis.*

aiyo *n.* small minnow-like fish with many sharp bones, caught in forest streams and eaten; *liklik bunpis i save stap insait long ol baret.*

akan *n.* **1.** arm; *han*; **Akanŋa imin**: underside of arm; *baksait bilong han.*

2. front leg of an animal; *lek bilong pik, dok, mumut, na ol kainkain animol.*

akan suman *n.* upper arm; *bikpela mit bilong han.*

akanbir *n.* forearm; *han.*

akandam *n.* crook made in arms bent to carry e.g. firewood; *han olsem yu brukim long en long karim paiwut i kam*; **Taruŋ akandamni warakkukuotet**: Put the firewood in your arms and bring it; *Kisim paiwut na karim i kam.*

akanŋa sokop *n.* elbow; *join bilong han.*

akápore *interj.* how can this be?; *aiye, olsem wanem?*

akatrik *n.* boil that develops in the armpit; *strongpela buk i save kamap long sangana bilong han.*

akirónda *n.* [*Adjora*], a kind of small green ground lizard; *wanpela kain liklik palai bilong graun.* Same lizard as **ŋgurbewat**.

akɨjim *n.* [*Kopar*], raincloud; *klaut bilong ren.*

akɨn *n.* **1.** cloud; *klaut.*
    2. sky; *antap.* **Akɨn tambutiek:** The sky is colored; e.g. at sunset; *Klaut i gat kalakala.*

akok *n.* spearshaft made of **wamb** (a strong *limbom* palm). Abandoned in the 1950s when iron became more accessible to villagers and the shafts of spears started to be made of bamboo; *spia bipo ol i wokim long strongpela limbom. Bihain long wo, ol tumbuna i lusim despela pasim long wanem ol i wokim spia long ain, na mambu ol i wokim long mambu.*

aku *v.i. irr.* be, stay; *stap.* (**ŋa kut/kuk; yu kut/kuk; ŋɨ kut; ŋgu wuk; yim wuk; yum kukem; ŋgɨ ŋgwuk, yim sene wuke**). **Ewar ŋa numnɨ kut:** Yesterday I was in the village; *Asde mi stap long ples.* **Epi ŋa numnɨ akunet:** Tomorrow I will remain in the village; *Tumoro bai mi stap long ples.*

am *n.* battle, fight; *pait.*

am *v.t.* (class 3), call out to summon a dog or pig; *singautim dok o pig.* **Ewar ŋa njenum kammbɨn mirinɨ kɨmbokɨnana, ŋgɨ mndatuko okɨnana.** Yesterday I called out to my dogs to go into the forest (to hunt), but they didn't come; *Asde mi singautim ol dog long igo ong bus tasol ol i les.*

ama *n.; voc.* mother; *mama.* See also **maya**.

amaye *interj.* expression used when speaker feels intense pain or shock; *hap tok ol man i save tok taim ol i karim bikpela pen.*

amai-(p)-i *v.t.* (class 1) search for something; *painim.*

amakato *n.* plant that grows in swamplands, traditionally used during divination rituals; *wanpela hap diwai ol saveman bilong bipo i save usim taim ol i holim stik bilong spia i gat powa bilong em.* See also **maies**.

ama kowot *n.; voc.* maternal aunt who is older than one's mother; *bikpela susa bilong mama.*

amamar *temp.* four days from now; *i go inap popela de.*

ama mosop *n.; voc.* maternal aunt who is younger than one's mother; *liklikpela susa bilong mama.*

amandukup *temp.* five days from now; *i go inap paipela de.*

amanep *n.* ground lizard; *palai bilong graun i gat kalakala.*

amasɨk[†] *n.* (*pl.* **amasɨkndodo** or **amasɨkɨmb**), ancestor; *tumbuna man o meri.*

amb *n.* **1.** place where pigs wallow; *hap bilong ol pik i save sindaun na slip long graun.*
    2. goiter; *buk long nek.*

ambagai *n.* men's house; *haus boi.*

ambɨn *interrog.* what?; *wanem?* **Ŋgu ambɨn orak?:** What is that? *Em wanem samting?*

ambɨn ana *interrog.* why?; *bilong wanem?*

ambɨkɨ *v.i. irr.* (*obsolete*), (**ŋa kambet/kambek; yu kambet/kambek, ŋɨ kambet, ŋgu ombak, yim kambek, yum kambɨkem; ŋgɨ omboko** or **ŋgombak, yim sene ombɨke**): be inside any kind of house; *stap insait long wanpela haus o haus boi.* **Munjenum oŋgarnɨ ŋgwoka aro ŋgombak:** The men have gone to the ceremonial house and are there inside; *Ol man i go istap insait long haus tambaran.*

ambɨrdadab *n.* small parrots; *liklik karangal* (*Birds of New Guinea* plate 21).

ambnor *n.* **1.** jowls of a male pig; *hap nek bilong pik man i save pundaun i godaun.*
    2. coil; *hip.*

ambonor *n.* large black python-like snake; *moran.*

ambrɨm *n.* [*Kopar*], **1.** basket sling; *han bilong basket ol meri i save wokim long* **maior**.
    2. wire on pot used to hang it up above fire; *waia bilong pot.* See also **numun**.

ambu *v.t.* (class 3), **1.** hide something; *haitim.*
    2. vomit something; *trautim.* **Ŋɨ kambwan kambukun:** He vomited vomit; *Em i traut;* **Ŋgu and ombukun:** She vomited blood; *Em i trautim blut.*

3. hang around neck; *hangampim long nek.*

ambukeni *interrog.* how?; *olsem wanem?*

ambukŋa *interrog.* which?; *wanem?* **Ambukŋa nim otitek?** Which tree fell? *Wanem diwai i pundaun?*

ambukŋa nanunkŋa *interrog.* what did it look like? (*lit.* 'what was its face?'); *em i luk olsem wanem?*

ambukŋa titimbŋa *interrog.* what color?; *wanem kala?*

ambukrani *interrog.* how many?, how much?; *haumaspela?, haumas?* **Kawat ambukrani yu ŋgunana pikwatan?** How much salt did you give her? *Yu givim haumas sol long em?*

ambruni *adv.* hiding, disguised; *i hait.* **Ŋgu ripim ambruni wuk, ene mborkini utok**: Before it was hiding, but now it has been revealed; *Bipo samting i hait na nau i kamap ples klia.*

ambwamki *v.i.* (**-net/-nak**), cook; *kuk.*

amen *temp.* three days from now; *haptumoro gen.*

amira *v.t. irr.* (class 3, **ŋi amirkakun, ŋgu omirokun**), bite something; *kaikaim.* **Ror aŋgu nderekeni waikar woka aramŋi amirkakun**: The child was walking along the path and a snake bit her; *Pikinini meri i wakabaut long rot i go na snek i kaikaim em.*

amku *v.i.* (group IIa intransitive verb; **ŋa kamiet/kamiek; ŋgu omiek; yum kamukem; ŋgi ŋgomiek** or **omko**), fight, *pait.*

amoiawin *n.* armpit; *sangana bilong han;* **amoiawinŋa pupur**: armpit hair; *gras bilong sangana bilong han.*

amor *n.* yam, several varieties of which have sharp needles; *mami, sampela i gat nil olsem redpela mami. Ol waitpela na ol pinkpela nogat nil.*

amurák(amurík)ku *v.t.* (class 5; the reduplicated part **amurík** isn't necessary but it often occurs with this verb as a kind of intensifier), **1.** swish something; *noisim.* **Sik amuráktukun awinni**: Swish the water around in your mouth; *noisim wara long maus.*

2. sway; *troimwe troimwe.* **Poŋgrom mir amurákamuríkkurar ekrukakutet!** You walk around with your big dick swaying to and fro! (*vulgar*); *Yu troimwe troimwe draipela kok bilong yu!* (*tok nogut*).

amwaw *n.* Twelve-wired Bird of Paradise, *kumul* (*Birds of New Guinea* plate 51, #8–9).

ana sokop *interrog.* when?; *wanem taim?*

ana(kni) *interrog.* where?; *long we?* **Ŋaŋan minjike ana?** Where is my betel nut? *Buai bilong mi we?* **Yu anakni mbot?** Where are you going? *Yu go we?* **Anakni iawni?** Where exactly? *(Istap/i kamap) we?*

and *n.* blood; *blut.*

and-(p)-o *v.t.* (class 1), wake somebody up; *kirapim.* **Ŋa ruru sene andpombinda**: I've woken up the two kids; *Mi kirapim pinis tupela pikinini.*

anda-(p/w)-o *v.t.* (class 2), **1.** miss or go past something or someone, without the object seeing the thing that missed it (e.g. two people go past one another in the bush without seeing one another); *abrisim, olsem tupela man i abris long bus na tupela i no lukim tupela yet,*

2. miss, in the sense of failing to hit something; *abrisim.* **Iryi mbor andapokun**: The spear missed the pig; *Spia i abrisim pik.*

anda-(p/w)-oki *v.i.* (**andapuwot/ andapuwok**): duck; *abrisim.* **Yunana ŋgigi taimbtukro, andawotet!** They're throwing a stick at you, duck! *Ol i troimwe wanpela hap diwai ia, abririm!*

andadiki *v.i.* (**-net/-nak**), yawn; *opim maus nating taim yu les.* **Andadikitet:** You'll yawn; *Bai yu opim nating maus bilong yu.*

andei-(p)-e *v.t.* (class 1), step on something; *krungutim.* **Kakámatik andeiŋarke, ndrikŋan apro aŋgi.** Don't step on a millipede, they are poisonous; *I no ken krungutim ol* **kakámatik***, i gat marasin nogut bilong em.*

andi *n.* **1.** crown of palm tree; *tel bilong kokonas, buai o saksak.*

2. palm tree seedling; *kru bilong kokonas, buai o saksak.*

andɨk *v.t.* (class 5), roof a house; *pasim haus*; **Ewar tukur aiki wákare ndɨ yim patɨr andɨkrɨkkun**: If it hadn't rained yesterday we would have roofed the house; *Sapos asde ren i no bin pundaun inap mipela pasim haus pinis.*

andɨkɨ *v.i.* (**ŋɨ kandiet/ŋgu ondiek**), swell, grow fat; *kamap patpela.* **Noŋor ondiek supwáspwa**: The woman is too fat; *Meri i pat nogut tru.*

andɨr *n.* cat's cradle; *pilai bilong rop ol mangi i save mekim.*

andŋan *adj.* raw, bloody (*lit.* 'has blood'); *i gat blut.*

androp *n.* thin white and green sugar cane; *suga i waitpela na grinpela na i no bikpela.*

andru-(w/p)-e *v.t.* (class 2), carry something on head; *karim long het.* **Mopokyi maniŋg andrupekun**: Mopok carried the bucket on her head; *Mopok karim baket long hed.*

andruku *v.i.* (group IIa intransitive verb: **ŋɨ kanduriet; ŋgu onduriek; yum kandɨkrem; ŋgɨ ŋgonduriek**), yelp, exclaim; *singaut.*

andu *v.t.* (class 3), **1.** follow a path; *bihainim rot.* **Ŋgu ewar ndereke aŋgo ondukuna wok**: Yesterday she followed this path; *Asde em i bihainim rot i go.*
2. gather leaf vegetables; *kisim tulip o aibika.*
3. roof a house; *pasim wanpela haus.* **Yim patɨr kandukun**: We roofed the house; *Mipela i pasim haus.*
4. follow someone else's advice; *bihainim tok bilong narapela man o meri.* **Ŋa ŋan nam kandukuna mbot**: I followed his talk and went; *Mi bihainim tok bilong em na mi go.*

andugur *v.t.* (class 4), **1.** squeeze out something, e.g. a boil, a banana, grated coconut; *bengim*; **Pap andugrɨtukun!** Squeeze the water out of the grated cocount! *Bengim kokonas!*
2. tie together the two sides of sago palm thatch on roof of a house at the top post running across the house; **Eirumŋa kokɨr kokarku andugrɨnkurem!** Close the roof of the house!; *Bungim hed bilong marota na pasim wantaim.*

andugur *v.t.* (conjugated like **ŋgur**) pump something; *pamim.*

ani *interrog.* (*pl.* **aniŋgro**), who?; *husat?*

animat *interrog.* whose?; *bilong husat?*

anire *interrog.* with whom?; *wantaim husat?*

aninde *dx. masc.* there, a bit further from speaker; *em ia, samting i no stap klostu tumas long husat i toktok i stap.*

aninɨ *n.* there, long hap; **Aninɨ ŋgrɨtukun**: Put it there; *Putim long hap*

aninɨnde *dx. masc.* over there, far away from speaker; *em ia long hap, samting i no stap klostu tumas long husat i toktok i stap.*

anomb *n.* **1.** groin; *sangana.* **Anombŋa pupur**: pubic hair; *gras bilong sem.*
2. lower belly; *hap bel man i save pilim pispis long en.*

anombi *temp.* later, afterwards; *bihain.* Cannot be used when narrating past events (there one would use **nunuk**); can only be used in present to designate a future occurrence. In addition, **anombi** highlights that the future action will be performed by the speaker(s) him/herself or themselves; *I no nap usim despela hap tok taim yu laik toktok long wanpela samting i bin kamap long asde o long taim bipo – yu laik toktok long taim bipo yu mas tok* **nunuk**. *Na tu* **anombi** *i miningim olsem husat man o meri yu toktok long en em yet bai mekim samting.* **Anombi ŋgu aikitaka namrutak**: Later on she herself will come and tell you; *Larim em yet bai kam tokim yu.*

antur *n.* human-like beings that look after particular areas of land. These beings are like **emári**, but less powerful, and they live on the ground and not in the water. The two most well-known in Gapun materialize in a two-headed snake, each head of which has a name, **Tareŋgéna** and **Matáŋgena**; *ol liklik masalai bilong graun, long Gapun olgeta i save long* **Tareŋgéna** *na* **Matáŋgena**, *em snek i gat tupela hed.*

anturŋa kandaw *n.* illness caused by **antur**, *sik ol* **antur** *i save giving long man.*

anumb *n.* sago palm with long fronds that are often used to make **iko** (funnel for leaching sago). It has short leaves, short needles and a very wide trunk. It produces a great deal of sago flour. *Saksak i gat ol bikpela pangal ol meri i save usim long wokim iko. Lip bilong em sotpela, i gat sotpela nil na namel bilong em bikpela. I gat bikpela muna.*

aŋ *v.t.* (class 3), pump something; *pulim.* **Awin kaŋkundara**: I pumped water; *mi pulim wara pinis.*

aŋgamgu-(p/w)-uku *v.i.* (**aŋgamgupuwot/aŋgamgupuwok**), bump into, collide with; *bamp. Balni emrarikar wokeya aŋgamgupukeya odiwoke*: The two men were playing soccer and they bumped into one another and fell down; *Tupela i pilai soka i stap na tupela i bamp na pundaun*; **Nim mbwar nderni wapakini otiteka wukŋa ŋi rarkru wákare mbota aŋgamŋgupuwota adimbot**: He didn't see the tree trunk that was lying across the path and he bumped into it and tripped; *Em i no lukim diwai i stap long rot na em wakabaut i go na em bamp long em na em pundaun.*

aŋge(de) *dx. pl. obj.* those, a bit further from speaker, *em ia, ol samting i no stap klostu long husat i wok long toktok i stap.*

aŋgeb *dx. pl.* these or those; *despela ol.* **Aŋgeb nje sene:** Those two dogs; *Despela tupela dok ia.*

aŋgi(de) *dx. fem. obj.* here, further from speaker, *em ia, samting i no stap klostu long husat i wok long toktok i stap.*

aŋgisukup *temp.* seven days from now; *i go inap sevenpela de.*

aŋgib *dx. pl.* those; *despela ol.*

aŋgo(de) *dx. fem.* here, close to speaker; *em ia, samting i stap klostu long husat i toktok i stap.*

aŋgok *dx. fem.* that; *despela.*

aŋgu *v.t.* (class 3), **1.** pull something; *pulim.* **2.** drag something; *pulim.* **Miŋgip aŋgo odiekŋan aŋgukwar kukumbot**: He dragged along his swollen knee and came; *Skru bilong lek i solap na em i pulim em na i kam.* **3.** dry something, absorb liquid from something; *draim wara o pulim wara long wanpela samting.* **Ŋgigi awin oŋgukuro**: They dried it; *ol i draim pinis.*

aŋgu(de) *dx. fem.* there, a long way from speaker; *em ia, samting i stap longwe liklik long husat i toktok i stap.*

aŋgudek *dx. fem.* that; *despela.*

aŋguraji *v.t.* (class 5), lure someone further on, e.g. further and further into the forest or up a tree; *grisim man i kam.*

aŋgurak *v.t. irr.* (class 5), throw something; *troimwe.* This verb can be inflected like a class 5 verb, but it is usually part of a complex construction. In such a construction, some speakers segment the final -ak as a dependent verb object and inflect it; others segment it as a fixed part of the verb and do not inflect it. **Ŋguyi aram aŋguraktiŋgen** (some speakers say **aŋgurattiŋgen**): She threw the snake away from her; *Em troimwe snek.* **Ror ainde nimŋat aŋgurakrukwankut**: That child is throwing a stick; *Pikinini ia i sut long hap diwai i stap.* **Kinda aŋgurakwe!:** Throw the tongs over here! *Troimwe kinda i kam!*

aŋgwar *n.* a kind of lethal sorcery carried out in the following way: a victim is ambushed in the rainforest by sorcerers who have often disguised themselves as flying foxes (**njakep**) or birds such as eagles (**kakar pwap**) or hornbills (**ondom**). These sorcerers hypnotize the victim, then disembowel him or her and replace the vital organs with leaves. They then resurrect the victim and whisper in his/her ear the exact time when he or she will die. Unaware of what has happened, the victim carries on his or her daily life, only to collapse and die at the time appointed by the sorcerers; *sanguma.*

aŋgwar munje *n.* man who enacts **aŋgwar**; *sanguma man.*

apik *v.t.* (class 5), open mouth in a yawn ; *opim maus long taim skin bilong yu i les*. **Ŋgu sik apiktukun**: She yawned (*lit.* 'she yawned mouth'); *Skin bilong em les na em opim nating maus*.

apirit *n.* waistbelt made from thread from a **pandim** tree; *let bilong ol tumbuna, ol i save wokim long* **pandim**.

apran *n.* poor thing, used when someone performs an act that one doesn't believe he or she had been capable of doing; *tarangu*. **Apran kawrikneta mborŋa pisikimb urakukumbet numni**: The poor thing summoned his strength and carried the pig back to the village; *Tarangu em i strong na kisim pik i kam long ples*.

apro *adj.* bad, *nogut, rabis*.

apro mir *intens.* really, incredibly; *nogut tru*. **Arawer mik apro mir**: The sun is incredibly intense; *San i hot nogut tru*.

apro sakar *vulgar intens.* (*pl.* **apri sakrem** (*obsolete*)), fucking; *blari pakin*. **Tokinema manŋa ŋgwab sawir manŋa apro sakar!**: Catfish cunt, fucking black hole cunt!; *Kan bilong yu i olsem wanpela bikmaus pis blari pakin bilakhul kan!*; **Mayama man kakunŋa apro sakar!**: Fucking eater of your mother's cunt! *Bastad kaikai kan bilong mama bilong yu!*

apu *v.t.* (class 3), **1.** burn something; *kukim*.
2. cook something by putting directly on fire or embers; *kukim long paia*.

apukor (also **akukor**) *n.* elves, little men and women of the forest who can capture the spirit (**mbunor**) of people who die. They can also capture the spirit of living people, who in that case soon die. They live in the tops of trees deep in the rainforest where people seldom travel. People know of their existence because the **apukor** whistle when they walk about; *ol liklik man i save kisim devil bilong ol sampela man long taim bilong indai. Ol i ken kisim devil bilong husat man i gat sik. Ol i kisim devil bilong yu long nait, moning bai yu pinis na devil bilong yu bai stap wantaim ol*.

apwisom *n.* fan; *win bilong winim paia*.

ar *v.t.* (class 3), **1.** chop down something; *katim i pundaun*. **Ŋgigi nim orkuro**: She chopped down the tree; *Em katim diwai i pundaun*.
2. marry someone; *maritim*. **Ŋguyi ŋi orŋgin**: She married him; *em (meri) maritim em (man)*; **Ŋiŋi ŋgu karkun**. He married her; *em (man) maritim em (meri)*.
3. emit urine; *pispis*. **Ŋgu nok orkun**: She urinated; *Em pispis*.
4. emit feces; *pekpek*. **Ŋi yiwir karkun**: He defecated; *Em pekpek*.
5. shave something; *sebim*. **Ŋi ŋgakreŋa purpur karkun**: He shaved his beard; *Em sebim mausgras bilong em*.

aram *n.* snake (*generic*); *snek (biknem)*.

arambwar *n.* small snake; *liklik snek*.

aramŋgor *n.* long, python-like snake; *draipela snek*.

aranj-(p)-e *v.t.* (class 1): singe leaves to make them pliable; *boinim*. See also **aianj-(p)-e**.

arawer *n.* **1.** sun; *san*.
2. a kind of small blue beetle with black markings; *liklik blupela binatang i gat ol bilakpela makmak*.

arawer sirŋgar taw *n.* west (*lit.* 'sun goes down side'); *hap san i save godaun long en*.

arawer wiŋgar taw *n.* east (*lit.* 'sun rising side'); *hap san i save kam antap long en*.

arei *n.* **1.** ginger root eaten to make a person angry and eager to fight; *kawawar bilong hatim bel*.
2. desire; *laik*. **Ŋa arei tari wákare, sisipot**: I had no desire (*lit.* 'desire didn't take me'), I was tired; *Laik i no kisim mi, mi les*; **Arei sumani tatin mum akrunana**: I have a huge desire to eat sago jelly; *Mi gat bikpela laik long kaikai* **mum**.

areini *adv.* quickly, hurriedly; *hariap*. **Yu ŋa areini namgarke**: Don't hurry me (*lit.* 'Don't tell me to hurry up'); *Yu no ken hariapim mi*.

areŋg *n.* a kind of tree from which floor supports are cut; *diwai ol i save katim long wokim* **tékduan**.

ari *pos.* below; *taunbolo.*

arik *intens.* really; *tru.* Can only be used with the word for 'little', 'small'; *taim yu laik tok olsem samting i liklik tru bai yu usim despela hap tok.* **Mokop arik aŋgo yu piatan:** You gave me a really small piece; *Yu givim mi liklik hap tru.*

arimb *n.* exhaustion; *bikpela les.* **Arimbi nitin:** I am exhausted (*lit.* 'exhaustion makes/does me'); *Bikpela les i mekim mi.*

ario *interj.* word used to scare small children into thinking that something is coming to get them. Uttered as a loud vocative to some threatening person or thing (a spirit, a pig), the word means 'Come now, come and get him/her'; *hap tok ol mama i save usim long mekim pret ol liklik pikinini.*

arimindai *n.* a betel nut with a watery nut; *buai i no mit tumas, mit bilong em i gat wara.*

ariŋgadew *n.* plant with large round leaves, put into sago jelly and fed to dogs, in order to get them to kill cassowaries; *diwai i gat bikpela raunpela lip, ol tumbuna i save tainim mum wantaim despela na givim long ol dok, bai ol i kaikai na kisim strong long kilim muruk.* See also **pap.**

arit *n.* **1.** saliva drooling from mouth, or slime from a vegetable like **ŋgat**; *spet i pundaun long maus o spet bilong aibika.*
  2. wing; *win.*
  3. part of a house: the **kotiw** that extends on from where the roof meets the walls of the house; *win bilong haus.*

ariuta *adv.* quietly, without noise or fuss; *isi, nogat kros.* **Ariutaki orak isiatan!**: Give it to me without making a fuss!; *Givim samting long mi long isipela we, i no ken kros.*

ariw *n.* spear thrower made of bamboo; *hap mambu bilong troimwe spia.*

arkar-(p)-eki *v.i.* (**arkarpet/arkarpek; ŋgi arkarpeko**): have a fever, a chill; *skin i kol.* **Toto arkarpek kadawi niritakana.** My skin is cold, I'm going to be sick; *Skin bilong mi kol, bai mi sik ia.*

arki *v.i.* (group IIa intransitive verb: **ŋa kariet/ kariek; yu kariet/kariek; ŋi kariet; ŋgu oriek; yim kariek; yum karikem; ŋgi ŋgoriek; yim sene orke**), **1.** go down by means of a waterway, e.g. to a village downriver; *godaun*; **Ewar ŋgi Moipre ŋgoriek:** Yesterday they went down to Watam; *Asde ol i godaun long Watam.*
  2. go inside; *go insait.* **Yim ewar Onai karieka prukŋa pin ninkun.** Yesterday we went inside the forest to Onai and did a bit of work; *Asde mipela i go insait long Onai na wokim liklik wok.*

arki *v.i. irr.* (**ŋa karot/karok; yu karot/karok; ŋi karot; ŋgu urok; yim karok; yum karkem; ŋgi ŋgurok; yim sene urke**), go inside, for example inside a mosquito net; *go insait, olsem long karambu.* **Ewar rorsem ewandni ŋguroka sapki sapki tako:** Last night the kids went into the mosquito net and slept all over the place; *Asde ol pikinini i go insait long karambu na ol i slip nambaut.*

arki *v.i. irr.* (**ŋa krit/krik; yu krit/krik; ŋi krit; ŋgu uruk; yim krik; yum krikem; ŋgi ŋguruk; yim sene uruke**), remain; *stap longpela taim.* **Ŋi mbota ŋan numni kritapi mbet:** He went and remained in his village a long time, then he came back; *Em i go istap longpela taim long ples bilong em, na em i kam.*

armbir *adj.* **1.** hot; *hat, hatpela.*
  2. *n.* heat, *hot.* **Armbir wuk ŋgon totoŋa, ŋgure minjikan aŋgwarke:** Heat is on her skin, you can't go close to her (i.e. heat generated a woman's blood, harmful and debilitating to everyone, but especially to men); *Hot i stap long skin bilong meri, i no ken go klostu long em.* See also **samba.**

aro 1. *n.* light; *lait*; **Arawerŋa aro:** Sunlight; *Lait bilong san.*
  2. day; *de.* **Arore arore ambukeni nirakut?** Every single day what is it you'll do?; *Olgeta de yu bai mekim olsem wanem?*
  3. *pos.* inside, enveloped in or covered by; *insait*; **aroŋa nam:** hidden, unexpressed talk; *insait tok.*

aroŋ-(p)-e *v.t.* (class 1), carry something inside an object such as a bag or a basket; *karim insait long wanpela samting olsem wanpela bilum o basket.*

aru *n.* ancient ancestor; *tumbuna bilong bipo bipo tru.* **Rɨpɨm ŋa arumandama tɨk tareŋgar wákare. Ene awoiŋgud ŋaŋan ŋgi tɨk ŋgurkwaŋgukre ŋa tankun.** Previously I didn't hear the stories of the ancestors. But my mother's brothers told them often and now I know them; *Bipo mi no save harim ol stori bilong ol tumbuna bilong bipo. Tasol ol kandere bilong mi i save stori na nau mi save pinis.*

aru-(p)-oi *v.t.* (class 1), wait for something or someone; *wetim.* **Ŋa yu aruoiakkut:** I'm waiting for you; *Mi wetim yu i stap.*

aruat *n.* thunder, *pairap bilong ren.*

arúmbatak *n.* fly, *rang.*

arúmbatak kunemb *n.* a kind of small bee; *liklik bi.*

arúmbatak wasow *n.* blue fly (*lit.* 'fly death'); *blurang.*

aru-(p)-okɨ *v.i. irr.* (**ŋa arupot/arupok; ŋɨ arupot; ŋgu arupok; yum arupokem; yim arupok; ŋgi arupoko; yim sene arupoke**), wait; *wet.*

asak-(p)-e *v.t.* (class 1), hop over something; *kalapim. Bal i* **nuwomb asakpekuna taw nonnɨ otɨtek**: The ball hopped over the creek and landed on the other side; *Bal i kalapim baret na pundaun long narapela sait.*

asáŋgo *n.* a tree whose leaves, which are red veined on the underside, are boiled and used to dye string and rope red; *diwai i gat lip na long baksait bilong despela lip i gat ol redpela rop. Boilim despela ol lip bai wara i kamap redpela, na despela wara ol manmeri save usim long putim redpela kala long ol samting bilong wokim pulpul o basket.*

asapoi *n.* close friend; *poro.*

ase *pos.* beside, on the edge of, on the periphery of; *klostu, long pron.*

askɨ *v.i.* (**ŋa kaset/kasek; yu kaset/kasek; ŋɨ kaset; ŋgu usek; yim kasek; yum kaskem; ŋgi ŋgusek; yim sene uske**), 1. come down from a place upstream to a place nearer the sea; *ikam daun, olsem yu stap long Sambaiag na yu kam daun long ples Gapun.*
2. appear, come outside, e.g. from inside the rainforest to outside on a path; *kam autsait.*

at *n.* 1. mosquito (*generic*), *natnat (biknem).*
2. half, part of; *hap.* **Nimŋat:** stick; *hap diwai.* **Tamwaiŋat:** bit of a sago pancake; *hap praim;* **At kut:** He's still alive (*lit.* 'half is there'); *Em i gat laip yet, i no indai.*

atarum *n.* forehead; *poret.*

atawo[†] *n.* (*dl.* **atawondodi**; *pl.* **atawondodo**) (*obsolete*), older sibling; *bikpela brata o susa.* See also **tata**.

atemb *n.* small tree python, can be yellow, green or brown; the one kind of snake that villagers used to eat; *snek bilong diwai, i gat yelopela, grinpela, braunpela. Bipo ol man i save kaikai.*

átiáti *n.* sudden intake of breath characteristic of babies. This is a sign that they are growing stronger and their liver is gaining strength; *liklik win ol nupela pikinini i save pulim long en, ol i wok long kisim strong, strongim lewa bilong ol.*

atiatir *v.t.* (class 4), hurry someone up; *hariapim narapela man.* **Atiatitiŋen!** Make him go faster! *Hariapim em!*

atikɨ *v.i.* (**ŋa katɨtet/katiek; yu katɨtet/katɨtek; ŋɨ katɨtet, ŋgu otɨtek; yim katɨtek; yum katikem; ŋgi ŋgotɨtek; yim sene otike**), 1. fall down; *pundaun.*
2. be completely without something; *lus long wanpela samting.* **Ŋa nda katɨtet, orak aŋgar wákare ŋayar.** I'm completely without anything, I really have no food; *Mi pundaun nau, mi nogat wanpela kaikai, nogat tru.*
3. be defeated; lose, *i no win;* **Yim katɨtek**: We lost [the soccer match]; *Mipela i no win [long soka], ol i winim mipela.*

atikɨ *v.i.* (**ŋa katot/ŋa katok; yu katot/yu katok; ŋɨ katot; ŋgu utok; yim katok;**

yum katikem; ŋgi ŋgutok; yim sene utike), 1. happen; *kamap*; **Nekan katot**: An earthquake happened (i.e. there was an earthquake); *Graun i guria*.
2. go outside; *igo autsait*.
3. go down; *igo daun*. **Ewar yim Potowre katok**: Yesterday we went down to Wongan; *Asde mipela i godaun long Wongan*.

atim *n.* spike made of bamboo that villagers insert into the ground in front of betel nut palms or other areas they want others to stay away from. If one steps on these spikes, they go up into the foot, causing injury and pain; *nil long mambu, ol manmeri i save haitim long as bilong buai o long ol rot ol i tambuim ol long en. Nogut husat i brukim despela tambu krungutim despela ol nil. Man i krungutim bai kisim bikpela pen*. See also **mandamandap**.

atir *n.* caterpillar; *binatang i save kamapim bataplai*.

ato *n.* 1. outside; *autsait*. **Atoŋa nam**: talk that is out in the open; *autsait tok*.
2. *dir*. down in the sense of downstream; *taunbolo*.

atokrim *n.* carbuncle; *strongpela skin long bel bilong leg, i save pen*.

ator-(p)-orki *v.i.* (**atorporiet/atorporiek**), appear in patches (used to describe e.g. rashes, mushrooms); *kamap nambaut (olsem bukbuk long skin, na ol talinga)*.

atunuŋ *n.* tree whose inner bark is processed to make basket slings and the fringed decorations on the sides of baskets; *diwai ol meri i save wokim long mekim ol han bilong basket na ol bilas bilong basket*.

atuŋgor *adj.* brown coat of animals; *kala bilong gras bilong ol pik o ol sampela narapela ol animol*.

awa *mood part.* word expressing expectation; *hap tok bilong tok olsem yu wetim wanpela samting*. **Ŋgu awa borsip tandiu pipiek?** Is the pork cooked well?; *Hap abus i tan ah?* **Ndamor awa?**: It must be Ndamor; *Nogut Ndamor*. See Section 7.6.1 of the grammar.

awaŋ *n.* owl; *taragau bilong nait* (*Birds of New Guinea* plate 26, #1–10 and #17–18). Villagers believe owls, which they say have the faces of men, to be the spirits of the dead, and they fear them accordingly. A favorite way of scaring a small child into submission is to point into the distance, clutch the child closer as though protecting him or her, and say urgently, "**Awaŋ**! **Awaŋ**! **Awaŋ** *i kam nau. Ye, lukim ai bilong em, em i kam nau!*" (Owl! Owl! The owl is coming! Ye look at its eyes, it's coming!)

awa-(p/w)-ar *v.t.* (class 4), be jealous about someone; *jelesim*. **Mbumeyi ŋgon omin awaparŋgin**. Mbume is jealous about her husband; i.e. she worries that he has affairs; *Mbume jelesim man bilong em*. See also **mwanambrir**.

awar *n.* wind from the swamp and the Sepik river, i.e. from the north; *win i kamap long tais na long Sepik wara*.

awar-(p)-e *v.t.* (class 1), decline to avenge someone's transgression, for example a person steals something from you and you do nothing about it; *ol manmeri i rongim yu, na yu no krosim ol o bekim*. **Ŋgigi ŋaŋan minjike ndagúni tatukrora, ŋayi ŋgi awarpembin**: They stole my betel nut and I did nothing to avenge the theft; *Ol i stilim buai bilong mi na mi no krosim ol o bekim bek rong bilong ol*.

awawarŋgar morasi *n.* jealousy (lit. 'jealous habit'); *jeles pasin*.

awesak *n.* fern (generic), *kumugras (biknem)*.

awin awin *adj.* watery, runny (lit. 'water water'); *i gat wara*. **Mum awin awin**: The sago jelly is runny; *saksak i wara wara*.

awin eiwir *n.* high tide; *haiwara*.

awin kapur *n.* well; *hulwara*.

awin *n.* 1. water; *wara*
2. liquid; *olsem wara*.
3. alcohol; *yawa*. **Awin okroya ŋar aŋgide nirkwanguk**: They've drunk alcohol and now they're making a lot of noise; *Ol i dring yawa na ol i wok long singaut i stap*.

4. a kind of tree like the **ŋgawro** tree, with very long leaves; *kain diwai olsem* **ŋgawro** *i gat longpela longpela lip.*

awin nanuk *n.* 1. reflection (*lit.* 'water face'); *piksa bilong pes i save kamap long wara o long wanpela glas bilong lukluk.*
2. mirror; *glas bilong lukluk.*
3. eyeglasses; *aiglas.*

awin ŋgorok *n.* traditional grass skirt covering the entire leg that was worn when women went into the water to fish, and also during mourning; *longpela pulpul ol meri bilong bipo i save putim long taim bilong ol long go insait long wara long umbenim pis. Na tu ol i save putim taim man indai na ol i save stap insait long banis.* See also **ŋgorok**.

awin pomɨŋ *n.* water energized by calling on the spirits of the dead, and then dipping the fingers of everyone present into it, then it will be spit into a circle; *wanbel wara.*

awin potaki *v.i.* be thirsty (*lit.* 'water throat + ERG.F'). A fixed verbal construction that remains the same regardless of pronoun or temporality, so **Ŋa awin potaki** (1SG + water + throat + ERG.F) means 'I am/was/will be thirsty'. **Yu awin potaki** (2SG + water + throat + ERG.F) means 'You are/was/will be thirsty', etc.; *laik dring.* **Ŋgɨ awin potaki**: They are thirsty; *Ol i laik dring.* See also **potak**.

awin tuwku *v.i.* (**-net/-nak**), give birth (*lit.* 'water bathe'); *karim.* **Yu mbadanɨ okɨtak awin tuwkutak ŋa yunɨ prukkɨnakana ɨnda**: You will go into the bush and give birth and I will have to work hard for you; *Yu bai go long bus na karim na mi bai wokhat long yu ia.* See also **tuwku**.

awin(nɨ) tuwŋgar patɨr *n.* maternity house (*lit.* 'water-bathing house'); *haus karim.*

awinnɨ tuwku *v.i.* (**-iet/-iek**), give birth; *karim.* **Ŋgu awinnɨ tutiekara?**: Has she given birth? *Em karim pinis?*

awinŋa naŋgatɨk *n.* tide; *tait.* **Awinŋa naŋgatɨki yimbar kukupuwok**: The tide lifted the canoe; *Tait i kisim kanu i go antap.*

awin *n.* Great-billed Heron (*Birds of New Guinea* plate 3, #3) and Egret (plate 3, #6–15).

awo *interj.* 1. expression of affirmation. Since the 1980s, this Tayap word has increasingly become replaced by the Kopar-language word **ore**. Now **awo** is most commonly used as an exaggerated or sarcastic affirmative, meaning something like "Yeah, right" or "Like I'm so sure"; *em tasol, em trupela, em nau.*
2. *emph.* when suddenly shouted, not in response to a question, the meaning is: I'm coming to hit you now; *Bai mi kam paitim yu nau.*

awoi† *n.* mother's brother; *kandere* (*obsolete*). See also **wow**.

ayáta *interj.* 1. never mind; *maski.* **Ayáta yu kandawŋan, memteta otet**: Never mind that you are sick, get up and go; *Maski yu sik, kirap na i go.*
2. *excl.* stop it; *inap.* **Ayáta!**: Stop it! *Inap!*
3. *excl.* forget it; *maski.*
4. *excl.* don't worry about it; *maski.*

D

du *n.* [*Adjora*], coil; *hip.* **Aramŋa du**: coiled up snake; *snek i hip i stap*; **Sokoi(ŋa) du**: cigarette (i.e. a rolled up piece of paper with tobacco in it); *smok.* In Tayap one would say: **Aram ambnor ŋgunkuna kut**: The snake is coiled up; *Snek i raunim em yet na istap.*

E

e *v.t.* (class 1), **1.** hold something or someone; *holim*; **Ndaram enkurem:** You all shake hands; *Yupela sekhan nau*.
  2. net fish; *umbenim pis*. **Ŋguyi ŋgomar sami pekun:** She netted a lot of fish; *Meri i kisim planti pis*.
  3. (*euphemism*), have sex with someone; *kwapim (tok bokis)*. **Ŋiŋi Mborakema noŋor pekun:** He had sex with Mborake's wife; *Em kwapim meri bilong Mborake*.

ei *n.* tearful cry; *krai*.

ei *v.t.* (class 1), **1.** peel something, e.g. bark from sago tree, the husk from a betel nut; *tekewe olsem skin bilong saksak o skin bilong buai*.
  2. scrape skin; *tekewe hap skin*. **Ŋa katiteta, toto peikun:** I fell and scraped my skin; *Mi pundaun na skin bilong mi tekewe*.
  3. wank, i.e. expose the glans penis or the inside of one's vagina; *skinim kok o skinim kan*. **Ŋi toto peikunŋan inde:** He's a wanker; *Em i save sikinim kok tasol*.
  4. skin an animal e.g. a lizard (**ŋgararik**) or cuscus (**enamb**); *tekewe sin bilong wanpela palai o kapul*.

eiakatiki *v.i.* (conjugated like **atiki**), pull away; *pulim na rausim*. **Otaka top aŋgi papŋa mbwareke puwokŋa eiakatetak maŋar utakkukuwe:** You go and pull away the betel ginger that is growing up the middle of the coconut palm and cut it and bring it; *Yu go na daka ia i go antap long namel long kokoas ia yu rausim na katim lip bilong em na ikam*.

eiamb *n.* large cluster of betel nut; *bikpela rop buai*. See also **aiamb**.

eiarki *v.i.* (**-net/-nak**), cry, *krai*.

eiki *v.i.* (**peiet/peiek**), **1.** become clear; *kamap klia*. **Ikur mit wuk aŋgo akin eiki wákare:** It's really dark, the sky isn't clear; *Bikpela tudak istap na klaut i no klia yet*.
  2. peel off, e.g. after a severe burn; *tekewe*. **Ngon toto eieira wok:** Her skin peeled off; *Skin bilong em tekewe*.
  3. wank (a calque of the Tok Pisin *sikinim kok/kan*, which means 'rub your prick/ cunt skinless'); *tekewe*. **Kwemŋa toto peiekŋa:** Wanker; *Skin bilong kok i tekewe long en*. See also **wetiki**.

eikuoki *v.i.* (conjugated like **oki**), pay no attention; *i no tingim, lusim*. **Ŋi ŋaŋan nam tankun, eikuwok:** He heard my talk and ignored it; *Em harim tok bilong mi tasol em i no bihainim, em lusim nating*. See also **utak**

eiro *n.* Paradise Kingfisher (*Birds of New Guinea* plate 24, #1–5).

eirum *n.* sago leaf shingle; *morota*.

eirumŋat kokir o *v.t.* exchange siblings in marriage (lit. 'pierce the head of sago palm leaf shingle'); *sens marit*. **Yim eirumŋat kokir pokure:** We are the exchanges for our siblings; *Mitupela i sens marit*. Refers to the Gapun tradition of exchanging males and females between groups so that when man A from one clan marries a woman B from another, a man C from the woman B's clan should marry man A's real or classificatory sister.

eitatiki *v.i.* (conjugated like **atiki**), peek, *stil lukluk*. **Ngogrodak eitatikar puwok aŋgi:** The frog is peeking around; *Prok i stil lukluk i go antap*; **Ŋi eitatikar rariar mbet:** He's following me and peeking at me; *Em bihainim mi na em stil lukluk long mi*.

eiwa *n.* a kind of sickness in which the stomach swells up and the body becomes emaciated; *splin*.

eiwir *adj.* **1.** young (referring to people). There is a plural form, **eiwiró**, but it is used only in reference to people, it cannot be used in speaking about fruit or trees; *yangpela (taim yu toktok long ol manmeri)*.
  2. unripe (referring to fruit or trees); *i no mau (taim yu toktok long ol laulau o popo o wanem samting bilong kaikai)*.

eiwireiwir *n.* immature, stupid act, as when a child defecates under the house even though he or she is old enough to go into the bush to defecate; *longlong, olsem pikinini i pekpek ananeat long haus taim em i kamap bikpela liklik na em i save go long long bus long wokim pekpek bilong em.*

eiwki *v.i.* (**peiwiet/peiwiek, ŋgi peiwko**), wash sago pith; *wasim saksak.*

eiwŋgar yimbar *n.* small canoe used since the 1990s to capture the water and sago flour that runs out from the **waris** (cocount fiber strainer) when women leach sago pith; *kanu bilong wasim pipia saksak.*

egon *adj.* reduced form **eŋgon**

ekop *n.* a hopscotch-like children's game; *wanpela kain pilai bilong ol pikinini.*

ekruka *v.i.* (conjugated like **a** 'be'; also pronounced **ikruka**), walk around; *wakabaut.* **Ŋa patirre patirre ekrukaŋwar noŋor wákare:** I'm not a woman who walks around visiting people (to gossip); *Mi no meri bilong raun raun nating long olgeta haus.*

emári *n.* **1.** powerful ancestral spirit of the rainforest, lives in rivers, swamps, large creeks and lakes; *masalai.*
  2. bone made of cassowary thighbone inserted through the septums of men in traditional times; *bun bilong muruk ol tumbuna man i save putim long hul long nus bilong ol.*

emárima ŋgino *n.* round scales on a crocodile near its head, these are eyes it uses to see underwater (*lit.* '**emári**'s eyes'); *ai bilong ol pukpuk ol i save lukluk long ol aninit long wara.*

emb *n.* morning; *moning.* **Embegon:** Good morning; *Gutpela moning.* **Note: egon** is a reduced form of **eŋgon**, 'good'.

emb *v.t.* (class 5), wave something away; *rausim.* **Arumbatak embtimbin!:** Wave away the flies! *Rausim ol rang!*

embátoto *n.* cloth; *laplap.* This word is derived from the Kopar word for 'white' (*embar*) and the Tayap word for 'skin' (**toto**) and reflects the fact that woven cloth was introduced to Papua New Guinea by white colonizers. *Em despela haptok i miningim olsem 'waitskin'. Em ol Wongan i laik tok long wanpela samting i wait bai ol i tok 'embar', na long Tayap* **toto** *em olsem skin. Em ol waitskin man i bin kisim ol laplap i kam long Papua Niugini – bipo nogat despela samting – na ol i putim despela nem i go long samting.*

embebre *n.* almost at the break of dawn; *klostu tulait.*

emra *n.* play; *pilai.* **Yu ambinŋa emra nirkwankut?** What kind of play are you making? *Yu mekim wanem kain pilai i stap?*

emrarki *v.i.* (**-pet/-pek**), play; *pilai.*

Emuto *n.* Mabuk village; *ples Mabuk.*

enamb *n.* cuscus; *kapul.*

endekar *n.* hunger; *hangre.* **Ŋa endekari** (*lit.* 'I hunger+ERG'), I'm hungry; *Hangre i mekim mi;* **Yu endekari:** You're hungry; *Hangre i mekim yu;* **Ŋgi endekari:** They are hungry; *Hangre i mekim ol.*

endekarŋa imin *n.* empty stomach (*lit.* 'hungry stomach'); *bel i nogat kaikai long en.*

endo *n.* traditional male waistbelt made from rattan; *tumbuna let bilong pasim malo.* See also **kapwasak.**

endurama *n.* Bowerbird (*Birds of New Guinea* plate 50).

ene *n.* **1.** today; *nau, despela de.*
  2. now; *nau.*
  3. nowadays; *nau.* **Ripim ŋa Sopak rarkwankut Potore, ene wákare rarkru:** Before, I used to see Sopak in Wongan, but now I don't anymore; *Bipo mi save lukim Sopak long Wonag, nau nogat.*

eno *n.* [*Kopar*], creek; *baret.*

eŋgeweŋgew *v.t.* (class 5), **1.** fondle something; *holim holim.* **Ŋi noŋor aŋgukma min eŋgeweŋgewnukwatan:** He was fondling that woman's breasts; *Em i holim holim susu bilong mer ia.*
  2. tickle; *holim sait bilong bel na mekim lap i kamap.* **Iminŋa taw eŋgeweŋgewŋagrke!** Don't tickle me! *I no ken holim holim sait bilong mi!*

eŋgin 1. *adj.* white, as pertaining to white people; *waitpela i miningim olsem ol waitman*. **eŋgin munje**: white man; *waitskin man*; **eŋginmandama morasi**: the habits and ways of white people; *pasin bilong ol waitskin man na meri*.
2. *n.* mythical founding ancestor; *kuskus*.
3. *n.* ginger root eaten to make men aggressive and successful in fights; *kawawar bilong pait na belhat*.

Eŋgin mer *n.* Tok Pisin (*lit.* 'white language'); *Tok Pisin*.

eŋginmandama mbatambur *n.* papaya (*lit.* 'white man's breadfruit'), *pawpaw*.

eŋgon (sometimes shorted to **egon**) **1.** *adj.* good, *gutpela*. **Ikur eŋgon**: Good evening; *Gutpela apinun*. **Emb egon**: Good morning; *Gutpela moning*.
2. *adj.* healthy, well; *gutpela*. **Ŋa eŋgon wákare**: I am not in good health; *Mi no gutpela*.
3. *n.* right (opposite of left), *i no kais, gutpela*; **Akan eŋgon**: right hand; *gutpela han, han sut*; **Ndow eŋgon**: right leg; *gutpela lek*; **Akan eŋgonŋa taw**: right hand side; *sait bilong gutpela han*. Compare **ŋgamgit**.

eŋgune eŋgune *n.* flattery, cajoling, persuasion; *gris*. **Epi aŋgi eŋgune eŋgune ŋgɨrgatinet**: Tomorrow I'm going to try to persuade him (through flattery and cajoling); *Tumoro bai mi grisim em*.

eŋguramat *n.* a spicy, chili-like leaf that men chew after they have performed various rituals to strengthen and heat up their bodies; *wanpela kawawar bilong ol man i save kaikai long strongim na hotim bodi bilong ol*.

eŋki[†] *n.* (*pl.* **eŋkindodo**), [*possibly Adjora*] (*obsolete*), husband of maternal aunts and nieces (male speaking); *man bilong kandere meri*.

ep *n.* long necklace of shells; *bilas, bis bilong ol liklik kina*.

ep *v.t.* (class 5), **1.** return an object; *bekim bek*.
2. give something in exchange for an object or service; *bekim*. **Ŋigi mbor epiati wákare**: They haven't given me anything in exchange for my pig; *Ol i no bekim pik bilong mi*.
3. respond to a letter, a threat or an insinuation; *bekim wanpela pas o bekim toktok o maus bilong narapela*. **Yu ambinana ŋgon sik eptukwatan?**: Why did you respond to her shouts by arguing back? (*lit.* 'why did you answer her mouth?'); *Yu bilong wanem bekim maus bilong em?* See also **sik ep**.

epi *n.* tomorrow; *tumaro*.

epɨŋgar *n.* **1.** a returned object or favor; *bekim*.
2. a thing given in exchange for something that one has already received; *bekim*. **Epɨŋgar ŋan ŋayi rarkru wákare**: I haven't received the thing he should have given me in exchange for what I gave him; *Mi no lukim bekim bilong em*.

eporaŋ *n.* **1.** large clam found in mangrove; *bikpela kina ol meri save kisim long mangoro*.
2. (*euphemism*) vagina; *sem bilong meri*.

epwaw *n.* a kind of grass that has a pleasant smell and is used to decorate armbands or necklaces; *gras i gat gutpela smel bai yu putim long ol bilas*.

er *v.t.* (class 1), **1.** tie something; *pasim*.
2. build a house; *kirapim haus*. **Yimŋi awin tuwŋgwar patɨr erkru wákare noŋor awinnɨ tuwkutakana aŋgo**: We didn't build a maternity house but the woman is going to give birth now; *Mipela i no kirapim haus karim na meri bai karim nau*.
3. braid something, e.g. hair, *pasim gras*. **Noŋor aŋgu kokɨrŋgrid perkunŋa patɨrnɨ wuk**: The woman with the braided hair is in the house; *Meri i pasim gras long en i stap long haus*.
4. fasten something, e.g. a traditional bucket made of **kondew** (sago palm sheaths); *pasim* **kondew**.
5. close something, e.g. a door; *pasim dua*.

eriŋeriŋkɨ *v.i.* (-net/-nak), rot; *sting*. **Kwem aproŋnan eriŋeriŋtakŋan, tumŋan aŋgo!** (vulgar): Bad rotten, maggot-eaten dick! *Rabis sting kok bilong yu i gat binatang!*

erɨk-(p/w) *v.t.* (class 2), agree; *pasim tok*. **Yim ewar erɨkputukun epi naw aprukru okɨnak**: Yesterday we agreed that tomorrow we would go put fire to the grassland; *Asde mipela i pasim tok olsem tumoro mipela i go kukim kunai.*

erki *v.i.* (**periet/periek; sene perke; ŋgɨ perko**), encoil, *raunim na pas wantaim olsem snek*. See also **woi**.

eroro-(p/w)-ar *v.t.* (class 2), carry in sling or in bag on back; *karim long baksait*. **Pasoyi Kiriŋ erorowarakkukuutok Potore**: Paso carried Kiriŋ on her back down to Wongan; *Paso i karim Kiriŋi godaun long Wongan*

erum *n.* leaves of several kinds of palm trees (*generic*); *morota (biknem)*. **Yamŋa erum epi utukrunaka, patɨr andukrunak**: Tomorrow we'll cut sago leaves and roof the house; *Tumaro bai yumi katim marota na pasim haus.*

erumo *n.* Fruit-Dove (*Birds of New Guinea* plate 17, all except #5).

et-(p)-o *v.t.* (class 1), imitate; *makim*. **Ŋɨ Kanako inde etoŋankut**: He is imitating Kanako; *Em makim Kanako i stap.*

ewar *n.* yesterday; *asde*.

I

i *v.t.* (class 1), **1.** give something; *givim*. **Nunuk iwatɨnet**: I'll give it to you later; *Bihain bai mi givim yu* (**Note:** when the meaning of the verb is 'give', the usual object morpheme is a BEN object morpheme; see Section 7.5 of the grammar).
2. realize something; *tingim*. **Ŋa numbwan pikunda ŋɨ ainɨ ende kut**: I realized that he is there; *Mi tingim nau em i stap long ia.*
3. emit a fart; *kapupuk*. **Kasekŋi pis pikun**: Kasek farted silently; *Kasek i kapupuk ia.*
4. (*euphemism*), hit someone; *paitim*. **Ŋa nda iwatɨnetana**: I'm gonna give it to you (i.e. hit you); *Bai mi paitim yu nau.*

ia *n.* poor thing; *tarangu*. **ŋɨ mbota ia orakaŋgar kakuna supwáspwanet**: The poor thing came and he ate the food and he fell sick; *Em i kam na tarangu i kaikai na em i kamap sik.*

iam *v.t.* (class 5), possess a skill; *save*. **Ŋɨ numŋa munjenetara, mer iamnukun, yimen aŋgwar morasi iamnukun**: He's become a villager, he knows our language and our ways; *Em i kamap pinis man bilong ples, em i save long tok ples na em i save long pasin bilong istap bilong mipela.*

iamɨr *v.i.* (-net/-nak) **1.** be sad about the loss of something; *wari*.
2. rumble (as in the sound of thunder rumbling); *paiarap*. **Aruat patorneta iamɨrneta mbot**: Thunder is rumbling; *Klaut i pairap i go.*

iapɨr *n.* fat; *gris*.

iar *v.t.* (class 5), shut someone up; *pasim maus bilong narapela*. **Ŋguyi mbioŋgi iartukuna min pikwatan**: She shut the baby up by giving it a breast (to suckle); *Em pasim maus bilong liklik bebi, em givim susu long em.*

ikɨn *n.* **1.** banana (*generic*); *banana (biknem)*
2. egg yolk; *yelopela bilong kiau.*

ikɨnŋan yandum *n.* a small, black earwig-like insect that lives in bananas (*lit.* 'banana centipede'); *liklik binatang i gat liklik kaŋgajin i save stap insait long ol rop banana.*

iko *n.* [*Kopar*], the palm leaf funnel into which the **tawar** is put to be leached and onto which the **waris** is nailed; *pangal bilong wasim pipia*. See also **ndadum**.

ikower-(p)-or *v.t.* (class 1), panicked sound pigs make when fighting or when they are speared or cornered by dogs; *singaut bilong pik taim dok i raunim em*; **Njei marŋgoni**

mbor poŋgŋina ikowerporkun. The dog hit the pig and the pig cried out; *Dok i kaikaim pik long tit na pik i singaut.*
ikruka see **ekruka**
ikur *n.* night; *tudak, nait.* **Ikur eŋgon**: Good night; *Gut nait.*
imbiki *v.i.* (**pimbiet/pimbiek**), fly; *plai.*
imikato *n.* lower intestine with feces in it, asshole; *hap bel i gat pekpek.* Frequently used in abusive language. e.g.: **Imin kato sawirŋa apro sakar!**, Fucking black asshole! *Pakin bilakpela as pekpek!*
imin i *v.t.* (class 1, this verb is **i** 'give'), impregnate someone or something (*lit.* 'give stomach'); *givim bel.* **Imin pikwatan**: He got her pregnant; *Em givim bel long em.*
imin *n.* 1. stomach, belly; *bel*
2. pregnancy; *bel.* **Ŋoŋor imin wospikun**: The woman got rid of her pregnancy (i.e. she aborted her pregnancy); *Meri i rausim bel.* **Ŋoŋor imin putukun**: The woman performed an abortion (*lit.* 'cut her pregnancy'); *meri i rausim bel.*
3. seat of emotion; *as bilong tingting.* **Ŋi imin pokembŋa munje**: He is a calm, restrained man (*lit.* 'cold-bellied man'); *Em bel isi man.*
4. apology; *tok sori.* **Imin isiŋgatan!** Tell him you're sorry (*lit.* 'Give him stomach'); *Tok sori long em.*
5. interior; *insait.* **Yimbarŋa imin**: The interior of the canoe; *Bel bilong kanu*; **Maraŋa imin**: The interior of the sea (i.e. under the surface); *Insait long solwara*; **Iminŋa nam**: hidden talk; *insait tok.*
imin sukumŋa grip *n.* umbilical cord; *rop long bel bilong ol nupela bebi, ol mama save katim em.*
iminni *pos.* inside, underneath; *insait, aninit.*
imisukum *n.* belly button; *beli batan.*
inaŋ *n.* 1. oar; *pul.* **Inaŋgŋa marit**: base of oar; *brait bilong pul*; **Inaŋgŋa marŋgop**: handle of oar; *handel bilong pul*; **Inaŋgŋa kokir**: top of oar; *hed bilong pul.*
2. shin; *bun bilong liklik lek.*

indagawr *n.* large white mosquito with a long proboscis, its bite hurts because its proboscis is splayed, not straight; *bikpela waitpela natnat. Em i gat longpela nus olsem supsup na em kaikaim yu bai yu pilim pen.*
Indam *n.* Singrin village; *ples Singrin.*
indiki *v.i.* (**pindiet/pindiek**), fuck (*vulgar*); *kwap* (*tok nogut*). **Yu pindietke mbet?** You just finished fucking and you've come here ah? *Yu kwap pinis na yu kam ah?*
indu *n.* depth, *dip.* **Ŋi patir mapitak kukupuwok, akin induni**: He's built the house too high, it's up in the clouds; *Em wokim haus i go antap tumas, em i go antap na insait long ol klaut.*
indu *v.t.* (class 1), fuck someone (*vulgar*); *kwapim* (*tok nogut*). **Ŋiŋi ŋgu pindukun**: He fucked her; *Em* (*man*) *kwapim em* (*meri*); **Ŋguyi ŋi pindigin**: She fucked him; *Em* (*meri*) *kwapim em* (*man*); **Manke pindukro yiwirgwabke pindukoya priek?** Did they all fuck your cunt or maybe your asshole before you arrived? *Ol i kwapim kan bilong yu o hulpekpek bilong yu na yu kam, ah?* **Maya pindukroŋan**: Mother fuckers! *Ol i save kwapim mama bilong ol!*
indurek-(p)-e *v.t.* (class 1), mix together, *miksim.* **Indurekpekoya ŋgwok**: They all mixed together (i.e socialized together) and left; *Ol i miks na igo.*
indub *n.* 1. seedling, shoot; *kru.*
2. sacred paraphernalia of the men's house; *ol samting bilong haus boi.* **Orak indub**: the things of the men's house; *ol samting bilong haus boi.*
induw *n.* the inner bark of a sago palm that is nearest to the outer bark, what is left when the **yamŋa mis** is pulverized; *insait bilong skin bilong saksak, skin nating.*
ipipir *n.* 1. fruit fly; *prut plai.*
2. (*obsolete*), small, nearly invisible gnats; *liklik bilakpela binatang i save kaikaim man.* This word to designate gnats has become replaced by the Koparlanguage word **mámaki**.
ipiki *v.i.* (**pipiet/pipiek**), burn; *kuk, kamap bilakpela long paia.*

ir *v.t.* (class 1), **1.** laugh at someone or something, *lap igo long wanpela man o long wanpela samting*. **Ŋayi ŋgu pirkun**: I laughed at her; *Mi lap long em*.
2. roll fibers against leg to bind them into rope; *wokim rop*. **Ewar ŋguyi tarŋa paŋgni merom pirkun**: Yesterday she rolled tar fibers into thread against her leg; *Asde em wokim rop*.

irar *v.t.* (class 4; **ŋi iranukun/ŋgu iratukun**), teach something; *lainim*. **Yu poror aŋgi ŋanana iratiatan!** Teach me that song! *Yu lainim mi long singsing!*

irik-(p)-e *v.t.* (class 1), twist something, wring something; *tainim*. **Kokokma potak irikétiŋgatan!**: Wring the chicken's neck! *Tainim nek bilong kakaruk ia!* **Ndow irikra woka adimbot**: My foot twisted and I tripped; *Lek bilong mi tainim na mi pundaun*. **Papŋa batep irikirikétukuna rukuatet!** Twist the coconut and throw it down! *Tainim tainim kokonas na troimwe i godaun*.

iroki *v.i.* (conjugated like **oki**), be submerged in water; *i godaun ananeat long wara*. **Munje kowot inde awinni katiteta irmbota sinieta wasownet**. The old man fell into the water and drowned (*lit.* 'sank and died'); *Lapun man i pundaun long wara na em i daun na em indai*. **Orem ainde purara ukar irokar mbet**: The crocodile is coming, bobbing its head up and down; *Pukpuk i apim na daunim hed bilong em na i kam*.

irki *v.i.* (**pirot/ pirok**), laugh; *lap*.

iro 1. *adj.* new; *nupela*.
2. *n.* laughter, *lap*.

iru *n.* **1.** seed; *pikinini bilong pawpaw, brus, gras, olgeta kain diwai*.
2. the point of anything, such as a spear, or a breast; *nus bilong olgeta samting i gat poin, olsem spia*; **Yirŋa iru**: point of a spear; *taget poin bilong spia*; **Minŋa iru**: nipple, *nus bilong susu*.
3. urethral opening; *nus bilong kok na nus bilong kan*.
4. clitoris; *hap nus bilong kan*.

iruiru *n.* **1.** fuzz; *mosong*. **Iruiruŋa**: fuzzy (*lit.* 'has fuzz'); *i gat mosong*. **Iruiruyi nitin, ŋa okinet tuwkunana**: The fuzz is making me (itchy), I'm going to go bathe; *Mosong i mekim mi, bai mi go waswas*.
2. male strength and power; *strong bilong man*. **Iruiru andakwakaŋgwarke**: Don't allow them (i.e. women) to crush your male strength (for example by letting them get close to you when they are menstruating); *Ol (meri) i no ken krungutim strong bilong yu*.

is *v.t.* (class 1), **1.** rub something or someone, *rabim*. **Ŋa sopni pisiŋgin ror ainde**; I rubbed the boy with soap; *Mi wasim pikinini long sop*.
2. remove something, e.g. clothing; *rausim koros*. **Trausis isitukun!**: Take off your trousers! *Rausim trausis!*
3. shed something, e.g. skin; *sensim skin*. **Aram toto pisukun**: The snake shed its skin; *Snek i sensim skin*.
4. slide out from a container or pouch; *kamautim*. **Yir pisukun mambirŋa**: I removed the spear from runner of the roof; *Mi kamautim spia long morota*. See also **ke-(p)-e**.

isiaiki *v.i.* (conjugated like **aiki**), be full; *pulap*. **Ŋa isimbet**: I (male) am full; *Mi pulap ia*. **Ŋgu isiwek**: She is full; *Em pulap ia*. **Mámbakir isiwek**: The netbag is full; *Bilum i pulap*. **Baket isiwek awinni**: The bucket is full of water; *Baket i pulap long wara*.

isirai *n.* a croton plant with a pleasant smell traditionally used as a decoration when people sing and dance; *gorngon bilong bilas long taim bilong singsing, i gat gutpela smel*.

isiraiki *v.i.* (conjugated like **aiki**), crouch; *lindaun*. **Ŋa kakatki isirimbeta siniet**: I quickly crouched down; *Mi hariap sindaun i godaun long lek*.

isirioki *v.i.* (conjugated like **oki**), **1.** deflate; *slek*. **Imin isiriwok, enderkari nitin, imin sindertak**: My stomach is empty I am hungry, I have no food in my stomach; **Munjesik isiriwok**: The boil has gone down; *Buk i slek*.

2. fall off or come off because the object is too large; *slek i pundaun*. **Pande isiriwoka naŋgir sindertak**: The axe fell off its handle; *Trausis* **isirisiriwok**: My trousers keep falling down (because they are too big); *Trausis i wok long slek i punduan pundaun.*

isiki *v.i.* (**pisiet/pisiek**), 1. rub on skin; *rabim o bilasim skin*. **Sopnɨ pisiet**: He washed with soap; *Em i waswas wantaim sop.* **Makatnɨ pisiek**: She decorated himself with red paint; *Em bilasim em yet wantaim redpela pen;* **Sumbwanɨ pisiet**: I rubbed dirt on my body (to decorate it); *Mi bilasim skin bilong mi long graun.*
2. be soiled with fluid, sap, or anything runny; *bagarap long wara o pen o pekpek o wanem samting i gat wara long en*. **Bioŋgi yiwirnɨ pisiet**: The baby was messy with feces; *Pikinini i bagarap long pekpek.*

iskuokɨ *v.i.* (conjgated like **okɨ**), 1. cut diagonally into a smaller piece; *katim long namel i go liklik.*
2. flatten grass; *krungutim gras*. **Ŋgwokara aŋgude ŋgusikrim isukuwoka ŋgwok**: They have gone, they went flattening the grass; *Ol i go na gras i ia ol i krungutim na i go.*

isuk *n.* 1. personal belongings of a deceased person; *ol deti samting bilong wanpela man o meri indai long en*. Traditionally these items, which usually consisted of the deceased's netbag and the possessions it contained, were burned after the funerary feast for the person had been held, signifying that the spirit of the deceased no longer hovered around the village, but was released into the rainforest forever. **Orak isuk(ŋan):** intimate possessions of a deceased person or someone who is to be ensorcelled; *deti samting.*
2. sorcery, *posin*. **Isuk werŋgar**: tie sorcery, i.e. tie and knot the leaves and other objects used to shoot sorcery into a victim's body (the verb is **er** but is pronounced [wɛr] here); *wokim posin.* **Isuk werŋgar munje**: sorcerer; *posin man* (lit. 'man who ties/knots sorcery'). The other word for sorcery in Tayap (**poisir**) is clearly derived from the Tok Pisin word *posin*, or *poisin* (pronounciation varies). **Isuk** is less used today in Gapun because it has for all intents and purposes been replaced by **poisir**, but it is likely the original precontact Tayap word for sorcery. **Toto isuk(ŋan)**: a body (*lit.* 'skin') that has been ensorcelled, which means that if you are bitten by a venomous snake or spider, you will die; *skin nogut, olsem sapos snek i kaikaim yu bai yu indai*. See also **poisir**.

isumbo *n.* horizontal runner supporting roof thatch; *sparen.*

itaw *n.* 1. vein; *rop.*
2. root of trees, plants; *ol rop bilong diwai.*

itrubaranɨ *adv.* sometimes, occasionally; *liklik*. **Yuwon maya prukaku itrubaranɨ? Wákare ŋayor**: Does your mother do some work occasionally? Not a bit; *Mama bilong yu i save work liklik? Nogat tru.*

itrukɨ *adv.* silently; *isi*. **Itrukɨ itrukɨ waikar ŋgusek**: They came down silently; *Ol i kamdaun isi isi.*

iu *v.t.* (class 1), 1. put liquid into a container; *pulamapim*. **Ŋa awin piukun**: I filled the container with water; *Mi pulamapim wara.*
2. use coconut shell to 'cut' (i.e. separate) sago jelly in the big pot in which it has coagulated and put it into smaller plates; *katim saksak long sel bilong kokonas long putim long ol plet.*

iurok *n.* a species of mosquito, yellow and bigger than **indagawr** mosquitoes; *wanpela kain mosquito, i yelopela na em i bikpela long* **indagawr**.

itum *n.* flea; *laus bilong dok.*

iwoŋ *n.* a kind of tree whose sap is collected and stored for a month. It eventually produces oil that rises to the surface. This oil is used to oil the point of a spear to lubricate it so that it doesn't remain in a pig that has been speared. The hope is that the spear will slide out of the pig's body and thus not be broken, and the pig will die from its wounds; *wanpela kain diwai ol man i save kisim wara bilong em na putim i stap. Wel bai kamap na ol man i save usim despela wel long welim spia bilong kilim pik.*

iwoŋgikin *n.* four-sided banana with yellow flesh, eaten boiled; *banana i gat yelopela mit, ol man i save boilim na kaikai.*

K

kai[†] *emph. part.* (*obsolete*), really – used only with the word **ayáta** 'enough'!; *olgeta, bai yu tok wantaim* **ayáta. Ayáta kai!** Stop it! *Inap olgeta!*

kaiknumb *n.* box; *bokis.* **Kaiknumbŋa nam**: talk that hides its true meaning (*lit.* 'box talk'); *tok bokis.*

kaikro *n.* [*Kopar*], landing place, where canoes are kept; *kastan.* The Tayap would be **yimbar worŋgar iaw**: place to go ashore; *ples bilong kanu igo asua.*

kaimwa *n.* Sulfur-crested Cockatoo; *koki* (*Birds of New Guinea* plate 20, #12).

kaindkɨ *v.i.* (**-pet**/**-pek**), miss, in the sense of fail to hit; *abris.*

kaind-(p)e *v.t.* (class 1), miss hitting or shooting something or someone; *abrisim.* **Ebianaŋi Saraki kaindpeŋgin sarepnɨ**: Ebiyana missed Saraki with the grass knife; i.e. when he swung the grass knife to cut him; *Ebiyana abrisim Saraki long grasnaip.*

kaiŋ *n.* a tree pod that looks like a very large cashew. The pod is cooked on a fire, and then broken open and eaten like a breadfruit seed. The meat is firm and white and tastes like yam. Standing in the smoke from the fire will result in blisters on skin; *wanpela bikpela pikinini bilong diwai, olsem bikpela mot. Yu laik kaikai bai yu kukim long paia, tasol nogut yu sanap long smok bilong paia long wanem smok i pas long skin bilong yu bai bukbuk i kamap.*

kaisar *n.* back of a canoe; *stia bilong kanu.*

kaitkait *n.* rotten shit (used to describe behavior one thinks is offensive); *pasin nogut.* **Kaitkait nirŋgarana, ayata!**: You can't do that shit, enough!; *I no ken wokim despela rabis pasin, inap!*

kaitut *n.* Nightjars (*Birds of New Guinea* plate 27).

kaiw *n.* a type of ginger whose leaves are used in sorcery and curing rituals; *smel gorngorn.*

kakámatik *n.* millipede; *longpela yelopela binatang i gat planti ol lek na skin bilong em i gat marasin. Sapos yu krungtim em na skin bilong yu i gat sua, despela marasin bai go insait long sua na givim bikpela pen long yu.*

kakarpwap *n.* Gurney's Eagle; *taragau* (*Birds of New Guinea* plate 8, #2–3).

kakrar *v.t.* (class 5), clear throat; *klirin nek. Krakrartɨmbɨna namtak*: "Yum aniŋgro?"; She cleared her throat and asked, "Who are you?"; *Em klirim nek na askim, "Yupela husat ia?"*

kamb *n.* croton plant; *plowa.*

kambagawr *n.* large round yam; *bikpela raunpela yam.*

kamban *n.* Australian Magpie (*Birds of New Guinea* plate 55, #9–10).

kambike *n.* area of chest around the collar bone; *hap bros bilong man klostu long bun kola.*

kambikeŋa niŋ *n.* collar bone; *bun bilong kola.*

Kambim *n.* Bien village; *ples Bien.*

kambobai *n.* black biting ants that build their nest in the middle of a tree; *ol bilakpela anis i save wokim haus bilong ol long namel long diwai, ol i save kaikai man.*

kambok *n.* seeds of a tree that villagers chew as a betel nut substitute when betel nut is scarce; *ol pikinini bilong diwai ol man i save kaikai taim ol i save lus long buai*.

kambrom *n*. small sticks inserted along the length of the **tandor** to secure it in place; *hap limbom bilong subim antap long pongan bilong haus*. See also **kapir**.

kambromtukur *n*. huge rainstorm; *bikpela ren tru*. **Kambromtukur suman aiakuk:** A massive rainstorm is coming; *Bikpela ren nogut tru i wok long kam*.

kambukar *n*. space between two vertical objects, e.g. the space between two legs or two poles; *spes namel long tupela samting i sanap, olsem namel long tupela lek o tupela pos*. **Kambukar sumanŋa munje:** a bow-legged man; *man i wakabaut na tupela lek bilong em i stap longwe longwe*; **Ewand seneŋa kambukarni aŋgi wuk:** It's in the space between the two mosquito nets; *Samting i stap namel long tupela taunamb ia*.

kambwan *n*. vomit, *traut*. **Ewar ŋgu kambwan ombukun:** Yesterday she vomited (lit. 'vomited vomit'); *Asde em i traut*; **Nje kambwanŋa nanukŋa munje ide namgi tower inde awnet:** Tell that man with the dog's vomit face there to shut up! (*vulgar*); *Tokim man i gat pes bilong traut bilong dok long stap isi!* (*tok nogut*).

Kamor *n*. a traditional deity to whom boys were introduced by way of short bamboo flutes, and prodigious cutting and scraping of their skin. The initiation rituals associated with this deity were celebrated for the last time in the early 1960s; *tamabaran bilong sikarap sikarapim skin bilong ol pikinini man*.

kamus *n*. 1. small termites; *ol liklik waitpela anis i save wokim haus bilong ol insait long kona bilong haus bilong man*.
  2. termite mound in which these termites live; men use them to lure bandicoots close to blinds they hide in to shoot them and women put them in baskets that trap fish; *haus bilong despela ol anis ol i save wokim long ol pos bilong haus. Ol man i save putim long banis mumut na ol meri i save putim igo insait long basket bilong kalabusim pis*.

kandam *n*. ass, buttocks; *as*. **Kandam sinder:** naked; *as nating*.

kanakai aramŋgor *n*. red, pythonlike snake; *snek i gat redpela kala*.

kandaŋ *n*. 1. clan; *klen, pamili*. **Orem kandaŋŋa munje:** man of the crocodile clan; *man bilong pamili pukpuk*.
  2. base, foundation; *as*. **Papŋa kandaŋ:** the base of the coconut palm; *as bilong kokonas*.

kandaŋni *pos*. under, at the base of; *ananeat, long as*.

kandap oŋgab (lit. 'pots of the **kandap**') *n*. a vine that produces massive brown seeds whose covering is the size and shape of pith helmets. This vine is notorious because it is used to make poison by collecting juice that has been caused to rot by perforating it, and mixing it with the liver of a **poketak** fish and a millipede; *wail rop ol man i save wokim posin long en.; rop i kamapim ol bikpela braunpela pikinini i luk olsem ol hat bilong ol kiap bilong bipo. Ol man nogut i save wokim wul long en na bihain em i sting pinis bai kisim wara na miksim wantaim lewa bilong* **poketak** *na kakamatik. Em nau em bai usim despela long kilim man*.

kandap *n*. (*pl*. **kandipeŋ**), 1. forest spirit, can be male or female, even though most villagers talk most commonly of them as females; *ol spirit bilong bus, i gat ol man na ol meri, tasol ol Gapun i save toktok planti long ol* **kandap** *meri*.
  2. mite; *liklik liklik redpela binatang i save go insait long skin bilong han na leg na skin i save sikarap*.
  3. large red ants that live in dry wood and can draw blood if they bite one; *bikpela redpela anis, ol i kaikaim yu bai blut i kamap, ol i save stap insait long diwai i drai*.

kandapat *n*. wild ginger pepper chewed with betel nut; *waildaka*.

kandapŋa niŋg *n.* a short bone that cassowaries have between the thigh bone and the hip; *sotpela bun bilong ol muruk i stap klostu long join bilong ŋgedɨk bilong em.*

kandaw *n.* illness; *sik.* **Kandawi nitin**: I am sick (*lit.* 'illness is affecting me'); *Sik i mekim mi.*

kandibwaŋ *n.* carving of a traditional figure; *kabing.*

kandip *n.* **1.** mangrove slug; *wanpela samting olsem* **pisik** *tasol nogat pinga bilong en i save stap long mangoro na ol meri i save kisim long wokim kaikai.*
2. Forest Kingfisher (*Birds of New Guinea* plate 24, #12).

kandiwara *n.* [*Kopar*], jellyfish; *samting i save stap long mangoro i luk olsem ol liklik* **njalat**. In Tayap one would say **toto tiwarŋgar orak awinŋa**: A thing in the water that hurts your skin; *Samting bilong wara i save bagarapim skin bilong man.*

kandigit *n.* a kind of wild ginger with long leaves that is used to make men aggressive and ready to fight, and dogs ready to kill pigs; *kawawar bilong hatim bel bilong ol man na ol dok.*

kandum *n.* **1.** a kind of tree with wide yellow leaves in which black ants live; *diwai i gat braitpela yelopela lip na ol bilakpela anis i save stap insait.*
2. the black ants that live inside the **kandum** tree; *ol bilakpela anis i save stap insait long* **kandum**.

kanimbit *n.* baldness, *kela.* **Kanimbitŋa munje**: bald man; *kela man.* See also **kokɨr**.

kanjaŋ *n.* tree whose leaves are dried and used as sandpaper and as a way of cleaning blackened pots; *mosong diwai ol man i save draim lip bilong en na usim olsem sandpepa long klinim skin bilong ol kabing na ol pot.*

kanjígogo (also **kanjígo**) *n.* a kind of bamboo whose shoots are frequently gathered and eaten; *wanpela kain mambu ol meri i save kisim kru bilong em na wokim kaikai long ol.*

kanuŋ-(p)-e *v.t.* (class 1), make a fork out of two sticks; *wokim pok.*

kanuŋ *n.* tree kangaroo; *sikau.*

kaŋ *n.* [*Kopar*], clam from the Sepik river; *kina bilong Sepik.*

kaŋan *n.* Tahitian chestnut; *galip.*

kaŋgajiŋ *n.* **1.** pincers of crustaceans like crabs or shrimp; *sapela pinga bilong ol kuka na kindam.*
2. the up-rounded tusks of boars; *tupela bikpela tit bilong pik.*

kaŋgior *n.* Spangled Drongo (*Birds of New Guinea* plate 54, #1).

kaŋgonase *n.* [*Kopar*], shark; *sak.* In Tayap, the name would be **rewɨnjan ŋgomar nimarŋa**: mangrove fish with teeth, but this phrase is never used; *long Tayap bai yu inap tok* **rewɨnjan ŋgomar nimarŋa**, *olsem pis i gat tit, tasol ol man i no save usim despela hap tok.*

kanjɨr *n.* **1.** dish made out of Areca palm sheath; *dis bilong limbum.*
2. one of the three species of trees which men use to make the floors of a house; *wanpela long tripela kain diwai ol man i save katim paitim long en na wokim ol plo bilong haus.* See also **kondew**, **serek**.

kap *v.t.* (class 5), gather together in arms; *hipim long tupela han.* **Pap samb kapnukuna kukumbet**: I gathered up the coconuts and carried them to the village; *Asde mi kisim ol kokonas i kam.*

kapa *mood part.* a word that encodes surprise, both positive and negative; *hap tok bilong tok long samting olsem yu no tingim na em i kamap.* **Ŋa kapa markar mbot, yu markɨ wákare**: I'm the only damned one who rowed, you didn't row; *Mi tasol i pul i go, yu no pul liklik.* See Section 7.6 of the grammar.

kapambɨnana *interj.* of course; *em tasol.*

kapar *adj.* mature, older; *bikpela.* **Kapar mɨr**: You're really mature (ironic, the meaning is: you're not mature, you're not growing up); *yu no kamap hariap.* **Omokaparma ror inde**: He's smart – he's the child of a man who had knowledge (opposite of **omosuama ror**); *Em i gat save – em pikinini bilong papa i gat save, em i no* **omosuama ror**. See also **sua**.

kapir *n.* small sticks used to support garden fence or inserted along the length of the **tandor** to secure it in place; *hap limbom bilong wokim banis bilong gaden o bilong subim antap long pongan bilong haus.* See also **kambrom**.

kapwakapi *n.* traditional axe used to carve wood; *ainsap ol tumbuna i save usim long makim ol kabing.*

kapwasak *n.* traditional girdle put around the **síw** (traditional loincloth). It was painted with **makat**, and also with blood from the wearer's penis; *let bilong síw ol tumbuna i save pasim. Ol tumbuna i save penim long* **makat** *na bilasim long blut bilong kok bilong ol.*

kar *n.* funerary feast to send a dead person's spirit on its way to the afterlife, usually conducted several months after a person's death; *pati.*

karam *n.* **1.** debt; *dinau.* **Karam nambar wuk aŋgi, yu epiati wákare:** There's a debt that you haven't paid me back; *Dinau i stap na yu no bekim bilong mi.*
   2. bark of sago tree; *skin bilong saksak.* **Ŋiŋi karam krankun:** He split the bark of the sago palm (to begin pulverizing it); *Em brukim skin bilong saksak.*

karamki *v.i.* (**-net/-nak**), present joking kin (**njakum**) with goods and decorations at the time of a funerary feast to decorate the corpse, as a kind of repayment for the life of the deceased; *hipim ol samting long ol njakum long taim bilong pati.*

karar *n.* **1.** parrot, **karangal** (*Birds of New Guinea* plate 20).
   2. *adj., n.* red, *redpela.*

karar ror *n.* newborn baby (*lit.* 'red child'); *nupela bebi.* **Ewarŋa karar ror ene aŋgi nda oŋgabni timbrak wiararkrunak:** I'm going to stuff this newborn baby in a cooking pot! (said by a mother in frustration when her 3-year-old daughter – whom she sarcastically refers to here as a newborn – wouldn't stop crying); *Bai mi holim pasim despela nupela bebi mi karim long asde na pulampaim em long pot!*

karat *n.* rattan; *kanda.*

karatukumb *n.* bowstring; *kanda bilong taitim banara.*

karep *n.* **1.** moon; *mun;* **Noŋor karep tatukun:** The woman is seeing the moon (i.e. the woman is menstruating); *Meri i lukim mun.*
   2. a small tree that grows in grasslands with white flowers; *liklik diwai i save kamap long kunai i gat ol waitpela plowa.*

karewa *n.* a kind of small, non-poisonous snake; *wanpela kain liklik snek.*

karuwa *n.* a large silver fish caught in the mangrove swamp; *pis bilong mangoro i waitpela, gutpela kaikai bilong em.*

kas *n.* sago palm leafstalk; *pangal bilong saksak.* See also **marŋgorŋa kas**.

katam *n.* dog-teeth decoration tied to forehead; *paspas bilong putim long poret, ol tumbuna i save wokim long tit bilong dok.*

katáwa *n.* scorpion; *skopion.*

katip *n.* Lowland Peltops (*Birds of New Guinea* plate 39, #2–3).

katip *v.t.* (class 5), **1.** cut something into small pieces; *katim liklik liklik.*
   2. be angry (*lit.* 'be with a cut-up stomach'); *i stap kros.* **Ŋi ewar imin katipra wok:** Yesterday he got angry; *Asde bel bilong em hat.*

katkat usually pronounced [kakat]; *adv.* quickly; *hariap.* **Katkat!** Hurry up! *Hariap!*

kato *n.* many colors; *kala kala.* **Ner katoŋa:** The grass skirt is colorful; *Pulpul i kalakala.*

katom *n.* a kind of rattan with small spines; *kanda i nogat strongpela nil.*

katurip *n.* Triller (*Birds of New Guinea* plate 33, #10–12).

kawat *n.* **1.** salt; *sol.*
   2. a kind of palm without spines that used to be burned in large heaps to produce ashes that were filtered for salt; *diwai ol tumbuna i save kukim sol long en.*

kawrik *adj.* tough, resistant, powerful, unashamed; *strongpela*; **Kokitok kawrik**: strong headed; *strongpela het*; **Nam kawrik**: direct, unashamed talk; *strongpela tok*.

kawrki *v.i.* (**-net**/**-nak**), howl; *singaut olsem dok*.

kawsomb *n.* [*Watam*], sailing canoe; *selkanu*.

kawt *n.* a painted cone-like hat made of rattan, habitually worn by adult men prior to WWII; *kanda kep bilong ol tumbuna*. See also **kokirat**.

ke-(p)-e *v.t.* (class 1), pull out or dig out something, e.g. **nono** (yams), **manduwar** (taro), **tat** (splinters embedded in skin); *kamautim long graun o long skin*. **Mborake kawadwi nitiŋgina kut, Antamawri mbeta totoŋan orak isuk kepeŋgatan**. Mborake was sick and Antamawri came and removed ensorcelled objects from his skin; *Mborake sik i stap, Antamawri i kam na kamautim ol posin long skin bilong em*.

ke-(p/w)-eki *v.i.* (**kepet/kepek**), fall out; *kamaut na pundaun*. **Mbor ainde amkwar mbot yirreki yir kepek**: The pig shook the spear [that had pierced it] and it fell out; *Pik i pait wantaim spia na em i kamaut na pundaun*.

keke *n.* (*dl.* **kekeŋgre**; *pl.* **kekeŋgro**), grandmother; *apa meri*.

kekékato *n.* **1.** worm; *liklik snek bilong graun*.
2. Maggi-brand noodles, or other kinds of dried manufactured noodles; *nudel*.

kemb *n.* **1.** carved front of a canoe; *poret bilong kanu*.
2. the two carved handles of a traditional plate (**paru**); *tupela handel bilong tumbuna plet*.

kembatik *n.* **1.** bow; *banara*.
2. gun (secret code); *gan (hait tok)*.

kemem *adj.* long; *longpela*.

kememni *adv.* lengthwise; *longpela*. **Ewand kememni ritukun**: Tie the mosquito net lengthwise; *Bihainim haus na taitaim taunamb*.

keŋgen *n.* tantrum; *krai na bikhed bilong ol pikinini taim ol i save les na ol i no harim tok*.

keŋgeŋki *v.i.* (**-net**/**-nak**), throw a tantrum; *krai na bikhed bilong ol pikinini taim ol i save les na ol i no harim tok*.

kerkwar *n.* horizontal roof support that rests on the tall **kóndrik**; *pongan*.

kewa oki *v.i.* (conjugated like **oki**), loosen; *kamaut*. **Yir kewa wok**: The blade of the spear is loose; *Ain i lus long mambu*.

keymare *n.* freshwater lobster; *draipela kinda i save stap insait long ol baret, i gat bigpela pinga bilong en*.

kik *n.* toy top made out of small coconut shell, traditionally spun with a string and played with by children; *sel bilong liklik kokonas, ol pikinini i save raunim long rop na troimwe, em bai raunraun*.

kikai *n.* Ground Robin (*Birds of New Guinea* plate 31, #3–4).

kikak *adj.* raw, uncooked; *i no tan*.

kikik *n.* small cicada whose cry signals the fall of evening; *liklik binatang i save singaut taim san i godaun*.

kimb *n.* Kingfisher (*Birds of New Guinea* plate 24, #6–9, #12–15).

kikiw *adj.* yellow; *yelopela*.

kikri *n.* large wasp that burrows in house posts; *bikpela bi i save drilim hul long ol hauspos*.

kikri-(p/w)-e *v.t.* (class 2), **1.** tickle the throat, like a bone stuck in the throat; *sikarapim long insait bilong nek*. **Ŋa mum akurar mbota, pinpin potakni krikripeiatande, mum werku wek**: I was eating sago jelly and a piece of something got stuck in my throat and I expectorated it; *Mi kaikai saksak i go na wanpela pipia i pas long nek bilong mi na mi rausim*.
2. gently rub a sore or a cut; *giaman sikarapim wanpela sua*.

kikriki *v.i.* (**-pet**/**-pek**), **1.** move around in a way that produces itching, like when a louse walks around in one's hair; *laus i wakabaut long hed*. **Pakind sami kikripekro kokirni**: Lots of lice are walking around on my head; *Planti laus i wakabaut long hed*.

2. dawdle; *wakabaut isi isi*. **Kikriwekar oŋgarke katkat katkat mbara otet:** Stop dawdling, hurry up a little! *Yu no ken wakabaut isi isi, i go hariap liklik*.

kim *n.* comb; *kom*.

kimirik *n.* sago grub; *binatang bilong saksak*. **Kutam kimirik kwarkwanuk:** Kutam is finding sago grubs (*lit.* 'Kutam is chopping sago grubs to extract them from the sago palm'); *Kutam brukim binatang bilong saksak i stap*.

kimitak *n.* floor of a house; *limbom*. Cut from one of three trees called **kondew**, **kaŋir** and **serek**; *ol man i save katim long despela tripela kain diwai*: **kondew**, **kaŋir** na **serek**.

kindit *n.* wall of house; *banis bilong haus*.

kind-(p)-o *v.t.* (class 1), **1.** close something; *pasim*; **Nek kindpokun:** I closed the door; *Mi pasim dua*.
 2. block something; *pasim*. **Ewar ŋgino kindpoiatan:** Yesterday he blocked my vision; *Asde em pasim ai bilong mi*.

kinda *n.* tongs; *sisis*.

kindip *n.* base of trees in mangrove swamp; *as bilong mangoro*.

kindit *n.* woven screen used as a wall, woven of bamboo and sago palm leafstalk; *blain ol i wokim long mambu na pangal*. See also **tandaŋ**.

kinj *n.* a tree with pleasant smelling bark; *diwai i gat gutpela smel*.

kiŋ *n.* ring; *ring*.

kip *n.* a kind of tree whose bark was traditionally used by women as a contraceptive. Consuming too much of this bark is believed to sterilize women, and this is the reason given in Gapun for female infertility; *kain diwai ol meri i save kaikai long pasim bel*.

kir *n.* heart; *lewa*.

kirat *n.* tobacco (*secret code*); *brus (hait tok)*. This is a secret word used in front of villagers from nearby villages who know **sokoi**, the usual word for tobacco. *Em wanpela hait tok ol Gapun i save usim long haitim tok long husat ol man na meri bilong narapela hap ol i save long* **sokoi** *tasol ol i no save gut long tok ples Gapun*.

kirawki *v.i.* (**-net**/**-nak**), be in a state of ritual seclusion, for example after one's spouse dies or when one has given birth, *tambu*. **Ŋgu kirawtaka wuk:** She's in ritual seclusion; *Meri tambu i stap*. See also **konimkikiraw** *v.t.* (class 5), **1.** know something; *save*. **Ŋayi kirawkru wákare:** I don't know; *Mi no save*; **Ŋayi kirawmbri wákare:** I don't know about them (i.e. I don't know where they are or where they went); *Mi no save long ol*; **Ŋayi kirawŋgar munjema nomb yuwon mbor pokunŋan:** I know the name of the man who killed your pig; *Mi save long nem bilong man i kilim pik bilong yu*. This first meaning of the word requires the use of ergative (see Section 4.3.1 of the grammar), other meanings do not; *Yu laik tok long save bai yu mas tok long* **ŋayi** *o* **ŋini** *olsem, i no ken tok long* **ŋa** *o* **ŋi** *tasol*.
 2. consider something; *skelim*. **Yu nam aŋgo kirawtukun ŋgo:** Consider this talk; *Yu skelim despela tok pastaim*.
 3. recognize something; *luksave*.
 4. feel, taste, or perceive something; *pilim, testim*. **Ŋi tomiktomik kirawnukun ŋan atarumeke ekrukukŋan:** He felt the spider that was crawling across his forehead; *Em i pilim olsem spaida i wakabaut long hed bilong em*.

kiskiski *v.i.* (**-tet**/**-tak**), fly in a downward arc or spiral; *plai i go na pundaun*. **Ŋayi tam tamaŋgani pokuna kiskistaka woka aini kemrak otitekara aŋgi:** I shot the bird with a slingshot and it must have soared and fallen somewhere over there; *Mi sutim pisin long katapel na em i mas land i go pundaun long sampela hap*.

kitkit *n.* mud; *graun*. **Sumbwa kitkit:** The ground is muddy; *Graun i warawara*.

kit *n.* pile, heap; *bung*. See also **sumbuŋ**.

kitiŋiŋ *adj.* short; *sotpela*.

kitip *n.* tree stump; *ol i katim diwai pinis na as tasol i sanap yet*. **Papŋa kitip:** stump of coconut tree; *as bilong kokonas*.

koi *n.* a kind of tree with large flat seeds that can be spun like tops; *diwai i gat ol bikpela pikinini ol mangi i save spinim ol long pilai bilong ol.*

koimbup *n.* a fuzzy tree with many seeds like coffee beans that birds frequent to eat. The tree is a popular place to build a bird blind, in order to shoot birds with arrows; *diwai i gat mosong na i save karim planti pikinini olsem ol sit bilong kopi. Ol pisin i save kam na kaikai, na olsem ol man i save wokim banis klostu long despela diwai.*

kokiparaŋ *n.* **1.** egg-cup shaped mortar used by old people without teeth to crush betel nut so that they can put it in their mouths and suck it; *liklik pilo bilong paitim paitim buai. Ol tumbuna man na meri bilong bipo i nogat tit long ol, ol i save paitim buai olsem;* **2.** headrest, traditionally made of wood, often **sanamb**; *pilo.* **3.** seat made of sticks on which men used to sit to pulverize sago pith; *liklik sia o pilo ol tumbuna bilong bipo i save wokim long sindaun paitim saksak.*

kokir i *v.t.* (class 1, the verb is **i**, 'give'): make someone do something they don't want to do, (*lit.* 'give head'); *pusim.* **Tamboŋ Naŋam kokir ikwatanuk wukinana Monei kotareŋgri minjikenana**: Tamboŋ is trying to coax Naŋam come down and ask Monei for betel nut; *Tambong i pusim Nangam long kam daun askim Monei long buai.*

kokir *n.* **1.** head; *hed*; **Kokir tuwtiek**: bald head (*lit.* 'head bathes'); *kela.* See also **kanimbit.** **2.** willfulness, stubbornness; *hed*; **Yu kokir sumanŋa ror aŋgo!** You're a stubborn, willful girl! *Yu wanpela bikhed mangi stret!* **3.** upper part of a location; *hed.* **Numŋa kokir**: the upper part of the village; *hed bilong ples.* See also **kokitok.**

kokirat *n.* a cone-like hat used by adult men prior to WWII; *kep bilong ol papa tumbuna.* See also **kawt.**

kokirŋa ror *n.* first born child (*lit.* 'head child'); *pesborn.* See also **mambirŋa ror.**

kokirŋan tawk *n.* skull (*lit.* 'head shell'); *sel bilong hed.*

kokirŋgrit *n.* head hair; *gras bilong hed.*

kokitok *n.* head; *hed.* Synonymous with **kokir**, but refers solely to the body part without any of the implications of willfulness and stubbornness invoked by that word.

kokok *n.* chicken; *kakaruk.*

kokokaraw *n.* long tailfeathers of rooster; *bilpela asgras bilong kakaruk man.*

kokosawir *n.* bad ways; *pasin nogut.*

kokosik *n.* medium-sized rat; *rat i bikpela tasol i no bikpela tumas.*

kokosuar *n.* Common Scrubfowl; *wailpaul* (*Birds of New Guinea* plate 1, #9a).

kokot *v.t.* (class 5), finish work; *pinisim wok.* **Pruk taman kokotnukundara**: He finished all the work; *Em pinisim wok pinis.* **Pruk kokotkru wákare, ŋa at orepekun**: I didn't finish the work, some is left; *Mi no pinisim wok, mi lusim hap i stap.*

Kokraŋa kup (or **Kokramat kup**) *n.* testicles, alluding to a myth about a man named Kokra; *bol bilong man.*

kokri *n.* sago jelly made with sago flour that has been mixed with with cane grass (*pitpit*) and shredded coconut; *saksak ol meri i tainim wantaim pitpit na kokonas.*

kokrow *n.* a kind of grass that resembles corn, the seeds of which are used in traditional decorations; *wanpela kain gras i luk olsem kon ol tumbuna i save kisim pikinini bilong em na wokim bilas long en.*

komand *v.t.* (class 5), disperse fire by removing burning firewood and embers one piece at a time, e.g. when people keep coming and taking firewood to go home and ignite their own fires; *kisim nambaut na pinisim paia.* **Ewar ŋaŋan otar komandtiatroya kukuŋwuk turo sindetia**: Yesterday they all came and took bits of my burning fire and left me with an empty hearth; *Asde ol i kam na pinisim paia bilong mi na turo bilong mi i stap nating.*

komb *adj.* deep; *i godaun.*

kombam *n.* group of four shelled coconuts tied together and put in men's house and distributed during meetings or food distributions; *ol hip long popela popela kokonas ol man i save putim long haus boi long givim long ol man bilong ol narapela hap. Ol inap dringim wara bilong despela ol kokonas long selekim nekdrai bilong ol long taim bilong bung o long taim bilong pati.*

kombin *n.* death adder, one of the two most venomous and feared snakes in the rainforest; *posin snek i save kilim man.* See also **mbumjor**.

kombobo *n.* clutter; *pipia nambaut.* **Patir komobobo sumanŋan:** The house is really cluttered and messy; *Haus i bagarap i gat ol pipia nambaut.*

komboj *adj.* dirty (used for water); *deti (taim yu laik toktok long wara).* **Komboj awin:** dirty water; *wara i no klinpela.*

komi *n.* a large edible larva found in rotten sago or **ndekik** palms; *bikpela binatang i save stap insait long drai saksak na long ndekik, ol man i save kaikaim em.*

kondew *n.* **1.** areca palm; *diwai limbom.*
   2. areca palm frond material used to make traditional buckets, mats, brooms and covers for various objects to protect them from the rain; *limbum i pundaun long graun. Ol meri i save samapim long kisim wara na mekim ol narapela kain ol wok.* **Ŋaŋan kondew putiatan?** Have you cut up my plate? (i.e. is this why you haven't brought me any food – said by a man to his wife or female relatives); *Yu katim plet bilong mi ah? Em olsem miningim bilong wanem yu kaikai pulap na mi stap hangre?*
   3. traditional bucket into which water is poured and in which the sago flour settles; *limbom.*

kondew yar *n.* thick red sugar cane; *bikpela redpela suga.*

kondikki *v.i.* (**-net/-nak**), become flaccid or soft; *kamap malomalo.*

kondikra oki *v.i.* (conjugated like **oki**; the **di** syllable can be reduplicated for emphasis), soft; *nogat strong, malomalo.* **Kiriŋmat mbioŋi kondidikra wakuk, kawrik wakare:** Kiring's baby is soft, it isn't hard (i.e. it is helpless and easily injured); *Pikinini bilong Kiring i malomalo i stap, nogat strong.* **Kwem yuwon kondidikra oŋgar!:** Your penis is flaccid! (*vulgar*); *Kok bilong yu nogat strong! (tok nogut).*

kondiŋ *n.* **1.** scrotum; *rop bilong bol i hangamap.* **Ŋaweiw kondiŋ sumanŋa!** Big testicles! (*vulgar*); *Draipela bol bilong yu! (tok nogut).*
   2. vine on which coconuts grow; *rop bilong bilong kokonas:* **Papŋa kondiŋ**.
   3. curved adze used to hollow out logs for canoes; *liklik eds ol man i save usim long sapim kanu.*

kondit *n.* ear lobe; *hap skin bilong yau.* See also **ndrig**.

kóndrik *n.* **1.** tallest post or posts holding up roof; *kingpost.*
   2. euphemism for penis; *wanpela we bilong toktok long sem bilong man.* **Erum otiteka kóndrik ŋayar puŋokawuk:** The thatch has fallen off but the king post is still standing (euphemism for 'He may be old and bald but his prick can still stand up'); *Marota i pundaun na kingpos i sanap i stap (olsem mining bilong em i olsem maski man i kela kok bilong em tait i stap yet).*

konemba *n.* sago palm with short fronds *pangal* (**ndadum**) and short leaves. It has no needles and has characteristic white fronds. *Saksak i gat sotpela pangal na sotpela lip. Nogat nil na pangal bilong em i waitpela.*

konenjarki *v.i.* (**-net/-nak**), float; *trip.* **Nimŋat konenjarkar wek:** The branch is floating towards us (*lit.* 'floating and coming'); *Hap diwai i trip i kam.* See also **purara oki**.

konimki *v.i.* (**-net/-nak**), be in a state of ritual seclusion, for example after one's spouse dies or when one has given birth, *tambu*. **Ŋgu konimtaka wuk:** She's in ritual seclusion; *Meri tambu i stap*. See also **kirawki**.

koŋgod *n.* hand-held hourglass drum; *kundu*.

koŋgon *n.* belongings; *kago, ol samting bilong wanpela man o meri*. **Kaiknumŋa koŋgon:** All one's boxes; *Ol bokis nambaut bilong man*.

koŋgrik *n.* bridge; *bris*. See also **nimirkokir**.

kopik 1. *adj.* streaky; *i gat makmak*. **Kopikŋa mum:** sago jelly with streaks of raw sago in it; *hotwara i gat ol haphap muna*; **Ŋguwur kopik kopik wokuk:** The rising smoke is black and white; *Waitpela na bilakpela smok i go antap*.

2. *n.* the liquid produced when **muna** (sago flour) is mixed with a little water to dissolve it, before a pot of boiling water is added to make the sago turn into **mum** (sago jelly); *wara i save kamap taim ol meri i save kapsaitim liklik wara long* **muna** *long redim em long wokim* **mum**.

kopiwok *n.* Palm Cockatoo; *koki* (*Birds of New Guinea* plate 20, # 14).

ko-(p)-o *v.t.* (class 1), extinguish something; *kilim olsem kilim paia*. **Ŋa otar kopokun:** I put out the fire; *Mi kilim paia*; **Ŋgan pwap kokru wákare:** His anger is not extinguished; *Kros bilong em i no indai*.

Koporot *n.* Kopar village; *ples Kopar*.

korar *v.t.* (class 4), gather together things; *bungim*. **Orasamb korankurem!** Everyone gather your things! *Yupela bungim ol samting!*

korareŋgar *n.* meeting; *bung*.

korareŋgar rumb *n.* slit-gong drum summons; *belo*.

koret *n.* foreign, not of Gapun village; *bilong narapela ples*. **Koretmandama morasi:** a foreign custom (*lit.* 'other people's custom'); *we bilong ol narapela*; **Yim koretŋa merni warakakuk:** We're speaking a foreign language; *Mipela i toktok long tok ples bilong narapela hap*.

korot *n.* net; *umben*.

kosep *n.* crab; *kuka*.

kosimb *n.* ash; *sit bilong paia*.

kosowak *n.* Oriole (*Birds of New Guinea* plate 33, #1–5; also plate 47, #15–20).

kotar-(p)-e *v.t.* (class 1), ask something; *askim*.

kotar-(p)-e-ki *v.i.* (**-pet/-pek**), ask; *askim*.

kotarŋgar *n.* question; *askim*. **Ŋa kotarŋgar non yu kotarerunet:** I have a question to ask you; *Mi gat wanpela askim long askim yu*.

kotiw *n.* vertical runner supporting roof; *sapnil*.

kotriŋ *n.* a kind of tree with fuzzy branches, its new leaves are boiled and eaten; *diwai i gat mosong olsem* **ŋgawro**, *ol man i no save kaikai kiao bilong em tasol ol nupela lip ol man i save boilim na kaikai*.

kowe *n.* **1.** the spongy white interior of a coconut that has begun to sprout. This is sweet and eaten; *kru bilong kokonas*.

2. the spongy core of a tree; *insait bilong diwai i no strong*.

kowir *n.* a tree pod that is cooked on a fire, and then broken open and eaten like a breadfruit. Tastes like corn; *wanpela kain pikinini bilong diwai ol man i save kukim long paia, brukim na kaikai olsem kapiak*.

kowmb *adj.* deep; *daun*. **Ŋgu numbwan pikun awin kowmb mera:** She thought that the water would be deep; *Em i ting olsem wara i mas daun*.

kowot *adj.* (*dl.* **kotiw**; *pl.* **koto**), mature, old. Used for people and animals. Can be used either to denote absolute age or in talking about someone who is older than the speaker or referent, for example in **ama kowot**, which literally means 'old mother', but which actually means 'mother's older sister'; i.e. older aunt – this contrasts with **ama mosop**, 'little mother', or 'younger aunt' (i.e. younger than the referent's own mother); *lapun ol manmeri na ol animol, na tu, bikpela susa bilong mama bilong yu bai yu kolim long* **ama kowot**. *O sas kowot bai yu kolim bikpela brata bilong papa bai yu*. **Noŋor kowot aŋgo ror non tatukunke?** Has that old woman ever had any children? *Despela lapun meri ia i bin karim sampela pikinini o?* See also **rowe**.

krakri *v.t.* (class 5), break, tear or fold something into small bits; *brukim brukim*.

krar *v.t.* (class 4), **1.** chop something; *brukim*. **Taruŋ kratukun!**: Chop the firewood! *Brukim paiwut!*
2. tear something; *brukim*. **Pendimorŋa pin kratukun ŋanana**: Tear off a piece of newspaper for me (to smoke); *Brukim hap pepa long mi*.
3. break something open; *brukim*. **Nam kratukun!** Talk openly; i.e. say what you mean!; *Brukim tok!*
4. look after something or someone; *lukautim*. **Ŋayi yu krarwankuta, sumantet**: Thanks to my care, you've grown (lit. 'I have looked after you and you have become big'); *Mi lukautim yu na yu bikpela*.

krar *v.t.* (class 4), care for domestic animals, making sure they have food; *lukautim ol pik o wanem kain ol animol bilong yu*.

krarara okɨ *v.i.* (conjugated like **okɨ**), break; *bruk*. **Tawk krarara wok**: The plate broke; *Plet i bruk*.

krimb *n.* **1.** small hard pellets; *ol liklik liklik kiau*. **Airŋa krimb**: small pellets in lime powder that pregnant women like to eat; men discourage this by saying that the women's babies will be born with sores; *kiaw bilong kambang, ol meri i gat bel save kaikai, o l man save krosim ol long wanem bebi bilong ol bai igat planti sua*.
2. hard round objects; *hatpela raunpela ol liklik samting*. **Papŋa krimb**: small hard coconuts without any water; *ol liklik liklik kokonas nogat wara long em*. **Moŋar krimb**: pebbles, money; *ol liklik ston*; *moni*.

krɨrkemb *n.* Tiger Parrot (*Birds of New Guinea* plate 21, #13–14).

kroi *v.t.* (class 5), completely consume something so that nothing is left; *pinisim olgeta*. **Mbor eirumgi yam kroitukurora**: The pigs ate all the sago; *Ol pik i pinisim olgeta saksak*.

krururkɨ *v.i.* (-net/-nak), buzz of mosquitoes; *pairap bilong natnat*. **Nekeni kururutak**: There's a mosquito buzzing in my ear; *natnat i pairap long iao bilong mi*; **At kuururakuk aŋgi**: The mosquito is buzzing; *Natnat i wokim pairap bilong em*.

kukutawaŋ *n.* hollowed out coconut shell attached to a stick, used to draw water from a well; *sel kokonas bilong rausim wara long hulwara*.

kum *n.* grave; *hul bilong planim bodi bilong man*.

kumb *n.* **1.** lethargy caused by sorcery or sadness; *bikpela les i kamap long wanem posin i mekim yu, o long indai bilong narapela*. **Kumbi nitiŋgina tatara**: Lethargy affected him and he slept; *Bikpela les i mekim em na em i slip*.
2. sadness and atmosphere of gravity caused by a serious illness or death; *hevi bilong indai*. **Maiwama kumb aŋgi woskru wákare**: The burden and sadness of Maiwa's death has not been resolved; *Hevi bilong indai bilong Maiwa ol i no rausim yet*. Compare **naimb**, which is a less serious kind of burden or sadness.

kumund *n.* **1.** a type of bamboo; *wanpela kain mambu*.
2. torch, flashlight; *tos*.

kumundat *n.* traditional pipe made out of bamboo; *paip bilong ol tumbuna*. **Kumundat aŋgikni sokoi waritukun!**: Fill the pipe with tobacco! *Pulamapim paip long brus!*

kunda *v.i.* (-net/-nak), disappear from view; *karamap, hait*. **Embatotoni ŋa kundanet**: I disappeared from view under a piece of cloth sheet; *Mi karamap long laplap*.

kundabebek *n.* Black Kite (*Birds of New Guinea* plate 8, #6–7).

kundar *v.t.* (class 4), cover something or someone up; *karamapim*. **Kundatiŋin embatotoni!**: Cover him with a piece of cloth!; *Karampim em long laplap!*

kunemb *n.* a kind of little bee; *wanpela kain liklik bi*.

kuŋun *n.* wave, in the sense of rough water; *si*. **Kuŋguni nɨm kepekun sumbwa kapurŋa**:

The waves dislodged a tree from the beach; *Si i kamautim diwai long nambis*; **Maraŋa kuŋgun**: waves on the sea; *si long si*.

kup *n*. **1**. cluster of something; *han*.
  2. a cluster of betelnut with some tobacco leaves, paper and leaves of a croton plant tied to it, given to people as part of a conflict settlement, during which the two shake hands, or given to ask someone to do something for you; *buai, brus, pepa na plowa ol man i save givim long taim bilong sekhan, o long taim yu laik askim narapela man long wokim sampela wok long yu*.

kurbi *n*. small green lizard that can stand on hind legs and run after people. This lizard is carved on slit gong drums and makes a characteristic chirping cry at night; *liklik grinpela palai i save sanap na ronim man. Ol man i save wokim kabing bilong em long ol garamut, na em i gat singaut bilong em bai yu harim long bus long nait*.

kuriŋ *n*. King Bird of Paradise; *kumul* (*Birds of New Guinea* plate 53, 10).

kurom *n*. **1**. back leg of a pig, *lek bilong pik* (see also **mburkow**).
  2. thighbone of cassowary, traditionally sharpened to make a knife used to kill people; *lek bilong muruk ol tumbuna i save wokim naip long en*.
  3. the knife made from a **kurom**; *naip ol i save wokim long* **kurom**.
  4. thighbone; *bikpela bun bilong lek*. **Kurom kememŋa**: a tall man; *longpela man*.

kuruk *n*. Kingfisher and Kookaburra (*Birds of New Guinea* plate 24, #13–21).

kutukutu *n*. the fork on which the **iko** stands; *pok bilong putim* **iko** *antap long en*.

k^v non-final *v*. (^{v} is a vowel that changes to harmonize with the vowel of the object). **1**. bring, *kisim i kam*. **Kukuwe!** Bring it! *Kisim i kam!* **Kiŋgiwe!** Bring him! *Kisim em (man) i kam!* **Kimbiwe!** Bring them! *Kisim ol i kam!*
  2. take, *kisim i go*. **Ŋaŋan sapwar kukuŋwokara**. They left with my basket; *Ol i kisim basket bilong mi igo pinis*.

k^v-X-(p/m)-emkɨ *v.i.* (serial verb construction in which X is an object suffix and ^{v} is a vowel that changes to harmonize with the vowel of the object suffix): build; *kirapim*. **Mbanu patɨr iro kukupemiekara**: Mbanu built a new house; *Mbanu wokim pinis nupela haus*.

kwai *n*. murder and the taking of heads during the pre-colonial era; *birua*. **Kwaiŋa orom**: the time of never-ending battle and murder (i.e. pre-colonial times, when clans were engaged in perpetual feuds, when people were killed in ambushes and raids, and their heads 'fed' to the spirits of the men's house); *taim bilong birua*. **Kwai kokɨr**: heads taken in ambush or battle in pre-colonial times and 'fed' to the **mɨrɨp** in the men's house; *hed bilong birua ol* **mɨrɨp** *i save kaikai insait long haus boi*. **Kwai ombrɨ ŋgok**: They have gone to kill people and take heads in battle; *Ol i go kilim birua*.

kwaw *n*. termite mound rising from the ground, made by **agu** (big termites). They are collected and put in fish traps and used to lure fish into them; *haus bilong ol waitpela anis i save stap long graun; ol meri na pikinini i save putim i go insait long ol banis bilong pis bai pis i go insait na kaikai*.

kwem *n*. **1**. penis; *kok*. **Kwem kememŋan!** Long prick!; *Longpela kok!*; **Kwem sawɨrŋan!** Black prick! *Bilakpela kok!*; **Kwemŋa nawŋa!** Useless prick! *Mit nating!* (all vulgar; *olgeta i tok nogut*).
  2. penis-like central root of some kinds of trees (such as papaya trees, **aikesim, tɨp, mayor, noni**) that grows straight down into the ground; *draipela rop bilong diwai i save grodaun long graun*: **Nimŋa kwem**.

kwem taro *n*. genital area of male pig, one of the few parts of a pig, along with the eyes and the gall bladder, that is not eaten; *kok bilong ol pik ol man i kilim long en, ol man i save rausim na troimwe*.

kwemŋa iru *n*. urethra; *nus bilong kok*.

kwemŋa toto *n*. skin of penis, including foreskin; *skin bilong kok*.

M

mambɨr *n.* large horizontal roof supporting beams that rest across the **towond**; *pilo.*

mai *interj.* Enough!, Stop it!; *Inap!, Maski!*

maies *n.* ceremonial, enchanted spear decorated with cassowary feathers traditionally used in men's house to ask spirits about sickness or deaths or inability to hunt. **Amakato**, a plant that grows in the swamps, then is brought to the men's house. The diviner spits on this plant with a chant connecting him to the spirits of the dead, and he calls to the spirits to enter into the spear, which will then act like a Ouija bord, shaking in answer to yes-no questions. The last man to know how to use a **maies** was Yuki Saragum, who died an old man in the 1990s; *spia i gat pawa. Ol tumbuna i save bilasim em long gras bilong muruk, na ol i save spetim **amakato** na singautim ol spirit bilong ol indai man. Ol spirit i save go insait long spia na husat man i gat save long askim bai holim spia na kisim save long ol sik o long sampela indai o bilong wanem ol sampela i no save painim abus. Nau nogat man i save long holim **maies**. Las man i gat save long despela em Yuki Saragum na em indai pinis.* **Yuki maies pekun, kotarpekun**: Yuki held the ceremonial spear and asked it; *Yuki holim spia na askim em.*

maikar *n.* shame; *sem.* **Ŋgu maikarŋgar wákare**: She is shameless; *Em i no save sem.*

maikarɨ *v.i.* (-**pet**/-**pek**), be ashamed; *sem.* **Ŋiŋi namŋat aŋgi supwáspwa ŋanana ninkunde, ŋa ŋgunana maikarpet**: He said something bad to me and I became ashamed; *Em i tokim mi long wanpela hap tok na mi sem.*

maikɨ *v.i.* (-**net**/-**nak**), be finished; run out; *i pinis.* **Muna maitakara**: There is no more sago; *Saksak i pinis.*

maimbog *n.* water that has run into the palm sheaths or canoe in which sago flour is settling. *Wara bilong saksak ol meri wasim long en.*

Mainamb *n.* Manam island; *ples Manam.*

mainye *n.* vine with stiff fuzz used by males until WWII to rid themselves of bad blood. It was dried and inserted into the urethra, then twisted and pulled out to cause copious bleeding; *rop i gat mosong ol tumbuna bilong bipo save putim i go insait long hul bilong kok, tainim tainim na rausim. Ol man i save kisim bikpela pen na rausim bikpela blut.* See also **ndabe.**

maisare *n.* comic act; *pani.* **Maisare ŋgunkun**: He performed a comic act; *Em wokim pani.* **Maisare ŋgrigar munje**: comic, funny man; *man i save wokim pani.*

makarkɨ *v.i.* (-**net**/-**nak**; r → ∅; so **makanet**/**makanak**), fall, used when referring to darkness, time or season; *taim.* **Ikur orom makatak**: It's the middle of the night; *Biknait nau.* **Tukur orom makarkɨ wákare**: It's not the rainy season; *I no taim bilong ren.*

makat *n.* 1. a tree that produces red, rambutan-like seedpods in which the seeds inside are embedded in a reddish sap used to paint the skin on festive occasions; *pen diwai i save karim redpela pikinini ol man i save brukim na bilasim skin long en.*
2. red earth dried in fire and made into a paint used to decorate skin; *redpela graun ol man i save kukim na wokim pen bilong bilasim skin.*
3. the red paint made from the seedpods and the earth; *redpela pen.* **Sumbwaŋa makat**: red paint from earth; *redpela pen bilong graun*; **Nɨmŋa makat**: red paint from seeds; *redpela pen bilong pikinini diwai*)

makatok *n.* stage three (of five) in coconut formation, a young green coconut full of water and ready to drink and eat; *kulau.*

makemake *n.* a kind of vine used to make **toriw** (arm bracelet); *rop ol man i save kisim na wokim paspas bilong han.*

makor *n.* implement made by village men to pulverize the inner bark of sago palm; *wanpela kain samting olsem tamiok o hama* *ol man i save wokim na usim long paitim saksak.* See also **yasuk**.

makorŋa rewi *n.* piece of iron at the head of a **makor** or **yasuk** that scrapes away the inner bark of the sago palm (*lit.* '**makor**'s teeth'); *ain bilong paitim saksak.*

malɨt *n.* tongue; *tang.*

malɨt mosop *n.* uvula (*lit.* 'little tongue'). This is what causes one to swallow, it pushes it into the throat to swallow. When a sick person can no longer eat, this is a sign that the 'little tongue' is not longer doing its work, and that the person will likely die; *liklik tang.*

mámaki *n.* [*Kopar*], gnat; *ol liklik liklik bilakpela binatang i save kaikai man.* This word is replacing Tayap **ipipir**.

mamanj-(p)-i *v.t.* (class 1), show something; *soim.*

mamar *n.* 1. small banana with yellow interior, usually eaten boiled; *wanpela kain banana i sotpela i gat yelopela mit, ol man i save boilim na wokim sup long en.*
2. (*obsolete*), rainbow, *renbo.*

mamba *v.t.* (class 3), lick something; *klinim long tang.* **Nje aŋgo toto mambokunda maritnɨ**: The bitch licked its skin with its tongue; *Dok meri ia i klinim skin bilong em long tang.*

mambadɨkɨ *v.i.* (**ŋɨ mambakadiet/ŋgu mambaodiek**), lick; *klinim long tang; lik.* **Nje ide mambadɨkut**: The dog is licking itself; *Dok i putim tang long em yet.*

mámbakɨr *n.* 1. netbag; *bilum.*
2. (*euphemism*) uterus, placenta; *bilum.*

mambɨr *adj.* (*pl.* **mambró**), young person, traditionally referred only to women, now it refers to both women and men; *yangpela man o meri.* **Noŋor mambɨrtak**: The woman has become young, (This is a euphemism meaning 'she is menstruating'); *Meri i lukim mun (tok bokis).*

mambɨrŋa ror *n.* first born, *pesbon pikinini.* See also **kokɨrŋa ror**.

Mambokor *n.* Marangis village; *ples Marangis.*

mambrag *n.* (*pl.* **mambɨgir**), spirit of dead person, ghost; *dewil.*

mambragegak *n.* a kind of vine used to affix the point of a spear or arrow to the shaft. Women use it as a contraceptive; *rop ol man i save usim long wokim paspas bilong wokim spia bilong sutim pisin. Ol meri i save usim long pasim bel.* **Ŋa toriwnɨ wot adukrunet**: I'm going to make a sling for the arrow; *Mi bai wokim paspas bilong* **wot**; a vine used as a contraceptive by women; *rop ol meri i save kaikai long stopim bel.*

mambragma num (also **mambɨgirma num**) *n.* cemetery (*lit.* 'village of ghosts'); *matmat.*

mamrai *n.* [*Kopar*], lightning; *laitning.* **Ŋan mayayi yɨwɨrŋan pomborrekɨ tatɨŋɨnŋan mamrairekɨ**: His mother gave birth to him together with a pile of shit, as lightning flashed (*vulgar*); *Mama bilong em i karim em wantaim pekpek na laitning i pairap (tok nogut).* The Tayap word, rarely used, is **urerŋgar**.

mamrarara okɨ *v.i.* (conjugated like **okɨ**), shake, shiver; *guria.*

mamrarkɨ *v.i.* (**-net/-nak**), flash; *lait.* **Aruat mamrartaka wok**: The lightning flashed (*lit.* 'the thunder flashed'); *laitning i lait.* See also **urekɨ**.

man *n.* vagina; *kan.* **Man sawirɨ!**: Black cunt!; *Bilakpela kan!*; **Man sumanɨ!**: Big cunt!; *Bikpela hul!*; **Man aprol**: Bad cunt; *Hul nogut!*; **Man pisimbŋa!** Rotten cunt! *Kan i sting pinis!* (all vulgar terms of abuse; *olgeta i tok nogut*).

manaw *n.* three; *tripela.*

mandamandap *n.* [*Kopar*], barb of a stingray. In the past, people used to camouflage these and place them at the base of their betel nut palms, so that if anyone attempted to steal the betel nut by climbing the palm, the barb would lodge in their foot; *nil bilong* **nakanaka**. *Bipo ol papa tumbuna i save putim despela long as bilong ol buai bilong ol, olsem stilman bai krungutim na kisim bikpela pen.* See also **atɨm**.

mandɨg *adj.* unripe; *i no mau.*

mandɨmep *n.* Ground Dwelling Pigeon (*Birds of New Guinea* plate 15, #1–7; plate 16. #1–3).

manduwar *n.* taro; *taro*.
mangɨm *n.* water rat; *rat i save kaikai pis na stap klostu long wara*.
manɨmbomo *n.* shelf fungus, sometimes used as a way of healing sores; *talinga i save kamap long pangal bilong kokonas o bilong saksak, ol tumbuna i save putim long sua bilong draim em.* See also **njogrob**.
manɨng *n.* 1. traditional bucket made out of sago palm leaf; *baket bilong ol tumbuna ol i save wokim long* **kondew**.
    2. urethra; *insait bilong kok o bilong kan*. **Ṇa oruneta, nok manɨng patorkɨtak**: If I hit you, you'll explode with piss; *Mi paitim yu olsem bai pispis i paiarap*.
manŋa iru *n.* clitoris; *nus bilong kan*.
manumbi *n.* a kind of tree, the leaves of which are boiled and used as a medicine to treat the illness **eiwa**; *diwai ol mama i save boilim lip bilong em na givim long husat pikinini i gat eiwa*.
maŋemaŋar *n.* grille; *gereray*.
maŋat *n.* tiny white shells like small cowries sewn into traditional decorations; *liklik ol kina ol tumbuna i save wokim bilas long en*.
mar *n.* 1. sago palm flowers; *plowa bilong saksak*.
    2. crown or top of felled sago palm; *tel bilong saksak ol man i wok long paitim em*.
mara *n.* ocean; *bikpela solwara*.
maraŋgap *n.* plant similar to **munjuko**, used to cover up sago flour and protect it from rain; *hap diwai olsem* **munjuko**.
markɨya okɨ *v.i.* (each verb conjugated separately; the first with the endings **-net/-nak**: **ŋɨ maneta mbot/ŋgu mataka wok/ŋgɨ matukoya ŋgok**), row; *pul i go*.
marŋgo *n.* a dog's sharp, canine teeth; *popela sapela tit bilong dok*.
marŋgop *n.* shaft of spear or oar; *as bilong spia o bilong pul*. **Yirŋa marŋgop wurotukun**: Raise the shaft of the spear (so that the spear doesn't stab me); *Apim as bilong spia*.
marŋgoram *n.* dog's teeth traditionally used as money; *ol tit bilong dok ol tumbuna i save usim olsem mani*.

marŋgorŋa kas *n.* sago frond that has been cut in a particular way (most leaves trimmed with only four left untrimmed, and the bottom leaf tied in a knot at the base) and decorated with dog's teeth arranged in a line along the spine in ten groups of three. Prepared as part of a conciliatory meal (i.e. a meal that is offered to resolve a fight or conflict) and carried by someone who stands at the head of the procession of food; *pangal saksak ol man i wokim long sekhan kaikai. Husat i go pes long sekhan kaikai bai katim lip bilong pangal na lainim tit bilong dok long bun bilong em. Despela pangal bai go wantaim kaikai long husat man ol man i laik stretim*.
marow *n.* short, narrow banana in two varieties, red and green; *liklik banana i gat tupela kain, redpela na grinpela*.
masipkakɨ *v.i.* (-**net**/-**nak**), (*obsolete*), resist, not want to do something; *nogat laik long wokim wanpela samting*. **Ŋgɨ Kono namtuko orakaŋgar nirkru, ŋgu masipkatak**: They told Kono to make food but she refused; *Ol i tokim Kono long wokim kaikai tasol em i no laik*.
masukondep *n.* small dark brown and blue lizard associated with mothers and newborn babies. Referred to as "mothers" by women in their maternity houses, and it is believed that they watch protectively over newborn babies. If you kill one, the baby will cry. *Ol liklik palai i save was long ol nupela bebi. Yu kilim wanpela bai bebi i krai*. **Mayaŋgro aŋgi bioŋginana wasakŋguk**: The mothers are watching over the baby; *Ol mama i was i stap long liklik bebi*.
matatak *n.* 1. dew; *wara i save stap long gras o long ol diawai long moning aua*.
    2. rain remaining on grass, tree branches and plants after a rainfall; *wara i save stap long gras o long ol diwai taim ren i pinis*.
maya *n.*; *voc.* (*dl.* **mayaṇre**, *pl.* **mayaŋgro**), mother; *mama*. See also **ama**.
mayar (also **maṇar**) *n.* leaf; *lip*.

mayor *n.* a tree whose bark is used to make the slings of a basket (**sapwarŋa numun**) and the fringed decorations on the sides of baskets; also used as a way of 'cooling' certain kinds of sorcery; *gomba ol meri i save katim na putim i go long wara long wokim ol* **sapwarŋa numun** *bilong ol basket na tu yu ken usim despela diwai long kolim sampela kain posin.*

mbába *n.* [*Kopar*], wooden pins used to hold the **waris** (coconut fiber strainer) in place; *nil bilong nilim laplap bilong kokonas.* See also **pandiŋ**.

mbababi *v.t.* (class 5; reduplicated form of **mbar**, used with plural objects), raise up to a standing position; *sanapim ol.*

mbábasak *n.* silly, crazy, disturbed; *longlong, paul.*

mbábasak *v.t.* (class 5), 1. misuse of something e.g. money; *paulim wanpela samting, olsem mani.* 2. confuse or 'bugger up'; *bagarapim.* **Munje ide numbwan mbabasaknukun orákaŋarana:** The man forgot to eat (*lit.* 'his thought about the food buggered up'); *Man ia i lus ting long kaikai.*

mbábasakkɨ *v.i.* (**-net/-nak**), confuse, mislead; *paul.* **Ŋaŋan numbwan mbabasaktak:** I forgot; *Tingting bilong mi paul.*

mbabuŋ *adj.* burned, scorched; *bilakpela long paia.*

mbabuŋkɨ *v.i.* (**-net/-nak**), burn, scorch; *kukim i go bilakpela long paia.*

mbada *n.* 1. rainforest; *bus.* 2. (*euphemism*), toilet; *toilet.* **Ŋa mbadanɨ mbot:** I'm going into the rainforest. If one is alone, this can mean that one is going to the toilet. If one is accompanied by dogs, this means that one is going hunting; *Mi go long bus. Em wanpela mining i olsem yu go long toilet tasol sapos yu go wantaim ol dok em miningim olsem yu go long painim abus.*

mbadaŋa patɨr *n.* euphemism for toilet and also for maternity house (*lit.* 'bush house'); *smolhaus o haus karim.*

mbadɨŋ *n.* bee; *bi.*

mbag *n.* riverbank; bank of creek; *sait bilong baret.*

mbainonoŋ *n.* [*Kopar*], casuarina trees on beaches near sea; *diwai yar.* The Tayap would be **sumbwakapɨrŋa nɨm**, *lit.* 'beach tree'.

mbaiskɨ *v.i.* (**-tet/-tak**), become tough and inedible, refers to taro; *kamap strong, em toktok bilong taro.*

mbákbak *n.* three-sided banana; *banana i gat tripela sait.*

mbakinono *n.* large, apple-shaped fruit; *bikpela laulau.*

mbankap *n.* cold wind in the morning, from the direction of Sanae village, i.e. rainforest wind; *kolpela win i save kamap long taim bilong moning i save kamap long bus.*

mbaŋ *v.t.* (class 5), bang against something; *bampim.* **Ŋa pande mbaŋkrunet kawrɨkkɨtak isurokɨ wákare:** I'll knock the axe against something so that the handle fastens and it won't loosen; *Bai mi bampim tamiok (long wanpela diwai o pos) long strongim em na em i no nap lus*; **Mbaŋku arotak!** Bang it (against the post) and it will go inside; *Bampim em na em bai go insait.*

mbaŋaw *n.* a kind of areca palm with large red seeds, used to make spear shafts, arrows. It is also used to make poison. One cuts the bark so that it forms a little bowl. After it rots, one collects the water in it, mixes it with a crushed millipede and uses it to poison someone; *wanpela limbum diwai i gat ol bikpela redpela pikinini, ol man i save katim long wokim banara o* **wot**. *Na tu. Ol man nogut i save usim despela diwai long posinim ol narapela man. Ol i save katim skin bilong diwai na larim em sting. Bihain bai miksim wanpela* **kakamatɨk** *na kilim ol man ol i paitim long en.* See also **pandɨm**.

mbar *v.t.* (class 4), make stand vertically; *sanapim.* **Sakɨnd wurotukuna mbatukun!** Lift the house post and stand it up! *Apim pos na sanapim!*

mbara *n.* garden where one grows food; *gaden.*

mbara(nɨ) *adv.* a little; *liklik*. **Pendimor kemem mbaranɨ utɨtukun:** Cut the paper so that it is a little bit long; *Katim pepa i longpela liklik*.

mbarmɨt *n.* thick, difficult to penetrate jungle; *bus i tik, hat long go insai long em*. See also **abar**.

mbarow *n.* a small blue, white and red fish that lives in forest streams. This fish is the one that went to tell the water-deity **Ŋgayam** that villagers were gathering his children in the dry creekbeds (see Tayap Text 2); *wanpela kain liklik pis bilong baret, blu, red na wait. Em despela pis i go tokim masalai Ŋgayam long ol man i wok long kisim ol pikinini bilong em*.

mbata *v.t.* (class 5), ruin or destroy something; *bagarapim*.

mbatak *n.* a kind of breadfruit in which only the seeds (**mot**) are eaten; *kapiak*.

mbatámbati *adj.* white and red mottled coat of an animal; *wait na redpela gras bilong kaskas o dok o kainkain animol*.

mbatambur *n.* a kind of breadfruit in which the interior fiber (**minj**) is eaten; *kapiak*.

mbatembatep *n.* **1.** small seeds; *ol pikinini bilong diwai*.
2. coins; *ol koins*.

mbateŋ *n.* club used by the ancestors to beat their loincloths out of bark; *stik bilong paitim malo*.
2. Nightjar (*Birds of New Guinea* plate 27).

mbatep *n.* [*Kopar*], one, one unit; *wanpela*, **Papŋa mbatep:** one coconut; *wanpela kokonas*; **Minjikeŋa mbatep:** one betel nut; *wanpela buai*; **Nonŋa mbatep:** one yam; *wanpela yam*.

mbatɨm *n.* rivulet; *liklik hanwara*.

mberɨg *n.* one of several trees from which **tékduan** (floor runners) are cut; *wanpela diwai ol man i save katim long wokim tékduan*.

mberowok *n.* bamboo used to make a knife that, in pre-colonial times, severed the heads of murdered enemies. This bamboo was first planted by Ombaŋ, a mythological ancestor; *mambu ol man bilong bipo i save wokim naip long rausim hed bilong ol birua, Ombaŋ i planim*.

mbibiknɨ see **mbiknɨ**.

mbidomo *n.* (*euphemism*), intercourse, *pasin nogut*. **Mbidomo nitukure:** The two of them had sex; *Tupela i wokim pasin nogut*.

mbiknɨ (also **mbini** and **mbibiknɨ**) *adv.* **1.** similar to, like; *olsem*. **Yarawin mbiknɨ:** It's like sugar water; *Em olsem wara bilong suga*. **Ŋɨ mbor mbiknɨ kakun:** He ate like a pig; *Em i kaikai olsem pik*; **Sopak munje ketukŋan mbibiknɨ warakakuk:** Sopak is talking like a man who coughs a lot; *Sopak toktok olsem man i save kus*.
2. like this; *olsem*. **Aŋgok mbiknɨ nitukun:** Do it like this; *Mekim olsem*.

mbímaŋ *n.* leech; *liklik snek i save stap long bikbus na i save pas strong long man na dring blut bilong em*.

mbin *n.* steam; *smok, hat bilong wara o wanem samting i boil long en*. **Mbin wokuk:** Steam is rising; *Hat bilong wara o wanem samting i go antap*.

mbini see **mbiknɨ**.

mbiodkɨ *v.i.* (-**tet**/-**tak**), flutter slowly; sputter; throb without pain; any weak recurring movement, such as the repeated clenching of a dog's anus while it engages in intercourse, the ticking of the second hand of a watch; *wok, pamp*. **Ŋɨ nok karkuna, kwem mbiodakuk:** He peed and is pumping out the last drops of urine; *Em pispis na em pampim liklik pispis i stap*.

mbióŋgi *n.* baby, until it laughs and sits, at which point it becomes a **ror** or **ror mokop**; *liklik nupela pikinini, i go inap em inap sindaun na lap, bihain long despela bai yu kolim em* **ror** *o* **ror mokop**.

mbirkraw onko *n.* big sago beetle; *bikpela binatang bilong saksak*.

mbiruŋa kɨt *n.* Pleiades; *yiar*. See also **ŋgudumŋa kɨt**.

mbirupa *v.t.* (class 3), **1.** suck or slurp something; *pulim long maus*. **Mum awin awin aŋgi utɨŋgarke tatarnɨ, mbirupatukun siknɨ:** The sago jelly is too watery, don't cut it with your spoon, slurp it up with your

mouth; *Saksak i wara wara i no ken katim putim tasol long maus na kaikai*;
2. inhale something; *pulim long maus*. **Yu ŋgo sokoiŋat isiatan, ŋa ŋgo pinni mbirupakrunet**: Give me your cigarette, I'll take a puff; *Givim hap smok long mi bai mi pulim liklik*.

mbibiu *v.t.* (class 5), to stretch something, e.g. a net, some material, talk; *pulim pulim*. See also **mbiu**.

mbid *n*. pain, ache; *pen*. **Aindet ror ainde mbid tarkrunet**: That boy is going to receive pain (i.e. I am going to hit him); *Despela mangi ia bai kisim pen*.

mbidki *v.i.* (most often takes beneficiary object forms): pain, ache; *pen*. **Ndow mbidtiatan**: My leg pains; *Lek bilong mi pen*; **Rewi mbidtukwatan**: Her teeth ache; *Tit bilong em pen*.

mbij *n*. copse; cluster of trees standing very close to one another; *hap long bus i gat ol as bilong diwai i bung klostu klostu*. **Yamŋa mbij**: a group of sago palms that grow very close together; *saksak ol i sanap grup*. See also **ŋgib**.

mbim *n*. Frogmouth and Nightjar (*Birds of New Guinea* plate 26, #11–18). The word is onomatopoetic, imitating the cries made by these birds.

mbin *n*. [*Kopar*], mud that appears in the mangrove and in creeks when water recedes; *graun i save kamap long mangoro o long ol baret long taim bilong draiwara*. The Tayap expression for this, not used by anyone but that I elicited specifically, would be the sentence **Awin odiwoka sumbwa sindertakara**: The water fell and the ground appeared uncovered.

mbir *n*. short piece of wood or short tree; *sotpela hap diwai o sotpela diwai*.

mbirat *n*. short stick; *sotpela hap diwai*.

mbiu *v.t.* (class 5), to stretch something, e.g. a fishnet, cloth, talk; *pulim olsem wanpela laplap o wanpela wumben o sampela tok*. See also **mbibiu**.

mbodaŋ *n*. 1. gill; *maus i staplong sait bilong pis*.

2. fin; *win bilong pis*. See also **naniŋg**.

mbodibodi *n*. Robin (*Birds of New Guinea* plate 37, #10; plate 39, #11–21). Being replaced by the Kopar-language word **mbodiŋeŋe**.

mbokak *n*. surface, *antap*.

mbokakni *pos*. on top of; on the surface of; *antap long*. **Mbokakŋani inde namakkut**: He's just talking on the surface (i.e. he's not saying what he really thinks); *Em tok i stap tasol, em i no brukim tok*.

mbókokir *n*. tadpole; *ol liklik ol pis i save kamapim ol prog*.

mbominj *n*. 1. fetus or stillborn child; *pikinini i no pinisim gut taim bilong em insait long bel bilong mama na em indai*.

2. newborn human, animal or bird; *nupela pikinini bilong man, na tu ol nupela pikinini bilong pik o dok o sasik o pisin o wanem kain ol animol*. **Man mbominjŋa!**: Hairless cunt! (vulgar); *Kan nating! (tok nogut)*.

mbonir *n*. Mannikin (*Birds of New Guinea* plate 48).

mbor *n*. (*pl*. **mboreirum**), pig; *pik*.

mbor mir *n*. boar; *pik man*.

mbor onko *n*. young, fertile female pig; *yangpela pik meri inap karim ol pikinini*.

mbor yam *n*. sago palm felled and cut open in order to lure a pig to eat it, so that one might spear it; *saksak bilong pik bai kaikai na bai yu inap sutim em long banis saksak*.

mborabaw *n*. wallow; place where pigs dig and sleep; *hap ol pik i save dikim long em na slip long em*.

mborbwaj *n*. large bamboo used to make walls; *bikpela mambu ol man i save wokim blain long em*.

mborgi *n*. large, salt-water shell that used to be draped around dancers at feasts, and around the neck of a corpse; *bikpela skin kina ol tumbuna save hangamapim long nek bilong ol long taim bilong singsing, na taim man indai bai putim long nek bilong bodi na planim wantaim*.

mbori *v.t.* (class 5), knock down so hard that the object of the punch writhes on the ground; *dropim*. **ŋayi aini ŋgratboriniŋin andni**

kararneta mbot inde: I knocked him down so hard that he writhed on the ground and was covered in blood; *Mi dropim em na em tainim tainim na em red long blut igo.*

mborirki *v.i.* (**-net/-nak**), flipflop; *tainim tainim.* **Mbarow sene mborimborikar woke awin motoreke**: The two fish were flipflopping along in the small puddles; *Tupela pis i tainim tainim igo long ol liklik wara.*

mboripki *v.i.* (**-net/-nak**), **1.** swell up as a result of sickness or sorcery; *solap;* **Munjema imin mboriptaka puwok patorkitakana**: The (dead) man's stomach has swollen up, it's about to break open; *Bel bilong man i solap i go antap pinis, em bai bruk nau.*
2. satiate, be filled up; *solap.* **Ndamori mum nitukuna kukuweka piatana, ŋa kakuna imin mboriptak**: Ndamor made the sago jelly and brought it and I ate it and was filled up; *Ndamor tainim saksak kisim i kam nau na mi kaikai na bel bilong mi pulap.*

mborkini *pos.* out in the open, unconcealed; *ples klia.* **Mborkini nam ŋgurkrundak**: They're going to talk openly; *Ol bai tokaut klia;* **Ŋaŋan man ewar mborkini ŋgutukro**: Yesterday they talked openly about my cunt (said about drunken men who cursed the female speaker); *Asde ol i putim kan bilong mi long ples klia (ol spakman toknogutim meri i makim despela toktok);* **Ŋgu mborkini utok, ripim ambruni wuk**: Now it's out in the open, before it was hidden; *Em kamap ples klia, bipo em i hait.*

mborŋa muna *n.* raw sago presented in a large palm sheath bucket to one's joking kin during a funerary feast, it is so large that it needs to be carried on a pole like the carcass of a pig (*lit.* 'pig's sago'); *saksak bilong pati bilong i go long ol wanpilai. Em bikpela tru na ol man bai putim insait long wanpela bikpela limbom na karim em i go long wanpela stik olsem ol i karim bodi bilong pik.*

mbormat *n.* kind of thick banana with red skin, eaten when ripe; *banana i gat redpela skin ol man i save kaikai mau.*

mbororki *v.i.* (**-net/-nak**), agree to murder someone; *pasim tok long kilim man.*

mborsip *n.* pork; *abus bilong pik.*

mbrat *n.* bare vine left when betel nut and other cluster fruit drop off, used by women as a broom; *ol rop bilong buai o bilong* **kondew** *o bilong kokonas taim ol buai i pundaun pinis, ol meri i save usim long brumin haus o graun.* **Minjikeŋa mbrat**: broom made of betel nut vine; *brum bilong buai;* **Kondewŋa mbrat**: broom made of **kondew** vine; *brum bilong* **kondew**.

mbreŋ-(p)-e *v.t.* (class 1), stir something; *tainim.*

mbua *n.* a kind of vine given to snakebite victims to eat raw, as a way of "cooling" the venom; *wanpela rop bilong gaden, ol man i save givim long husat man snek i bin kaikaim em. Em sapos long kolim posin bilong snek.*

mbubow *n.* a new shoot on a betel nut tree and several other kinds of trees that produce clusters of seeds or nuts. The shoot emerges covered with a **kondew** (sheath), which later opens, releasing the cluster of seeds or pods; *kru bilong buai na sampela ol narapela kain diwai.*

mbubujiram *n.* bubbles from fish, crocodiles, turtles emerging from underwater; *win bilong ol samting i stap ananeat long wara, i kam antap na ol man save lukim olsem wara i boil.*

mbubuk *n.* pouch-like sheath made from the tender offshoot of betel nut palms; *liklik kontaina bilong putim ol sampela samting, ol i save wokim long limbom bilong buai.* **Sokoiŋa mbubuk**: pouch for storing tobacco leaves; *liklik kontaina bilong putim ol lip brus ol i draim pinis.*

mbuga *n.* a type of banana; *wanpela kain banana.*

mbumjor *n.* extremely venomous black snake with shiny black skin and blue stripes; *bilakpela posin snek.* See also **kombin**.

mbun *n.* 1. air, breath; *win*. **Mbun aŋgukwankut**: He's breathing; *Em pulim win i stap*; **Mbun tarkru wåkare**: He's stopped breathing; *Em i no pulim win*.
2. remains, *bun, samting i bagarap pinis*. **Patirŋa mbun**: abandoned, collapsed house; *ol pos na ol narapela samting bilong haus i bruk na pundaun*. **Nawŋa mbun**: burnt grassland; *kunai bihain long paia i kukim long em*. See also **pora**; **war**.

mbunbun *n.* mosquito with bluish coloring and long legs that are especially active in the late afternoon; *mosquito i blupela na i gat ol longpela pinga, em save kamap long apinun*.

mbunim *n.* wind from the mangrove swamp, i.e. north wind; *win i save kamap long mangoro*.

mbunoŋ *n.* a banana similar to **oremai ikin** except it is bigger; *banana i olsem oremai ikin tasol em i bikpela long en*.

mbunor *n.* 1. spirit; *spirit, dewil*.
2. power; *pawa*. **Ambagai mbunorŋan**: men's house with power – i.e. a men's house that retains its connections to ancestral spirits and forest deities, and can therefore cause illness and channel power to succeed in hunting or battle; *haus boi i gat powa*.

mbur-(p)-e *v.t.* (class 1), bend something; *taitim, krungutim*. **Ewar kembatik mburpekunde, ŋgu odiwok**: Yesterday he bent his bow (to shoot it), and it broke; *Asde em i taitim banara bilong em, na banara i bruk*.

mburai *v.t.* (class 5), sweep something; *brumim*. Synonymous with **mburai-(p)-i**.

mburai-(p)-i *v.t.* (class 1), sweep something, *brumim*. Synonymous with **mburai**.

mburararakki *v.i.* (**-net**/**-nak**), rot to the point of being completely decayed; *sting olgeta*.

mburko *n.* 1. foot of bird; *pinga bilong pisin*.
2. hoof; *pinga bilong lek na han bilong pik*. **Mborma mburkow**: pig's footprints; *mark bilong lek bilong pik*. See also **sikrim**.

mburuw *n.* stomach; *namba wan bel*.

mbus-(p)-i *v.t. irr.* (class 1, conjugated as class 1 verb in realis, but the irrealis stem form is **mbudji**), 1. send someone or something; *salim*. **Ewar ŋayi siw sene mbuspikwatan**: Yesterday I sent her two pieces of skin; *Asde mi salim em tupela hap skin*; **Epi ŋayi siw sene mbudjikwatinet**: Tomorrow I will send her two pieces of skin; *Tumaro bai mi salim em tupela hap skin*; **Yu mbustimbina Potore ondak, nunuk yu wetet ŋaŋan patirni**: Send them on their way to Wonga, then come to my house; *Salin ol i go long Wongan, bihain yu kam long haus bilong mi*.
2. sell something; *salim*.

mbutak *n.* large skink; *bikpela palai i save pait*.

mbutup *adj.* blunt; *i no sap*.

mbutupki *v.i.* (**-tet**/**-tak**), become blunt; *kamap olsem nogat sap*.

mbwag *n.* 1. spine of a leaf; *bun bilong brus o aibika o banana*.
2. braid to which the strands of a traditional skirt are attached; *hap bilong pulpul ol meri i save pasim* **tar** *long en*.
3. an old sago palm that has lost all its leaves; *lapun saksak nogat moa lip*: **yam mbwag**.
4. long, sharp black quills on cassowary wings; *pinga bilong liklik win bilong muruk*.

mbwagki *v.i.* (**-tet**/**-tak**), shed leaves; used only when talking about sago palms; *saksak i plowa olgeta, nogat lip*.

mbwaj *n.* bamboo (*generic*); *mambu* (*biknem*).

mbwajorom *n.* gun; *gan*. **Eŋgin mandama mbwajorom patorŋar**: White men's guns make an explosive noise. *Gan bilong ol waitman i save pairap*.

mbwak-(p)-o (class 1), smush together two vaginas; *tupela meri i kwap na mekim pairap*. **Iru mir sapkini mbwakoku ekrukakutak!**: You walk around with your big clitoris banging against other cunts! (*vulgar*); *Draipela nus bilong kan wakabaut bengim nating ol kan!* (*tok nogut*).

mbwantaw (from **mbwajŋa taw** 'bamboo's side') *n.* **1.** bamboo razor; *tumbuna reza ol isave wokim long mambu.*
2. (*euphemism*) grass knife; *grasnaip (tok bokis).*
mbwar *n.* **1.** back; *baksait.* **Mbor mbwarŋan**: Pig with meat on it (*lit.* 'pig with a back'); *Pik i gat bikpela mit.*
2. tree trunk; *namel bilong diwai.* **Makatok papŋa mbwarŋa otitek**: The young coconut fell down from the coconut tree-trunk; *Kulau i stap antap long diwai kokonas na i pundaun.*
3. surface of body of water, *antap bilong wara.* **Yimbar awinŋa mbwarni purarapuwok**: The canoe is floating on the water; *Kanu i trip antap long wara.*
4. surface of ground, *graun.* **Ŋgritukun ainini sumbwaŋa mbwarni**: Put it here on the ground; *Putim long ia long graun.*
mbwarni *pos.* behind; *baksait.*
mbwarpasinderni *adj.* content, without worry, happy (*lit.* 'back light'); *hamamas.*
mbwarpasinderki *v.i.* (**-net/-nak**), be worry free, happy; *i stap hamamas.* **Ŋa mbwarpasinderki wákare, imin naimbtiatan**: I'm not content, I'm weighed down with worry (*lit.* 'my belly has been made heavy'); *Mi no hamamas bel bilong mi i hevi.*
memki *v.i.* (**ŋa pemiet/pemiek, yu pemiet/pemiek, ŋi pemiet, ŋgu pemiek, yim pemiek, yum pemkem, ŋgi pemko, yim sene pemke**), **1.** get up, stand up; *kirap.*
2. start, for example when talking about a fire or an outboard motor; *kirap, olsem paia o moto o wanem samting yu laik statim.* **Tukur aiki wákare ndi, otar memrikrak**: If it hadn't rained, the fire would have started; *Sapos ren i no bin i kam, paia i mas kirap pinis.*
menjikan *pos.* nearby, close to; *klostu.*
meŋemeŋe *n.* **1.** itch; *samting i sikarap.*
2. sexual desire, orgasm; *pilings, sikarap.*
meŋemeŋeki *v.i.* (**-net/-nak**), awaken sexual desire, turn on; *kisim pilings.* **Ŋgu meŋemeŋera wek**: Her sexual desire was awakened; *Pilings bilong em i strong na i kam.* **Yu meŋemeŋetetke?**: Are you turned on? *Yu sikarap o?*
meŋgini *adv.* slowly; *isi.* **Ŋi meŋginiki ŋayar prukakkut**: He is working really slowly; *Em i wok i stap isi tru ia.*
mer *n.* language; *tok ples.* **Tayap mer**: Tayap language; *tok ples Gapun*; **Eŋgin mer**: Tok Pisin; *Tok Pisin.*
mera *mood part.* a word that marks the epistemic status of an action or event as something that has been assumed but that the speaker or the referent believes did not correspond to what actually happened; *hap tok i laik tok olsem yu ting olsem wanpela samting bai kamap, tasol i no kamap.* **Ŋa namnet ŋi Potore okinet mera**: I thought he would go to Wongan (but he didn't); *Mi ting olsem em bai go long Wongan (tasol nogat).* See Section 7.6.2 of the grammar
Merew *n.* Sanae village; *ples Sanae, Mangum.*
merom *n.* thread; *tret.*
meruk *n.* sago and scraped coconut, boiled in a banana leaf; *saksak na kokonas ol i save putim i go insait long wanpela lip banana na boilim.*
met *n.* braided rope; *rop.*
metawr *n.* wasps or bees that make honey; *ol bi i save wokim switpela wara.*
metawrŋa naŋaŋa awin *n.* honey (*lit.* 'the water of the eggs of **metawr**'); *wara bilong ol kiau bilong ol* **metawr**.
mimb *n.* coconut cream; *wara bilong kokonas i sikarapim na bengim long en.*
min *n.* breast of women and female animals, including cassowaries; *susu.* See also **ŋgatma min**.
mindia *n.* stone axe; *ston tamiok bilong ol tumbuna.* See also **poŋgrom**.
minj *n.* the meat of a breadfruit; *mit bilong kapiak.* **Batamburŋa minj**.
minjia *v.t.* (class 3), chew something; *krungutim long tit.*
minjike *n.* betel nut; *buai.*
minjinai *n.* pancreas; *laplap bilong karamapim bikpela bel.*

minŋa iru *n.* nipple (*lit.* 'breast's point'); *nus bilong susu*.

mintumb *n.* chest muscle; *bros*.

mipat *n.* **1.** fleshy rear parts of birds, crustaceans or other animals that do not have tails; *as bilong pisin na ol sampela narapela samting*. **Ŋgatma mipat**: cassowary tail; *as bilong muruk*; **Pisikma mipat**: hermit crab tail; *as bilong pisik*; **Kanipma mipat**: flesh of mangrove slug; *mit bilong kandip*.
  2. bottom; *as*. **Kontainaŋa mipat**: Bottom of the container; *As bilong kontaina*.

mis *n.* **1.** meat; *abus*.
  2. meaning; *as*.
  3. inner bark of sago palm that is pounded and leached for sago flour; *mit bilong saksak*.

misikap *n.* wisdom, good sense, good knowledge learned from ancestors (i.e. how to be generous, how to fulfill social obligations, etc.); *skul, gutpela pasin bilong ol tumbuna bilong bipo*. **Koto taman waswituko, omosew, neningro, ŋgigi misikap taman kukuŋgwok**: All the old ones have died, the fathers, the grandfathers and they took all their wisdom with them; *Olgeta lapun indai pinis, ol papa na ol tumbuna na ol i kisim ol gutpela save bilong ol na i go wantaim*.

misisiŋ *n.* breast milk of women or animals; *susu*. **Misisiŋ kikiu** (*lit.* 'yellow milk') and **misisiŋ apro** (*lit.* 'bad milk'): colostrum, which is expressed and discarded by most women; *yelopela susu i save kamap pes, planti ol meri i save bengim na rausim*.

miw *n.* ground cuscus; *kuskus bilong graun*.

mik *adj.* **1** sharp; *sapela*.
  2. intense, hard; *strongpela, hatpela*. **Awarer mik**: The sun is intense; *San i hot*. **Pruk mik**: intense, hard work; *hatpela wok*. **Nim mik**: hard wood; *strongpela diwai*; **Imin mikŋa**: furious (*lit.* 'stomach sharp'); *belhat*.

min *n.* **1.** the chewed husk of **minjike** (betel nut), **yar** (sugarcane) or **kanjigogo** (bamboo shoots); *meme bilong buai, suga o kru mambu*.
  2. grated coconut once all the milk has been squeezed out of it; *pipia bilong kokonas bihain long yu bengim em na rausim olgeta wara*.

minda *n.* be tired or sick of something, or unwilling to do something; *les*. **Ŋa minda!** I don't want to! **Ŋa mindarakkut yumon pindiŋana!** I'm sick of listening to your noise! *Mi les long pairap bilong yupela!*

mindiki *v.i.* (**pindiet/pindiek**), **1.** work sago; *wok saksak*; **Yum mindikinana mbokem?**: Are you all going to work sago? *Yupela i go wok saksak ah?*
  2. pulverize sago pith; *paitim saksak*.

minimbki *v.i.* (**-net/-nak**), wrinkle, *skin i slek*.

minjikki *v.i.* (**-net/-nak**), make a 'tsk' sound; *tok olsem 'tsk, mi les'*.

minjurup *n.* kissing sound; *nois olsem tupela man i kis*.

minjurupki *v.i.* (**-net/-nak**), make a kissing sound; *pairapim maus olsem yu laik kis long wanpela pikinini*.

minuomb *n.* round pool of water in the swamp where **emári** (water deities) may live; *raun wara i gat masalai*.

miŋan *adj.* male; *man*. **Miŋanke? Noŋor?**: Is (the newborn baby) a boy or a girl? *Pikinini man o meri?*

miŋandor *n.* a contraction of **miŋan ror**, 'male child', the word is used to designate a newly born male child in reponse to the question: "**Miŋanke? Noŋor?**": "Is it a boy or a girl?". However, mostly it is used by parents and other caregivers to shame girls who don't obey or do things of which the caregivers disapprove. The message, phrased as an assertion (**Miŋandor!**) or an upbraiding question (**Miŋandorke?!**) is that the girl is acting gender inappropriately; *pikinini man (em narapela we long kolim* **miŋan ror**: *pikinini man*). *Ol man na meri i save kolim taim ol i laik toktok long nupela pikinini man o taim ol sampela i askim "Pikinini man o meri" na yu laik tok* "pikinini man". Tasol planti taim ol man na meri i save usim long givim sem long ol pikinini meri. Taim ol pikinini meri i save wakabaut as nating, o taim ol i no save harim tok, husat i laik givim sem long ol bai tok **Miŋandor!** o bai askim: **Miŋandorke?!**

miŋanŋa kup n. small intestine; bel.

miŋg n. a knife tied to a stick to cut fruit or something else in a tree that one can't reach; naip ol man i save pasim i go antap long diwai long katim buai o wanem samting i stap antap long diwai. **Miŋg nitukuna mbatambur uritukun:** Tie a knife to a stick and cut down the breadfruit! Pasim naip antap long diwai na sakim kapiak!

miŋgip n. knee; skru. **Ewar ŋgu miŋgip odukun:** Yesterday she kneeled; Asde em i brukim skru. See also **adu**.

miŋgipŋa sokop n. knee cap; sel bilong skru.

miŋgŋa bwar n. long piece of bamboo that used to be laid on the grave of a recently buried body. After several hours, the spirit of the deceased enters it, and it is carried around the village and asked questions about who killed the person; hap mambu bipo ol tumbuna i save putim antap long hul ol i bin planim man long en. Spirit bilong man bai go insait long despela hap mambu na ol man inap kisim em bek na askim em long indai bilong papa bilong spirit.

minminki v.i. (-net/-nak), speak indistinctly, to murmur; toktok isi tru olsem guria.

mir intens. really; bikpela. **Suman apro mir:** really huge; bikpela nogut tru; **Naimb apro mir:** really heavy; hevi nogut tru; **Arawer mir:** huge, hot sun; bikpela hotpela san; **Kandap mir apro sakar:** [You're a] big fucking elf! [Yu] wanpela blari spirit nogut ia!

miri n. rainforest; bus.

miriŋmiriŋ n. noise; pairap. **Ŋare miriŋmiriŋ nirkwanaŋwarke!** Stop making noise here! I no ken mekim nois long hap bilong mi!

miriŋa at n. tiny black mosquitoes endemic to the rainforest; ol liklik liklik bilakpela natnat i save stap insait long bus. **Miriŋa ati mbatati:** The little mosquitos in the jungle made me miserable; Ol liklik natnat bilong bus i bagarapim mi.

miriŋa awin n. (euphemism), secret male rituals in the rainforest (lit. 'rainforest water'); wara bilong bus ol man i save waswas long en. **Miriŋan awinni tuwku okinak:** Let's go wash in rainforest water; Mipela i go waswas long wara bilong bus.

miriŋa munje n. uneducated, rural hillbilly (lit. 'rainforest's man'); buskanaka.

miriŋan toto puwas n. (lit. 'rainforest's skin white'), albino; wait skin man o meri bilong Papua Niugini, i no waitskin man bilong ol kantri.

mirip n. traditional men's cult deities, embodied in flutes and other sacred objects; tambaran. The names of the most important of the deities are **Empantur, Sopak, Kairaban, Esawaŋ, Ogarbi, Ogarpa, Akrontsim**; Ol nem bilong ol bikpela tambaran **Empantur, Sopak, Kairaban, Esawaŋ, Ogarbi, Ogarpa, Akrontsim.** See also **mokit; timbar noŋor**.

mit adj. dense, thick; bikpela. **Ŋi ewar ikur mitni mbet:** Yesterday he came in the middle of the night; Asde em i kam long biknait.

mitimap n. Zoe Imperial Pigeon (Birds of New Guinea plate 19, #2–3).

moimbir n. white mushroom. This word is increasingly rarely used, villagers call the mushroom by the Adjora name **tambawa**; talinga, planti long Gapun i no save long despela hap tok na ol i save kolim long tok ples Sanae, **tambawa**. Whenever one spots a patch of mushrooms, if one chants the following (non-Tayap) words, more patches will appear close by: **tambawano ramawano tawi tawi tawi tawi tawi tawi**. Taim yu lukim sampela talinga yu mas wokim despela singsing na bai yu lukim planti talinga i kamap klostu long yu.

Moip n. Watam village; ples Watam.

mokir n. seedling; kru.

mokit n. sacred flutes, tambaran. See also **mirip**.

mokop *adj.* (*dl.* when referring to people: **mopri**; *pl.* when referring to people: **mopro**), little, small; *liklik*. Used interchangeably with **mosop**.

mokwa *n.* **1.** multi-pronged spear used to shoot birds, bandicoots and fish; *supsup*. **2.** whistle; *wisil*. **Mokwa ninkun**: He whistled (*lit.* 'made a whistle'); *Em wisil*.

mom *n.* a popular kind of banana that one can eat ripe, as opposed to cooking it like a plantain. Newly introduced to Gapun, the name is from an unknown Sepik language; *wanpela kain banana i swit long kaikai mau. Nau tasol em i kam long Gapun, nem bilong em bilong wanpela tok ples long Sepik*.

mombi *n.* a kind of tall grass that has no sharp edges; *wanpela kain kunai i no save katim skin bilong man*.

momik *n.* Western Crowned Pigeon; *guria* (Birds of New Guinea plate 15, #8–11).

momor *n.* [Kopar]. **1.** sago grub; *binatang bilong saksak*. **2.** euphemism for penis; *kok* (*tok bokis*). **Momor utingatindak**: They'll cut off his prick; *Ol bai katim katim kok bilong em*.

momorik *n.* **1.** sago pancake made on a **pambram** (pot shard); *praim ol i wokim long wanpela hap kanaka sosbin*. **2.** flour mixed together with scraped coconut and smoked in banana leaves, made for funerary feasts; *mixim saksak wantaim kokonas. Putim i go insait ol lip bilong banana na smokim long paia. Ol man i save wokim despela kaikai long taim bilong pati*. See also **tapak**.

mond *n.* penis; *kok*. **Mond sumanŋa!** Big cock! (vulgar); *Bikpela kok bilong yu!* (*tok nogut*).

mondki *v.i.* (**-net/-nak**), become hard; *kamap strong*. **Kwem nim mbibikni mondtak**: His penis became as hard as a tree; *Kok bilong em i kamap strong olsem diwai*.

mondra oki *v.i.* (conjugated like **oki**), become hard; *tait i go*. **Ror ende kwem mondra wok nok arkunetana**: The child's penis is getting hard, he wants to pee; *Kok bilong pikinini i tait i go na em i laik pispis*.

monjuko *n.* plant with long green leaves with a core that can unravel like sheets of paper; used to make different kinds of decorations; *hap diwai i gat longpela lip ol man i save usim long wokim bilas*.

moŋapat *n.* **1.** kidney; *tupela kiao i stap insait long bel*. **2.** shooting star; *suting star*. **3.** hard black stone used as a hammer; *strongpela bilakpela ston*.

moŋar krimb *n.* **1.** pebbles, *ol liklik ston*. **2.** money (specifically 'coins', but is also used to refer to money more generally); *ol koins, moni*.

moŋom *n.* a species of wild yam; *wanpela kain wailyam*.

moprindag *n.* rash; *bukbuk long skin*. **Moprindag atorporiek sami ŋayar**: A rash appeared all over; *Bukbuk i kamap nambaut*.

mor-(p)-e *v.t.* (class 1), force or coerce someone; *pusim*. **Ŋiŋi morpeinde, ŋa nim karkun**: He forced me to chop the tree; *Em pusim mi long katim diwai*.

moramori *n.* **1.** twins; *tuins*. **2.** anything double, such as two bananas inside one skin or two nuts inside one shell; *tupela samting i pas wantaim, olsem tupela banana i stap insait long wanpela skin banana*. **Moramori ŋgirkar wekŋan**: There are two of them, like twins; *Tupela olsem tuwins i stap*. See also **takrot**.

moramorik *n.* bud; *kru*. **Moramorik utok**: A bud appeared; *Kru i kamap*. **Nim moramorik ŋgutukun**: The tree flowered (*lit.* 'put buds'); *Ol kru i kamap long diwai*.

morasi *n.* **1.** habit, way of doing things; *pasin*. **2.** deed, action; *pasin*. **Yuwon morasi apro**: It's your fault; *Asua bilong yu*.

Moreng *n.* Murik village; *ples Murik*.

morip *n.* Pigeon; *balus* (Birds of New Guinea plate 18, all except #2–3).

moser *v.t.* (class 4), buy something; *baim*.

mosop *adj.* little, small; *liklik*. Used interchangeably with **mokop**.

mot *n.* **1.** the seed of breadfruit tree; *pikinini bilong kapiak*: **mbatakŋa mot**.
  2. knot. Before the advent of the Western calendar, meetings between people who resided in different, far-way villages were arranged by sending a string of knots to the person with whom one wanted to meet and exchange items (say, sago for fish). At the beginning of each day, that person would cut off a knot. When the last knot was cut, the person would know that the meeting was to take place on the following day. This tradition no longer exists, but it is retained in the third meaning of **mot**; *Long taim bilong ol tumbuna sapos yu laik makim de wantaim narapela man o meri i save stap long narapela ples bai yu taitim wanpela rop na salim igo long despela narapela. Olgeta de bai despela narapela i katim wanpela hap rop, na taim em katim las hap rop em bai save olsem tumoro bai mi go bung wantaim man ia i bin salim rop long mi.*
  3. an agreed upon day of exchange with another village or people from another village; *de ol i makim long en long ol man o meri long narapela ples long bung na sensim ol samting, olsem ol Singrin bai makim de wantaim ol Gapun na bai ol i kisim kina na pis na ol Gapun bai sensim long kru mambu o abus bilong pik*. **Mot ŋgunkundara**: We marked a day for our exchange to take place; *Mipela putim de pinis*.

motikXoki *v.i.* (serial verb construction conjugated like **oki**. Note: X here stands for an object suffix), swallow; *daunim long maus*. **Ŋgi awin motikkuwok**: They swallowed the water; *Ol i daunim wara*.

motini *adv.* again; *gen*. **ŋi motini ninkun aŋgo**: He's doing it again. *Em wokim gen nau*.

moto *n.* debris in water that makes the water dirty; *ol detipela samting i stap insait long wara*. **Awin moto**: puddle; *liklik pipia wara*.

mow *n.* **1.** meat of coconut; *mit bilong kokonas*: **pap mow**.
  2. white of egg, *waitpela wara bilong kiau* (also **pap mow**).
  3. flesh of a young animal; *mit bilong yangpela pik o kapul o mumut o muruk*. **Njenumgi mowana kekepeŋrora**: the dogs stripped the flesh (off the young pig or cassowary); *Ol dok i kamautim pinis olgeta mit (bilong yangpela pik o muruk)*.

muk *n.* clot; *strongpela samting olsem ston o wanem samting i strongpela liklik*. **Neŋgirŋa muk**: hard snot; *kus i kamap strongpela*; **Andŋa muk**: blood clot; *blut i go hatpela*; **Ketukŋa muk**: phlegm; *strongpela spet bilong man i kus*.

mukúki *n.* a man or woman who doesn't say much and doesn't get angry often; *daunpasin man o meri i save stap isi tasol na i no save krosim ol narapela o toktok planti*.

mum *n.* sago jelly, the staple food of Gapun, served in basins with something boiled placed on top, such as a small piece of **mborsip** (pork), or **kimirik** (sago grubs), or, at last resort, only a few leafy greens. On top of this will be poured a **wawan** (soup), which is the liquid, usually made of milk squeezed from grated coconut, in which the pork, sago grubs or vegetables has boiled; *saksak ol meri i save tainim long en*.

mumuk *n.* butterfly or moth; *bataplai*.

muna kokir *n.* ball of raw sago flour put on a fire and eaten (*lit.* 'sago head'); *hap saksak yu brukim long* **muna** *na kukim long paia*.

muna *n.* sago flour; *saksak*.

munakatar *n.* a cake of sago flour; *wanpela hap saksak*.

munakumund *n.* sago flour cooked in bamboo; *saksak ol i putim i go insait long wanpela hap mambu na kukim long paia*.

mundumindiki *v.i.* (-net/-nak) **1.** hum; *singsing* **Mundumidini pororkar mbet**: He is coming humming a tune; *Em singsing i kam*.

2. murmur; *toktok isi* **Mun sene mundumɨndirakkukem**: The two men are murmuring; *Tupela man i wok long toktok isi istap.*

munjar *n.* [*Kopar*], handle of **makor** (sago pounder); *stik bilong* **makor**.

munje *n.* (*dl.* **mun** or **muŋro**; *pl.* **munjenum**), 1. man; *man.*
2. husband; *man meri i maritim em.* **Ŋgon munje kut inde**: Her husband is here; *Man bilong em i stap.*

munjeki *v.i.* (**-net/-nak**), become a man; *kamap man.* **Ene yu munjetet**: Today you've become a man; *Yu kamap man pinis.*

munjesik *n.* 1. boil; *buk.*
2. banana frond/seedling that has not yet sprouted leaves that one plants to grow a new banana plant; *kru bilong banana i nogat lip yet.* See also **oraw**.

munjewatkɨ *v.i.* (**-net/-nak**), become extremely cold; *igo kol olgeta.* **Toto munjewattak**: The skin is really cold (i.e. the person will soon die or is already dead); *Skin i go kol olgeta.* **Awin munjewattak**: The water is really cold; *Wara i kol olgeta.*

munji *n.* pointing motion; *makim.* **Munji aŋgo nirkwankut**: He is pointing; *Em makim wanpela samting i stap.*

munjuko *n.* plant similar to **maraŋgap**, used to cover up sago flour and protect it from rain; *hap diwai olsem* **maraŋgap**.

muntatak *n.* Hanging and Pygmy Parrot (*Birds of New Guinea* plate 21, #1–5).

muŋap *n.* sling made of vines, for carrying firewood; *sling bilong karim paiwut.*

muŋgit *n.* 1. the day before yesterday, *hap asde.*
2. recently; *i no longtaim.*

muŋgit orom *n.* 3 days ago; *hap asde bipo.*

muŋguku *v.i.* (**puŋgot/puŋgok, yim sene puŋguke; ŋgɨ puŋgwok**), stand; *sanap.*

murkɨ *v.i.* (**-net/-nak**), low humming growl made by wild pigs who smell a hunter; *paiarap bilong ol wailpik taim ol i smelim skin bilong man.*

muta *n.* 1. hole dug by a crab; *hul kuka i dikim long en.*
2. narrow hole dug to accommodate a house post; *hul bilong putim hauspos.*

mwanambrir *v.t.* (class 4), [*Kopar*], be jealous about someone; *jelesim.* **Mbumeyi ŋgon omɨn mwanambritɨŋgɨn**: Mbume is jealous about her husband; i.e. she worries that he has affairs; *Mbume jelesim man bilong em.* See also **awa-(p/w)-ar**.

mwanambrirgar morasi *n.* [*Kopar*], jealousy (*lit.* 'jealous habit'); *jeles pasin.*

mwaniŋ *n.* yaws; *sik yaws, strongpela sua.*

mwarmbwam *n.* bark of tree chewed as substitute for wild ginger; *rop daka.*

N

nai-(p)-i *v.t.* (class 1), hit someone hard; *solapim.*

naimb *adj.* 1. heavy; *hevipela.*
2. *n.* sorrow, worry; *hevi.* See also **kumb**.
3. *n.* trouble or conflicts resulting in anxiety and fear of death, *hevi.* **Num naimbŋan**: The village is wracked by conflicts that may result in people's deaths through sorcery or violence; *Ples i stap long hevi.*

nak *v.t.* (class 5), count something; *kauntim.*

nakanaka *n.* [*Kopar*], stingray; *pis i gat win na i gat nil long tel bilong em.*

nam *v.t.* (class 5), 1. tell or say something, *tokim.*
2. shout something, be angry; *krosim.* **Sopakyi Mairum namtukun awinnɨ tuŋgwar patɨrana**: Sopak yelled at Mairum about the maternity house; *Sopak krosim Mairum long haus karim.*

namasapi *n.* whisper; *isipela toktok.*

namasapikɨ *v.i.* (**-net/-nak**), whisper; *tok isi.* **Yum ambinana namaspɨrakkukem?**: Why are you all whispering? *Bilong wanem yupela i toktok isi i stap?*

nambar *n.* 1. one; *wanpela.*

2. alone; *wan*.

nambarkɨ *v.i.* (**-net/-nak**), become as one; agree; *kamap olsem wanpela*. **Yim imin nambartak**: We've become in agreement (*lit.* 'our stomachs have become one'); *Mipela i kamap wanbel.*

nambe *n.* [*Kopar*], small, silver-dollar like fish caught in the mangrove swamp and eaten; *liklik waitpela pis bilong mangoro.*

nambɨr *n.* **1.** chest; *bros.*
    2. towards; *pesim.* **Naw nambɨni ŋgunkuna mbot**: I'm going in the direction of the grassland (*lit.* 'I've put my chest towards the grassland and am going'); *Mi pesim kunai i go nau.*

namkɨ *v.i.* (**-net/-nak**), **1.** say, talk; *tok.* **Ŋa yunana namkɨ wákare**: I wasn't talking about you; *Mi no tok long yu.*
    2. think; *tinting.* **Ŋa ndi namnak Ŋgemanɲi mera**: I thought Ŋgeman did it; *Mi ting olsem Ŋgeman i wokim.*

nande(n) *adv.* thus; *olsem.* **Nande nitukun**: Do it like this; *Wokim olsem.*

nanɨŋ *n.* [*Kopar*], **1.** fin; *win bilong pis.*
    2. fish or crocodile scale; *gereray bilong pis o bilong pukpuk.* See also **mbodaŋ**.

nanjag *n.* traditional body decoration made out of dog's teeth; *bilas ol tumbuna i save wokim long tit bilong dok.*

nanuk *n.* **1.** face; *pes*; **Nje kambwanŋa nanukŋa munje ide namgɨ tower inde awnet**: Tell that man with the dog's vomit face there to shut up! (*vulgar*); *Tokim man i gat pes bilong traut bilong dok long stap isi! (tok nogut).*
    2. appearance; *luk.* **Ambukŋa nanukŋa?**: What did it look like? (*lit.* 'what face did it have?'); *Em i luk olsem wanem?* **Yir ŋaŋan yuwon nanuk nambarŋa**: My spear looks like yours; *Spia bilong mi i luk olsem wankain bilong yu.*
    3. shadow; *devil.* **Samak ɲiŋano nanuk tankun**: Samak saw his own shadow; *Samak lukim devil bilong em yet.*

naɲa *n.* egg; *kiau.*

naŋgak *n.* wild sago palm. This kind of sago plam has not been planted, as most other kinds of palms are, and it has many needles. *Wailsaksak i gat planti nil.*

naŋatik *n.* **1.** flow, force, power; *powa.* **Kwemɲa naŋatik utiŋgarke**: You shouldn't cut your male power (by sleeping with women); *I no ken katim powa bilong kok bilong yu, i no ken prenim ol meri.*
    2. virginity; *pestaim yu stap wantaim meri pestaim tru, o yu merit pestaim yu stap wantaim man.* **Naŋatik utukrunet**: he is going to lose his virginity (*lit.* 'cut his flow').
    3. length of skin on the underside of the penis that determines growth. If this is severed, one will not grow (this may be a new meaning of this word, older men do not know this meaning, it seems to have originated with a man now in his mid-40s); *rop i stap long baksait bilong kok bilong man. Yu katim despela rop bai gro bilong yu i stop.*
    4. hymen (probably a novel meaning of the word, cited only by some male speakers in their twenties and thirties); *rop i stap insait long sem bilong meri, despela rop i bruk na blut i kamap bai gro bilong meri i stop.*
    5. tide; *tait.* **Awinna naŋatik**: tide; *tait.*

naŋatikku *v.t.* (class 5), extract a sliver from a coconut husk in order to make a sling to carry it; *sutim skin bilong kokonas, apim hap skin bilong wokim rop na ropim.*

naŋɨr *n.* **1.** handle of axe or **makor** (sago pounder).
    2. frame of a net; *hap mambu bilong umben*: **korotŋa naŋɨr**.

naŋgo *n.* **1.** large wooden hook to hang things on inside a house; *bikpela wuk ol man i save hangamapim ol samting long em i go insait long haus.*
    2. a kind of marking carved into hourglass drums and slit-gong drums; *mak ol man i gat save bai makim long kundu na long garamut.*

nao *n.* **1.** genital flesh; *skin bilong sem*; **Kwemɲa nao**: penis flesh; *skin bilong kok*; **Manŋa nao**: vulva; *skin bilong kan*.

2. clam meat; *mit bilong kina*. **Eporaŋ nao:** clam meat or vulva; *mit bilong kina o mit bilong kan*. **Nao sumanŋa!** Big genitals! (*vulgar*); *Bikpela sem bilong yu!* (*tok nogut*).

napo *n.* camouflaged blind in which men hide to shoot wild pigs, *banis bilong sutim pik*. **Yamŋa napo:** Blind made by men to wait for pig that will eat at a sago palm that has been cut and stripped to lure the pig; *Banis saksak*.

naw *n.* grasslands; *kunai*.

naw o *v.t.* (class) trample the grass on the periphery of a grassland before setting fire to it, to make a path that the fire-setters can walk on to set the fire to the grassland; *krungutim kunai*.

ndabai-(p)-i *v.t.* (class 1), help or support someone; *helpim, givim sapot*. **Ndabaitukun!** Help her! *Helpim em!* **Ewar Agranaŋi Kwaŋa dabaipiŋgina rumb tambungatan:** Yesterday Agrana helped Kwaŋa carve his (Kwaŋa's) slit-gong drum; *Asde Agrana i helpim Kwaŋa makim garamut bilong em (bilong Kwaŋa)*.

ndabaiki *v.i. irr.* (**yim ndabaipiek, yum ndabaipikem, ŋgi ndabaipiko, yim sene ndabaipiké**), disperse; *go nambaut*. **Yim nda ndabaipiek:** Let's go our own ways now; *Mipela i go nambaut nau*. **Ndabainkem!** Break it up! *Igo nambaut nau!*

ndabe *n.* a tree with branches that have short thorns. Until the early part of the 1900s, was used during female initiation, placed on the ground and inserted into a young woman's vagina, causing her to bleed profusely (compare **mainye**); *diwai i gat ol liklik nil. Ol tumbuna meri bilong bipo tru save putim ol liklik han bilong despela diwai insait long sem bilong ol nupela meri, long wanem ol i laik rausim blut nogut long bodi bilong em (em wankain olsem* **mainye**).

ndabo *n.* cheek; *sait bilong wosket*.

ndaburak *n.* tree with red sap, used to make frames for blinds in houses; *diwai i gat redpela blut, ol han bilong em i no hevi na ol man save putim long haus na nilim ol blain antap long ol*.

ndadab *n.* **1.** peel; *skin bilong wanem samting ol man i bin tekewe long en*.
2. bark of tree; *skin bilong diwai*. See also **ŋgakraw**.

ndadar *n.* a piece of limbum palm the size and shape of a large dustpan used to pick up what one has swept into a pile; *hap pangal ol man na meri i save usim long rausim ol pipia*.

ndadibwaŋ *n.* lip, *skin bilong maus*.

ndadum *n.* sheath cut from the base of a sago palm leaf, used to carry things like sago flour in, and also used as a funnel for washing sago pith; *pangal bilong saksak, ol man i save yusim long karim* **muna** *na ol meri i save usim long wokim* **iko**.

ndag *n.* top-middle part of felled sago palm; *namel i go antap bilong saksak ol man i paitim mit bilong en*.

ndagro *n.* roof shingle made of sago palm leaf; *morota*.

ndagu *n.* theft; *stil*. **Ŋgume ndaguŋan nam ayata.** Enough of that talk about stealing; *Despela totok bilong stil inap nau*.

ndagúni *adj.* furtively; *stil*.

ndagúni tar *v.t.* (class 4), steal something; *stilim*. **Ŋaŋan ta ndagúni tatiatro:** They stole my knife. *Ol i stilim naip bilong mi*.

ndagurai *n.* Dollarbird (*Birds of New Guinea* plate 25, #3)

ndagurgar munje/noŋor *n.* thief (lit. 'steal man/woman'); *stilman o stilmeri*.

ndagurki *v.i.* (**-net/-nak**; **r → Ø** in realis, so **ŋgu ndagutak**; **ŋi ndagunet**; **yum ndagunkem**): steal; *stil*. **Ndagutuko:** They stole; *Ol i stil*.

ndagurni *adv.* without permission; *stil*.

ndadrar *v.i.* (**-net/-nak**), swim; *swim*.

ndakin *n.* package, envelope; *karamap*.

ndakin-(p)-o *v.t.* (class 1), wrap up something in a container or package; *karamapim*.

ndakop *n.* together; *wantaim*. **Ndakop okitike:** Let's go the two of us. *Mitupela wantaim bai go*. **Ndakop onkem!** Go together! *I go wantaim!*

ndakruk *n.* Hooded Butcherbird (*Birds of New Guinea* plate 55, #6).

ndakur *n.* large, green olive-like seeds of the **ŋgimraw** tree, boiled and eaten; *ol pikinini bilong tulip ol man i save boilim na kaikai.*

ndam *n.* cluster on one vine of betel nut or betel nut substitute like **ndekik**; *han buai o* **ndekik**.

ndamɨr *n.* **1.** food remains, i.e. crumbs and stains and bits of food on plates or clothes; *pipia bilong kaikai.*
   2. dirty in the sense of poor personal hygiene; *deti olsem man i no save waswas gut.* **Munje ainde ndamɨr sumanŋa, tuwŋgar wákare**: That man is really dirty, he doesn't bathe; *Man ia skin bilong em save deti, em i no save waswas.*

ndar *n.* bird's beak; *nus bilong pisin.*

ndaram bwar *n.* back of hand; *baksait bilong han.*

ndaram *n.* **1.** arm; *han.*
   2. hand; *han.* **Orakaŋgar ninkurema ndaram enkurem**: They made food and shook hands (in conciliation); *Ol i wokim kaikai na sekhan.* **Ndaram tawainukurem!**: You all applaud! *Yupela paitim han!*

ndaramŋa adadɨt *n.* wrist, *join bilong han.*

ndaramŋa imin *n.* palm of hand (*lit.* 'belly of hand'); *insait bilong han.*

ndarúpadɨgar *n.* (secret code), the word used by women to name a freshwater fish called **kut** when they see one and want to net it. If they say the word **kut**, it will elude them; *hait tok bilong ol meri taim ol i lukim wanpela* **kut**. *Ol i kolim nem tru bilong pis em bai bikhet na ol i no inap wumbenim em.*

ndaw *v.t.* (class 5), stir or shake something; *noisim.*

ndedeŋ *n.* bedbug, *liklik binatang i save stap insait long bedsit na kaikaim ol man long taim bilong slip.*

ndebodam *n.* Rail (*Birds of New Guinea* plate 10).

ndebom *n.* Purple Swamphen (*Birds of New Guinea* plate 10, #14).

ndederkɨ *v.i.* (**-net/-nak**; /r/ → Ø in realis, so **ndedenet/ ndedenak**): roll; *tainim tainim i go.* **Pap otɨteka ndedetaka oriek tokronɨ**: The coconut fell and rolled down the slope; *Kokonas i pundaun na tainim tainim i godaun long ples daun.*

ndegib *n.* rib, side; *bun bilong sait.*

ndekik *n.* **1.** tree from which **tak** (supporting floorboard runners) are cut; *diwai ol man save usim long katim* **tak**.
   2. the nut of this tree, eaten as betel nut substitute; *pikinini bilong despela diwai, ol man i save kaikai taim ol i lus long buai.*

nder *n.* path, road; *rot.* **Nderŋa noŋor**: promiscuous woman (*lit.* 'road woman'); *pamuk meri*; **Nderŋa ror**: out-of-wedlock child; (*lit.* 'road child'); *bastad pikinini.*

ndidi yam *n.* a kind of **yam** sago palm with few needles and a very hard interior. *Saksak i nogat planti nil na mit bilong em i strong tru.*

ndirmar *n.* river; *wara Sepik.*

ndɨ *emph. part.* particle that emphasizes or focuses attention on the word that precedes it; *hap tok bilong strongim narapela hap tok.* See Section 3.11 of grammar.

ndɨdɨk *n.* **1.** hiccup. Believed to make children grow faster; *win ol man i pulim hariap hariap; ol pikinini i pulim win olsem ol man i tok bai grow hariap.*
   2. scar, *sua i drai pinis tasol mak long skin i stap yet.*

ndɨdɨk *v.i.* (**-net/-nak**), hiccup; *pulim win hariap hariap.*

ndɨdɨkdɨdɨk *adj.* lumpy, bumpy; *kiao kiao, i gat ol liklik bukbuk.*

ndɨdɨmaŋ *n.* eel-like fish with hard shell on head; *pis i luk olsem malio tasol i gat hatpela sel long het bilong em.*

ndɨdɨnoŋko *n.* Wampoo Fruit Dove (*Birds of New Guinea* plate 17, #5).

ndɨrɨrɨ-(p/w)-ar *v.t.* (class 2), stick together with someone or something; *pas wantaim.* **Mun sene aŋge mbwar ndɨrɨrɨparkureya tutukeya wuke**: The two men are sitting back to back; *Tupela man i givim baksait na tupela pas na i stap.*

ndiriri-(p/w)-arki *v.i.* (**ndiriripariet/ndiriripariek, sene ndiririparke**), copulate; *kwap*. **Nje sene ndiririparkeya wuke:** The two dogs are copulating; *Tupela dok i pas wantaim na istap*.

ndok *n.* decoration; *bilas*.

ndok *v.t.* (class 5), decorate; *bilasim*.

ndokdok *n.* chisel; *sisel*.

ndokop *n.* Meliphagas and Honeyeaters (*Birds of New Guinea* plate 46).

ndokopndokop *v.t.* (class 5), make clicking sound to call puppies; *singautim ol pikinini dok*.

ndow kawrik *n.* bunion (*lit.* 'tough foot'); *skin i kamap strongpela long lek*.

ndow *n.* **1.** leg; *lek*.
  2. foot; *lek*.
  3. shoe; *su*.

ndowbir *n.* ankle; *join bilong lek*.

ndowbwar *n.* top of foot; *skin i stap antap long lek*.

ndowni o *v.t.* (class 1), kick something (*lit.* 'strike with foot'); *kikim*.

ndowŋa imin *n.* sole of foot (*lit.* 'foot+POSS belly'); *ananeat long lek*.

ndowŋa ku *n.* heel; *as bilong lek*.

ndowŋan sokop *n.* ankle; *join bilong lek*.

ndrik *n.* venom; *marasin bilong bagarapim man*. **Kakámatikma ndrik:** millipede venom; *marasin bilong* **kakámatik**; **Kaiŋŋa ndrik:** venom in the smoke produced when a **kaiŋ** nut is burned, that affects human skin like poison ivy; *marasin bilong kaiŋ*. **Tatakkutre ikurre kakámatik ewandni uroka pepeika puwoka ŋginoŋa tawni wospikunde ŋgon ndrikyi ŋgino opiatan:** Last night as as I was sleeping in my mosquito net a millipede slithered in and crawled up to the side of my eye; I brushed it away but its venom burned my eye; *Asde mi slip istap na wanpela* **kakámatik** *i go insait long taunamb na igo insait na wakabaut i go antap long sait bilong ai, mi rausim em na marasin bilong em i kukim ai bilong mi*.

ndrig *n.* lobe, cartilage; *hap skin, hap bun*. **Nekeŋa ndrig**: earlobe; *hap skin bilong yau*. **Rawŋa ndrig**: nostril or septum; *sait bilong nus o bun bilong nus*. See also **kondit**; **rawŋa sokop**.

ndugubar *n.* spine; *bun bilong baksait*.

nduko *n.* branch; *han bilong diwai*.

ndukup *temp.* six days from now; *nau i go inap sixpela de*.

ndum *v.t.* (class 5), clear undergrowth, e.g. to prepare a garden; *brasim*.

ndúmdum *n.* poison; *posin*.

ndumki *v.i.* (**-net/-nak**), clear undergrowth; *brasim*.

nek *n.* **1.** ladder, i.e. notched pole used to go up into houses, which are always raised at least 1.5 meters off the ground; *lada*.
  2. door; *dua*.

nekan *n.* **1.** earthquake; *guria*.
  2. walking stick insect; *binatang i luk olsem han bilong diwai*.

neke *n.* ear; *iau*.

nekénduko *n.* tall grass found in **naw** (grasslands). Avoided because its three-cornered, sharp stems slice skin like razors; *trikona*.

nekenekeki *v.i.* (**-tike**), divorce; *stap wanwan*. **Omindeominde ndakopke wuke? Wákare, nekeneketikera**: Is the couple still together? No, they're divorced. *Tupela marit i stap wantaim yet? Nogat, tupela i stap wanwan*. The verb is a reduplication of **neker** 'alone'.

nekeni warakki *v.i.* (**-net/-nak**), talk on mobile phone (*lit.* 'talk against ear'); *toktok long mobail*.

neker *adv.* alone, by oneself; *wan*. **Yu neker otet!**: You go by yourself!; *Yu wan i go!*. See also **ŋayar**.

neni *n.* **1.** (*dl.* **neniŋgre**; *pl.* **neniŋgro**), grandfather; *apa man*.
  2. ancestor; *tumbuna man*.

neŋgib *n.* genital fluids of both sexes; *wara bilong kok o bilong kan*. **Neŋgib utok:** Genital fluid appeared; *Wara bilong kok o bilong kan i kamap*; **Neŋgib kwemŋa aprol:** Runny dick! (*vulgar*) *Kok bilong yu i pulap long wara! (tok nogut)*. **Yu aini enda aikitak neŋgib rukrutak!** You dare come here, your cunt juice will fly out all over the place (because I will hit you)! (*vulgar*); *Yu kam bai wara bilong kan bilong yu sut i go! (tok nogut)*.

neŋginiki neŋginiki *adv.* very slowly, gradually; *isi isi*. **Awin wek neŋginiki neŋginiki**: The water came (i.e. the tide came in) very slowly; *Wara i kam isi isi*.

ner *n*. **1.** short traditional grass skirt that went down to above the knee. Cut in layers (**patɨrkɨ patɨrkɨ**) like the stepladder to a house; *pulpul. Ol i save katim* **patɨrkɨ patɨrkɨ**.

2. long tail feathers of bird of paradise; *pulpulbilong ol kumul*. See also **ŋgorok**; **pesaw**.

níme *adv*. thus, like this; *olsem*. **Ŋa níme teuniɛtre ŋgu okɨ wákare Merewre**. I'm afraid of that, that she didn't go to Sanae; *Mi pret olsem em i no bin i go long Mangum*.

nímera *mood part*. expression of surprise that something occurred contrary to expectation; *hap tok bilong tok olsem yu ting wanpela samting bai kamap na i no kamap tu*. **Yum nimera akunana mbekem**: So you've all come to do nothing, is it?; *Yupela kam long istap nating, ah*? See Section 7.6.4 of the grammar.

nimɲa pap *n*. love magic; *marira, pupuru*. **Ŋa nimɲa pap apukrunet**: I'm going to make some love magic; *Mi bai kukim marira*.

niɲan *adj*. like; *olsem*. **Ewar yim aram taniŋgin. Aram Ndairɲi peŋginɲan, niɲan me nɨpɨsɲa kemem**: Yesterday we saw a snake as long as the one that Ndair caught; *Asde mipela i lukim snek i bikpela olsem narapela snek ia Ndair i bin holim em*. **Niɲan noɲor aŋgo eŋgon wákare**: This kind of woman isn't good; *Despela kain meri i no gutpela*.

nirkɨ *v.i.* (-net/-nak; r → Ø in realis, so **ninet/ ninak**), **1.** do; *mekim*. **Ŋɨ ninet** (sticks out tongue): He went (sticks out tongue); *Em mekim olsem (soinim tang)*.

2. have sex with; *mekim samting wantaim man o meri*. **Ŋɨ ŋgunana ninet**: He had sex with her (*lit.* 'he with her made'); *Em (man) i mekim em (meri)*. **Ŋgu ɲinana nitak**. *Em (meri) i mekim em (man)*.

nir *v.t.* (class 4), **1.** do something; *wokim*.

2. make something; *mekim*.

3. signal something; *mekim*. **Ŋginoni ninin**: He signalled to me with his eyes; *Em i mekim mi long ai*.

4. say something, *tok*. **Ŋɨ pemietre niniet, "Tsk"**. He got up and went "Tsk" to me; *Em kirap i tokim mi olsem, "Tsk"*.

5. look after; *lukautim*. **Eneke nirmankukeŋan?** Is it only now you've been looking after us? (wailed over an old woman's corpse, meaning "You've looked after us for many years"); *Nau tasol yu save lukautim mipela?*

nireŋgar munje *n*. boyfriend; *pren man*.

nireŋgar noŋor *n*. girlfriend; *pren meri*.

nirere *temp*. a little while ago; *nau tasol*. **Nirere ŋgwok**: They just left; *Nau tasol ol i go*.

nɨkɨr *n*. lap; *lek ol pikinini i save sindaun long en*.

nim iru *n*. **1.** seeds of tree; *sit bilong diwai*; *pikinini bilong diwai*.

2. rice; *rais*.

3. cocoa beans; *kakau*.

nim *n*. **1.** tree (*generic*); *diwai (biknem)*.

2. wart; *liklik buk long skin*.

nimaniadɨ *v.t.* (class 3: **nimanɨkadɨŋgin** 'he beat him'/ **nimanɨodɨŋgin** 'she beat him'), hit, strike or slap someone; *kilim*. **Ror mosok aŋgukyi air woreku woka mayayi nimanɨodukun**: The little child spilled the lime and her mother hit her; *Liklik pikinini i kapsaitim kambang na mama i paitim em*.

nimaniadɨkɨ *v.i.* (group IIa intransitive verb: **ɲa nimanɨkadiet/nimanɨkadiek**; **ŋgu nimanɨodiek, yum nimanɨkadikem, ŋgi nimanɨgodiek**), hit, slap; *pait*. **Ŋiɲano nimanɨkadiet**: He hit himself; *Em i paitim em yet*.

nɨmar *n*. mangrove swamp; *mangoro*.

nimbɨja *n*. [*Kopar*], a person or animal who is extremely skinny; *man o pik i bun nating*.

nimbisim *n.* lemongrass; *smel kunai.*

nimbup *n.* **1.** rotten log or tree; *diwai i sting pinis na i go malomalo.*
  2. corpse of person; *bodi bilong man indai long en.*
  3. phosphorescent fungus that grows on rotten trees; *wanpela kain mosong o talinga i save stap long ol diwai na i save lait long nait.*

nimbup kotar-(p)-e *v.t.* (class 1), ask a corpse; *askim bodi.* A tradition, last practiced in the mid-1980s, of carrying a corpse on a bier just before burial and whispering in its ear, asking it to reveal who killed it through sorcery. The corpse then moves its bearers to walk to various houses and people, bumping against them, leaving villagers to interpret the message; *wanpela we bilong painim aut husat i kilim man o meri long poisen. Ol man bai askim bodi husat i poisenim em na em bai mekim ol man i karim em i go nambaut na bamp long ol haus na long ol man o meri. Em nau, ol man bai lukim na tingim. Ol man i lusim despela we bilong askim bodi long ol yia long 1986 nambaut.*

nimir *n.* stick for carrying things such as bananas, coconuts, the carcass of a dead pig or cassowary; *hap diwai ol man i wokim long karim ol samting olsem banana, kokonas, bodi bilong pik man i kilim long en.*

nimirkokir *n.* bridge; *bris.* See also **koŋgrik.**

nimnimki *v.i.* (**-net/-nek**), be taut; *tait.* **Ŋgrip nimnimtak**: The rope is tight; *Rop i tait.* **Ror aŋgo oraki asakpekuna nimnimtak**: The child was frightened by a spirit and was paralyzed; *Wanpela samting i kalapim pikinini ia na skin bilong em i tait olgeta.*

nimŋat *n.* branch, stick; *hap diwai.*

niŋ *n.* bone; *bun.* **Yu niŋŋake amugar?** Are you strong enough (*lit.* 'do you have the bones') to fight? *Yu gat bun bilong pait ah?*; **Ŋiŋ sinder**: skinny, without fat; *bun nating.*

niŋgar *v.t.* (class 4), portion out; *skelim, dilim.* **Ewar orakaŋgar niŋgatukuro**: Yesterday they portioned out the food; *Asde ol i dilim kaikai.*

niŋgasin *n.* furry caterpillar; *pikinini bilong bataplai i gat gras, yu holim em bai skin bilong yu bai pen.*

niŋgir *n.* snot; *kus.* **Niŋgir rawŋa!** Snotty nose! *Kus nus yu!*

niŋgirŋan *adj.* sticky, *bai pas long skin.*

niŋgirarik *n.* stage two (of five) in coconut formation, the coconut has meat, but it is watery, like egg white; *yangpela kokonas i gat mit tasol mit bilong em i warawara.*

niŋir *n.* **1.** sap; *blut bilong diwai.*
  2. glue; *glu.*

niŋir aram *n.* species of smallish snake said to omit a sticky fluid when touched or held (*lit.* 'glue snake'); *snek i gat glu long skin bilong em na bai pas long skin bilong yu.*

niŋirŋan *adj.* sticky (*lit.* 'has sap'); *i gat glu na i save pas long han o long wanem samting.*

nipis 1. *adv.* enough; *inap.* **Yu nipis wákare ŋaŋan nam epeŋgar:** You don't have it in you (i.e. you aren't strong enough or clever enough) to respond to my talk; *Yu no inap bekim maus bilong mi.* **Ŋa nipis enda:** I'm up to it, I can do it; *Mi pitman, mi inap;* **Yuwon patir nipiske?** Is your house big enough? *Haus bilong yu inap ah?*
  2. *adv.* almost; *mak.* **Ŋa nipis wasowŋgar, wákare**: I was ready to die but I didn't; *Mi kisim mak bilong indai tasol mi no indai.*
  3. *adv.* the same, *wankain.* **Yu nipis nambar inde kut**: You're still the same; *Yu stap wankain yet.*
  4. *n.* sufficiency; *inap.* **Nipis wákare**: There isn't enough; *I no inap.*
  5. *n.* imprint; *mak bilong han o lek.* **Ndowŋan nipis**: footprint; *mak bilong lek.*

nir *n.* **1.** clump; *strongpela samting.* **Kawatŋa nir**: a clump of salt; *sol i go strongpela.*
  2. tree with hard wood; *diwai i strongpela na hat long katim.*
  3. the remains of a tree when it is stripped of branches, leaves and bark and made into a housepost; **Sakindŋa nir**: bare house post; *bun diwai ol i wokim long pos bilong haus.*

nja-(p)-o *v.t.* (class 1), **1.** peel or shave off something; *sapim, tekewe, rausim skin, olsem long taro*.
  2. remove spine from tobacco leaf; *rausim bun bilong ol lip brus*.
njajak *n.* brown grasshopper; *braunpela grashopa*.
njakep *n.* flying fox; *bilak bokis*.
njakep oraw *n.* a kind of flying fox, big with white and red fur on its neck; *bikpela bilak bokis i gat waitpela na redpela gras long nek*.
njakep ror *n.* poor thing, someone who has nothing (*lit.* 'flying fox child'); *tarangu man, rabis man*.
njakepma arit *n.* small black mosquitoes that appear in the late afternoon and early evening; *ol liklik liklik bilakpela natnat i save kamap long apinun klostu tudak*.
njakum *n.* traditional 'joking' kin, which are inherited kin relations to members of the clans into which one may not marry; *wanpilai*.
njalat *n.* a kind of tree with soft bark that has leaves like poison ivy that inflame the skin. The red shoots of the tree are gathered and mixed with bamboo fuzz and meat, put in a bamboo tube and roasted. This mixture, when cooled is given to dogs to eat, to 'heat' their stomachs so that they can fight successfully with and kill pigs. Men use this same mixture to 'heat' their own stomachs in preparation for fighting; *kain diwai i gat ol lip bilong em man i tasim bai pen i kamap bihain. Ol man i save kisim redpela kru bilong em wantaim mosong bilong mambu na mixim wantaim wanpela abus, putim igo insait long wanpela hap mambu na kukim, na givim long dog bilong hatim bel bilong em long pait wantaim pik. Man tu i ken wokim na kaikai long hatim skin bilong em*.
njam *n.* hurriedly-assembled bush house with only one half of a roof; *bus haus ol man i save wokim hariap na i gat hap marota tasol antap*. **Yu njam waksiretak!**: Make a bush house! *Wokim wanpela bus haus!*

njame *n.* the dregs of the **tawar** that remain in the **iko**; *pipia saksak olsem das i stap long iko*.
njanimb† *n.* (*pl.* **njanimbeda**) (*obsolete*), great-grandchild; *pikinini bilong pikinini bilong pikinini*.
njapar *n.* an edible green vegetable with leaves that look like large mint leaves and that when boiled tastes like spinach; *aupa*.
njawap *adj.* wet, *i gat wara*.
njawap *v.i.* (**-net/-nak**), become wet; *wara i wasim*.
nje *n.* (*pl.* **njenum**), dog; *dok*.
njegagip *n.* tree from which the handle of an axe is carved; *diwai ol man i save wokim* **pandeŋa naŋgir** *long en*.
njem *n.* **1.** spittle; *spet*.
  2. magical chant; *singsing i gat pawa bilong em*.
  3. foam; *spet*.
njem ru *v.t.* (class 4), spit on something; *troimwe spet*. **Mbeka njem tunkun**: I came and spit; *Mi kam na mi troimwe spet*.
njemni andu *v.t.* (class 3), spit magic chant on; *spetim*.
njemuk *n.* metal scraper the size and shape of serrated spoon affixed to a small stool used to grate coconut; *sikarap bilong kokonas*.
njeŋa rewi *n.* dog's teeth, traditionally used as a kind of money; *tit bilong dok ol tumbuna i save usim olsem moni*. See also **marŋgoram**.
njeyewir at *n.* mosquito with red coloring (*lit.* 'dogshit mosquito'); *redpela mosquito*.
njijerik *n.* Lorikeet (*Birds of New Guinea* plate 19, #8–18). Being replaced by the Koparlanguage word **njijeriŋ**.
njijiriŋ *n.* bubble, *babol*. **Njijiriŋ wukar wok**: Bubbles are rising; *Babol i go antap*.
njim *n.* **1.** haze; *smok*.
  2. water made of scraped base of the **arit** tree, used to wash carvings before they are painted; *wara bilong kil bilong diwai* **arit** *ol man i save boinim long paia, sikarapim, na putim long laplap bilong kokonas na wasim. Wara bilong em bai yu usim long wasim ol kabings, bihain*

bai yu putim pen long ol. **Ajiragiɲi kandibwan njɨmnɨ pokun**: Ajiragi washed the carvings in **njim**; *Ajiragi i wasim ol kabings long* **njim**.

njiɲai *n.* soft stone; *wanpela kain ston i no hat tumas.*

njip *n.* mouse; *liklik rat.*

njogrob *n.* shelf fungus that grows on **mberig** trees; boiled and eaten; *talinga i save kamap long ol diwai* **mbergig**, *ol man i save boilim na kaikai wantaim mum*. See also **manɨmbomo**.

njojok *n.* green grasshopper; *grinpela grashopa.*

nkɨnkɨm *n.* [*Adjora*], fatty, end part of a cassowary's tail; *as bilong muruk*. The Tayap equivalent is **ŋgatma mipat**.

nkɨrkɨr *n.* [*Adjora*], sorcery that has been rubbed on something a person ingests; *poisin ol man nogut i rabim long wanpela samting na narapela man i kaikaim em*. **Nkɨrkɨr kakun**: He ingested an ensorcelled object; *Em i kaikai o em i smok wanpela samting i gat poisin long en.*

nok *n.* urine, *pispis.*

nok nder *n.* bladder (*lit.* 'urine path'). Sometimes removed from the bodies of animals killed in a hunt and blown up like a balloon for children to play with; *insait long bodi pispis i save kamap long en*; *ol man i save rausim na winim long ol pikinini bai hamamas long pilai wantaim em.*

nom *n.* a kind of wild taro; *wanpela kain wailtaro.*

nomb *n.* name; *nem*. **Anima nomb?** What is (your) name? (*lit.* 'Whose name [is yours]?'); *Wanem nem bilong yu?*

noni *n.* small tree with yellow inner bark, people dig up the roots, mix them with coconut and make oil that they use to oil their skin; *liklik diwai i gat yelopela mit bilong en, ol man na ol meri save dikim ol rop bilong em na wokim wel bilong welim skin.*

nono *n.* yam; *yam.*

nonódadáb *n.* dragonfly. Children capture these in nets and tie them to a string and play with them; *binatang i save kamap planti long apinun. I gat bikpela win na ol pikinini save kisim na taitim long string na pilai long en.*

noŋge *n.* white clay that pregnant women often crave to eat; *waitpela graun ol meri i gat bel i save laikim long kaikai.*

noŋor *n.* (*dl.* **naŋaw**; *pl.* **naŋro**), 1. woman; *meri.*
2. wife; *meri bilong man.*
3. *adj.* female; *meri.* **Nje noŋor**: female dog, bitch; *dok meri.*

noŋorkɨ *v.i.* (-**net**/-**nak**), become a woman; *kamap meri*. **Ŋgu kapa weka numŋa noŋortakara**: She's really become a village woman (said of a women who moved to Gapun from another village); *Em kamap meri bilong ples pinis.*

noŋorŋa kup *n.* lower intestine, *bel.*

nop *n.* boil; *sua*. **Nop utok**: A boil appeared; *Sua i kamap.*

num *n.* 1. village; *ples*. **Tayap num**: Gapun village; *ples Gapun*.
2. Great-billed Heron (*Birds of New Guinea* plate 3, #3–4).

numat *n.* 1. ground, *graun*. **Mbaso bal rukotɨtek numatnɨ**: Mbaso threw the ball on the ground. *Mbaso i troimwe bal i godaun long graun.*
2. area around one's house; *hap bilong man long arrare long haus*. **Naŋan numwatŋa oromnɨ emrariakaŋremke**! You can't play in the area around my house! *Yupela i no ken pilai long hap bilong mi!*

numbutik *n.* small cockroach; *liklik kokros.*

numbwan i *v.t.* (class 1, the verb is **i**, 'to give'), 1. think something; *tingim*.
2. realize something, *tingim*. **Ŋa ndɨ numbwan pikun yu mbotmera**: I thought you had gone; *Mi ting olsem yu go pinis.*

numbwan mbabsakkɨ *v.i.* (-**net**/-**nak**), forget; *lus ting*. **Numbwan mbabsakgarke!** Don't forget! *I no ken lus ting!*

numbwan *n.* 1. thought; *tinting*.
2. desire; *laik*. **Ŋgu ŋgon numbwannɨ wok**: She went because she wanted to; *Em i go long laik bilong en.*

3. knowledge, sense; *save*. **Yu numbwan wákare**: You have no sense; *Yu nogat save*.
4. intention; *laik*. **Ŋa numbwan wákare tawk krarŋgar**: I didn't mean to break the plate; *Mi no brukim plet long laik*.
5. happiness, contentedness; *skin i hamamas*; **Numbwan memki wákare, totoŋan naimb suman**. My thoughts aren't getting up, my skin is really heavy (i.e. I am unhappy); *Mi no hamamas, skin bilong mi i hevi tru*.

numbwan reki *interj*. watch out, be careful (*lit*. 'with thought'); *lukaut*. **Numbwan reki adigarana ŋaŋan orak**: Be careful not to break my thing; *Lukaut long brukim samting bilong mi*.

num-(p)-o *v.t*. (conjugated like **o**). Usually followed by the conjunction **-a** or **-ya** and a fully inflected verb of motion): appear in a group; *ikam o igo grup*. **Numokruya aiki wákare**: They didn't come in a group; *Ol i no kam grup*.

numun *n*. 1. basket sling; *sling bilong basket*: **sapwarŋa numun**.
2. wire on pot used to hang it up above fire; *handel bilong pot*: **oŋgabŋa numun**. See also **ambrim**.

nunuk 1. *temp*. later, afterwards; *bihain*.
2. *n*. behind, *baksait*.

nunukni *adv*. 1. behind; *baksait*; **Mukar ŋaŋan nunukni tutotakut**: Mukar is sitting behind me; *Mukar i sindaun long baksait bilong mi*.

2. *adv*. after; *bihain*. **Ŋgu woka Wewak wukre, ŋgon nunukni omin wasownet**: She went to Wewak and while she was there, after she had gone, her husband died; *Em i go istap long Wewak na man bilong em indai bihain long igo bilong em*.

nunukŋa orom *n*. future; *bihain taim*.

nunukŋa ror *n*. last born (*lit*. 'afterwards child'); *lasbon, las pikinini*.

nunum *adv*. go quickly, *ron*. Inserted into commands to emphasize the need for speed; *hariap*. **Kukununumwetet!**: Bring it right now, fast! (*lit*. 'bring it running'); *Kisim i kam hariap!*

nunum-(p)-oki *v.i*. (ŋa nunumpot/-pok; yu nunumpot/-pok; ŋi nunumpot; ŋgu nunumpok, yim nunumpok; yum nunumpokem; ŋgi nunumpoko; yim sene nunumpoke). Usually followed by the conjunction **-a** or **-ya** and a fully inflected verb of motion): go quickly; *ron*. **Ŋi nunumpota mbet**: He came running; *Em ron i kam*. **Ŋgi nunumoki wákare**: They didn't run; *Ol i no ron i go*. **Aram inde nunumpota mbot**. The snake went quickly; *Snek i ron i go*.

nuŋgŋa orom *n*. dry season; *draisisen*.

nuruw *n*. ironwood tree from which slit-gong drums and **ŋgúnbara** (house posts) are cut; *diwai garamut*. See also **sakind**.

nuwomb *n*. creek; *baret*.

Ŋ

ŋa *pro*. 1. I; *mi*.
2. me; *mi*.

ŋan *pro*. his; *bilong em (man)*.

ŋano *pro*. oneself or itself; *yet*. **Ŋa ŋano taniet awin nanukni**: I see myself in the mirror; *Mi lukim mi yet long glas*. **Ŋgi ŋano rarekutikeya tutukeya wuke**: They are sitting looking at each other; *Tupela i sindaun lukluk pes tu pes na istap*. **Ŋa ŋanoki okineta tarkrunet**: I myself will go and get it; *Mi yet bai mi go kisim*.

ŋaŋan *pro*. mine; *bilong mi*.

ŋat *n*. piece; *hap*. **Mborsipŋat kukuwe**: Give me a piece of pig meat; *kisim hap abus i kam*; **Tamwaiŋat kukuwe**: Give me a piece of sago pancake; *Hap praim i kam ia*.

ŋaumb *n*. large shell ring traditionally hung around neck as decoration during singing and dancing; *bikpela sel kina ol tumbuna i save hangamap long nek long taim bilong singsing*.

ŋawmb *n.* rings that decorated **toriw** (traditional bracelets); *ol liklik ring i save hangamap long ol paspas.*

ŋawmbi *n.* large white stone ring with hole in the middle, traditionally used both as decoration and as valuable object; *bikpela waitpela ston ring bilong ol tumbuna.*

ŋayar (also **ŋayor**) *adv.* **1.** really, truly; *tru.* **Suman nayar**: really big; *bikpela tru.*
  2. by oneself; *tasol.* **Ŋa ŋayar okinet**: I'm going alone; *Mi tasol bai go.* See also **neker**.

ŋayor See **ŋayar**

ŋgabugar *n.* the biggest kind of rat; *bikpela rat.*

ŋgabugrip *n.* a large brown or black beetle that lives in breadfruit trees, its larvae are **urukuruk** and both the larvae and the adults are eaten; *mama bilong ol urukuruk i save stap long ol kapiak. Ol man i save kaikai despela ol mama na ol pikinini tu.*

ŋgadan *n.* sore; *sua.*

ŋgadir-(p)-i *v.t. irr.* (class 1; behaves like a class 1 verb in realis, but has no **i** in irrealis; so **ŋgadirpikun** 'he passed by her', but **ŋgadirkru wákare** 'he didn't pass by her'): pass someone or something by; *abrisim.*

ŋgadir-(p)-i *v.t. irr.* (class 1; behaves like a class 1 verb in realis, but has no **i** in irrealis; so **ŋgadirpimro** 'they defeated us', but **ŋgadirmri wákare** 'we were not defeated'): defeat someone; *winim.*

ŋgado *adj.* bent, crooked; *krungut.* **Man ŋgado!** Crooked cunt! (*vulgar*); *Kan i krungut! (tok nogut).*

ŋgadogadi *adj.* really bent, really crooked; *krungut tru.* **Ngadogadiŋa munje**: Stooped over old man who cannot stand up straight; *Man i krungut.*

ŋgadogadi *v.t.* (class 5), twist or bend something; *tainim na krungutim.*

ŋgadoki *v.i.* (-**net**/-**nak**) bend; *krungut.*

ŋgaga-(p/w)-eki *v.i.* (-**pet**/-**pek**), tip; *i sait.* **Oŋgab aŋgi ŋgagapek, Tarakwetak!** The pot is tipping over, put it right! *Pot i sait, stretim em!*

ŋgagar *n.* side; *sait.* **Yimbarŋa ŋgagar**: side of a canoe; *sait bilong kanu;* **Turoŋa ŋgagar**: side of the hearth; *sait bilong hap ol meri i save sindaun i kuk long en;* **Kumŋa ŋgagar**; the side of a grave; *sait bilong hul ol i save planim bodi bilong man long en.*

ŋgagaweni *pos.* on its side; *sait.* **Oŋgab aŋgi ŋgagaweni puŋgok aŋgi wuk, tarakmemebatukun!** The pot is lying on its side, take it and right it! *Pot is em i sait i stap, yu stretim na sanapim!*

ŋgagit *n.* smallest digit on hand or foot; *liklik pinga bilong han o bilong lek.* **Ndaramŋa ŋgagit**: little finger, *liklik pinga bilong han.* **Ndowŋa ŋgagit**: little toe; *liklik pinga bilong lek.*

ŋgagobit *n.* the cut of pork around the tail. This is the choice cut that usually goes to the men who helped the hunter carry the dead pig from the rainforest into the village. It can also be given to the man who speared the pig, if it was speared in someone else's **napo** (sago palm pig trap); *as bilong pik. Ol man i save laikim despela hap abus, na papa bilong pik i save dilim despela long ol man i helpim em karim bodi bilong pik ikam long ples. Sapos wanpela man i sutim pik long banis saksak bilong wanpela narapela man, papa bilong despela banis saksak i save givim despela hap abus long husat man i bin sutim pik long en.*

ŋgagon *n.* tail of all animals, including fish; *tel bilong olgeta animol na bilong pis tu.*

ŋgagrini *adv.* out of the corner of one's eye; *lukim long hap ai.* **Ngagrini taniŋgin**: I saw him out of the corner of my eye; *Mi lukim em tasol long hap ai.*

ŋgagwak *n.* [*Kopar*], crack, crevice; *wul.* **ŋgagwak mir, njemat man nimŋat ngagwak mbini nitakŋa!** You big hole, your dog's cunt makes like a hole in a tree! (*vulgar*); *Wul yu, hul bilong yu olsem bilong dok, i save mekim olsem wul bilong diwai! (tok nogut).*

ŋgaibo *n.* **1.** the tough skin around the jawbone of a pig once one has removed the jawbone; *strongpela skin bilong pik bilong wosket.*
  2. (*vulgar*) cunt; *kan.* **Ngaiboŋa taw suman!** Big cunt! *Draipela kan bilong yu!*

ŋagir *v.t.* (class 4), enumerate; *kolim ol samting*. **Yu ŋgo ŋgagitimbɨn!** You enumarate! *Yu kolim ol!*

ŋakraw *n.* peel; *skin bilong ol samting bilong tekewe*. See also **ndadab**.

ŋakraw-(p)-o *v.t.* (class 1), **1.** peel something, e.g. bananas, sugar cane, breadfruit seeds, eggs, sores; *tekewe skin long banana, suga, pikinini bilong kapiak, kiao, ol sua*.
  2. shell something, such as coffee beans; *selim kopi na ol kain bin olsem*. **Kopi tarak masinni ŋakrawokwankuk**: We used to take coffee to the machine to shell it; *Mipela i save kisim kopi na putim long masin long selim*.

ŋakrawmunjik *n.* **1.** a newly formed coconut with no meat, stage one (of five) in coconut formation; *nupela kokonas tru i nogat mit*.
  2. vine with sharp spines. Before WWII, this vine was dried and wrapped into bundles. It was used to beat male initiates in the men's house; *rop i gat nil. Ol tumbuna save paitim ol yangpela man insait long haus boi wantaim despela rop*.

ŋakre *n.* jaw; *wisket*.

ŋakreŋa pupur *n.* beard (*lit.* 'jaw hair'); *mausgras*.

ŋamai *n.* wind from the mountain, i.e. south wind; *win i save kamap long maunten*.

ŋamamb *n.* **1.** upper back; *antap bilong baksait*; **Ror inde ŋaŋan ŋamambni kut, yim weke nɨmɨrkokɨrnɨ otɨtike awinnɨ**: The child was (being carried) on my back, we went and on the bridge we fell into the water; *Pikinini ia i stap long baksait bilong mi, mitupela i go na long bris mitupela i pundaun long wara*.
  2. the spaces in the front and back of a house under the pinnacles of the roof; *kona bilong haus*.

ŋamambat *n.* the cut of pig meat that is on either side of the bone that connects the head to the spine; *abus bilong bun bilong nek bilong pik*.

ŋamamber *n.* a green and brown acorn-like nut that is cooked and eaten; *pikinini bilong diwai i gat grinpela na braunpela kala ol man i save kukim na kaikai*.

ŋamgit *n., adj.* left; *kais*. **Ŋamgitŋa munje**: left-handed man; *kaisman*; **Ŋamgitŋa akan**: *left hand, kaishan*; **Ŋamgitŋa ndow**: left leg; *kaislek*; **Akan ŋamgitŋa taw**: left side; *sait bilong kaishan*. Compare **eŋon**.

ŋan *pro.* theirs; *bilong ol*.

ŋanokaw *v.t.; inv.* let or allow someone do something; *larim*. **Ŋanokaw waraka-kawndak**: Let them keep talking; *Larim ol toktok i stap*. **Ŋanokaw Sunum atotak Potore**: Let Sunum go down to Wongan; *Larim Sunum i godaun long Wongan*.

ŋanokeya *n.* poor thing; *tarangu*.

ŋapar *n.* handle of **koŋgod** (hour-glass drum); *han bilong kundu*.

ŋaptaw *n.* small coconut that has fallen to the ground because a cockatoo has chewed a hole in it to drink and eat; *kokonas i stap long graun ol koki i drilim wul long en long dring wara bilong en*.

ŋar *n.* call, shout; *singaut*.

ŋar orom *n.* windpipe, *nek*.

ŋar *v.t.* (class 4), call or shout out something to someone or something; *singautim*. **Ndamor ŋatukun!**: Call out to Ndamor; i.e. shout her name to get her attention; *Singautim Ndamor!*

ŋararik *n.* large black and white monitor lizard. Its skin is used to make hourglass drums and its flesh is eaten; *bikpela palai ol man i save tekewe skin bilong ol na wokim kundu long en. Abus bilong despela palai ol manmeri i save kaikai*.

ŋaratgarat *n.* cicada; *binatang i save pas long diwai na i save singaut taim san i laik godaun*.

ŋarɨr *n.* burp, belch; *win i pas long bel i kamap*; **Ŋarɨr puwok**: He burped (lit: 'a burp came up'); *Em i rausim win i pas insait long bel*.

ŋarorak *n.* yellow land crab; *yelopela kuka i save stap long graun*.

ŋgat *n.* **1.** Northern Cassowary; *muruk* (*Birds of New Guinea* plate 1, #1).
2. commonly eaten plant with edible green leaves that becomes slimy when boiled; *aibika*.
3. praying mantis; *bikpela grinpela binatang*.

ŋgat ndow *n.* cuts under the foot where the toes meet the sole of the foot, a condition similar to athletes' foot that afflicts people during the dry season (*lit.* 'cassowary foot'); *ol liklik liklik sua i save kamap long lek long taim bilong draisisen*.

ŋgat ner *n.* (*lit.* 'cassowary grass skirt'), feather-duster like implement made out of the feathers of cassowaries, carried by big men and used to swat away mosquitos and flies; *liklik brum ol bikman i save wokim long gras bilong muruk na ol i save usim long rausim ol natnat na ol rang*.

ŋgat tuwaw *n.* immature cassowary whose feathers have not yet turned black; *yangpela muruk i nogat bilakpela gras yet*.

ŋgatma min *n.* small nipple on the throat of a cassowary through which cassowaries are believed to feed their young with breast milk. The number of young determines the number of nipples; *susu bilong muruk*.

ŋgatnimŋa pupur *n.* stiff bristles on the back of a pig; *strongpela gras i sanap long baksait bilong pik*.

ŋgatwaw *n.* baby cassowary; *liklik pikinini muruk* (*Birds of New Guinea* plate 1, #2b-c).

ŋgaweiw *n.* testicles; *bol*.

ŋgawgarak *n.* Golden Myna (*Birds of New Guinea* plate 49, #1–2).

ŋgawŋki *v.i.* (-net/-nak), bark; *singaut bilong ol dok*.

ŋgawriŋki *v.i.* (-net/-nak), growl; *mekim nois olsem dok i laik pait*.

ŋgawro *n.* a nut-like fruit eaten with salt; *kombi*.

ŋgawrokukum *n.* immature fruits of the **ŋgawro** tree; *ol liklik pikinini bilong ŋgawro*.

ŋgem *n.* large eel; *malio*.

ŋgesiŋe *n.* flying squirrel, one of the few mammals in the rainforest not eaten, because of its unpleasant smell; *wailpusi, ol man i no save kaikai,i gat smel nogut*.

ŋgido *n.* white pus-like secretion from eyes; *waipela susu nogut i save kamap long ai*.

ŋgimraw *n.* a kind of edible tree leaves; *ol lip diwai olsem tulip*.

ŋgino mbod *n.* bone above eyes; *bun bilong ai*.

ŋgino mbodŋa pupur *n.* eyebrow; *gras bilong bun bilong ai*.

ŋgino *n.* **1.** eye; *ai*. **Ŋginoni ninin**: He signaled to me with his eyes; *Em tokim mi long ai*. **Ŋginoni tikwankut ŋanana**: He is winking at me; *Em i mekim mi long ai*.
2. head or tip of something, *ai*; as in **ŋgadanŋa ŋgino**: head of boil; *ai bilong sua*.
3. be alive; *i gat laip*. **Aram ŋginoŋanke?** Is the snake alive? *Snek i gat ai o?*
4. base of fingernail; *as biling kapa bilong pinga*: **ndaramŋa ŋgino**.

ŋgino rerem *n.* eyeball; *waitpela long ai*. **Ŋgino rerem sumanŋan apro mir!**: Big eyeballs! *Draipela ai bilong yu!* Said to children to shame them.

ŋginoŋa toto *n.* eyelid (*lit.* 'eye's skin'); *skin bilong ai*.

ŋginoŋa totoŋa pupur *n.* eye lash; *gras bilong ai*.

ŋgi *pro.* **1.** they; *ol*
2. them; *ol*.

ŋgib *n.* immature plant, sapling; *kru bilong ol diwai*. **Minjikeŋa ŋgib**: betel nut sapling; *kru bilong buai*; **Papŋa ŋgib**: coconut sapling; *kru kokonas*.

ŋgidik *n.* hips; *bun bilong baksait*.

ŋgidiŋ *adj.* blue, *blupela*.

ŋgigiŋki *v.i.* (-net/-nak), walk without being able to see; *wakabaut long bikpela tudak*. **Ŋa ewar ikur mitni ŋgigiŋkar mbota nimni aŋamgupuwot**: Yesterday in the pitch darkness I walked along and bumped into a tree; *Asde long bikpela tudak mi wakabaut i go na mi bamp long diwai*.

ŋgigregoki *v.i.* (conjugated like **oki**), turn and look around, for example when searching for something; *tainim tainim na lukluk*. **Ŋgu ŋgigregoyakuk**: She's looking around; *Em wok long lukluk long sait sait i kam*; **Ŋi ewar**

ŋgigregokar mbot: He looked around him as he went; *Em luk luk i go long pron, long sait sait na igo.*

ŋginana (also ŋgiŋana) *adv.* therefore, for that reason; *long despela.* Yim ŋgume nam nirkwankukre, pirok. Ŋginana pirok. We were talking about that and we laughed. For that reason we laughed. *Mipela mekim toktok olsem na mipela i lap. Long despela mipela i lap.*

ŋgir *n.* stick framework of sago palm leafstalk that holds the limbom sheath buckets upright; *bet bilong pangal bilong putim limbom.*

ŋgire *adv.* therefore; *na olsem.* Ewar ŋa prukni kuta, ŋgiré yure tutuku wákare: Yesterday I was at work, so therefore I didn't sit down with you; *Asde mi stap long wok na olsem mi no sindaun wantaim yu.*

ŋgit-(p)-o *v.t.* (class 1), **1.** tie tightly; *taitim strong.* **2.** strangle someone; *taitim nek.* Yu kokɨr nirŋgar ror potak ŋgitowatinet! You disobedient child, I'm going to strangle you! *Yu bikhed pikinini bai mi taitim nek bilong yu!*

ŋgiti-(p/w)-ar *v.t.* (class 2), tie two or more pieces of rope into a knot; *joinim sampela hap rop.* Ŋgitiwaritukun!: Tie the knot! *Joinim rop!*

ŋgo *dm.* then, in the sense of 'in that case'; *pastaim.* Yu ŋgo otet: You go then (i.e. you've said you are going to go, so it's OK, you can leave now); *Yu go pastaim.*

ŋgo wákare *adv.* yet; *yet.* Ŋa oki ŋgo wákare: I haven't gone yet; *Mi no go yet.*

ŋgodɨr-(p)-u *v.t. irr.* (class 1; behaves like a class 1 verb in realis, but has no i in irrealis; so ŋgodirpukun 'he requested it', but ŋgodirkru wákare 'he didn't request it'): request something; *askim.*

ŋgogrodak *n.* small bright green lizard that lives inside houses; *grinpela palai i save stap insait long ol haus.*

ŋgogrok *n.* a kind of bamboo like yiŋg, traditionally eaten, but not eaten any more; *wanpela kain mambu olsem yiŋg, ol tumbuna i save kaikai tasol nau ol man i no save kaikai.*

ŋgoijam *n.* morning star; *star i save kam antap klostu long tulait.*

ŋgomákokɨr *n.* small freshwater minnow; *ol liklik liklik pis i save stap insait long baret.*

ŋgomar *n.* fish (*generic*); *pis (biknem).*

ŋgomaroŋgar *n.* index finger; *pinga bilong han ol man i save usim long poinim ol samting.*

ŋgomkokɨrŋa *adj.* white hair; *waitpela gras.* Munje ide ŋgomkokɨrŋa mbet inde. The man with the white hair is coming; *Man i gat waitpela gras i kam ia.*

ŋgon *pro.* hers; *bilong em (meri).*

ŋgop *adj.* young, used for plants and breasts; *yangpela – ol man i save usim long toktok long ol diwai na long susu bilong meri.* Minjike ŋgop: a young, small betel nut tree; *yangpela, sotpela buai;* Pap ŋgop: a young coconut palm; *yangpela kokonas;* Min ŋgopŋa: young, firm erect breasts; *susu i sanap.*

ŋgoram *n.* Sacred Ibis (*Birds of New Guinea* plate 2, #6–9).

ŋgoriŋsua *n.* tree, the leaves and shoots of which are boiled and used to cure colds; *diwai ol man i save boilim kru bilong em na kru bilong em long pinisim kus.*

ŋgoriw *n.* shredded sago pancakes mixed with coconut water to form a kind of cold, sweet soup. Eaten on special occasions, such as the night before setting fire to a grassland plain; *brukim brukim ol praim na putim i go insait long wara bilong kokonas. Ol man i save kaikai despela long taim bilong bung long wokim sampela wok, olsem taim bilong pasim tok long kukim kunai.*

ŋgorok *n.* long traditional grass skirt that went down to about the calf, all the strands were one length; *longpela pulpul.* See also awin ŋgorok; ner.

ŋgoromai *n.* Ecletus Parrot (*Birds of New Guinea* plate 20, #4, female).

ŋgot *n.* yellow cartilage inside cassowary hip socket where the leg connects to the hip; *join bilong lek bilong ol muruk.*

ŋgow *n.* taste, sweetness; *swit.* Ŋgow eŋonke? Is it tasty? (lit. "is the taste good?"); *Swit ah?*; **Ikin ŋgowŋa**: The bananas are sweet, *banana i switpela.* **Ŋgow urok**: It was sweet (*lit.* 'sweet went inside'); *Swit ia.*

ŋgrag *n.* early evening, from about 5–7 pm.; *apinun.* **Ŋgrag eŋgon**: Good afternoon; *Apinun.*

ŋgrag arawer *n.* late afternoon, from about 4–5 pm.; *apinun.*

ŋgrukkɨ *v.i.* (**-net**/**-nak**), snore; *pulim nus.*

ŋgu *pro.* **1.** she; *em (meri).*
  2. her; *em (meri).*

ŋgudum *n.* **1.** star; *star.*
  2. firefly, considered to be a messenger of the dead. If a **ŋgudum** falls straight into the fire, a future death is foretold. If it flies around you, goes to the top of the house, then disappears thought a crack in the floor, someone is going to die; *star. Ol man i save tok olsem despela ol liklik binatang i gat save long ol indai man. Sapos wanpela star i raunim yu pastaim na bihain em pundaun long paia, em nau bai wanpela indai i kamap. O sapos em raunim yu, plai i go antap long haus, na bihain em i go daun na i go lus ananeat long haus, em tu bai wanpela indai i kamap.*

ŋgudumŋa kɨt *n.* Pleiades (*lit.* 'heap of stars'); *yar.* See also **mbiruŋa kɨt.**

ŋgugrub *n.* large red biting ants; *bikpela redpela anis i save kaikai man.*

ŋgugugrai *n.* sleepiness; *slip.* **Ŋa ŋgugrugaii (ŋgugugrai + ERG)**: I'm sleepy; *Slip i kam nau.*

ŋgume *adv.* thusly, such; *despela kain.* **Ŋgume morasi oretukun!** Stop always doing that! *Lusim despela kain pasin!*

ŋguméŋi *interj.* (contraction of **ŋgume aŋgi**), that's right, that's it, of course; *em tasol.*

ŋgúnbara *n.* short, squat vertical post on which the floor runners rest; *sotpela belpos.*

ŋgur *v.t.* (class 4), put or set something down; *putim.* **Note:** the vowel in this verb stem undergoes vowel harmony to harmonize with the vowel in the object morpheme that follows it; so **Ŋayi sapwar ŋgunkun**: I put down the basket, but **Ŋayi Njime ŋgɨngɨn**: I put down [the male baby] Njime; **Ŋayi ŋgurkru wákare**: 'I didn't put her down', **Ŋayi ŋgɨrgrɨ wákare**: 'I didn't put him down', **Ŋayi ŋgɨrmbrɨ wákare**: 'I didn't put them down'.

ŋgurbewat *n.* green ground lizard, *liklik grinpela palai i save stap long graun.*

ŋgurpan *n.* black mosquito, smaller than **aiawaŋgar**; *bilakpela natnat, liklik bilong* **aiawaŋgar.**

ŋgurub *n.* a kind of plant with big tough leaves that are used as parcels into which sago can be put and roasted directly on a fire; *wanpela kain hap diwai i gat strongpela lip bilong kukim* **paŋgip.**

ŋgurum *n.* speed; *spit.* **Ŋgi ŋgurum tatukreya weke**: The two of them picked up speed and came; *Tupela i spit i kam.*

ŋgusikrim *n.* grass; *gras.*

ŋguwur *n.* smoke; *smok bilong paia.*

ŋgwab *n.* **1.** hole, *hul.*
  2. cave; *hul bilong ston;*
  3. (*vulgar*) vagina; *sem bilong meri (tok nogut).*
  4. (*vulgar*) anus; *hul pekpek (tok nogut).*

ŋgwar *n.* **1.** marsupial pouch; *bilum bilong ol kapul na mumut.*
  2. kind of tree whose sap is used as a glue; *kain diwai ol man save kisim blut bilong em na usim olsem glu.*

ŋi *pro.* **1.** he; *em (man).* **Ŋi mbet inde**: Here he comes; *Em i kam.*
  2. him; *em (man).* **Ŋguyi ŋi poŋgɨn**: She hit him; *Em (meri) paitim em (man).*

O

o *v.t.* (class 1), **1.** strike someone or something; *paitim.* **Rumb pokun**: He beat the slitgong drum; *Em paitim garamut.*
  2. spear, stab, or shoot something; *sutim.* **Ŋiŋi mbor pokun**: He speared a pig; *Em sutim wanpela pik.*

3. strike (for example when talking about snakes); *snek i sutim man.* **Aramɲi Sakanup poŋgin**: The snake bit Sakanap; *Snek i sutim Sakanup.*
4. kill someone or something; *kilim indai.*
5. weed a garden or plot of land by hand, cut away grass with grass knife; *widim gras long han.*
6. make a sago pancake or **ŋgoriw**; *wokim praim o wokim* **ŋgoriw**.
7. tramp on grassland grass; *slipim kunai:* **naw pokun.**

obiman† *n.* ex-husband (used by the ex-in-laws of the man) (*obsolete*); *meri i lusim man bai mama na papa bilong meri kolim ex-man long despela nem.*

oike *n.* mango; *mango.*

oimbatak *n.* ring of rattan that surrounds the lizard skin on an hourglass drum; *kanda ol i save putim long kundu long pasim skin bilong palai.*

oiŋga† *n.* (*pl.* **oiŋgabidib** or **oiŋgandodo**) (*obsolete*), daughter-in-law (female speaking); *meri bilong pikinini man (mama bilong man bai tok).*

óiraraoki *v.i.* (conjugated like **oki**), go missing; *igo lus.* **Yu ŋa namgar pime yuwon pitiŋar oirarawokŋa tumbni, nipis yim amairiknuwanak**. If you had told me that your bush knife had gone missing on the mountain, we would have been able to find it for you; *Sapos yu bin tokim mi olsem busnaip bilong yu i bin go lus long maunten, inap mipela i painim long yu.*

ojirror *n.* [*Adjora*], small piglet; *liklik pikinini pik.*

okemki *v.i.* (**-net/-nak**), screw, in the sense of 'have sex'; *pamuk nambaut.* **Ɲiɲi ŋguɲana okemkinet**: He will just have sex with her, he has no desire or plans to marry her; *Em i laik kwap wantaim meri tasol, em i no gat tingting long maritim em.* **Okemŋgar noɲor**: Promiscuous woman; *Pamuk meri.*

oki *v.i. irr.* (**ŋa mbok/mbot; yu mbok/mbot; ɲi mbot; ŋgu wok; yim mbok; yum mbokem; ŋgi ŋgwok; yime sene woke**), go, *igo.*

Ombági *n.* Pangin village; *ples Pankin.*

ombare† *n.* nephew's wife (male speaking) (*obsolete*).

ombre† *n.* (*pl.* **ombrendodo**) (*obsolete*), father-in-law (male speaking); *man bai kolim papa bilong meri bilong em.*

ombuto *n.* a tree from which the bark to make traditional waistbelts is cut; *diwai ol man i save katim skin bilong em long wokim ol kapwasak.*

omgande omgande† *n.* (*obsolete*) 1. two or more wives of one man; *tupela meri bilong wanpela man.*
2. two or more female-in-laws; *tupela tambu meri.*

omin *n.* spouse; *man bilong meri o meri bilong man.*

ominde-omninde *n.* married couple; *tupela marit.*

omo *n.* (*pl.* **omosew**), father; *papa.* See also **sas**.

onaw *n.* 1. Brush-turkey; *bikpela wailpaul* (*Birds of New Guinea* plate 1, #4–6).
2. egg of this bird; *kiau bilong despela pisin.*

ondar *v.t.* (class 5), collect or gather together something, e.g. fruit that falls at the base of a tree or things scattered about the house; *bungim.* **Ondanukuna kukumbeta kit parkun**: I collected my things and brought them together to make a pile; *Mi kisim ol samting bilong mi na bungim long wanpela hip.*

ondir *v.t.* (class 4), pierce or shoot something many times; *sutim sutim.* **Mborɲi munje odingin, ŋgadan samiɲan**: The pig pierced the man many times (with its tusks), he has many wounds; *Pik i sutim sutim man na em i gat planti sua.*

ondim *v.t.* (class 5), delay or procrastinate to do something; *wokim isi isi.* **Yum patir ondimnukurem**: You've all built the house really slowly; *Yupela i wokim haus isi isi tru.*

ondir *n.* 1. hostility, refers to the time before the arrival of white people in Papua New Guinea, when villagers were engaged in never-ending warfare; *birua.* **Ondirŋa orom**: the pre-colonial time of eternal warfare; *taim bilong birua.*

2. custom of murdering a child of one's own matrilineal kin (for example a niece or nephew), last practiced in the 1920s. A murder of this kind was committed if a man's wife left him for another man. In retaliation, the wronged husband could kill a child belonging to one of his own siblings, or some other matrilineal kin (in a matrilineal society like Gapun and neighboring Sanae, these children are regarded as a man's true kin, unlike the man's own children, which belong to his wife's clan). Killing one's own matrilineal relative forced the man who married one's wife to compensate by killing one of *his* matrilineal relatives. If this happened, the matter was regarded as settled. If the man did not kill one of his own matrilineal relatives, then he could legitimately be killed, either by sorcery or by being murdered with a spear; *pasin bilong kilim indai wanpela kandere bilong yu. Sapos man i kisim meri bilong yu bai yu kirap kilim wanpela kandere bilong yu. Em nau, man i kisim meri bilong yu ia bai i mas kilim bilong em long stretim rong bilong em. Em kilim bilong em pinis bai samting i pinis. Nogat, em bai yu kilim em long poisen o long spia. Las taim ol man i wokim despela pasin em long taim bilong Amani, long taim bilong ol waitman i kam pinis long Papua Niugini.*

ondir ror *n.* (*lit.* 'ondir child') poor thing; *tarangu.*

onjaɲnoɲor *n.* a kind of small black lizard with different colored markings that lives at base of trees; *liklik bilakpela palai i gat makmak i save stap long ol as bilong diwai.*

ondom *n.* Blyth's Hornbill; *kokomo* (*Birds of New Guinea* plate 25, #8).

oŋgab *n.* traditional pot made of clay; *kanaka sosbin.*

oŋgar *n.* departure; *igo.* **Ŋan oŋgar kirawkru wákare:** I don't know when he left; *Mi no save long igo bilong em.*

oŋgarŋa patir *n.* traditional men's cult house that was situated outside the village in the rainforest. Not built in Gapun since the 1950s; *haus tambaran bilong bipo ol man i save kirapim insait long bus. Ol papa i kirapim wanpela long taim bilong istap long Sambaiag, tasol long taim bilong lusim Sambaig na kirapim nupela ples ol i nomoa wokim wanpela haus tambaran.*

oŋgisu *n.* [*Adjora*], large white mushroom; *bikpela waitpela talinga.*

oŋki *n.* small bamboo with fuzz, used as a tube into which raw sago is inserted and cooked on the fire; *liklik mambu i gat mosong ol man i save pulamapim em long saksak na kukim* **munakumund.**

oŋko *n.* fattest digit of hand or leg; *bikpela pinga bilong han o bilong lek.* **Ndaramŋa oŋko:** thumb; *bikpela pinga bilong han;* **Ndowŋa oŋko:** big toe; *bikpela pinga bilong lek.*

oŋgwan[†] *n.* (*pl.* **oŋgwabidig**) (*obsolete*), sister in-law (female speaking); *tambu meri em meri i tok.*

okinokin *n.* a palm sheath container onto which one attaches a handle, used to pour water into the **iko;** *liklik limbom ol meri samapim bilong kisim wara.*

opam[†] *n.* (*pl.* **opamndodo**) (*obsolete*), son-in-law; *man bilong pikinini meri.*

orai *n.* state of readiness; *redi.* **Ŋa orai nirkrunet:** I'm going to get ready; *Mi bai redi.*

oraiki *v.i.* (**-net/-nak**), be ready; *redi.* **Ŋa nda okinana orainetakut:** I'm ready to go; *Mi redi i stap long igo.*

orai *v.t.* (class 5), present someone with gifts, bestow; *givim ol sampela samting.* **Turuŋwadgi oraitimbroya kandipŋa nimir sene reki buspimbroya nda ŋgi prike.** The people of Turuŋwad presented them with gifts and sent them on their way with two sticks of (dried and smoked) hermit crabs; *Ol* **Turuŋwad** *i givim tupela stik i gat* **kandip** *long tupela na ol i salim tupela i go.*

orak *n.* (*pl.* **orasamb**), thing, object; *samting.*

orákaŋgar *n.* food (*lit.* 'thing for eating'); *kaikai.*

oraw *n.* banana frond/seedling that has sprouted leaves that one plants to grow a new banana plant; *kru bilong banana i gat lip*. See also **munjesik**.

orma[†] *n.* (*pl.* **ormabɨdib**) (*obsolete*), younger sibling; *liklik brata o susa*.

oré [*Watam*], **1.** *n.* yes, *yes*.
   2. *adv.* that's right; *em nau*. This word is replacing Tayap **awo**. *Ol Gapun i nomoa save tok awo olsem ol papa tumbuna. Ol i save tok long despela hap tok long ol man bilong nambis*.

ore-(p)-e *v.t.* (class 1), **1.** let go of something; *lusim*.
   2. leave something behind; *lusim*.
   3. forget something; *lus ting*. **Ŋa yunana numbwan orepekun**: I forgot all about you; *Mi lus ting long yu*.

orem *n.* crocodile; *pukpuk*.

oremai ikin *n.* green banana with white interior most often eaten roasted in skin directly on fire, *banana i gat waitpela mit ol man i save putim long paia na kaikai*.

orewir[v]**-X-oki** *v.i.* (serial verb construction conjugated like **oki**. Note: the X is an independent object suffix and [v] is a vowel that changes to harmonize with the vowel of the object morpheme), throw down; *troimwe i godaun*. **Ŋa orak aŋgo orewirukuokɨtak**: I'm going to throw this stuff down; *Bai mi troimwe despela samting*.

orɨkatɨrkɨ *v.i.* (-**net**/-**nak**; **r** → ∅ in realis, so **orɨkatɨnet**/**orɨkatɨnak**). be insane; *stap longlong*.

orimb *n.* loud audible fart; *kapupu i pairap*. **Yuyi orimb pikun**: You farted an audible fart; *Kapupu bilong yu i paiarap*.

orimb *n.* **1.** agemate, i.e. someone born near the same time you were; *wanlain*. **Ŋa orimbŋan yu nɨrɨ wákare**: I'm not your agemate; *Mi no wanlain bilong yu*.
   2. men initiated at the same time; *ol lain bilong lukim tambaran o pasim* **síw** *long sem taim*. **Siwŋa orimb**: fellow initiate; *ol lain bilong pasim* **síw** *long sem taim*.

orɨnd *n.* long, eel-like fish; *longpela pis i luk olsem maliau*.

oriŋárak *n.* large vine that, when cut, drips copious amounts of drinkable water. Looked for while walking through the rainforest during the dry season when one is far from water. It is also drunk as a cure for snake venom; *rop i gat bikpela wara. Ol man i save painim despela taim ol i wakabaut long bus long draisisen. Snek i kaikaim yu bai yu dring wara bilong despela rop*.

orka sene *n.* two guys; *tupela man*. **Ŋgɨ namtuko orka sene ŋgwokara**. They said the two guys had gone; *Ol i tok olsem tupela i go pinis*. Can be used for either gender, but always in this idiomatic form, so **orka manaw** (three guys) is not possible.

orom *n.* **1.** time; *taim*. **Ŋa yu aruoiwankuta orom kememtak**: I've waited for you for a long time; *Mi wetim yu longpela taim pinis*; **Emrarɨŋgar oromki ŋgo wákare!**: It isn't time to be playing! *I no taim bilong pilai!*; **nunukŋa orom**: the future; *taim bihain*; **taŋgar orom**: time to sleep; *taim bilong slip*.
   2. middle; *namel*. **Nɨmŋa orom**: the middle of the tree, *namel bilong diawai*.
   3. lower back; *baksait*. **Orom bɨdɨatan**: My lower back hurts; *Baksait bilong mi i pen*.
   4. amongst; *namel*. **Ŋa nambar inda yumon oromnɨ kut**: I'm all alone amongst you all; *Mi wan istap long namel long yupela*.
   5. near, in the vicinity of, around; *klostu long*. **Wotŋa orom**: the section of a felled sago palm just above the base section; *hap i stap klostu long as bilong saksak ol man i laik paitim long en*.

oror *v.t.* (class 4), **1.** surround something or someone; *raunim*.
   2. stir something; *raunim raunim*.

ororŋgar *adj.* round; *raunpela*.

orwo *n.* **1.** tiny spines on the two sides of sago palm leaves; *liklik ol nil i save stap long sait bilong ol lip bilong saksak*.
   2. boil resulting from burn; *sua i save kamap sapos yu kukim skin bilong yu long paia o long hotpela wara*.

osi *adv.* the other side, the opposite side; *hapsait*.

osiki *v.i.* (ŋa posiet/posiek, yu posiet/posiek, ŋi posiet, ŋgu posiek, yim posiek, yum posukem, ŋgi posuko; yim sene posuke): **1.** cross over to other side; *katim i go long hap*. **Ngi nuwombŋan taw nonni posuko**: They've gone over to the other side of the creek; *Ol i go long hapsait long baret*. **2.** be obstructed; *pas*. **Nder posiek**: The path is blocked; *Rot i pas*. **3.** spread, in the sense of catching something from somone else; *kalap long*. **Toto apro ŋani posiek**: The bad skin (e.g. grille) has spread to me; *Skin nogut i kalap long mi*; **Kandaw aŋgi ŋani osiŋgarana**: I hope that illness doesn't spread to me; *Nogut despela sik i kalap long mi*. **4.** dry out; *drai*. **Ngadan posiek**: The sore is dry; *Sua i pas nau*; **Awin kapur posiekara**: The well is dry; *Hulwara i drai pinis*.

osiŋgir *n.* pig tusks that are so developed and upward-turned that they form a circle, valued for traditional decorations; *bikpela tit bilong piki go raunpela olgeta*.

osos *n.* Hook-billed Kingfisher (*Birds of New Guinea* plate 24, #17–18)

otan⁺ *n.* (*pl.* **otinimb**) (*obsolete*), grandchild; *pikinini bilong pikinini*.

otar kut *n.* piece of wood (usually from the **koimbup**, **ŋgawro**, **kotriŋ**, or **awin** trees) used as a lighter. It is lit and carried around to light fires and cigarettes; *hap paiawut bilong laitim paia o bilong laitim smok*.

Husat i nogat wanpela geslaita bai karim despela taim yu wakabaut.

otar *n.* **1.** fire; *paia*. **2.** (*euphemism*), anger; *kros*. **Yu munje nonana mamrara wakakkutak, yuwonana otar rorikakkutak**: You quiver in your boots whenever anyone else asks you for things but when your own family asks you for anything, a fire gets lit! (i.e. you get angry and begin shouting); *Yu save guria i stap wantaim ol narapela, tasol ol lain bilong yu i laikim wanem samting bilong yu, paia i save lait! (olsem yu save kros na bikmaus)*. **3.** torch, flashlight; *tos*. **4.** fever, *bikpela hot long skin*. **Toto otar sumanŋa**: Skin is burning up; *Skin i hot nogut tru*.

otiŋgar *n.* a kind of light or lightning that is said to come up and make a thunderous sound when a man or woman dies; *lait i save kamap taim man o meri i laik indai*.

otre⁺ *n.* (*pl.* **otrendodo**) (*obsolete*), mother-in-law (male speaking); *nem man bai kolim mama bilong meri bilong em*.

oyaŋ *n.* [*Kopar*], **1.** small clam in mangrove with red meat; *liklik kina bilong mangoro i gat redpela mit*. **2.** (*euphemism*), vagina; *sem bilong meri*.

oyeŋ⁺ *n.* (*pl.* **oyeŋgud**) (*obsolete*), in-law (in the widest sense, including brother-in-law, sister-in-law, etc.); *tambu*.

P

paindakki *v.i.* (**-net/-nak**), become barren, unable to become pregnant. Can be used for dogs and pigs too; *pasim bel, stopim bel. Ol pik na dok tu yu ken tok* **paindaktak**. **Noŋor aŋgu paindaktak, motini awinni tuwku wákare**. That woman is barren, she'll never have another child; *Meri ia i pasim bel na em i no nap karim moa*.

pakas *adj.* dry; *drai, nogat wara*. **Mum pakasgarana, aŋgode wawan**: Don't let your sago jelly get dry; here's some soup; *Nogut* **mum** *i drai, sup ia*.

pakaski *v.i.* (**-net/-nak**), dry out; *i go drai*.

pake *n.* python; *draipela snek*.

pakind *n.* louse; *laus*.

pakras *n.* noise, like the sound of rustling leaves or far-off approaching rain; *pairap, olsem win i save pas long ol diwai o ren i stap longwe na pairap i stap*. See also **pindiŋ**.

palusemb *n.* Swallow (*Birds of New Guinea* plate 29).

pambram *n.* part of broken **oŋgab** (clay pot) used as a kind of frying pan on which to make **tamwai** (sago pancakes); *hap* *kanaka sosbin ol meri i save usim long kukim praim.*

pambram sikrim turtle (*secret talk*); *paup* (*hait tok*).

pamiŋgap *n.* top part of a **makor** (sago pounder); *hap i stap antap long makor.*

panap (or **panapanap**) *n.* large green grasshopper; *bikpela grinpela grashopa.*

pande *n.* axe; *tamiok.*

pandiŋ *n.* 1. a kind of large needle made out of **sekund**. Used to pierce a hole in bundles of sago palm leaves in order to fasten them to a frame to make roof shingles; *nil ol i save wokim long* **sekund**. *Ol man i save usim long samapim morota long pasim haus.*
2. wooden pins used to hold the **waris** (coconut fiber strainer) in place; *nil bilong nilim laplap bilong kokonas.* See also **mbába**

pandim *n.* a kind of *limbom* tree, the seeds of which are gathered and used by children as ammunition for slingshots. It is also used to make poison. One cuts the bark so that it forms a little bowl. After it rots, one collects the water in it, mixes this with a crushed millipede and then uses it to to kill someone; *wanpela kain limbom ol mangi i save kisim ol pikinini bilong em long sut long katapel. Na tu ol man nogut i save wokim posin long despela diwai. Ol i save katim skin bilong diwai na larim em sting. Bihain bai miksim wanpela wanpela* **kakámatik** *na kilim ol man.* See also **mbaŋaw.**

pandiripiŋ *n.* stringy fiber in yams or sago palms; *strongpela pipia i stap insait long saksak o long taro.*

pandiri(pi)ŋ war *v.t.* (class 2), provoke someone; *sikarapim nating bel bilong narapela man o meri.* **Ambin orakana Kruniɲi Sakre sapkini pandiriŋ parkun?**: Why did Kruni provoke Sake?; *Bilong wanem Kruni sikarapim nating bel bilong Sake?*

paŋg *n.* fiber from **tar** tree that women roll into thread; *tret bilong tar ol meri i save wokim tret long em.* See also **piŋg.**

paŋgip *n.* sago wrapped in a leaf and cooked on a fire. Usually mixed with something, such as sago grubs, fat or the membrane enclosing the inner organs of a pig; *saksak ol i save karamapim long lip na kukim long paia.*

pap *n.* 1. coconut; *kokonas.*
2. coconut palm; *diwai bilong kokonas.*
3. earwax; *pekpek bilong iao;* **Nekeŋa pap wostukun!** Get rid of your ear wax! *Rausim pekpek bilong iao!*
4. another kind of tree, the seedling of which is shredded and added to sago jelly and fed to dogs to get them to kill cassowaries; *narapela kain diwai ol man i save sikarapim kru bilong em na putim i go insait long mum. Bai ol i givim despela mum i go long ol dok na ol dok bai kaikai na igo kilim muruk.* See also **ariŋgadew.**

papo *n.*; *voc.* maternal uncle's wife; *meri bilong kandere.*

pap taw *n.* the final stage (of five) of coconut formation, a coconut that has fallen to the ground; *drai kokonas.*

papakndam *n.* a kind of tree, the leaves of which are used to tie together brooms bristles and tobacco leaves; *wanpela kain diwai ol man i save usim lip bilong em long ropim ol brum na ol lip bilong brus.*

papembir *n.* dry coconut palm leaves used to light fires or as a torch at night; *drai bombom.* **Yu papembir ruŋgrakkukuwetak ŋanana**: You pull off some dry coconut palm leaves and bring them to me; *Rausim sampela bombom na kisim i kam long mi.*

papetraw *n.* coconut husk fiber, used to get fires started, to wipe things up from floor, and as toilet paper; *skin bilong drai ol man i save usim long statim paia o long rausim samting i pundaun long graun insait long haus, o long klinim as.*

papkrim *n.* small coconut; *liklik kokonas.*

papku *v.i.* (**-iet/-iek**) pierce; *sut.*

papndaw *n.* wild coconut, a palm tree with very large, round leaves that can be used like big umbrellas to hide from the rain. The wood is strong and used to make bows; *wail kokonas i gat bikpela raunpela ol lip, ol man i save usim long wokim* **kembatik.**

paru *n.* traditional long canoe-shaped plate for eating, carved out of wood. By the early 1990s, these had all been replaced by plastic or tin store-bought plates and basins and are no longer made; *plet bilong ol tumbuna*.

pasákeke *n.* frog (*generic*); *prok* (*biknem*).

pasinder *adj.* light (in the sense of weightless); *i no hevipela*. **Taruŋg pasinder, naimb wákare**: The firewood is light, it isn't heavy; *Paiawut i no hevipela*.

pasuwer *n.* Great Cuckoo Dove (*Birds of New Guinea* plate 16, #4)

patarík *n.* Swift (*Birds of New Guinea* plate 28).

patirki patirki *adv.* method of cutting a **ner** (grass skirt) in layers; *we bilong katim pulpul olsem bai luk olsem ol step bilong lada bilong haus*.

patorki *v.i.* (-**net**/-**nak**), explode, make an explosive sound; *pairap*. **Mbwaj patortak**: The bamboo made an explosive sound (when it was burned in the fire); *Mambu i pairap*. **Ŋa oruneta, nok maniŋg patorkitak**: If I hit you, you will explode with piss; *Mi paitim yu olsem bai pispis i paiarap bai yu sutim pispis i go autsait*.

pawkpawk *n.* horizontal roof support placed on top of the **kerkwar**; the highest point of the roof; *namba tu pongan*.

pawp *n.* turtle (*generic*); *trausel* (*biknem*).

pawrik 1. *n.* strength; *strong*.
  2. *adj.* strong, tough, resistant, unbending; *strongpela*. **Ŋan numbwan pawrik ŋime oŋgrinana**: His mind is made up, he's going to kill that man; *Em i gat strongpela tingting long kilim despela man*.

pendimor *n.* **1.** a kind of tree with wide leaves; *wanpela kain diwai i gat ol braitpela lip*.
  2. the leaves of this tree, traditionally used to roll tobacco and smoke; *mangas, ol lip bilong despela diwai ol tumbuna i save usim long wokim smok bilong ol*.
  3. sheet of newspaper to smoke; *wanpela hap pepa bilong wokim smok*.
  4. book; *buk*.

pendo *n.* a kind of taro with a sacklike base, with large flowers that smell like rotting flesh when they decay; *wanpela kaim wailtaroi gat bikpela lip na taim despela lip bilong em i save sting wanpela smel nogut olsem bilong man indai i save kamap*.

peiki *v.i.* (-**tet**/-**tak**), boil; *boil*. **Awin peitak-ara**: The water has boiled; *Wara i boil pinis*.

perei *v.t.* (class 5), **1.** say something insulting; *tok bilasim*. **Ŋa yu pereiru wákare**: I didn't say anything to insult you; *Mi no tok bilas long yu*.
  2. oppose someone; *egensim*. **Yu ŋaŋan nam pereiŋgarke**: Don't oppose my talk; i.e. don't argue against me; *I no ken egesnim tok bilong mi*; **Pereiŋgar nam**: insult; *tok bilas*.

pereipereiki *v.i.* (-**net**/-**nak**), race; *resis*. **Pereiperekitike!** Let's race!; *Resis!*

perumb *n.* tree with soft bark used for carvings, traditional plates (**paru**) and canoes, two kinds, one white and one yellow; *diwai ol tumbuna i save usim long wokim kabing o **paru** o kanu, i gat tupela kain, wanpela i waitpela na narapela i yelopela*.

perumb orem *n.* yellow freshwater crocodile; *pukpuk i gat yelopela skin i save stap insait long ol baret*.

pesaw *n.* Lesser and Greater Birds of Paradise, *kumul* (*Birds of New Guinea* plate 51, #2–8 and #1–6 in the lower plate are females). **Pesawma ner**: long tailfeathers of bird of paradise; *pulpul bilong kumul*; **Pesawma sind**: two extended tail feathers of some species of bird of paradise; *tupela longpela gras i godaun long pulpul bilong sampela kain ol kumul*.

piar *n.* a kind of grass that makes one itch. Used to reanimate the ability to hunt: if a man has hunted unsuccessfully a number of times, he can eat a **paŋgip** made with the seeds of this grass in order to "heat" his skin and make him able to hunt again; *wanpela kain gras i save sikarapim skin bilong man. Sapos wanpela man i save go long banis saksak o em i save go wantaim ol dok na em i no save painim abus, em bai kaikai wanpela **paŋgip** ol i wokim long pikinini bilong despela gras. Olsem bai skin bilong em kamap hotpela gen na em bai go painim abus*.

pinumb *n.* snout, muzzle of animal, including crocodiles; *nus bilong olgeta kain animol*. See also **poŋgip**.

piɲin *n.* **1.** clitoris; *liklik hapnus bilong kan*.
   2. urethral opening. Speaker opinions differ on whether or not there is a **kwemɲa piɲin**; a urethral opening in the penis. Some say this opening cannot be referred to with **piɲin**; *hul bilong kan na hul bilong kok. Sampela i tok olsem yu ken toktok long* **kwemɲa piɲin**. *Na sampela i tok olsem em despela i kranki, piɲin em bilong meri tasol*.
   3. red sores that appear on the genitals of dogs; *redpela sua i save kamap long sem bilong ol dok*.

piokpiokkɨ *v.i.* (**-tet/-tak**), throb; *pamp*. **Itaw piokpiokakuk:** The vein (in my head) is throbbing; *Rop bilong hed i pamp i stap*.

pipiŋgabu *n.* hook; *wuk*.

piriŋ *n.* the two protrusions at the two ends of a slit-gong drum on which a **mɨrɨp kokɨr** (carving of a traditional deity) is carved above and a **kurbi** lizard below; *hed bilong garamut i gat mak*.

pis *n.* soundless fart; *kapupu i nogat pairap*. **Yuyi pis pikun:** You farted silently; *Yu kapupu na nogat pairap*.

pisaipisai *adj.* [*Kopar*], soft; *malomalo*. This word is replacing the Tayap complex construction **kondikra okɨ**.

pisik *n.* hermit crab; *guma*.

pisikimb *n.* corpse of a person or animal; *bodi bilong man indai long en, o bilong pik o mumut o wanem kain animol indai long en*.

pisimb *n.* **1.** rot, decay; *sting*.
   2. pus; *susu i kamap long sua*.

pisimbkɨ *v.i.* (**-net/-nak**), rot; *sting*.

pit *n.* Sunbird and Honeyeater (*Birds of New Guinea* plate 45).

pitatak *n.* small branches; *ol liklik liklik han bilong diwai*.

piwiukɨ *v.i.* (**-net/-nak**), chirp; *singaut olsem pikinini pisin*.

pɨk *n.* **1.** traditionally: veranda of house or men's house that projects from head of house; *bipo em miningim veranda bilong haus boi*.
   2. now: any veranda; *nau em miningim olgeta kain veranda*.

pɨn *n.* a little; *liklik*.

pɨndɨŋ *n.* noise, louder than **pakras** and intentional, for example children laughing and talking; *pairap. Bai yu harim strongpela liklik olsem ol mangi i lap na toktok wantaim*. See also **pakras**.

pɨnni *adv.* just a little while; just a minute; *liklik*. **Aruotak pɨnni:** Wait just a little while; *Wet liklik*.

pɨnimb *n.* lemon, grapefruit, citrus fruit; *muli*.

pɨnjɨrip *v.t.* (class 5), **1.** throw something away, *rausim*. **Ŋgu awin moto pɨnjɨriptukun:** She threw away the dirty water; *Em rausim wara i gat pipia*.
   2. spurt something; *sut*. **Nok pɨnjɨriptukun:** Urine shot out; *Pispis i sut i go*.

pɨnpɨn *n.* rubbish; *pipia*.

pɨŋ *n.* thread; *tret*. **Tarɲa pɨŋ:** thread taken from the pandanus tree; *tret bilong tar*. See also **paŋ**.

pɨŋgrɨm *v.t.* (class 5), scrape off something, e.g. the skin of a corpse of a pig or other animal that has been singed by fire to burn off its fur, sap from a breadfruit from your hands, sago from inside a pot; *sikarapim, olsem skin bilong pik taim ol i kukim bodi bilong em long rausim gras, blut bilong kapiak i pas long han, saksak i pas insait long wanpela sosbin*.

pɨŋkɨ *v.i.* (**-net/-nak**), jump up; *kalap*. **Ndamor pɨŋtaka warakɨtak:** Ndamor is going to jump up and talk; *Ndamor bai kalap na toktok*; **Samek pwɨŋra posieta pombɨn:** Samek jumped up and went over and hit them; *Samek kalap i go long hapsait na paitim ol*.

pɨrimat *n.* rag; *hap koros o malo o pulpul i brukbruk*. **Siwɲa pɨrimat:** a ragged loincloth; *malo i brukbruk long en*.

pɨt *v.t.* (class 5), wash objects like dishes, pots or clothes; *wasim ol samting*.

pɨtɨɲar *n.* machete, bush knife; *busnaip*.

pokemb *adj.* cold; *kolpela*.

pokembkɨ *v.i.* (**-tet/-tak**), become cold; *kamap kolpela.*

poketak *n.* [*Kopar*], a little fish with a large stomach and sharp teeth; poisonous, not eaten. Its venom is supposedly used by people to poison others; *bikbel pis ol man i no save kaikai. Ol man i save draim marasin bilong en na putim long kaikai o long buai bilong ol narapela ol man long bagarapim ol.* The Tayap, which no one ever uses, would be **ŋgomar imin suman**: big-stomach fish; *bikbel pis.*

pom *n.* handle of knife or machete; *handel bilong naip o busnaip.*

pombor *n.* heap of shit; *hip pekpek.* **Ŋan mayayi yɨwɨrŋan ŋgwabekenɨ pomborrekɨ tatɨŋɨŋan mamrairekɨ**: His mother gave birth to him through her asshole with a pile of shit, while lightning flashed (*vulgar*); *Mama bilong em i karim wantaim pekpek long hul pekpek taim laitning i pairap* (*tok nogut*).

pomɨŋ *n.* conch; *taur.*

pomɨŋsua *n.* snail; *liklik taur bilong graun.*

ponjame *n.* **1.** maturity and strength in late puberty. For men this is the appearance of a beard and hair on chest; for women breasts. Traditionally associated with maturity enough to marry; *strong bilong man na meri i save kamap taim mausgras i kamap long ol man na susu i kamap long ol meri.* **Ponjame sisiek**: He (or she) is strong and mature; *em kisim strong.*

2. maturity and strength in pigs, made visible by growth of tusks; *pik i gat kaŋgajin* (*draipela tit*). **Mbor aŋgo ponjame sisiekŋa**: This pig is tusked and mature; *Pik ia i bikpela na strong bilong em i kamap pinis.*

3. orgasm (probably a novel meaning of the word, cited only by some male speakers in their 20s and 30s); *kapsaitim wara bilong kok o bilong kan* (*em ol sampela yangpela man tasol i toktok long despela mining*).

poŋgip *n.* crocodile snout; *nus bilong pukpuk.* See also **pinumb**.

poŋgrom *n.* **1.** stone axe; *ston tamiok bilong ol tumbuna.* See also **mindia**.

2. (*vulgar*) penis, *kok* (*tok nogut*). **Poŋgrom sumanŋan!** Big dick! (*vulgar*); *Bikpela kok!* (*tok nogut*). **Nenima poŋromŋan amasik poŋgromŋan apro sakar!** Fucking grandfather dick, ancestor prick! (*vulgar*); *Yu paken bastad lapun kok, kok bilong ol tumbuna!* (*tok nogut*).

popro *n.* **1.** lungs; *namba tu lewa.*

2. early evening star; *star i save kam antap long apinun.*

por *v.t.* (class 5), **1.** beat something, as in beating a drum; *paitim olsem man i paitim garamut o kundu.*

2. the cooing sound made by crowned pigeons; *singaut ol guria i save mekim*: **Momɨk rumb porkwankut**: The crowned pigeon is cooing (*lit.* 'beating the slit-gong drum'); *Guria i singaut i stap.*

pora *n.* **1.** wind, breath; *win.* **Pora tarkru wákare**: He's not breathing; *Em i no pulim win.*

2. rest, *malolo.* **Yɨm ŋgo pora tarkunak ŋgo**: Let's take a rest; *Yumi malolo pastaim.* See also **bun**.

poisir *n.* sorcery; *posin.* **Poisirŋa munje**: sorcerer; *posinman.* This is certainly a borrowing from Tok Pisin, but it has been thoroughly incorporated into Tayap. See also **isuk**.

porimb *n.* [*Kopar*], floor support that runs cross-wise, from **ŋgúnbara** to **ŋgúnbara**; *rola.* See also **tékdwan**.

poror *v.i.* (**-net/-nak**), sing; *singsing.*

potak *n.* **1.** neck, throat; *nek.*

2. meat of wild animal, *abus.* **Potak tombetŋan seknɨ aŋgi wuk**: The meat is under the shelf; *Abus i stap ananeat long bet.*

potakɨ *v.t. inv.* crave something to drink, eat or smoke; *nek i bagarap long dring o smok o kaikai wanpela samting.* **Yu awin potakɨ?** Are you thirsty? *Nek bilong yu i bagarap long dring ah?*; **Ŋgu sokoi potakɨ**: She wants to smoke; *Nek bilong em i bagarap tru long smok*; **Ŋa mum aŋgar potakɨ**: I'm craving sago jelly; *Nek bilong mi i bagarap tru long kaikai* **mum**.

potakɨr *n.* small talk, conversation; *toktok nambaut.*

Potow 1. *n.* Wongan village; *ples Wongan.*

2. *adj.* Wongan, *Wongan.* **Potow mer**: Wongan language; *tok ples Wongan.*

powow *n.* whistle loudly with fingers in mouth, wolf whistle; *strongpela wisil.* **Powow nitukun!**: Wolf whistle! *Wisil strong!*

prak *v.t.* (class 5), untie something, *lusim.*

pramat *n.* small cluster of betel nut; *liklik rop buai.*

prerikɨn *n.* sweet potato; *kaukau.*

prɨk *adj.* ripe; *mau.*

prɨk *v.t.* (class 5), clear undergrowth; *brosim.* **ŋa mbara prɨkkru wákare**: I haven't cleared my garden; *Mi no brosim gaden.*

pruk *n.* work; *wok.* **Yum prukŋa pɨnpɨn nɨrkwankukem ŋgo**: Finish the little bit of work you have left; *Yupela wokim liklik wok bilong yupela pastaim.*

prukkɨ *v.i.* (**-net**/**-nak**), work; *wok.*

punatkɨ *v.i.* (**-net**/**-nak**), mourn, miss; *wari.* **Munje kowot ainde ŋan noŋorana punatnet**: The old man is mourning his wife. *Lapun man ia i wari long meri bilong em.* See also **wur-(p)-ekɨ.**

punat *v.t.* (class 5), mourn, miss; *wari.* **ŋayi nɨ punatɨŋena eiarte**t: I missed him and I cried; *Mi wari long em na mi krai.* See also **wure.**

pundidip *n.* **1.** pea shooter; *mambu ol pikinini i save kisim sit bilong diwai na sut long en.*
   2. bamboo pipe that used to be inserted into grave, to act as a tunnel to allow the spirit of the dead person to emerge from the grave; abandoned as a practice in the 1990s; *hap mambu ol tumbuna i save planim antap long kum. Hap i stap antap long graun, na hap ol i save subim i godaun insait long hul. Em olsem lada na dewil bilong man i indai long en inap go ikam long despela lada.*

punim *n.* Greater Black Coucal (*Birds of New Guinea* plate 23, #12, 14–19).

puŋg *n.* New Guinea Flightless Rail (*Birds of New Guinea* plate 10, #16).

puŋgup *n.* large metal dish that people keep on their verandas. Filled with earth and used to hold **otar kut** (slow-burning lighted branches or pieces of firewood) so that people can easily light their cigarettes. In houses with no hearths, women suspend pots over these, light firewood and cook on them; *bikpela dis bilong putim paia.*

puŋun *n.* wild Malay apple tree; *wail laulau.*

pura *n.* blind for killing birds that come to drink water or eat seeds on ground; *banis pisin.*

puraraokɨ *v.i.* (conjugated like **okɨ**), float; *trip.* **Yimbar awinŋa mbwar purarapuwok**: The canoe floated on top of the water; *Kanu i trip antap long wara.* See also **konenjarkɨ.**

purikɨ *v.i.* (**-tet**/**-tak**), splatter, splash; *kapsait olsem man i spetim wara long haus boi.* **Pap taw otɨtek sumbwanɨ awɨn purɨtaka puwok**: The coconut fell on the ground and its water splattered out; *Drai kokonas i pundaun long graun na wara bilong em i kapsait olsem man i dring wara long* **awɨn pomɨŋ** *na spetim man.*

purkɨ *v.i.* (**ŋa punet/punak, yu purtet/purtak; nɨ punet; ŋgu putak; yim punak; yum punkem; ŋgɨ putuko; yim sene putuke**), rest; *malolo.* **Ŋa nda purkɨnetana**. I'm going to rest; *Mi laik malolo nau.*

purpur *n.* feather, *gras bilong pisin.*

puwai *n.* **1.** dust; *das, olsem kar i ron na kamapim das.*
   2. sand; *welsan.*

puwaiorom *n.* beach; *welsan.* See also **sumbwa kapɨr.**

puwas *adj.* white; *waitpela.*

pwak-(p)-o *v.t.* (class 1), open up something, e.g. a box, basket, netbag; *opim wanpela bokis o basket o bilum.*

pwap 1. *n.* anger; *kros.* **Pwapŋar noŋor**: a woman who is always cross; *meri bilong kros.*
   2. *adj.* large, used only with certain animals, such as **enamb pwap** (cuscus); **kakar pwap** (Gurney's Eagle), **kanuŋ pwap** (tree kangaroos) and **ŋgararɨk pwap** (lizards); *bikpela, taim yu toktok long kapul, taragau,* **kanuŋ** *o ol palai.*
   3. *n.* skinned, exposed flesh; *mit nating.* **Pwap sinder**: a skinned corpse; *mit nating.*

pwapkɨ *v.i.* (**-net**/**-nak**), get angry; *kros.* **Yukɨre pwapakkut**: He's angry with Yuki; *Em kros wantaim Yuki.*

pwapwag *n.* tip of nose; *poin bilong nus.*
pwar *v.t.* (class 4), sprout a shoot or blossom; *kamapim kru.* **Minjike pwatukun:** The betel nut sprouted a new vine; *Nupela rop buai i kamap.*

pwiki *v.i.* (**-net/-nak**), roll around, as in a child who rolls around in a mosquito net while sleeping; *tainim tainim olsem pikinini i tainim tainim insait long taunamb taim em i slip i stap.*

R

ramaŋ *n.* **1.** enclosure erected outside the men's house to seal it off from view when the sacred flutes are played inside; *banis tambaran.*
  2. a fence made to seal off an area so that only people who pay can go inside to dance or watch DVDs; *geit.*
ramb *n.* carving on a slit gong drum, hourglass drum, or on a **kandibwaŋ** (traditional carving); *makmak.*
ramborgar *adj.* white and black mottled coat of an animal; *kalakala gras bilong kaskas o pik o wanem kain animol.*
rambu *v.t.* (class 4), mark something by carving or painting it, *makim.*
ramu *n.* small banana, eaten when ripe; *liklik banana ol man i save kaikai mau.*
rar *v.t.* (class 4, both **r**'s change in realis), **1.** see; *lukim.* **Ŋayi yu raru wákare:** I can't see you; *Mi no lukim yu.*
  2. help someone, *sapotim, helpim.* **Rurumgri ŋgweka ŋa tatioya patirni pruktuko:** My nephews came and helped me with the work on my house; *Ol liklik kandere i kam na helpim mi long wok bilong haus.*
  3. (*euphemism*), have sex; *kwapim (tok bokis).* **Noŋori aindet munje ainde tatŋgin:** The woman had sex with that man; *Meri i kwapim man ia.*
  4. *v.i.* look. As part of a serial verb construction with any verb of motion, this means 'look in X direction'. So **rarpuwot** (**rar** + realis form of **wurku**, 'go up') means 'he looked up'. **Rarosikinet** (**rar** + the future form of **osiki** 'go across') means 'he will look across'; **rarposiet** (**rar** + realis form of the same verb, **osiki**, means 'he looked across'; *lukluk olsem yu putim despela haptok long wanem narapela haptok i miningim*

olsem i go long wanpela hap o i go antap o kain mining olsem, em bai yu tok long husat ia i lukluk i go antap, o em bai lukluk i go long hapsait, despela kain mining.
raraiki *v.i.* (conjugated like **aiki**), become visible; *kamap.* **Karep rarwek:** The new moon has appeared; *Nupela mun i lait.*
rarer *n.* appearance, sight; *luk.* **Rarer eŋgon wákare:** It doesn't look good; *I no luk smart.*
rarekurki *v.i.* (**-net/-nak**), support, provide help; *sapot.*
rarki *v.i.* (**-pet/-pek**), keep an eye out, look around; *lukluk.* **Ŋa yunana rarpet yu aiki wákare:** I was keeping my eye out for you but you never came; *Mi lukluk long yu na yu no kam.*
raw *n.* nose; *nus.*
rawmitki *v.i.* (**-net/-nak**), be serious, stoic, without reaction; *pes drai.*
rawni **1.** *adv.* first, previous; *pes.*
  2. *pos.* in front of; *pron long* **Aŋgude turoŋa rawni wuk:** It is there in front of the fireplace; *Samting i stap long pron bilong hap bilong kukim kaikai.*
rawŋa sokop *n.* septum; *bun bilong nus.* **Rawŋa sokop timirbirni rowandparkro:** They pierced the septum; *Ol i drilim bun bilong nus.* See also **ndrig.**
re(ki) *per. case.* with; *wantaim.* **Yu anireki mbet?** Who did you come with? *Yu kam wantaim husat?*
rembow *n.* a kind of seashell, sometimes used to make traditional spoons; *sel ol man i save usim sampela taim long wokim spun bilong tumbuna.*
rerem *n.* **1.** ember; *sit bilong paia:* **otar rerem.**
  2. eyeball; *waitpela bilong wanpela ai:* **ŋgino rerem.**
rew *n.* fear, *pret.*

rewki *v.i.* (ŋa tewniet/tewniek, yu tewtiet/ tewtiek; ŋi tewniet; ŋgu tewtiek; yim tewniek; yum tewnkem; ŋgi tewtuko; yim sene tewtike), **1.** fear; *pret.* **Ŋanana tewtuko:** They are afraid of me; *Ol i pret long mi.*
    2. run away, get out of here, piss off; *ranawe, pisop.* **Yu makatni iskitetre, ŋa rewkinet:** If you decorate yourself with that red paint, I'll run away (or: I'll be afraid); *Yu putim despela redpela pen bai mi ranawe (o bai mi pret).* Note that this verb in this meaning of 'get out of here' has a regular, intransitive Group I imperative form: **rewtet** (to a male), **rewtak** (to a female), **rewnkem** (to more than one addressee). All mean "Get out of here!", "Piss off!".

rewi *n.* tooth, teeth; *tit.*

rewiŋgun *n.* gums; *skin bilong tit.*

rewitoto *n.* black ants (*lit.* 'teeth-skin'), smaller than **kambobai**. They live in the ground and are encountered when people cut grass. They deliver painful bites; *Ol bilakpela anis i liklik long kambobai i save stap long graun. Taim man i katim gras sapos yu distebim haus bilong ol bai ol i kam autsait na bai yu kisim pen.*

riri *v.t.* (class 5), roll something between hands vigorously, for example clothes one is washing; *wiruwuim.*

rimb *n.* traditional decoration made of fragrant leaves and hung around neck and back during times of singing and dancing; *tumbuna bilas ol i save wokim long ol lip na ol plowa igat smel, ol man i save hangamapim long nek long taim bilong singsing.*

ripam *temp.* before, in olden times; *bipo.*

ripamŋa orom *n.* past; *taim bipo.*

ripiki *v.i.* (**tipniet/tipniek**), lead, in the sense of walking first in a line; *go pas.*

ripim *temp.* previously; *bipo.* **Ripim ŋa naŋro manaw armbrinana, ŋa numbwan pikun pruk mik, ŋa mndanet:** Previously I wanted to marry three women but I realized that it would be hard work and so I changed my mind; *Bipo mi laik maritim tripela meri tasol mi save olsem hatwok tumas na olsem mi les.*

rir-(p)-or *v.t.* (class 1), throw a spear or shoot an arrow; *sut long ain o long banara.*

rir-(p)-orki *v.i.* (**rirporiet/rirporiek**), kick legs in all directions, like what a child does during a tantrum or what a cassowary does when it throws itself on its back to fend off dogs and hunters; *sutim sutim lek olsem pikinini i keŋgen o muruk i laik sutim dok o sutim man.*

rit *adv.* used only with verbs of motion: without pausing; *hariap.* **Ŋgu rit ŋayarni puwoka patirni otar kukusisiek:** She rushed up into the house and brought down some fire; *Em hariap tru i go antap long haus na kisim paia i karim i godaun.*

riwind *n.* surprise, start; *kirap nogut.* **Riwind isukwa!** Give her a start! *Mekim em kirap nogut!*

riwindra aiki *v.i.* (conjugated like **aiki**), be startled; *kirap nogut.* **Ŋi riwindra mbet, pemieta, rarikut:** He got startled, got up and was looking around; *Em kirap nogut em sanap na em i lukluk i stap.*

romb *n.* Starling (*Birds of New Guinea* plate 54, #5–7).

romgar[†] *n.* (*pl.* **rurumgri**) (*obsolete*), sister's child; nephew or niece; *pikinini bilong susa.*

roŋgiki *v.i.* (**toŋginiet/toŋginiek**), be blocked; *pas.* **Yimbar toŋgitiek:** The canoe is unable to pass (because a tree has fallen into the creek); *Kanu i pas.*

roŋgur *v.t.* (class 4; both **r**'s change in realis, so **toŋgunkun**), **1.** remove yams from ground; *kamautim yam o mami.*
    2. prevent, constrain; *pasim.* **Orak sene aŋgikmeŋgi ŋan roŋgrikutŋan:** Those two things are his constraints; i.e. they are what is preventing him from doing what he wants; *Em despela tupela samting em i save pas long em.*

ror *n.* (*dl.* **ruru**; *pl.* **rorsem**), child; *pikinini.*

rorki *v.i.* (**toriet/toriek**), ignite; *lait.*

rorŋa niŋ *n.* back leg joint of pig; *join bilong lek bilong pik.*

rowand-(p/w)-ar *v.t.* (class 2), pierce something; *sutim.*

rowe *adj.* old, used for inanimate objects; *olpela ol samting*. **Num rowe**: the old village; *olpela ples*; **Nder rowe**: the old path; *olpela rot*. See also **kowot**.

ru *v.t. irr.* (class 4 but does not take the first part of the discontinuous subject marker), 1. throw or propel something; *sutim*. **Yir tukun**: He threw a spear; *Em i sut long spia*. 2. eject or expel something; *sutim*. **Munjenum aŋge tewtukoya nok tukro**: The men were so afraid they peed themselves; *Ol man i pret na sutim pispis*.

ruX-arikɨ *v.t. irr.* (conjugated like **arkɨ**. X here stands for the BEN object markers. The vowel in the first part of the verb undergoes assimilation to harmonize with the vowel in the object morpheme that follows it, so **rukuarikɨ wákare** [feminine object not thrown out], **riŋgarikɨ wákare** [masculine object not thrown out]), 1. throw something away, empty something; *rausim*. **Pɨnpɨnŋa kondew rukuaritak!** Empty that rubbish bucket!; *Rausim ol pipia i stap insait long kondew*.

ruk *n.* 1. smell; *smel*. **Ŋan totoŋa ruk pisikmat ruk mbibikŋa**: His skin smells fishy, like a hermit crab; *Skin bilong em i gat smel olsem wanpela* **pisik**. 2. crown of tree; *tel bilong diwai*. 3. anal glands in possums and bandicoots; see also **warniŋg**.

rukana tar *v.t.* (class 4), smell something; *smelim*. **Mbawi ruakana orakaŋgar tankunde, endekari nitiŋgin**: Mbawi smelled the food and became hungry; *Mbawi smelim kaikai na hangre i mekim em*.

rumb *n.* slit-gong drum; *garamut*.

rumbruku *v.i.* (-tet/-tak), sag; *pundaun*. **Ŋgwab mɨr rumbrutak otɨtekŋa apro sakar**: Your big cunthole is fucking sagging! (*vulgar*); *Draipela hul bilong yu i pundaun i godaun olgeta!* (*tok nogut*).

ruŋgu *v.t.* (class 4), pluck something, e.g. a leaf, the feathers from a chicken; *rausim olsem lip o rausim gras bilong kakaruk*. **Ŋa kokokma pupur tuŋgunukun**: I plucked the feathers off the chicken; *Mi rausim gras long kakaruk*.

rupu *v.t.* (class 4), tie a grass skirt, skirt, piece of cloth or traditional waistbelt around the body. To specify a part of the body other than the waist, you would say, e.g. **potaknɨ** (around the neck); *pasim pulpul, siket, laplap o malo*.

rur *v.t.* (class 4, both **r**'s change in realis, so **ŋa tunukun/ŋgu tutukun**): sharpen something; *sapim*.

rurur-(p)-e *v.t.* (class 1), crumple or fold something up; *brukim*. **Ewand rurueku sapwarnɨ parkun**: I crumpled up the mosquito net and put it in the basket; *Mi brukim taunamb na putim i go insait long basket*.

rurur-(p)-ekɨ *v.i.* (-pet/-pek), adhere; *pas na i strong*.

ruwond-(p)-i *v.t.* (class 1), smoke (i.e. cure) something; *smokim*.

ruX-(p)-osikɨ *v.i.* (conjugated like **osikɨ**. Note: X here stands for a non-final object suffix. The vowel in the first verb in this series, **ru**, undergoes vowel harmony to harmonize with the vowel in the object morpheme that follows it), hang up on two forks pitched into ground; *hangamapim long pok*. **Mbor riŋgosikitike**: Let's hang up the boar; *Yumi hangamapim pik*.

S

saim *n.* basket with one string that women put on their heads to carry things like vegetables, or fish that they catch; *liklik basket igat wanpela han tasol. Ol meri save hangamapim long hed na pulampim long ol kumu bilong bus o long pis*.

saiput *n.* basket that until the 1970s used to be used wash and leach sago pith; *basket ol mama bilong bipo i save usim long wasim saksak*.

sak *n.* earring; *ring bilong putim long yau*

sak *v.t.* (class 5), embrace, kiss; *kis*.

saki(nɨ), see **sapki(nɨ)**.

sakɨnd *n.* a kind of ironwood tree; *kwila*. See also **nuruw**.

samba (also **sambaŋa kandaw**) *n.* illness caused by women's vaginal heat. Everyone is susceptible, especially men, but also women who have recently given birth themselves; they must eat their food using tongs or a spoon to avoid ingesting their own heat and giving the illness to themselves. Symptoms are shortness of breath, coughing, pain in skin and joints, especially the knees, and especially in the afternoon. If one eats just a little one's stomach swells up. One boils the leaves of the **manumbi** or **ŋgoriŋsua** tree as part of a cure; *sik i save kamap long hot bilong ol meri. Bai sotwin, kus, bun bai pen, skin bai pen, yu bai kaikai liklik na skin bai solap. Bai yu kisim ol lip bilong ol* **manumbi** *or* **ŋgoriŋsua** *na dring*.

samba mɨr *n.* ignorant person, stupid person; *man o meri i nogat save*. Compare **sua mɨr**.

sambai oremai ikin *n.* same kind of banana as **oremai ikin**, except that it is half the size and has a yellow interior; *wanpela kain banana olsem* **oremai ikin**, *tasol em i gat yelopela mit bilong em*.

sambaŋa njem *n.* a magic chant sung to help pregnant women who are having difficulty giving birth. It involves calling the names of other women who have recently given birth, and swearing at them; *singsing bilong helpim husat meri bel bilong em i pas na em i no go insait long bus tasol i no karim. Bai yu kolim nem bilong ol nupela mama na bai yu tok nogutim ol*.

sambap *n.* **1.** pointed stick used to remove the husk from coconuts; *stik bilong selim kokonas*.
  2. digging stick; *stik bilong dikim graun long gaden*.
  3. molar; *bikpela tit i stap long baksait bilong bun bilong maus*.
  4. (*euphemism*) penis; *kok* (*tok bokis*).

sambi *n.* a small tree that has leaves that smell pleasantly; *liklik diwai i gat gutpela smel*.

sambo *n.* a sago palm that has a watery interior, containing little sago starch; *saksak i nogat strongpela mit, warawara tasol*. **Yam sambo, muna wákareŋan**: The sago palm is **sambo**, it has no sago starch; *Sakasak i warawara, nogat* **muna**.

sambona *interj.* [*Kopar*], never mind, stop it; *maski*.

sambwaŋmond *n.* Cormorant (*Birds of New Guinea* plate 2, #1–4).

sami *n.* many; *planti*.

sanamb *n.* a tree with soft wood like cork that floats when put in water. It used to be used for making traditional carvings, plates, headrests and sometimes canoes, also used in secret male rituals to stay healthy and grow tall; *trip diwai ol man bilong bipo i save usim long wokim ol kabing o ol pelet na sampela taim ol i save usim long sapim kanu; ol man tu i save usim long wok bilong ol long kamap strongpela na longpela*.

sandaw *n.* falsetto shout of happiness that is repeated over several beats, like 'o-o-o-o'. The shout is given when to announce a laudible or desirable act, such as spearing a pig or cassowary, carrying a large house post, catching sight of someone one hasn't seen in a long time, or glimpsing a new moon; *gutpela singaut bilong hamamas*. **Rorsemgi sandaw pokure**: The two children shouted **sandaw**; *Tupela mangi i wokim* **sandaw**.

saŋrɨwat *n.* noose, trap made of rope to capture birds ; *rop i redi long taitim samting*.

saŋudam *n.* a wrack made of sago palm leafstalk for smoking fish; *samting ol i wokim long pangal bilong smokim pis*.

sapki *adv.* **1.** good, agreed; *gutpela, em tasol*. **Sapki yu ŋgume orak piatan**: It's good you gave me this thing; *Gutpela na yu givim despela samting long mi*.
  2. happy; *hamamas*. **Ŋa sapki aŋgi**: I am happy (lit. 'I good here'); *Mi hamamas ia*.

sapki(nɨ) (also **saki(nɨ)**) *adv.* **1.** just; *nating, tasol*. **Sapkinɨ utok**: It just appeared; *Em*

i kamap nating; **Ŋa sapkini nam aŋgi aroni ŋgunkun:** I'm just saying (*lit.* 'I'm just putting the talk outside'); *Mi putim nating tok i go autsait*; **Yu saki tarŋgar aku wákare:** You didn't just sit there and listen; *Yu no laik harim na istap tasol.*
2. for no reason; *nating.* **Arore arore noŋor aŋgu sapkini pororakawkuk:** Every day that woman is always singing for no reason; *Oltaim oltaim despela meri i save singsing nating.*
3. haphazardly, without goal or purpose; *nambaut.* **Sapki sapki rirporkun:** He's just shooting randomly with no purpose; *Em i sut nambaut.*

saprew *n.* belly stuffed full of food or shit; *bel i pulap long kaikai o long pekpek.* **Yiwir saprew sumanŋa mbor aŋgo:** That pig shits everywhere; *Pik i save pekpek long olgeta hap.*

sapwar *n.* basket (*generic*); *basket* (*biknem*). **Simbergar sapwar:** everyday basket for carrying around one's belongings, such as one's supply of betel nut and lime; *liklik basket bilong putim ol liklik samting bilong yu olsem ol samting bilong kaikai buai*; **Miriŋa sapwar:** large basket for carrying supplies and food to and from the rainforest; *bikpela basket long karim i go long bus*; **Karatum sapwar:** basket with traditional decorations belonging to the crocodile clan; *basket i gat makmak bilong ol pukpuk*; **Maŋai sapwar:** basket with traditional decorations belonging to the dog clan; *basket i gat makmak bilong ol pik.*

sarep *n.* grass knife; *grasnaip.*

sas *n.* [Adjora], father, *papa.* In the speech of most villagers, this word has replaced the Tayap equivalent **omo.**

sasápoke *n.* black land crab; *bilakpela kuka bilong graun.*

sasawraŋ *n.* large cockroach; *kokros.*

sasik *n.* bandicoot; *mumut.*

sasma ror *interj.* my goodness (lit. 'father's child'); *oyo.* Expression used to convey surprise or dismay.

sasu *n.* shrimp, small lobster; *kinda.*

sasupat *n.* small shrimp; *ol liklik kinda.* This word is being replaced by the Kopar-language word **nap.**

sawáraŋa *n.* traditional fighting mace; *bikpela tumbuna naip bilong pait na kilim man.*

sawrek-(p)-e *v.t.* (class 1), mix something together; *miksim.* **Munareki papreki sawrekekuk.** We are mixing the sago and the coconut; *Mipela miks saksak na kokonas i stap.*

sawir *adj.* black; *bilakpela.*

sek *n.* underside; *ananeat.*

sekni *pos.* below, *long ananeat.* **Patir sekni sirewuk:** It's under the house; *Em i stap ananeat long haus.*

sekund *n.* a kind of palm tree similar to a betel nut palm; *wanpela kain diwai i wankain olsem buai.*

semaya *n.* Tagula Butcherbird (*Birds of New Guinea* plate 55, #4).

semb *n.* eel larva; *liklik pikinini malio.*

send *n.* banyan tree; *pikus.*

sendam *n.* name of song that used to be played and sang by men when they arrived in the village bearing the severed heads of their enemies (**kwai kokir**); *singsing ol man i save wokim taim ol hed bilong birua i kam long haus tambaran.*

sene *n.* two; *tupela.*

seŋgrim *adj.* without accompaniment; describes for example sago jelly with nothing on it; *nogat abus o kumu long mum.* See also **sinder.**

serek *n.* one of the three species of trees which men use to make the floors of a house; *wanpela long tripela kain diwai ol man i save katim paitim long en na wokim ol plo bilong haus.* See also **kondew, kaŋir.**

ser-(p)-e *v.t.* (class 1), 1. hold something in one hand; *holim long wanpela han.*
2. hold something by cradling it in arms or supporting it, as in holding up person who is drunk or has fainted; *Holim long han, olsem yu sapotim wanpela man i hap indai long en*

seser-(p)-e *v.t.* (class 1), 1. hold several things in one hand; *holim long wanpela han.*

2. hold several things by cradling in arms or supporting, as in holding up person who is drunk or has fainted; *Holim long han, olsem yu sapotim wanpela man i hap indai long en.*

sesu *n.* mossy green plant with sharp herbal smell, placed on corpses during the night of mourning to disguise the smell of decay; *liklik hap diwai i gat gutpela smel, ol man i save putim long bodi bilong man indai long karamapim smel nogut bilong bodi.*

sik ep *v.t.* (class 5), respond to or answer to accusations; *bekim maus.* **Ŋa Wandima sik epkwatɨnet**: I'm going to answer Wandi's accusations; *Mi bai bekim maus bilong Wandi.* See also **ep**.

sik *n.* mouth; *maus.* **Awinŋa sik**: bullshit (*lit.* 'water mouth'); *mauswara*.

sikesike *n.* tiny betel nut; *liklik liklik buai.* **Yu ŋanana sikesikeŋa mbatep non isiatan, ŋa simberkɨnet**: Give me a little betel nut, I want to chew betel nut; *Yu givim liklik buai long mi bai mi kaikai buai.*

sikin *n.* **1.** brain; *kru*.
  2. sharp scraper attached to the end of a **makor** or **yasuk** (sago pounder), traditionally made of bamboo, now made of a sawn-off pipe; *sapela hed bilong makor o bilong yasuk.*

sikɨp *n.* large lump of sago pith that has not been pulverized; *bikpela hap hap mit bilong saksak.* **Tawar aŋgo sikipŋan tandiw tawaitukun ŋgo!**: The **tawar** has a lot of unpounded bits, pulverize it better!; **Tawar** *i gat planti bikpela hap i stap, paitim gut pastaim!*

sikrim *n.* **1.** finger; *pinga bilong han.*
  2. toe; *pinga bilong lek.*
  3. finger or toenail; *kapa bilong pinga bilong han o bilong lek.* **Ndaramŋa sikrim**: fingernail; *kapa bilong pinga bilong han*; **Ndowŋa sikrim**: toenail; *kapa bilong pinga bilong lek*;
  4. insect leg; *lek bilong ol liklik binatang.* **Pakɨndma sikrim**: louse's leg; *lek bilong laus.*
  5. hoof; *pinga bilong lek na han bilong ol sampela animol.* **Mborma sikrim**: pig's hoof; *lek bilong pik.* See also **mburkow**.

simb *v.t.* (class 5), **1.** organize something; *stretim.* **Orasamb simbtukun!** Get your things together! *Stretim ol samting!*
  2. settle or agree on something; *stretim.* **Nam simbtukroyapi, ndabaituko**: They settled the talk (i.e. they agreed on their plans), and they went their separate ways); *Ol i stretim tok na go nambaut;* **3** smooth out, *stretim.*

simbébi *n.* Quail (*Birds of New Guinea* plate 1; #12–15).

simberkɨ *v.i.* (**-net/-nak**), **1.** chew betel nut; *kaikai buai.*
  2. (*euphemism*), menstruate; *karim blut, lukim mun* (*tok bokis*). **Noŋor Njari simbertak**: The woman is menstruating; *Meri i karim blut.*

simber *n.* the wad of masticated red betel nut that betel nut chewers spit out after it has exhausted its usefulness; *buai i stap long maus.*

símbu *n.* **1.** vein that connects the testicles to the body; *rop bilong bol.*
  2. maggot; *liklik binatang i gat longpela tel olsem liklik snek i save stap insait long hul bilong toilet na long as bilong saksak.*

simpak *v.t.* (class 5), stretch something, straighten something out; *stretim.* **Orom simpaknukun mbɨd utok nunuk**: I stretched my back and later it began to hurt; *Mi stretim baksait na pen i kamap bihain.*

simpaknɨ *adv.* directly, straight; *stret.* **Yu simpaknɨ otaka wetak**: You go straight there and come back! *Yu go stret na i kambek.*

sind *n.* **1.** needle, spine, quill; *nok*.
  2. antenna; *nok bilong ol binatang o wanem ol narapela ol samting.* **Sasuma sind**: shrimp's antenna; *nok bilong kinda.*
  3. two long tail feathers of some species of bird of paradise, for example the **kuriŋ**; *tupela longpela gras bilong pesaw.*

sinder *adj.* **1.** empty, bare; *nogat samting.* **Num sinder**: empty village; *ples nating.* **Kandam sinder**: bare-assed, naked; *as nating*; **Muna wákare patɨr sinder ŋayar**: There's

no sago in the house, it's completely empty; *Nogat saksak, haus nating olgeta.*
2. without the expected or appropriate accompaniment; *nating.* **Mum sinder**: sago jelly without any meat, insects or vegetables on top of it; *saksak nating. Kap sinder*: an empty cup; *kap nating.* See also **seŋgrim**.

sindibam *n.* (contraction of **sind** + **yimbam**: 'quill' + 'bundle'), broom; *brum.*

sindip *v.t.* (class 5), stretch something; *stretim, taitim.* **Ŋa ŋgo orom sidipkrunet**: I'm going to stretch out my back; *Mi bai stretim baksait bilong mi.*

sindir *v.i.* (-**net**/-**nak**; r → Ø in realis, so **sindinet/ sindinak**), slip; *wel.* **Pande sinditakre miŋgip wakaipiŋgatan**: The axe slipped as he was chopping and struck his knee; *Tamiok i wel na paitim skru bilong em.*

siŋ *v.t.* (class 5), peel something off, strip away; *brukim, tekewe.* **Yum munjenum koto wenkem karat siŋkrunana!**: All you old men come and peel away rattan (to make rope in order to roof a house); *Yupela ol lapun man i kam na brukim kanda!*

siŋki *v.i.* (-**net**/-**nak**), be pleased, happy; *hamamas.* **Ŋgu siŋki wákare**: She isn't pleased; *Em i no hamamas.*

sip *n.* meat, usually only used in the collocation **mborsip**: pig meat; *abus, ol man i save kolim abus bilong pik* **mborsip**.

sire *pos.* down, below, under; *taunbolo.* **Sire aŋgi wuk**: It's down there; *Em i stap taunbolo.*

sireŋ *n.* Cuckoo Shrike (*Birds of New Guinea* plate 32).

sirki *v.i. irr.* (ŋa siniet/siniek; yu siniet/siniek; ŋi siniet; ŋgu sisiek; yum sinkem; yim siniek; ŋgi sisiko; yim sene sisike).
1. go down, descend; *godaun.* **Ŋa aruowankuta kuta kuta arawer siniet**: I waited for you for such a long time that the sun set; *Mi wetim yu igo igo igo na san i godaun.*
2. step into; *kalap.* **Ŋgu sisiek yimbarni**: She got into the canoe; *Em i kalap long kanu.*

sisir *v.t.* (class 4), sew something; *samapim.*

sisiw *n.* 1. laziness; *les.* **Munje ainde sisiw sumanŋa**: That man there is really lazy; *Man ia wanpela lesman stret.*
2. fatigue, stupor; *hap indai, nogat rot bilong kisim win.* **Nimanikadukuna sisiw ninkun**: He beat her until she was completely spent; *Em kilim em hap indai.*

sisiwoki *v.i. irr.* (ŋa sisipot/sispok; yu sispot/sisipok; ŋi sispot; ŋgu sisipok; yim sisipok; yum sisipokem; ŋgi sisipoko; yim sene sisipoke), tire, be lethargic; *les.* **Kruni kandawŋa wákare, ŋi sapkini sisipot**: Kruni isn't sick, he's just tired; *Kruni i no sik, em les tasol;* **Ŋa sisipot ewar prukakkutŋa arimbi nitin**: I'm worn out, yesterday's work exhausted me; *Mi les, asde mi wok na skin bilong mi les.*

siw *n.* 1. strips of skin of butchered large game, such as pigs or cassowaries; *skin bilong ol pik o ol muruk man i katim na dilim.*
2. traditional loincloth; *malo.*
3. ground possum; *kapul bilong graun.*

siwididimra oki *v.i.* (conjugated like **oki**), have a body part fall asleep; *hap bodi inda long eni.* **Ndow siwididimra wok**: My leg is asleep; *Lek bilong mi indai ia.*

siwir *n.* ant (generic); *anis (biknem).*

siwirdidim *n.* tiny red ants; *liklik liklik redpela anis.*

siwir kararkarar *n.* red ants that live in **koi** trees at the edge of the grasslands; *redpela anis i save stap insait long ol koi diwai long sait bilong kunai.*

sokoi *n.* tobacco; *brus.*

sokoidu *n.* cigarette; *smok.*

sonai *n.* (obsolete), first pubic hair; *nupela gras bilong sem i save kamap long ol nupela man na meri.* **Sonai manŋa!** Hairy cunt! (vulgar); *Kan i gat gras! (tok nogut).*

Soŋgodo *n.* Mangan village; *ples Mangan.*

soroŋ *n.* cowrie shell; *liklik kina i gat makmak.*

sowo *n.* Pitohui (*Birds of New Guinea* plate 42, #7–13).

sowor-(p)-o *v.t.* (class 1), boil a small amount of something; *boilim liklik samting.*

soworoŋgab *n.* little soup pot; *liklik sosbin bilong boilim sup.*

sua *n.* **1.** ignorance (antonym of **yam**), without skill, without power; *nogat save, nogat powa*. **Omosuama ror:** You are the son of a man with no knowledge, i.e. your father was stupid and so are you!; *Yu pikinini bilong wanpela man i nogat save!*; **Mayasuama ror:** You're the child of a stupid woman i.e. your mother was stupid and so are you!; *Yu pikinini bilong wanpela stupid meri stret!*; **Aram sua:** a poisonous snake whose venom doesn't have the power to kill, for example because one has blocked this power by reciting a magic spell or a prayer, or a non-venomous snake); *Snek i nogat poisin*. **2.** *adj.* useless, rubbish; *rabis.* **Yuwon pruk sua aŋgi kakat nitukun!** Hurry up and finish your stupid work! *Pinisim hariap despela rabis work bilong yu!* See also **kapar**.
sua mir *n.* person without any skills or talents; *man o meri i nogat save long wokim wanpela samting.* **Sua mir!:** You have no skills or knowledge, you are stupid!; *Yu nogat save olgeta!* Compare **samba mir**.
suawuk *n.* a tree whose bark is peeled off and given to snakebite victims to eat raw, as a means of "cooling" the venom; *wanpela kain diwai ol man i save givim skin bilong em long husat man o meri snek i bin kaikaim em. Skin diwai bilong despela diwai bai kolim poisin bilong snek*.

suk *n.* accusation; *sutim tok*. **Yu ŋanana sapkini suk ŋgitiatan:** You're accusing me without reason; *Yu saspektim mi nating*.
sum-(p)-or *v.t.* (class 1), chop something into small pieces; *katim liklik liklik*.
suman 1. *adj.* big; *bikpela*.
 2. *n.* the first inhabitants of the ground, such as the mythical ancestors **Karatum** and **Yamdar**; *kukurai, kuskus olsem* **Karatum** *na* **Yamdar**.
sumbuŋ *n.* [*Kopar*], pile, heap; *hip*. See also **kit**.
sumbwa kapir *n.* beach; *nambis*. See also **puwaiorom**.
sumbwa *n.* **1.** ground, dirt, mud; *graun*.
 2. sago flour (*secret code*); **muna** (*hait tok*).
sumusumu *n.* bat; *liklik bilakbokis*.
supwáspwa *adv.* badly; *kranki*. **Ŋi supwáspwa pruknet:** He is working badly; *Em i wok kranki*.
sura *n.* reeds used to make baskets; *gras bilong mangoro ol meri i save usim long wokim ol basket*.
suwir *n.* sago palm with long leaves and needles. Its leaves are not tough and are not used for house thatch. This kind of sago palm is easy to pound because its interior is not hard and it produces a lot of sago flour. *Saksak i gat longpela lip na longpela nil. Lip bilong em i no strong na ol man i no save usim ol long pasim haus. Mit bilong em i no strong na i gat bikpela* **muna**.

T

ta *n.* knife; *naip*.
taimb *n.* club; *hap diwai bilong paitim samting*. **Sura taimb:** bowling pin shaped club used to beat **sura** (reeds) flat in order to be able to make them into baskets; *hap diwai ol meri i save usim long paitim* **sura**. See also **nimŋat**.
tak *n.* floor support that runs lengthwise, placed on top of the **porimb**; the bark floor (**kimitak**) is placed on top of these; *limbom*.
taki *v.i. irr.* (**ŋa tat/tak, yu tat/tak, ŋgu tak, ŋi tat, yim tak, yum takem, ŋgi tako, yim sene také**), sleep; *slip*.

takrot *n.* [*Kopar*], twins, double, e.g. a betel nut with two seeds, a banana with two bananas in one skin; *tuins, tupela samting i stap insait long wanpela karamap, olsem tupela banana i stap insait long wanpela skin bilong banana o tupela buai i stap insait long wanpela skin buai*. See also **moramori**
takwat *n.* lie, *giaman*.
takwat *v.t.* (class 5), lie to someone; *giamanim*.
takwatki *v.i.* (**-net/-nak**) lie, *giaman*.
tam *n.* bird (*generic*); *pisin* (*biknem*).

taman 1. *n.* all, everything, everyone; *olgeta*. **Taman waswituko**: They all died; *Olgeta indai pinis*. **2.** *adj.* inexperienced; *nogat save*. **Akan taman**: inexperienced hand, said of someone who doesn't know how to carve or perform some other skill with his or her hands; *Han i nogat save*; **Ndow taman**: inexperienced leg, said of a person who tires or gets lost as they walk somewhere; *Lek i no save gut long wakabaut*; **Raw taman**: face without experience, unknown face – this expression is used in the context of preventing **kandap**, tree spirits from stealing the souls of babies. Women carrying small children may call out to the tree beings and say **"Ŋa koret wákare, ŋa raw tamanŋa wákare"**: I am not a foreigner, I don't have an inexperienced face, i.e. a face that doesn't know this jungle and that you haven't seen before; *Pes i nogat save – em bai yu tok long ol kanap i laik kisim pikinini bilong yu bai yu singaut olsem:* **"Ŋa koret wákare, ŋa raw tamanŋa wákare"**: *Mi no bilong narapela ples na i no namba wan taim mi kam long despela hap, yupela lukim pinis pes bilong mi planti taim.*

tamanki *v.i.* (-tet/-tak), **1.** become closed, blocked; *pas*. **Nuwomb tamantak**: The creek is blocked; *Baret i pas*; **Neke tamanŋan**: deaf (*lit.* 'ears blocked'); *iaopas*. **2.** become certain; *tingting i pas*. **Mbowdima numbwan tamantak Arut wokmera Merewre**: Mbowdi is certain that Arut went to Sanae; *Tingting bilong Mbowdi i pas strong long Arut i mas i go pinis long Sanae.*

tamaŋga *n.* slingshot; *katapel*.

tamb *n.* bier on which a corpse is carried to the graveyard and buried; *bet bilong putim bodi bilong man*.

tambar *n.* group of people, team; *grup, tim*. **Yim rumbŋa tambarni kuk**: We were part of the group working on the slit-gong drum; *Mipela i stap insait long grup bilong wokim garamut.*

tambawa *n.* [*Adjora*], mushroom; *talinga*. This word is replacing the Tayap **moimbir**. *Planti ol Tayap i no save toktok long* **moimbir** *moa, ol i save kolim long despela nem.*

tambrak *n.* shelf, platform, table; *bet, tebol*. **Waw tambrak**: raised platform of floor material outside a house where people sit to socialize; *haus win*.

tambuno *n.* temporary makeshift house made to protect one from a sudden downpour of rain; *liklik haus ol man i save kirapim long bus taim ren i pundaun.*

tambur *n.* dream; *driman*. **Tamburni tak**: She dreamed (*lit.* 'she slept on a dream'); *em i driman.*

tamburni taki *v.i.* (conjugated like **taki**): dream; *driman*. **Ŋa tambuni tata yu tanun**: I dreamt of you (*lit.* 'I dreamed and I saw you'); *Mi driman long yu.*

tambiroro *n.* Yellow-billed Kingfisher (*Birds of New Guinea* plate 24, #10).

tamburni tar *v.t.* (class 4, conjugated like **tar**), perceive something in a dream; *driman*. **Mokakaiyi tambuni tatŋgin munaŋa saiput kukumbet**: Monakai dreamed that he came carrying a sago basket; *Monakai i drimanim olsem em i kam wantaim liklik basket bilong saksak*

tamriware *adv.* first time; *pestaim*. **Ŋgandu tamriware akan tamanni mbor pokun**: Ŋgandu shot his first pig; *Em namba wan taim long Ŋgandu sutim pik.*

tamro *n.* **1.** orange fruit, the size and shape of a tennis ball, traditionally hung in the men's house to signify the number of pigs given during a funerary feast; *wailbal, bipo ol tumbuna i save ropim na hangampaim long haus boi long makim ol pik i bin igo long haus boi long taim bilong pati.* **2.** crest of cassowary or rooster; *redpela bilas i stap antap long hed bilong ol muruk na bilong ol kakaruk man.* **3.** vaginal fistula; *waipela sua i save kamap long sem bilong meri.*

tamroŋa kup *n.* wattle; *redpela samting i save hangamapa long nek bilong ol muruk na ol kakaruk.*

tamropirup *n.* chili pepper; *lombo*.

tamwai *n.* sago pancake; *praim*.

tandaŋ *n.* woven screen used as a wall, woven of coconut leaves and sago palm leaves; *blain ol i wokim long lip bilong kokonas na bilong saksak.* See also **kindit**.

tandimirit *n.* small broom for swatting mosquitos; *liklik brum bilong rausim ol rang.*

tandiw *adv.* **1.** well; *gut.* **Tandiw siretak!** Descend well (i.e be careful not to fall)! *Godaun gut!*
   2. correctly, *gut.* **Ŋi tandiw namnet**: He said it right; *Em i tok gut.*

tandor *n.* braided mat of palm leaves placed across the **pawkpawk**, to seal the crown of the house from rain; *kapa bilong marota.*

taŋa *n.* **1.** insect eggs such as lice eggs in hair; *ol liklik kiao bilong ol binatang olsem ol kiao bilong ol laus.*
   2. tiny seeds inside certain fruits (the seeds inside a kiwi fruit would be **taŋa**); *ol liklik kiao i save stap insait long sampela ol prut.*

taŋgar *n.* **1.** nest, burrow, or dwelling of any sort of animal or insect; *haus bilong ol pisin, ol binatang o wanem kain ol animol.*
   2. home; *haus bilong man em i save stap long en.*

tap *v.t.* (class 5), **1.** carry something or someone on shoulders, e.g. a child sitting on one's neck; *karim long sol, olsem pikinini i sindaun antap long sol.*
   2. carry something by hanging from head, as in a basket or a netbag carried by draping the sling across the forehead and letting the load rest on one's back, *karim long hed, olsem hangamapim long poret han bilong basket o bilong bilum.*

tapak *n.* [*Kopar*], flour mixed together with scraped coconut and smoked in banana leaves, made for funerary feasts; *mixim saksak wantaim kokonas. Putim i go insait ol lip bilong banana na smokim long paia. Ol man i save wokim despela kaikai long taim bilong pati.* This word has replaced the Tayap equivalent, **momorik**, in the speech of most villagers.

tapetak *n.* large green gecko with white stripes on tail; *bikpela grinpela geko i gat makmak long tel bilong em.*

tapiam *n.* a kind of vine used to ease headaches by twisting it so that the sap emerges. It is then put on the forehead. Its sap is also inhaled as a decongestant; *rop ol man i save putim long hed bilong daunim hed i pen o ol i save pulim marasin bilong em long daunim kus.*

tapran *n.* fork; *pok.* **Nderŋan tapran**: fork in path; *pok long rot.*

tapraw *adj.* broad, wide; *braitpela.*

tapraw *v.t.* (class 5) **1.** open up or widen something; *opim.* **Taprawtukun ndow!**: Open your legs! *Opim lek!*
   2. unfold or unravel something; *opim* **Embatoto taprawtukun!**: Unfold the cloth!; *Opim laplap!*

tapur *n.* foam; *spet.* **Nok tapurreki werambotitekŋa!**: You were pulled out of your mother's cunt along with the foam of her piss! (vulgar); *Mama bilong yu i karim yu long pispis bilong em! (tok nogut).*

tapurmanj *n.* **1.** bubbles that appear on the surface of water when it rains; *spet i save kamap long wara taim ren i pundaun long en.*
   2. bubbles that appear when an oar pulls the water; *spet i save kamap long wara taim man i pul igo.*
   3. bubbles blown by children from soap water; *bal ol pikinini i save winim long wara bilong sop.*

tar *n.* pandanus tree; *diwai ol meri i save brukim na wokim rop long wokim bilum.*

tar *v.t.* (class 4): **1.** take something, get something; *kisim.*
   2. have sex with someone, *kwapim.* **Ŋguyi munje ainde tatiŋgin**: She had sex with that man; *Meri i kisim man ia.*

tar *v.t.* (class 4), **1.** hear or listen to something or someone; *harim.*
   2. smell something, *smelim.* **Ŋgu ŋgomarma ruk tatukun**: She smelled the smell of the fish; *Em i smelim smel bilong ol pis.*
   3. believe something; *bilipim.* **Ŋayi ŋan nam tarŋgati wákare**: I didn't believe his talk; *Mi no bilipim toktok bilong em.* Differentiated from the verb 'take' by

stress in realis forms (**tánkun** = I heard it; **tankún** = I took it) and by different imperative forms (**tatukun!** = you listen!; **taretukun!** = you take it!). See Sections 2.5 and 7.1.2.2 in the grammar.

tarmbwar *n.* pendulous areal roots of the pandanus tree, the interior of which is used to make thread; *ol rop bilong* **tar** *i save hangamap, ol meri i save brukim despela na wokim tret*.

taruŋg *n.* firewood; *paiwut*.

tat *n.* spine, splinter; *nil*.

tata *n. voc.* older sibling; *bikpela brata o susa*. See also **atawo**.

tataimaŋg *n.* boil that can develop in the tender part of the inner thigh where it meets the groin; *buk i save kamap long sangana bilong lek*.

tatak *n.* traditional decoration made of rattan tied around forehead during singing and dancing; *bilas long kanda ol tumbuna bilong bipo i save taitaim long poret long taim bilong singsing*.

tatar *n.* **1.** finger or toenail; *kapa bilong pinga bilong han o bilong lek*. **Ndaramŋa tatarni sind urok**: A splinter went into my fingernail; *Nok i go insait long kapa bilong pinga*. **2.** traditional spoon; *spun bilong ol tumbuna*.

tatikem (*secret code*) *n.* small betel nut; *liklik buai (hait tok)*. Used in the company of foreigners who know the Tayap word **minjike** in contexts where Tayap speakers want to hide the fact that they are talking about betel nut. See also **sikesike**.

taw *n.* **1.** half or part; *hap*.
  2. pieces, sips or spoonfuls; *hap*. **Ŋa wawaŋŋa taw sene tarkrunakana ŋgo**: I'm just going to take two spoonfuls of soup; *Bai mi kisim tupela hap sup pastaim*.
  3. side; *sait, arere*. **Man taw**: Side or part of vulva (vulgar); *Hap kan (tok nogut)*. **Baso patirŋan tawni tutotakut**: Baso is sitting on the side of the house; *Baso i sindaun i stap long arere bilong haus*.
  4. behind one's back; *baksait*. **Ŋaŋan oŋgwan nambar tawŋan warakeŋgar wákare**: You're my only relative who never talks behind my back; *Yu wanpela tambu bilong mi i no save tok baksait*.

tawai *v.t.* (class 5), **1.** thump someone or something; *paitim*. **Ŋiŋi ndaramni nambir tawainiŋgatan**: He thumped him on the chest with his hand; *Em paitim bros bilong em long han*.
  2. pound or hammer something; *paitim*. **Ŋgu sura tawaikrutakana**: She is going to pound the reeds (to make a basket); *Em bai paitim rop bilong wokim basket*.

tawaŋgeni *adv.* **1.** be minding one's own business, *stap nating*. **Ŋa tawaŋgeni kut**: I'm minding my own business; *Mi stap nating*.
  2. be ignorant; *nogat save long samting i kamap*. **Tawaŋgeni inde mbota prukkar mobotara inde**. He went off to work and wasn't aware [of what had happened]; *Em i go wok na em i no save long samting i kamap*.

tawar *n.* pulp or pith of sago palm once it has been pounded into what looks like sawdust. This is what one washes to leach it of sago flour. *Mit bilong saksak ol man i paitim long en*.

tawar mbup *n.* the washed and leached pith of the sago palm; what **tawar** is called once it is washed and all the sago flour has been extracted from it; **tawar** *ol i wasim na nogat moa saksak long en*.

tawaromo *n.* mushrooms that grow on the washed and discarded **tawar** of sago; *ol talinga i save kamap long* **tawarmbup**.

tawek-(p)-e *v.t.* (class 1), knead something, *miksim*.

tawk *n.* **1.** coconut shell; *sel kokonas*.
  2. plate, dish; *pelet o dis*.
  3. any breakable outer shell; *sel inap bruk long en*. **Kokirŋa tawk**: cranium; *sel bilong hed*. **Ŋginoŋa tawk**: top of a coconut; *ai bilong kokonas*.

tawki *v.i.* (-**tet**/-**tak**), become dried out; *igo drai*. **Minjike tawtakara**: The betel nut is all dried out; *Buai i drai pinis*. **Awin tawakuk**: The tide is out and the water is receding; *Draiwara nau*.

tawni *pos.* beside; *long sait*.

Tayap mer *n.* Tayap language; *tok ples Gapun*.

tayap *n.; adj.* villagers' name for themselves; *nem bilong ol Gapun ol yet ol i kolim long tok ples.* **Tayap munjenum naŋro:** Gapun men and women; *Ol man na meri bilong Gapun.*

Tayap num *n.* Gapun village; *ples Gapun.*

tékduan *n.* floor support that runs cross-wise, from **ŋgúnbara** to **ŋgúnbara**; *rola.* See also **porimb.**

temiŋ *n.* **1.** stick with which slit-gong drum is hit; *stik bilong paitim garamut.* **2.** euphemism for penis; *kok (tok bokis).*

tep *n.* the wooden support on which a slit-gong drum rests; *pilo bilong garamut.*

tete-(p)e *v.t.* (class 1), desire or want something; *mangalim.* **Ŋayi sapwar aŋgi tetepekun:** I desire that basket; *Mi mangalaim despela basket.*

tetei *n.* biting horsefly; *binatang i luk olsem draipela rang i save kaikai man.*

ti *n.* a kind of narrow bamboo used to make a **mokwa** (multi-pronged spear); *mambu bilong wokim supsup.*

titi *n.* the inner shoots of sago or **papakdam** saplings that are peeled open and made into festive decorations; *ol lip bilong saksak o bilong* **papakdam** *ol man i save opim na wokim bilas long en.*

ti *adv.* too, also; *tu.* **Ŋa ti okinetana ide:** I too intend to go; *Mi tu bai go ia.*

ti-(p/w)-ar *v.t.* (class 2), sting someone or something, used for jellyfish and stinging caterpillars; *pas long skin bilong yu na givim pen, bai yu tok long* **niŋgasin** *na* **kandiwara.**

tik ŋgur *v.t.* (class 4), tell a story; *stori.*

tik *n.* story, narrative; *stori.*

tik *v.t.* (class 5), **1.** suppress something, such as anger; *daunim.* **Imin yuwon tiktukuna siretak!** Suppress your anger (*lit.* 'suppress your stomach and go down'); *Daunim bel bilong yu!.* **2.** step on something; *krungutim.* **Ŋayi sasawraŋ tiknukuna wasotak:** I stepped on the cockroach and it died; *Mi krungutim kokros na em indai.* **3.** blink or wink an eye; *pasim pasim ai.* **Ŋginoni tikkwankut:** He is blinking; *Ai bilong em i op op.*

timbar *n.* swamp; *tais.*

timbar noŋor *n.* (*euphemism*), swamp woman, i.e. **mirip** (men's cult deity); *tambaran (sait tok).*

timbi/tumbu *v.t.* (class 5; **Note:** the vowels in this verb stem undergo vowel harmony to harmonize with object morpheme that follows it), **1.** Capture someone or something; *holim pasim*; **Timbitiŋin!** Capture him! *Holim pasim em!*; **Ŋa mbor ror wemperkuna kukumbota tumbunkun:** I chased the small pig captured it; *Mi ronim pikinini pik na mi holim pasim em*; **Ŋginoŋa aram timbitiŋin:** She captured the snake alive; *Em holim pasim snek i gat ai.* **2.** arrange or spread something out on a flat surface, as in lay a floor or lay a mattress flat on a floor; **Kimitakni timbitukun!** Spread it out on the floor!; *Putim i godaun long gran!*

timbraXoki *v.i. irr.* (serial verb construction conjugated like **oki**, **Note:** the X is a non-final object suffix), **1.** Humiliate or embarrass someone or something; *daunim.* **Yu numŋa nomb timbrakwok yuwon morasi aproni:** You're giving the village a bad name with your bad ways; *Yu daunim nem bilong ples long despela ol pasin nogut bilong yu.* **2.** defeat; *winim.* **Yim kamieka ŋgigi yim timbramwok:** We fought and they defeated us; *Mipela i bin pait na ol i winim mipela.* **3.** inhibit, restrain; *daunim.* **Ndagúni morasi timbrakotak!** Stop stealing!; *Daunim pasin bilong stil!*

timbrioki *v.i.* (conjugated like **oki**), bend over, lean down; *godaun, lindaun.* **Timbrioteta arotet!** Lean down and go inside! *I go daun na go insait!* **Timbrotet kandam pituwatinak:** Bend over and I'll wipe your ass (said to a small child); *Lindaun bai mi klinim as bilong yu (mama i tok long liklik pikinini bilong em).*

timir *n.* **1.** needle traditionally made of cassowary bone to sew a netbag, bracelet or arm decoration, and traditional buckets made of sago fronds; *nil bilong wokim bilum, paspas o limbom, ol tumbuna i save wokim long bun bilong muruk.*

2. any kind of sharp needle or wire; *waia*. **Timɨrnɨ poŋgro:** They shot him with an ensorcelled needle; *Ol i sutim em long waia*.

tɨmɨrbɨm *n*. needle used to make a basket or a fan, traditionally made out of the bone of a flying fox; *nil bilong wokim basket o win bilong winim paia, ol tumbuna i save wokim long bun bilong bilak bokis*.

tɨndra *n*. wooden steps leading up into a house; *lata i go antap long wanpela haus*.

tɨŋg *n*. small fence around a garden, or to fence in pigs; *liklik banis i save raunim gaden o bilong putim ol pik i go insait*.

tɨp *n*. tall tree with hard wood with few branches, used for different kinds of house posts; *longpela diwai nogat han ol man i save usim long wokim* **kerkwar** *o* **mambɨr**.

tɨrɨri-(w/p)-ar *v.t.* (class 2), join something together; *joinim*. **Otarŋat at aŋgi tɨrɨriwarkurarwe, otar wasoŋgarana:** Join together the two pieces of firewood so that the embers don't go out. *Joinim despela tupela hap paiwut i kam, nogut paia indai*.

tɨrkɨ *v.i.* (**-net/-nak**), blossom, bear fruit; *karim, olsem diwai i save karim*.

tɨrkɨ *v.i.* (**ŋa tɨniet/tɨniek; yu tɨtiet/tɨtiek, ŋgu titiek, ŋi tɨniet, yim tɨniek, yum tɨtikem, ŋgi tɨtukó; yim sene tɨtike**), itch; *sikarap*. **Toto tɨrɨkuk:** My skin is itchy; *skin bilong mi sikarap*.

tɨt *n*. shoot or tip of plant, e.g. coconut or bamboo; *kru bilong kokonas o mambu o kanjigogo i nogat strong*.

tɨtimb *n*. 1. color or pattern; *i gat kalakala o i gat makmak*.

  2. tattoo; *makmak*. **ŋgu tɨtimb totoni ŋgututkun**. She put a tattoo on her skin; *Em makim skin bilong em*.

tɨtipreŋ *n*. wood louse; *liklik binatang i save stap insait long ol sting diwai*.

tokɨ *v.i. irr.* (**ŋgu tok, ŋgi toko**), give birth, used only for animals; *karim, bai yu yusim despela hap tok taim yu laik toktok long ol animol tasol i karim, i no bilong toktok long ol meri*.

tokine *n*. catfish; *bikmaus*.

tokɨmot *n*. breast bone; *bun bilong bros*.

tokro *n*. 1. shortness of breath; *sotwin*.

2. slope; *hap mounten o baret o wanem samting i godaun*.

3. a small amount of food for your **njakum** (joking kin), given as an immediate return for the larger amount of food you have received from them; *liklik kaikai yu givim long wanpilai bilong yu long wanem ol i bin putim bikpela kaikai bilong ol long yu*; **Orak tokroengar ninkurem:** They made the little joking kin food; *Ol i wokim liklik kaikai bilong wanpilai*.

4. a kind of tree that has fuzz and seeds that stick to the skin. One can remove these seeds from their husk, wash them and eat them with betel nut; *wanpela kain diwai i gat mosong na ol pikinini i save pas long skin bilong man. Sapos yu laik kamautim despela ol yu ken wasim ol na kaikai wantaim buai*.

tombet *n*. shelf; *bet*.

tombirkɨ *v.i.* (**-net/-nak**; **r → Ø** in realis, so **tombinet/ tombinak**), stay awake; *i stap na i no slip*.

tombtomb *n*. plant like a pineapple that grows in the middle of tree with long green leaves. Women used to rub this plant on the bodies of their newborn babies to strengthen their bones, and then hang it in their maternity house; *diwai olsem painapel i gat longpela lip i save kamap long namel bilong diwai, bipo ol mama i save usim long strongim bun bilong ol nupela bebi*.

tomɨktomɨk *n*. spider; *spaida*.

tomɨktomɨk sumbwaŋa *n*. large tarantula-like spider that lives in tunnels in the ground (*lit*. 'spider of the ground'). These spiders are poisonous and are known to result in the deaths of children they bite; *bikpela spaida i save stap insait long wul bilong graun. Marasin bilong em inap kilim man indai*.

tomɨr *n*. base of tree; *kil bilong diwai*.

ton *n*. 1. joint connecting two sections of bamboo; *join bilong mambu*.

  2. (*vulgar*) scrotum; *bol bilong man*. **Ton sawɨrŋan!** Black scrotum! *Bilakpela bol bilong yu!*

toŋgeb *n.* upper Sepik; *Sepik antap.* **Toŋgeb munjenum aŋge ŋgwek**: Men from somewhere in the upper Sepik are coming; *Ol man bilong Sepik antap i kam nau.* **Toŋgeb kokɨr**: source of the Sepik river; *hed bilong Sepik antap.*

toŋgodip *n.* Malay apple tree and fruit; *laulau.*

top *n.* ginger to chew with betel nut (*generic*); *daka* (*biknem*).

toremb *n.* individual slit-gong drum signal; i.e. a specific beat, like a Morse code signal, used to call to specific individuals when they are far away; *waris bilong garamut, bipo ol man i gat pairap bilong garamut bilong em stret.* **Toremb ŋgon nitukwatan!**: Hit her garamut signal!; *Paitim garamut bilong em!*

torɨw *n.* traditional bracelet; *paspas.*

toromb *n.* green vegetable (*generic*) *kumu* (*biknem*).

toto *n.* **1.** skin; *skin.*
  2. shame; *sem.* **Toto mɨr aŋgo nitukun**: You are shameful; *Yu wokim sem pasin.* **Toto aŋgo atɨtɨkɨ wákare**: You are shameless (lit. 'shame doesn't arise on you'); *Yu no save sem.*
  3. the part of a cake of sago immediately under the ashes that are poured on it so that it will dry. This is eaten; *skin bilong saksak.*

totrɨk *n.* traditional decoration made with small shells and dogs' teeth, worn on forehead above **tatak**; *bilas bilong singsing ol man i save putim long poret antap long tatak.*

tower *adv.* quietly; *isi.* **Yum tower awnkem! Ŋa yumon pɨndiŋana mndarakkut!**: You all be quiet (lit. 'be quietly')! I'm tired of hearing your noise! *Yupela i stap isi! Mi les long pairap bilong yupela!*

towerkɨ *v.i.* (**-net/-nak**), shut up, be quiet; *pasim maus.* **Yum towenkem!** You all shut up! *Yupela pasim maus!*

towoi *v.t.* (class 5), **1.** try to do something; *traim.* **Towoitukun!** Try it! *Traim!*
  2. test or challenge someone; *testim.* **Towoiŋgrɨnet**: He will challenge him; *Em bai traim testim e.*
  3. make a sexual advance to someone; *traim.* **Ewar ikurre Kakɨpaɲi Sombaŋ towoinukun.** Yesterday evening Kakɨpa tried to have sex with Sombaŋ; *Asde long nait Kakɨpa traim Sombaŋ.*

towond *n.* large post on each of the four corners of a house; *saitpos.*

towotowo *n.* four; *popela.*

trai *v.t.* (class 5), blood let; *rausim blut.* Villagers cut themselves to bleed frequently for many reasons, for example to ease pain – so a prolonged headache will be treated by cutting the temples and letting blood flow. Mothers also also have female specialists cut the faces and bodies of children who cry too often, in the belief that 'bad blood' is making them cry and that releasing it will stop them from crying. *Ol man na meri i save rausim blut long kamap gutpela, olsem hed bilong yu i pen yu ken katim skin long said bilong hed bilong yu na rausim blut. Ol mama tu i save tokim ol meri i gat save long katim skin bilong pikinini bilong ol i save kraikrai tasol, long wanem blut nogut i save mekim despela ol mangi na taim ol i rausim ol mangi bai pinisim krai bilong ol.*

trar-(p)-o *v.t.* (class 1), boil a large amount of something; *boilim bikpela samting olsem planti abus.*

trɨrɨ-(p/w)-ar *v.t.* (class 2), join something together; *joinim.* **Trɨrɨwarɨtukun taruŋŋat sene!** Join together the two pieces of fire (i.e. move the two pieces of firewood so that their ends butt up against one another); *Joinim tupela hap paiwut.*

tromtrimb *n.* Fantail (*Birds of New Guinea* plate 37).

tu *v.t.* (class 5), **1.** Sharpen something, e.g. a knife; *sapim naip, tamiok, grasnaip.*
  2. scratch something, e.g an itch; *sikarapim.* **Ŋgadan ŋaŋan meŋemeŋera wekre, ŋa tunkun**: My sore kept itching, and I scratched it; *Sua bilong mi sikarap na mi sikarapim.*

truku *v.i. irr.* (**ŋa tuniet/tuniek; yu tutiet/ tutiek, ŋgu tutiek, ɲi tuniet, yim tuniek, yum tunkem, ŋgɨ tutuko; yim sene tutuke**), dance; *singsing long lek.*

tu-(p)-o (or **tutu-(p)-o**) *v.t.* (class 1), plant something; *planim.* **Ŋgi ikin tutupokrore, ŋa nunukni kaset**: They had planted the bananas when I arrived; *Ol i planim pinis ol banana taim mi kamap.*

tuemb *n.* the day after tomorrow; *haptumaro.*

tukur *n.* rain; *ren.* **Tukur aikitakke?** Will it rain? (*lit.* 'will rain come?'); *Ren bai kam o?*

tukursim (also **tukursum**) *n.* drizzle; *liklik ren.*

tum *n.* beetle; *wanpela kain binatang igat strongpela sel na i gat win tu.* **Tum kwemŋa apro sakar!** Maggot prick! (*vulgar*); *Kok bilong yu i sting na i gat binatang!* (*tok nogut*).

tumb 1. *n.* mountain; *maunten.*
    2. *adj.* thick; *tik.*

tumb(ŋa) bwar *n.* peak (*lit.* 'back') of a mountain; *tel bilong mounten.*

tumbigir *n.* a type of wild cane grass with white flowers; *pitpit nogat strong long en na i gat ol waitpela plowa.*

tumbiŋye *n.* mold; *das olsem mosong.* **Tumbiŋye mbatatukun**: it's moldy (*lit.* 'Mold has ruined it'); *das i bagarapim.*

tumbuno *n.* makeshift house built in a hurry to protect one from rain; *liklik haus ol manmeri i save wokim hariap long hait long ren.*

tumbur *n.* shoulder; *sol.*

tur *n.* traditional song and dance; *tumbuna singsing.*

tur *v.t.* (class 4), **1.** remove husk; *selim.*
    2. empty something; *kapsaitim.*
    3. have sex with someone; *kwap.* **Ŋgu okitaka pap turkrutak ŋan sambapni**: She is going to go remove a coconut husk on his sharp stick (i.e. she is going to go have sex with him); *Em bai go selim kokonas long stik bilong em (em miningim olsem: em bai go kwap wantaim em).*

turara oki *v.i.* (conjugated like **oki**), empty something out, e.g. out of a basket; *kapsait i godaun.*

turaw *n.* coconut husk; *skin bilong kokonas.*

turaw pakas *n.* stage four (of five) in coconut formation, an old **makatok** that has begun to dry out; *kulau i wok long drai.*

turkopki *v.i.* (**-net/-nak**), miss one's step or lose one's grip; *wel.*

turo *n.* fireplace inside house, hearth; *hap bilong kuk.*

turuw *n.* scale of fish, snake, lizard, or person afflicted with grille; *gereray bilong pis o snek o palai na tu bilong husat man gereray i kamap long bodi bilong em.* **Muna turuw**: old sago; *olpela saksak.*

tutuk *n.* sweat; *tuhat.* **Tutuki nitin**: I am sweating (*lit.* 'sweat makes me'); *Mi tuhat ia.*

tutuku *v.i. irr.* (**ŋa tutot/tutok, yu tutot/tutok, ŋgu tutok, ŋi tutot, yim tutok, yum tutukem, ŋgi tutuko, yim sene tutuke**), sit; *sindaun.* **Tutuŋarke!** Don't sit! *I no ken sindaun!*

tutumb *n.* beetle (*generic*); *bikpela binatang.*

tutuw *n.* opening, where something opens; *maus bilong wanpela samting.* **Nuwombŋa tutuw**: place where creek meets the mangrove lake; *maus baret.* **Saimŋa tutuw**: opening of a little basket; *maus bilong liklik basket.* **Kwemŋa tutuw**: urethral opening on penis; *maus bilong kok.*

tuw *v.t.* (class 5), wash a person or animal; *wasim man o wanpela samting i gat ai olsem dok o liklik pik.*

tuwku *v.i.* (**tuwniet/tuwniek**; **ŋgi tuwtuko**), bathe; *waswas.* **Ewar Njimeŋi noŋor sene tanimbin tuwrukukeŋa**: Yesterday Njime saw two women bathing; *Asde Njime lukim tupela meri i waswas i stap.* See also **awin tuwku**.

U

um *n.* crumb, *liklik pipia.* **Munaŋa um**: crumbs from sago; *ol pipia muna*; **Mborsipŋa um**: tiny bits remaining from pig meat; *ol pipia abus bilong pik.*

umb *n.* **1.** crown of sago palm; *tel bilong saksak.*
    2. young shoot of papaya, tobacco, sago or pumpkin, *kru bilong popo, brus, saksak o pankin.* **Waruŋa umb adigarke**: Don't break off the pumpkin shoot! *I no ken brukim kru bilong pankin!* See also **indub**.

undiki *v.i.* (**pundiet/pundiek**), dig for brush turkey eggs; *dik long yamiŋe.*

undir-(p)-o *v.t.* (class 1), dig for brush turkey eggs; *dikim yamiŋe.* See also **undu**.

undu *v.t.* (class 1), **1.** dig away dirt to find a **yamiŋe** (brush turkey egg); *painim kiao bilong waipaul.* **2.** pulverize sago palm pith; *paitim saksak.* **Ŋa yamŋa orom kemem pundukun**: I pulverized a large section of the sago palm; *Longpela hap saksak mi paitim.* See also **undir-(p)-o**.

uran *adj.* dirty; *deti.*

uráŋgeba *n.* bullfrog; *bikpela prok.*

urar *v.t.* (class 4; final **r** changes in realis), shake water off skin like a wet dog; *skin olsem ol dok save wokim long rausim wara long skin.* **Awinŋa toto urariruku wok**: The dog shook its skin to get rid of the water; *Dok i noisim skin long rausim wara.*

urek-(p)-e *v.t.* (class 1), **1.** turn something around; *tainim.* **2.** turn an object, for example a **nek** (house ladder) so that people either can or can't walk up it, because the notches to walk up are either turned outwards or inwards, or turn something over (earth; a piece of wood that is upside down); *tainim.* **3.** translate something; *tainim tok.* **Mer ureketukun**: Translate! (*lit.* 'turn language'); *Tainim tok!.* **4.** change one's mind; *sensim tingting.* **Ŋi numbwan urekpekun**: He changed his mind; *Em i sensim tingting bilong em.*

urerki *v.i.* (**-tet/-tak**), flash lightning, *pairap long klaut.* **Aruat urerakut**: Lightning is striking (*lit.* 'the thunder is lightning-ing'); *Laitning i lait.* **Yewirreki ureruotitekŋa**: You fell out (of your mother's ass) with shit and lightning (*vulgar*); *Mama bilong yu karim yu long as wantaim laitning (tok nogut).*

urerŋgar *n.* lightning, *pairap long klaut.* See also **mamrai**.

uretikimb *n.* spearshift; *mambu bilong spia.* **Uretikimbni yir waptukun**: Put the point of the spear into the spearshaft; *Putim spia i go insait long mabu.*

urukuruk *n.* large edible larva of the **ŋgabugrip** beetle; *pikinini bilong ŋgabugrip ol man i save kaikai.* This word is being replaced by the Kopar-language word **wanuwanu**; *despela hap tok ol Gapun i wok long lusim, ol yangpela i save kolim* **wanuwanu** *long tok ples Wongan.*

usik *n.* shushing sound; *hap toktok bilong stopim man long toktok o singsing.* **ŋiŋi usik ninkun**: He made a shushing sound; *Em tok 'shhhh'.*

usikki *v.i.* (**-net/-nak**), shush, *tok 'shhh' long stopim man long toktok o singsing.* **Yu ambinana usiktet?**: Why are you shushing?; *Yu bilong wamen tok 'shhhh'?*

ut *n.* cane grass; *pitpit.*

utak *v.t.* (class 5), **1.** ignore or disobey someone; *sakim.* **Nam utakŋgarke!**: Don't disobey (this talk)! *I no ken sakim tok!* **2.** push someone; *sakim.* See also **eikuoki**.

utakatiki *v.i.* (conjugated like **atiki**), loosen something, e.g. the top of a container; *slekim kontena* **ŋa ŋgino utakatotaka ketukun!**: Take off the lid! *Opim ai bilong kontena!*

utak-(p)-osiki *v.t.* (**utakposiet/utakposiek**), move across; *katim i go long hapsait.*

utaroror *v.t.* (class 5), block something or someone by surrounding it or them; *banisim long ring.*

utaw *v.t.* (class 5), dislodge coconuts and fruits like papayas from their trees; *sakim.*

utaXru *v.t.* (serial verb construction with class 4 final verb. **Note:** the X is a non-final object morpheme, and final vowel of stem undergoes vowel harmony to harmonize with the vowel in the object morpheme that follows it): push someone; *sakim.* **Sopakyi Waiki utatriŋri wákare**: Sopak didn't push Waiki; *Sopak i no sakim Waiki.* **Ewar Masitoyi Sopak utaktukuna awinni otitek**: Yesterday Masito pushed Sopak into the water; *Asde Masito sakim Sopak i pundaun long wara.*

utiki *v.i.* (**putiet/putiek**), become pure, purified, clear; *kamap klinpela.* **Papŋa yapir**

putiek: The coconut oil became free from impurities; *Wel bilong kokonas i kamap klinpela*.

utɨr-(p)-or *v.t.* (class 1), cut something into small pieces; *katim liklik*.

utɨtɨoki *v.i.* (conjugated like **oki**), be angry; *belhat*. **Ŋa imin utɨtɨokɨtak**: I'm going to be angry; *Mi bai belhat ia*.

utukutuk *v.t.* (class 5): shake something insistently; *noisim strong*.

W

wa-(p/w)-ar *v.t.* (class 2), tuck something in or under; *putim i go ananeat*. **Ŋgu ewar ewand waparkun**: Yesterday she tucked in the mosquito net; *Asde em i putim taunamb i go ananeat long mat*.

wagurmos *n.* Milky Way; *waitpela smok i save kamap long skai long nait*.

wai 1. *n.* sago swamp where people go to work sago; *hap tais i gat saksak*.
    2. *excl.* exclamation used to convey disapproval and that the addressee should stop doing whatever he or she is doing; *singaut long tokim narapela olsem inap o no ken mekim olsem*.

wai-(p)-e *v.t.* (class 1), make threatening move to hit someone; *mekim eksen long paitim man o pikinini*. **Mayayi ror aŋgo okrunana waipekunde, rɨwindra wek**: The mother pretended to hit the child and the child became startled; *Mama i wokim eksen long paitim pikinini na pikinini i kirap nogut*.

waikɨ *v.i.* (**wainet/wainak**; **ŋgɨ wiatuko** or **waindak**), walk around; *wokabaut*.

waiŋgrikɨ *v.i.* (**-niet/-niek**), conceal talk, lie; *hait tok, giaman*. **Yu nda waiŋgrikut inde**: You are concealing something you know; *Yu wok long giaman na haitim tok*; **Ŋgu waiŋgitiek**: She lied; *Em giaman*; **Yuyi waiŋgurkwankut**: You're hiding talk; *Yu wok long haitim tok*.

wak-(p)-ekɨ *v.i.* (**-pet/-pek**), lodge, become jammed; *pas*. **Ŋgomar kakunde, niŋ potaknɨ wakpekre, werak wek**: I was eating fish and a bone lodged in my throat and I expectorated it. *Mi kaikai pis na bun i pas long nek bilong mi na mi kamautim*.

wakai-(p)-i *v.t.* (class 1), smack; *paitim*. **Ŋayi ror aŋgi ndaramnɨ wakaipikuna ŋgu eiarkar wok**: I smacked that kid and she's crying; *Mi paitim pikinini ia na em krai i go*.

wákare 1. *interj.* no; *nogat*. **Yu mum akrutetke? Wákare, ŋa inda mai inda**: Will you eat some sago jelly? No, I've had enough; *Yu laik kaikai saksak? Nogat, mi kaikai inap pinis*.
    2. negation word, the word used to negate a statement; *we bilong tok nogat*. **Ŋgɨ aku wákare**: They are not here; *Ol i no istap*. **Ŋa sokoi aŋgar wákare**: I don't smoke; *Mi no save smok*. **Ŋgu aikɨ wákare**: She isn't coming; *Em i no inap kam*.

wákarekɨ *v.i.* (**-tet/-tak**), run out, be finished; *nogat, pinis*. **Wákaretakara**: It's all finished, there is no more; *Em pinis, nogat moa*.

wákare rekɨ *adv.* still, yet; *yet*. **Ŋa mum akru wákare rekɨ ŋgɨ ŋgwek**: I still hadn't eaten sago jelly and they arrived; *Mi no kaikai mum yet na ol i kam*. **Nɨ aikɨ wákare rekɨ ŋgɨ ŋgok**. He still hasn't arrived and they have left; *Em i no kam yet na ol i go pinis*.

wak-(p/w)-uwku *v.i.* (conjugated like **wuwku**), raise; *putim i go antap*. **enamb non tutoka wuk nimnɨ ŋa rarkrunana *tos* wakpuwok**: A possum was sitting in the tree and to see it, I raised the torch/flashlight; *Kapul i sidaun i stap long diwai na mi putim tos i go antap long lukim em*.

waksirkɨ *v.i.* (conjugated like **sirki**), **1.** turn something upside down; *tainim*; **Paru aŋgo waksiretak!**: Turn the plate over! (said to male or female); *Tainim pelet!*.

2. lower something; *putim i go taunbolo.* **Tos waksiniek**: I lowered the torch/flashlight; *Mi bengim tos taunbolo.*
3. put on a shirt; *putim siot. Siot* **waksirkitak**: I'm going to wear the shirt (male or female speaker); *Mi bai werim siot ia.*

wakwik *v.t.* (class 5), shake; *seksekim.* **Towond aŋgi wakwiknukurema kekuwotak!** Shake the housepost back and forth and lift it out! *Noisim noisim pos na kamautim!*

wakwikkɨ *v.i.* (**-net/-nak**), tremor, shake; *seksek.*

wakwikŋgar kandaw *n.* a hereditary disease that since the 1960s has affected one specific kin group of villagers, causing them to shake, stumble and have slurred speech, ultimately resulting in incapacitation and death. The reason for this illness (which in Tok Pisin is called *sik muruk*, 'cassowary illness'), is because a man in this kin group shot and killed another village man in the 1960s. He later used the same gun to shoot a cassowary, and the illness was transmitted when he then ate the meat of the cassowary. Probably Huntington's disease; *sik muruk.*

wamar *n.* sago palm similar to the **konemba**, except that its fronds are long and green. *Saksak em wankain olsem konemba, tasol pangal bilong em i longpela na grinpela.*

wamb *n.* **1.** fontanelle; *hap bilong sel bilong het i malomalo long en.*
2. a kind of tree with strong wood that used to be used to make bows; *strongpela diwai ol tumbuna i save sapim na workim banara.*
3. a betel nut substitute that looks like a betel nut but has a beige and nut-like interior; *wanpela samting ol man i save kaikai taim ol i lus long buai. I luk olsem buai.*

wamb kosowak *n.* Helmeted Friarbird (*Birds of New Guinea* plate 33, #1–5).

wand *n.* (pl. **wanjmeŋg**), cross-sex sibling; *susa bai kolim brata bilong em* **wand** *na brata bai kolim susa* **wand.**

wap *v.t.* (class 2), insert something; *putim i go insait.*

wapaki-(p/w)-arkru *v.t.* (class 2), put or lay something across; *putim akros.*

wapakinɨ *adv.* cross-wise; *akros.* **Yu wapakinɨ tatet**: Sleep crosswise (i.e. at the head or base of the mosquito net, at other sleepers' heads or feet); *Yu slip akros.*

wapatúŋgro *n.* swarm of lightning bugs that live in treetops; *ol ŋgudum i save stap antap long tel bilong diwai na troimwe lait long nait.*

war *n.* thigh; *lek.*

war *v.t.* (class 2), **1.** bury something; *graunim.* Traditionally this verb was only used to refer to the burial of human bodies and yams; *Long taim bilong ol tumbuna ol i save usim despela hap tok long toktok long graunim ol bodi bilong man na graunim ol yam tasol.*
2. put something inside, e.g. a basket; *pulamapim long basket o long narapela samting.* **Ŋgu tatar parkun sapwarnɨ**: She put the spoon in her basket; *Em putim spun i go insait long basket*; **Ndadumnike waratkɨŋgɨkatot Potowre?** Did he put him in a sago palm leaf sheath and carry him down to Wongan? *Em i putim em i go insait long wanpela pangal na karim em i godoun long Wongan?*
3. scrape or grate something, e.g. coconut; *sikarapim kokonas.*
4. fill something up; *pulamapim* **Awin warɨtukun oŋabnɨ**: Fill up the pot with water; *Pulamapim wara long pot.*
5. breathe air; *pulim win.* **Ŋgu mbun warkru wákare.** She's not breathing; *Em i no pulim win.*

warakkɨ *v.i.* (**-net/-nak**), talk, converse; *toktok.*

waram *n.* traditional shield; *hap pangal ol tumbuna i save holim long abrisim ol spia long taim bilong birua.*

waramkɨ *v.i.* (**-net/-nak**), shield; *banis.*

waram taw *n.* the layer of sago left close to the bark of the palm when one is almost done pulverizing it; *liklik hap mit bilong saksak i stap klostu long skin bilong saksak.*

warɨs *n.* screen made of coconut fiber; *laplap bilong kokonas.*

warɨs orɨm *n.* membrane covering the inner organs; *bilum i karamapim lewa na ol* *narapela samting i stap insait long pik o mumut o wanem kain ol animol.*

warkɨ *v.i.* (**pariet/pariek**), fish by setting a net; *umben.*

warmis mokop *n.* calf (*lit.* 'thigh little'); *mit bilong baksait bilong lek.*

warmis *n.* thigh muscle; *mit bilong lek.*

warnɨŋŋa *n.* (*obsolete*), **1.** anal glands in arboreal possums and bandicoots that have a strong, unpleasant fishy smell if accidentally cut while butchering the carcass. This word is no longer known by most speakers, who call these glands **ruk** (*lit.* 'smell'); *tupela liklik bol i save stap long as bilong ol kapul na mumut. I gat smel nogut. Ol bikpela man na meri bilong nau i no save gut long despela hap tok, ol i laik kolim samting bai ol i tok long smel.* **Warnɨŋŋa man!**: Smelly cunt! (*vulgar*); *Kan bilong yu sting ia! (tok nogut bilong bipo).* **2.** genital fluid from both women and men; no longer known by most speakers; *wara bilong sem bilong meri na bilong sem bilong man tu.*

waru *n.* pumpkin; *pankin.*

waruk-(p)-ekɨ *v.i.* (**-pet/-pek**), turn back; *tainim bek.*

wasowkɨ *v.i.* (**-net/-nak**), die; *indai.* **Ŋɨnɨ munje ide poŋgɨna wasownet**: He shot the man and he died. *Em sutim man na em indai.*

wasowra aikɨ *v.i. irr.* (conjugated like **aikɨ**), faint; *hap indai.*

waswirkɨ *v.i.* die *en masse*, die like flies; *indai nambaut.* **Ŋgɨ taman waswirtuko** or **waswindak**: They all died; *Olgeta indai pinis.* **Waswirkɨnkemana taman**: You're all going to die like flies; *Bai yupela indai nambaut ia.*

watakep *n.* a kind of wild taro with tough, long leaves that one can use as an umbrella to shelter from the rain; *wanpela kain waitaro i gat ol bikpela lip. Long taim bilong ren ol man i save usim despela ol lip long hait long ren.*

waw *n.* **1.** fog, morning mist; *smok.* **Waw otɨtek**: The fog came in (*lit.* 'fell'); *Kol i kam.* **2.** coldness caused by weather, like fog in the morning or rain, *kol.* **Wawɨ nitɨn**: I'm cold (*lit.* 'cold+ERG does me'); *Kol i kisim mi.* **Wawŋa tambrak**: raised platform of floor material outside a house where people sit to socialize; *haus win.* **3.** web; *haus bilong spaida.* **Tomɨktomɨkma waw**: spiderweb; *haus bilong spaida.*

wawan *n.* [*Kopar*], soup; *sup.* This word has replaced the Tayap **kawatŋa awɨn** (*lit.* 'water with salt'). *Long tok ples Gapun bai yu kolim sup olsem* **kawatŋa awɨn** *tasol ol man i no save tok olsem, ol i save kolim long tok ples Wongan.*

wawar-(p)-eɨ *v.t.* (class 1) hang up something, for example an **oŋgab** (pot) or **potak** (butchered meat); *hangamapim, olsem sosbin o abus.* **Ŋa yu wawareirunet nɨmnɨ**: I'm going to hang you up in a tree; *Bai mi hangamapim yu long diwai.*

wawar-(p)-eɨkɨ *v.i.* (**wawarpet/wawarpet**), hang; *hangamap.*

wawar-(p)-oskɨ *v.i.* (conjugated like **oskɨ**), climb, *hangamap long ol diwai na go nambaut olsem kapul.* **Noŋor aŋgu enambbi wawaroskar ekrukuk munjenum sami aramb orembanuk**: That woman is like a cuscus, she hangs from many trees (i.e. many men), she's married and left many men; *Meri i olsem kapul, i wok long kalap kalap (long planti diwai), em maritim planti man na lusim ol.*

wawku *v.i.* (**pawiet/pawiek**), **1.** stick to, adhere; *pas long.* **Mbɨmaŋ ŋaŋan ndownɨ pawiek**: The leech stuck to my leg; *Liklik snek bilong bus i pas long lek bilong mi;* **Ror ainde pawiet totonɨ!**: This boy is sticking to me; i.e. is sitting pressed right up against me)! *Pikinini ia i pas long skin bilong mi!* **2.** fasten in or be caught in e.g. a net; *pas long.* **Ŋgomarsam pawko korotnɨ**: The fish were caught in the net; *Ol pis i pas long wumben.*

wekaŋgu *v.t.* (class 3), pull in, *pulim i go insait.* **Paup kokɨr wekoŋgukuna odukun**: The turtle pulled its head and and hid it;

Trausel i pulim hed bilong em i go insait na haitim.

wekaŋ-(p)-or *v.t.* (class 1), stretch something out, e.g. when one is tired; *taitim skin*. **Toto wekaŋgorkru wákare:** I didn't stretch out; *Mi no taitim skin*

wekok *n.* obscenity, vulgarity; *tok nogut*.

wekokni adi *v.t.* (class 3), swear at or curse someone (*lit.* 'break obscenity'); *tok nogutim*. **Nguyi ŋgi wekokni odibin:** She cursed them; *Em tok nogutim ol*.

wekwareŋgar *adj.* narrow; *i no braitpela*.

wemb-(p)-er *v.t.* (class 1), chase something; *ronim*.

wepiki *v.i.* (**pepiet/pepiek**), creep, used to describe the locomotion of snakes, centipedes, millipedes, spiders, crabs; *wakabaut bilong ol* **yandum, kakámatik,** *kuka na snek*.

wer *v.t.* (class 2), pull out, remove or extract something; *pulim*. **Ŋayi tatar sapwarŋa perkun:** I took the spoon from my basket; *Mi kamautim spun long basket*; **Ŋayi ta ewandŋa werkru wákare, aro wuk aŋgo:** I didn't take the knife out of the mosquito net, it's there inside; *Mi no kamautim naip long taunamb, em i stap insait*. **2.** castrate an animal; *kamautim bol*. **Mborma gaweiw krimb perkrora:** They removed the pig's testicles; *Ol i kamautim bol bilong pik*.

werki *v.i.* (**periet/periek; ŋgi perko**), dig around, snuffle (most commonly used for pigs); *dikim graun long nus (ol man i save tok long ol pik)*. **Mbor periek:** The pig snuffled around; *Pik i dikim graun long nus bilong em*; **Mbor werikuk:** The pig is snuffling around; *Pik i dik i stap*.

werki *v.i.* (-**net**/-**nak**), look good, be in order; *luk gut, istap gut* **Nder werki wákare:** the road isn't in order; *rot i no gutpela*; **Yum tandiw wernkem, ŋa mborsip wákare:** You're all fine but I have no pig meat; *Yupela i stap git, tasol mi nogat abus*.

wepokki *v.i.* (-**net**/-**nak**): crawl; *wakabaut long skru*. **Ewar ŋgu wepoktaka wok:** Yesterday she crawled; *Asde em wakabaut long skru*; **Ror ainde wepokkar katot inde ŋgwabre minjikannet inde,** **atitiŋgarana!**: The child is crawling out and is close to the hole (in the floor), watch out that he doesn't fall (through the hole)! *Pikinini i wakabaut long skru i kam autsait klostu long hul, nogut em i pundaun!*.

werki *v.i.* (-**net**/-**nak**): **1.** be straight; *stap stret*. **Ŋgu wertaka aŋgi wuk:** It's straight (referring to a line, or a post that has been raised); *Em stret i stap*.
2. look good, be comfortable, have enough to satisfy one; *kamap gut*. **Yum tandiw wernkem, ŋa mborsip wákare.** You all are content and have enough, but I don't have anything to eat (*lit*. 'I don't have any pig meat'); *Yupela i kamap gut, mi tasol nogat bilong kaikai*.

werandru *v.t.* (class 3), dig ground to plant things; *dikim graun long planim ol samting*. **Nguyi ewar sumbwa werondrukun sambapni:** Yesterday she tilled the ground with a digging stick; *Asde em dikim graun long stik bilong dikim graun*.

weri-(p/w)-uku *v.i.* (**weripuwot/weripuwok**), dry up; *drai*. **Nuwomb weripuwok:** The creek is almost dry; *Baret i no moa dip*.

weraXoki *v.i.* (conjugated like **oki**), pull something loose or pull something out, like when a strong wind uproots a tree; *kamaut na pundaun*. **Naŋro kosepyi manŋa iru utipormbatanŋan rorsem ŋgime werambotiteknan yiwirgwabekeni!:** They were pulled out the assholes of women whose clits are snipped at by crabs! (*vulgar*); *Ol i pulim rausim ol long hul pekpek bilong ol meri husat ol kuka i save katim nus bilong kan bilong ol!* (*tok nogut*).

wetiki *v.i.* (**petiet/petiek**), wank; *skinim kok o skinim kan*. **Kwem petieknan munje:** Wanker; *Man i save sikinim kok*. See also **weiki**.

weu *v.t.* (class 2), lay in hiding and wait for a pig to eat at a sago trap, so that one can spear it; *was long saksak long sutim pik*. **Ŋaŋan omo weukrunana wakut:** My father used to go lay in hiding to kill pigs at a sago trap; *Papa bilong mi i save go was long saksak long sutim pik*.

weX-(p/m)-uŋguku *v.i.* (conjugated like **muŋguku**), corner something or someone; *sanapim.* **Njeŋi mbor wemperŋgina kiŋgimbota wetpuŋgot**: The dog chased a boar and cornered him; *Dok i ronim pik man igo na sanapim em.* **Njeŋi mbor wemperkuna kukumbota wekpuŋgot**: The dog chased a female pig and cornered her; *Wanpela dok i ronim pig igo na sanapim em.*

wiki *v.i. irr.* (**ŋa pwiet/pwiek; yu pwiet/pwiek, ŋgu pwiek, ŋi pwiet, yim pwiek, yum piukem, ŋgi piuko, yim sene piuke**), rise, come up (e.g. from Wongan); *kam antap.* **Karep pwiek**: The moon rose; *Mun i kam antap.* **Arawer pwiet**: The sun rose; *San i kam antap*; **Awin pwiek**: The water is rising; *Haiwara nau*; **Arawer wikinetre, am atikitak**: When the sun rises, a fight is gonna break out; *San i kam antap bai pait i kirap.*

wi-(p/w)-o *v.t.* (class 2), **1.** put something up; *putim i go antap.* **Mumŋa paru wiwokru wákare tombetni, yu sapki oreku wuka mbokre njei okun**: You didn't put the plate of sago jelly above on the shelf, you left it and went away and the dog ate it; *Yu no putim plet bilong saksak i go antap long bet, yu lusim nating igo na dok i kaikai;*
2. wear clothes; *putim koros o su.* **Ngi ndow wiwkru wákare**: They weren't wearing shoes; *Ol i no putim su.*

wind *n.* tree whose grated bark is used to try to cure an ensorcelled person whose stomach swells to alarming proportions; *diwai bilong kolim posin bilong bel i solap. Bai yu sikarapim skin bilong despela diwai na givim long husat man i gat despela sik.*

wir *n.* watch; guard; *was.* **Ewar ŋi mbot yam wir ŋgurkrunana**: Yesterday he went to watch the sago palm (that he had prepared for a wild pig to come and eat it); *Asde em i go long putim was long saksak.*

wira *n.* Lorikeet (*Birds of New Guinea* plate 19, the word refers to the larger ones).

wirar *v.t.* (class 3; **ŋi wirkarkun/ŋgu wirorkun**): put something inside; *putim i go isait.*

wis *v.t.* (class 5), put something down, lower something; *putim i godaun.* **Ror aŋgo wisnukun subwani**: I put down the child on the ground; *Mi putim pikinini ia i godaun long graun.*

wiswis *n.* **1.** . Goshawk and Falcon (*Birds of New Guinea* plate 5, plate 6). This word is an onomatopoetic rendering of the sound made by the beat of these birds' wings.
2. euphemism for sorcerer; *poisin man.* **Wiswis inde mbet**: A sorcerer is coming; *Poisin man i kam ia.*

wit-(p)-i *v.t.* (class 1), string something together, e.g. **sokoi** (tobacco leaves), **toŋgodip** (*laulau* fruits), **tamro** (big orange seeds used to signify how many pigs were given at a funerary feast and hung in the men's house); *ropim, olsem brus, laulau, wailbal.*

wiwir *v.t.* (class 4), blow on, fan or inflate something; *winim.*

wo *pos.* above; *antap.* **Wo aŋgi wuk**: It's there above you; *Em i stap antap.*

woi *v.t.* (class 2), **1.** sweep; *brumim.*
2. roll; *rolim.* **Ŋanana sokoiŋa pin kukuwe, ŋa sokoidu woikrunet**: Bring me a bit of tobacco, I'm going to roll it into a cigarette; *Kisim brus i kam long mi bai mi rolim smok.*

woiki *v.i.* (**poiet/poiek; yim sene poike/ŋgi poiko**), intertwine; *raunim*: **Aram sene poikeya aŋgi wuke**: The two snakes are intertwined; *Tupela snek i raunim tupela yet na istap.* See also **erki**.

wor *v.t.* (class 2), **1.** put a canoe aground; *pasim kanu.* **Yimŋi yimbar porkure**: the two of us put the canoe aground; *Mitupela pasim kanu.*
2. forbid something; *tambuim.* **Ŋa naŋan minjike porkun. Ndagúni ekwaŋgukre ŋginana porkun.** I've forbidden people to take my betel nut. People have been stealing it and for this reason I've forbidden it; *Mi tambuim buai bilong mi. Stil i kisim na long despela mi tambuim.*

worer *v.t.* (class 5), spill something; *kapsait.* **Aindet ror ainde awin worerkru wákare**: That child can't pee (*lit.* 'can't spill water'); *Pikinini i no inap rausim wara.*

worerXokɨ *v.i.* (serial verb construction conjugated like **okɨ**. Note: X here stands for an object suffix), capsize something, pour something out, *kapsaitim*.

workɨ *v.i.* (**poriet/poriek; ŋgɨ porko**), 1. go ashore; *go asua*. **Yim ŋgo ainɨ workɨnak ŋa nokɨ imin putiatan:** Let's go ashore here, I'm dying for a piss (*lit.* 'urine is cutting my stomach'); *Yumi pas long ia, pispis i kilim mi.* 2. engage in certain secret male activities; *wokim ol sampela wok bilong kamap strong na skin i lait.* **Workɨ okɨnak?:** Shall we go do the secret activities? *Bai mipela i go long bus wokim samting?* 3. be blocked, as in water that won't go through a strainer; *pas.* **Ewar ŋa mboka peiwieka awin workɨ wákare:** Yesterday I went and washed sago and the water wouldn't go through the strainer; *Asde mi go wasim saksak na wara i no godaun long* **waris.**

wormbɨt *n.* socket into which the back leg joint fits, in pigs, bandicoots, possums and dogs. Cassowaries don't have this, they have a **ŋgot** and a **kandapŋa niŋg**; *join bilong ol pik, sasik, kapul na dok. Ol muruk nogat despela, ol i gat* **ŋgot** *na* **kandapŋa niŋg.**

wos-(p)-i *v.t.* (class 1; irregular in that the irrealis verb stem is **wos**, not **wosi**), throw something away, get rid of something; *rausim.* **Pɨnpɨn aŋgo wostukun!** Throw away that rubbish! *Troimwe pipia!*; **Pɨnpɨn aŋgo wosŋgarke!** Don't throw away the rubbish! *I no ken rausim pipia!* **Aŋge rowesamb ange wosmbɨ ondak:** Get rid of those old people and make them go away; *Rausim despela ol lapun i go.*

wot *n.* 1. arrow; *spia bilong sutim long banara.* 2. base of a felled sago palm; *as bilong saksak ol man i katim long en.*

wow *n.; voc.* maternal uncle; *kandere.* See also **awoi.**

wu *n.* liver; *namba wan lewa.*

wuŋa nok *n.* gall bladder; *hap lewa i gat marasin.*

wupitapikɨ *v.i.* (**-net/-nak**), warp to look rippled or waved like a swell on the sea; *taim wanpela samting olsem diwai i lapun na brukbruk na i go 'ap and daun'.* **Kɨmɨtak wupitapitakara:** The floor is warped; **Kɨmɨtak** *i ap and daun.*

wur *v.t.* (class 2), 1. dislodge something, e.g. when one goes up a coconut palm and kicks the coconuts down with one's feet; *sakim.* 2. remove or extract something; *kamautim.* **Tat wurɨtukun!:** Extract the splinter! *Kamautim nil!.* 3. hook something with a hook, e.g. a fish, a coconut, a breadfruit; *wukim, olsem pis o kokonas o kapiak.* 4. strain sago; *wasim* **muna** *wantaim wara long wokim* **mum**: **Ŋgu kopik purkun:** She strained the water mixed with sago flour; *Em strenim saksak na wara.* 5. name something; *kolim nem.* **Tayap mernɨ nomb wurɨtukun!:** Say the name of this in Tayap! *Kolim nem bilong despela long tok ples Gapun!* 6. braid a grass skirt; *wokim pulpul.* **Ŋayi ner purkun:** I braided a grass skirt; *Mi wokim wanpela pulpul.*

wur-(p)-ekɨ *v.i.* (**wurpet/wurpek**), worry, miss, be concerned about; *wari.* **Ŋa yunana wurekɨnet:** I'm going to miss you and worry about you; *Mi bai wari long yu.* See also **punatkɨ.**

wur-(p)-o *v.t.* (class 1), lift something up; *apim.* **Wurotin!** Lift me up! *Apim mi!*

wure *v.t.* (class 5), worry about something, be concerned about something; *sore long o wari long wanpela man o long sampela lain.* **Ŋa wurembrɨ wákare:** I'm not worried about them; *Mi no wari long ol.*

wureŋgar *n.* worry; *wari.* **Ŋɨ wureŋgar suman pikwatan maya ŋanana:** He makes his mother very worried; *Em i givim bikpela wari long mama bilong em.*

wurɨ *dir.* up, in the sense of upstream; *antap.*

wurkɨ *v.i. irr.* (**ŋa priet/priek, yu priet/ priek, ŋgu priek, ŋɨ priet, yim priek, yum prikem, ŋgɨ pɨrko, yim sene pɨrke**), go up; *go antap.* **Yum prɨkema mbokemre, ŋguwur pemiek:** You all went up (the mountain) and had gone when the smoke started rising; *Yupela i go antap i go pinis taim smok i kirap.*

wuw *v.t.* (class 2), **1.** carry something on one shoulder; *karim long sol.* **Ŋa munŋa ndadum puwkuna kukumbet:** I came carrying the sago flour in a palm sheath on my shoulder; *Mi karim saksak long pangal na mi kam* **2.** butcher something; *katim.* **Aionŋi ewar mbor non pokuna, puwkun.** Yesterday Aion killed a pig and butchered it; *Asde Aion sutim wanpela pik na katim.* **3.** cut slices out of coconut meat in its shell; *katim kokonas.* **Pap mow wutukun!** Slice the coconut! *Katim kokonas!* **4.** dig a hole; *dikim wul.*

wuwku *v.i. irr.* (ŋa puwot/puwok, yu puwot/puwok, ŋi puwot, ŋgu puwot, yim puwok, yum pukem, ŋgi puko, yim sene puke), ascend, *go antap.*

wuwur *n.* charcoal; *bilakpela sit bilong paia.*

Y

yakaiya *interj.* oh my goodness; *aiye.*

yakua *n.* Catbird (*Birds of New Guinea* plate 49, #6).

yam 1. *n.* sago palm. Used as the generic, but it is also a specific kind of sago palm with short fronds and long spikes. One of the most desirable palms to pound for sago; its leaves are used as thatch for houses; *saksak. Em despela em biknem, tasol yam tu em wanpela kain saksak i gat sotpela pangal na longpela nil. Gutpela saksak long paitim na pangal bilong em ol man i save kisim long pasim haus.* **2.** *adj.* knowledge of a skill; *igat save long wokim wanpela wok.* **Ŋa yam:** I am skilled; *Mi gat save long wokim samting;* **Ŋgi yam:** They are skilled; *Ol i gat save long wokim samting.*

yam mbatim yam *n.* a kind of **yam** sago palm characterized by being short, having short needles, and an interior that is soft and easy to pound. *Saksak i sotpela na i gat sotpela nil. Mit bilong em i no strong.*

yamiŋe *n.* egg of **kokosuar** (Common Scrubfowl) or **onaw** (brush turkey), a local delicacy; *kiao bilong waipaul, ol man i save laikim nogut tru.*

yamiŋe tumb *n.* **1.** nest of brush turkey; *haus bilong wailpaul.* **2.** mound of dirt prepared to plant **prerikin** (sweet potato) or **nono** (yam); *hip graun bilong planim kaukau o yam.*

yamŋa mis *n.* pale inner bark of sago palm before it is pulverized; *mit bilong saksak.*

yam síw *n.* a kind of **naŋgak** sago palm that grows to great heights and has long fronds. It has needles, but in very tall ones the needles will fall off and leave a bare palm. *Wanpela kain naŋgak i save gro na kamap longpela moa. I gat nil tasol long ol longpela ol nil i save pundaun na namel bilong em bai stap nating.*

yandum *n.* centipede; *sentipit.*

yandumtit *n.* a small centipede-like insect that secretes a liquid that sticks to skin and glows at night; *wanpela liklik binatang olsem* **yandum** *i gat* **niŋir***, na sapos yu krungutim em samting bai pas long skin bilong yu na long nait em bai lait olsem sta.*

yaŋgaro *n.* carved representation of a man costumed to represent a spiritual deity (**mirip**); *tumbuan.*

yar *n.* sugar cane; *suga.*

yasuk *n.* sago pounder that villagers traditionally used to chip away at and pulverize the interior bark of the sago palm while sitting down. It is made out of a single piece of wood, as opposed to a **makor** which is made of two pieces; *ain bilong paitim saksak ol man bilong bipo i save wok long en. Ol man i save wokim em long wanpela hap diwai.*

yaw *n.* place; *hap.*

yim *pro.* **1.** we; *mipela.* **2.** us; *mipela.*

yimbam *n.* bundle; *mekpas.*

yimbram *n.* clove tree; *kain diwai ol man i save kaikaim skin bilong em.*

yimen *pro.* ours; *bilong mipela.*

yio *n.* fence around a garden; *kain banis olsem i save raunim wanpela gaden.*

yir *n.* **1.** spear; *spia.*
   2. matrilineal kin group; *lain.*
   3. group of people in a line; *ol lain bilong man.* **Munjeŋa yir aŋge ŋgwok naw okrunana**: A line of men has gone to stamp down the grassland (to light fire to it); *Ol lain man i go long krungutim kunai.*

yir pwap *n.*, claw of a cassowary or chicken (*lit.* 'spear anger'); *sapela pinga bilong muruk o bilong ol kakaruk.*

yit *n.* **1.** base of tree; *as bilong diwai.*
   2. mouth of stream, where it enters the swamp, *tel bilong baret.* **Saŋgiwar yitni wurkitike**: Let's go up to the mouth of the stream; *Mipela i go antap long tel bilong Saŋgiwar baret.* **Manŋa yit sumanŋa!** Big cunt mouth! (*vulgar*) *Draipela hul kan! (tok nogut).*

yiwir ar *v.t.* (class 3), defecate feces; *pekpek.*

yiwir ariŋ *n.* diarrhea; *pekpek wara.*

yiwir ariŋ pinjirip *v.t.* (class 5), expel diarrhea; *pekpek wara.*

yiwir *n.* feces; *pekpek.* **Yiwir iminŋa apro!** Shit ass! (*vulgar*); *Bel bilong yu i pulap long pekpek! (tok nogut).*

yiwirgwab *n.* asshole (*vulgar*; *lit.* 'shit hole'); *hul pekpek (tok nogut).*

yum *pro.* **1.** you all (subject); *yupela.*
   2. you all (object); *yupela.*

yumon *pro.* yours (*pl.*); *bilong yupela.*

Animals, insects, fish and birds

Note: With the exception of the words for some fish, all Tayap words below for animals, insects and fish are listed and defined separately in the Tayap-English-Tok Pisin dictionary.

Tayap has relatively few names for the various species of wildlife found in the rainforest. This paucity is partly explained by the fact that the Papua New Guinean rainforest is not particularly rich in mammal species. Pigs are the largest mammals, there are no monkeys or apes, and few species of deer (none of which live in the area around Gapun). The mammals named by the villagers are pigs (**mbor**), domesticated dogs (**nje**), tree possums and cuscus (**enamb**), ground possums (**síw**), bandicoots (**sasik**), rats and mice (**ŋgabugar, kokosik, njip, mangɨm**), sugar gliders (**ŋgesiŋe**), flying foxes (**njakep**) and bats (**sumusumu**). The name of a species of tree kangaroo that used to be hunted is remembered (**kanuŋg**), but those animals have not been encountered by villagers for two generations.

Some villagers these days have cats. They want their cats to catch the rats that happily make their homes in the thatched roofs of the village houses. More often than not, however, cats find it easier to steal meat and fish that villagers leave to smoke above hearths. For that reason, for every villager who likes cats, there are many more who hate them and kill them and sometimes eat them if they find them prowling in or around their house. There is no word for 'cat' in Tayap. They are called by the Tok Pisin name *pusi*. They were introduced to the area by white missionaries, colonial officials and businessmen, and they came to Gapun so recently that the oldest villagers in 2009 still remembered the first village cat: it was a big black cat named Kaŋgrámse. The cat came from Watam village and was brought into Gapun in the late 1950s by Masambe Njagur.

There is a generic word for crocodiles (**orem**) and snakes (**aram**), and snakes are further differentiated into a variety of species: **ambonor, arambwar, aramŋgor, atemb, karewa, kanakai aramŋgor, niɲɨr aram, pake**, and the two feared venomous species **mbumjor** and **kombɨn**. At least eleven species of lizard are distinguished (**agin, akirónda, amanep, mbutak, ŋgararɨk, ŋgogrodak, ŋgurbewat, kurbi, masukondep, onjaɲnoŋor, tapetak**). The generic word for frog, **pasákeke**, refers to all frogs except one, a large brown water bullfrog called **uráŋgeba**. Tadpoles are **mbókokɨr**, a word derived from **kokɨr**, which means 'head'.

There are certainly more insect names than I know. My knowledge is limited mostly to the insects that children and others brought me to see while I was living in the village. Undoubtedly there are some I missed because no one found any, thought to bring them to me, or could think of them when I asked them to name insects (*ol binatang* in Tok Pisin).

The insect names I did collect are as follows. Mosquitoes, unsurprisingly in swampy Gapun, have both a generic word (**at**) and the most named species (**aiawaŋgar, indagawr, iurok, mbunbun, miriŋa at, njakepma arit, njeyewir at, ŋgurpan**). Ants have both a generic name (**siwir**) and six named species (**kandap, ŋgugrub, kambobai, rewitoto, siwirdidim, siwirkararkarar**). Termites are **agu** and **kamus**. Spiders are abundant in the village and the surrounding rainforest both in numbers and varieties (I had at least 6 different species living in my outhouse toilet at any one time), but there are few names for them. Spiders are called by the generic reduplicated form **tomiktomik**, which can be compounded with a noun to specify it. So for example, **tomiktomik sumbwaŋa** (*lit.* 'spider of the ground') is the name of the poisonous, tarantula-like spider that lives in burrows. One of these spiders is believed to have caused the death of a village teenager in 2005. **Tomiktomik patirŋa** (*lit.* 'spider of the house') is the name given to the hairy, outstretched-hand-sized brown spiders that live in the walls and roofs of people's houses and that scuttle around on the walls noisily at night.

Butterflies and moths are all **mumuk**. Caterpillars are divided between those without fur, **atir**, and those with fur, **niŋgasin** (there is disagreement among older speakers about whether this latter word was Tayap or a borrowing from the Kopar language). Several beetles, the largest of which are eaten, are named: **tutumb** (which is also the generic), **arawer, mbirkraw onko**, and **ŋgabugrip**. Beetle grubs, all of which are eaten, are **kimirik, komi** and **urukuruk** (this last word increasingly being replaced by the Kopar-language **wanuwanu**).

Other insects with names in Tayap are the feared and despised centipedes (**yandum**), the beloved fireflies (**ŋgudum**), which are considered to be avatars of dead villagers, bees (**mbadiŋ**, which is the generic word, also **kunemb, arúmbatak kunemb, metawr**), wasps (**kikri**), flies (**arúmbatak**), biting horseflies (**tetei**) and blue flies (**arúmbatak wasow**; which literally means "fly death", in recognition of their rapid appearance at the death of an animal or person), fruit flies and gnats (**ipipir**), scorpions (**katáwa**), millipedes (**kakámatik**), walking sticks (**nekan**), praying mantises (**ŋgat** – the same word as 'cassowary'), worms (**kekékato**), earwigs (**ikinŋan yandum**), wood lice (**titipreŋ**); cicadas (**ŋgaratgarat, kikik**); grasshoppers (**njojok** and **njajak**), cockroaches (**sasawraŋ** and **numbutik**), bedbugs (**ndedeŋ**), fleas (**itum**), lice (**pakind**), leeches (**mbímaŋ**) and mites (**kandap**).

Villagers name a number of shellfish and fish. Unlike fish (**ŋgomar**), shellfish have no generic name. Shellfish include shrimps (**sasu**), small shrimp (**sasupat**), freshwater lobster (**keymare**), crabs (**kosep, ŋgarorak, sasápoke**), hermit crabs (**pisik**), shelled slugs (**kandip**) and two varieties of clams (**eporaŋ** and **oyan** – both these words are also euphemisms for 'vulva'). While shrimp and crabs are found in the freshwater creeks that flow through the rainforest, the clams, slugs and hermit crabs live in the large mangrove swamp that lies between Gapun and Wongan. Their names, like the names of all fish caught in the mangrove swamps, are probably Kopar language borrowings, and for that reason, the words used by villagers to identify most of the fish caught in those waters are not included in the dictionary. Before WWII, villagers would have acquired these foodstuffs by trading pork, cassowary meat and other "bush" items with villagers from Wongan. After WWII, Gapuners began making canoes and venturing into the mangrove swamps themselves.

Tayap also has names for several species of small freshwater fish that women and children catch with hooks and nets (**aiyo, ndɨdɨmaŋ, ŋgomákokɨr, orɨnd, semb**). There are also large fish in the rainforest streams, and men and women fish for these with hooks and nets during the dry season. With the exception of catfish (**tokine**) and large eels (**ŋgem**), I never saw an intact specimen of those fish, and villagers' descriptions of them were not enlightening – when I asked people to tell me what the named varieties looked like, I would receive some version of "It's big. (Pause). But really not so big" (*em i bikpela. Tasol i no bikpela tumas*) or "It's brown. (Pause). But some of them are white" (*Em i braunpela. Tasol sampela i waitpela*).

Here are the names I collected, but they are not included in the dictionary because I never managed to identify them: **irawr, kambɨŋeŋ, kandapoŋgap, konop, kut, mbaimat**.

Bird names

Names for birds are an important exception to Tayap's otherwise relatively modest wildlife vocabulary. The extent of Tayap's bird vocabulary is surprising. The rainforest is full of birds, certainly. But it is also full of other kinds of wildlife, such as frogs, bats, spiders, and insects that the villagers do not distinguish lexically. Even large mammals such as the different species of tree possums and cuscus look very different from one another in terms of size and fur-color, but Tayap classifies them all with the same word, **enamb**.

Birds (**tam**) do not make up any particularly noticeable percentage of the villagers' diet. Boys kill small birds with slingshots or arrows and roast them to eat as snacks. During the dry season, young men set traps or build blinds (**pura**) in which they hide at dawn and dusk, hoping to shoot large birds like the turkey-sized crowned pigeon (**momɨk**) when those fly down to drink at the few streams and ponds that retain water. Villagers eat cassowary (**ŋgat**) meat with gusto, but those big birds are elusive and fierce, and they were killed only rarely until about 2012, when one village man learned to set rope traps for cassowaries and has subsequently killed scores of the birds – so many, in fact, that they are now becoming increasingly rare throughout the area.

Cassowary eggs are boiled and eaten whenever they are found, and women and girls regularly dig into the mounds made by scrubfowls (**kokosuar**) and brush-turkeys (**onaw**), searching for their large red eggs (**yamiŋe**), which are prized as a delicacy, regardless of what stage of development the egg happens to be in when it is eaten. Some villagers raise a few domestic chickens (**kokok**), but those leathery fowl are only killed on special occasions to impress and honor visitors, or as part of a conciliatory or funerary feast.

With a few exceptions (cassowaries, eagles and a few small birds), birds do not feature in the village's myths and traditional stories. Nor is the plumage of birds collected, at least nowadays, to make into decorations to wear on festive occasions.

Despite their relative lack of importance in the villagers' diet, myths or daily life, many birds have names in Tayap. I collected more than 70 words for different bird species. I was able to do this thanks to the marvelous book, *Birds of New Guinea*, by Bruce M. Beehler, Thane K. Pratt and Dale A. Zimmerman, illustrated by Dale A. Zimmerman and James Coe (Princeton University Press, 1986). This invaluable field guide contains 55 illustrated plates, most in color, depicting every species of bird known to exist in New Guinea.

Villagers of all ages loved this book. I had others that I used to help me elicit words for animals, such as *Mammals of New Guinea* by Tim Flannery (Cornell University Press, 1995). Those books, though, had photographs of animals, rather than drawings. Villagers turned out to be much less interested in the photographs than they were in drawings. My impression was that villagers had a hard time recognizing many animals from their photographs. Many of the photos in a book like *Mammals of New Guinea*, it must be said, are not particularly clear. They are taken from angles, or from distances – for example, in extreme close up – from which villagers would normally not ever view the animals. There were also numerous photographs of animals like small bats that villagers call by the same word, and have little interest in differentiating. Villagers quickly became bored looking at this book.

The plates in *Birds of New Guinea* elicited a completely different response. Older men and women repeatedly returned to the drawings to recognize and name different kinds of birds. Younger people and children used the drawings to test each others' knowledge of bird names.

The following is a list of all the names of birds I was able to elicit from villagers. The English names are from *Birds of New Guinea,* and for easy identification, the relevant plate number and drawing number in that book is given in parentheses after the English translation (anyone wishing to know the classificatory Latin name of the birds will find it there). If no drawing number is given, the Tayap word refers to all birds depicted on that plate.

The overwhelming majority of the birds with names in Tayap have no names in Tok Pisin, which means that the most convenient way to talk about them is to use a vernacular language name. Villagers under thirty, especially females, who do not hunt birds like boys and young men do, generally do not know the names of birds that are rarely encountered. But for commonly seen birds, the vernacular names are still known, even by children. Because there are no Tok Pisin equivalents, many of the words for birds are likely to endure long after many other parts of the language have been forgotten.

On the rare occasions when the bird has a name in Tok Pisin, that is also noted in the entry.

aikeitam : Black Bittern (plate 3, #1–2, 5, 7, 10).

ambirdadab: small parrots; *liklik karangal* (plate 21).

amwaw: Twelve-wired Bird of Paradise, *kumul* (plate 51, #8–9).

awaŋ: Owl; *taragau bilong nait* (plate 26, #1–10 and #17–18). Villagers believe owls, which they say have the faces of men, to be the spirits of the dead, and they fear them accordingly. A favorite way of scaring a small child into submission is to point into the distance, clutch the child closer as though protecting him or her, and say urgently, "**Awaŋ! Awaŋ! Awaŋ** *i kam nau. Ye, lukim ai bilong em, em i kam nau!*" (Owl! Owl! The owl is coming! Yes, look at its eyes, it's coming!)

awin: Great-billed Heron (plate 3, #3) and Egret (plate 3, #6–15).

eiro: Paradise Kingfisher (plate 24, #1–5).

endurama: Bowerbird (plate 50).

erumó: Fruit-Dove (plate 17, all except #5).

kaimwa: Sulfur-crested Cockatoo; *koki* (plate 20, #12).

kaitut: Nightjars (plate 27).

kakarpwap: Gurney's Eagle; *taragau* (plate 8, #2–3).

kamban: Australian Magpie (plate 55, #9–10).

kandip: Forest Kingfisher (plate 24, #12).

kaŋgior: Spangled Drongo (plate 54, #1).

karar: Parrot, *karangal* (plate 20).

katip: Lowland Peltops (plate 39, #2–3).

katurip: Triller (plate 33, #10–12).

kikai: Ground Robin (plate 31, #3–4).

kimb: Kingfisher (plate 24, #6–9, #12–15).

kokok: Common Domesticated Chicken; *kakaruk*.

kokosuar: Common Scrubfowl; *wailpaul* (plate 1, #9a).

kopiwok: Palm Cockatoo; *koki* (plate 20, #14).

kosowak: Oriole (plate 33, #1–5; also plate 47, #15–20).

krirkemb: Tiger Parrot (plate 21, #13–14).

kundabebek: Black Kite (plate 8, #6–7).

kuriŋ: King Bird of Paradise; *kumul* (plate 53, 10).

kuruk: Kingfisher and Kookaburra (plate 24, #13–21).

mandimep: Ground Dwelling Pigeon (plate 15, #1–7; plate 16. #1–3).

mbateŋ: Nightjar (plate 27).

mbim: Frogmouth and Nightjar (plate 26, #11–18). The word is onomatopoetic, imitating the cries made by these birds.

mbodibodi: Robin (plate 37, #10; plate 39, #11–21). Being replaced by the Kopar-language word **mbodiɲeɲe**.

mbonir: Mannikin (plate 48).

mitimap: Zoe Imperial Pigeon (plate 19, #2–3).

momik: Western Crowned Pigeon; *guria* (plate 15, #8–11).

morip: Pigeon; *balus* (plate 18, all except #2–3).

muntatak: Hanging and Pygmy Parrot (plate 21, #1–5).
ndagurai: Dollarbird (plate 25, #3)
ndakruk: Hooded Butcherbird (plate 55, #6).
ndebodam: Rail (plate 10).
ndebom: Purple Swamphen (plate 10, #14).
ndidɨ́noŋko: Wampoo Fruit Dove (plate 17, #5).
ndokop: Meliphagas and Honeyeaters (plate 46).
njijerik: Lorikeet (plate 19, # 8–18). Being replaced by the Kopar-language word *njijeriŋ*.
num: Great-billed Heron (plate 3, #3–4).
ŋgat: Northern Cassowary; *muruk* (plate 1, #1).
ŋgatwaw: baby cassowary; *liklik pikinini muruk* (plate 1, #2b-c).
ŋgawgarak: Golden Myna (plate 49, #1–2).
ŋgoram: Sacred Ibis (plate 2, #6–9).
ŋgoromai: Eclectus Parrot (plate 20, #4, female).
onaw: Brush-turkey; *bikpela wailpaul* (plate 1, #4–6).
ondom: Blyth's Hornbill; *kokomo* (plate 25, #8).
osos: Hook-billed Kingfisher (plate 24, #17–18).
palusemb: Swallow (plate 29).
pasuwer: Great Cockoo Dove (plate 16, #4).
patarík: Swift (plate 28).

pesaw: Lesser and Greater Birds of Paradise, *kumul* (plate 51, #2–8 and #1–6 in the lower plate are females).
pit: Sunbird and Honeyeater (plate 45).
punim: Greater Black Coucal (plate 23, #12, 14–19).
puŋg: New Guinea Flightless Rail (plate 10, #16).
romb: Starling (plate 54, #5–7).
sambwaŋmond: Cormorant (plate 2, #1–4).
semaya: Tagula Butcherbird (plate 55, #4).
simbébi: Quail (plate 1; #12–15).
sireŋ: Cuckoo Shrike (plate 32).
sowo: Pitohui (plate 42, #7–13).
tam: bird (*generic*); *pisin* (*biknem*).
tambiroro: Yellow-billed Kingfisher (plate 24, #10).
tromtrimb: Fantail (plate 37).
wamb kosowak: Helmeted Friarbird (plate 33, #1–5).
wira: Lorikeet (plate 19, the word refers to the larger ones).
wiswis: Goshawk and Falcon (plate 5, plate 6). This word is an onomatopoetic rendering of the sound made by the beat of these birds' wings.
yakua: Catbird (plate 49, #6).

Kin terms

Obsolete kin terms are marked with †.

The dual and plural forms of those kin terms still in use are not generally known by speakers under 50.

abambi† *n.* ex-wife (used by the ex-in-laws of the woman); *man i lusim man bai mama na papa bilong man kolim ex-meri long despela nem.*
agampɨ *n.; voc.* (*pl.* **agampɨndodo**), mother's mother's brother; *brata bilong mama bilong mama.*
ama *n.; voc.* mother; *mama.* See also **maya**.
ama mosop *n.; voc.* maternal aunt who is younger than one's mother; *liklikpela susa bilong mama.*
ama kowot *n.; voc.* maternal aunt who is older than one's mother; *bikpela susa bilong mama.*

amasik† *n.* (*pl.* **amasikndodo** or **amasikimb**), ancestor; *tumbuna man o meri.*
atawo† *n.* (*dl.* **atawondodɨ**; *pl.* **atawondodo**), older sibling; *bikpela brata o susa.* See also **tata**.
awoi† *n.* mother's brother; *kandere.* See also **wow**.
eŋki† *n.* (*pl.* **eŋkindodo**), [*possibly Adjora*], husband of maternal aunts and nieces (male speaking); *man bilong kandere meri.*
keke *n.* (*dl.* **kekeŋre**; *pl.* **kekeŋgro**), grandmother; *apa meri.*

maya *n.* (*dl.* **mayaŋre**, *pl.* **mayaŋgro**), mother; *mama*. See also **ama**.

neni *n.* (*dl.* **neniŋre**; *pl.* **neniŋgro**), grandfather; *apa man*.

njanimb[†] *n.* (*pl.* **njanimbeda**), great-grandchild; *pikinini bilong pikinini bilong pikinini*.

obiman[†] *n.* ex-husband (used by the ex-in-laws of the man); *meri i lusim man bai mama na papa bilong meri kolim ex-man long despela nem*.

oiŋga[†] *n.* (*pl.* **oiŋgabidib** or **oiŋgandodo**), daughter-in-law (female speaking); *meri bilong pikinini man (mama bilong man bai tok)*.

ombare[†] *n.* nephew's wife (male speaking).

ombre[†] *n.* (*pl.* **ombrendodo**), father-in-law (male speaking); *man bai kolim papa bilong meri bilong em*.

omgande omgande[†] *n.* **1.** two or more wives of one man; *tupela meri bilong wanpela man*. **2.** two or more female-in-laws; *tupela tambu meri*.

omin *n.* spouse; *man o meri bilong em*.

ominde ominde[†] *n.* married couple; *tupela marit*.

omo *n.* (*pl.* **omosew**), father; *papa*. See also **sas**.

oŋgwan[†] *n.* (*pl.* **oŋgwabidig**), sister in-law (female speaking); *tambu meri em meri i tok*.

opam[†] *n.* (*pl.* **opamndodo**), son-in-law; *man bilong pikinini meri*.

orma[†] *n.* (*pl.* **ormabidib**), younger sibling; *liklik brata o susa*.

otan[†] *n.* (*pl.* **otinimb**), grandchild; *pikinini bilong pikinini*.

otre[†] *n.* (*pl.* **otrendodo**), mother-in-law (male speaking); *nem man bai kolim mama bilong meri bilong em*.

oyeŋ[†] *n.* (*pl.* **oyeŋgud**), in-law (in the widest sense, including brother-in-law, sister-in-law, etc.); *tambu*.

papo *n.*; *voc.* maternal uncle's wife; *meri bilong kandere*.

romgar[†] *n.* (*pl.* **rurumgri**), sister's child; nephew or niece; *pikinini bilong susa*.

sas *n.*; *voc.* father; *papa*. See also **omo**.

tata *n. voc.* older sibling; *bikpela brata o susa*. See also **atawo**.

wand *n.* (*pl.* **wanjmeŋ**), cross-sex sibling; *susa bai kolim brata bilong em* **wand** *na brata bai kolim susa* **wand**.

wow *n.*; *voc.* maternal uncle; *kandere*. See also **awoi**.

The adjectives **mokop/mosop** (little) and **kowot** (senior) are used with many of the most common terms both in reference and address to modify the kin term, on the pattern of **ama mosop** and **ama kowot** above; **mokop/mosop** designating 'younger', **kowot** meaning 'elder'. The point of reference is the speaker or the person whose kin the speaker is talking about.

Parts of a house

arit *n.* the **kotiw** that hang as extensions from where the roof meets the walls of the house; *win bilong haus*.

isumbo *n.* horizontal runner supporting roof thatch; *sparen*.

kambrom *n.* small sticks inserted along the length of the **tandor** to secure it in place; *hap limbom bilong subim antap long pongan bilong haus*. See also **kapir**.

kapir *n.* small sticks inserted along the length of the **tandor** to secure it in place; *hap limbom bilong subim antap long pongan bilong haus*. See also **kambrom**.

kerkwar *n.* horizontal roof support that rests on the tall **kóndrik**; *pongan*.

kimitak *n.* bark floor of house; *limbom*.

kindit *n.* wall of house; *banis bilong haus*.

kóndrik *n.* **1.** tallest post or posts holding up roof; *kingpost*. **2.** euphemism for penis; *wanpela we bilong toktok long sem bilong man*. **Erum otiteka kóndrik ŋayar**

puŋgokawuk: The thatch has fallen off but the king post is still standing (euphemism for 'He may be old and bald but his prick can still stand up'); *Marota i pundaun na kingpos i sanap i stap (olsem mining bilong em i olsem maski man i kela kok bilong em tait i stap yet)*.
kotɨw *n*. vertical runner supporting roof; *sapnil*.
mambɨr *n*. large horizontal roof supporting beams that rest across the **towond**; *pilo*.
ŋgúnbara *n*. short, squat vertical post on which the floor runners rest; *sotpela belpos*.
pawkpawk *n*. horizontal roof support placed on top of the **kerkwar**; the highest point of the roof; *namba tu pongan*.
porimb *n*. [*Kopar*], floor support that runs cross-wise, from **ŋgúnbara** to **ŋgúnbara**; *rola*. See also **tékdwan**.
tak *n*. floor support that runs lengthwise, placed on top of the **porimb**; the bark floor (**kɨmɨtak**) is placed on top of these; *limbom*.
tandor *n*. braided mat of palm leaves placed across the **pawkpawk**, to seal the crown of the house from rain; *kapa bilong marota*.
tékdwan *n*. floor support that runs cross-wise, from **ŋgúnbara** to **ŋgúnbara**; *rola*. See also **porimb**.
towond *n*. large post on each of the four corners of a house; *saitpos*.

Words pertaining to sago processing

Sago is the staple food of Gapun. It is eaten every single day of the year, ideally at least twice a day; once in the morning and once in the late afternoon. Its raw form is a flour that resembles compacted corn starch. This flour (**muna**) can be made into a kind of rubbery pancake (**tamwai**) by heating it on a broken pot shard (**pambram**) or a frying pan, it can be tossed onto the fire raw in a tennis ball-sized chunk (**muna kokɨr**, which literally means 'sago head'), it can be wrapped in a leaf and cooked in on a fire (**paŋgɨp**), or it can be crumbled into a bamboo tube and thrown onto a fire to congeal (**munakumund**). Its most common and most appreciated form, though, is as what, in English, is usually misleadingly called 'sago pudding' or 'sago jelly'. Both designations are misleading because they imply (a) that said food item that has the consistency of pudding or jelly, and (b) that said food item is appetizing.

Both these implications are false. In fact, the texture of sago referred to by 'sago jelly' is much closer to slime or phlegm than it is to jelly or pudding. Its consistency is such that some of a mouthful will be in your mouth; at the same time some of it will be hanging down into your throat, like a long thick sputum. And appetizing, alas, 'sago jelly' is not – unless, of course, one happens to be a Sepik villager raised on it from birth (villagers in Gapun start feeding their babies sago jelly only a few days after they are born). The color of 'sago jelly' varies from light pink to dark red or even black, depending on the quality and character of the water in which it was leached.

'Sago jelly' (**mum**) is served in plates or washbasins in big viscous globs. On top of such a glob, women will place a few leaves of some vegetable, or a small piece of fish or tiny chunk of meat – like a cherry on top of an ice cream sundae (although, again, that image is deceptive because it suggests something tasty). On top of that, a few spoonfuls of 'soup' (**wawan**) will be poured. 'Soup' consists of coconut milk (i.e. the liquid produced when a coconut is grated and squeezed in cold water) in which the vegetables or meat served on top of the **mum** has been boiled. If the villagers have salt, they will use copious amounts of it to flavor the soup. Aside from salt, no flavorings, spices or herbs of any kind are used in Gapun's cuisine.

Villagers produce sago in a process so complicated that it makes one wonder how human beings could possibly ever have discovered it. Most sago palms, to begin with, are far from inviting: they have have long sharp needles covering their trunks and their leaves. Nevertheless, people somehow, at some point in the distant past, discovered that an edible starch can be wrested from the inner bark of those spine-covered palms, according to the following steps.

First, men fell the sago palm and use bush knives to strip it of its needles. The outer bark of the palm is then slit open with an axe, lengthwise down the palm. This outer bark is pried open on both sides of the cut with axes and bush knives, producing a gash which men widen until the outer bark lies open like a shell. Men then begin chipping away at the exposed pale inner bark with an instrument that looks like a cross between an axe and a large chisel (**makor** or **yasuk**). They start at the base of the tree (**wot**) and work their way upwards towards the crown of the palm (**mar**). The scraped-away inner bark looks like coarse pink sawdust.

This sawdust (**tawar**) is taken away by women to a place from which they can draw water – ususally a rough well dug somewhere near the sago palm (because sago palms grow in swamps, there is usually plenty of water on hand). Women take the sawdust and put handfuls of it into a long funnel (**iko** or **ndadum**) that they make out of the base of one of the sago palm leaves. They attach a coconut fiber strainer (**waris**) to the end of this funnel and they pour water into it. They then squeeze and knead the sago pith in the funnel, thereby releasing the flour it contains. The flour runs through the strainer along with the water, and is collected in buckets made of palm fronds (**kondew**) placed on the ground below the funnel. The sago pith, once it has been leached of its flour in this manner, is tossed away. Each handful of sago pith is washed 4–5 times to ensure that it has been completely leached.

The sago flour that has run through the strainer with the water settles on the bottom of the palm frond buckets and the water rises to the top. When this settling process is completed, the water that has risen to the top of the sago is poured off, and what remains are firm cakes of wet flour. These are dried by covering them with leaves and putting hot ashes on top. The heat generated by these ashes extracts the remaining water. The cakes of sago flour (**munakatar**) are then carried to the village and used to prepare the villagers' meals.

'Sago jelly' is made from this raw sago by breaking off a mound of sago flour, putting it in a pot and diluting it in a small amount of cold water. This produces a watery paste that is strained so that most of the remaining impurities (insects, twigs, ashes) are removed. Next, the cook pours a large amount of boiling water onto the paste, stirring vigorously all the while. The boiling water and the stirring cause the sago paste to coagulate and become the viscous mass so beloved by villagers. This pot of gummy mucous is twisted like taffy onto people's basins, it is topped with the requisite few leaves or small chunk of meat and fish, and *voilà*, *Bon Appetit*.

The sago-processing work described above is protypically done by a married couple. In practice, both men and women can and do perform all steps in the process by themselves or with same-sex friends or same-sex kin. This might happen, for example, if a mother sends her teenage girls or boys off to work sago, or if a person's spouse is ill and the household supply of sago has run out. But despite the fact that sago processing can be done alone or in same-sex groups, it is strongly associated with conjugal couples. In Gapun, there is no ceremony surrounding marriage – nothing is exchanged, bought or given by anyone involved in a marriage. The only surefire sign that a couple is married is that they go off together to work sago. This time in the rainforest producing sago is also the time when a married couple often have sex. In their house, a husband and wife are seldom alone – and if they have children they are never alone. And what goes on in the house is audible to anyone walking by, as well as visible to anyone stopping to peek through the braided bamboo or sago palm leaves that villagers use as walls.

The entire sago-production process, from felling the sago palm to producing the cakes of sago flour, takes an entire day, from about 8 am to 3 or 4 o'clock in the afternoon, for two people to complete. And this day's work will usually only result in half the sago palm being processed – the other half remains for the following day. One day's work produces between 5–8 large cakes of sago. Depending on how much of that sago one distributes to relatives, this amount of sago will last a family of eight 2–4 days.

Traditionally, Gapuners processed sago like their Adjora-speaking neighbors to the east. Men pulverized sago pith in a seated position, sitting on small benches made of branches (**kokɨparaŋ**) and using a short sago-pounder made of a single piece of wood (**yasuk**). Women leached sago in a basket (**saiput**) that they hung from a frame and squeezed with both hands. In the mid-1960s, Gapuners moved their village from its former site on top of a small mountain down to its present site in a swampy clearing in the rainforest. At the same time, they began to adopt the sago-processing methods used by the villagers of Wongan and other people who live near the coast. Women abandoned the sago-leaching basket and men started to stand up to pound the pith. This method of sago processing has remained the one used by all villagers. The only innovation since the 1960s occurred in the 1990s, when villagers began to abandon the sago frond buckets into which the water containing the sago flour settled after the pith had been washed. Again copying the villagers of Wongan, Gapuners began to carve large canoe-shaped receptacles and using those instead of the sago-frond buckets. They did this because the wooden canoes are more durable than the buckets, which fall apart after only a few weeks' use.

Kinds of sago palms

anumb *n.* sago palm with long fronds that are often used to make **iko** (funnel for leaching sago). It has short leaves, short needles and a very wide trunk. It produces a great deal of sago flour. *Saksak i gat ol bikpela pangal ol meri i save usim long wokim* **iko**. *Lip bilong em sotpela, i gat sotpela nil na namel bilong em bikpela. I gat bikpela muna.*

konemba *n.* sago palm with short fronds *pangal* (**ndadum**) and short leaves. It has no needles and has characteristic white fronds. *Saksak i gat sotpela pangal na sotpela lip. Nogat nil na pangal bilong em i waitpela.*

naŋgak *n.* wild sago palm. This kind of sago plam has not been planted, as most other kinds of palms are, and it has many needles. *Wailsaksak i gat planti nil.*

ndidi yam *n.* a kind of **yam** sago palm with few needles and a very hard interior. *Saksak i nogat planti nil na mit bilong em i strong tru.*

suwir *n.* sago palm with long leaves and needles. Its leaves are not tough and are not used for house thatch. This kind of sago palm is easy to pound because its interior is not hard and it produces a lot of sago flour. *Saksak i gat longpela lip na longpela nil. Lip bilong em i no strong na ol man i no save usim ol long pasim haus. Mit bilong em i no strong na i gat bikpela muna.*

wamar *n.* sago palm similar to the **konemba**, except that its fronds are long and green. *Saksak em wankain olsem konemba, tasol pangal bilong em i longpela na grinpela.*

yam mbatim yam *n.* a kind of **yam** sago palm characterized by being short, having short needles, and an interior that is soft and easy to pound. *Saksak i sotpela na i gat sotpela nil. Mit bilong em i no strong.*

yam *n.* 1. sago palm (*generic*); *diwai saksak* (*biknem*).
2. specific kind of sago palm with short fronds and long spikes. One of the most desirable palms to pound for sago; its leaves are used as thatch for houses; *kain saksak i gat sotpela pangal na longpela nil. Gutpela saksak long paitim na pangal bilong em ol man i save kisim long pasim haus.*

yam síw *n.* a kind of **naŋgak** sago palm that grows to great heights and has long fronds. It has needles, but in very tall ones the needles will fall off and leave a bare palm. *Wanpela kain* **naŋgak** *i save gro na kamap longpela moa. I gat nil tasol long ol longpela longpela ol nil i save pundaun na namel bilong em bai stap nating.*

eiwki *v.i.* (**peiwiet/peiwiek**, **ŋgi peiwko**), wash and leach sago pith; *wasim saksak*.

eiwŋgar yimbar *n.* canoe used since the 1990s to capture the water and sago flour that runs out from the **waris** (cocounut fiber strainer) when women leach sago pith; *kanu bilong wasim pipia saksak*.

iko *n.* [*Kopar*], the palm leaf funnel into which the **tawar** is put to be leached and onto which the **waris** is nailed; *pangal bilong wasim pipia*. See also **ndadum**.

induw *n.* the inner bark of a sago palm that is nearest to the outer bark, what is left when the **yamŋa mis** is pulverized; *insait bilong skin bilong saksak, skin nating*.

karam *n.* bark of sago tree; *skin bilong saksak*. **Ŋiŋi karam krankun:** He split the bark of the sago palm (to begin pulverizing it); *Em brukim skin bilong saksak*.

kokiparaŋ *n.* small bench that men used to use to sit on and pulverize sago pith; *pilo bilong sindaun na paitim saksak*.

kondew *n.* sheath of limbom tree, used to make buckets into which water is poured and in which the sago flour settles; *limbom*.

kutukutu *n.* the fork on which the **iko** stands; *pok bilong putim iko antap long en*.

maimbog *n.* water that has run into the palm sheaths or canoe in which sago flour is settling. *Wara bilong saksak ol meri wasim long en*.

makor *n.* [*Kopar*], sago pounder with long handle; *ain bilong paitim saksak*. See also **yasuk**.

makorŋa rewi *n.* piece of iron at the head of a **makor** or **yasuk** that scrapes away the inner bark of the sago palm; *ain bilong paitim saksak*.

mar *n.* crown or top of felled sago palm; *tel bilong saksak ol man i wok long paitim em*.

mbába *n.* [*Kopar*], wooden pins used to hold the **waris** (coconut fiber strainer) in place; *nil bilong nilim laplap bilong kokonas*. See also **pandiŋ**.

mindiki- *v.i.* (**pindiet/pindiek**), pulverize sago pith; *wok saksak*. **Yu mindikinana mbotke?:** Are you going to work sago? *Yu go wok saksak ah?*

muna *n.* sago flour; *saksak*.

munakatar *n.* a cake of sago flour; *wanpela hap saksak*.

munjar *n.* [*Kopar*], handle of **makor** (sago pounder); *stik bilong* **makor**. See also **naŋgir**.

naŋgir *n.* handle of axe or **makor** (sago pounder); *stik bilong* **makor**. See also **munjar**.

ndadum *n.* long, hard palm frond used to make **iko** (funnel) and also to carry sago once it is dried into sago flour; *pangal bilong wokim* **iko** *na bilong karim* **munakatar**.

ndag *n.* top-middle part of felled sago palm; *namel i go antap bilong saksak ol man i paitim mit bilong en*.

njame *n.* the dregs of the **tawar** that remain in the **iko**; *pipia saksak olsem das i stap long* **iko**.

ŋgir *n.* stick framework of that holds the limbom sheath buckets upright; *bet bilong pangal bilong putim limbom*.

okinokin *n.* a palm sheath container onto which one attaches a handle, used to pour water into the **iko**; *liklik limbom ol meri samapim bilong kisim wara*.

pamiŋgap *n.* top part of a **makor** (sago pounder); *hap i stap antap long* **makor**.

pandiŋ *n.* wooden pins used to hold the **waris** (coconut fiber strainer) in place; *nil bilong nilim laplap bilong kokonas*. See also **mbába**.

saiput *n.* basket that until the 1970s used to be used wash and leach sago pith; *basket ol mama bilong bipo i save usim long wasim saksak*.

sambo *n.* a sago palm that has a watery interior, containing little sago starch; *saksak i nogat strongpela mit, warawara tasol*. **Yam sambo, muna wákareŋan:** The sago palm is **sambo**, it has no sago starch; *Sakasak i warawara, nogat muna*.

sikin *n.* sharp scraper attached to the end of a **makor** or **yasuk** (sago pounder), traditionally made of bamboo, now made of a sawed-off pipe; *sapela hed bilong* **makor** *o bilong* **yasuk**.

sikɨp *n.* large lump of sago pith that has not been pulverized; *bikpela hap hap mit bilong saksak.* **Tawar aŋgo sikɨpŋan tandiw tawaitukun ŋgo!**: The **tawar** has a lot of unpounded bits, pulverize it better!; *Tawar i gat planti bikpela hap i stap, paitim gut pastaim!*

tawar *n.* pulp or pith of sago palm once it has been pounded into what looks like sawdust. This is what one washes to leach it of sago flour. *Mit bilong saksak ol man i paitim long en.*

tawar mbup *n.* the washed and leached pith of the sago palm; what **tawar** is called once it is washed and all the sago flour has been extracted from it; *tawar ol i wasim na nogat moa saksak long en.*

unduku *v.t.* (class 1), pulverize sago palm pith; *paitim saksak.* **Ŋa yamŋa orom kemem pundukun**: I pulverized a large section of the sago palm; *Longpela hap saksak mi paitim.*

wai *n.* sago swamp where people go to process sago; *hap tais i gat saksak.*

waram taw *n.* the layer of sago left close to the bark of the palm when one is almost done pulverizing it; *liklik hap mit bilong saksak i stap klostu long skin bilong saksak.*

waris *n.* screen made of coconut fiber; *laplap bilong kokonas.*

worki *v.i.* (**poriet/poriek**), be blocked, e.g. water that doesn't drain through the **waris** (coconut fiber strainer); *i pas.* **Ewar ŋa mboka peiwieka awin worki wåkare**: Yesterday I went and washed sago and the water wouldn't go through the strainer; *Asde mi wasim saksak na wara i no godaun.*

wot *n.* base of a felled sago palm; *as bilong saksak ol man i katim long en.*

yamŋa mis *n.* pale inner bark of sago palm before it is pulverized; *mit bilong saksak.*

yasuk *n.* sago pounder that villagers traditionally used to chip away at and pulverize the interior bark of the sago palm while sitting down. It is made out of a single piece of wood, as opposed to a **makor** which is made of two pieces; *ain bilong paitim saksak ol man bilong bipo i save wok long en. Ol man i save wokim em long wanpela hap diwai.*

Processing sago

wot	wotŋa orom	orom	ndagŋa orom	ndag	marŋa orom	mar

Parts of a felled sago palm from the base (**wot**) to the crown (**mar**). The word **orom** means 'in the vincinty of', so **wotŋa orom** is 'the part near the **wot**', **ndagŋa orom** is 'the part near the **ndag**', and so on.

English-Tayap finder list

This list is intended to assist English-speakers who wish to find a particular word in Tayap.[1] It lists all the words associated with a particular topic, usually without providing any closer definition of the words. The definitions are found under the Tayap entry in the Tayap-English-Tok Pisin section of the dictionary.

A

abort: **imin wuw**
above: **wo**
    wurɨ
absorb *v*.: **aŋgu**
ache *n*.: **mbɨd**
accompaniment (without): **seŋgrim sinder**
adhere *v*.: **wawku**
    rurur-(p)-ekɨ
adorn *v*.: **ndok**
adornment: **atunuŋ**
    emári
    ep
    isikɨ
    isirai
    kapwasak
    kokrow
    maies
    makat
    maŋgat
    monjuko
    nanjag
    ndok (generic)
    rɨmb
    tatak
    titi
    totrɨk
affirmation: **awo**
    ore
after: **nunuknɨ**
afternoon: **ŋgrag**
afterwards: **nunuk**

again: **motinɨ**
age mate: **orimb**
agree *v*.: **nambarkɨ simb**
agreed: **sapki**
air: **mbun**
a little: **mbara**
alcohol: **awin**
alive: **ŋginoŋa**
all: **taman**
allow: **ŋganokaw**
almost: **nɨpɨs**
alone: **nambar neker**
also: **tɨ**
amongst: **oromnɨ**
anal gland: **warniŋ** (possums and bandicoots)
ancestor: **aru**
    eŋgin
anger: **otar**
    pwap
angry *v*.: **nam**
    pwapkɨ
    utɨtɨo
animal coat: **atuŋgor**
    mbatɨbati
    ramborgar
animal hide *n*.: **sɨw**
ankle: **ndowbɨr**
    ndowŋan sokop
answer back *v*.: **sik ep**
ant: **sɨwɨr** (generic); *see special section on "Animals, insects, fish and birds"*
antenna: **sind**

---

[1] I am grateful to Ahmad Qadafi, who helped me by preparing the first draft of this wordlist, which I then edited.

anus: **yiwirgwab**
apology: **imin**
appearance: **nanuk**
applaud: **ndaram**
arm: **akan suman** (upper arm)
    akanbir (forearm)
    ndaram
armpit: **amoiawin**
    amoiawinŋa pupur (armpit hair)
arrival: **aiŋgar**
arrow: **wot**
ash: **kosimb**
ask v.: **kotar-(p)-e**
    kotar-(p)-e-ki
ass: **kandam**
assemble v.: **korar**
asshole: **yiwirgwab**
assumption: **awa**
athletes' foot:
    ŋgat ndow
awhile ago: **nirere**
axe: **mindia**
    pande

B

baby: **átiáti**
    isiki
    krimb
    masukondep
    mbioŋgi
    miŋan
    taman
    tombtomb
back: **mbwar**
    ŋgamamb (upper)
    orom (lower)
backbone: **ndugubar**
backside: **nunuk**
bad ways: **kokosawir**
bad: **apro**
badly: **supwaspwa**
bald head: **kokir tutiek**
baldness: **kanimbit**
bamboo: **kanjigogo**
    mberowok

    mbwaj (generic)
    mbwantaw
    miŋgŋa bwar
    oŋki
    ti
banana earwig: **ikinŋan yandum**
banana: **ikin** (generic)
    iwoŋgikin
    mamar
    marow
    mbákbak
    mbuga
    mbormat
    mbunoŋ
    mom
    munjesik (frond)
    oraw (seedling)
    oremnai ikin
    ramu
    sambai oremai ikin
bandicoot: **sasik**
bang against: **mbaŋ**
bank of stream: **mbag**
barb: **mandamandap**
bark v.: **ŋgawŋki**
barren v.: **paindakki**
base of tree: **tomir**
base: **kandaŋni**
basket sling: **ambrim numun**
basket: **Karatum sapwar** (crocodile clan)
    Maŋai sapwar (dog clan)
    miriŋa sapwar (for carrying supplies and food)
    saim (carried on head)
    saiput (for sago processing)
    sapwar (generic)
    simbergar sapwar (for carrying one's belongings)
bastard child: **nder**
bat: **sumusumu**
bathe v.: **tuwku**
beat v.: **por**
be careful: **numbwan reki**
be full: **isioki**
be happy v.: **siŋki**
be v.: **adaiki**
    aku

English-Tayap finder list — 457

    ambkɨ
    arkɨ
beach: **puwaiorom**
    sumbwa kapɨr
beak: **ndar**
bean sprout: **mbua**
beard: **ŋgakreŋa pupur**
become a man *v*.: **munjekɨ**
become a woman *v*.: **noŋork**
become one: **nambarkɨ**
become overgrown *v*.: **abarkɨ**
become purified *v*.: **utikɨ**
bedbug: **ndedeŋ**
bee: **kunemb** (generic); *see special section on "Animals, insects, fish and birds"*
beetle: **tutumb** (generic); *see special section on "Animals, insects, fish and birds"*
before: **rawnɨ**
    rɨpam
behind: **mbwarnɨ**
    nunuknɨ
believe *v*.: **tar**
belly button: **imin sukum**
belly: **imin**
belongings: **koŋgon**
below: **ari**
    seknɨ
    sire
bend over *v*.: **tɨmbrio**
bend *v*.: **mbur-(p)-e**
    ŋgadogadikɨ
bent: **ŋgado**
beside: **ase**
    tawnɨ
bestow *v*.: **orai**
betel nut smasher: **kokɨparaŋ**
betel nut: **adu-**
    aiamb
    arɨmɨndai
    atɨm
    ei
    eiamb
    kambok
    kandapat
    kokɨparaŋ
    kup
    mandamandap

    mbatep
    mbrat
    mbubow
    mbubuk
    minjike (generic)
    minjikeŋa ŋgɨb
    mɨn
    moramori
    ndam
    ndekik
    ŋgɨb
    ŋgop
    pramat
    sapwar
    sikesike
    simberkɨ (*v*. chew betel nut)
    takrot
    tatikem
    top
    wamb
bier: **tamb**
big toe: **ndowŋa oŋko**
big: **mɨr**
    suman
bird: **tam** (generic)
bitch (female dog): **nje noŋor**
bite *v*.: **amɨra**
black: **sawɨr**
bladder: **nok nder**
blink *v*.: **ŋgino**
    tɨk
block *v*.: **kɨnd-(p)-o**
    oskɨ
    roŋgikɨ
    utaroror
blocked: **taman**
blood clot: **muk**
blood let *v*.: **trai**
blood: **and**
bloody: **andŋan**
blossom *v*.: **pwar**
blow on *v*.: **wiwir**
blue: **ŋgɨdɨŋ**
blunt: **mbutup**
boar tusk: **kaŋgajɨŋ**
    osɨŋgir

boil n.: **munjesik**
  nop
  orwo
boil v.: **peikɨ**
  sowor-(p)-o
  trar-(p)-o
bone: **adaradɨ**
  emárɨ
  kambɨkeŋa nɨŋ
  kandapŋa nɨŋ
  kurom
  ndugubar
  nɨŋ (generic)
  ŋaibo
  ŋakre
  ŋamambat
  ŋgino mbod
  tɨmɨr
  tɨmɨrbɨm
  tokɨmot
  tombtomb
bottom: **yit**
bow n.: **kembatik**
bow-legged: **kambukar**
bowstring: **karatukumb**
box: **kaiknumb**
boyfriend: **nireŋar munje**
bracelet: **tɨmɨr**
  torɨw
braid n.: **met**
braid v.: **wur**
  er
brain: **sikin**
branch: **nduko**
  nɨmŋat
  pitatak
breadfruit: **mbatak**
  mbatambur
  minj
break open: **kra**
break v.: **adádadɨ**
  adur
  adurɨokɨ
  krakrɨ
  krarara okɨ
breast bone: **tokɨmot**
breast milk: **misisiŋ**

breast: **min**
  min ŋgopŋa
breath: **mbun**
  pora
  tokro
breathe v.: **mbun**
  war
bridge: **koŋgrik**
  nɨmɨrkokɨr
bring v.: **kᵛ**
bristles: **ŋatnɨmŋa pupur** (on pig's back)
broad: **tapraw**
broom: **sindibam**
  tandímɨrit
brush turkey: **onaw**
bubble: **njijɨriŋ**
  mbubujiram
  tapurmanj
bucket: **maniŋ**
bud: **moramorik**
build: **er**
bullfrog: **uráŋgeba**
bullshit: **awinŋa sik**
bumpy: **ndɨdɨkdɨdɨk**
bundle: **yɨmbam**
bunion: **ndow kawrik**
burn v.: **apu**
  ipɨkɨ
  mbabuŋkɨ
burned: **mbabuŋ**
burp n.: **ŋarɨr**
burrow n.: **taŋar**
bury v.: **war**
bush knife: **pitɨŋar**
butcher v.: **wuw**
butterfly: **mumuk**
buy v.: **moser**
buzz v.: **krururki**

C

cajoling n.: **eŋune eŋune**
cake of sago flour: **munakatar**
calf of leg: **warmis mokop**
call n.: **ŋar**
call out v.: **ŋar**

call v.: **ŋgar**
   ndokopndokop (call puppies)
calm person: **mukúki**
cane grass: **tumbɨgir**
   ut
   nekénduko
canoe: **kaikro**
   kaisar
   kemb
   yimbar
capture v.: **tumbu**
carbuncle: **atokrim**
care for domestic animals v: **krar**
carry v.: **wuw** (on one shoulder)
   andru-(w/p)-e (on head)
   aroŋg-(p)-e (inside something)
   eraro-(p/w)-ar (in sling on back)
   tap (on shoulders)
cartilage: **ndrɨg**
   ŋot
carve v.: **rambu**
carving: **kandibwaŋ**
   tumbuan
cassowary: **emári**
   kurom
   maies
   mbwag
   mipat
   nkɨnkɨm
   ŋat (cassowary)
   ŋat ndow
   ŋatma min
   ŋatwaw
   ŋot
   rɨr-(p)-orki
   tamro
   tamroŋa kup
   tɨmɨr
   yir pwap
castrate v.: **ke-(p)-e**
catch v.: **wuru** (with hook)
caterpillar: **atɨr**
   nɨŋasin
cave: **ŋgwab**
cemetery: **mambrag num**
centipede: **yandum**
   yandumtɨt

challenge v.: **towoi**
change mind v.: **urek-(p)-e**
chant n.: **njem**
   sambaŋa njem
charcoal: **wuwur**
cheek: **ndabo**
chest: **kambɨke**
   mintumb
   nambɨr
chestnut: **kaɲan**
chew v.: **minjia**
chew betel nut: **simberkɨ**
chicken: **kokok**
child: **nder**
   ror
chili leaf: **eŋuramat**
chili pepper: **tamropirup**
chirp v.: **piwiukɨ**
chisel n: **kapwakapi**
   ndokdok
chop down: **ar**
chop v: **kra**
   sum-(p)-or
cicada: **kikik**
   ŋaratgarat
cigarette: **sokoidu**
citrus fruit: **pinɨmb**
clam: **eporaŋ**
   kaŋ
   oyaŋ
clan: **kandaŋ**
claw: **yir pwap**
clay: **noŋge**
clear undergrowth v.: **ndum**
   ndumkɨ
   prɨk
climb v.: **wawaroski**
clitoris: **iru**
   piɲin
close to: **minjikan**
close v.: **er**
   kɨnd-(p)-o
closed: **taman**
clot: **muk**
cloth: **embátoto**
cloud: **akɨjim** (raincloud)
   akɨn

clove tree: **yimbram**
club: **mbateŋ**
    sawáraŋga
    taimb
clump: **nɨr**
cluster: **kup**
    mbɨj
    ndam
    pramat
clutter: **kombobo**
cockroach: **numbutik**
    sasawraŋ
coconut cream: **mimb**
coconut formation: **makatok** (stage three)
    niŋgirarik (stage two)
    ŋgakrawmunjik (stage one)
    pap taw (final stage)
    turaw pakas (stage four)
coconut palm: **andi**
    pap
    papembɨr
coconut shell : **kukutawaŋ**
    tawk
coconut shredder: **njemuk**
coconut: **meruk**
    mɨn
    mow (meat)
    pap
    papetraw (husk fiber)
    papkrɨm (small)
    papndaw (wild)
    papŋa ŋgɨb (sapling)
    turaw (husk)
coerce *v.*: **kokɨr i**
    mor-(p)-e
coil: **ambnor**
    du
coin: **mbatembatep**
cold: **arkar-(p)-ekɨ**
    imin
    mbankap
    pokemb
    pokembkɨ
    munjewatkɨ
    waw
collapse: **adɨokɨ**
collarbone: **kambikeŋa niŋg**

collect *v.*: **ondar**
colorful: **titɨmb**
comb: **kɨm**
come *v.*: **aikɨ**
come off *v.*: **isiri okɨ**
come up *v.*: **wikɨ**
    wurkɨ
comedian: **maisare ŋgrɨgar munje**
comic act: **maisare**
complete *v.*: **kokot**
concealed talk: **wai**
conch shell: **pomɨŋ**
cone hat: **kawt**
    kokɨrat
confuse: **mbábasakkɨ**
consider: **kiraw**
constrain *v.*: **roŋ**
construct: **er**
consume: **a**
    kroi
conversation: **potakɨr**
coo *v.*: **por**
cook *v.*: **ambwamkɨ**
    apu
copulate: **ndɨrɨrɨ-(p/w)-arkɨ**
corner of eye: **ŋagrɨni**
corner *v.*: **weX-(p/m)-uŋgu**
corpse: **nɨmbup**
    pisikɨmb
correctly: **tandiw**
count *v.*: **nak**
couple *n.*: **omɨnde-omnɨnde**
cover up *v.*: **kundar**
cover: **pura**
crab: **kosep** (generic)
    kaŋgajiŋ
    ŋarorak
    sasápoke
crack: **ngagwak**
crave *v.*: **potaki**
crawl *v.*: **wepɨkɨ**
    wepokɨ
crazy: **mbábasak**
creek: **eno**
    nuwomb
crest: **tamro** (of cassowary or rooster)
crevice: **ngagwak**

crocodile: **orem**
   perumb orem
crooked: **ŋgado**
   ŋgadogadi
cross *v.*: **osiki**
crosswise: **wapakini**
croton plant: **kamb**
crouch down *v.*: **isisraiki**
crown: **ruk**
   mar
   umb
crumb: **um**
crumple up *v.*: **ruru-(p)-e**
crush *v.*: **ririr**
cry *n.*: **ei**
cry *v.*: **eiarki**
cult house: **oŋgarŋa patir**
   ambagai
cunt: *see* vagina
curse *v.*: **adu**
cut across *v.*: **utak-(p)-oski**
cut *v.*: **katip**
   imin
   iskuo
   trai
   utir-(p)-or
   wuw

D

dance *v.*: **truku**
dawdle *v.*: **kikriki**
day after tomorrow: **tuemb**
day before yesterday: **muŋgit**
day of exchange: **mot**
day: **aro**
deaf: **tamanki**
debris: **moto**
debt: **karam**
decorate: **isiki**
   ndok
decoration: **katam**
   nanjag
   ndok (generic)
   rimb

   tatak
   totrik
deed: **morasi**
deep: **kouwmb**
defeat *v.*: **ŋgadir-(p)-i**
   timbrXoki
defecate *v*: **yiwir ar**
departure: **oŋgar**
descend *v*: **sirki**
descendant: **otan**
   njanimb
desire *n.*: **arei**
   meŋemeŋe
   numbwan
   tete-(p)e
destroy: **mbata**
dew: **matatak**
diarrhea *n.*: **yiwir ariŋ**
die *v.*: **wasowki**
   waswi
diety: **mirip**
dig out *v.*: **ke-(p)-e**
dig *v.*: **werki** (snuffle)
   undiki (for eggs)
   unduku (for eggs)
   wuw (a hole)
   werandru (plant things)
digging stick: **sambap**
directly: **simpakni**
dirt: **kitkit**
   sumbwa
dirty: **komboj**
   ndamir
   uran
disappear *v.*: **kunda**
dish: **kanjir**
   puŋgup
   tawk
dislodge: **wur**
disobey: **utak**
disperse: **ndabaiki**
disturbed: **mbábasak**
dive in: **iroki**
do *v.*: **nir**
dog: **marŋgoram**
   nje
   njeŋa rewi

door: **nek**
double *n*.: **moramori**
　　takrot
down: **ato**
　　sire
dragonfly: **nondadab**
dream *n*.: **tambur**
dream *v*.: **tamburni ta**
drink *v*.: **a**
drizzle *n*.: **tukursim**
drool *n*.: **arit**
drum: **koŋgod** (hourglass drum)
　　rumb (slit-gong drum)
dry *adj*.: **pakas**
dry season: **nuŋgŋa orom**
dry *v*.: **pakas**
dust: **puwai**
dwelling: **taŋgar**

E

eagle: **kakar**
ear: **neke**
　　pap (earwax)
earlobe: **ndrɨg**
earring: **sak**
earthquake: **nekan**
east: **arawer sirŋgar taw**
eat: **a**
eel: **ŋgem**
　　semb
egg white: **mow**
egg yolk: **ikin**
egg: **naŋa** (generic)
　　onaw
　　taŋa
　　yamiɲe
eject *v*: **ru**
elbow: **miŋgip**
　　miŋgipŋa sokop
elf: **apukor**
elves: **apukor**
embarrass: **tɨmbrXokɨ**
ember: **rerem**
embrace *v*.: **sak**
emotion: **imin**

enclosure: **ramaŋ**
enough: **ayáta**
　　nɨpɨs
　　nɨpɨs wákare
envelope: **ndakɨn**
enveloped: **aro**
evening star: **popro**
everyone: **taman**
everything: **taman**
exchange *v*.: **ep**
exclaim: **andruku**
exhaustion: **arimb**
explode: **patorkɨ**
exposed: **mborkɨnɨ**
extinguish: **ko-(p)-o**
extract *v*.: **ke-(p/w)-ekɨ**
　　er
　　wur
eye: **ŋgino**
eyeball: **ŋgino rerem**
eyebrow : **ŋgino mbod**
eyeglasses: **awin nanuk**
eyelid: **ŋginoŋa toto**

F

face: **nanuk**
facing: **rawnɨ**
faint *v*.: **wasowra aikɨ**
falcon: **wiswis**
fall down *v*.: **atɨkɨ**
fall off *v*.: **isiri okɨ**
fall out *v*.: **ke-(p/w)-ekɨ**
false accusation: **suk**
fan *n*.: **apwisom**
fan *v*.: **wiwir**
fart *n*.: **pis** (soundless)
　　orimb (explosive)
fart *v*: **i**
fasten *v*.: **er**
fat: **iapɨr**
father: **omo**
　　sas
fatigue *n*.: **sisiw**
fault *n*.: **morasi**
fear *n*.: **rew**

fear v: **rewki**
feather: **purpur**
feces: **yiwir**
feel v.: **kiraw**
fence: **ramaŋ**
   tiŋ
   yio
fern: **anumb**
   awesak
fetch v.: **k**ᵛ
   tar
fetus: **mbominj**
fiber: **paŋ**
fight v.: **amku**
fight: n. **am**
fill up v.: **war**
   mboripki
fill v.: **iu**
filter v.: **utiki**
fin: **mbodaŋ**
   naniŋ
finger: **ŋgagit** (little)
   ŋgomar oŋgar (index)
   oŋko (thumb)
fingernail: **ndaramŋa ŋgino**
   sikrim
finish v.: **kokot**
   komand
   kroi
   maiki
   wákareki
fire: **otar**
firefly: **ŋgudum**
   waptuŋgro (swarm)
firewood: **taruŋ**
first born: **kokirŋa ror**
   mambirŋa ror
first: **rawni**
   tamriware
fish: **ŋgomar** (generic); *see special section on "Animals, insects, fish and birds"*
flaccid: **kondikki**
   kondikra oki
flash: **mamrarki**
flatten grass: **iskuoki**
   naw o
flattery: **eŋgune eŋgune**

flea: **itum**
flee: **rewki**
flesh: **mow**
   pwap
   toto
float v.: **konenjarki**
   purara oki
floor: **kimitak**
flow: **naŋgatik**
flute: **mokit**
fly n.: **arúmbatak** (generic)
   arúmbatak wasow (blue fly)
   ipipir (fruit fly)
fly v.: **imbiki**
flying fox: **njakep**
   njakep oraw
flying squirrel: **ŋgesiŋe**
fly swatter n: **tandímirit**
foam: **njem**
   tapur
fog: **waw**
fold v.: **adádadi**
   krakri
follow advice v.: **andu**
follow v.: **andu**
fondle: **eŋgeweŋgew**
fontanelle: **wamb**
food: **orákaŋgar**
   tokro
foot: **ndow**
   ndowbwar
   ndowŋa imin (sole)
   ndowŋa ku (heel)
footprint: **ndoŋan nipis**
force n: **naŋgatik**
force v.: **mor-(p)-e**
forehead: **atarum**
foreign: **koret**
forget: **numbwan mbabsakki**
fork: **tapran**
four: **towotowo**
frame: **naŋgir** (of net)
friend: **agídada**
   asapoi
frog: **pasákeke**
frond: **kondew**
   mbaŋaw

ndadum
pandɨm
front: rawnɨ
frying pan: pambran
fuck v.: indɨkɨ
indu
funerary feast: kar
airuramb
fungus: manɨmbomo
nɨmbup
njogrob
tombtomb
funnel: iko
fur: atuŋgor
mbatɨbati
ramborgar
furious: mɨk
fuzz: iruiru
fuzzy: iruiruŋa

G

gall bladder: wuŋa nok
Gapun: Tayap num
gather : andu- (leaf vegetables)
gather together v.: ondar
gecko: agin
tapetak
genitals: iru
kwem
kwem taro
man
nao
neŋgib
ŋgaibo
piɲin
get into: sirki
get stuck: waku
get up: memkɨ
ghost: mambrag
gill: mbodaŋ
ginger pepper: kandapat
top (generic)
ginger root: arei
eŋgin
kaiu

girdle: kapwasak
girlfriend: nireŋgar noŋor
give birth v.: awinnɨ tuwku (humans)
tokɨ (animals)
give: i
glue: niɲir
gnat: ipipir
mamaki
go across: oski
go ahead: rɨpɨkɨ
go ashore: worki
go down v.: arki
aski
sirki
go inside v: arki
arki
go outside v.: atiki
go up v.: wurki
rar
go: okɨ
good sense: misikap
good: eŋgon
émb egon (good morning)
ikur eŋgon (good evening)
ŋgrag eŋgon (good afternoon)
sapki
gossip: ikruk
gradually: neŋginiki neŋginiki
grandfather: neni
grapefruit: pinɨmb
grass knife: sarep
grass skirt: awin gorok
ner
ŋgorok
grass: mombi
nekénduko
nɨmbɨsim
piar
tumbɨgir
ut
grasshopper: njajak
njojok
panap
grassland: nawŋa mbun
naw
grate v.: war
grave: kum

grease: **iapɨr**
grille: **maŋemaŋar**
groin: **anomb**
ground cuscus: **miw**
ground: **numat**
    sumbwa
group: **tambar**
growl *v*.: **murkɨ**
grub: **kɨmɨrɨk**
guard *v*.: **wɨr**
gums: **rewiŋgun**
gun: **mbwajorom**

H

habit: **morasi**
half: **at**
    taw
hammer *v*: **tawai**
hand: **ndaram**
    ndaramŋa adadit
    ndaram bwar
    ndaramŋa imin
handle: **munjar**
    naŋgɨr
    ŋapar
    pom
hang up *v*.: **wawar-(p)-ei**
hang *v*.: **adu**
    wawar-(p)-ei
    wawar-(p)-eikɨ
haphazardly: **sapki(nɨ)**
happen: **atikɨ**
happy *adj*.: **sapki**
hard: **mɨk**
hard-headed: **kokɨrŋan**
hat: **kawt**
    kokɨrat
have sex: **mbidomo**
    okemkɨ
haze: **njim**
he: **ŋɨ**
head hair: **kokɨrŋgrit**
head: **kokɨr**
    kokɨtok

    kokɨrŋgrit
    ŋgino
headrest: **kokɨparaŋ**
healthy: **eŋgon**
heap: **kit**
    pombor (of shit)
    sumbuŋ
hear *v*.: **tar-**
heart: **kir**
hearth: **turoŋa ŋagar**
heavy: **naimb**
heel *n*.: **ndowŋa ku**
help *v*.: **ndabai-(p)-i**
    rarekurkɨ
    rar
her: **ŋgu**
here: **ai**
    ainde
    aŋgo(de)
hermit crab: **pisik**
hers: **ŋgon**
hiccup *n*.: **ndɨdɨk**
hiccup *v*.: **ndɨdɨk**
hide *v*.: **ambu**
high tide: **awin eiwɨr**
hillbilly: **mɨriŋa munje**
him: **ŋɨ**
hips: **ŋgɨdɨk**
his: **ŋan**
hit *v*.: **adu**
    o
    nai-(p)-i
    nɨmaniadi
    nɨmaniadɨkɨ
hold *v*.: **e**
    ser-(p)-e
hole: **ŋgagwak**
    ŋgwab
    muta
home: **taŋgar**
honey: **metawrŋa naŋaŋa awin**
hoof: **mburko**
    sikrim
hook: **pipiŋgabu**
hopscotch: **ekop**
horsefly: **tetei**

hostility: **ondir**
hot: **armbir**
hourglass drum: **koŋgod**
hourglass drum: **oimbatak**
house post: *see special section on 'Parts of house'*
house: **ambagai** (men's house)
    ambagai mbunorŋan (with power)
    kimitak (floor)
    njam (hurriedly assembled)
    oŋgarŋa patir (mens cult house situated in rainforest)
    patirŋa mbun (abandoned, and collapsed)
    tambuno (makeshift for protection from rain)
how many: **ambukrani**
how: **ambukeni**
howl *v*.: **kawrki**
huge: **mir**
hum *v*.: **mundumindiki**
humiliate: **timbrXoki**
hunger: **endekar**
hunting blind : **napo pura**
hurriedly: **areini**
hurry: **katkat nunum**
husband: **munje**
husk: **min turaw**
hygiene: **ndamir**

I

I: **ŋa**
ignite: **rorki**
ignorance *adj*.:**sua**
ignorant: **samba mir**
ignore: **eikuoki utak**
illness: **kandaw**
imitate *v*.: **et-(p)-o**
immature *n*: **eiwireiwir tuwaw**
impregnate: **imin i**

imprint: **nipis**
incredibly: **apro mir**
index finger: **ŋgomar oŋgar**
inexperienced: **taman**
inflate *v*.: **wiwir**
in-law *n*.: **oyeŋg**
insect: *see special section on "Animals, insects, fish and birds"*
inside: **aro iminni**
insult *n*.: **perei**
insult *v*.: **perei**
intense : **mik**
intension: **numbwan**
intercourse: **mbidomo**
intertwine *v*.: **erki woiki**
intestine: **imikato miɲanɲa kup noŋorŋa kup**
intoxicate: **adu**
itch *n*.: **meŋemeŋe**
itch *v*.: **tiriki**

J

jaw: **ŋgakre**
jealous *v*.: **awa-(p/w)-ar mwanambri**
jealousy: **mwanambrirgar morasi**
jellyfish: **kandiwara**
join *v*.: **tiriri-(p/w)-ar**
joint: **adadit**
    rorŋa niŋg (back leg of pig)
    ton (connects two sections of bamboo)
jump up *v*.: **piŋki**
jump *v*: **piŋra oki**
just: **sapki(ni)**

K

kick *v*.: **ndowni o rir-(p)-orki**
kidney: **moŋapat**
kiss *v*.: **sak**

kissing sound *v*: **mɨnjurupkɨ**
kissing sound: **mɨnjurup**
knecklace: **ep**
knee cap: **mɨŋɨpŋa sokop**
knee: **mɨŋɨp**
kneel: **adu**
knife: **kurom**
    mbwantaw
    mɨŋ
    pom
    sarep
    ta
knock *v*.: **mbaŋ**
knot *n*.: **mot**
knot *v*.: **ŋgɨtɨ-(p/w)-ar**
know: **kɨraw**
knowledge: **mɨsɨkap**

L

lack *v*.: **atɨkɨ**
ladder: **nek**
    pundɨdɨp
    tɨndra
ladle: **kukutawaŋ**
lake: **mɨnuomb**
landing place for canoes: **kaɨkro**
language: **mer**
lap: **nɨkɨr**
large: **mɨr**
    pwap
    suman
larva: **kɨmɨrɨk**
    komɨ
    urukuruk
later: **nunuk**
laugh *v*: **ɨr**
    adu
    ɨrkɨ
laughter: **ɨro**
lay out *v*.: **tumbu**
laziness: **sɨsɨw**
lead *v*.: **rɨpɨkɨ**
leaf spine: **mbwag**
leaf: **mayar**

leaf: **ŋgɨmraw** (edible)
    papakndam
    sokoɨ (tobacco)
lean down *v*.: **tɨmbrɨo**
leave behind: *v*.: **ore-(p)-e**
leech: **mbɨmaŋ**
left: **ŋgamgɨt**
leg: **akan**
    ndow
    mburkow
lemon : **pɨnɨmb**
lemon grass: **nɨmbɨsɨm**
let go *v*.: **ore-(p)-e**
lethargic *v*: **sɨsɨwokɨ**
lethargy: **kumb**
lick: **mamba**
    mambadɨkɨ
lie *n*.: **suk**
    takwat
    waɨ
lie *v*.: **takwat**
    waɨŋgrɨkɨ
lift up *v*.: **wur-(p)-o**
    wure
light *n*: **aro**
light *v*.: **ror**
lightening *n*: **mamraɨ**
    otɨŋgar
lightening *v*.: **mamraɨkɨ**
    urerkɨ
like: **mbɨknɨ**
    nɨme
    nɨŋan
lime (for chewing betel nut): **aɨr**
line: **yɨr**
lip: **ndadɨbwaŋ**
listen *v*.: **tar**
little: **mokop**
liver : **wu**
lizard: *see special section on "Animals, insects, fish and birds"*
lobe: **ndrɨg**
lobster: **sasu**
lodge *v*.: **wak-(p)-ekɨ**
log: **nɨmbup** (rotten)
loincloth: **sɨw**
long: **kemem**

look after: **krar**
look v.: **ŋgigregoki**
  rarki
  rar
look for v.: **amai-(p)-i**
loosen v.: **utakatiki**
lose grip v.: **turkopki**
lose v.: **atiki**
  óiraraoki
louse: **kikriki**
  pakind
low tide v: **tawki**
lower intestine: **noŋorŋa kup**
lumpy: **ndidikdidik**
lung: **popro**

M

machete: **pitiŋar**
maggot: **símbu**
make plans to kill someone: **mbororki**
make v.: **nir**
Malay apple tree: **puŋun**
  toŋgodip
male: **miŋan**
man: **munje**
mango: **oike**
mangrove swamp: **nimar**
  kindip
many: **sami**
mark v.: **rambu**
married couple: **ominde-omninde**
marry: **ar**
marsupial pouch: **ŋgwar**
maternal uncle: **atawo**
  wow
maternity house: **awin(ni) tuwŋgar patir**
mature: **kapar**
  kowot
  ponjame
me: **ŋa**
meat: **mborsip** (pig)
  minj (breadfruit)
  mis
  mow (coconut)

potak (wild animal)
  sip
meeting: **korareŋgar**
  mot
men's house: **ambagai**
  oŋgarŋa patir
  pik
menstruate: **karep**
  simberki
mess up v.: **isiki**
middle: **orom**
Milky Way: **wagurmos**
millipede: **kakámatik**
mine: **ŋaŋan**
mirror: **awin nanuk**
mislead v.: **mbábasakki**
misstep v.: **turkopki**
miss v.: **anda-(p/w)-oki**
  kaind-(p)-e
  ŋgadir-(p)-i (pass by)
  punatki
  wur-(p)-eki
  wure
misuse v.: **mbábasaki**
mite: **kandap**
molar: **sambap**
money: **marŋgoram** (dog teeth)
  moŋar krimb
moon: **karep**
morning star: **ŋgoijam**
morning: **emb**
mortar: **kokirparaŋ**
mosquito: *see special section on Animals, Insects, Fish and Birds*
moth: **mumuk**
mother: **ama**
mountain: **tumb**
mourn: **punatki**
mouse: **njip**
mouth: **sik**
mud: **kitkit**
  mbin
  sumbwa
murder: **kwai**
murmur v.: **minminki**
muscle: **mintumb** (chest)
  warmis (thigh)

English-Tayap finder list — **469**

mushroom: **moimbɨr**
  oŋgisu
  tambawa
  tawaromo
mushroom: **moimbɨr**
  tambawa
muzzle: **pinumb**

N

nail: **tatar**
naked: **kandam sinder**
name *n.*: **nomb**
name *v.*: **wur**
narrate *v.*: **tɨk ŋgur**
narrative: **tɨk**
narrow *adj.*: **wekwareŋgar**
nearby: **minjikan**
neck: **potak**
necklace: **ep**
  rɨmb
needle: **pandiŋ**
  sind
  tɨmɨr
  tɨmɨrbɨm
nest: **taŋgar**
  yamiɲe tumb
net *n.*: **korot**
  naŋgir
  net *v.*: **warkɨ**
netbag: **mambakɨr**
never mind: **ayáta**
new: **iro**
newborn *n.*: **karar ror**
  mbomɨnj
night: **ikur**
  makarkɨ
nipple: **minɲa iru**
  ŋgatma min
no: **wákare**
noise: **mɨriŋ**
  pakras
  pɨndiŋ
noodle: **kekékato**
noose: **saŋgriwat**
nose: **raw**

now: **ene**
nowadays: **ene**
nut: **kaiŋ**
  ndekik
  ŋgamamber
  ŋgawro
  wamb

O

oar: **inaŋg**
obscenity: **wekok**
obstructed *v.*: **oski**
ocean: **mara**
of course: **kapambínana**
  ŋguméŋgi
old: **kowot**
  rowe
on top: **mbokaknɨ**
  wo
one : **nambar**
  mbatep
oneself: **neker**
  ŋano
  ŋanokɨ
open *v.*: **kra**
  pwak-(p)-o
  siŋ
  tapraw
opening: **tutuw**
oppose *v.*: **perei**
opposite side: **osi**
organize *v.*: **simb**
orgasm *n.*: **meɲemeɲe**
  ponjame
ours: **yimen**
out of wedlock: **nder**
outside: **ato**

P

package *n.*: **ndakin**
package *v.*: **ndakin-(p)-o**
pain *n.*: **mbɨd**
pain *v.*: **mbɨdkɨ**

paint v.: **rambu**
palm of hand: **ndaramŋa imin**
palm frond: **kondew**
    mbaŋaw
    pandim
pancake: **momorik**
    tamwai
pancreas: **minjinai**
pandanus: **tar**
papaya: **eŋginmandama batambur**
parrot: **karar**
part n.: **at**
    taw
pass by v.: **ŋgadir-(p)-i**
patterned: **titimb**
peak: **tumb(ŋa) bwar**
peek: **eitatiki**
peel n.: **ndadab**
    ŋakraw
peel v.: **ei**
    njaw-(p)-o
    ŋakraw-(p)-o
penis: **Kokraŋa kup**
    kondikra oki
    kóndrik
    kwem
    momor
    mond
    mondki
    nao
    ŋaweiw
    piŋin
    sambap
    temiŋg
    tutuw
perceive v.: **kiraw**
persuasion: **eŋgune eŋgune**
phlem: **muk**
pierce v.: **ondir**
    papku
    rowand-(p/w)-ar
pig: **agráŋkar** (skinny)
    akan (front leg)
    amb (place where they wallow)
    ambnor (jowls)
    ikower-(p)-or- (sound they make when panicked)
    kaŋgajiŋ (tusks)
    kurom(back leg)
    kwem taro (genitals)
    mbor (pig)
    mborabaw (wallow)
    mbor mir (male)
    mbor onko (young, fertile, female)
    mborsip (meat)
    mbwar (fat)
    murki (growl)
    nimbija (skinny)
    ŋaibo (skin around jawbone)
    ŋamambat (cut of meat)
    ŋatnimŋa pupur (back bristles)
    ojirror (small pig)
    osiŋgir (tusks)
    ponjame (maturity)
    sip (meat)
    werki (snuffle)
pile: **kit**
    sumbuŋ
pillow: **kokiparaŋ**
    tep
pincers: **kaŋgajiŋ**
pine tree: **mbainonoŋ**
pipe : **kumundat**
    pundidip
place: **yaw**
placenta: **aiawaŋg**
    mambakir
plant v.: **tu-(p)-o**
    werandru
plant n.: **amakato**
    ariŋgadew
    amakato
    isirai
    kamb
    njalat
    ŋat
    ŋgib
    ŋgop
    ŋgurub
    sambi
    sesu
    tit
    tombtomb
    yamiŋe tumb

plate: **paru** (traditional wooden) **tawk**
platform: **tambrak**
play v.: **emrarki**
pleased v.: **siŋki**
Pleiades: **mbiruŋa kit** **ŋgudumŋa kit**
pluck v.: **ruŋgu**
plunge v.: **mbar**
point v.: **munji**
poison: **ndumdum**
poor thing: **apran** **njakep ror** **ŋanokeya** **ondɨr ror**
pork: **mborsip** **ŋagobit** **ŋamambat**
portion v.: **nɨŋgar**
possessions: **koŋgon**
possum: **enamb** **warniŋ** (anal glands)
pot: **oŋgab** (made of clay) **soworoŋgab**
pouch: **mbubuk** **ŋgwar** (marsupial)
pour v.: **worera okɨ**
power: **mbunor**
powerless: **sua**
praying mantis: **ŋgat**
pregnancy: **imin**
prevent v.: **roŋgur**
previous: **rawnɨ**
previously: **rɨpɨm**
prick: *see* penis
promiscuous: **nder okemkɨ**
puberty: **ponjame**
pubic hair: **anombŋa pupur** **sonai**
pull out v.: **ke-(p)-e** **ke-(p/w)-e** **wer**
pull v.: **aŋgu**
pummel v.: **adádadɨ**
pump v.: **andugur** **aŋ**

pumpkin: **waru**
purposeless: **sapki(nɨ)**
pus: **ŋgido** (from eyes) **pisimb**
push v.: **utak** **utaXru**
put v.: **ko-(p)-o** (put out) **moramorik** (buds) **ŋgur** (generic) **tumbu** (put down) **waksirki** (put on) **wapaki-(p/w)-arkru** (put across) **war**(inside) **war** (put inside) **waraX** (inside) **wi-(p/w)-o** (put above) **wis** (put down) **wirar** (put inside) **wor** (put aground) **wor**(aground)
python: **pake**

Q

question: **kotarŋgar**
quickly: **areinɨ** **katkat**
quietly: **arɨutanɨ** **tower**
quill: **mbwag** **sind**

R

race v.: **pereipereiki-**
rain storm: **kambromtukur**
rain: **matatak** **tukur**
rainbow: **mamar**
rainclouds: **akɨjim**
rainforest: **mbada** **mɨri**
raise up: **mbababin**
rash: **moprɨndag**

rat: **kokosik**
   mangim
   ŋabugar
rattan: **karat**
   katom
   oimbatak
raw: **andŋan**
   kikak
ready *v.*: **orai**
really: **ɲayar**
recently: **muŋgit**
recognize *v.*: **kiraw**
reconsider *v.*: **urek-(p)-e**
reed: **sura**
reflection: **awin nanuk**
refuse *v.*: **masipkaki**
   mnda
remain: **arki**
remains: **mbun**
remove *v.*: **is** (clothing)
   wer (pull out)
   wur (extract)
   ke-(p/w)-e (extract)
   nja-(p)-o (spine from tobacco leaf)
   roŋur (yams)
   sambap (husk)
   tur (remove husk)
request *v.*: **ŋodir**
resist *v.*: **masipkaki**
resistant: **kawrik**
respond *v.*: **ep**
   sik ep
response: **ep**
rest *v.*: **purki**
restrain *v.*: **timbraXoki**
return *n.*: **epiŋgar**
rib: **ndegib**
right hand side: **akan eŋgonŋa taw**
right hand: **akan eŋgon**
right leg: **ndow eŋgon**
right(direction): **eŋgon**
ring: **kiŋ**
   ɲawmb
   ɲawmbi
ripe: **prik**
rise *v.*: **wiki**
river: **ndirmar**

riverbank: **mbag**
rivulet: **mbatim**
road: **nder**
roll *v.*: **ndederki**
   riri
   woi
roll around *v.*: **pwiki**
roll fibers: **ir**
roll up *v.*: **woi**
roof *v.*: **andu**
roof shingle: **ndagro**
rooster: **tamro** (crest)
   kokoaraw
root: **itaw**
rot *v.*: **eriŋeriŋki**
   mburararaki
   pisimbki-
rotten: **nimbup** (tree or log)
round *adj.*: **ororŋgar**
row *v.*: **markiya oki**
rub *v.*: **kikri-(p/w)-e**
   isiki
   is
   tombtomb
rubbish: **pinpin**
ruin *v.*: **mbata**
run out: **maiki**
   wákareki
run *v.*: **nunumoki**
runny: **awin awin**

S

sadness: **naimb**
sago flour: **muna**
   muna kokir
   munakatar
sago frond: **kondew**
sago grubs: **kimirik**
   komi
sago jelly: **kopikɲa mum**
   mum
sago palm sheaths: **kondew**
sago palm: *see special section on "Words pertaining to sago processing"*

sago pancake: **momorɨk**
    paŋgɨp
    tamwai
    tamwaiɲat
sago swamp: **wai**
sago: *see special section on "Words pertaining to sago processing"*
salt: **kawat**
saltwater shell: **mborgi**
sand: **sumbwa kapɨr**
sap: **nɨɲɨr**
sapling: **ŋgɨb**
    titi
say *v*.: **nam**
scale: **turuw**
scar: **ndɨdɨk**
scorch *v*.: **mbabuŋkɨ**
scorpion: **katáwa**
scrape off *v*.: **pɨŋgrɨm**
scrape *v*.: **war**
    e
scratch *v*.: **tu**
scrotum: **kondɨŋ**
    ton
search for *v*.: **amai-(p)-i**
secret talk: **kɨrat** (tobacco)
    sumbwa (sago flour)
    tatikem (betel nut)
secretion: **ŋgido** (from eyes)
see *v*.: **anda-(p/w)-o** (not see something or someone)
    rar-
seed: **iru**
    mbatembatep
    mot (breadfruit)
    piɲin
    taŋa
seedling: **andi**
    indub
    mokɨr
    munjesik
    oraw
send: **mbus-(p)-i**
Sepik river: **ndirmar**
septum: **rawɲa sokop**
serious *v*.: **rawmɨtkɨ**
settle *v*.: **simb**

sew: **sisir**
sexual desire: **meŋemeŋe**
shaft: **marŋgop** (oar)
    uretikimb (spearshaft)
shake *v*.: **ndaw**
    wakwikkɨ
    utukutuk
shake hands: **ndaram**
shake water off like a do *v*.: **urar**
shallow: **mbokaknɨ**
    pwai
shame *v*.: **maikar**
shap needle: **tɨmɨr**
shark: **koŋganase**
sharp: **mɨk**
sharpen *v*.: **rur**
    tu
shave *v*.: **ar**
    mbwantaw (razor)
    njaw-(p)-o
she: **ŋgu**
sheath: **kondew**
    mbubuk
    ndadum
shed *v*.: **is**
shelf: **tambrak**
    tombet
shell: **mborgi**
    pomiŋg
    tawk (coconut)
shield *v*.: **waramkɨ**
shield: **waram**
shin: **inaŋg**
shit: **yɨwɨr**
shiver *v*.: **arkar-(p)-ekɨ**
    mamrarara okɨ
shiver: **mamrarara okɨ**
shoe: **ndow**
shoot *n*.: **indub**
    mbubow
    tɨt
    titi
shoot *v*.: **mbwajorom** (gun)
    o
    ondir
    rɨr-(p)-or
shooting star: **momorɨk**

short: **kitiŋiŋ**
shortness of breath: **tokro**
shoulder: **tumbur**
shout *n*.: **ŋgar**
shout *v*.: **nam**
    ŋgar
show *v*.: **mamanj-(p)-i**
shrimp: **sasu**
shut up *v*.: **towerki**
sick of: **mnda**
side: **ndegib**
    ŋgagar
    taw
signal *n*.: **toremb** (by slit-gong drum)
signal *v*.: **nir**
silly: **mbábasak**
similar: **mbikni**
sing *v*.: **poror**
singe *v*.: **ainaj-(p)-e**
sip *n*.: **taw**
sit *v*.: **tutuku**
skill: **yam**
skin *n*.: **air** (white, unhealthy skin)
    siw (strips of animal skin)
    toto
skin *v*.: **ei**
    wetiki
skink: **mbutak**
skinned: **pwap**
skinny: **agraŋkar**
    nimbija
    niŋ sinder
skull: **kokirŋan tawk**
sky: **akin**
slap *v*.: **nimaniadi**
    nimaniadiki
sleep *v*.: **taki**
sleepiness: **ŋgugrugai**
slide out *v*.: **is**
slingshot: **tamaŋga**
slip *v*.: **sindir**
slit gong drum: **korareŋgar rumb** (summons)
    piriŋ
    rumb (drum)
    temiŋg

tep
toremb
slope: **tokro**
slowly: **ariutaki**
    meŋgini
    neŋginiki neŋginiki
slurp: **mbirupa**
smack *v*.: **wakai-(p)-i**
small intestine: **miɲanna kup**
small talk: **potakir**
smear *v*.: **undiki**
smell *n*.: **ruk**
smell *v*.: **rukana tar**
smoke *n*.: **ŋguwur**
smoke *v*.: **a**
    ruwond-(p)-i
smooth out *v*.: **simb**
snail: **pomiŋgsua**
snake: *see special section on 'Animals, insects, fish and birds'*
snap fingers *v*.: **adu**
snore *v*.: **ŋgrukki**
snot: **muk**
    niŋgir
snout: **pinumb**
snuffle *v*.: **werki**
socket: **wormbit**
soft: **pisaipisai**
soften: **kondidikra oki**
soiled: **ndamir**
sorcerer: **isuk werŋgar munje**
    poisirɲa munje
    wiswis
sorcery: **aŋgwar**
    isuk
    isuk werŋgar
    mayor
    nkirkir
    poisir
sore: **ŋgadan**
    piɲin
sorrow : **naimb**
soup pot: **soworoŋgab**
soup: **ŋgoriw**
    wawan
speak *v*.: **minmiŋki** (indistinctly)
    namki

spear *n.*: **maies**
   marŋgop
   mokwa
   yir
spear *v.*: **o**
spearshaft: **akok**
spearthrower: **ariw**
speech: **nam**
speed: **ŋguruŋ**
spider: **tomiktomik**
spike: **atim**
spill *v.*: **worer**
spine: **sind**
   tat
   orwo
spirit beings: **emári**
   kandap
   mambrag
   mbunor
spit *v.*: **njem ru**
   njemni andu
spittle: **arit**
   njem
spleen: **eiwa**
splinter: **tat**
spouse: **omin**
spread out *v.*: **tumbu**
spread *v.*: **oski**
sprinkle *v.*: **risriski**
sprout *v.*: **pwar**
sputter: **mbiodki**
squeeze out *v.*: **andugur**
stand *v.*: **mbababi**
   mbar
   muŋguku
star: **ŋgudum**
   ŋgoijam
   popro
start (as in 'startle'): **riwind**
startle : **riwindra aiki**
stay awake *v.*: **tombirki**
stay *v.*: **arki**
steal *v.*: **ndagúni tar**
steam: **mbin**
step on *v.*: **andei-(p)-e**
step on *v.*: **tik**
stick for beating slit-gong drum: **temiŋg**

stick out tongue: **nirki**
stick to: **wawku**
stick: **mbir**
   nimir
   nimɲat
   sambap
   temiŋg
sticky: **niɲirɲan**
still born: **mbominj**
still: **reki**
sting *v.*: **ti-(p/w)-ar**
stingray: **mandamandap**
   nakanaka
stir *v.*: **ndaw**
   oror
stomach: **endekarŋa imin**
   imin
   mburuw
stone axe: **mindia**
stone: **moŋapat**
   njiɲai
   ŋawmbi
stone-faced *v.*: **rawmitki**
stop it: **ayáta**
storm: **kambromtukur**
story *n.*: **tik**
straight: **simpakni**
straighten *v.*: **simpak**
strain *v.*: **wur**
strangle: **ŋgit-(p)-o**
streaky: **kopik**
strength: **niŋg**
   pawrik
   ponjame
stretch *v.*:
   wekaŋg-(p)-or
string together *v.*: **wit-(p)-i**
strip away *v.*: **siŋ**
strongheaded: **kokitok kawrik**
stubbornness: **kokirɲan**
stump: **kitip**
stupid: **eiwireiwir**
   samba mir
   sua
stupor: **sisiw**
suck *v.*: **mbirupa**
sufficient: **nipis**

sugarcane: **yar**
sun: **arawer**
sunlight: **arawerŋa aro**
support v.: **rarekurki**
suppress v.: **tik**
surface n.: **mbokakni**
    mbwar
surround v.: **oror**
swallow v.: **malit mosop**
    motikXoki
swamp: **nimar**
    timbar
    wai (sago swamp)
swarm: **waptuŋgro** (fireflies)
swear v: **wekokni adu**
sweat: **tutuk**
sweep v.: **woi**
    mburai
    mburai-(p)-i
sweet potato: **prerikin**
sweetness: **ŋgow**
swim: **ndarar**

T

table: **tambrak**
tadpole: **mbokokir**
tail: **mipat**
    ŋgagon
talk n.: **aroŋa nam** (unexpressed talk)
    atoŋa nam (out in the open talk)
    kaiknumbŋa nam (talk that hides its true meaning)
    potakir (small talk)
    wai (concealed talk)
talk v.: **nekeni warakki** (talk on a mobile phone)
    namki-
    waiŋgriki
    warakki
tantrum n.: **keŋgeŋ**
tantrum v.: **keŋgeŋki**
taro: **manduwar**
    nom
    pendo
    watakep
taste n.: **ŋgow**
taste v.: **kiraw**
tattered: **pirimat**
tattoo: **titimb**
teach v.: **irar**
team: **tambar**
tear v.: **kra**
    krakri
teeth: **njeŋa rewi** (dog teeth)
    rewi
termite: **agu**
    kamus
termite hill: **koaw**
termite mound: **kamus**
    kwaw
test v.: **towoi**
testicle: **momor**
    ŋgaweiw
    poŋgrom
    simbu
that's right: **ore**
theirs: **ŋgan**
them: **ŋgi**
then: **ŋgo** (in that case)
there: **ainde**
    aninde
    anininde
    aŋgo(de)
    aŋgi(de)
    aŋgu(de)
therefore: **ŋginana**
    ŋgire
these/those: **aŋgeb**
they: **ŋgi**
thick: **tumb**
thief: **ndagurgar munje/noŋor**
thigh: **tataimaŋg**
    warmis
thigh: **war**
thighbone: **kurom** (cassowary)
thing: **orak**
think v.: **namki**
    numbwan i
thirsty: **awin potaki**

thought: **numbwan**
thread: **merom**
    pɨŋ
threatening action *v*.: **wai-(p)-e**
three: **manaw**
throat: **potak**
throb *v*.: **piokpiokkɨ**
throb without pain: **mbiodkɨ**
throw away *v*.: **pɨnjɨrip**
    wos-(p)-i
throw *v*.: **aŋgurak**
    arɨw (spear thrower)
    rɨr-(p)-or (a spear)
    ru
thumb : **ndaramŋa oŋko**
thump *v*.: **tawai**
thunder: **aruat**
thus: **nɨme**
    nande(n)
thusly: **aike**
tickle *v*.: **kɨkri-(p/w)-e**
tide: **awinŋa naŋgatik**
tie *v*.: **andugur**
    er
    isuk
    mɨŋ
    ŋgit-(p)-o
    ŋgiti-(p/w)-ar-
    papakndam
    rup
tighten *v*.: **nɨmnɨmkɨ**
time: **orom**
tip *n*.: **iru**
    ŋgino
    tit
tire *v*.: **sisiwokɨ**
tired: **mnda**
tobacco: **sokoi**
    kirat
today: **ene**
toe: **mburko**
    ndowŋa gagit
    ndowŋa oŋko
    sikrim
together: **ndakop**
toilet: **mbadaŋa patɨr**

Tok Pisin: **eŋgin mer**
tomorrow: **epi**
tongs: **kinda**
tongue: **malɨt**
too: **tɨ**
tooth: **rewi**
top *n*.: **kik**
    koi
torch: **papembɨr**
tough: **kawrɨk**
traditional knowledge: **misikap**
trample *v*.: **naw o**
    naw okɨ
translate *v*.: **urek-(p)-e**
trap: **saŋgrɨwat**
tree bark: **aikesim**
    atunuŋg
    ei
    induw
    karam
    kɨmɨtak
    kinj
    mayor
    mbaŋaw
    mis
    mwarmbwam
    ndadab
    njalat
    noni
    ombuto
    pandɨm
    perumb
    suawuk
    waram taw
    wind
    yimbram
tree kangaroo: **kanuŋg**
tree pod: **kaiŋ**
    kowir
tree: **areŋg**
    asáŋgo
    atunuŋg
    awin
    itaw
    kandum
    karam

karep
kɨndɨp
kɨnj
kɨtɨp
koi
kondew
kotrɨŋ
kowe
maior
mayor
mbaŋaw
mberɨg
mbɨj
mbwar
ndabe
ndaburak
ndadab
ndekɨk
nɨm (generic)
nɨmbup
nɨr
njegagɨp
nuruw
ŋgɨmraw
ŋgoriŋsua
ombuto
orom
pandɨm
pap
pendimor
ruk
sanamb
send
serek
suawuk
tar
tokro
tomɨr
toŋgodɨp
wamb
wind
yɨt
tremor v.: **wakwɨkkɨ**
trip v.: **adɨokɨ**
truly: **ŋayar**
    ŋayor

try v.: **towoi**
tuck v.: **wa-(p/w)-ar**
turn back v.: **waruk-(p)-ekɨ**
turn upside down: **waksɨrki**
turn v.: **urek-(p)-e**
turtle: **pawp**
tusk: **kaŋgajɨŋ**
    osɨŋgir
twin n.: **moramori**
    takrot
twist v.: **irik-(p)-e**
    ŋgadogadi
two: **sene**

U

umbilical cord: **imin sukumŋa grɨp**
uncle: **atawo**
    wow
unclean: **ndamɨr**
unconcealed: **mborkini**
uncooked: **kikak**
under: **kandaŋnɨ**
    sire
underneath: **imɨnnɨ**
underside: **sek**
uneducated: **mɨrɨŋa munje**
unexpected adj: **sinder**
unit: **mbatep**
unripe: **eiwɨr**
    mandig
unskilled: **sua**
untie: **prak**
up: **wurɨ**
upper back: **ŋgamamb**
urethra: **iru**
    kewmŋa iru
    kwemŋa tutuw
    manɨŋg
    piɲin
urinate: **nok ar**
urine: **nok**
us: **yɨm**
useless: **sua**

uterus: **mambakɨr**
uvula: **malɨt mosop**

V

vagina: **eporaŋ**
  man
  mbominj
  ndabe
  ŋgado
  ŋgaibo
  ŋgwab
  nao
  piɲin
  oyaŋ
  sambaŋa kandaw
  sonai
  warnɨŋ
  yit
vaginal fistula: **tamro**
vegetable: **andu** (gather)
  njapar
  ŋgat
  saim (basket for carrying)
  toromb (generic)
vein: **itaw**
    sɨmbu
veranda: **pɨk**
village: **Emuto**
  Indam
  Kambin
  Koporot
  Mambokor
  Merew
  Moip
  Moreŋ
  num
  Ombági
  Potow
  Soŋgodo
vine: **kandap oŋgab**
  maiɲye
  makemaka
  mambragegak
  muɲap

  ŋgakrawmunjik
  orŋarak
vomit *n*.: **kambwan**
vomit *v*.: **kambwan ambu-**
vulgar language: **eporaŋ**
  eriŋeriŋkɨ
  kondikra okɨ
  kwem
  man
  mbominj
  nao
  neŋgib
  ŋgado
  ŋgaibo
  ŋgwab
  oyaŋ
  patorki
  eikɨ
  wetɨkɨ
  piɲin
  sambaŋa njem
  sonai
  tutuw
  warnɨŋ
  yit
vulva: **ŋgado**
  man taw
  manŋa nao

W

waistbelt: **apɨrɨt**
  endo
wait *v*.: **aru-(p)-oi**
  aru-(p)-okɨ
wake someone *v*.: **and-(p)-o**
walk around *v*.: **ikruk**
  waikɨ
walking stick: **nekan**
wall: **kɨndɨt**
  tandaŋ
wallow *n*: **amb** (where pigs wallow)
wank: **eikɨ**
  wetɨkɨ

want *v.*: **arei**
    tete-(p)e
warp *v.*: **wupitapikɨ**
wart: **nɨm**
wash *v.*: **pɨt**
    tuw
    tuwku
wash sago *v.*: **eiwkɨ**
wasp: **kɨkri**
watch *n.*: **wɨr**
watch out: **numbwan rekɨ**
water deity: **emári**
    mɨnuomb
water: **awin**
    awin pomiŋ (energized by the spirits of the dead)
wattle: **tamroŋa kup**
wave away: **emb**
wave on sea: **kuŋgun**
way of doing things: **morasi**
we: **yim**
wear *v*: **wɨ-(p/w)-o**
well *adv.*: **tandiw**
well for drawing water: **awin kapur**
west: **arawer sɨrŋgar taw**
wet *adj.*: **njawap**
wet *v.*: **njawapkɨ**
what: **ambin**
    ambukŋa nanunkŋa (what does it look like?)
    ambukŋa tɨtɨmbŋa (what color?)
when: **ana sokop**
where: **ana(knɨ)**
which: **ambukŋa**
whisper *n.*: **namasapi**
whisper *v.*: **namasapikɨ**
whistle *n.*: **mokwa**
    powow
whistle *v.*: **mokwa nir**
white hair: **ŋgomkokɨrŋa**
white man: **eŋgin munje**
white people: **embátoto**
    eŋgin
white: **puwas**
who: **ani**

whose: **animat**
why: **ambin ana**
wide: **tapraw**
widen *v.*: **tapraw**
wild ball: **tamro**
willingfulness: **kokɨr**
wind: **awar**
    mbankap
    mbunim
    ŋgamai
    pora
windpipe: **ŋgar orom**
wing: **arɨt**
wink *v.*: **ŋgino**
    tɨk
wire: **ambrɨm**
    numun
    tɨmɨr
wisdom: **misikap**
with: **anire**
wolf whistle: **powow**
woman: **noŋor**
wood louse: **tɨtɨpreŋ**
wood: **mbɨr**
    otar kut
work *n.*: **pruk**
work *v.*: **prukkɨ**
worm: **kekékato**
worry *n.*: **naimb**
    wureŋgar
worry *v.*: **wur-(p)-ekɨ**
    wure
wrap up *v.*: **ndakɨn-(p)-o**
wring *v.*: **irɨk-(p)-e**
wrinkle *v.*: **minɨmbkɨ**
wrist: **ŋgomar oŋgar**

Y

yam: **amboboaŋ**
    amor
    moŋom
    nono

yawn *v.*: **andadɨkɨ apɨk**
yellow: **kɨkɨuw**
yelp *v.*: **andruku**
yes: **awo**
   ore
yesterday: **ewar**

yet: **ŋgo**
   wakare rekɨ
you: **yu**
you PL: **yum**
young person: **mambɨr**
yours SG: **yuwon**
yours PL: **yumon**

Appendix 1

English translation of Georg Höltker 1938. **Eine fragmentarische Wörterliste der Gapún-Sprache Newguineas.** *Anthropos* 33: 279–82

Translated by Agnes Brandt, edited by D. Kulick

EDITOR'S NOTE:
In his transcriptions of Tayap words, Höltker used "the Anthropos alphabet", which was a catalogue of phonetic symbols employed by German missionaries and anthropologists at the time Höltker was writing. This alphabet is handily summarized in an article by Kirschbaum and von Führer-Haimendorf (1934: I-IV).[1] The symbols have not been used for over 40 years, but with the exception of one symbol – a̧, which denotes what the International Phonetic Alphabet (IPA) would render /ɛ/ – they should be intelligible to anyone familiar with the IPA. The lavish diacritics denote phonetic phenomena such as place of articulation, stress and vowel length.

The numbering of the examples in this translation corresponds to the numbering in the original article.

A fragmentary word list of the Gapún language of New Guinea

In August-September 1937, when I was spending some time with the missionary P. Josef Much, S.V.D., in the village of Wátam, the first coastal village South of the Sepik outlet in New Guinea, in order to collect ethnographic and anthropographic observations, we also had the opportunity to go on a day trip to the village of Gapún. On 6 September, we first travelled in a dugout canoe across the big Wátam lagoon from Wátam to the village of Wánggan (approximately three hours travelling time). Wánggan shares the same language as the villages of Kópar and Síngrin located at the lower Sepik river, a language completely different to the Wátam language. The next morning (7 Sept.), we crossed the lagoon towards the

---

[1] Kirschbaum, Franz J., and Christoph von Führer-Haimendorf 1934. *Anleitung zu ethnographischen und linguistischen Forschungen mit besonderer Berücksichtigung der Verhältnisse auf Neuguinea und den umliegenden Inseln.* Mödling bei Wien: Verlag der internationalen Zeitschrift Anthropos. I-IV.

Note: I gratefully acknowledge the director of the Anthropos Institut, Prof. Dr. Joachim Piepke, for granting me permission to publish a translation of Höltker's article as well as his two photographs of Gapun, and also for kindly providing me with the above text on the Anthropos alphabet.

https://doi.org/10.1515/9781501512209-013

Southern side and went on a good two-hour, rather arduous hike through forest and marshland until we reached Gápun.

Gapún is situated on top of a hill-crest, which on this side rises almost unexpectedly from the low-lying sago marshland up to a height of some 500 m. From the hill-crest the eye has a free view over the lower Sepik lowlands. One can also see the Marienberg [mission] station. According to the official census, Gápun has only 33 inhabitants. The few and poor village houses are randomly scattered across the hill-top, wherever the bare rock offers a couple of square meters of building ground. The building structure, which makes skilful use of the existing rock-formations as "stairs" or "house posts", reminds me of similar conditions in the villages on the island of Ubrúb.

Unfortunately, we only had that one day (7 Sept.) for our Gapún trip, since we wanted to be back in Wánggan by evening. We went to the "spirit cave" famous among all the local natives, which is situated a good one-hour walk Southwest of Gapún. Apparently, no Kanaka [Ed. note: 'no native'] has set foot inside this cave out of fear of the spirits who are supposed to dwell there in snake form. We found a small cave measuring a couple of square metres of ground area and of approximately 1.5m of height. It seems to have been formed by washouts. The walls consist of clay-coloured sedimentary rock. We did not find any traces of artefacts or human settlement. Supposedly, it used to be bigger in the past and it used to have a second opening, as P. F. J. Kirschbaum, S. V. D., told me recently, who years ago also visited the cave, something that all Kanakas still talk about with admiration. Our visit will probably become similarly famous among the natives in the foreseeable future, for even our relatively enlightened black carriers and cook boys did not dare to enter the cave with us.

As the above details imply, P. Much and I unfortunately only had time for a rest of some three hours in the village of Gapún itself. During this rest, we recorded the following word list of the Gapún language with the help of some older men. Consequently, we are not only aware that this list is of fragmentary coverage; we also know that the individual words lack the desired level of certitude. Even though we made every effort to record and write down the data, as any fieldworker knows, speech recordings are hardly ever free from fault at first transcription and unless they are frequently counter-checked at a later point in time. Nevertheless, it appears to me that the publication of this short word list is not without value. According to the natives, the Gapún language is spoken only in Gapún and has no relation whatsoever with other languages. With the necessary reservations, the word list may thus provide comparative linguistics with substantial research material, which may provide some clues, even if only a hint, as to the classification of this language. What is more, it seems unlikely that another researcher will "stumble across" Gapún any time soon, if only because of the small chances of worthwhile academic yields in this small village community, and also because of the inconvenient and arduous route leading to this linguistic island. The publication of the word list at this point and in this form is thus reasonable and justified. The reproduction of the stock of phonemes follows the conventions of the Anthropos Alphabet.

Word list of the Gapún language.

World.

1.	sky	ǰim	3.	moon	karếb
2.	sun	aráve̜ř[2]	4.	star	gudúm

Elements.

5.	fire	otár	13.	northwester	ăvár[3]
6.	firewood	tarúŋ	14.	southeaster	gamaį̯[4]
7.	hearth	tu̱ró̱r	15.	north wind	buním[5]
8.	sea	makás	16.	forest wind	báŋkap
9.	water	avín	17.	cloud	akữn
10.	rain	tukúr	18.	lightning	ure̜ráku[6]
11.	river	nu̜óm	19.	thunder	ărúăt[7]
12.	wind	porá			

Time.

20.	day	aró	23.	yesterday	evár
21.	night	ikúr	24.	tomorrow	epí
22.	today	ĕné			

Numbers.

25.	one	nambár	30.	six	daram-nambar-táu̯ne̜-nambár
26.	two	se̜ná̜			
27.	three	manáu̯	31.	seven	daram-nambar táu̯ne̜-se̜ná̜
28.	four	tovo̱tovó̱			
29.	five	daram-nambár[8]			

---

2 Cf. Nubia language: ra^u, ra^w; Bosngun language: ła̜u̯ .
3 Cf. Nubia-Bosngun: var; Wátam language: o̜ár.
4 Cf. Nubia: gémi; Bosngun: gáme; Wátam: ga̜me̜į̯.
5 Cf. Pidgin: punim; Nubia: bunúm; Wátam: búnim.
6 Verb.
7 Verb.
8 "Hand-one".

32.	eight	*daram-nambar-táu̯nę̄-manáu̯*	35.	eleven	*daram-sę̄ná̜-nambár*
33.	nine	*daram-nambar-táu̯nę̄-tovo̱tóvo*	36.	twenty	*daram-sę̄ná̜-ndo-sę̄ná̜* [10]
34.	ten	*daram-sę̄ná̜* [9]			

Plants.

37.	garden	*mbará*	47.	coconut palm	*pab*
38.	digging stick	*naŋgár*	48.	coconut (ripe)	*ntáu̯*
			49.	coconut (unripe)	*makátok*
39.	fence	*nyo̱r*	50.	banana	*ikı́n*
40.	tree	*ŋa̱m*	51.	yam	*nonór*
41.	trunk	*ŋa̱m-oró̱m*	52.	taro	*măndu̯ár* [11]
42.	root	*ŋa̱m-tomó̱t*	53.	sago palm	*nyam*
43.	branch	*ŋa̱m-ŋgan-du̱kó̱r*			
44.	twig	*ŋa̱m-du̱kor-motšóp*			
45.	leaf	*ŋa̱m-ayár*			
46.	flower	*ŋa̱m-i̱rú*			

Fauna.

54.	pig	*mbo̱r*	60.	kangaroo	*kanúŋ*
55.	boar	*mbo̱r-mŭr*	61.	rat	*kokó̱tsik*
56.	sow	*mbo̱r-ŋoŋgó̱r* [12]	62.	bird	*tam*
57.	dog	*ŋdžar*	63.	cassowary	*ŋgad*
58.	dog tooth	*márŋgor*	64.	crocodile	*orém*
59.	dog's-tooth necklace	*márŋgó̱r-am*	65.	fish	*ŋgo̱már*

Body Parts.

66.	head	*ko̱kḗr*	70.	cheek	*ndabóṙ*
67.	brain	*zikı́n*	71.	scalp hair	*ko̱kḗr-ŋgrι*
68.	forehead	*atárum*	72.	body hair	*pupúr*
69.	temple	*ginómbo̱t*	73.	hair shaft	*káu̱t* [13]

---

9 "Hand-two".
10 "Hand-two-foot-two".
11 Cf. Wátam; *mandún*. – It should be noted that the designation of crop plants etc. remained inconclusive insofar as it could not be determined whether collectives or varieties were given. The Kanakas often distinguish an alarming wealth of individual varieties.
12 "Pig-female".
13 Melanesian loan word; cf. Manam language: *káu̱ta*; Biem language: *káu̱t*; also e.g. in Nubia and Bosngun: *kóu̱t* as loan word.

74.	eye	ŋginó	94.	palm of hand	darăm-imín[14]
75.	eyelid	ŋgino-mbǫ́rt	95.	back of hand	darăm-bǫár̃[15]
76.	eyebrow	ŋgino-mbǫ́rt-pupúr	96.	finger	darăm-sikrím
77.	eyeball	ŋgino-rẹrẽ́m	97.	arm	akán
78.	eyelash	ŋgino-rẹrẽ́m-na-pupúr	98.	elbow	akan-burnăd-tsokǫ́rb
79.	mouth	ⁿsik			
80.	lip	dadẽ́mbo̱aŋ	99.	shoulder	tumbúr
81.	tongue	maríd	100.	foot	ndo
82.	tooth	ndévi	101.	leg	bǫár
83.	throat	garoróp	102.	knee	muŋgíp
84.	chin	ŋgakra̱	103.	lower leg	bǫar-mosǫ́p
85.	neck	potá̆ᵏ	104.	toe	ndo-sikrím
86.	nose	ráuⁿ	105.	chest	nambúr
87.	nasal wing	rau̱-ndër̃ík	106.	breast	min
88.	nasal septum	rau̱-nakúr̃	107.	belly	imín
89.	nostril	rau̱-ŋgǫáb	108.	back	bǫár
90.	ear	nekéi̱	109.	buttocks	kăndám
91.	earhole	nekéi̱-ŋgǫáb			
92.	earwax	nekéi̱-napab			
93.	hand	darắm			

Some Other Words.

110.	man	mundžǫ̱r	119.	spirit house	o̱ŋgár
111.	old man	mundžǫ̱r-ko̱vǫ́t	120.	door	na̱k
112.	boy	mundžǫ̱r-ŋrǫ́rẹ	121.	roof	patër-gámu̱r
113.	woman	no̱ŋgór	122.	saucepan	o̱ŋgáb
114.	old woman	no̱ŋgór-ko̱vǫ́t	123.	wooden bowl	parú
115.	girl	no̱ŋgór-ŋrǫ́rẹ			
116.	child	ŋrǫ́rẹ	124.	limbum container	kăŋgér̃
117.	house	patḗr			
118.	men's house	ămbágeɪ̱	125.	club	tsau̱váraŋga

GEORG HÖLTKER, currently Bogia (New Guinea)

---

[14] "Hand-belly".
[15] Cf. numbers 101, 103, 108.

Appendix 2

Two photographs of Gapun village taken in 1937 by Georg Höltker

Figure 1: Gapun village in 1937, photograph by Georg Höltker.

Note: Many thanks to Harald Grauer for finding these two photographs in Höltker's archived papers and alerting me to their existence.

Figure 2: Gapun village in 1937, photograph by Georg Höltker

References

Note: several of the books/articles listed below refer to discussions found in the dictionary section of this work.

Aikhenvald, Alexandra. 2006 Serial verbs constructions in a typological perspective. In: Aikhenvald, A.Y, and Dixon, R.M.W., (eds.) *Serial verb constructions: A cross-linguistic typology*. Oxford University Press, Oxford, UK., pp. 1–68.

Aikhenvald, Alexandra Y. 2007. Typological distinctions in word-formation. In Timothy Shopen (ed.) *Language typology and syntactic description (2nd ed)*. Vol 3. 1–65. Cambridge: Cambridge University Press.

Aikhenvald, Alexandra Y. 2015. *The art of grammar: A practical guide*. Oxford: Oxford University Press.

Aikhenvald, Alexandra Y., Yuamali Ala Jacklyn, and Luma Laki, Pauline Agnes. 2008. *The Manambu Language of East Sepik, Papua New Guinea*. Oxford: OUP Oxford.

Andrews, Avery D. 2007. Relative clauses. In Timothy Shopen (ed.) *Language typology and syntactic description (2nd ed)*. Vol 2. 206–236. Cambridge: Cambridge University Press.

Beehler, Bruce M., Thane K. Pratt and Dale A. Zimmerman, illustrated by Dale A. Zimmerman and James Coe. 1986. *Birds of New Guinea*. Princeton, N.J.: Princeton University Press.

Bruce, Les. 1984. *The Alamblak language of Papua New Guinea (East Sepik)*. Canberra: Pacific Linguistics C-81.

Dahl, Östen. 2004. *The growth and maintenance of linguistic complexity*. Amsterdam: John Benjamins.

Diessel, Holger. 1999. *Demonstratives: Form, function and grammaticalization*, Amsterdam: John Benjamins Publishing Company.

Dixon, R. M. W. 1994. *Ergativity*. Cambridge: Cambridge University Press.

Dorian, Nancy. 1981. *Language death: The life cycle of a Scottish Gaelic dialect*. Philadelphia: University of Pennsylvania Press.

Evans, Nicholas. 2010. *Dying words: Endangered languages and what they have to tell us*. UK: Wiley-Blackwell.

Flannery, Tim. 1995. *Mammals of New Guinea*. Chatswood, NSW: Reed Books.

Foley, William A. 1986. *The Papuan languages of New Guinea*. Cambridge: Cambridge University Press.

Foley, William A. 1991. *The Yimas language of New Guinea*. Stanford: Stanford University Press.

Foley, William A. 2000. The languages of New Guinea. *Annual Review of Anthropology* Vol 29: 357–404.

Foley, William A. 2018. The languages of the Sepik-Ramu basin and environs. In Bill Palmer (ed.) *The languages and linguistics of the New Guinea area: A comprehensive guide*. 197–431. Berlin: Mouton de Gruyter.

Haspelmath, Martin. 1995. The converb as a cross-linguistically valid category. In Martin Haspelmath and Ekkehard König (eds.). *Converbs in cross-linguistic perspective*. 1–55. Berlin: Mouton de Gruyter.

Haspelmath, Martin. 2016. The serial verb construction: Comparative concept and cross-linguistic generalizations. *Language and Linguistics* 17(3): 291–319.

Henty, E. E., (ed.) 1985. *Handbooks of the flora of Papua New Guinea, Volume II*. Melbourne: Melbourne University Press.

Höltker, Georg. 1938. Eine fragmentarische Wörterliste der Gapún-Sprache Neuguineas. *Anthropos* 33: 279–82.

Krauss, Michael. 1992. The world's languages in crisis. *Language* 68(1): 4–10.

Kulick, Don. 1992. *Language shift and cultural reproduction: Socialization, syncretism and self in a Papua New Guinean village*. Cambridge: Cambridge University Press.

Kulick, Don. 1993. Speaking as a woman: Structure and gender in domestic arguments in a Papua New Guinean village. *Cultural Anthropology* 8(3): 99–129.

Kulick, Don. 2019. *A death in the rainforest: How a language and a way of life came to an end in Papua New Guinea*. New York: Algonquin Books.

Kulick, Don and Christopher Stroud. 1993. The structure of the Taiap (Gapun) language. In Tom Dutton, Malcolm Ross and Darrell Tryon (eds.) *The language game: Papers in memory of Donald. C. Laycock*. 203–226. Canberra: Pacific Linguistics C-110.

Laycock, D.C. 1973. *Sepik languages checklist and preliminary classification*. Canberra: Pacific Linguistics B-25.

Laycock, D. C. 1975. Observations on number systems and semantics. In Stephen A. Wurm (ed.), *New Guinea area languages and language study Vol 1. Papuan languages and the New Guinea linguistic scene*. 21–236. Canberra: Pacific Linguistics C-38.

Laycock, Donald C. and John A. Z'graggen. 1975. The Sepik-Ramu Phylum. In Stephen A. Wurm (ed.), *New Guinea area languages and language Study Vol 1. Papuan languages and the New Guinea linguistic scene*. 731–764. Canberra: Pacific Linguistics C-38.

Longacre, Robert E. 2007. Sentences as combinations of clauses. In Timothy Shopen (ed.) *Language typology and syntactic description (2nd ed)*. Vol 2. 372–420. Cambridge: Cambridge University Press.

McGregor, William B. 2010. Optional ergative case marking systems in a typological-semiotic perspective. *Lingua* 120: 1610–1636.

McWhorter, John. 2001. The world's simplest grammars are creole grammars. *Linguistic Typology* 5: 125–166.

Mihalic, F. 1971. *The Jacaranda dictionary and grammar of Melanesian Pidgin*. Milton, Queensland: The Jacaranda Press.

Nettle, David and Suzanne Romaine. 2001. *Vanishing voices: The extinction of the world's languages*. Oxford: Oxford University Press.

Obata, Kazuko. 2003. *A grammar of Bilua: A Papuan language of the Solomon Islands*. Canberra: Pacific Linguistics 540.

Pawley, Andrew K. 2006. Where have all the verbs gone? Remarks on the organisation of languages with small, closed verb classes. 11th Biennial Rice University Linguistics Symposium, http://www.ruf.rice.edu/~lingsymp/Pawley_paper.pdf.

Payne, Doris and Immanuel Barshi. 1999. External possession: What, where, how, and why. In Payne, Doris and Immanuel Barshi (eds.). *External possession*. Philadelphia: John Benjamins. 3–31.

Reesink, Ger. 1993. "Inner speech" in Papuan languages. *Language and Linguistics in Melanesia*. 42: 217–225.

Reesink, Ger. 2002a. A grammar sketch of Sougb. In Ger Reesink (ed.). *Languages of the eastern Bird's Head*. 181–275. Canberra: Pacific Linguistics 524.

Reesink, Ger. 2002b. Clause-final negation: Structure and interpretation. *Functions of Language* 9(2): 239–268.

Reesink, Ger. 2003. The North Papuan linkage: A hypothesis. Paper for the workshop Pioneers of Island Melanesia, Cambridge, April 2003.

Reesink, Ger. 2014. Topic management and clause combination in the Papuan language Usan. In Rik van Gijn, Dejan Matić, Jeremy Hammond, Saskia van Putten and Ana Vilacy Galucio (eds.). *Information structure and reference tracking in complex sentences*. 231–261. Amsterdam: John Benjamins.

Roberts, John. 1997. Switch reference in Papua New Guinea. In Andrew K. Pawley (ed.) *Papers in Papuan linguistics No. 3*: 101–241. Canberra: Pacific Linguistics A-87.

Ross, Malcolm. 2005. Pronouns as a preliminary diagnostic for grouping Papuan languages. In Andrew Pawley, Robert Attenborough, Jack Golson and Robert Hide (eds.) *Papuan pasts: Cultural, linguistic and biological histories of Papuan-speaking peoples*. 15–65 Canberra: Pacific Linguistics 572.

Sanders, Arden and Joy Sanders. 1980. Defining the centers of the Marienberg language family. *Papers in New Guinea Linguistics 20*. 171–196. Canberra: Pacific Linguistics A-56.

Sankoff, Gillian. 1980. *The social life of language*. Philadelphia: University of Pennsylvania Press.

Schachter, Paul and Timothy Shopen. 2007. Parts-of-speech systems. In Timothy Shopen (ed.) *Language typology and syntactic description (2nd ed)*. Vol 1. 1–60. Cambridge: Cambridge University Press.

Schieffelin, Bambi. 1990. *The give and take of everyday life: Language socialization of Kaluli children*. Cambridge: Cambridge University Press.

Schmidt, Annette. 1985. *Young people's Dyirbal: An example of language death from Australia*. Cambridge: Cambridge University Press.

Spencer, Andrew and Anna R. Luís. 2012. *Clitics: An introduction*. Cambridge: Cambridge University Press.

Suter, Edgar. 2010. The optional ergative in Kâte. In John Bowden, Nikolaus P. Himmelmann and Malcolm Ross (eds). *A journey through Austronesian and Papuan linguistic and cultural space: Papers in honour of Andrew Pawley*. 423–437. Canberra: Pacific Linguistics 615.

Terrill, Angela. 2003. *Lavukaleve*. Berlin: Mouton de Gruyter.

Van Valin, Robert D. Jr. and Randy J. La Polla. 1997. *Syntax: Structure, meaning and function*. Cambridge: Cambridge University Press.

Volker, Craig, Russell Jackson, Susan Baing and Brian Deutrom. 2008. *Oxford Tok Pisin-English dictionary*. Melbourne: Oxford University Press.

de Vries, Laurens. 2005. Towards a typology of tail-head linkage in Papuan languages. *Studies in Language* 29(2): 363–384.

Wilkins, David. 1999. The 1999 demonstrative questionnaire: "This" and "that" in comparative perspective. In D. Wilkins (ed.) *Manual for the 1999 Field Season* 1–24. Nijmegen: Max Planck Institute for Psycholinguistics.10.17617/2.2573775

Womersley, John S. 1978. *Handbooks of the flora of Papua New Guinea, Volume I*. Melbourne: Melbourne University Press.

Wurm, Stephen A. 1982. *Papuan languages of Oceania*. Tübingen: Gunter Narr Verlag

Index

adjectives 25, 66–71, 88, 91, 105, 132–133, 223, 268
Adjora language 52, 336, 348, 349, 450. *See also* Sanae
adverbial subordinate clauses 250, 258–268, 275
adverbs 72–84, 102, 160, 179, 212, 274, 275, 278
Aikhenvald, Alexandra 44, 59, 137, 239
alcohol 15, 287. *See also* brawls, drunken
Andrews, Avery D. 268
Angoram 11, 12
animacy in nouns 53–54, 62, 112, 119, 120, 125
article, indefinite 92–93
aspect 21, 39, 136, 137, 147–149, 150, 156–157
– progressive 40, 176, 177, 213, 242, 245
– habitual 118, 246–249
– in young people's Tayap 324–325, 328
aspiration 27
Austronesian languages 140

Barshi, Immanuel 217
betel nut 11, 12, 17, 92, 203
Bien village 15
Bilua language 60
bivalve shells 12
borrowings. *See* loan words; Kopar language; Tok Pisin
brawls, drunken 3, 15, 16
Bruce, Les 59
Bungain language 9, 10

Catholicism 4, 23, 24
Chambri language 11, 12
clitics 17, 25, 53, 54, 105, 110–111, 121
cognates 12, 13
collapse of morphological classes 21, 93, 176, 188, 197. *See also* young people's Tayap
common nouns 49
complex predicates 26, 136, 229–249, 276, 286
consonant inventory 26, 27

coordination 252, 253–257
cosubordinate constructions 252, 274–280
counterfactual 25, 40, 65–66, 146–149, 244, 262–266
– in young people's Tayap 263, 264

Dahl, Östen 25
deixis 93–96, 235
– in young people's Tayap 62
Diessel, Holger 95
discontinuous subject markers 25, 64, 147, 164, 167, 183. *See also* subjects
ditransitive verbs 64, 218
Dixon, R. M. W. 112
Dorian, Nancy 20

echo pronouns. *See* pronouns
either/or 96–97
elevation 72, 80–84
ergative 25, 84–85, 87, 109–120
– in young people's Tayap 119–120, 326, 327, 328
Evans, Nicholas 4

feminine gender 58–61, 93–94, 112, 156
– in young people's Tayap 120
finite nominalizations 26, 271
Foley, William A. 10, 11, 13, 55, 58, 60, 112, 179, 218
fusional 25, 136
future tense 141–142, 149, 150–153, 164, 171–178, 183–184, 187, 190–191, 212, 249

Gapun (people and place) 1–9, 12, 20, 22–24, 47, 55–56, 61, 81, 118, 156
Gapun sub-phylum level family 10
gender 8–9, 25, 49, 55–62, 69, 85–86, 93, 115, 145, 202–203
– principles of gender assignment 57–60
– in young people's Tayap 61, 62, 317, 326, 327
genericness in nouns 25, 53–55, 112. *See also* animacy

habituals/habituality 26, 107–109, 148–149, 150, 242–249
harangues 16, 60
Haspelmath, Martin 231, 236, 240, 242, 254
Höltker, Georg 8, Appendix 1, Appendix 2

interrogatives. *See* questions

Karawari language 10
Kawri Kruni 14
kinship and kin terms 24, 52–53, 446–447
Kopar language 10, 12, 47, 166, 344, 348, 349. *See also* Wongan village
Krauss, Michael 4
kros (vituperative displays of anger) viii, 91, 118, 336
Kruni Ayarpa, viii 14, 344
Kulick, Don 2, 3, 5, 7, 13, 14, 15, 22, 24, 92, 118, 283

land rights 1, 15, 22
language death 3–7, 21. *See also* young people's Tayap
language shift. *See* young people's Tayap
La Polla, Randy J. 274
Laycock, Donald C. 8, 9, 10, 13, 15, 87
"let's do X", 41, 126, 214, 215
lexical loss 79, 325, 326–335. *See also* young people's Tayap
loan words 12, 52, 98. *See also* Kopar language; Tok Pisin
locational nouns 49–51, 126–127
Longacre, Robert E. 254, 274
Luís, Anna R. 111

malaria 14
Marienberg Hills language family 10
Marienberg mission station 23
masculine gender 25, 58–60, 62, 93–94, 115
maternity huts (language use in) 3, 18, 19
McGregor, William B. 112
McWhorter, John 25
medial-final clauses 26, 239, 252, 254, 258, 274–279
men's house cult 3, 14
Mihalic, Francis 135

Monei Mbanaŋ 14, 15, 215
moribund forms 52, 69, 91, 160, 198, 212, 262, 342. *See also* young people's Tayap
morpho-phonemic rules 41–44, 47
motion verbs 80, 190, 235–238, 274–279, 282, 286
– in young people's Tayap 20, 21, 80, 198–199, 241, 317, 328
multiplicity 252, 282–283
Murik language 10, 11–12

Ndamor Monei viii
near future 77, 149, 153–154, 215
negation 98, 138–144, 147–149, 239, 254, 275, 277, 279, 283
Nettle, Daniel 4, 5, 6
non-final object suffixes 85, 230, 233–234
non-final verbs 85, 230–236
non-future tense 141–142, 148, 154–155
– in young people's Tayap 21, 246
number marking
– in adjectives 25, 68, 69
– in nouns 25, 51–55
– in verbs 25, 57, 85, 183, 191, 201, 203
– in young people's Tayap 326–327

Ŋgero Sair, viii 15, 24

Obata, Kazuko 60
objects 64
– benefactive 217–223
– multiple objects 282–283
– non-final object suffixes 232–234, 340–341
– object suffixes 144–145
opacity in verbal morphology 25, 112, 163–199
optionality of grammatical features. *See* ergative
orthography 27, 35, 37, 45–48

Papua New Guinea 1, 3, 5, 13, 14, 220
Papuan languages, common features in 9, 11, 25, 55, 58, 59, 112, 140, 212, 240, 275, 280
participles 107–109, 138

particularity in gender assignment 57–58, 60, 61, 62
passive active bilinguals 21, 241, 282, 283, 307, 315
passive bilinguals 20, 21
Pawley, Andrew K. 179
Payne, Doris 217
perception, clauses of 26, 117, 130, 270, 271–274
perfect aspect 39, 148, 155–158, 163, 181, 286
peripheral cases/oblique arguments 39, 50, 53, 121–129
– in young people's Tayap 134–135
positional adverbs 80–84
possession 26, 53, 130–134, 217–220
predicate structure 136, 229, 250
prenasalization 26, 28, 35, 43, 46, 47
progressives 26, 43, 147–148, 190, 213, 242–246
– in young people's Tayap 176–177, 328
pronouns 25, 84–86, 105, 107, 145–147
– echo 107
– resumptive 268

quantification. See number marking
questions 96–98

Ramu river 1, 2, 13, 60
Raya Ayarpa viii, 14, 289
reduplication 38, 44, 79, 158–161
Reesink, Ger 37, 55, 59, 94, 140, 179, 212
reflexive/reciprocals 162
relative clauses 21, 26, 105, 106, 130, 250, 268–271, 273, 274
– in young people's Tayap 283
repeated actions 77, 160–161
resumptive pronouns. See pronouns
Roberts, John 240
Romaine, Suzanne 4, 5, 6
Ross, Malcolm 8, 9, 13

sacred flutes 4
sago 448–453
Samek Wanjo viii, 15, 299
Sanae 53, 118, 224, 349. See also Adjora language
Sanders, Arden 10

Sanders, Joy 10
Sankoff, Gillian 1
Schachter, Paul 236
Schieffelin, Bambi 31
Schmidt, Annette 62, 220
schooling 2, 6, 7, 24
semantic reduction 21, 158, 325, 328
semi-speakers 20, 21. See also passive active bilinguals; passive bilinguals
Sepik-Ramu phylum 8
– Lower Sepik language family 10, 11, 12
– Sepik languages 9, 10, 13, 59–60
Sepik river
– and Tayap 1, 2, 10, 25, 81
– geology 8
serial verb constructions 26, 83, 136, 229–240, 269, 275
– in young people's Tayap 241–242
Shopen, Timothy 236
simple sentences 250–252
Singrin village 348. See also Kopar language
social conflict 1, 14, 16
Solomon Islands 60
Sougb language 37
Spencer, Andrew 111
stori (narrative)
– characteristics of 315–316, 322–324
– in young people's Tayap 315–316, 322–324, 327–328
Stroud, Christopher 15, 46
subjects 63–64, 86, 105, 109, 112–119, 136, 137–139, 145–148
– in young people's Tayap 21, 61, 316, 324, 327, 334. See also ergative; discontinuous subject markers
subjunctive 41, 149, 200–212
subordinate constructions 26, 250, 252, 258–265, 280
– in young people's Tayap 21, 283–287
suppletion 25, 52, 56, 69, 138, 177, 248, 265, 266
Suter, Edgar 119
S.V.D. (Societas Verbi Divini) 8
switch-function 239–240

tail-head linkage 250, 280–281
– in young people's Tayap 283

Tayap language
- as an isolate language 10–13
- location 1–2
- number of speakers 1–2
- past linguistic research on 8–13
- villagers' attitudes towards 3, 17–21, 282, 342–345
- villagers' way of writing 45–48
tense 136–138, 147–155
- in young people's Tayap 21, 156–157, 163, 174, 176–177, 180, 188, 197, 323
Terrill, Angela 15
Tok Pisin 1, 3, 4, 7, 17, 19, 45, 48, 53, 264
- linguistic influence on Tayap 21, 87, 134, 135, 157–158, 160, 214, 235, 285, 323–326, 327–335
Torricelli phylum 10
Transitivity 25, 63, 64, 136, 138

Van Valin, Robert D. Jr. 274
verb classes 25, 64, 154, 163–189, 190–195, 337–340
- in young people's Tayap 21, 57, 166–167, 173–176, 180–182, 188–189, 196–199, 324- 325, 327–335
verbalization 62–63, 70, 71
verbless clauses 251–252
Volker, Craig 349
vowel harmony 35–37, 44
vowel inventory 26, 30
vowel length 31, 32
de Vries, Laurens 280

Watam language 98, 481, 483
Watam village 8, 48, 299, 441, 481
Wilkins, David 94
Wongan village 1, 7, 8, 16, 80, 81, 210, 226, 242, 344, 348. *See also* Kopar language

wordhood 44
Wurm, Stephen A. 9

Yimas language 11, 12
young people's Tayap 17–21, 125, 327
- aspect 324–325
- complex constructions 241–242, 263–264, 283–289
- counterfactual 263–264
- deixis 62
- dual 126, 199
- ergativity 119–120, 326, 327
- gender 61–62, 120, 317, 326, 327
- lexical loss 79, 325, 326–335
- motion verbs 20, 21, 80, 198–199, 241, 317
- non-future tense 21, 246
- number marking 326–327
- peripheral cases/oblique arguments 134–135
- progressives 176–177, 328
- relative clauses 283
- *stori* (narrative) 315–316, 322–324, 327–328
- subjects 21, 61, 316, 324, 327, 334
- subordinate constructions 21, 283–287
- tail-head linkage 283
- tense 21, 156–157, 163, 174, 176–177, 180, 188, 197, 323
- verb classes 21, 57, 166–167, 173–176, 180–182, 188–189, 196–199, 324–325, 327–335
- verb morphology 57, 154–158, 163, 166–168, 173–177, 180–182, 188–189, 196–199, 324, 325, 327–335

Z'graggen, John A. 10

www.ingramcontent.com/pod-product-compliance
Lightning Source LLC
Chambersburg PA
CBHW020603300426
44113CB00007B/485